Eric Moon

Eric Moon

The Life and Library Times

by KENNETH F. KISTER

with a foreword by John N. Berry III

McFarland & Company, Inc., Publishers

Jefferson, North Carolina, and London

About the front cover

One can discern in this insouciant 1945 RAF photograph
(in Comilla, East Bengal, India — now Bangladesh)
the sportsman Eric is. Win the game is what he does,
define the game as well — and try to leave wrongfooted
all opponents. In middle age, he was often quick
to disagree with anyone who agreed with him,
and equally quick to agree with someone
who thought they were disagreeing with him.
Whatever it took, like soccer, he'd feint,
he'd swivel, and wherever *your* foot was,
the ball was no longer.
—*Robert Franklin (publisher)*

Back cover

Eric Moon at the banquet
celebrating his inauguration as president of the
American Library Association, Detroit, 1977

Frontispiece

Eric Moon in 1977 before his inauguration —
photograph, inscribed "to my friend Eric Moon,"
by John Mitchell Carter

Library of Congress Cataloguing-in-Publication Data

Kister, Kenneth F., 1935–
Eric Moon : the life and library times / by Kenneth F. Kister ;
with a foreword by John N. Berry III
p.   cm
Includes bibliographical references and index.

ISBN 0-7864-1253-4 (sewn softcover : 50# and 70# alkaline paper)

1. Moon, Eric, 1923–   2. Librarians — Biography.
3. Library journal — History — 20th century.
4. American Library Association — History — 20th century.
I. Title.
Z720.M678K57   2002
020'92 — dc21

2001007509

British Library cataloguing data are available

Manufactured in the United States of America

*McFarland & Company, Inc., Publishers
Box 611, Jefferson, North Carolina 28640
www.mcfarlandpub.com*

For Ruth Shaw Leonard,
who first introduced me to library history

Foreword

by John N. Berry III

I have known the author of this book and its subject for decades. We have been friends and we have worked together. We have shared good times and bad, and watched each other go through the changes that measure a life. They are tough lessons and landmarks, triumphs and tragedies for the one who is going through them, yet they seem typical steps in the process of maturing and aging for those who only observe them. I feel lucky that in the case of both Moon and Kister, I have lived and observed many of these changes.

I worked with Ken Kister before I met Eric Moon. The director of the Beatley Library at Simmons College to whom we reported, Kenneth Shaffer, is one of the last of a generation of bookmen. They are and were mostly men. Their position and status was based more on their personal knowledge and style than on their academic credentials. They were an idiosyncratic lot. To me it seemed that their talents and expertise were the accumulated wisdom and authority of a life of reading, and of running things pretty much as they saw fit. Shaffer hobnobbed with librarianship's greats, and saw to it that those for whom he was mentor, librarians like Kister and me, were introduced to the great men. My favorite of that generation, and I think he was Shaffer's, was Jesse Shera.

Eric Moon was in the next generation, sharing characteristics of his predecessors and of those to come. More than once, Shaffer told me how much he disapproved of Eric Moon's editorship of *Library Journal*. I think my interest in Moon started then.

Ken Kister was there when I outgrew my boyhood Republican politics, as I met and was radicalized by faculty and friends from the old and new left at Simmons and around Boston. He was there when I first met Eric Moon. As one mentored by Shaffer, I was given a very firm foundation in the strategy and tactics of library administration, and a deep appreciation of the history of librarianship in America, especially its great leaders of the 20th century. I am truly grateful for that important education and friendship. In our idealism, both Kister and I occasionally violated the rules, or over-stepped the boundaries of Shaffer's librarianship at Simmons—sometimes inadvertently, sometimes not.

From Eric Moon, however, I got a very different set of tools. Some of them were simply techniques for editing others and myself. Yet he gave me the more crucial tools by which to gain confidence (sometimes by enlarging one's ego), and the tools to make fundamental career and life decisions. His lessons in how not to be afraid to take risks also taught me that one's principles are a better reason to take risks than tactics or strategy.

It was the experience of Simmons and Shaffer that got me started toward the liberalism that is the ideology of librarianship. I became a Democrat at Simmons. It was Moon, by introducing me to his combative, English working-class ideology and style, who transcended that safe liberalism, taking me through the transition that finally completed my liberation from my roots in the narrowly proscribed provinces of the Republican, conservative culture of New England.

In the process he gave me the toolkit that I have used for my work ever since we began working together in 1964. He also gave me my most helpful support. Moon is the most honest editor for whom I ever wrote. When we began, he delighted in deleting what I thought was "my best stuff," usually those opening paragraphs, and those elaborate and fiery endings over which a writer tortures himself. I still use that quick fix on my own writing and on that of others. Since those early days, I always write for Eric, and while I write I think about how he would react to an editorial or a line of prose. Often, I wish he was still editing my stuff. So this foreword is my long-overdue "thank you" letter to him. Thanks, Eric, for equipping me to handle the enjoyable career I have had.

From the beginning, Moon and I argued our way through our friendship. At first the arguing scared me. He was the boss and I was new to *Library Journal.* He never gave me any explicit reassurance, and often we both got very angry. Still, somehow, either by letting the issue stand, or in the rare compromises, I grew to understand that we both used the arguing to strengthen our views, and to improve our methods. For example, in an editorial about me written before I joined *LJ*, a four-pager which still stands as the longest he ever wrote, Moon attacked me for raising the question of whether or not a group of Southern libraries were integrated without having researched the answer. Yet in the end his editorial praised me for uncovering an injustice in libraries, and in the way the American Library Association gave award money.

The episode led to a meeting when he came to Boston on other matters and took me out for a night of heavy drinking, argument, and ultimately a job offer to join him in New York. I realized that he liked to argue. I learned from him that adversaries can be good friends. As far as I could see, Moon never held a grudge. I'm sure there are people he doesn't like, and I know there are many with whom he disagrees. What has always surprised me is that he could always find a reason to praise someone, even those who saw him as an enemy.

Eric Moon is the most competitive person I ever met. He has beaten me at every game and every kind of competitive event we could dream up. I don't remember one victory. At our first card game he won every cent I had. He didn't brag when he beat me, so he was always able to get me to compete. Once when he quit a competition, letting me think I had beaten him, I heard him tell a friend that he wanted me to know that while winning is fun, the fruits of victory can be disappointing. He was right too, I was disappointed!

While he always enjoyed winning, and would show it, he never ridiculed those who lost to him. He used the same tactics in business that he used in games, and both at *Library Journal,* and later at Scarecrow Press, he delivered results that proved his competitive victories. I was always glad I didn't have to compete with him in anything more than games and private events. Still I developed a strong love for competition from the experience.

Moon's willingness to take risks was contagious. He hired outspoken editors and debated them through the publication process. He understood the uses of controversy, its limits, and its place in a magazine. He understood those things far better than most who worked for him or for whom he worked. He was as pleased as any of us when controversy increased interest and readership in *Library Journal,* but he wouldn't use it only for that. Controversy was and is a regular contributor to the magazine, thanks to Moon. To this day, because of Moon, controversy in *LJ* is based on issues, not sales. It is part of that belief he shared and taught, that principle is more important to editorial decisions than profit.

Moon was quite willing to take risks for profit too. He convinced the Bowker Company to risk heavy investment in books like Lawrence Clark Powell's *Fortune and Friendship*, when others who didn't know of Powell couldn't see any business return in the book. He was instrumental in the sale of the Bowker Company to the Xerox Corporation, despite the misgivings of the CEO. At the time I was outraged at the decision, but ultimately lived to see that merger take the Company to a golden period of growth in both profits and benefits to employees.

Moon bailed me out financially several times. Once he put up his own stock in the Company as collateral on a loan to get me out of deep financial problems. I think that it was part of his risk-taking nature. At the time I felt he was willing to invest in me, both as a friend and as a working colleague. It gave me confidence to continue the work, and relief from the urgent if extraneous issue of creditors at the door.

So there it is, a deep friendship and an enduring partnership that has given this partner his editorial toolkit, his ideology, his attitudes toward risk and controversy, and a kind of generous loyalty that few ever receive.

For me, it has been joyous to read and be reminded of so much in this biography of a man so important to my life. For it to be the creative effort of my long-standing friend and colleague, Ken Kister, doubles the reward. It also adds two more purposes to this Foreword. Thanks Ken, for writing so creatively and in such detail about Eric Moon. Thanks as well, for giving me a chance to write to him and, as always, for him.

John N. Berry III
Editor-in-Chief
Library Journal

Contents

Foreword by John N. Berry III   vii

Preface   xv

Abbreviations   xx

Acknowledgments   xxi

1 — Growing Up in Southampton   1

2 — Entering Librarianship   21

3 — Defending Home and Country   32

4 — Learning at Loughborough   44

5 — Advancing in British Libraries   62

6 — Ruffling Establishment Feathers   86

7 — Rabble-Rousing in Canada   109

8 — Reviving Library Journal   129

9 — Exploding the Silent Subject   152

10 — Remaking Library Journalism: Techniques   177

11 — Remaking Library Journalism: Triumphs   207

12 — Capturing Ilse's Heart   253

13 — Feeding a Scarecrow   287

Between pages 314 and 315 are 16 plates containing 57 photographs

14 — Moving from Backbench to President   315

15 — Taking Sherry at Westminster Abbey   360

16 — Reforming the American Library Association   370

17 — Retiring in the Sun   388

18 — Summing Up Eric Moon   405

Notes   411

Bibliography   421

Index   431

What is memory but the repository of things doomed
to be forgotten, so you must have History.
— Joyce Carol Oates, *Foxfire*

Life can only be understood backwards;
but it must be lived forwards.
— Soren Kierkegaard, *Life*

Preface

On the face of it, preparing a biography seems a reasonably straightforward undertaking. First decide on a subject, then conduct the necessary research, and finally write it all up in a tidy chronological narrative, shepherding the great man or woman from birth to death or, in the case of a living subject, to the present. But as anyone knows who has done the work, the road to a finished biography can be — usually is— a bumpy one, filled with potholes, speed traps, cul-de-sacs, barricades, detours, and other assorted hazards. Lytton Strachey, author of the classic *Eminent Victorians* and one thoroughly suited by temperament to the biographical form, doubtless spoke from the heart when he observed, "It is perhaps as difficult to write a good life as to live one."

The quintessential problem for the biographer is truth and how to get at it.

Sometimes people central to the story refuse to talk or, if they do, they speak in conundrums or platitudes, revealing precious little that is relevant. Others slant the truth, either subtly or flagrantly. Still others lie outright. Sometimes the biographee or his or her minions try, one way or another, to silence those who might furnish potentially embarrassing or less-than-flattering revelations. Sometimes important documents no longer exist, having been either lost or purged, as happened with Eric Moon's school records.

The writing of biography, welcomed by the subject or not, is a conscious invasion of privacy. Janet Malcolm, author of a life of Sylvia Plath, suggests the biographer is metaphorically akin to "the professional burglar, breaking into a house, rifling through certain drawers that he has good reason to think contain jewelry and money, and triumphantly bearing his loot away." James E.B. Breslin, biographer of the artist Mark Rothko, feels much the same way: "Voyeuristic and invasive, biography transgresses."

In the case of a living, cooperative subject, how much should the biographer trust the subject? People's memories naturally became blurred and less reliable as time goes by. After being confronted with several patently mistaken recollections during the preparation of this book, Eric Moon confessed, "I am beginning to understand how truly cloudy a thing memory has become." The flip side of dim memory is self-aggrandizement, wherein people deliberately embellish their lives and accomplishments, seeking to skew history's judgment, if ever so slightly. Everyone wants to be remembered well; few willingly expose their shortcomings, real or imagined.

No biographer can hope to discover the whole truth. The best that can be achieved in most instances is an honest albeit surface inquiry into the subject's persona and life's work. Truth is often too fluid, too amorphous, too relative, too complex, too scatty, too cryptic, too distant, too private to be captured except inexactly and inconclusively. There is simply too much to be known about any individual who has lived a life worth telling. The biographer cannot ferret out every secret motivation, every ambivalent action, every fib masquerading as fact. At some point the biographer must call a halt to the information-gathering and get down to sifting, organizing, and eventually recording the life at hand.

Several new problems now confront the biographer, the foremost being how best to relate the story. Should the writer merely present the known facts and let them speak for themselves in an effort at impartiality? Or should the teller of the tale provide analysis and risk becoming not only an advocate for or against the subject but an intellectual player — some would say contaminating specter — in the story?

Prior to the 20th century, biographers customarily maintained a discreet distance from their subjects, remaining an unobtrusive presence behind the scenes without a discernible point of view. The author simply assembled the illustrious person's bona fides and let the book more or less compose itself. But in modern times biographers have frequently shed their anonymity and put their interpretative stamp on events and behaviors. Robert Caro, Lyndon Johnson's biographer and proponent of the activist approach, contends that "biography is not merely the recording and regurgitating of interviews. It's important to try to assess the impact of someone's life on political and social history." Again, Lytton Strachey: "Uninterpreted truth is as useless as buried gold."

A related problem for the biographer concerns how much of the story to tell. How candid can or should the author be? What is the biographer's obligation, within the bounds of the libel laws, to reveal all that he or she has discovered about the subject? What is the reader's or public's right to know? On the other hand, what is the biographee's right to have certain material kept private? Ultimately who decides? These questions become all the more acute when the subject is alive.

Today biographies come in all sizes and guises. Some are puff jobs; some are snow jobs; some are hatchet jobs. Some are detached and objective studies while others (like the one you have in your hand) offer judgments, positive and negative; still others reek of sensationalism and exposé— more "pathography" than biography, to borrow a Joyce Carol Oates coinage. While the current plethora of biographies hardly validates Emerson's famous pronouncement that "there is properly no history; only biography," it does suggest how rich and diverse a source of knowledge biography has become.

This biography of Eric Moon (born in 1923) — a 20th-century librarian who for more than fifty years served his profession as practitioner, journalist, publisher, association leader, and mentor — intends to be an honest, readable account of the man's life, including his beliefs, ambitions, accomplishments, failures, methods, and demons.

The aim is a flesh-and-blood Moon, not hagiography. No subject is taboo, including sex, booze, and the clownish antics of library association grandees. Every reasonable effort was made to solicit input from Moon's adversaries and detractors as well as his friends, loyal colleagues, and family.

This biography seeks not only to tell the story of Eric Moon but to be a history of his times as a librarian. Obviously the book is not, nor could it be, a systematic account of postwar library developments, but it does attempt to limn the main currents of Anglo-American librarianship during the past half century through the prism of Moon's career. A competitive man with bedrock beliefs and an enormous appetite for argumentation, Moon was at the center of almost every important debate involving the shape and direction of the library profession in North America from the late 1950s to well into the 1990s and before that for some years in England. He knew and worked or jousted with practically all of the key people (and many not so key) who deliberated, quarreled, bickered, shouted, cried, connived, and figuratively spilled blood over the great issues that have preoccupied the profession in recent decades: civil rights, social responsibility, intellectual freedom, collection development, information policy, computerization, public funding, and association governance.

As readers will quickly discover, much of this work is told in the words of the participants, including, of course, Moon himself. As such, the biography serves as an oral history of the man and his times. The book complements Moon's *A Desire to Learn: Selected Writings* (Scarecrow Press, 1993), as well as two earlier compilations, *Book Selection and Censorship in the Sixties* (R.R. Bowker, 1969) and *Library Issues: The Sixties* (R.R. Bowker, 1970), which reprinted many of his *Library Journal* editorials and surveys.

The book also plumbs the question of what makes a leader. Why and how did Eric Moon, born in obscure Yeovil, England, in 1923 of equally obscure parents, come to have so vital an impact on American librarianship? What techniques did he employ? Were his leadership skills innate or learned? If the latter, where did he acquire them and who were his teachers and what were their methods? Most important, what does his experience tell us, if anything, about developing a better grade of library leader for the future?

This is an unauthorized biography, meaning that I initiated the project and am entirely responsible for the book's contents, as well as any and all deficiencies it might have. Though Eric Moon read the manuscript and at my urging commented on various passages, the final product represents my work and conclusions and no one else's. Eric understood and agreed to this at the outset.

Eric and his wife, Ilse, assisted the project by sitting for well over 100 hours of interviews between them. Suffice it to say that without their active cooperation the book would not have been attempted. In addition, they provided access to professional and personal papers in their immediate possession, though I did not get so much as a peek at their love letters, which are extant. The Moons also furnished names and addresses of people considered likely sources of information to help me piece the story together.

I did not seek nor did I receive any outside financial support in connection with the project, heeding Lytton Strachey's sage advice that a principal responsibility of the biographer is "to maintain his own freedom of spirit." From beginning to end, I insisted on complete freedom to learn what I could about Eric Moon and his times and to report the findings in my own manner and time.

The only perks I accepted were Ilse's lunches. Interview sessions with the Moons took place at their home in Sarasota, Florida, and I admit to tucking into omelets, cheeses, ploughman's specials, and other comestibles that Ilse brought forth with the *élan* of a junior Julia Childs; if this sounds sexist, I can only say that Eric made an agreeable busboy. Did these repasts compromise my integrity or eat away (so to speak) at my freedom of spirit? Had I sold my biographer's soul for an omelet? Was Moon, whom some view with good reason as a latter-day Svengali, trying to butter up his biographer? Such questions illustrate how devilishly sticky the ethics of making a biography, especially of a living person, can be.

During the course of the project I contacted numerous people who figured one way or another in Eric's life and career. Many responded, most proving to be interested, helpful, and wonderfully generous with their time and knowledge. (See the Acknowledgments, following) Some people particularly close to Eric were interviewed in person or by phone, but the majority answered my questions either in writing or via audiotape.

Of course, some people refused to cooperate. In one instance, a well-known staffer at the American Library Association and Moon antagonist chided me in a telephone conversation for relying too much on Eric's professional friends and the so-called "Moon Mafia," but in the next breath said she could not possibly respond to my questions because of her position in the Association. In another case, an aging pooh-bah who had once worked fairly closely with Eric on ALA business wrote me as follows: "This sounds like a very valuable project, and I wish you all success in it. I regret, however, that I cannot be available to work with you on it. Very Truly yours." I was especially sorry that Eric's first wife (of 23 years), now Diana McMorrow, declined to be interviewed.

As a first-time biographer I made many mistakes, some doubtless not yet apparent to me. Of those I know about, the most egregious was losing a tape of an interview with E.J. Josey somewhere in the Hyatt Regency Hotel in Atlanta. In another instance I indiscreetly told an interviewee that a colleague of hers said she had acted like "a shit" during the infamous *Speaker* affair. In the case of the Josey tape I was able to reconstruct most of the conversation from my notes, but the latter incident left a wound not yet completely healed. Boswell surely had it right when he observed that biography occasions "a degree of trouble far beyond that of any other species of composition."

A vow: Though I enjoy words and word play as much as the next person, I promised myself early on that I would resist the temptation to pun on Eric's surname. In one of our first interview sessions he mentioned that someone had once proposed doing an article about him to be called "The Luminous Mr. Moon." We both laughed and immediately thereafter I silently took the "no pun" pledge.

Some, perhaps many, will disagree with my assessment of Eric Moon as the 20th-century embodiment of Melvil Dewey. Whatever one's opinion, it is my hope that this book will stimulate increased interest in and appreciation of the rich history of the library profession in both North American and the United Kingdom.

Kenneth F. Kister
Tampa, Florida
February 2002

Abbreviations

AAL ... Association of Assistant Librarians
ACRL ... Association of College and Research Libraries
AECT ... Association of Educational Communications and Technology
ALA ... American Library Association
ALISE ... Association for Library and Information Science Education
APLA ... Atlantic Provinces Library Association
ASIS ... American Society for Information Science
BIP ... *Books in Print*
BLS ... Bachelor of Library Science degree
BSL ... *Bay State Librarian*
CFC ... Congress for Change
CLA ... Canadian Library Association
COA ... Committee on Accreditation of the ALA
FETS ... Further Education and Training Scheme
FLA ... Fellow of the Library Association
GLD ... Greater London Division of the AAL
IFC ... Intellectual Freedom Committee of the ALA
IFLA ... International Federation of Library Associations
JMRT ... Junior Members Round Table of the ALA
LA ... Library Association (British)
LAR ... *Library Association Record*
LC ... Library of Congress
LJ ... *Library Journal* (Lj, no italics, was used during the 1960s)
MLA ... Medical Library Association
MLS ... Master of Library Science degree
MP ... Member of Parliament
NCLIS ... National Commission on Libraries and Information Science
NFFL ... National Freedom Fund for Librarians
NLW ... National Library Week
OIF ... Office for Intellectual Freedom of the ALA
PW ... *Publishers Weekly*
SLA ... Special Libraries Association
SLJ ... *School Library Journal*
SRRT ... Social Responsibilities Round Table of the ALA
TLS ... *Times Literary Supplement*
VLA ... Virginia Library Association
WHCLIS ... White House Conference on Library and Information Services
WLB ... *Wilson Library Bulletin*

Acknowledgments

My gratitude to Eric and Ilse Moon is boundless. I am indebted to both for their help and cooperation, which were crucial to the project. They allowed me to invade their lives, test their patience, and write about them with freedom and candor. Only strong, secure individuals would agree to this.

I am likewise grateful to the many other people who shared their thoughts, opinions, experiences, and recollections about Eric Moon and his times with me, either in person, by telephone, in writing (snail mail or e-mail), or on audiotape. My heartfelt thanks to:

Ben Bagdikian, Johnnie Givens Barnes, Ed Beckerman, Ronald Benge, Sanford Berman, John N. Berry III, Fay Blake, Lee Bobker, Al Bowron, Miriam Braverman, Dorothy Broderick, Richard Buck, Richard E. Bye, Harry Campbell, Mary K. Chelton, Stan Crane, Arthur Curley, Al Daub, Robert Delzell, Ernest A. DiMattia, Dick Dougherty, Edward Dudley, William (Esh) Eshelman, Helena Estes, Rice Estes, Robert (Robbie) Franklin, Jack Frantz, Sidney Gadsden, Elizabeth Geiser, David Gerard, T.W. (Bill) Graham, Shirley Havens, T. Mark Hodges, Edward Holley, Zoia Horn, Norman Horrocks, Jeanne Isacco, Arthur Jones, Clara Jones, Wyman Jones, E.J. Josey, Bill Katz, Alan Moon, Belinda Moon, Bryan Moon, Pearce Penney, Art Plotnik, Lawrence Clark Powell, Charles E. Reid, Pat Rom, Patricia Glass Schuman, Judith Serebnick, Russell Shank, Gerald R. Shields, Harold Smith, Ken Stockham, Carla J. Stoffle, Roy Stokes, Ron Surridge, John Taylor, Jana Varlejs, Esmé Clarke Vesey, Gawan Vesey, John Wakeman, Ted Waller, Robert Wedgeworth, George Wieser, Evie Wilson-Lingbloom, and Donald Yelton.

Special thanks are due to:

T.W. (Bill) Graham — one of Moon's oldest friends, a coworker at Southampton (England) Public Library, a classmate at Loughborough College School of Librarianship, and a sterling reference librarian (now retired) — for providing valuable background information on the city of Southampton and its library, along with his recollections of Eric's years in England;

David Bromwich, local history librarian at the Somerset (England) County

Library, for his perusal of the March 1923 issues of *The Western Gazette*, which reported events in Yeovil, Moon's birthplace, at the time of his birth;

Peter Munro, deputy principal at Taunton's College (successor to Taunton's School, Eric's grammar school in Southampton), for his efforts (unsuccessful) to locate Moon's school records;

A.J. Meadows, professor and dean of education and humanities at Loughborough University (in Loughborough, England), for his efforts (also unsuccessful) to track down Moon's records at what was then Loughborough College and for supplying an informative history of that institution;

Charles Cameron, manager of the Newfoundland (Canada) Provincial Resource Library, for detailed information about library service in the province during Moon's time there and for providing or verifying numerous facts about people and events;

Wendy Scott and Tom Schulte-Albert of the National Library of Canada for uncovering articles by and about Moon published during his brief period in Newfoundland;

Jean Peters, librarian at Cahners Publishing Company, current publisher of *Library Journal*, for searching her archives for material about the Moon years at *LJ*, including the magazine's circulation statistics;

Betty Havrylik, library assistant, Simmons College Graduate School of Library and Information Science, for some much appreciated emergency library service;

Elizabeth Cardman, assistant archivist of the American Library Association Archives at the University of Illinois at Urbana-Champaign, for locating and furnishing pertinent documents from the archives;

David Gerard — British librarian, teacher, poet, and memoirist — for reading with a critical eye chapters 5 and 6 in manuscript form; and

James Carmichael, library historian and educator (professor, Department of Library and Information Studies, University of North Carolina at Greensboro), for reading and commenting on that part of the book's preface dealing with the nature of biography.

Finally I am ever grateful to Clarice Ruder — spouse, colleague, and best friend — for her support and understanding. It was she with her persistent question, "Is he born yet?" who kept me focused and ever mindful that the biographer has only so much time to tell a life.

– 1 –

Growing Up in Southampton

Prologue

Like practically all of us, Eric Moon is best understood within the context of time, place, and lineage.

In Moon's case, appreciation of the central fact of his life — birth into the British working class in the 1920s — requires at least a nodding acquaintance with the modern socialist movement in Great Britain, an evolutionary response to inequitable social and economic conditions created or exacerbated by runaway capitalism in the 19th century. Thus the quest for Eric Moon and the formative influences on his development, both personal and professional, begins at what might seem an unlikely point in history: the reign of Queen Victoria, when the British Empire was at its zenith.

Under Victoria's long rule (1837–1901) Great Britain experienced unparalleled success, the empire at one time comprising nearly a quarter of the world's land and population. Despite poverty and hardship among vast numbers of people at the lower end of the social scale, the Victorian Age was a time of prosperity and comfort for Britain's elites. The arts and sciences flourished, and progress, a key word in the Victorian vocabulary, was fueled by technology, an irresistible, seemingly omnipotent force that generated untold wealth and changed how people lived, worked, traveled, and thought. The Crystal Palace, a revolutionary glass and iron structure encompassing 19 acres at the Great Exhibition of 1851 in London, exemplified the expansive spirit of the age.

During this optimistic time many upper-class Englishmen (women hardly mattered, the queen notwithstanding) believed they had achieved, or were on the verge of achieving, the best government, the best economic system, the best language, the best schools, the best manners and morals, indeed the best society the world had ever known. Self-confidence, a spirit of adventure, a general earnestness about life, and a messianic urge to share the fruits of Englishness with the rest of planet were hallmarks of the Victorian personality. But there was a darker, inverted side too, characterized by the less attractive traits of arrogance, smugness, primness, prudery, and hypocrisy. A social

1

system based on rigid class distinctions dictated how Britons spoke, how much education they received, when and what they ate, what type of work they did, where they lived, whom they married, who their friends were, what clothes they wore. In short, class-consciousness determined their essence as human beings, with ordinary working people and the poor trapped like detritus at the bottom of the heap. As the whim of history would have it, Victoria, the formidable presence who presided over the empire for almost 65 years, died on January 22, 1901, just as the new century was ushered in.

Aside from lamentations for the dead queen and hand-wringing over a costly war with the Boers in South Africa, the 20th century in Britain began as if nothing had changed, as if Britannia would continue to rule the world (or a sizable chunk of it) forever. The new monarch, Edward VII, Victoria's aging son, represented continuity and familiarity. Coming to the throne late in life, the king personified the complacent materialism and fashionable patina of the privileged classes; the nation's underclasses remained largely subdued and unnoticed, figuratively "below stairs." But beyond the polished exterior, doubts about the country and its institutions began to be sounded in influential quarters. Thoughtful people — mainly artists, writers, and intellectuals such as H.G. Wells, Bernard Shaw, Roger Fry, Virginia and Leonard Woolf, D.H. Lawrence, E.M. Forster, and Beatrice and Sidney Webb — pointed to disturbing signs of moral mendacity, social discontent, economic injustice, and political myopia. Upstart Germany, which had been a unified power only since 1870, increasingly threatened British imperial interests. By 1914, to the surprise of almost no one except obtuse politicians on both sides, Great Britain and Germany were at war, a protracted conflict that enveloped all of Europe and eventually much of the world, including the United States.

World War I and its aftermath had a devastating effect on Great Britain and its people. Approximately 750,000 British soldiers died in what is still called the Great War and a million more were wounded, many gassed, grotesquely maimed, or psychologically traumatized. In addition to producing horrendous battlefield casualties, the war exhausted Britain's economy and weakened its mercantile base, diminished the nation's political and military stature as a world power, fractured the Victorian/Edwardian value system that had guided the society for nearly a century, and opened the way for the British proletariat — a boisterous, energetic, often indecorous lot — to achieve political power for the first time.

By early 1924, less than six years after the war had ended, the Labour Party, a new force in British politics representing working-class aspirations and grievances, formed its first government. Committed to policies based loosely on ideas advocated by a group of high-minded socialists called the Fabian Society, Labour replaced the increasingly ineffectual Liberal Party as the main challenger to the Conservatives (or Tories), long the party of the entrepreneurial and upper classes in Britain. Predictably, Labour's fledging government was short-lived, falling after just eleven months. Still, this assertion of working-class power signaled the beginning of momentous events that would change British society in ways unthinkable during Victoria's heyday: in 1926 a bitter and disruptive General Strike shocked the capitalist ruling class; in 1928 women achieved the vote; a year later Labour, now Britain's largest party, was returned to power, only to be frustrated again, this time by the Great Depression.

It was into this milieu of social and political upheaval that Eric Moon was born and grew up, a self-described "poor boy from the working class."

March 6, 1923

Eric Edward Moon arrived in this world inconspicuously on Tuesday, March 6, 1923, in Yeovil, an old market town in the south of England about 60 miles west of Southampton, the large port city where he went to elementary and secondary school, found his first job, and met and married his first wife, Diana.

By historical standards March 6, 1923, was not a memorable day. No dreadful wars began or ended, no celebrated personages died or were murdered, no great ships sank, no crowded trains crashed, no hideous plagues broke out, no calamitous earthquakes or other natural disasters occurred, no wondrous new inventions or discoveries were announced. Yet the day's news did contain ominous foreshadowings of occurrences, foreign and domestic, that would dominate the British national mood during Moon's youth and early manhood:

In France, the government extended the period of military service for draftees: "The Cabinet decided today that the class of 1921, due to finish eighteen months' military service the first week in April, will be kept under the colors until May 3," *The New York Times* (March 7, 1923) reported in a boxed front page dispatch datelined Paris, March 6. "If German resistance continues in the Ruhr," the article went on, "it is possible that a part of the class will be kept on duty until the class of 1923 joins its regiments in September. To have liberated the 1921 class in April would have been to reduce the French effectives by more than 200,000 at a time when France has much use for her troops."

In Germany, Chancellor Wilhelm Cuno delivered a "stiff" speech to the Reichstag denouncing recent French actions in the Ruhr and their plans to unilaterally revise the Treaty of Versailles and impose a new agreement. According to a London *Times* correspondent on the scene, the French viewed the present treaty as "inadequate" to resolve such recalcitrant problems as war reparations and border security.

Also in Germany, the newspaper *Vorwärts* reported that the nation's cost of living rose an astronomical 136% between January and February 1923, far outstripping wages. Asked the paper editorially, "If we have foreign prices, why not foreign wages, too?"

In Italy, the Archbishop of Messina, following a trip to the Vatican, stated in a pastoral letter to his flock that Pope Pius XI "is well satisfied with Premier Mussolini," the flamboyant fascist leader who had come to power the previous October.

In Great Britain on March 6, 1923, the Conservative government of Prime Minister Bonar Law suffered a humiliating by-election defeat in Liverpool's Edgehill constituency: John Waller Hills, Financial Secretary of the Treasury, lost what was considered a safe seat in Parliament to the Labour candidate, J.H. Hayes. Edgehill was the third by-election lost by the Conservatives in as many days, all involving top-level cabinet ministers, a reversal unprecedented in British parliamentary history.

Also in Great Britain on that day, J. Ramsay MacDonald, leader of the increasingly confident Labour opposition, condemned French policy in the Ruhr as "rewriting the Treaty of Versailles without consultation with her allies." MacDonald warned in the House of Commons that the situation "could end in war"— between Britain and France. He chastised Bonar Law's government for indecision and delay in its handling of this grave situation.

Also in Great Britain, the Chancellor of the Exchequer announced that his country could not, or would not, tap dollar reserves in Canada to help repay its large American debt, accrued during the Great War.

And in faraway America on March 6, 1923, the United States president, Warren Harding, and his ailing wife Florence and various top government officials were in the midst of a leisurely excursion by train from the capital in Washington to Florida, where the presidential party planned to spend the next four or five weeks cruising the inland waterways between St. Augustine and Miami on a houseboat. "The purpose of the trip," informed *The New York Times*, "is to build up Mrs. Harding's health with absolute quiet and Florida sunshine."

Working-Class Stock

According to his birth certificate, Eric Moon was born at home at 3 Westlands Road, Yeovil, in the county of Somerset. Somerset was then, and still is, principally an agricultural area in southwestern England, similar to Dorset, a neighboring county famous as the setting for Thomas Hardy's brooding Wessex novels. In his adult life Moon claimed an intellectual kinship with the writer based on the geography of birth. "I'm a great Hardy fan. I like to be thought of as from Hardy country. The first present I ever gave Ilse [his second wife] was a Hardy novel. Read this, I said, and if you don't understand it you'll never understand me." However, he spent only a brief period in Somerset as an infant before his parents moved on to Southampton (in Hampshire), hardly enough time to assimilate much "Hardy country" aura. Later, when pressed on the point, Moon conceded his alleged bond with the novelist was "a manufactured one."

Moon's birth certificate identifies his father as Francis Edward George Moon, occupation "Mechanical Engineer (Fitter) (Journeyman)," and his mother simply as Grace Emily Moon, "formerly Scott." Little is known of Francis Moon's ancestry, other than that his father, Edward George Moon (Eric's grandfather), was born in 1869 and worked at various times as a general laborer, trapper, and fish salesman somewhere in the south of England, most likely in or near Yeovil. Francis's mother, Louisa Ann Moon, née Sumsion (Eric's grandmother), was born in 1874 in Yeovil, where her father worked as a glove cutter. The union of Edward and Louisa Moon produced eight children (six boys and two girls), Francis being the oldest.

Grace Emily Moon's roots were equally humble. Her father, James Albert Scott, was a tea salesman in Southampton; his father, also named James, was born in East Dereham in Norfolk (a county northeast of London) and worked as a servant; his father, William (Grace's great-grandfather), also came from East Dereham and was a laborer; Grace's mother, Clara Ellen Scott (maiden name unknown), was a housewife. Though scant, the evidence suggests that Moon descended from sturdy if undistinguished English working-class stock.

His parents' marriage certificate reveals that the couple were married on Christmas day, December 25, 1919, in Shirley, a Southampton neighborhood, in the local parish church "according to the rites and ceremonies of the Established Church." Francis, born in 1895 in Yeovil and called Ted by family and friends, was 24 years old at the time and a "bachelor"; Grace, born in 1902, was 17 and a "spinster." After they married, Ted and Grace lived in Yeovil until shortly after the birth of Eric, their first child, when they moved to Southampton. Though Moon was and continues to be a familiar surname in Yeovil, the couple never lived there again. Years later, after Eric had come to live and work in the United States, he passed through Yeovil without a flicker of interest or sentiment. He recalled that he and Ilse and their friends Bill Eshelman and Pat Rom "toured all down through Devon and Cornwall and came back through Somerset. I was asleep in the back of the car when we went through Yeovil. Esh woke me up and asked if I wanted to stop. 'No, drive on,' I said, and went back to sleep."

Ocean Island

In late 1924 Ted Moon, his wife Grace, and young son Eric, then about a year and half old, sailed from Southampton to Ocean Island in the central Pacific, where Ted had secured a job with the British Phosphate Commission, a huge government-sponsored mining concern. Ocean Island, just 2.2 square miles in size, was discovered by English explorers in 1804, and in 1915 it became part of the Gilbert and Ellice Islands Colony, one of the last outposts of the British empire. (Today Ocean Island, renamed Banaba, is part of Kiribati, an independent republic comprised of several central Pacific island groups, including the Gilbert chain.) The island, the only one of the Gilberts created by volcanic action, contained massive phosphate deposits, which the British began mining after World War I, an operation that continued for 60 years, until 1979. Ted Moon — by trade a "fitter," or mechanic who assembles and maintains machinery — was one of thousands of British workers employed on Ocean Island during this period.

The Moon family remained on Ocean Island for two or at most three years, returning to England sometime in 1927 — probably early in the year but certainly no later than December, as Eric's only sibling, his brother Bryan, was born in Southampton in January 1928. Understandably, Moon, a mere nipper at the time, had only murky recollections of Ocean Island as an adult. He did recall playing with some native children and learning a few words of Gilbertese, the local language, but remembered none of the vocabulary in later years. He also had no memory of living conditions on the island — a hot, dusty, isolated, claustrophobic speck of land in the middle of a huge ocean where the chief activity was extracting a smelly mineral from the ground. In the 1920s, before air conditioning, television, and jet travel, daily life on Ocean Island must have been a hellish experience for workers and their families.

The adult Moon, however, spoke of "growing up in the South Seas" as if Ocean Island were some sultry paradise. The embellished words themselves—"growing up in the South Seas"—are ripe with the romance of exotic places. Despite remembering practically nothing about it, he liked to convey (delicately, subtly, offhandedly) the notion that life on the island was, at least for him, a grand adventure, one that gave his childhood the cachet of a Somerset Maugham tropical tale.

The conceit that "growing up" on Ocean Island made him special doubtless took root after he returned to England and started school, where he had "a feeling that I was behind the other kids, having lived overseas for all those years." At school he was, if only in his own mind, the little boy from "the South Seas," set apart from his peers by virtue of this experience. He possessed knowledge — intriguing knowledge — they did not and could not have. Ultimately, Moon's unremembered couple of years on Ocean Island when a toddler became a vehicle to assert a needed sense of superiority toward others—a need that would play out in similar fashion again and again throughout his life.

The Mystery of Ted Moon

When the Moons returned to England from Ocean Island in 1927 (via Melbourne, Australia), their ship docked in Southampton and there at least two of them remained — Grace for the rest of her life and Eric until he started his professional career. As for Ted: until Eric's 78th year no one knew what became of him.

Southampton was a logical place for Ted and Grace to drop anchor. They knew the area, having married and previously lived there; also Grace's parents lived in the city, and it was natural she would want to be near them, especially after having been far away for several years. In addition, Southampton's bustling port offered plenty of job opportunities for experienced mechanics like Ted. For instance, work on the city's huge Western Docks complex, which took half a dozen years to complete, had just begun in 1927. A further motivation prompting Grace to settle down in Southampton was the fact that sometime before leaving Ocean Island or soon thereafter she became pregnant with her second (and last) child, Bryan. But no doubt the most compelling reason she stayed put was the unexpected — and apparently unexplained — disappearance of her husband. Not long after Bryan's birth on January 13, 1928, or possibly before, Moon *père* vanished and was never heard from again (as far as is known) by Grace or either of her sons. "He apparently left us about the time I was born," Bryan remembered. "No connection I hope."

For years, Ted Moon's sons speculated about why their father abandoned them and their mother and what had become of him. Perhaps he grew tired of his responsibilities as husband and father and took off for another country or Pacific island? Perhaps he fell in love with another woman and established a new household somewhere in England or abroad? Perhaps he was murdered, his body weighted and dumped off a Southampton dock and never recovered? Perhaps he was abducted by an underworld cartel in need of the services of an expert fitter?

Over the years Grace Moon, who died in 1975, offered conflicting versions of her husband's sudden disappearance, including the claim that he was lost at sea while still working at the Ocean Island site. But British Phosphate Commission records, which report Francis Moon "departed from our service on arrival Melbourne [Australia] 12th January 1927," contradict this account. Eric too dismissed the lost-at-sea story, suggesting it was a face-saving white lie told by a woman unable to admit that her husband had deserted her. Instead, he believed his father did not return to England with him and his mother but remained somewhere in the Pacific region, working on another job: "My father was sort of an itinerant civil engineer or something like that. Almost from birth he traveled pretty continually, in South Africa, Australia, all over the place." In Eric's imagination his father became a dashing figure roaming the world *à la* Phileas Fogg; he was a "civil engineer," not a prosaic fitter.

Finally, after nearly three-quarters of a century, the mystery of Ted Moon's disappearance was solved, though some details still remain unclear or unknown. In 1999, Chris Moon, Bryan's son, hired an investigator to look into what had become of the wayward family patriarch. The inquiry, aided by two nephews of Ted Moon in England (one living in Yeovil), revealed that Ted eventually settled down in the tiny Australian Outback town of Quorn (pop. 924) north of Adelaide, where he supervised the local electricity company until his death of intestinal problems in 1957 at age 62. In 1931, several years after abandoning Grace and his two English sons, Ted married a woman named Gladys and fathered three more children, all boys: Michael (*b.* 1934), David (*b.* 1939), and Ron (*b.* 1949). Ted Moon's whereabouts between 1927, when he left Ocean Island, and 1931, when he married Gladys in an Australian registry office, are still unexplained, as is the lack of evidence of a divorce from Grace back in England. What is known is that Ted Moon loved to be on the move, and while in Australia he and his second family lived in many places, including the states of Victoria, New South Wales, and South Australia (where Quorn is located), as well as Alice Springs in the Northern Territory.

So it was that late in life Eric and Bryan Moon gained a whole new family halfway around the world.

Jock and the Southampton Boardinghouse

After losing her husband, Grace Moon, a spirited young woman in her mid-twenties limited by the disadvantages of minimal education and no vocational experience other than as mother and housewife, faced the daunting prospect of supporting herself and two small sons. She soon resolved the problem by renting a semi-detached house (or duplex), which she turned into a small boardinghouse, providing rooms and meals for three or four male lodgers, usually dock workers. Located in a rough section of Southampton, the boardinghouse was the first of five or six such establishments she operated in the city during her lifetime. Eventually her parents and a brother, Stanley (nicknamed Scott), came to live with her and the boys.

Some of Eric's earliest memories were of the first Southampton boardinghouse and its denizens. A Diogenes-like character made an especially strong impression: "I remember there was a crazy Welshman among the lodgers who was a lamplighter who used to go out on his bicycle with a long pole over his shoulder about four or five o'clock every morning. For many years I couldn't get out of my head a song that he used to sing, because I would wake up in the morning singing this song."

In time Grace married one of her lodgers, a man named Alexander (Jock) Beatson. Beatson, a Scotsman with an honors degree from Edinburgh University, worked by choice as a carpenter at the Southampton docks, preferring manual labor to a more genteel career. "He liked using his hands as well as his mind," recalled Eric, who was nine or ten when Jock came on the scene. Jock became the father the boy had never known. The two got on famously, compatible as fish and chips. Moon: "We were great friends. Jock spent much time working with me to improve my knowledge in a variety of areas, not all intellectual. For example, he taught me how to play darts; we played on teams in pubs." Skill at darts later proved useful to Moon when in library school he sometimes played for and won his lunch or supper.

A sandy-haired man of average height and slight build who loved literature and was good at mathematics, Jock gave Grace's first son a much needed male role model and authority figure. He encouraged Eric — a bright, thin, wiry, competitive, rambunctious lad — to explore the world around him, to value education, to read, to think, and, when necessary, to stand and fight. Moon's recollection of how Jock encouraged him to take on a local bully remained with him for the rest of his life:

I was a little skinny kid who used to get beaten up a lot. There was this tough Irish kid on the block who would give me a lot of trouble. Eventually Jock said, 'No more of this. Get out there and beat him up!' 'That's not a very good idea, I said.' But with Jock's encouragement I joined the local boys' club and took boxing lessons. Eventually there was a showdown with the Irish kid — I beat him up and that was the end of my getting beaten up on the way to school.

Jock was, in Moon's words, a "strong left-wing Labour man" and an "old Scottish socialist," and he had a conspicuous hand in shaping young Eric's basic political attitudes, which became fixed early on. From adolescence until the time he left England, Moon identified emphatically with the Labour Party: "I would never think of voting Conservative; there was never a question in my mind." His (and Jock's) views corresponded closely to those espoused by the Fabian Society, an early think tank that achieved prominence in British political circles soon after its founding in the 1880s. Taking their name from the Roman general Fabius Maximus Cunctator renowned for his cautious tactics, the Fabians sought creation of a socialist state through gradual, democratically induced reforms; they rejected the way to power — violent revolution — preached by Karl Marx and his Bolshevik disciples. Eric's first real sense of political ideology occurred as a teenager in the 1930s when the Spanish Civil War broke out, pitting a coalition of leftist groups against a strong fascist force led by General Francisco Franco in what became a dress rehearsal for World War II. The boy's sympathies naturally lay with the intellectuals, trade unionists, and communists who opposed Franco. "I'm sure," Moon observed years later, "that this is where my political awareness first began, as it did for many of my contemporaries. It was a period when the far left was a very respectable position, because the alternative was fascism, which was intolerable."

Not a tub-thumper, Jock seldom talked much about politics per se. Instead, he quietly encouraged his stepson to question orthodox values and traditional methods. This meant viewing the Establishment with skepticism and challenging those who venerate the status quo; it meant taking on those who resist or disparage reform; it meant confronting those who prefer that decisions be made behind closed doors rather than in the light of day; it meant opposing those who seek to perpetuate themselves in power for the sake of power itself; and, above all, it meant doing battle with those who lack passion for justice and equality. In short, Jock sought to instill in his stepson a political compass for life. For his part, Moon always acknowledged his stepfather's role in his personal development: "I would have to say that in the early years the most powerful influence on me was Jock, certainly more influential than any teacher."

A Birthday to Remember

One incident involving Jock stood out above all others in Moon's adult mind. Months before Eric turned 13, his stepfather offered him an irresistible birthday "bribe." Moon tells the story:

If I could bring off some unprecedented (unprecedented for me) feat of scholarship — I believe the requirement was that I had to finish at the top of my class in at least four subjects that year — I should receive for my thirteenth birthday a present, Jock said, I would remember all my life.

Powered by visions of a bicycle that was at least two-thirds chrome, I conquered my usual laziness and a few time-consuming passions and somehow achieved the impossible goal. On the morning I was to receive my Oscar, I raced around the house searching for the gleaming vehicle that was to be the materialist envy of my friends, and even more particularly of my enemies. Nothing was in evidence except a square brown-paper package on the kitchen table. In those days, bicycles came from the shop all in one piece, so I knew my saddled dream could not be compressed into any packet so unprepossessing. What that package did contain, though I did not know it then, and would not for some time, consumed as I was by chagrin and the certainty that I had been well and truly had, was however a vehicle that would take me much further than ever the gleaming two-wheeler of my fantasies could. It was a volume containing the complete plays of Bernard Shaw.

That was the day my education really began. As my anger and frustration cooled, curiosity started to do its insidious work. I had to find out what my stepfather (whom I regarded with a certain affection and respect) thought was so special about that fat brown volume, and for weeks I ploughed doggedly through its pages.

Some months later, my English teacher, surprised on several occasions by my penchant for quoting the irascible Irishman, invited me home for tea, and we talked Shaw for an hour or two. The next day he asked me if I would give a talk to the class on Shaw. That was one of the terror events of my life but it gradually began to dawn on me that the square brown-paper package might indeed be more valuable than the chrome-plated bicycle. It had already given me a kind of grudging status and recognition among my fellows as the possessor of something more mysterious than a bicycle: I knew something none of them knew. What I had was knowledge. A little piece, to be sure, but the genuine article nevertheless.

Not only did Jock's initially disappointing birthday present teach the adolescent Eric a potent lesson, it introduced him to George Bernard Shaw, one of the great writers and radical thinkers of his day. A founding member of the Fabian Society and winner of the Nobel Prize for Literature, Shaw (1856–1950) was an unrelenting critic of the Victorian and Edwardian hypocrisies that pervaded much of British society at the time. Many of his plays, especially the earlier ones, contained broadside attacks on conventional thinking. For example, *Mrs. Warren's Profession*, written in 1893, mocked conformist attitudes about prostitution, and public performance of the play was banned in England for more than thirty years. Opinionated and argumentative, Shaw questioned everything, believing that vigorous debate was the most effective way to discover the truth. Shaw "influenced my way of looking at things," Moon wrote years later, "perhaps more profoundly than anyone else."

Mum

But no matter how well Jock and Eric got along, no matter how much bonding occurred between them, Moon's deepest, most intuitive relationship while growing up was with his mother —"Mum" to her boys. Both her sons loved and admired her unconditionally. They saw her as a secure pillar — an affectionate, outgoing, hardworking woman who was always there for them when they needed her. "I don't remember her as a powerful intellectual influence," said Eric, "but I do remember her as a great, beautiful, benign presence; I always felt a kind of warmth there and support. She was very kind, not hard; she was terrific, just terrific."

Clearly, times were difficult for Grace after the family returned from Ocean Island, nor did they improve much during the long years of economic depression in the 1930s. Brother Bryan recalled, "We were relatively poor although never hungry. Our house was modest but always clean. An extravagance was a visit to the cinema." Both Moon boys remembered their mother as an indefatigable worker, always scraping to make ends meet. "To us," said Bryan, "she was the protective mother, caring, patient, terrific cook and, it often seemed, tireless. She cooked the most voluminous meals, especially for breakfast, which was good for business as many of her customers at the guest house were regulars." Eric put it more succinctly: "She worked her ass off."

In addition to operating a number of boardinghouses during her years in Southampton, Grace once ran a bakery, worked in a butcher shop (during World War II), and in her later years was a stewardess on Cunard passenger ships sailing out of Southampton. She did what she had to do, often under difficult circumstances, to keep her family together. Tall and lean, she was, in Eric's mind, "very British looking," a gregarious woman who loved company, often talking at length with her boarders and neighbors. According to Bryan, she could also be "a feisty lady to anyone who crossed her and was very vocal about it." Happily for her sons, she never begrudged them any maternal or material support she could provide, even as they grew older and became of working age. Bryan: "When I came out of the RAF at 21, I went back to the Southampton College of Art and lived with my mother. She put up with me for the four years I was studying and supported me in every way. I always knew I could rely on Mother if I was in any need and she was always there."

On the other hand the household the Moon brothers grew up in was not always a tranquil one. Relations between Grace and Jock were often contentious and grew more so with the passage of time. The two quarreled, usually over money, the arguments exacerbated by Grace's parents, James and Clara Scott, who lived with her, Jock, and the boys. According to Bryan, "There was always turmoil in the house, domestic fights between Mother and Jock, never any prolonged period of domestic 'bliss.'"

Eric and Bryan frequently found themselves trying to restore harmony during a family row. Before leaving home, Eric, being the elder son, took primary responsibility for refereeing disputes between his mother and stepfather. After Eric left, Bryan recalled his mother would ask him "to intervene on her behalf" in fights with Jock: "It was very difficult to keep any balance between them." In order to cope, both young men were forced to develop interpersonal skills that later served them well in their work as adults. Certainly in Eric's case his early experience as a neophyte mediator at home helped him become an effective negotiator between hostile parties in professional situations. Those who knew him might not think of Moon as a conciliator, yet throughout his career as librarian, editor, publisher, and association leader he often tried (not always successfully) to bring people together in an effort to achieve a common goal, a compromise solution, or simply a lessening of tensions. Just as he had done as a teenager caught between warring parents.

Sometime after Eric left home to join the Royal Air Force (RAF) in 1941, Grace and Jock separated and eventually divorced, and Jock, who remarried, lost touch with his stepsons. Years later Eric heard Jock had died, though he could not remember the particulars (where, when, how, or who told him). Toward the end of her life Grace took up with a man named Archie Donkin, another of her lodgers. In addition to being her lover, Donkin helped Grace run her business (her last), a little bed-and-breakfast on Burlington Road in Southampton. Archie was much younger than Grace — in fact younger than Eric — but this hardly surprised those who knew her well. Grace's attitude toward sex had always been open and, by any standard, relaxed or permissive. Eric: "I think she was pretty easy about stuff like that. I think she was pretty active sexually all her life. She married Jock and then wound up in later years living with this guy who was younger than me. So down to the end she was always kind of lively."

Brother Bryan

A five-year age difference separated Eric from his younger brother Bryan. The two also had different interests and personalities and, as a result, were not close as youngsters or as adults, though in their later years they grew closer. As a child, Bryan had the feeling of being the smaller, weaker, and seemingly less accomplished of the two:

Eric and I had little in common. He was tall, I short, he extroverted, I introverted (at that time), he academically successful, I a slow starter except in art, he graduated to high school, something I never expected to accomplish. I can remember at that time wishing I was more like my brother, a desire that changed as the years went by!

I don't recall that we did much together except occasionally fool around, usually at Eric's instigation. I do remember that we were "playing" in front of the family room coal fire one day. As usual, I got the worst of the play and fell into the fire knocking a kettle of hot water over my knees. This sent me to my first hospital visit and generated into scarlet fever. But Eric was bigger than I and there wasn't too much I could do about it! But I admired his success at school, his freedom of movement (he seemed to have much more latitude to do as he wished than I), his easy way of making friends, all qualities I lacked.

Eric was never a "good" brother. On the other hand, he was never "bad"—except perhaps that fireplace incident! We simply had little in common and events separated us at an early age so we grew accustomed to watching each other's progress from afar as it were. However, the two occasions I really needed Eric's advice and help, he came through without any questions being asked. Around 1953–54, I was applying for my first executive position in London. My boss-to-be was eccentric; he asked me to write an article from which he would judge my acceptability for the position. I was not good at writing at that time but Eric was. Big brother rewrote my draft and I got the job. It was a turning point in my career.

Later, Eric emigrated to the States and kept telling me to do the same. Some years later I decided he was right (again) but entry to the States could be expedited by a sponsor. By then, big brother was an American citizen and he became my sponsor. Another milestone for Moon junior. So Eric was there when I most needed help and we would come together for any family crisis. Our mother went through some difficult years toward the end of her life and, between us, Eric and I tried to make her life more comfortable. We were together when she died and for her funeral. But other than this, our lives took their own course.

Bryan's consuming professional passions were aviation and art. Like Eric, he served in the RAF during World War II. Upon return to civilian life he studied art for four years and then spent a long period in the airline business, first as advertising director for the British Aircraft Corporation, then as an executive with Aloha Airlines out of Honolulu, and finally for twenty years (1968–1988) as a vice president of Northwest Airlines, during which time he became an American citizen.

In 1986, Bryan and his son Chris spent three weeks in Africa with the late George Adamson of *Born Free* fame. Bryan, who never completely gave up his art, wanted to do a series of paintings of lions: "So I wrote to George Adamson, the legendary conservationist who raised orphaned and abandoned lion cubs in the Born Free Compound in Kenya. Adamson responded with an invitation to his 'Camp of Lions.'" The following year, Bryan and Chris produced a one-hour television documentary, *Father of the Lions*, recording their stay at the camp and featuring interviews with Adamson, then an old man on the verge of giving up the Kenya operation.

In 1988 Bryan retired early from Northwest to paint full time. He then embarked on various art odysseys, which took him to Pitcairn Island, where prints of his painting

HMS Bounty Approaches Pitcairn Island celebrating the 200th anniversary of the famous mutiny, were signed and stamped by descendants of the mutineers; to the North Pole with an expedition led by Will Steger; to China in search of lost aircraft that were part of the raids led by Colonel Jimmy Doolittle in 1942; to Romania, where he found and retrieved the remains of an American bomber shot down over the Ploesti Oilfields during World War II; and to New Guinea, where he lived with a native family while searching for yet another missing World War II warplane. When not traveling the world looking for new subjects to paint, Bryan works out of his studio in Frontenac, Minnesota, creating originals, prints, and stamps based on his research. On April 12, 1992, the *CBS Sunday Morning* television show with Charles Kurault carried a segment on his work with the Doolittle Raiders.

Though different people, both Moon brothers succeeded spectacularly well in life. As Alan Moon, Eric's younger son, has observed, "Despite coming from a very poor household, and having their father run away when they were very young, these two brothers beat the odds and were able to create very successful lives for themselves." What were the chances in the 1930s that these two lads from an unpromising working-class environment in Southampton, England, would grow up to achieve great success in their chosen fields? Are their attainments a matter of brains? Or diligence? Or luck? Or is there a biological imperative at work? Was the genetic mix created by the union of Ted Moon and Grace Scott so potent, so robust, so dynamic that any offspring would have been blessed innately with exceptional talent and vitality, virtually assuring success? No one has yet fully sorted out the nature-versus-nurture controversy, but it's difficult to resist the conclusion that the Moon-Scott gene pool contained the right stuff.

Grandparents and Uncle Scott

Grace's parents, James and Clara Scott, were also very much part of the Southampton household in which the Moon boys grew up. James, who sold tea for many years, died in 1940 and Clara followed some years later. Eric and his grandparents were chalk and cheese, completely lacking rapport. Moon: "They were terrible bastards, a royal pain in the ass, always bitching about me. My impression is that they always liked Bryan better than me. The old man I remember once coming at me with a knife. He had gone crazy by then, but the mother lived on for a long time. She was one of the real problems for my mother and her relationship with Jock; she never liked Jock and was constantly trying to drive a wedge between them and she eventually succeeded, breaking up their marriage." As might be expected, Bryan's memories of his grandparents differed sharply from Eric's: "I just remember our grandfather with great kindness. I was also devoted to our grandmother. It seems to me that they paid more attention to me than to Eric and my impression is that he did not feel as close to them as I did. Perhaps I was enjoying youngest member status."

Another member of the family was Grace's brother, known as Scott or Scotty, a play on his surname. As in the case of their grandparents, the Moon brothers had contradictory recollections of their uncle. Eric remembered him as "a real bum" who was "always at odds with Mother." He was also a bit daft, "a real kookie character. Once he took a job as a chauffeur when he didn't have a driver's license!" But the worst mark against Uncle Scott was his alleged pro–German sympathies in the 1930s. Though probably not a member of the British Union of Fascists (then the foremost fascist organization in Britain, led by the Hitlerite Sir Oswald Mosley), Scott became involved with a German woman just before the outbreak of war, prompting authorities to question his loyalty. Bryan, who loved his uncle, was distressed:

Scott was the father I never knew, but for reasons never clear to me Scott and Eric were distant. Just before World War II, Scott developed a relationship with a German lady. I think I met her once. It turned out she was a German agent and on the first day of World War II, Scott was arrested and taken away by two British Special Branch officers. I was devastated. He was interned without trial on the Isle of Man throughout the war with other suspected "sympathizers." While there, he married another German lady and soon after his release, they went to Canada. Scott taught me to paint. His wife died some years later and he lived an artist's life in Canada until he began to drink. I was able to rescue him from this and eventually he went to live in an old people's home in Hope, Canada.

Lucky Eric

Over the years Moon had more than his share of physical mishaps, both as man and boy, with nary a broken bone. As an adult he was in some scary automobile accidents in Canada, New Jersey, and Georgia, and in each instance he emerged — remarkably — with only cuts and bruises and no serious injuries. Lucky Eric's misadventures began as a youngster in Southampton: "I would have accidents that seemed so terrible that you couldn't image how I could emerge from them, and yet would never break a bone or anything. Mother said I would drive her to an early grave with the things I did." On one occasion he was at a boys' club camp during the summer at Exmouth in Devon on the south coast of England:

I had joined the boys' club and was very active in it. I was doing quite a bit of boxing then. One day some of us boys decided to climb a huge cliff that overlooked the ocean and the pavement at the beach. We were climbing and I got almost to the top — it must have been 300 feet — and grabbed a root and it came out in my hand. I fell all the way down, 300 feet, all the way through bushes, rocks, bouncing all the way down, and wound up unconscious on the sidewalk. I was taken off in an ambulance. I was absolutely covered with cuts, bruises, and had a hole in my shoulder. When I went home I didn't say a word to Mother. She said, "My God, what's happened to you? What did they do to you at this camp?" I told her I tripped over a tent peg. I never did tell her that I fell over a cliff.

Another time he was injured in a gang fight: "We were living in a pretty tough area of Southampton. I was part of a gang there. There was a rival gang around the corner, and on one occasion we had a 'showdown at OK Corral.' The other gang carried a huge pole, like a telephone pole. One of the kids heaved it, hitting me and knocking me into a ditch; blood was streaming everywhere. A woman came along and picked me up and carried me home. That was the end of my gang life." Yet another time, when out playing with some other boys, he cut his thumb severely with a Swiss Army knife while peeling a pear and was rushed to the hospital for treatment. His mother, who had not heard about the injury, saw one of the boys he had been with and asked where Eric was. "Oh, he cut his thumb off," was the casual answer, sending Mum into a state of near apoplexy.

Southampton: Gateway to the World

Southampton lies between the estuaries of two rivers, the Test and the Itchen, and has been a major British seaport since the Middle Ages. Located on the southern coast of England some 70 miles southwest of London, the city originated as a Roman settlement in A.D. 43. In Anglo-Saxon times its port served nearby Winchester, then the capital of England. In 1620 the Pilgrims embarked for America on the *Mayflower* from Southampton, and nearly 300 years later, on April 10, 1912, another historic ship, the *Titanic*, set sail for New York from the same waters on its doomed maiden voyage. For years the port, which boasts extensive dock facilities, shipyards, marine engineering works, and oil refineries, has been Britain's main conduit for transatlantic commercial and passenger traffic. Southampton's population —circa 200,000 — has remained relatively stable for more than a century.

The city prospered during the 1920s, principally because of a booming overseas trade and large-scale construction projects, including the Western Docks complex built between 1927 and 1933. Eric's stepfather worked at the docks and possibly his father after returning from Ocean Island — if Ted Moon actually did return. Early in the 1930s, however, the Depression set in and unemployment hit Southampton as hard or harder than the rest of the country. On October 19, 1932, for instance, 1,400 angry and dispirited men gathered outside Audit House (then the seat of city government) to protest the lack of work, some carrying signs proclaiming "Work Not Dole" and "No Work No Rates."

Despite hard times, Southampton proved an agreeable place for Eric to grow up. "It was a kind of marvelous town," he observed years later, looking back with affection on the city of his youth. Southampton's mix of raw commercialism, dockside coarseness, and cosmopolitan vistas gave it an allure and sense of expectation that quickened the spirit of an inquisitive, high-spirited lad like Eric, who dreamed of someday becoming someone — though who or what he was not at all sure. "I knew Southampton like the back of my hand," he remembered. During his boyhood and adolescence he and his family lived in several different sections of the city, including Millbrook down by the docks. There he could see the great cruise ships looming in the background like mammoth sea monsters, a sign over the entrance to the docks announcing: THE GATEWAY TO THE WORLD. Young Eric was awed: "I can remember riding on my bike along some of the roads there where the big ships were docked and seeing this enormous ship coming up out of what looked like the roadway, not far from our house. It was an overwhelming feeling."

Beyond Southampton's vast docks along the waterfront are the city's various neighborhoods with plangent names like Shirley, Northam, Redbridge, Bitterne Park, Woolston, the Polygon, and the aforementioned Millbrook. While the city suffered massive bomb damage during World War II, some medieval structures remain, including the Bargate, part of a 14th-century wall that enclosed the town during Norman times and is now one of its most prominent landmarks. In the middle of the city is the Common, a large park where Eric spent many hours as a boy and young man larking about on his bicycle and playing football — soccer to Americans. He never forgot one distinctive fact about the Common: "Its exact size was 365 acres, an acre for every day of the year."

He also got to know some of Southampton's pubs, especially those where he and Jock played darts; later as a young man he discovered others, including the Old Red Lion Inn, one of the city's best known watering holes. Another local landmark was the Dell, a football field very near Grace Beatson's last establishment on Burlington Road. "Mother had to put up with lots of ruffians on the way to and from games," he recalled. He and Bryan bought the house from their mother — the only one she ever owned — before she died in 1975, a kindness that relieved her of financial worries toward the end of her life.

Boys and Their Bicycles

Before automobiles became commonplace in England, "Southampton was very much a cycling town. Almost everyone had a bike," wrote local historian Eric Wyeth Gadd. He describes the scene in the early 20th century:

The bobby, in peaked cap and greatcoat, rode his high-framed Sunbeam. The dignified professional man pedaled along the Avenue between home and down-town shop or office. The doctor sped on two wheels between patients. The parson leaned his machine against his elderly parishioner's front garden wall. The awesome headmaster and his cap-touching pupil, "with satchel and shining morning face," dismounted together at the school gate as the summoning bell approached 9 o'clock. The suburban lady sat demurely behind her capacious wicker basket, her skirts protected by smart black chain-case and strings radiating from the rear hub. The lively young blade, crouching low over drop handle-bars, wove expertly in and out between horse-drawn vehicles and tramcars.

Motor cars ceased to be a rarity during Eric's teens, but many Sotonians — Southampton folk — continued their love affair with the bicycle well into the 1930s and beyond. Certainly most boys, even poor ones, had some sort of bike, and all ached for a shiny new one, young blade Eric Moon being no exception. Of course he never did receive the gleaming chrome-plated cycle from Jock for his 13th birthday, but his old battered wheels got lots of hard use. Moon: "Gangs of us boys would scream around on our bikes. I was involved with a group of guys who loved dirt track racing. We built a circular track with cinders in the middle of the Common. We had wild races and would rack up our bikes like crazy, tearing up tires, and so on." Eric's gang was known as the "dirt track crowd."

Early Sex

The pubescent Moon developed a strong and healthy interest in sex early on. One of Southampton's grammar schools for girls was just across the Common from where Eric spent much of his free time and where his own grammar school was located. This proximity naturally encouraged a certain amount of exploration between the sexes. "We boys would do whatever we could get away with," admitted Moon. "We did what teenage boys did."

The hypocritical sexual mores that characterized the Victorian and Edwardian Ages were still much in evidence in Britain during Eric's adolescence, but some men, especially working-class males, laughed at the rules; others had enlightened parents. Moon:

I never really felt that I was living in any repressive atmosphere as far as sex was concerned. I was very interested in girls very early. I think I even went to Sunday school one time because there was a girl I was very interested in — this was not a conversion to religion but purely sexual interest. This was when I was about ten. I don't remember my first sex, but it couldn't have been later than 13. And the first big love affair was right after I started at the library at 16. Girls were of great interest to me all the way through the teens.

Mum, said Eric, was "extremely permissive, liberated. Anything I did was OK, it was right. I don't remember her laying down the law about things. She was not difficult with me about things like that. I used to have a gramophone player in my bedroom and occasionally would have a girlfriend around, ostensibly to listen to music. Mother used to comment on the fact that sometimes one record seemed to be playing forever."

Taunton's School

Moon's formal education began at the Regent's Park Elementary School in Southampton. As an adult he had few specific recollections about the school. Only one teacher — Mr. Gale, who taught math and was known as "Blower" Gale — made an impression. Mostly he sensed that he was at a disadvantage at school due to having "lived overseas for all those years." But this memory does not square with the fact that he returned to England from Ocean Island at about age four, well before enrollment at Regent's Park.

Of major concern in elementary school was the "Eleven-Plus" examination, a one-day nationwide test given at the time to all students at age 11 to assess their potential for further education and suitability for scholarship assistance. Moon remembered, "I only had a few years to get through the exam, which determined your fate forever. If you did not pass that exam, you continued on in the regular schools and you emerged from those at 14 or 15 and became a working-class stiff or laborer or something like that." Fortunately Eric passed the exam, which allowed him to attend grammar (or secondary) school courtesy of the state on a means-tested scholarship. Of the several grammar schools for boys then in Southampton, Taunton's School was, according to

Moon, "thought to be the best of the lot." His boyhood friend, Bill Graham, went to King Edward VI School, another first-rate grammar school in the city, though it was decidedly second-best in Eric's competitive mind.

He spent five years (1934–1939) at Taunton's, entering at age 11 and leaving at 16. At that time the school, now called Taunton's College, was situated near the Southampton Common, familiar territory to Eric: "I used to travel across the Common on my bicycle to Taunton's, which was set almost at the back of the Common. I then lived at the other end of town." The boys all wore similar jackets to class and looked both scholarly and angelic at picture-taking time, though out of camera range some, Eric among them, required regular disciplining by the headmaster. "I was always in trouble," recalled Moon, thinking back on his mischievous exploits. At one point he was expelled from both art and music classes: "There was no possibility that I would ever learn anything in either of those subjects," so he made trouble until he got the boot. On another occasion, "I was thrown out of woodwork because this other student kept bugging me, so I hit him with a mallet. I was hauled up on the carpet by the headmaster for that one."

Of his teachers at Taunton's, Dr. Horace M. King was most memorable. An accomplished musician and dynamic personality, King later went into politics, serving in Parliament where he became Speaker of the House of Commons and ending his career in the House of Lords as Lord Maybray-King. Moon: "He was a big Labour Party man and a marvelous entertainer who played the piano. A great, great character." Interestingly, it was King who first encouraged Benny Hill, the British comedian best known for his off-color humor, to pursue a career as a funny man. Alfie Hill—he did not become Benny until he launched his career—was also a working-class kid from Southampton who attended Taunton's around the same time as Eric, though apparently their paths never crossed.

Despite his checkered deportment, the teaching staff at Taunton's quickly recognized Eric as a student with enormous potential, especially in the areas of language and math. He possessed excellent cognitive skills, a prodigious memory, and the ability to ace any test with minimal study. As his school days at Taunton's flew by, his biggest problem was not lack of academic promise or intellectual capability. It was sports, specifically tennis, which became an obsession:

I was always a pretty good student when I put my mind to it, but I could easily get distracted. In grammar school, I was supposed to be a star student, a candidate for a scholarship to Oxford or Cambridge or someplace like that, but later on I decided that tennis was my life. From 13 or 14 on, my whole focus was Wimbledon. I was a pretty good player, won a couple of tournaments, and for the last two years at Taunton's I spent many more hours bashing a furry white ball across a net than cracking the covers of books.

During one summer of tennis madness, he had the good fortune to find a partner in a young Frenchman, an exchange student at Taunton's. He not only played some demanding tennis with his new friend from across the Channel, he greatly expanded his French vocabulary: "I learned more French from him than I have learned any other way, especially about cussing and swearing in French." But excessive devotion to the sport took its toll academically, and his once auspicious matriculation at Taunton's School ended on a sour note:

> When school certificate results came in, I got hauled over the carpet again by the headmaster. He said I should have done much better had I not wasted all my time on tennis. I had probably the best marks in the school in German, French, English, and math. These were my strengths; everything else was incidental. But I had to have two other subjects to get my school certificate, so I got a pass in history and a weak pass in chemistry and physics, which meant I had only just scraped through."

Books and Reading

Because of his later prominence in the library world it might be assumed that Moon read widely as a youngster, that he knew and loved the classics of children's literature. Not so. When not studying or playing tennis or riding his bicycle or engaged in activities with girls, he was boxing or playing darts or football or otherwise horsing around with his friends. He was not keen on reading when young, nor were books abundant in the home, though Jock had done his bit with the plays of Bernard Shaw.

Most of what Moon read as a boy he later described as "junky kid's stuff," such as juvenile magazines and especially Billy Bunter comic books. The latter were weekly illustrated stories by Frank Richards (a pseudonym for Charles Hamilton) about a fat boy's irreverent adventures at school. They achieved wild popularity among young people in England in the 1930s, but were condemned by educators as a bad influence on youth. Still, Eric was in good company: "At my private school," recalled Evelyn Waugh, "the Billy Bunter stories were contraband and I read them regularly with all the zeal of law-breaking."

Later Moon graduated to Leslie Charteris mysteries featuring the Saint. He did not become a serious reader until after going to work at the Southampton Public Library, when he became part of a group of young people concerned with serious ideas and better literature. Moon always maintained that reading "junk lit" in his youth did him no harm, and who is to dispute the claim? Certainly not the thousands upon thousands of other successful people in England, who cut their literary teeth on schoolboy comics. From young man through his retirement years, Moon remained a devoted fan of the detective story, the novels of Florida author John D. MacDonald and his creation, Travis McGee, particular favorites.

Why Not University?

While at Taunton's, Moon accepted the fact that he, an impecunious scholarship student from a working-class home, realistically had little chance for a university education in the Britain of the late 1930s, no matter what his academic record:

> If I had wanted to go on to university, I would have had to stay two more years at Taunton's. I was in the upper fifth form when I left; had I stayed, I would have gone into

the upper sixth form, then taken the exam for university. The headmaster urged me to continue in school and then take the exam, but I said my mother had been supporting me for a long, long time and was not in the kind of circumstances that would allow her to support me for another two years and then on to university for four more years.

At the time he had only an inchoate sense of the unfairness of the system, which excluded some of the brightest people in the country from higher education. It was the way things were; it was the way the system worked; it was the only way he knew and he had no means to change it. Besides, as a teenager, he had more to worry about than life's cosmic inequities. His concern was to find a job, to earn his keep, to be on his own. Only later, as an adult with mature political sensibilities, did Moon comprehend the harm the class-bound British educational system caused him and others in his situation. Whereas society's privileged few — those born with wealth and position — would go on to Oxford and Cambridge more or less automatically regardless of intellectual capacity or academic achievement, he was forced into the workplace, taking a job that earned next to nothing.

In a speech in 1977 at a seminar sponsored by the State Library of New York, Moon engaged in a bit of autobiographical reminiscence that goes to the heart of the matter: "These were the thirties and a poor boy from the working class, no matter what his academic and scholarship potential, could rarely afford the extravagance of elite and expensive institutions like Oxford and Cambridge. His early contribution to the family budget — or the removal of his drain upon it — was mandatory." Only after World War II and the election of a Labour government with an overwhelming mandate for social change did the educational system in the UK finally become more egalitarian. But by then it was too late for Moon and his generation.

On the bright side his forced entry into the real world at age 16 meant that Moon went to work in a library. Had he gone on to university, as doubtless he would have today, he almost certainly would not have become a librarian, thus denying the profession one of its most creative and influential figures since James Duff Brown's day in Britain and Melvil Dewey's in North America.

– 2 –

Entering Librarianship

September 4, 1939

In the summer of 1939 young Moon prepared to leave Taunton's armed with his school certificate and the good wishes of his headmaster ("I wasn't entirely in the doghouse at school"). He was determined to find work in Southampton, but jobs were scarce, the worldwide Depression hanging on like a stubborn canker. In addition, many believed Europe was on the road to war, which created even more economic uncertainty. Germany, now under the domination of Adolf Hitler, the fascist leader who came to power in 1933, seized Austria in March 1938 without a struggle. Six months later the Germans annexed the Sudetenland in western Czechoslovakia, a diplomatic coup engineered at a meeting of major European heads of state in Munich where Hitler gave assurances that after the Sudetenland he had no further territorial ambitions. Relieved, the British prime minister, Neville Chamberlain, rushed home to declare that "peace in our time" had been secured. But in March 1939 (the month Moon turned 16) the German dictator gobbled up the rest of Czechoslovakia and then turned his attention, ominously, to Poland.

Moon looked to the public sector for work. "Jobs were not easy to come by," he recalled. "Among the most desirable in those years were those occasionally offered by local government departments. The pay was awful, but they offered what seemed then equally valuable attractions—security and respectability." His first job interview took place in August: "I was sent off by the headmaster with a recommendation to the Southampton borough treasurer," who had a junior clerkship open. Because of his proficiency with numbers, Moon seemed a promising candidate, but he apparently made a bad impression and failed to get the job: "By some stroke of fortune I failed to get past the interview. I think the pin-striped gent who conducted it regarded my passion for tennis as a sign of instability which would surely lead to some future violation of his black-bound ledgers."

His next interview, however, not only landed him the job, a junior library assistant position paying a meager £56 a year (about $225 at the time), it determined the type of work he would do for the rest of his life. Obviously in 1939 he had no inkling that a momentous choice — if choice it really was — had been made. What interested him most at the time was the politics of the hiring process:

Back at school my initial failure in the job market was met with resignation, but a couple of days later I was sent off with another letter of recommendation — this one on the basis of my second subject strength, English — to the Southampton borough librarian. When I arrived for the interview I discovered there were 13 candidates for four jobs, and one of the candidates was the chief librarian's son. I doubt that I knew the word nepotism then but my instincts told me I had only a one-in-four chance. However, I hadn't yet learned about sexual discrimination. Apart from the chief librarian's son, I was the only other male candidate — perhaps because librarianship was thought of by many as a "sissy" job, a matter that caused me, the macho sportsman, some little disquiet. At any rate we were both, the chief's son and I, appointed, along with what we both agreed were the two best looking of the other 11 candidates.

Though pleased to have found a job so quickly, Moon had little time to reflect on his good fortune. He was instructed to report for work at the library on the first Monday in September. Meanwhile, the nation watched anxiously as Hitler struck again. On Friday, September 1, Germany invaded Poland, using surprise, superior weaponry, and lightning speed to overwhelm an antiquated Polish army. Two days later, on Sunday morning, September 3, Britain and France, both pledged to defend Poland, declared war on Germany: BRITAIN AND FRANCE IN WAR AT 6 A.M.; HITLER WON'T HALT ATTACK ON POLES; CHAMBERLAIN CALLS EMPIRE TO FIGHT screamed the front page of *The New York Times*.

The next day — Monday, September 4, 1939, the day after World War II broke out — Eric Moon began his library career.

Of course he had no idea what lay ahead on that dark day. On the most superficial level he was gratified to be alive and employed. Deeper down he wondered what the war would mean for him, his family and friends, his country. Being young, he found it impossible not to be optimistic. Like a fly in sugar he was poised to partake of the bounty life had to offer. Despite the perilous times he did not think about dying — he was still immortal. Viscerally he sensed that life would go on, war or no war, and that the job he was about to start might, with luck, allow him to recoup some of what he had forfeited by not continuing in school and competing for a place at university: "I left school at 16 — and it was perhaps more than coincidence that I became a librarian, because I already knew, with instinctive conviction, that it was only on those dim and dusty old shelves that education, or my only chance at it, really lay."

Southampton Public Library

Prior to 1938 Southampton's main public library was located in a large Carnegie-style brick building at the junction of London Road and Cumberland Place. Built in 1892 the Victorian edifice "had long outgrown its usefulness and was staffed mainly with unqualified staff," according to Bill Graham, Southampton's reference librarian for many years until his retirement in 1974 and Moon's oldest friend and professional colleague. In 1938 the main library moved to the city's new Civic Centre, an imposing white Portland stone structure that housed all departments of local government, along with an art gallery and the Southampton School of Art. Located in the heart of the city, the new library pleased most users though the public service staff had a few reservations. Bill Graham: "Although clean and new, the library was in some ways unsatisfactory, being too small from the start. For example, the reference library was a light, airy room with many windows (to conform to the overall Civic Centre design), but the room lacked wall space for books; much staff time was spent ferrying books to and from the stacks."

During this time Southampton Public Library was one of the larger and better regarded municipal libraries in England, consisting of the central library at the Civic Centre and half a dozen or so branches in neighborhoods throughout the city. The system had about 50 employees, ranging from the chief librarian and professional staff down to clerical and maintenance personnel. It was, Moon remembered, "a pretty exceptional staff. In retrospect, I recognize that I was lucky to start at Southampton, because it was one of those key libraries in the country that many of the future leaders went through, like Manchester, Sheffield, and Westminister. My impression was that the stars of the library were the departmental people."

The reference department particularly impressed junior assistant Moon, who even at that early point had a sharp eye for library talent. Eric Clough, head of the department and the number three man in the library's administrative hierarchy, was a nationally known figure in British librarianship, eventually serving as president of both the Library Association and the Association of Assistant Librarians, the UK's two most important library organizations. When Moon became president of the American Library Association in 1976, Clough wrote proudly to remind him that "the Reference Library at Southampton now has the unusual distinction of having had on its staff a President of both the American and British Library Associations."

Other members of the reference department included Bill Graham, who was a year older than Moon and started working at the library in 1938 directly out of grammar school; Terry Delaney, a dashing Irishman who sported great locks of wavy reddish hair and later became a BBC producer; Hubert (Bumble) Humby, a short, dark, intelligent fellow with a theatrical flair; and Joe Morant, described by Graham as "a lovable man with an acid wit and a fondness for drink; after a liquid lunch he would return to work smelling of cachous to sweeten his breath." Moon remembered Morant not so much for his drinking habits as his potent pipe tobacco: "Joe was older than most of the others. He smoked this navy plug tobacco—black stuff soaked in rum. The staff was very impressed with that. So I went to him for advice when I decided I wanted to smoke a pipe. He advised me to get some strong stuff, and I got very sick the first time I smoked."

The cataloging (or technical services) department was headed by H.V. (Harold) Bonny, who later achieved international recognition for his work with UNESCO setting up demonstration libraries in developing countries. Moon received a lesson in attention to detail from Bonny when he briefly worked in the department: "My only memory of Bonny is that I was given a whole bunch of catalog cards to type. At the end of the day he came over and looked through my cards one by one and tore up about every third one because it wasn't perfect. 'We will have nothing but perfection in this department,' he said. 'Do them again.' And I did. There was no choice." After the war, John Bristow, an up-and-coming young librarian, replaced Bonny as head cataloger. Another shining light in the department was Paddy Martin, a bright, lively young woman who became Bill Graham's wife.

The library's deputy director was Lawrence (Larry) Burgess, then arguably England's foremost authority on the Bliss Classification, a method of organizing library materials similar to the better known Dewey Decimal Classification. First introduced in 1908 by Henry Evelyn Bliss, an American librarian, and now little used, the Bliss system gained modest acceptance in Britain during the first half of the century when approximately 50 libraries adopted it. A retiring figure, Larry Burgess came across, in the words of Bill Graham, as "a brilliant scholar and an eccentric, more suited for academic work than the harsh realities of public libraries." Still, his expertise added luster to the Southampton staff.

Not so impressive, at least in the opinion of junior assistant Moon, was the library's chief, Robert (Bob) Lynn. Well before Moon's arrival on the scene, Lynn had been appointed director over Burgess, a source of lasting friction between the two men. Bill Graham: "The animosity engendered was to remain between them through all the years they served together. For the most part Lynn ignored Burgess and very often bypassed him, working straight to the heads of departments." A private man, Lynn rarely interacted with members of the clerical staff except when they were summoned to his upstairs office. For Moon this usually meant trouble: "The intercom would say, '*Send Moon up*,' and I knew that was not good." He did, however, become friends with Ron Lynn, the director's son. They were roughly the same age and had started at the library on the same day. "I spent some time at the Lynns' house because of Ron and was therefore probably better known to the chief librarian than any other junior assistant in the system, aside from Ron. But I think for that reason he always leaned on me kind of hard, because he didn't want to show any favoritism toward his son's friend."

Junior Assistant Moon

Almost from the beginning Moon decided he would work toward professional qualification in the field of librarianship, which in the United Kingdom (unlike North America) did not require a college or university degree. The first step in this lengthy process involved passing the Elementary (or Entrance) Examination, a standard test administered by the Library Association to determine mastery of basic library principles and procedures. To prepare, Moon completed several correspondence courses offered by the Association of Assistant Librarians and easily passed the exam in late 1940. But the following March, after turning 18, he enlisted in the air force, thus placing any career goals on hold indefinitely. Not until seven years later, after the end of the war and after he had married, would Moon again turn his attention to becoming a librarian.

When he started at Southampton Public on that cheerless September day in 1939 he was the lowest form of British library life, a junior assistant (or entry-level clerk). He first worked in the lending (or circulation) department of the central library at the Civic Centre where a principal duty was checking books in and out. He became intimately familiar with the Browne Charging System, then the most popular circulation system in British libraries. An entirely manual operation, Browne was slow and cumbersome, entailing working with small, tatty paper tickets in long wooden trays. Many years ago this author worked in an English public library and remembers Browne with distaste: "The system ... works by issuing little pocket-like tickets to readers, and when a book is borrowed the book's card is placed in the reader's ticket. Filing these tickets and, worse, finding them when the book is returned, is incredibly slow business. Staff time is wasted in endless grubbing around in endless trays of little tickets; all the while, the patron is stoically waiting, sometimes in a seemingly endless queue. The whole process would drive a time-and-motion study man 'stark staring bonkers,' as the English say."

Moon also spent a fair amount of time shelving books, donkeywork that he came to view as valuable training for apprentices in the library field: "Much of my time was spent shelving books. I think personally it would benefit all librarians if they had to spend a good part of their early career doing just that. They might learn more about their book stock than most of them seem to know now. That's how I learned about book stock — I would go around the shelves with these great armfuls of books, shelving."

Not all his time and energy went into such productive work. As happened at Taunton's, Moon regularly got into trouble with his superiors. His friend Bill Graham remembered one particular personality clash: "Eric spent his time in the central lending library, which was ruled by an unqualified middle-aged spinster — the daughter of a former chief librarian who was short on librarianship but strong on petty discipline. Obviously the sparks flew between her and Eric." On one occasion he came to work in a turtleneck sweater instead of the required shirt and tie. He tried to bluff his way out of this rule violation. Moon: "The lending librarian, an older lady named Miss Hopwood, thought this was most improper. Apparently my infraction got back to the chief librarian, Bob Lynn, and I was sent upstairs for a scolding. I tried to talk my way out of it by telling him that I had only two shirts and both were in the wash, but he didn't buy that." (Years later, when Moon was a deputy chief librarian in the London area, he had to deal with a clerk who claimed to own only *one* shirt!)

Another time he got into the proverbial soup over some mischievous reader's advisory work:

When I was shelving, this old lady used to bug me all the time. She would always say, "Have you got a nice book for me, son?" I would try to find her something, but after awhile I became impatient and frustrated by her. I'm going to get her, I thought. So I gave her *Forever Amber*! The juiciest novel of the day! Well, she came in and created hell. I was hauled up on the carpet before the chief librarian, who asked, "Didn't I have better judgment than that?" I said I thought it was a nice book.

Moon worked too for short periods in the reference and cataloging departments, but as his transgressions piled up he was eventually transferred — exiled — from the central library to the branch at Woolston, a dangerous neighborhood at the time. He had no illusions why he was banished to Woolston:

I was sent to Woolston with Dickie Denton, who was the best man at my first marriage. We were both sent there as punishment. It was really a crummy old branch right on the banks of the river within sight of the Spitfire factory in Southampton. Because of that, the Germans practically bombed Woolston into oblivion; the library was never hit, but everything around it looked like pictures of Berlin after the allied bombing. I remember Dickie and I used to come in every morning and every book in the library would be on the floor. We'd spend practically all day getting them back in some order and the next morning they would be back on the floor again. So it was a real punishment being sent to Woolston.

Later, before enlisting in the RAF, he also worked briefly at the Shirley branch.

Wild and Wonderful Readers

In some respects public libraries have changed little since Moon worked at Southampton Public more than half a century ago. Certainly patrons—"readers" or "borrowers" in British library parlance — have remained much the same. As in Moon's day, most are reasonably sane, literate people who go about using the library without fuss or fanfare. On the other hand there are always a few who stand out for one reason or another. Every librarian who ever worked with the public has "war" stories, and Moon, an accomplished raconteur, loved telling his:

There was a man called Willy Painter, who was an habitué of the central reference library. A little man with Coke-bottle thick glasses, he had a passion for the largest books in the library, like back volumes of the London *Times*, which were physically huge. He would sit there and just turn the pages; he never read anything but he loved to turn the pages.

Another "marvelous character" was a man whose real name was Julius Caesar:

Julius was definitely a little cracked. Somehow during the early months of the war he got himself enrolled in the auxiliary police. He would come into the library in his new uniform, complete with cape, and announce in a loud voice that "Caesar is here!" On one particular day, Julius came into the library, announced "Caesar is here!" and threw open his cape — he didn't have a stitch on underneath!

And then there was a memorable incident involving a dropped "h" that occurred during Moon's short stint at the Shirley branch:

We got a bulletin from the central library saying too many errors were being made in pulling out the Browne tickets when checking in books — tickets were being given to the wrong readers. In order to counteract this problem, when we discharged a book we were instructed to look at the ticket and say the reader's name aloud before we gave it back, as a double check. I was a young lad on the desk at the branch and about the second day we were doing this, this rather raunchy looking older woman came in and I pulled her ticket and said "Adcock?"— the name on the ticket. And she said with a great twinkle, "Yes, son, and I've loved it."

The Battle of Britain and the Blitz

All the while young Moon was learning the rudiments of library work in Southampton, the United Kingdom was at war, standing alone against the Nazis. During his first seven months at the library, the belligerents remained deceptively quiet. Then World War II began in earnest.

After Britain and France declared war on Germany in September 1939, the two sides avoided direct military confrontation until the spring of the following year—a period the press dubbed the "Phony War" and Evelyn Waugh, the writer, described as "that odd, dead period before the Churchillian renaissance, which people called at the time the Great Bore War." But by April and May of 1940, Hitler was on the march, invading and conquering Denmark, Norway, Belgium, Luxembourg, and the Netherlands in quick succession. On May 10 Winston Churchill began the renaissance Waugh spoke of, replacing Neville Chamberlain as prime minister. Between May 26 and June 4 the Germans drove the British military from continental Europe, forcing evacuation of more than 300,000 troops from the beaches of Dunkirk, a seaport on the English Channel in northern France. Days later France fell, the vaunted Maginot Line a dud in the face of blitzkrieg; the Nazis goose-stepped into Paris on June 14. Hitler then went after Britain full-bore, ordering the German air force, the Luftwaffe, to bomb the island nation into submission as prelude to a seaborne invasion.

The Battle of Britain began in mid–June 1940 and continued well into the fall of that year. The Luftwaffe conducted daylight attacks against the RAF and its bases around the country in an all-out effort to destroy British air power. When the RAF prevailed (thanks mainly to first-class fighter planes and effective use of radar), Hitler reluctantly called off the planned invasion but not the air assault. The Luftwaffe continued its attacks, switching to mostly night raids, blasting both military and civilian targets in London and other major cities, including Southampton. Soon, Hitler reckoned, the British would become weary and demoralized and sue for peace. This was the Blitz—thunderous sorties that continued without let up until May 1941.

Southampton was among the most heavily bombed cities during the Blitz, not only because of its strategic importance as a major port but also because the main plant that manufactured the Spitfire fighter plane was located on the banks of the Test river in the Woolston area. Without the Spitfire—renowned for its speed, rapid acceleration, and tight turning capability—the RAF would not have been able to stymie the Luftwaffe during the Battle of Britain, and increased production of the plane was vital to continuing the war effort. Fortunately, though the Germans blasted Woolston repeatedly and with great intensity, the Spitfire factory survived intact. Moon was an eyewitness: "The Germans made every effort they could to bomb that thing; they didn't seem to be very good because they bombed the shit out of both sides of the river but never hit the factory."

At the height of the Blitz in November and December 1940 the Luftwaffe unloaded on Southampton around the clock. Moon recalled the center of the city was "completely decimated by the air raids. You have to remember that England during the early stages of the war had very little in the way of defense. The Spitfire was only just beginning to go into large-scale production. Defense was quite fragmentary. We had these barrage balloons all over town; they were the main things we had to keep the German bombers off a bit." Barrage balloons—large inflated devices that floated on long steel wires—helped prevent German aircraft from flying low over the city and ships in the harbor. The scene resembled a Macy's Day Parade from hell. Moon participated directly in another defensive measure, fire-watching: "During the early years of the war, all library staff enrolled in fire-watching duty. This meant you spent some nights actually sleeping in one of the libraries so that if it got hit by a bomb or something, someone was there to report the damage and get help. I fire-watched at several libraries, and was also on duty at the top of a tower at the Civic Centre the night the first land mines were floated down over Southampton."

The Blitz touched the lives of everyone in Southampton one way or another. The incessant bombing terrorized the people, indiscriminately killing and injuring civilians and destroying property all over the city. Moon, who continued to live at home while working at the library, vividly remembered his parents' home being hit by an incendiary bomb that "landed in the middle of Mother's bed" around Christmastime in 1940. He ran about half a mile to borrow a ladder, needed to put out the fire. Later someone "snatched the ladder right out from under Jock, who was left hanging from the bedroom window." Owing to the government's foresight, thousands of youngsters, including Eric's brother Bryan, then 12, were evacuated to safe areas in the countryside.

Hands Across the Clock

Toward the end of 1940 an observer described Southampton as "broken in spirit," and an official government report dated December 9, 1940, bluntly stated, "The strongest feeling in Southampton today is the feeling that Southampton is finished. Many will not say this openly, but it is a deep-seated feeling that has grown in the past fortnight." Such conclusions were wrong; the city refused to quit. But for a time it was touch and go. Perhaps the darkest hour was when the Civic Centre received a direct hit. The library came through the ordeal relatively unscathed but the art gallery and art school were partially destroyed and many people, mostly young students, lost their lives. Moon was on duty at the library that awful afternoon:

As far as I'm concerned, this was the most traumatic incident of that whole period. I was on the desk in the middle of the afternoon and the sirens went off and we were all ordered down to the shelters below. The library was on one side of the Civic Centre, while the art gallery and art school filled the other whole wing of this huge building. I was in the shelter toward the end of the library section when, about half a dozen yards beyond me, everything collapsed. I went to see what I could do to help. I was in there, oh, all afternoon and evening and through the night, helping to dig out bodies, most of them children in the art school. It was gruesome. We could see them down the line, some of them drowning because the pipes had burst; the water was flooding in before we could get to them. It was absolutely gruesome.

When I came up to the library the next morning, the clock over the circulation desk had stopped with its hands at a quarter to three, the exact time of the attack the day before. Later, I wrote a piece called "Hands Across the Clock" describing the incident, but unfortunately it never got published.

Another regret: "Hands Across the Clock" no longer exists, a casualty of Moon's peripatetic life during and after the war.

The Group

Between the time he started at the library in September 1939 and entered the military in March 1941 Moon's life changed dramatically in several ways. First, he went from grammar school student to wage earner — boy to man — practically overnight, a big adjustment for any young person. Actually Eric relished earning his own way, even if his salary was small. In the same vein he welcomed leaving behind the regimentation and discipline of the classroom — though he soon discovered the library workplace had its own rules that, while different from those at school, were often just as irksome. Second, he found himself in the midst of a terrifying war, a conflict with seemingly no end and a relentless enemy that sought to blast him and all those he cared about into oblivion. The war's oppressive proximity engendered adult feelings of apprehension, confusion, and revulsion new to him. And third, this was the time he became part of a circle of friends in Southampton passionately interested in the arts, particularly literature and the theater. As a core member of this lively group, which consisted primarily but not exclusively of library staff members, he began thinking seriously for the first time about things literary and cultural. Not since Jock had conned him into reading Shaw at age 13 had Moon felt so alive intellectually.

The group — which quickly metamorphosed into the Group — read and discussed contemporary writers, many of them new to Moon, including such diverse voices as D.H. Lawrence, André Malraux, W.H. Auden, and Christopher Isherwood. For the first time he read Thomas Hardy, who impressed him mightily, and became acquainted with cutting-edge American authors, Steinbeck, Hemingway, and Faulkner among the most esteemed. Favorite playwrights were Elmer Rice, Clifford Odets, and Maxwell Anderson (for whom Moon's first son was named). Each of these writers articulated a spirit of revolt against the values of the previous generation, a theme the Group found appealing. Called the "pylon boys" by disapproving critic Stephen Spender, writers favored by the left-leaning Group emphasized the most unattractive features of life in the 1930s — regimented, dehumanizing factories; ugly, ubiquitous towers (or pylons) strung together with electric power cables; rampant despoilment of the natural landscape; industrial greed and insensitivity to workers — while idealizing the proletariat and laboring-class values. Spender complained the pylon boys had "ganged up and captured the decade."

Members of the Group encouraged one another to write stories and poetry, which were sometimes read aloud when the gang got together at a pub or someone's home. For Moon, who possessed a solid grammar school education but previously had not read widely nor been inclined to write creatively, becoming part of the Group "was like emerging into a new world." Though he still enjoyed sports, playing tennis and boxing when he could and developing a wicked game of table tennis, his new friends opened up a wider vista: for the first time he could appreciate the possibilities of the life of the mind.

In addition to Moon, principal members of the coterie included Terry Delaney, Bill Graham, Paddy Martin, Bumble Humby, and Joyce Rackham, all from the library, and a fascinating fellow named John Arlott, then a youthful police constable in Southampton. Nine years older than Moon, Arlott later achieved considerable fame as a cricket announcer and poetry presenter for the BBC. Moon remembered him vividly:

> Arlott was a policeman at the time we first met him, but he was a very heavy library user, so he became known to all of us and became part of the Group. We would write poetry and read it to each other. Bill Graham thought Arlott was the worst poet of the bunch, but he was the one who got published. He also gave Workers' Educational Association lectures all over town. He would ride his bicycle, which had a basket at the front with books in it, and read on his way to a lecture.
>
> With the money he made from his lecturing, he bought first editions of English poetry, which he would send to the authors and ask them to sign; so he built up the greatest collection in England of signed first editions of English poets, and in this process became known to publishers and poets. He used this connection to publish a poetry anthology. As a result of that John subsequently became a poetry producer for the BBC, after which he became the greatest sportscaster and cricket commentator the BBC ever had. He became quite a celebrity.

Arlott, who died in 1991, never changed his distinctive Hampshire "burr" (or accent), which became his trademark, an obituary in *The Guardian* (December 16, 1991) noting that he had "probably the most celebrated British voice after Churchill's."

It was Terry Delaney, however, who had the strongest influence on Moon at the time: "Terry, along with Paddy Martin, did the most to indoctrinate me into a great enthusiasm for American literature. This is when I started reading Farrell, Steinbeck, Faulkner, Hemingway. Terry was thoroughly knowledgeable about American literature." In fact, he idolized Delaney, summed up in Arlott's autobiography, *Basingstoke Boy*, as a bon vivant "addicted to beer, football, cricket, and the young life." Like Arlott, Delaney was older than Moon, and he knew how to manage himself socially, had plenty of women, and was politically on the far left — important measures of a man's character in the eyes of the still impressionable teenage Moon.

The Group also put on skits and plays to help boost morale among Southampton's war-weary residents. Eric usually had a prominent role in these amateur productions:

> In those early war years when Southampton was being heavily bombed, we started to put on shows in some of the big air-raid shelters where people were living — actually living — because they had been bombed out of their homes. We would put them on in the

shelters and in small halls around the bombed areas. They were kind of fun; we put on corny Victorian melodramas, hammy stuff. In one play, Bumble replaced an actress who had fallen ill backstage; when he appeared on stage, I had to make up the dialogue for the next five minutes!

This sort of experience later proved invaluable when Moon became a stage entertainer in the RAF.

People in the Group cared about literature, theater, poetry, and writing, but they also liked to have fun. Moon and Bill Graham sometimes went on a pub crawl and then to the soccer game to watch the Saints, Southampton's football team. Sex and romance also figured in the Group's activities. Moon later recalled that his "first big love affair was right after I started at the library at 16," Joyce Rackham, a library assistant and member of the Group, his "first serious girlfriend in libraries." He also had a close, albeit platonic, relationship with an older woman on the staff named Patsy Quinn. "She was an Irish lady with a great biting sense of humor who took me under her wing for awhile. I liked her a lot, but she wasn't part of my social group."

Goodbye to the Library—for Now

As soon as he turned 18 Moon enlisted in the RAF, leaving his job at the Southampton Public Library where he had worked for a year and half. This initial period at the library had been an eventful and fruitful time for him. His position as a junior assistant, lowly though it was, gave him a glimpse of a professional future. His first-hand encounters with war instilled in him a fatalism that would remain strong for the rest of his life. And his new-found interest in literature and the stage, kindled by a company of spirited friends, started him on the road to intellectual maturity.

– 3 –

Defending Home and Country

Lucky Eric Goes to War

Moon made it through World War II without so much as a scratch, except perhaps scuffed knees suffered on the soccer fields of India. Not only did he not engage a single enemy, he never actually saw one. In fact, Moon's wartime experience after volunteering for military service following his 18th birthday in March 1941 consisted as much of fun and games as it did soldiering: "I was either acting or playing table tennis or soccer throughout most of the war. For me, it was not altogether an unpleasant war. I was as concerned as anyone about the outcome, but I was never involved in any fighting. The nearest I got to it was in Calcutta where the Indian independence movement was beginning to be rather rambunctious." Paradoxically, during the war years he was in greater danger as a civilian at home in Southampton than at anytime while in uniform.

Moon chose to serve in the RAF (pronounced either R-A-F or Raff), enlisting as an Aircraftman Second Class, the force's lowest rank. A number of his coworkers at Southampton Public did the same, with Bill Graham leading the way: "I think I was the first to leave, being called up in October 1939," remembered Graham. "Eric Moon, Eric Clough, and John Bristow all followed into the RAF. Bob Lynn's son, a friend of Eric's, was also called into the RAF." Initially Moon wanted to be a RAF pilot — they were the stars of the Battle of Britain, forever memorialized in Churchill's stirring tribute, "Never in the field of human conflict was so much owed by so many to so few" — but for reasons no longer clear he did not become one. Moon: "I can't remember why I didn't get accepted for pilot training. They told me they would consider me for navigator, but I didn't want to be a navigator, so I turned it down and became just part of the ground crew." The decision probably saved his life: a RAF pilot's longevity averaged about three months in the early 1940s and a navigator's chances weren't much better.

Instead of flying, he became a wireless (or radiotelegraphy) operator, receiving his training at a base in Blackpool, a seaside resort described many years later by a thoroughly Americanized Moon as "the Atlantic City of England." Though wireless operators obviously lacked the chic of the chaps who flew the Spitfires and the Hurricanes, everyone in the air force enjoyed a certain cachet. The RAF mystique, he discovered, "rubbed off to some extent on everybody else. The uniforms were blue instead of khaki. There was a certain status."

Eastern Brothers

Royal Air Force or no, like many new recruits Moon disdained the military culture, particularly its petty rules and discipline. Ronald Benge, a well-known British librarian and Moon contemporary, articulated the antagonism felt by many young soldiers in his memoir, *Confessions of a Lapsed Librarian*: "My individualism had rendered me almost unfit for military consumption. Automatically, when they said turn right, I turned left. It was all symbolized by boots: formerly I had worn sandals and now there were these enormous weights, which had to be not only worn but polished and, if one did it properly, spat upon." Moon got a taste of this spit-and-polish mindset in basic training and decided that not only didn't he care for it, he bloody well was going to find a way around it:

Before we went to Blackpool we spent some weeks doing that kind of drill in basic training. I learned very quickly that was not the kind of shit I wanted to be doing very much of. As soon as I got to Blackpool I found a way out of that. The way out was to have rather more important things to do. I decided that if I was going to get anything out of this war, the thing to do was to find some pursuit other than the usual crap that goes on in the services where the mentality was that if you're not busy we'll find something useless for you to do.

Once in Blackpool, Moon settled into the business of training as a wireless operator, which included mastering Morse code, while at the same time hitting on the "pursuit" that, he hoped, would enable him to escape the usual military dreck: he became an entertainer to the troops. Harkening back to the hammy plays he and his friends in the Group had put on in bomb shelters in Southampton, he hooked up with a fellow airman, whose name is lost to history, to form an act called the Eastern Brothers, a take-off on the Western Brothers, then a popular British comedy team of two chinless upper-class types who specialized in raunchy humor. There were, explained Moon, "all kinds of little entertainments going on encouraged by the RAF. Most of the troopers were rather bored, there being very little to do outside of training. Things were pretty much shut down, remember, because of the blackouts due to the bombing. They asked for volunteers to do a show, and I got together with this guy and we worked out a routine."

Recalled as "pseudo-sophisticated comedy," the routine involved a mixture of songs, jokes, send-ups, and repartee, much like an old-time English music hall act. Moon and his partner wrote their own material, drawing on light news of the day and topics of universal interest to servicemen — sex and lavatory habits were staples. The Eastern Brothers' early efforts received good notices and before long they were invited to perform at the big Sunday RAF show held at the Blackpool opera house, a spacious theater that seated more than 3,000. Moon was ecstatic; this was the big break; stardom beckoned!

"The show was full of big-name pros at the time: Henry Hall's orchestra; Max Miller, the Cheeky Chappie, who was a famous, very dirty comedian of the day; lots of other big-name people. The whole thing was run by the head of RAF Entertainment, who used to be a very famous organist; he's the guy who booked us."

But the muses did not smile on the Eastern Brothers that Sunday at the big RAF show before a packed house of fighting men seeking a little lighthearted relief from their circumscribed lives. Severe stage fright on the part of Moon's sidekick sank the act. Moon: "The curtain went up, the music started, and my partner's mouth was opening and closing but nothing was coming out—*nothing* at all. This continued, I believe, for two or three minutes. I was dying, and this guy is beside me and nothing is coming out, until finally it emerged. When we walked off, sweat was dripping off my fingers, I was so scared."

A number of British comedians (Tommy Cooper and Dick Emery among them) discovered their calling on similar stages at military bases during World War II. Like Moon, they started as amateurs, young servicemen with a flair for creating and acting in home-made entertainments, and progressed from there. After the war Moon briefly considered acting as a career, until marriage and dicey nerves dissuaded him. But while based at Blackpool he put his natural histrionic talents to good use. Though the debacle at the Sunday RAF show left a painful memory, he decided to carry on, sans his tongue-tied partner. Being an entertainer had too many perks for him to quit just because of one bad performance: "One of the great things about being in show business was that I got all kinds of exemptions from usual discipline. For example, I used to carry chits, one of which said, 'This airman does not have to have his hair cut.' I had another chit saying I didn't have to be in by curfew and so on. So it had its advantages."

Chorus Girls

Moon sometimes missed wireless classes due to "all the showbiz stuff." One time shortly after the demise of the Eastern Brothers he "went on the road for awhile with a line of chorus girls, emceeing shows around the Blackpool area." During this gig he became friendly—in the biblical way—with one of the girls, which ended in a farce worthy of a B movie. When they got back to Blackpool Moon discovered his lady love "lived in a sumptuous apartment overlooking the ocean. I was up there one evening with her and in walks a wing commander! Her husband!! So I'm saluting and then I got out of there as fast as I could. I couldn't see spending the rest of the war in the brig."

During his five-plus years in the service he had "quite a few" relationships with women—"crumpet" in the male vernacular of the day. Most were typical casual wartime encounters though several became serious, at least for the nonce. "I had a spell," he confessed, "where I had a habit of getting engaged and somehow getting disengaged again." In any event, he made it through the war without losing his heart — or his bachelorhood.

Machrihanish

By the time he finished his wireless course in early 1942 the war had entered a new, more hopeful phase. Hitler's air assault on Britain had failed to bring the country to its knees and the threat of invasion receded, at least for the moment. On the eastern front the Germans, who invaded the Soviet Union in June 1941, were stalled outside Moscow, hampered by severe winter weather and unexpectedly stiff Russian resistance. And the entry of the United States into the war in December 1941 dramatically altered the balance of power: within a few months the British and Americans were busy mapping plans to launch ground attacks on German positions in northern Africa. Aircraftman Moon soon found himself a tiny cog in these plans.

Despite the "showbiz" distractions, he developed into a highly proficient wireless operator, skilled at both transmitting and receiving Morse code. After Blackpool he was posted to a base in Kirkcaldy, Scotland, on the Firth of Forth not far from Edinburgh. Shortly thereafter each of the services (army, navy, air force) were ordered to select two or three of their best operators for an experiment involving high-speed radio transmission in connection with the upcoming invasion of North Africa. Moon was one of those chosen by the RAF and before he could say Samuel F.B. Morse he found himself seconded (temporarily transferred) to Fleet Air Arm, the aviation wing of the Royal Navy, which had responsibility for communications for the North Africa campaign.

Fleet Air Arm conducted the wireless experiment at remote Machrihanish, remembered by Moon as "a dreadful little place" located on a rainy, blustery, sparsely populated peninsula on the west coast of Scotland where the wind howled like wild dogs. Used to the relatively mild climes of southern England he hated Machrihanish's weather from day one. The work was even worse.

This is how Moon described it:

It was always raining and blowing like hell. I remember stepping out of the bus when we arrived at Machrihanish and going into mud up to my knees. We were there ostensibly to man a high-speed radio network in preparation for the North African invasion. We were on duty continuously for three months—four hours on, eight hours off, four hours on, eight hours off. At the end of it they sent you home for rest and comfort—you were almost mad by then. They had selected all of us on the basis of whether we could handle very high-speed messages for a long period of time, both receiving and sending. They discovered that there were very few people who could do that, although some of the old navy pros who were with us were incredible; they had been doing it for 35 years.

This experience was "the one tough spot" Moon endured in the service during World War II.

Back in Blighty

After the Machrihanish experiment ended he returned to the RAF, working as an instructor in Morse code at an air force base in Calne, a town in Wiltshire in the south of England less than 50 miles from Southampton. Happy to be back in reasonably warm England and close to home, he remained at Calne for roughly two years, until the fall of 1944. Teaching Morse was routine, uneventful work, though two experiences stood out during this period. The first forced him to learn a new skill — how to type — which proved enormously valuable later in civilian life:

While I was at Calne another experiment came up. They decided to see if it was possible to receive Morse directly on a typewriter at even higher speeds. So they picked half a dozen operators like me who were very fast but had never touched a typewriter, and half a dozen who were just ordinary operators but who had real typing skills, and put them in a course together, starting from scratch, with Morse coming through first at low speeds and then increasingly faster.

Interestingly, at the end of the course, which lasted about six weeks, out of the 12 operators, five of the top six were the ones who were the fast operators who had never touched a typewriter before. We learned to type better than they learned to decode Morse. So that was how I learned to touch type, which became very useful later when I became a journalist.

The other experience that made a lasting impression on him was a visit to an American air force base in Lincolnshire, where he spent several weeks teaching U.S. airmen how to operate a new radio system in their bombers. "The Americans discovered they didn't know how to use the new equipment, and I was sent to make sure they learned how to use it." This was Moon's first encounter with real, live Americans; he recalled, "The food at the American base impressed me mightily."

Sometime after the D-day invasion in June 1944 he was transferred from Calne to Morecambe, a port north of Blackpool where he waited to be shipped overseas, destination India. To pass the time in he played table tennis, a game he enjoyed and had gotten good at in Southampton prior to enlisting. He played regularly with a couple of mates at a Morecambe service club, never dreaming that this casual recreation would land him a spot in an international competition:

The guys I played with weren't particularly good, whereas I had been playing in a fairly heavy league in Southampton before I joined the RAF. There was a guy watching me play for a couple of nights from the sidelines, a rather studious guy who eventually came over to me and said, "You think you can play this game, don't you?" and I said "Well, I'm not bad. Why?" He said, "We've got a guy in our billet who claims that he's an English international, one of the top players in the country, and frankly I think he's full of bullshit and I'd like to bring him down to play you." "Sure, bring him along," I said, "but if he *is* an English international, he's going to beat my ass."

So this guy walks in the next night, this so-called English international, with six rackets under his arm. And we start just knocking the ball back and forth and before we play I know I've got something here. He beats me 21-3, 21-1, 21-4. Turns out he not only played for England but he was a top player in the Lancashire league, which was then the best table tennis league in the country. Fortunately, he and I went on the boat together to India.

They had a table on the boat and I played with him almost every day, and by the time we got to India I'm up to 21-17, 21-18. That's how you learn, you play someone better than you are. Subsequently, when we got to India, he arranged an international match between England and India and asked me to play for the English team, which is the only time I've ever played at the international level. I lost, of course, but it was kind of fun playing at that level.

India

Moon's ship arrived in Bombay in early 1945 just as the war was winding down both in Europe and Asia. From Bombay he traveled east across India to a RAF station south of Calcutta in Cuttack in the state of Orissa, where he was assigned to an all–Indian meteorological unit as head of signals, which required overseeing radio communications. "I was the only Englishman in the unit," he remembered. "They had Indian officers and Indian personnel. There was very little for me to do; I would check in every morning and see that the signals operation was going fine, instruct everybody in what to do, and then I was free."

Happily for Moon the station boasted a first-class soccer (i.e., English football) team comprised of RAF personnel: "The rest of the time I worked out with the soccer team, which was one of the starring teams in India at that time. We played local teams and occasionally visiting professional teams from England, which were sent out for the entertainment of the troops. I played against some of the best professional soccer players in England and Scotland during that period." Just as Moon the schoolboy dreamed of Wimbledon and tennis fame, so Moon the young soldier now fantasized about a soccer career. He loved the competition, the camaraderie, the opportunity to stand out, to show his stuff, to be a cynosure, a star.

Soccer's other attraction was gin — liters of it. A lot of drinking took place in the service but the soccer players, according to Moon, were a special case:

As far as the soccer team was concerned, we used to have privileges that others didn't have because we represented the RAF and the country all over Asia. One of the things everybody had to take in India was mepacrine to avoid malaria — mepacrine is a horribly bitter quinine-like synthetic drug. But most of the soccer players didn't take it — they drank so much gin that it killed everything! I don't think anybody on the big representative soccer teams ever took mepacrine and I don't think any of them ever got malaria, so there must be something medicinal about gin! Not that we drank enormous quantities, but we drank enough. We were playing in 100 to 120 degree heat and you could lick your arm and taste the gin coming out of the sweat.

The officers' mess always had plenty of booze but we peons couldn't get too much, so we would arrange for a sergeant who worked in the officers' mess to smuggle the stuff out to us. The soccer team after all had to be looked after — it was an important part of the war effort!

After some months in Cuttack Moon's meteorological unit was transferred to a station at Comilla (or Kumilla; now in Bangladesh), a city in eastern Bengal near the Burma border. On the way to Comilla the unit stopped for a time at a transit camp in

Calcutta, then a hotbed of anti–Raj feeling. Here he came to empathize with the Indian people's desire for independence: "It was during this time that I finally really realized the impact of the Gandhi revolution. Things were very tense in Calcutta in that transit camp. Whenever a truck was sent out anywhere in the city, they put guys on the back with guns to protect themselves. I personally felt very sympathetic to the Indian cause."

Moon's unit traveled part of the way to Comilla via the river Ganges. During the trip his competitive juices got him involved in another sports challenge: "There was a Sikh on the boat who was reputed to be the best drafts—checkers— player in the world. The guys in my unit kept saying, 'You've got to play him.' I said, 'I don't think I want to play him.' 'But you have to play him,' they said. So I played him, and he just beat my ass. I wasn't bad at chess and thought that checkers would be easy. Within three moves this guy would tell you you were done, finished. It was really incredible."

On to Singapore

Moon had been at the Comilla station only a few months when his unit received orders to proceed to a faraway place called Hanoi. He had heard about Hanoi and salivated at the prospect:

We were supposed to be posted to what was then called French Indochina, later known as Vietnam. We were going to a little town called Hanoi. Before we left we heard rumors that if you had American cigarettes, Hanoi was yours— women, watches, whatever you wanted. So all of us invested practically every nickel we had buying cheap American cigarettes in Comilla. We had stacks of them, hundreds of packs of them. So we got on the boat headed for Hanoi, but then we heard that a revolution had broken out in Indochina and that we're being sent on to Singapore instead. We arrived in Singapore to find that American cigarettes were cheaper there than they were in Comilla!

By the time Moon arrived in Singapore in early 1946 the war was long over in both Europe and Asia, and he spent several lackadaisical months at a RAF base in the Changi section of the island waiting for orders to be transported home. Changi — the site of a notoriously squalid prison during the Japanese occupation of Singapore in the 1940s— was one of those World War II place-names, like Auschwitz and Hiroshima, that became infamous. But when Moon got to Changi the Japanese and their horrible jail were gone. In fact, for him the name became associated with not imprisonment but liberation, for it was at the base in Changi, of all places, that he learned to drive. Few people have ever had a more unorthodox introduction to driving a motor vehicle:

Our base was right near Changi jail. We got there before the base was set up in any organizational way. I was only a corporal but was in charge of the entire signals unit. There were no officers, no sergeants, nothing. So here I am, running the whole signals show, and to my delight we find that there's a huge armored Japanese signals wagon that had been left behind when they departed. And it was at my disposal; nobody else needed a signals wagon. The thing had about six gears and I decided that I was going to learn to drive on it, which I did.

I used to drive the wagon up and down the air field; I took it over as my personal vehicle. Subsequently, we learned that an officer was coming in to take over the signals unit. Somebody had to meet him at the boat and bring him back to the base, so I drove down to the docks in this huge machine and drove him back to the base. When we got there he said, "Corporal, that is the most hair-raising ride I've ever had in my life. You are banned from that vehicle from now on."

Years later, after emigrating to North America, Moon raised more hair, as well as eyebrows, with his cavalier driving habits, but never again did he drive anything as bizarre as the hulking Japanese signals wagon he commandeered at the RAF base in Changi.

The Happy World Cabaret

While waiting for orders to return home he played more soccer and won a service championship in table tennis. Also, being a randy young chap, he kept an eye out for and on the ladies: "Because there was little to do on the base — there was practically no message traffic and practically nobody else had arrived — I got involved in a nightclub in downtown Changi run by a Chinese family with five or six gorgeous daughters. It was called the Happy World Cabaret. I became sort of the unofficial manager of the cabaret in my spare time for a few months before coming back to England. Ilse always calls it a whorehouse but it was in fact some sort of cabaret." Pressed for elucidation, Moon defined a cabaret as "one step above a brothel." And his relationship with the gorgeous daughters? "Good friends."

Churchill Out, Labour In

While Moon was defending his country in the Far East a watershed election took place in Great Britain following Germany's surrender in May 1945. The prime minister and Conservative party leader, Winston Churchill, acclaimed by many patriotic British subjects as the architect of the allied victory over fascism, wanted to postpone national elections until after the defeat of Japan, then imminent. But the Labour Party, led by Clement Attlee, insisted on an immediate referendum on the postwar future of the nation. The election, held on July 26, 1945, shocked many Britons and others around the world, including Americans who revered "Winnie": the voters decisively rejected Churchill and the Conservatives, Labour ending up with a massive 146-seat majority in Parliament and its first prime minister since the Depression era.

Corporal Moon naturally and enthusiastically had cast his vote (by absentee ballot) for Labour, as did an overwhelming number of young people at home and overseas. At the time there was a general feeling the country needed a radical change in political direction. Cyril Connolly, editor of the influential magazine *Horizon*, spoke for many when he informed readers he intended to vote for Labour. Why? Because the time had come for "a levelling up which socialism alone can provide; we cannot continue to maintain two utterly different standards of living." In Moon's case, his political sympathies had been formed years earlier as an adolescent in Southampton. A product of the British working class and an adherent of the socialist principles espoused by the Fabians, he adamantly believed a Labour victory held the key to a more just and humane future:

The war years left me, like many other young servicemen, with the conviction that we wanted not the kind of the England that we had left. We were all part of that movement that led to Churchill's quick demise after the war and the election of the Labour Party. Many people in the U.S. thought this a great ingratitude on the part of the British people to this great man, but we knew Churchill as a son of a bitch and a bastard and we wanted him out of there. There was a feeling among many of the people I was stationed with, particularly in the later years of the war, that while Churchill's bombast had been useful and perhaps even inspirational during the early part of the war, we didn't want to go back to a government that operated on his kind of terms. We wanted a government that would recognize the needs of people generally. There was a feeling that we had to throw out the Tories if there were going to be any reasonable arrangements made for us to catch up the five or six years of our lives we had lost.

Mustered Out and Back Home

After being discharged from the RAF in the summer of 1946, Moon returned to Southampton to try as best he could to pick up the pieces of his life and somehow start making up for the years "lost" to the war. He found a country ravaged by bomb damage, economic deprivation, and social disruption. Between the outbreak of the war in 1939 and its conclusion in 1945, approximately 60 million changes of address occurred among the 48 million people that comprised Britain's civilian population. Many soldiers returning home agreed with Ronald Benge: "I felt empty, exhausted and alone.... I was once again a new recruit to an alien world."

Instead of going to work immediately Moon, now 23 years old, took a few months off to begin the adjustment process. He wanted to refamiliarize himself with Southampton while taking stock of his situation and options. Though not overjoyed at having spent more than five years of his young life in the military he realized that countless others had made the same sacrifice; he was not alone in feeling disadvantaged by the war. Ultimately, he harbored no great bitterness or regret about the years spent serving his country. After all, he had learned, done, and seen much that, had there been no war, he would have missed. True, he had not risen to exalted heights within the RAF, mustering out as a mere corporal. But he did not seek high rank: "I didn't want to be anything else. I had too much freedom with my various activities, which got me all kinds of privileges anyway. I was asked a couple of times if I had any interest in becoming an officer; I said no, I like it this way. I just didn't want to be an officer."

Most of all he felt a sense of urgency about getting on with a career and establishing himself professionally. He would have to decide what type of work he wanted to do and decide quickly, because others who had not spent years in the military would be ahead of him, and still others returning from the service would be battling alongside him for those places that were available, no matter what occupation he chose. Pulled this way and that, Moon weighed his career options as carefully and realistically as a child in a candy store who could have but one piece:

The war years gave me some choices when I came out of the service. When I came back to England I had the potential of signing on as a professional soccer player; of becoming a professional actor—I had offers from a couple of repertory companies to go and do theater full-time; and of course there was always the library to go back to. This was an interesting turning point for me—I could have gone either of several directions. I was very torn at the time. If I had gone into pro soccer, that might have led to a broadcasting career, like John Arlott, which I would have loved to have done.

He had also once wanted to be a writer, a notion that grew out his association with the Group before entering the RAF. While in the service his interest in literature did not dissipate; he still harbored dreams of someday expressing himself with the same power and urgency as his favorite authors—Hardy, Malraux, Steinbeck, Hemingway, Faulkner, Maxwell Anderson, and the rest. But by the time he returned to Southampton in 1946 the idea of earning his living as a creative writer had passed: "The period of 1941 to 1946 was very much a growing up period for me. Everybody carries around certain dreams. In my case, for years I wanted to be a writer. That's what I really wanted to be. I wrote poems, short stories; I think I even kept a diary at one stage; I started a novel at one point, which I later burned."

Finally, in the fall of 1946, Moon returned to his old job at the Southampton Public Library, albeit reluctantly:

I decided to go back to the library for a spell and see how things were there. I don't know if I can recall how I felt, other than perhaps a bit confused about where I might now be going. I had had such a varied, indeed almost an entertaining life for five years that going back to a life in Southampton and working in the library seemed really pretty mundane. I wasn't sure whether I was going to be able to handle that. That was why I kept thinking about those other alternatives—theater and soccer—and whether I should actually pursue them.

He found the library intact physically, the main facility in the Civic Centre and the branches having survived the war without major structural damage. Other members of the staff who had been in the military were also returning to their jobs, including his friend Bill Graham, who resumed his duties in the reference department. Tragically, Ron Lynn, the director's son and Eric's friend, was killed while serving in the RAF. "It may be my imagination," observed Graham years later, "but I think it hurt Robert Lynn to see us all return from the war while his son did not." Promoted to senior library assistant, Moon was assigned to the central lending library again, "doing perfectly routine stuff, managing the circulation desk, working with Browne tickets."

Slowly he readjusted to the rhythms of daily life in Southampton and commonplace duties at the library. More than five years of adventure—Blackpool, Kirkcaldy, Machrihanish, Calne, Morecambe, Cuttack, Calcutta, Comilla, Singapore, Changi—would never be forgotten. But now the war was over, and there was a vast, unpredictable future waiting. Fretting over or living in the past was not Moon's way; he was too competitive to waste his time on what might have been. Besides, he fell in love — seriously in love — with an attractive young woman almost as soon as he returned to the library. As he put it, "Life and biology reasserted themselves and normality wasn't that hard to take after awhile."

First Marriage

Moon eagerly observed that there were "a lot of new young women on the library staff" when he returned to work in the fall of 1946: "They seemed to have been waiting for all us guys to come back from the service, because there must have been four or five of us who came back and all were married within six months. And that put paid to other occupational choices for me. Obviously, repertory on the road or soccer on the road is not a good start for any marriage."

She was Diana Mary Simpson, a junior library assistant from the Bitterne section of Southampton and, in the opinion of Bill Graham, "easily the prettiest girl on the library staff." Eric was 24 and Diana — or Di, as she was called by friends and family — was in her late teens when they were married in May 1947. Dickie Denton, Moon's old mate from the Woolston Branch before the war, served as best man. The wedding was a modest affair, followed by a reception at the Cowherd's Inn, a pub in Southampton. Later in the day a bit of unpleasantness occurred when Eric and Dickie went out to buy more beer but failed to return promptly, stopping to hoist a few more on the way. Not to worry, the day ended happily enough, as the young couple took off for a brief honeymoon in Brighton, a coastal resort town some 60 miles east of Southampton. Unfortunately, Eric had not made reservations in Brighton and he and his bride were turned away from several hotels because no one believed they were married. Finally, exhausted, the newlyweds found a place to spend the night and start their union. Although they did not live happily ever after, they would remain married for the next 23 years.

Aside from physical attraction, Moon was not certain what drew him to his first wife. "We went dancing a lot, but I can't remember any other shared interests." He did recall that the Simpson house in Southampton was "pretty primitive" and that "the old man," Diana's father, "was a character — he came on like Colonel Blimp, a very pompous, jingoistic blowhard." Despite this personality flaw, Moon and his father-in-law "actually got along fairly well; we used to go to the pub together periodically and drink beer and play dominoes." Diana had two brothers, one named Brian, whom he liked, and another named Peter, whom he did not.

Off to Library School

Once married, Moon wasted no time making librarianship his chosen field, which meant passing the Library Association's rigorous Registration Examination, the chief hurdle to qualifying as a librarian in the UK. Because it was important to get his professional stripes as soon as possible ("to catch up on those lost years") he decided to attend one of the new library schools created after the war specifically to prepare returning veterans like himself for the exam. So, a few months after the wedding, he was off to Loughborough College in the Midlands as a full-time student. Moon: "Once the decision was made to go the library route, the next decision was to go to library school, because it was the only way to close that gap. Bill Graham and I both went to see Lynn and said that we wanted to go to library school beginning in the fall of 1947, and we both wound up going to Loughborough."

– 4 –

Learning at Loughborough

Library Education in Postwar Britain

Moon attended library school at Loughborough College in England for two years between September 1947 and June 1949, but his academic experience differed markedly from that of his counterparts in North America, where he would spend the better part of his career. To begin with, he lacked an undergraduate education when he entered library school, having left grammar (or high) school at 16 to go to work. Furthermore, once finished with library school he was not required to earn (nor did he) a baccalaureate degree in order to qualify as a library professional. American and Canadian librarians, who customarily go from high school to college or university and then on to graduate school for a degree in library science, might find Moon's path to professional qualification unconventional, but it was the norm in postwar Britain.

Not only did the library school at Loughborough not require an undergraduate degree for admission, it offered no credits for courses completed, gave no final examinations, issued no grades, and granted no degrees. Rather, the school provided a course of study intended to prepare students—most of them, like Moon, ex-servicemen and women returning from the war—for written examinations that, if passed, would culminate in professional status. Significantly, these all-important exams were constructed, administered, graded, and in all other respects controlled by the Library Association (LA), the principal library organization in the UK.

The rationale for this approach to qualification (or accreditation) rested on a simple but compelling premise: admission to the professional ranks of librarianship should be determined by members of the profession itself, and not by some governmental agency or group of academics or other outside sanctioning body. The LA, through powers granted it by royal charter, strictly regulated who became a librarian in Britain and who did not. Candidates who met all the LA's requirements, including successful completion of its exams, became "chartered" members of the association—meaning that they were officially certified as professionals in the library field. In North America the system was quite different: anyone with a degree from a library school accredited

44

by the American Library Association possessed the presumption of professional status.

When Moon went to work at the Southampton Public Library as a junior assistant in 1939 the time-honored method of becoming a chartered librarian was through an apprenticeship system based on supervised experience and qualifying exams. After working in a library or libraries for a time, assistants (clerks responsible for nonprofessional tasks) who demonstrated an aptitude for the work and desired advancement were encouraged to take the LA's Elementary Examination, which tested for comprehension of library basics and was the first step toward becoming a librarian. Assistants studied for the exam in their spare time either on their own or more likely through correspondence courses offered by the Association of Assistant Librarians, an organization affiliated with the LA that catered mainly to the interests of younger library workers.

Moon passed the Elementary Exam before entering the RAF in 1941, and had the war not intervened he almost certainly would have then begun studying, again in his spare time, for the LA's Registration Examination, the gateway to chartered membership in the association. Normally taken over a period of time, this rigorous, multipart exam required extensive knowledge in six broad areas of librarianship, including reference work, bibliography, cataloging and classification, and administration. Aspirants who passed all parts of the exam, and who met conditions concerning age, job experience, and foreign language proficiency, became chartered librarians with the title Associate of the LA.

For most librarians the Associateship was sufficient, but for those who wished to go further there was the Fellowship, the LA's highest distinction. Becoming a Fellow of the LA (or FLA) entailed mastering a specialty within the field, sitting for another grueling exam, and submission of an acceptable thesis.

The British approach to library education underwent a major change after the war when the Labour government, in concert with the LA, established seven library schools in colleges in different areas of the UK. Prior to World War II only the University of London offered a library science curriculum, and it was aimed almost exclusively at students with a university degree who planned to work in academic libraries. The main goal of the new schools was to speed up the qualification process, particularly for those whose careers had been interrupted by military service. War veterans who wished to become librarians were advised to enroll one of the schools, where they would devote their full energies to preparing for the LA exams with knowledgeable tutors (as opposed to the old way of studying part-time on one's own). The brightest and most eager students could be chartered in a year or so.

The government offered veterans incentives to attend library school in the form of financial assistance authorized under the Further Education and Training Scheme (FETS), a program similar to the GI Bill in the United States. Moon received FETS grants during both his years at Loughborough; otherwise he (and many of his classmates) could not have afforded full-time study. Still, the grants were modest, and years later he groused that they were "not nearly so luxurious" as those afforded American vets under the terms of the GI Bill.

Birth of a Library School

The Loughborough College Moon knew—founded in 1909 as Loughborough Technical Institute—no longer exists. By the mid–1960s it had evolved into a large university complex consisting of four quite separate institutions: Loughborough University of Technology, Loughborough College of Education, Loughborough College of Art and Design, and Loughborough Technical College. The college Moon attended, known today as "old" Loughborough College, had an enrollment of some 1,300 students when he arrived on campus in the fall of 1947. Located on the western edge of Loughborough, a midsized community in central England between the larger cities of Nottingham and Leicester, the college was best known for strong programs in science and technology, especially engineering, and for its emphasis on sports. The latter naturally impressed Moon, a serious athlete who had played soccer and table tennis at a major league level during the war: "When I was there, Loughborough had some of the best sports facilities of any academic institution in England. In fact, many of the British Olympic teams trained at Loughborough because the facilities were so good. They had umpteen soccer fields and cricket pitches—great facilities."

The driving force behind Loughborough College was Herbert Schofield, an extraordinary man who presided over the institution for 35 years, from 1915 to 1950. A Yorkshire native known as an American-style entrepreneur with little tolerance for bureaucratic cock-ups and inefficiency, Dr. Schofield built Loughborough into one of Britain's top technical colleges between the world wars. Called approvingly an "educational buccaneer" by some and denigrated as an opportunist by others, he was constantly on the lookout for new programs that would enhance the college's stature as well as boost its enrollment. Despite a reputation as a penny-pincher, Schofield believed the best education possible required the best faculty available, and he was willing to spend to get it.

In early 1946 the British Ministry of Education and the LA set up a joint committee, chaired by none other than Loughborough's Schofield, to develop a new approach to educating librarians in the postwar era. The committee recommended creating half a dozen or so schools of librarianship at technical and commercial colleges situated around the country. Not unexpectedly, Loughborough College was selected as one of the sites, along with similar colleges in Brighton, London, Manchester, Leeds, Newcastle, and Glasgow. If possible, the new schools were to be operational by the fall and Schofield, always quick off the mark, wasted no time launching Loughborough's program, appointing R.B. (Roy) Stokes as senior lecturer and head of the school and Alfred (Fred) Johnson as assistant lecturer.

Stokes and his colleague got cracking immediately and before long they were ready for opening day. Stokes described the scene in an article in a leading library periodical: "On the morning of Saturday, September 21, 1946, the tutors of the School of Librarianship pushed a wheelbarrow along one of the main roads of Loughborough. Inside it were the textbooks which had been gathered together from all quarters and with their arrival we felt that everything was more or less ready." The school's initial class consisted of 41 students about equally divided between men and women. All came to Loughborough with at least one year's work experience as a library assistant and the recommendation of a chartered librarian, usually the chief where they were employed.

Dr. Schofield's eye for academic quality did not fail him when he recruited young Roy Stokes to head Loughborough's new library school. An FLA who was then just 30 and not much older than most of his students, Stokes would remain at Loughborough for nearly a quarter of a century, during which time he achieved near-legendary prominence as a library educator in Britain and abroad. From the beginning he set out quite deliberately to create a school that not only prepared students for the LA exams but instilled in them a desire to change the face of British librarianship, then a stodgy profession mired in the past and hostile to new ideas and innovation. A measure of Stokes's success can be seen in the careers of his most able students, among them Eric Moon, who became arguably the most influential library activist of his day.

Why Loughborough?

Stokes was the first to concede that "many people regarded Loughborough as a very curious site in which to start a school of librarianship." Neither the town nor the college had anything approaching adequate library resources to support such a program. Stokes: "At the time, Loughborough was a small town of only 30,000 population with virtually no public library in it at all. It was a very, very small library, which was distinguished by the fact that it had an alligator hanging in the entrance hall and, what always intrigued the students, a stuffed snowbird in a case, which it said underneath had been run over at Nanpantan, a small village just on the outskirts of Loughborough." Of course, those who wondered why Loughborough had a library school when other, better equipped colleges in larger places did not were either unaware of or failed to take into account Dr. Schofield's considerable influence with the Ministry of Education as well as his relentless determination to push Loughborough College onward, ever onward.

There is also the question of why Moon and his friend Bill Graham decided to attend library school in Loughborough instead of, say, Brighton or London. Especially Brighton, which was in southern England and not all that far from Southampton, Moon's hometown and where his wife lived with her parents while he was off at library school. Loughborough, on the other hand, was 150 miles north of Southampton in the Midlands, a region considered barbarian territory by some born and bred in the south of England. Later Moon had no recollection of how or why Loughborough had been chosen: "Why Loughborough? I don't know. I honestly don't know. I don't remember whether we [he and Graham] picked it or whether we were assigned to it." Graham likewise has no memory of how he and Moon ended up at Loughborough.

Perhaps Robert Lynn suggested, or maybe even decreed, they go there. Perhaps Moon and Graham, sports-minded men who often went to soccer and cricket matches together in Southampton, chose the school because of its reputation for athletics. Norman Horrocks, a British-born librarian who came to know Moon well after they both came to America in the 1960s, suggested another possible reason. He remembered Moon once remarking that he had picked Loughborough because it was a "residential school"— that is, the college was in a small place where practically all the students came from elsewhere and therefore lived on campus or in digs (rooms) in the town, whereas students at colleges in larger places tended to be from the area and live at home. Horrocks himself was from Manchester and attended library school at the Manchester College of Science and Technology.

In the long run it mattered little how or why Moon got to Loughborough. What did matter was that once there he had the enormously good fortune to study with the charismatic Roy Stokes, and the intuitively good sense to internalize the core of the Stokesian message: "Ask the right questions, the probing questions, the kind of questions children ask when they're learning for the first time: Why? Why? Why? Why?" Bill Graham agreed: "I cannot remember any logic behind the choice of Loughborough, but it turned out to be a good one as we came under the influence of Roy Stokes and Alfred Johnson."

Classmates

Moon and Graham arrived in Loughborough in late September 1947, part of the second wave at the new library school. Their class had approximately 30 full-time students, most of them war veterans in their mid-to-late twenties. "There were some women, some of whom had been in the service, some not. We were generally an older group than the rest of the college per se," remembered Moon. Ron Surridge, another member of the class, recalled, "There were a few locally based students but most were drawn from all over the place, though on reflection I can't remember any from Ireland, Scotland, or Wales. We were in fact a fairly closely knit group—there wasn't anything much to do in Loughborough, which meant a lot of socializing and a lot of work."

Roy Stokes handled the school's administrative affairs and between them he and Fred Johnson taught all the courses and served as faculty advisers. Stokes was impressed by the students, whom he found to be mature, inquisitive, and self-motivated:

The school had just completed its first year of life and the second year had a very similar intake. The majority of those coming in at that time were men and women who were returning from war service of some kind. They were, of course, of an age which meant that they had considerable maturity both of personality and library experience.

Two things distinguished students at that time. First, they were more than anxious to get on again with their professional lives; they wanted to get on with things quickly; there was no question of hanging around and wasting time; there was a great degree of urgency in everything that everyone was doing. And second—and this made such a world of difference—they were so critical, so inquiring about everything they saw and everything they read. Many of them had spent the war years in situations that they found were sometimes less than obviously clear as to what the intent was, and they were determined that now they needed to establish very firm guidelines for themselves; they weren't anxious to be told things so much as to inquire and find out. This is exactly the spirit one hopes to find in a professional school—that people are motivated to try and discover the situations, the problems, the solutions for themselves.

Except for Bill Graham, Moon knew none of his classmates prior to arriving at Loughborough. During his two years at the school he got on well with most people, but it was with Ronald Surridge, a bright, likable Londoner, that he formed a lifelong friendship. Surridge—born "within the sound of Bow bells," that is, a true Cockney—was on leave from a branch library job in London's East End while attending Loughborough. Like Moon, he loved sports, enjoyed the occasional pint, was married, and had served in the RAF during the war. The two men hit it off smashingly from the beginning, their relationship cemented by common interests, the camaraderie of studying together, and many sociable hours spent in pubs. Both men opted for a second year at the school to study for the FLA and naturally they shared digs. Surridge: "This is where we really got to know one another. It was often a quite hilarious and wonderful year. The Blacksmith's Arms was just around the corner from our rooms, and this little pub with a devoted clientele and some wonderful British ales became a happy second home to us. We were on the darts team and many a gregarious evening slipped easily into the small hours."

Another classmate Moon found congenial was John Taylor, a tall, wiry fellow with a quick and witty tongue. Unlike Moon and Surridge, Taylor spent just one year at Loughborough. After passing the Registration Exam and getting his Associateship he had a long and distinguished career as a public library administrator in Nottingham and Nottinghamshire. Moon never forgot one of Taylor's lines: "It lived with us for years. Everytime we saw a very tall and rather fashionable young woman walking down the street we would all come out simultaneously with Johnny Taylor's phrase: 'Look at that, a long bodied woman'"—the words "long bodied" drawn out with delicious exaggeration.

Other students in Moon's class during the first year included Tony Rowberry, John Colgan (his roommate), Esmé Green, Carol Smith, Jimmy Matthews, Maureen Precious, Dora Armstrong, Sted Ashmore, Derek Austin, Gawan Vesey, Esmé Clarke (later Esme Vesey), Ric Taylor, Htan Htutt (who was from Burma and became a library leader there), and Mona (Jeff) Jefferson, who eventually married Roy Stokes, a made-in-heaven union broken only by his death in 1995.

Much to Moon's chagrin he was forced to live in a hall (or dormitory) his first year at Loughborough while his old Southampton chum, Bill Graham, lived in digs in town because, explained Graham, "I was older"—though older by only one year, which further rankled Moon. He disliked living on campus not only because roommate Colgan had a bad case of smelly feet and a tendency to leave "his stinky socks all around the room," but because the college's housing regulations seemed excessively silly to a man of the world like himself: "Except for Bill, we were all housed in college dorms that first year, which was very peculiar because we were sort of old mature men compared with all these kids that we were living with. They had restrictions that we were not prepared to live by—you had to be in by certain hours and so on. We said the hell with that. So we were a very rambunctious crowd, and the college had a hard time learning to live with us." How rambunctious were they? An example: late one evening, Moon, Surridge, and Jimmy Matthews boozily returned to the campus from a local pub to find the doors to their hall locked. The best solution at the time seemed to be to throw Matthews, a small guy, through one of the plate glass doors so they could get in. And they did that. (Fortunately, Matthews survived the incident with no permanent scars.)

More decorous social events sponsored by the library school, such as parties at Christmas and end of term, brought the whole class together, with Moon usually the center of attention, or trying to be. "Those were the times when we were still small enough as a school to have parties," recalled Stokes. "I particularly remember the Christmas parties that were held in an upstairs room at the old Boot Hotel in Loughborough's marketplace, and I can vividly recall Eric, an extremely thin and tall young man, who seemed in fact almost emaciated, looking somewhat excited and perhaps slightly disheveled come the end of the Christmas eve party evening."

Pioneering Spirit

Inasmuch as Dr. Schofield wanted his school of librarianship up and running as quickly and economically as possible, minimal attention was devoted to classroom amenities in the early years. In fact, the school's facilities during Moon's first year were strictly makeshift, most classes conducted in two drafty, dilapidated huts set in the middle of a large sports field. Though nowhere nearly as bad as Machrihanish during the war, the frigid classrooms remained in Moon's memory for the rest of his life: "We were in very primitive quarters. We were in Nissen [or Quonset] huts on the playing fields of Loughborough. It was quite cold in the winter, so we would sit in class in our overcoats and scarves and gloves." But, according to Ron Surridge, the spartan conditions hardly mattered: "There were no individual desks—just tables and chairs. There was no equipment that I can remember. For reference studies it was a frequent hustle to the larger libraries of Nottingham and Leicester. But I don't think the shortage of equipment mattered a jot." John Taylor euphemistically characterized the spirit of the school as "pioneering."

While the students roughed it, the head of the school coped as best he could with unexpected difficulties. Stokes was nonplussed, for instance, by the college library:

The library in the college itself was in one quite small room, with furniture which was absolutely magnificent because it was all made by the department of teachers in training, and the great strength of that department was its woodwork. So the woodwork was all superb, the most magnificent chairs and desks, but everything had been made in order to show off the prowess of the woodworkers. For example, the card catalog was a magnificently built-in unit, but the drawers were of a size that fit absolutely no known size or shape of catalog card that was on the market, so every card had to be cut down to size to fit into the catalog cabinet. The librarian was appointed by just taking one of the girls from one of the offices, giving her a copy of *Dewey* as a kind of badge of office, and saying that from this moment on you are the librarian, the one and only person on the library staff, and this is it.

Stokes remembered too the college dining room, a source of both mirth and suspicion among the library school students:

The group as a whole got quite a deal of amusement out of the dining room. This was the time that Loughborough was still being run very much as a private institution, and it was always alleged that the dining room was one of the places in which Herbert Schofield and his cooperators made quite a bit of their profits. To ex-servicemen and women coming back after wartime and remembering that rationing was still in force at this time and was to remain so for a number of years yet, they looked at food very critically. I recall that one of the allegations most often made about the dining room was that if one held a piece of Spam — that curious product of the postwar years in England, a meat product of rather unknown origin — one could read the newspaper through it, the slices being cut so thinly.

School for Revolution

Whereas the library school's physical facilities were often deficient or eccentric or both, the intellectual content of the curriculum was just the opposite, the courses infused with substantial, demanding, and, in the eyes of some, radical material. Stokes and Johnson emphasized those subjects covered in the LA's exams, but beyond that the tutors had considerable leeway to teach what they thought students about to become British librarians in the postwar period needed to know and hear. For instance, students learned about Britain's library trailblazers, men like James Duff Brown, an English Melvil Dewey who introduced the concept of open access in the UK, authored the most famous text in the field (the oft-revised *Manual of Library Economy*), and founded and edited the *Library World* (now the *New Library World*), the leading British independent library magazine. But they also studied the careers of contemporary librarians in Britain and abroad. Moon captured the flavor of the school's expansive approach to library education in his foreword to Lawrence Clark Powell's memoir, *Life Goes On*:

I thought back to my own days in library school in Britain and realized that one would have to have slept through almost every class to have emerged into the profession without an awareness of the achievements, not only of such figures of British library history as Panizzi or James Duff Brown but also of such more recent, then still practicing giants as Lionel McColvin, Ernest Savage and Frank Gardner. More importantly, in the context of our professional heritage, in our pantheon there were also many names from across the Atlantic. They included not just the obvious lions of the past — Dewey and Cutter and Winsor and Dana and Putnam — but more recent giants, like Joe Wheeler, or then emerging ones such as Powell, Shera, and Shaw.

The person most responsible for the range and vitality of Loughborough's library school curriculum in those days was — no surprise here — Roy Stokes. It's hardly an exaggeration to say the school was Stokes and Stokes was the school. Fred Johnson, the other faculty member, was a capable lecturer but lacked the commitment to library education Stokes had. Johnson left Loughborough after only a couple of years, replaced by a young man, John Cox, who remained at the school well after Stokes had been lured away from Loughborough by Canada and the University of British Columbia.

By all accounts Stokes was a masterly teacher, a Mr. Chips with an edge. He possessed knowledge and experience in many areas of librarianship, with a special passion for bibliography. But more important than *what* he taught was *how* he taught. He had the rare pedagogic gift for using the Socratic method effectively: he prized questions over answers, dialectic over certitude. Gawan Vesey, a Moon classmate, described Stokes as a "brilliant tutor," and Ron Surridge, impressed by his ability "to inspire enthusiasm in a very diverse group of people," summed up Stokes the teacher this way:

He was opinionated, he could irritate, he could certainly excite; but the beauty of it all to me, and I'm sure Eric, is that he questioned virtually everything in and about librarianship — and literature too for that matter. His techniques too were unusual. Sometimes the lecture was simply reading an article or even a series of articles from the *Times Literary Supplement*. This sounds prosaic but not the way Stokes read them — his rich, fruity voice extracting every nuance it could from the printed word. And he did his lectures not infrequently lying down on the table in front of the class.

Another of Stokes's favorite techniques involved day trips to libraries around central England. These excursions were serious learning experiences, not a day off for sightseeing or horsing around. Stokes:

When we went around to visit libraries there was a very critical atmosphere. I recall very clearly — and I'm pretty certain it was during Eric's time at the school — that we visited a medium-sized library in the Midlands, one which shall be nameless as shall the librarian at the time, and towards the end of the visit after we'd looked around and spent sometime with the system, he said that he liked to do all the classification of the books himself because it was the only kind of intellectual pastime which he had.

And I can recall now so clearly the students rounding on him and saying that he had absolutely no right whatsoever to be doing something just for his own personal taste and fulfillment. His job was to run the library as whole, to plan it, not to seek refuge in some job that he happened to find pleasing; anyone could classify the books at a much lower salary than that which he was being paid. Our relations with that library were quite strained for a number of years afterwards. But this is the kind of questioning that was so common throughout all our visits and with all our visitors. Yet at the same time I think we always maintained, I hope we always maintained, a sort of basic professional courtesy.

Stokes believed too in creating a collegial atmosphere at the school, which included relaxed get-togethers with students at his home. Looking back years later Moon remembered these sessions as an important part of his education at Loughborough:

We had only two faculty members — Roy Stokes, who was head of the school, and a man called Johnson, who taught cataloging and classification. I don't remember what else he taught but it seemed to me that Roy taught almost everything else. One of the nice things I remember is that Roy would have some of the students back to his house in the evenings — just talking about books and what have you. I found among other things that he introduced me to some American books that I hadn't known; he introduced me, for example, to Leo Rosten and all that marvelous stuff he's written. Stokes was a very good teacher. We would have these literary chats and everything. I really thoroughly enjoyed it.

Moon believed Roy Stokes was a "revolutionary" and Loughborough a "school for revolution." Stokes demurred, insisting that all he ever tried to do was "confront students with situations to which they were expected to react." Revolution or confrontation? Either way, Loughborough could be a mind-bending experience.

Saturday Mornings

The teaching technique Stokes valued above all others was debate, a form of civilized confrontation. In his final years, after retiring as head of the library school at British Columbia, he lamented, "There is so little debating in North America. I think it is much more an English tradition than it is either a Canadian or an American one, and I think we lose a lot not having good, well constructed debates." Not surprisingly, Loughborough held student debates regularly on Saturday mornings. "Saturday Mornings," as the debates came to be known, were central to the educational experience at the school. Stokes had no doubt they helped students become more articulate, more poised, more confident:

I frequently arranged for debates among ourselves. This was for several reasons. Debating is an art, skill, whatever you like to call it, in which I have a very profound belief. It teaches people to think on their feet in a way that no other practicable exercise does; it gives people a chance to marshal their ideas quickly; and when it's with people who meet week in and week out, day in and day out, it overcomes some of the problems that people feel about speaking before an unknown audience. I've always been concerned about this because I've been distressed right to my retirement that we are such an incredibly inarticulate profession. We are not terribly good at writing but we are even worse at speaking. I can think of very, very few speakers in the library field whom I would ever listen to with pleasure. And if you don't listen to a speaker with pleasure, then on the whole you get very little from their talk.

Saturday Morning debate topics usually focused on professional issues, the more controversial the better, including political questions if they in some way affected libraries or related subjects, such as literacy, literature, or publishing. Occasionally, Stokes chose a subject merely to improve students' forensic skills: "I often used to quote what I think is the finest topic of all for a debate, which is on the motion that 'In the opinion of this house this house has no opinion.' I would use any topic that would get the students to become accustomed to standing on their feet, hearing the sound of their own voices, of countering arguments, of putting forward ideas no matter how ridiculous those ideas might be."

Sometimes Saturday Mornings featured a guest speaker, usually a librarian in the area or one willing to travel to Loughborough from London or Liverpool or Sheffield or wherever. Stokes: "We had a very wide range of librarians who came to us in those early days when there was a certain novelty still in the schools." He sought to attract practicing librarians "who stood out a little bit in terms of professional controversy. I remember that many of them, some of the leading figures in the profession, were subjected to a great deal of close questioning and scrutiny, so that in one sense I think that we were beginning to practice what one might call 'confrontation.'"

Indeed, Saturdays Mornings sometimes got quite heated, students and guest tangling like scorpions in a bottle — though reasonably courteous scorpions who observed Marquis of Queensberry rules in the clinches. Stokes abhorred nor would he tolerate boorish behavior on the part of his students:

I never invited anyone to come and talk with the students unless he or she was prepared to be open and honest, and to take criticism, if it be necessary, all in good part. I avoided the stuffy figureheads who I thought would not enter into the spirit of the game. I think over the years I was very selective. We had some extremely good Saturday Mornings. I told the visitors of my belief that this was a time to come and be absolutely honest, that I told the students to be absolutely honest in return in both their questions and their comments, that it should be in one sense a "no holds barred" contest. But at the same time I always reminded the students that all debate at all times and in all places should be conducted within the bounds of civilized behavior. We never under any circumstances got into anything that resembled a verbal brawl, but we did have a lot of very, very sincere questioning.

A Bug Named Moon Confronts the Great McColvin

A good illustration of confrontation methodology as practiced at Loughborough during Moon's student days occurred when Lionel McColvin came to speak in Nottingham in 1948. McColvin — longtime chief librarian of the City of Westminster in London and author of the landmark 1942 survey, *The Public Library System of Great Britain* (aka the *McColvin Report*) — was universally regarded as one of the two or three top British public librarians of that era. When Stokes learned the great McColvin would be speaking at a library meeting in Nottingham, an easy run from Loughborough, he decided to take the whole class to hear him. Moon remembered well what happened:

Stokes said to us, you all know about Lionel McColvin's strengths, one of the great figures of the profession, and you can tell us all the great things he's done. However, like all great figures, he has his weaknesses; they are — and Stokes would go through a list. Now that's where I want you to get him. And Stokes would do this consistently; he wanted us to go in and challenge these big-name people and find out what it was like being with them *tête-à-tête*.

Stokes said, "Moon, you're going to be the first one up to challenge him." McColvin was the guest speaker at this meeting, which was being chaired by Duncan Gray, who was the chief librarian at Nottingham at the time and probably the stuffiest individual who ever lived. The only equivalent I can think of is the former librarian at Boston [Massachusetts], Milton Lord. Duncan Gray was the English Milton Lord. Anyway, I stood up and challenged McColvin, I'm sure quite rudely because there wasn't much couth among us ex-servicemen at the time. And Duncan Gray gave McColvin no chance to answer but immediately got up to the microphone and stamped on me as if I were a bug to be squashed. At which point Roy Stoke leapt to the microphone and thoroughly pummeled Duncan Gray. And then he asked McColvin to respond to my remarks. It was that kind of thing that made library school terribly exciting and interesting, plus the fact that Stokes was interested in exploring issues well beyond the purview of the examinations we were studying for.

Moon the Library Science Student

There's no question Loughborough was an exceptional school of librarianship in those early, heady years after the war, but what about Eric Moon? What sort of student was he? How well did this cocky, 24-year-old veteran fit into the Loughborough landscape? How was he perceived by others at the school, including Roy Stokes? Was he up to the high standards Stokes demanded?

Clearly, Moon's style and persona played well at Loughborough. Though obviously intelligent and blessed with a first-rate memory, he was not an especially scholarly or studious individual. He was not a grind or, in today's parlance, a nerd, with his head stuck in a deep tome. Much of his time at library school was spent schmoozing in pubs, playing sports, talking politics, generally having a jolly good time. His approach to the academic side of life at Loughborough tended to be nonchalant — until crunch time, when he would put his brain into high gear and, like a powerful sports car, take off. Grades were a driving force; competitive to the core, he always strived to be the best in his class. Bill Graham recalled that he (Graham) and Ron Surridge were "plodders who had to assimilate the information passed on to us at lectures in small doses gradually working towards the exams. This was not Eric's method. For a fortnight before an exam he would concentrate and sweat both day and night with a wet towel round his head. He would then produce the results on the day — usually top of the class."

On one memorable occasion he got fed up with school and went home to Southampton for a week. It was toward the end of the first year, a short time before the Registration Exam was scheduled, when he informed Surridge, "'Ron, I'm cutting out.' Ron said, 'You can't do that, we got the exams in a couple of weeks.' I said, 'Screw the exams, I'm going home,' and I went home for a week or so just to get away from it all." Remarkably, this capricious little rebellion had no adverse effect on his performance at exam time: "The exams went fine. In fact, I got really rather terrific results in the exams. I think I had honors in about three separate parts of the Registration Exam, which was pretty unusual."

Classmate John Taylor viewed Moon as a coldly competitive person endowed with great, if unpredictable, energy. Taylor wondered if Moon was really cut out for a career as a librarian:

From the first day, we were conscious of "Shiner" Moon, as he was generally known ["Shiner" being a play on Moon's surname, a popular British practice; Moon had no recollection of being called "Shiner" at Loughborough]. Eric always played to win. This was equally true with sports (I remember playing tennis with him) or the Library Association examinations. I don't know whether he played cards but if so I wouldn't have played with him for money.

At that time he had the look, with his thin mustache, of a rather undernourished secondhand car salesman and probably something of the manner of one. I can remember him discussing American novels — Wolfe, Steinbeck, Dos Passos, etc. — but never any English ones. There was something in his general go-getting attitude that made you feel that conventional British librarianship would never hold him — in fact you wondered if any librarianship would.

Ron Surridge, his closest friend at Loughborough, admired Moon's ability to make difficult tasks look easy: "This, of course, showed itself in our studies. Eric was a top grade student, passing his examinations seemingly without effort but as a good all-rounder was as conscientious in his studies as in his sports. He showed brilliantly in debates and even then exhibited a characteristic even more pronounced in his later years—that of keeping cool under fire. He needed to—he created a lot of heat."

Though he lacked the temperament of a scholar, other qualities stood Moon in good stead at Loughborough, where resourcefulness, inventiveness, quick-wittedness, incisive argumentation, and high exam scores were prized over erudition and contemplation. In addition to being a quick study who normally acquitted himself well under pressure, he possessed strong communication skills. "Eric was articulate in speech and persuasive in his use of the written word," observed Stokes, who believed these talents were key to his success as a student and later in the field. For his part, Moon believed the papers he wrote for Stokes at Loughborough helped lay the foundation for his eventual career as a library journalist. He also credited discussions in Stokes's classes with teaching him the fundamentals of polemics: "I was probably one of the most argumentative in class. I did argue quite a lot."

Playing Fields of Loughborough

In the late 1940s Loughborough College ranked among the top sports schools in England, and Moon and Surridge lost no time letting the coaches know that the School of Librarianship had a couple of phenoms ready and able to play—tennis, soccer, cricket, badminton, whatever. Moon:

Only two library school students ever made any of the college teams—Ron Surridge and me. I played for the college tennis team and the soccer team, and Ron played for the college cricket and badminton teams. On the badminton team he was the only non–Malayan player. One year the captain of the soccer team was the captain of the English Olympic team, so we had pretty high-class teams. Also, that year tennis was interesting. I had been number one on the college tennis team and a guy from South Africa came along who just beat the living daylights out of me, and he became number one on the tennis team. He subsequently went down to Wimbledon where he qualified but lost in the first round. So I discovered how far my old dreams of Wimbledon had gone down the drain.

Surridge added these recollections: "Eric represented the college in tennis and football, I in cricket and badminton. Loughborough was then, and probably still is, Britain's foremost athletic training ground and such was the quality of Eric's play that I thought he could easily have made a career success in either sport. As a natural athlete with a keen eye for the ball he shows it now in tenpin [tenpin bowling] and golf." Though not as accomplished an athlete as Moon or Surridge, Bill Graham also found relief from the rigors of study through sport: "At every opportunity between lectures we would move out onto the playing fields and play endless games of cricket. In hindsight, the sun seemed to shine every day."

Goodbye to Southampton Public—Forever

In the summer of 1948 Moon and Graham returned to their jobs at the Southampton Public Library in the lending and reference departments respectively. There they awaited the results of the Registration Exam and weighed their professional futures. Graham had pretty much decided to stay put at the library, but Moon had a strong desire to return to Loughborough the following September for a second year —called the finals year —*if* all went as he hoped:

After taking the Registration Exam we had to wait for the results, which took quite sometime coming through. As you can imagine the Library Association does not work with great speed any more than the American Library Association does. Roy Stokes, meanwhile, had been in touch with me and said he hoped that I'd be coming back for the finals year. I said, "Roy, I don't know whether I can; I don't know whether I can afford it; I don't know whether I can get another year's leave of absence; I don't know whether I can get another government grant." And he said, "We'll take care of that. Just come." But I said, "I don't know if I passed," and he said, "You will pass."

As it turned out both Moon and Graham passed the exam with flying colors and subsequently became chartered librarians. They were now professionals with the right to call themselves Associates of the LA. They now had their library union card. Graham, who found everything he ever wanted in his hometown, remained at Southampton Public for the duration of his career, serving for many years as head of the reference department before retiring in 1974. Moon, however, was determined to return to Loughborough in the fall to study for the FLA, especially after Stokes called to let him know he would get a FETS grant for the second year. Ambitious and impatient, Moon hankered after success, but not ordinary success. He wanted to be the next Lionel McColvin, or at the very least among the top librarians in the country: "It seemed to me that going for the finals year was my one chance for a crack at this and that I better take it and the risk be damned. If I didn't do it now it meant being confined to a somewhat pedestrian middle-level life in the profession forever."

In this mood Moon went to see Bob Lynn, telling him that he planned to return to library school for another year. Regrettably, Lynn was uncooperative. According to Moon, "Lynn said I cannot spare you for another year, and I cannot guarantee you a professional position when you come back at the end of the year. So I said, 'I will have to take my chances, won't I,' and went anyway." Graham's version of the Lynn-Moon meeting is livelier: "Eric asked for further leave of absence to continue his studies and after a desk-thumping episode Eric stood up for his principles, resigned, and went back to Loughborough to complete his qualifications." Quite possibly Lynn, remembering Moon as something of a problem employee, was happy to see his back. Or perhaps Moon reminded the chief librarian too much of his son who did not return from the war.

Finals Year

A defiant but upbeat Eric Moon returned to Loughborough in September 1948 for a second year to study for the Fellowship, or FLA. Of the approximately 30 students in his original class less than a dozen came back for the finals year. Moon: "My finals year was similar in many ways to the first year except that we were a smaller, more elite group. We spent much more time with Stokes." Along with Moon, those returning included Ron Surridge, Tony Rowberry, John Colgan, and Derek Austin.

They spent the year studying for the LA's advanced exam and working on a thesis. The exam covered all the essential subjects (reference, bibliography, cataloging and classification, book selection, and so on) in great detail, plus there was a literature component that required in-depth knowledge of standard authors. "We had a very heavy literature exam," Moon explained. "It was an exam in which you could get asked anything about any major author over a period of several centuries. The idea was that library students should know authors." He recalled Stokes used a "cunning" technique to prepare his charges for this part of the exam:

> I remember particularly that in preparation for the finals literature exam Roy got us to learn through teaching. He would assign each of us to teach certain authors, but the cunning thing he did was he would never have you teach anybody you knew much about. He knew I was the American expert, so he would not let me near Steinbeck or Wolfe or Faulkner or Hemingway. Instead, he gave me Mrs. Gaskell and George Gissing. Of course, you had to learn about them if you were going to teach the class about them. So I was spending all this time reading goddamn Mrs. Gaskell!

Moon's thesis topic — the American writer John Steinbeck — was obviously more to his liking. He had begun reading Steinbeck soon after going to work at Southampton Public as a teenager, and his interest had never waned: "I was onto Steinbeck pretty early. I remember being greatly enamored with *In Dubious Battle*, which is his most labor union conscious novel, at least before *Grapes of Wrath*. You have to remember that I was essentially an English socialist, so Steinbeck struck a great chord with me, particularly after *In Dubious Battle*. He is also kind of sentimental, which appeals to young people. I was still sentimental then, not cynical as I became later on." He finished his thesis, "The Position of John Steinbeck in the Contemporary American Novel," prior to leaving Loughborough in June 1949.

Much to his relief, Moon escaped "all the silly little college restrictions" during his finals year by sharing a room off-campus with Ron Surridge and Tony Rowberry. They lived at a guest house or inn about two miles from the college in a small village called Quorn, which Moon described as "in the middle of foxhunting country, a very upper-class area, very county." But despite their swell surroundings the three roomies were poor as characters in a Gissing Grub Street novel. Their government grants barely covered basic expenses, and Moon and Surridge each had a wife and child back home. Eric's firstborn, a son, Maxwell David, arrived in April 1948 and Surridge's wife delivered a daughter around the same time. "Because we were sharing we could just about afford the room," Moon remembered. Beyond that things were extremely tight:

> We had very little money left over for food and stuff, so we had to do some entrepreneurial things to help out. I remember that Ron and I worked the young ladies in the grocery shops around town rather hard, because rationing was still on and we didn't have rationing books or anything else, so we had to work stuff under the counter with the help

of some friendly young ladies in these shops. One of the other things that helped out enormously was some of my early training with Jock at darts. Ron and I played for two darts teams in Quorn and the pubs would feed us a lot of free beer and sandwiches and things like that, so that helped out with the food expenses.

Moon and Surridge also turned lunches at the school into adventures in culinary frugality. Library science classes no longer met in the old Nissen huts, having moved to a building in town. The new classroom had an electric fire (or heater) that provided a modicum of warmth during the winter months, and the impoverished duo used it to fix tasty treats. Moon: "Ron and I would frequently during the lunch hour toast sandwiches on this electric fire with Gorgonzola cheese and God knows what else, and Stokes would come in and wrinkle up his nose and say, 'Moon and Surridge have been at it again.' We were famous for the cooking sessions, and everybody noticed what we had for lunch."

Bibliographic Perfection

The second year at Loughborough flew by faster than Moon could think up terrible things to say about Mrs. Gaskell. Before he knew it, it was time to take the advanced exam, a tense but exhilarating time. Psychologically, he and his classmates ceased to be students, becoming instead candidates for the Fellowship, the Holy Grail of British librarianship. No longer were they answerable to their mentor, the good Stokes; their fate now rested with anonymous LA examiners, all of whom possessed the FLA and were considered among the best and brightest librarians in the UK. These personages would prepare, administer, read, and grade the exam Moon and his mates were about to take—a multifaceted test famous as the ultimate measure of a librarian's breadth of knowledge and depth of understanding of his or her profession. That the failure rate was high was no secret. "I don't think that more than 30 or 40 percent passed," recalled Moon, "and you could pass certain sections and fail in others. The person who passed everything the first time was very unusual."

Moon and Surridge crammed together as the exam period approached. According to Moon, "Ron was a great worrier. He used to worry about the exams coming up, and he would sit up and study for all hours. Tony Rowberry was the most laid back guy you could imagine, and would say 'For God's sake, you guys, go to sleep.' And Ron would keep me up before the exams for hours, wet towels around the head and asking questions so he could keep answering questions until he got it into his head. So he had to be mothered a lot, but he was a good guy to live with."

Candidates typically sat for the exam over a period of several days; altogether it required from 18 to 20 hours or more to complete. Moon took the exam in a hot, noisy room, obviously not ideal conditions for such business, but per usual he rallied his faculties and did amazingly well. Not only did he pass all sections of the exam on the first try, he earned an honors certificate in historical bibliography. Only later did he learn from Stokes that he had received a perfect score on the bibliography exam — and that, even more incredibly, his examiner had been Arundell Esdaile, then the foremost

British authority on the subject. Moon was stunned: "It blew my mind. Getting a perfect grade from Esdaile was like being sanctioned by God." What's more, Moon was apparently the only candidate ever to receive a perfect score on an LA exam. Roy Stokes talked to Esdaile about Moon's accomplishment:

> Perhaps my main memory of Eric academically is that in the final examination in historical bibliography he received a mark of 100, a perfect grade. The examiner for historical bibliography was Dr. Arundell Esdaile, who at that time had only recently retired from his lifetime of work in the library of the British Museum. I spoke to him at a meeting just after the exam results came out and said that I didn't know of an occasion when anyone had received a mark of 100 in any examination. And Esdaile said, "I can't recall ever having given a perfect mark before but the paper that was submitted had no mistakes in it whatsoever, so there was nothing that I could do but give it the highest mark." That was no mean achievement.

After passing the advanced exam in the summer of 1949 Moon submitted his Steinbeck thesis to the LA as the final requirement for the Fellowship. Then he waited. Months later, in May 1950, the association's Registration and Examinations Executive Committee, after reviewing the thesis and finding it satisfactory, voted to elect Eric Edward Moon a Fellow of the Library Association. Now, with the impressive initials FLA behind his name, Moon was among the UK's library crème de la crème — at least on paper.

Married Life

Soon after marrying Diana Simpson in May 1947 he hied off to library school in faraway Loughborough for the better part of two years, seeing his wife, who remained in Southampton, only at infrequent intervals during that time. Moon believed that Diana, who lived with her parents and continued to work at the public library as a junior assistant, had no problem with this arrangement:

> I went home very, very rarely. I didn't have the money for one thing. Diana was understanding; she knew I had to get through this; she was supportive. She was OK; she was in good hands. My first son, Max, was born while I was at Loughborough, in April 1948, around the beginning of the last term. I was not home when that took place, but the birth was a breeze, right on time, it was routine. I do remember, however, that Ron Surridge's daughter was being born around the same time, and he was frantic because she was late in arriving. I had to mother Ron for several weeks during this traumatic period.

Did newlywed Diana Moon possibly resent the fact that her husband was rarely home? That he led the life of a virtual bachelor for the first two years of their marriage? That he failed to be with her during the "routine" birth of their first child? Moon insisted there was no problem: "The marriage was OK. Maybe she harbored some resentments about this, but I don't remember any problems arising. I would get home between terms and periodically at other times, but not very often because I simply couldn't afford it."

Valedictory

Moon always looked upon his time at Loughborough with satisfaction and gratitude. The library school, and particularly Roy Stokes, had an enormous influence on his development as both a librarian and human being. The school and Stokes systematically introduced him to the body of knowledge that comprised the field of library and information science. The school and Stokes prepared him to confront the onerous Library Association examinations with confidence. Finally, the school and Stokes imparted a set of core convictions—ask questions, think for yourself, challenge orthodoxy, insist on change when change is necessary and right—that served him well throughout all facets of his career.

Moon, who grieved when Stokes died in February 1995, remembered his mentor as a magnetic individual as well as a superb teacher: "He taught everything in sight—bibliography, reference work, literature, administration, you name it. And he was clearly committed to his students and committed to turning out people who were going to make a difference. You felt that. I've described Loughborough as a 'school for revolution.' That, it seems to me, is what we were doing there. Stokes was trying to turn out people who would challenge the status quo, question what was done, why it was done, why it couldn't be done better. That was behind the teaching all the time."

Stokes encouraged his students to look for "the heart and core of it all," which to him meant questions, not answers:

I've always said that nobody should leave library school thinking that they know the answers to anything at all, that no one on the faculty knows what answers to give, nor does the profession as a whole. The ideal state in which to leave a school of librarianship on graduation is that you have some darn good questions. If you know the right questions, then at least you know what lines to pursue in order to find some tentative answers. This has always been my feeling about debates. Ask the right questions, the probing questions, the kind of questions children ask when they're learning for the first time: Why? Why? Why? Why?

Moon left Loughborough in June 1949, his formal education concluded. The time had come to put theory into practice. As might be expected, Stokes played a central role in helping his star pupil land his first job as a professional. "Roy was scouting for us," recalled Moon. "As I remember it, Mary Austin had just recently been appointed county librarian at Hertfordshire, just outside London. She was a friend of Roy's and said to him, 'I've got several jobs coming up in the county—send me some of your good students.' I know several us went down there; I don't know how many, but Derek Austin [no relation to Mary Austin] and I were both appointed straight out of library school."

– 5 –

Advancing in British Libraries

Fizz in the Air

In late summer 1949 Moon — 26, thin, angular, cheeky, fresh out of library school, brimming with bright ideas and buoyant expectations, married with one child — went to work for the county library system in Hertfordshire as a regional (or branch) librarian, his first professional job. Hertfordshire, a geographically large county in the south of England on the outer rim of the Greater London area, lay within easy reach of the central city via rail or motorway and was an integral part of the London commuter belt. Greater London then had a population of roughly 8.5 million and was even more of a political warren than it is today, comprising 90 separate and widely diverse local government authorities, including 28 metropolitan boroughs, all of which, for instance, had autonomous public library systems. Historically, London had pushed outward in every direction, and by the time Moon arrived in Hertfordshire the city stretched higgledy-piggledy for 35 miles north to south and 40 miles west to east.

It was in this huge, sprawling, still war-weary but very much alive metropolis that Moon would spend the next nine years of his life, remaining at Hertfordshire for a little more than two years, then moving ever closer to the heart of London, first to Finchley, then Brentford and Chiswick, and finally Kensington, which he left in June 1958 for a job abroad in Newfoundland, Canada. During the London years he worked enormously hard and in the process gained valuable practical experience in every major area of professional library work. Tireless, he also spent vast amounts of time and energy on library association business, plus writing articles and reviewing books for the library press. These collateral activities helped advance his career by getting his name around and providing him with opportunities to put forth his ideas while at the same time taking potshots at the old, ingrained ways of doing things. To his credit he did not shrink from telling the truth as he saw it, be it in person or in print, though his confrontational style was not always appreciated. Many of his colleagues — especially older librarians who had been in place before and during the war — found him overbearing and bad-mannered and dismissed him as an *enfant terrible*.

The London that emerged from World War II bore little resemblance to the self-satisfied city that had flourished in the previous century during Victoria's long reign, when it was not only the capital of the nation but of the empire and, many believed, the world. Rather, thanks to Hitler and the Luftwaffe, parts of London had been blasted to rubble, and for a long time after the war the city was plagued by varying degrees of disruption and turmoil, the landscape pockmarked with disfiguring craters, bomb-scarred buildings, and stressed-out citizens. The words of the poet Shelley—"Hell is a city much like London"—seemed eerily prophetic. Moon's recollection of London at the time lacked poetry but was vivid: the place "was a fucking mess."

And yet, notwithstanding its physical and psychological wounds, postwar London was an exhilarating place to be, particularly if you were, like Moon, a young, spirited, go-getting professional starting an interesting career. The end of hostilities meant reconstruction of the city's damaged roads, bridges, buildings, communications, and other infrastructure, a massive undertaking that put the accent on the future rather than the past. But more than that, London after the war was the locus of a peaceful revolution that promised much needed and long overdue changes in British society. After its crushing election victory over the Tories and Winston Churchill in 1945, the Labour Party finally emerged as the dominant political power in Britain after decades of false starts. In the words of historian A.J.P. Taylor, the war "had changed the very spirit of the nation. No one in 1945 wanted to go back to 1939." Responding to a clear mandate for social and economic renewal, Labour nationalized various industries and embarked on an energetic program aimed at creating a better, more equitable, more caring state, the cornerstone of which would be free health service for all.

Young fire-eating socialists like Moon idolized the chief architect of the new National Health Service, Aneurin (Nye) Bevan, a Welsh-born politician who for years had been a leading member of the left wing of the Labour Party. A staunch antifascist, an uncompromising champion of working-class aspirations, a man of unflinching principle, a spellbinding orator capable of making mincemeat of any opponent (he once called the House of Lords "vermin in ermine"), Bevan kept postwar politics roiling. His enemies detested him — the British Medical Association sarcastically dubbed him "the Minister of Disease"—but partisans believed that he and not Clement Attlee, the low-key prime minister, represented the true heart and soul of Labour's revolution. (Churchill memorably skewered Attlee as "a sheep in sheep's clothing.")

Nye Bevan appealed directly to Moon's innermost political convictions: an abiding faith in democratic processes and socialist solutions coupled with a deep-seated distrust of elites. For Moon and numerous of his contemporaries who had grown up poor during the Depression and then had been plunged into a bitter world war, voting out the hated Tories, who had run the country seemingly forever and had mucked it up seemingly royally, was almost as sweet as defeating Hitler and his cohorts. And then seeing their own political agenda put forward — and implemented!— was better than all the clotted cream in Devonshire — a dream come true. It was a heady time in the land of hope and glory.

Libraries in the UK understandably were in bad shape in 1945, having been neglected during the years of economic privation and war. There had been relatively few new libraries built since the 1920s, books and materials were in short supply, and librarians often acted like relics of the Edwardian Age. Happily, public libraries—the people's libraries—experienced a strong resurgence under the policies of the postwar Labour government. Established in the 19th century as part of the movement toward universal education, public libraries offered every citizen the possibility of a better life through reading, self-education, and unfettered access to knowledge and information. For the working class especially, Labour's prime constituency, libraries represented tangible hope for an improved tomorrow. Moon and other reform-minded librarians—mainly young practitioners who had been in the war and had only recently qualified—embraced the concept of the public library as a vital institutional force for social progress. Energized by a national government willing to invest heavily in public services, these librarians set about reviving the nation's libraries and, equally important, changing British librarianship to reflect their own dynamic vision of the future.

Harold Smith, then a London librarian and part of Moon's circle of acquaintances, recalled the period after the war as "one of the golden eras of British librarianship. Libraries were, without a doubt, on the upswing, popular, and in demand. All over London—and all over the country—libraries were opening, expanding, trying new ideas." Ron Surridge too noted the optimistic spirit of the times: "These were the days when there was a tremendous fizz in the air of librarianship here. Things were really on the move after the years of war." Because it had the largest concentration of libraries and librarians in the country, the Greater London area was naturally the hub of this renaissance. Moreover, the Library Association, the embodiment of the British library Establishment, had its headquarters in central London (in the Bloomsbury area), which added the froth of politics to the fizz of change.

Moon and his compatriots thrived in this intoxicating atmosphere. Surridge described the scene: "In London there was usually some library connected activity every weekday night and Eric and I were usually involved—duties permitting. And afterwards almost invariably the meeting of minds in the Marlborough pub, just by Chaucer House, the old LA HQ, where my memory is of Eric with pint in hand and pipe of St. Bruno in mouth." Edward Dudley, an up-and-coming librarian who also worked in the London area and knew all the key players, remembered another Moon constant: a propensity for backroom machinations as a means to gain his ends.

Just as he had adapted readily to the military and then student life at Loughborough, Moon felt comfortable in London and environs from the beginning. He quickly became the leader of a band of like-minded colleagues, ambitious men who were not shy about promoting their views, agitating for change, getting noticed, and doing their bloody best to discomfort the old guard. Moon relished the competitive beat of the big city, which suited his style. He liked being at the center of things. He was, at least in his mind's eye, a young Nye Bevan doing combat with the troglodytes. Some others, however, saw him as a junior Machiavelli.

London was a stage large and consequential enough to accommodate his manifold ambitions. On the most prosaic level Moon wanted to be a chief librarian—not in 15 or 10 or five years but soon, very soon, ASAP. But chiefships were at a premium, so he drove himself to make his mark on the profession as rapidly and incisively as possible, lest he not be properly positioned for the big opportunity when it came, if it came. Constantly calculating his chances he worried that someone else — most likely one of those many other war veterans in their mid-to-late twenties who had also raced through library school and who were now busily climbing the job ladder right along with him — might snare the choice positions, leaving him behind, stuck in a run-of-the-mill job, part of the undistinguished pack. That would be intolerable. After all, he was special. Wasn't he? All during the London years he was dogged deep down by the question, Would there be room at the top for him?

Hertfordshire

In 1949 Hertfordshire was a county in transition with a growing population that would soon reach 500,000 (and well over a million by the beginning of the 21st century). The county's largest city at the time was Watford, an industrial community of 75,000 located about 15 miles north of central London. Numerous smaller towns and villages dotted the 632-square-mile county. Prior to World War II the county had been overwhelmingly rural and agricultural, known for good pasturelands, arable farms, and picturesque parks and woods. This bucolic picture began to change after the war, due mainly to the construction of large housing estates and new towns throughout the county, including Hemel Hempstead in the west, Hatfield in the east, Stevenage in the north, and Oxhey (now South Oxhey) in the south. Created under the auspices of the New Towns Act (1946) and Town and Country Planning Act (1947) and built on land acquired by the London County Council, these instant communities were designed to relieve urban congestion and provide comfortable, affordable suburban housing for thousands of people from the inner city who had been displaced during the war. Because Hertfordshire had abundant open space and easy proximity to commercial London, it seemed an ideal place for such development.

Hertfordshire's public library system boomed after the war, the result of both the county's sudden population swell and government policies promoting libraries. In many ways the Hertfordshire system typified county libraries all over Britain at the time, which were just then coming into their own. Before the war an estimated six million Britons living in counties (as opposed to municipalities) lacked library service of any kind, whereas by the end of the 1950s virtually all county residents had access to either a main library, a branch, or a bookmobile. According to Ken Stockham, a Moon contemporary and authority on the subject, county libraries in Britain grew dramatically during the postwar period and soon became "the dominant force in the development of British public libraries." Because county libraries were where the action was, said Stockham, "Many of us who began our careers in municipal libraries transferred to the county services."

Moon agreed with this assessment, grateful that his first professional experience came in a county library: "In the period after the war the county systems, contrasted with the city systems, were growing more rapidly and had the larger per capita support.

They were also ahead of the city libraries in hiring women as head librarians. And on the whole, county libraries were more progressive and much less traditional and stuffy than city libraries. That's why I was happy to start off in a county system." In the case of Hertfordshire its library service was well funded, possessed a reasonably good book collection, and had a director, Mary Austin, who proved to be a forward-looking, service oriented librarian not at all reluctant to delegate real authority to her professional staff, many of whom, including Moon, were in branches far from the headquarters library in Hertford, the county seat.

Moon's job at Hertfordshire involved two very different responsibilities. The first involved overseeing an established branch library at Bushey, a residential town a few miles down the road from Watford, and the second required the creation of a brand-new library service for Oxhey, a housing estate just south of Bushey that was still being construction in 1949. The challenge for Moon entailed meeting the library needs of Oxhey's new arrivals—mostly working-class families relocated in the Hertfordshire countryside from devastated areas of central London — while at the same time maintaining expected levels of service at the Bushey branch, which catered to a predominantly affluent readership. With the ink on his Associateship barely dry and no prior knowledge of the communities involved, he plunged into this challenging assignment with high hopes. He immediately sized up Oxhey as a heaven-sent opportunity to showcase himself an innovative, committed librarian. And Bushey? Well, Bushey was another matter altogether.

Opposition at Bushey

Like a hound sniffing for the scent of fox but getting only skunk, Moon never connected with the people of Bushey or the locals who worked at the branch library. An old, well-to-do town of (then) 15,000 with a 13th-century church and a large historic hotel, Bushey was politically and socially conservative and doubtless had been since the days of Ethelred the Unready. Moon, a son of the working class and an ardent Labourite, was repelled by Bushey's bourgeois attitudes and snobby manners. He denigrated the town as "a retired colonel community," a dwelling place of reactionaries.

"My immediate job," he recalled, "was to plan a library service for Oxhey while at the same time trying to keep Bushey happy." But conflict at Bushey was evident from the outset:

When I went there, Bushey had a nice branch library with a pretty conservative staff. I was informed almost immediately upon my arrival that the staff let it be known that they had not requested my appointment, that they did not particularly want me. I had been imposed upon them by the county. There was a woman on the staff who had been there for many, many years who was related to a board member who was the person they really wanted. But I had been bestowed upon them. So it was a great beginning for someone straight out of library school. A nice situation to be faced with.

Moon retaliated, albeit obliquely. He had to let the Bushey community know that he was in charge, that he was not a Milquetoast to be pushed around:

Bushey was established as a library service so there weren't too many things that had to be changed there, though I did attempt to change the tenor of the book collection. One of my early encounters with censorship was at Bushey. We had a collection of art that was changed periodically, the pictures rotated every so often. The pictures were always very good, quiet delightful Vermeers and the like hung around the library. The first opportunity I had to choose the pictures I asked for a batch of Gauguins. And I got enormous flak from the board and some readers about all these naked women around the library.

"I didn't do it on purpose," he said years later, a wink in his voice. "I just like Gauguin. I thought, hell, wouldn't it be nice to have a change, and so we had our first big explosion." Over time, Moon came to view the Bushey experience as a valuable lesson in library management: "It was an interesting political exercise for a first job. I think that this was one of Hertfordshire's chief contributions to my career. It was an early exercise in dealing with opposition — opposition right at the heart of what I was doing. I was fortunate that I had Mary Austin's total support and encouragement, otherwise the job would have been quite unbearable."

Moon also looked for political support in the Bushey community. Austin allowed him considerable leeway to conduct the job as he saw fit, within the constraints imposed by the local library board, a cautious, tweedy body that usually opposed him and his ideas. "One of the things I did quite early," explained Moon, "was go out and look around at the Labour Party people in the area to see if there was someone who might be able to get elected to the library board, so that I would at least have an ally. And I did succeed at this after a year or so." Nevertheless, antagonism between Moon and Bushey continued throughout his time at Hertfordshire, the community wishing its brash branch librarian would just go away and he mentally cocking a snook at the town's straitlaced borrowers whenever they came to mind.

Innovation at Oxhey

His positive energies at Hertfordshire went into fashioning a rudimentary library service for the new housing estate at Oxhey, whose people he understood and empathized with. When he arrived in 1949, "Oxhey was not much more than a whisper. At first there was nothing much in Oxhey, a huge area much larger than Bushey. Then suddenly it built up and became full of city people living in council houses." Gawan Vesey, a classmate of Moon's at Loughborough and his successor as regional librarian at Bushey-Oxhey, recalled Oxhey's early history:

Building at Oxhey began in 1947 and was virtually completed in 1952 with over 4,000 dwellings housing a population of 17,000. It must have been a strange experience for families, many of whom had lived in quite close-knit communities in the crowded streets of London, to find themselves living in an area surrounded by fields and woods. In the estate's early days there were very few amenities and only a few shops. Most of the residents were young and working class. Oxhey is now called South Oxhey, to distinguish it from the much older urban district of Oxhey which lies some distance to the north.

Most Britons, Moon among them, welcomed the Labour government's creation of new towns and estates like Oxhey as enlightened social policy, but many people in the communities themselves suffered terrible adjustment problems, especially during the early years. A major complaint concerned the dearth of services, both public and private. Moon: "What we had was an inner-city population dumped down into what they regarded as a rural atmosphere with no services. It led to a lot of frustrations and dislocations. It was a trying, difficult period." From the start he recognized that his top priority was to get some sort — any sort — of library service operational in Oxhey as quickly as possible. Consequently, no one was happier than Moon when in the spring of 1950 a county library bookmobile began making its rounds on the estate. Moon's bookmobile service, which brought the public library to the fledgling community, was seen as both a practical step forward for the often dispirited residents and a symbol of hope for the community's future. Already Moon was making a difference in people's lives. He relished the feeling.

Some unexpected help getting the bookmobile on the road came his way in the person of a young, adventuresome Canadian librarian named Al Bowron, holder of a library science degree, who just happened along as a *deus ex machina* in early 1950. Moon was elated to have an intelligent sidekick about his own age with library experience who was not adverse to working under less than perfect conditions:

Clearly, the only way I could begin serving Oxhey was through a mobile library. Just about the time I was planning this service, this Canadian, Albert Wilson Bowron, apparently came over to England on his own and waltzed into the Library Association in London and said, "Look, I'd like to work over here for a spell. Can you recommend a library in the area where interesting things are happening where I would be welcome." Bernard Palmer, who was then education officer of the LA, said, "Well, there's this guy Eric Moon out at Bushey-Oxhey in Hertfordshire who's setting up a whole new system to run these London County Council housing estates, so why don't you go out and see him." So Al came out and I liked him. I called up Mary Austin and asked if I could hire him for a spell — six months or a year — and she said sure.

So Al and I set up the mobile service. We went out and tramped the empty streets of Oxhey, which still had no sidewalks or street signs. The houses were there, the people were coming, but it was very primitive. We had to make our own maps with Xs on. We went to the schools and sent home notices with the kids about the new mobile service. It was the first social service in Oxhey.

Fiction traditionally has accounted for a high percentage of books circulated by public libraries in Britain, and light novels—in Britspeak, "thrillers," "loves," and "cowboys"—have been by far the most popular. Moon and Bowron, however, decided to defy convention when stocking the Oxhey bookmobile collection. Instead of larding the mobile's shelves with "lights," they selected "higher quality" fiction and then closely monitored borrowers' reactions. Moon believed, given the option, library users would more often than not choose better literature over pap.

We decided to develop a mobile collection of higher quality fiction — usually mobile collections aimed at the lowest common denominator. We decided our bottom-level fiction would be around the Somerset Maugham level. At first we didn't know how readers would respond, but they responded very favorably, with surprisingly little demand for lower-level fiction. In fact, we found the general reading level was quite high. Mary Austin at HQ was impressed by our requests for serious fiction, asking "What are you guys doing with all this stuff?" I said, "We're putting it on the Oxhey bookmobile." She could hardly believe it.

Al and I used our personal taste and knowledge of authors to decide what was better fiction. Many of us saw this as our primary work. If we weren't good at developing such a collection, then what were we doing calling ourselves librarians? We learned that it was important to match the collection with the readership. For example, we knew we couldn't try such an experiment at Bushey, because of the snobbery and antagonism. In fact, within a year Oxhey's circulation per capita was double or triple that of Bushey's. We couldn't keep the fiction collection stocked.

While the bookmobile was heavily used and a notable success, it had the inherent drawbacks of any mobile service, such as restricted hours, limited number of books in the collection, lack of space for study and browsing, and minimal opportunity to provide reference assistance. Only a branch library, Moon was convinced, could offer the sort of comprehensive service Oxhey's residents needed and deserved. The county at the time lacked the money for a new branch, but he was not dissuaded. In early 1951, his last year at Hertfordshire, he came across an abandoned, dilapidated farmhouse built in the 1860s on the edge of the Oxhey estate and, with Austin's blessing, converted it into a temporary branch library. The people of Oxhey responded positively to their improvised branch, despite constant problems with the building: "There was dry rot under the floor boards and parts of the roof leaked, but it was better than nothing," observed Gawan Vesey. Indeed it was. The "temporary" branch served Oxhey's library users for more than a decade, until finally replaced in 1962 with a permanent building in the center of town.

The farmhouse-cum-library is early evidence of one of Moon's great professional strengths: a natural talent, displayed throughout his career, for finding workable solutions to thorny or seemingly intractable problems. Transforming an old, broken-down building into a branch library when the alternative was no branch at all might not sound all that impressive in hindsight, but at the time it required a combination of good judgment, unclouded vision, resolute commitment, bounteous energy, and a touch of audacity — qualities not every neophyte librarian has. But Moon had them in abundance, and later his gift for problem-solving contributed significantly to his success on the American library scene.

Al Bowron remained in Hertfordshire for more than a year, assisting Moon with the bookmobile service and working in the Bushey and Oxhey branches, where his chief memory is of being cold: "I arrived to begin my duties in the winter and found the library at least a little warm after a very drafty ride on the bus from Edgware Station. My enjoyment of the heat was always shortlived. Eric on arrival at the branch would throw open wide the windows 'to let the fug out.' I've never forgiven him for his cruelty to a poor subservient, underpaid Canadian librarian!" Bowron returned to Canada in 1951 and went on to work at the Toronto Public Library, direct the Scarborough (Ontario) Public Library, and finally become Canada's first full-time library consultant.

At Last a Place of Their Own

Eric Moon and Diana Simpson became husband and wife in May 1947, but prior to his going to work at the Hertfordshire Public Library in the summer of 1949 the couple had never had a home of their own, nor had they even lived together for any length of time. Now, finally, the Moons—Eric, Diana, and year-old son Max—were together as a family for the first time. But they had little money, and Eric was forced to borrow from his friend Bill Graham to set up housekeeping.

At first the couple rented a bedsitter in the Oxhey area, where they had a furnished bedroom and shared a kitchen and sitting (or living) room with the owner of the house, an arrangement that "wasn't very pleasant," recalled Eric, annoyed by the lack of space and privacy.

Around this time Hertfordshire authorities acquired a private estate a few miles north of Watford in the tiny village of Langleybury with an eye to fixing up the property and using it for county services and employee housing. The estate included a mansion (later a school) and, behind that building, stables, which were to be converted into modern flats, or apartments. Eric put his name on the list for one of the new flats and approximately six months later the Moons at last had a place of their own. They lived in Langleybury until Eric left Hertfordshire for Finchley near the end of 1951.

The Moons' home life was ordinary, uneventful, prosaic. Diana, described by Norman Horrocks as "slim, attractive, very pleasant, and easy company," occupied herself as housewife and mother while Eric pursued his budding career with the intensity of a young lion on the prowl, the job and association activities keeping him out late most weekday evenings and sometimes weekends too. For Moon, work definitely came before family. While at Langleybury he did manage to find time to play some soccer, helping start a village team with two neighbors who were also hotshots at the game. "After recruiting a team and training them, we joined a local league and finished first in our division the first year. That was kind of fun," he recalled. The Moons did experience one memorable domestic misfortune while at Langleybury. One cold winter evening when Diana and Max were visiting her family in Southampton, Eric returned to the flat to find that the water pipes had frozen and burst. The place was heavily flooded, he remembered, "a terrible mess." This was but the first of several floods in his life. A few years after Langleybury a large water tank ruptured at his Brentford and Chiswick library, inundating the building and ruining a priceless collection of small press books. Later, after coming to the United States, the Moons suffered through two nasty floods in New Jersey where they lived in the 1960s. "Floods seem to be part of my life," he reflected, apparently wondering if these events had some mystical meaning or were simply chance occurrences.

On a brighter note, Diana became pregnant with their second child while at Langleybury. A boy, Alan Richard, was born on November 18, 1951, soon after Eric left Hertfordshire for Finchley. Just as she had done when Max was born, Diana returned to Southampton and her parents for Alan's birth, and again Eric "didn't get down to Southampton that evening."

On to Finchley

By mid–1951 Moon had been at Hertfordshire for two years and was eager to move on and up. His main mission at Hertfordsire — to bring basic library service to Oxhey — had been accomplished, and he found no joy at snooty Bushey. Besides, he could now tack the prestigious initialism FLA behind his name, having been elected a Fellow of the Library Association in 1950. Again, Roy Stokes played an instrumental role in promoting his career, mentioning Moon's name to J.D. Reynolds, director of the Finchley Public Libraries in north London, who was looking for an enterprising young librarian to run his North Finchley branch. Moon applied for and got the job of district (or branch) librarian, starting at Finchley in October 1951 and staying until the summer of 1954, when he left to become deputy chief at nearby Brentford and Chiswick.

Located north and west of central London about eight miles from Charing Cross, Finchley in the 1950s was a residential municipal borough with a population of nearly 70,000. Unlike Hertfordshire, Finchley was urban in character, the community made up largely of older middle-class homeowners, about a quarter of whom were Jewish. (Finchley became famous in the 1980s as Margaret Thatcher's parliamentary district, though when Moon was there Mrs. Thatcher was a politically green, 26-year-old research chemist who had just lost her first bid for Parliament as the Conservative candidate not for Finchley but industrial Dartford in Kent, a county south of London. It was not until 1959, after Moon had left England for Canada, that the future prime minister first stood for and was elected MP for Finchley, long a safe Tory seat.)

When Moon arrived at Finchley the library system consisted of three facilities — Central Finchley, East Finchley, and North Finchley — each roughly equal in terms of collection size and population served, though Central, nominally the headquarters library, had the largest reference collection. John Reynolds, the chief librarian, believed in providing an active reference service, so much so that he encouraged his staff at Central to come to his office, strategically located behind the circulation desk, whenever they had queries they couldn't handle: "If I don't have the answer," he said, "who's going to have it?"

Among the three libraries, the North Finchley branch, Moon's new bailiwick, normally circulated the fewest books each month. Reynolds gave Moon carte blanche to try anything within reason to boost the branch's performance, a charge that appealed to the new district librarian's robust competitive instincts. Reynolds told Moon in so many words that he was on his own at North Finchley; that he should use his initiative and make whatever changes he felt were necessary; that he, Reynolds, would not be an obstacle but would furnish unconditional support for whatever Moon tried, short of some moral lapse, like dropping his drawers on Finchley Common. Reynolds was Moon's kind of boss.

Moon's second in command — or "number two" — at North Finchley, John Wakeman, turned out to be a smart, sensitive, hardworking, likable chap in his early twenties. Wakeman, who would go on to work at the Brooklyn Public Library in the United States, edit the *Wilson Library Bulletin*, produce a standard reference work (*World*

Authors, 1950–1970), and write poetry, initially begrudged Moon's appointment, grumbling that "he usurped my job." But in no time at all, Wakeman remembered, the two men were great buddies, working together as harmoniously as bangers and mash:

Fresh out of library school, I'd been appointed assistant branch librarian at North Finchley. A few months later my boss moved on rather abruptly to higher things and I was left in charge. I coped amazingly well. It amazed me, at any rate, and I couldn't see why the arrangement should not become permanent. But the job was advertised and went to this bumptious whiz kid with the ridiculous name.

Consequently, I disliked Eric Moon even before we'd met, though once we had it got harder. For one thing, he had ideas about the purpose and possibilities of librarianship beyond the wildest dreams of my library school instructors, if they had wild dreams. And yet he listened to my own half-baked theories as if I was Moses down from the mountain. He seemed to be under the delusion that he was supremely fortunate to have me as his assistant, and this warmed me to him.

"John and I struck a chord," recalled Moon. "It was clear that we felt like a good working team. I said to him, what we're going to do here is play a lot, and we're going to work a lot, and we've going to experiment a lot, and we'll see what works and what doesn't. But for sure what we're going to do is make this the best of the three Finchley libraries." This pep talk — unadulterated Moon — outlined his game plan for victory at Finchley. Competitive from head to toe, he always sought to win, to be first, to be best, to beat the other guy, no matter how consequential the business at hand, be it circulating the most books in Finchley, running for elected office in a library association, or playing a board game with brother Bryan or son Alan.

Library Salesmanship

The North Finchley branch, which had about a dozen full-time staffers at the time, was a substantial, traditional building that looked like a library should look in the 1950s. Inside, the large, high-ceilinged reading room had heavy dark wood shelving with a big open space in the middle. Solid and durable, the library was inviting in a quiet, subdued way. Moon, however, thought the place too dark, too somber, too unwelcoming. Immediately he and Wakeman began, in his words, "to jazz up the library." He warned the staff, "We're going to launch into salesmanship," by which he meant use modern promotional techniques to market the library and its wares:

So we made directional signs painted bright yellow and red and generally jazzed the place up. We went to a couple of art schools in the area, asking for their help in designing and making a whole slew of portable display cases — essentially boxes with shelves and glass doors. We set up six or eight of these in different areas of the library, stocked with books on different subjects, and we put some around in the community, in shops and so on. We also got a store up the road that sold kitchen equipment to lend us an oven in which we displayed cookbooks. We did crazy stuff.

We were always on the lookout for ideas that would move stock. John and I read magazines from other trades and professions in search of ideas. One of us came up with the discovery that stock at eye-level moves better than that placed anywhere else. So one Monday morning we came into the library and said to the staff, OK, we want everybody on board, we want to go all around the library and move all the books on the bottom shelves to eye-level and vice versa, the whole way down the line. What about the Dewey order, said the staff? Screw the Dewey order, we said. And at the end of the week we found that books that had not circulated for a year had gone out like wildfire—that it was working.

Along the same lines Moon put "bottom-shelf" books in some of the display cases, labeling them "Books Nobody Will Read," and borrowers eagerly snapped them up, perhaps simply to prove the sign wrong. "There were a couple of glass-fronted display cases in the lobby," Wakeman remembered. "We began to churn out subject reading lists and devised exhibits to go with them, featuring surprising objects borrowed from friends, food shops, movie theaters, museums. If a news story broke of national or local interest, we junked our current theme and overnight produced a tie-in book list and display." The campaign to sell the library was infectious: "We kept experimenting like this and soon the whole staff joined in the spirit of the thing," recalled Moon, mover of stock.

Saturation Buying

One of Moon's most inventive experiments at North Finchley involved what he called "saturation buying," a systematic effort to satisfy public demand for standard titles, especially fiction:

John and I sat down and said there are certain books people come into this library asking for but they are never on the shelves. What can we do about this? Clearly, we don't have enough copies of these books. So why don't we see how many copies it takes before a reader has a good shot at finding the book on the shelves. So we set up a list of titles and authors, some classics, some very popular, such as Hemingway, Faulkner, Thackeray, Somerset Maugham, Nevil Shute. We decided that on the first week of the month we would check the shelves and any titles on our list that were not in the library we would immediately buy three additional copies. One month later we would do the same and buy three more copies if needed.

We made some interesting discoveries, though today they seem so damned obvious. One was that libraries are wrong in assuming that all books by an author have equal appeal. For instance, in the case of Jane Austen you need many more copies of *Pride and Prejudice* than you do *Northanger Abbey*. In the case of Thackeray there was only one title—*Vanity Fair*—that was in heavy demand all of the time; other Thackeray titles you can forget about. Another thing we learned was how many copies a library needs in order to get reasonable saturation—that is, to have at least one copy on the shelves most of the time. In the case of *Pride and Prejudice*, for instance, in our branch library it was 42 copies! We found it was practically impossible to saturate anything by Nevil Shute; the same with Hemingway.

In one instance, saturation buying appeared to backfire, almost embarrassing Moon in front of Finchley's deputy director. Only hastily arranged defensive action saved the day. Moon:

There was much interest in what we were doing at North Finchley by other librarians in the system, often with a critical eye. One morning the branch was hosting the weekly meeting of the top brass, including the deputy director, a nice but conservative fellow named Tommy Tomlinson. He came to me before the meeting and said, "Eric, I thought you and Wakeman were the great salesmen, movers of stock. I've just looked at your shelves and there are *six* copies of *War and Peace* sitting there. Now you know nobody needs that many copies." And I said, "Tommy, you just don't realize how things move around here. Those six copies will all probably be in circulation by the time we finish this meeting." He said, "Ah come on, I don't believe that." I said, "You want to bet half a crown on it?" He said, "Right."

Before I went into the meeting I told Wakeman those six copies of *War and Peace* had better be in circulation by the time I got out of the meeting. John immediately got the six copies and quickly set up a prominent display. In the staff room he got bright yellow paper and vivid red paint and scrawled MARLON BRANDO'S FAVOURITE BOOK on the paper, and placed it across the top of the display. Incidentally, playing at the cinema on the corner of our street was *A Streetcar Named Desire*, starring you know who. When we came out of the meeting two hours later, Tommy went over to the fiction section and found no copies of *War and Peace*. He said, "Where did you stash them?" I said, "Let's ask the desk if they have any circulation records on them," and they produced six Browne tickets holding book cards for all six copies of *War and Peace*.

As part of the saturation buying program Moon and Wakeman examined all copies of classic fiction titles in the collection for physical condition, weeding out those that were old and dog-eared and replacing them with new editions with glossy jackets and inviting covers. Moon believed the classics "weren't competing on an even field with the current stuff. People would say you don't need all those classics because they don't circulate, but the reason they didn't circulate was that they were in tatty condition. If you have a shop of clothes and some are new and others look secondhand, obviously the new will sell while the others won't. So we went out and got glossy jacketed editions of the classics and they went out like wildfire."

Dear M. Malraux

Moon also brashly created a reference service at North Finchley where none had existed before. Brashly because, although today all but the smallest or most moribund public libraries in the UK routinely provide reference assistance to users, such was not the case prior to World War II or in the immediate postwar period. The new library schools, including Loughborough, offered courses in reference work—called "assistance to readers"—but many library directors of the day, products of an earlier time and philosophy, resisted the notion of actively helping borrowers, viewing the library's role primarily as custodial. Edward Dudley, who worked at the public library in the London borough of Hampstead in the 1950s and later became a prominent library educator, remembered how difficult it was to change the old ways:

Not only old systems but old modes of thought. Our chiefs were varied, some of them were progressive, but the general tone was authoritarian — male authoritarian — and, above all, hierarchical. There was, in a sense, a professional intellectual gap between senior public librarians and middling characters such as Eric and myself. One way in which it showed itself was that most of the new library types had a much sharper sense of the importance of what we called assistance to readers. It's strange to look back now but the concept of the reference or information desk in a lending library was rare. The concept of a whole staff organized so that readers had immediate and direct access to someone who could help sort out their problems was rare.

Moon installed North Finchley's reference (or enquiry) desk smack in the middle of the reading room. The librarian at the desk — usually Wakeman or another young professional, Margaret Amor, or Moon himself—fielded all requests for information other than directional questions, a function that had previously been handled by circulation assistants as best they could. Library users were also encouraged to telephone the branch for reference information; just call Hillside 4081 and have your questions answered! Like his experiments with promoting and developing the book collection, the new reference service shook up everyone involved, changing old habits and patterns and creating a sense among staff and patrons alike that the library was a lively, service-conscious enterprise concerned as much with shaping the future as preserving the past. Moon knew, of course, that he had the full support of John Reynolds, a progressive chief who needed no convincing about the importance of helping borrowers find books and information. Still, a reference desk at a branch library in Britain in the early 1950s was both uncommon and unconventional, and some of Moon's more conservative professional brethren pointed to it as yet another example of his radical notions.

Prior to Moon's coming to North Finchley, reference service at the branch consisted of a small, motley collection of fact-finding books and little else. "Searchers after knowledge were satisfied with this or, more often, told to get a bus to Finchley's Central Library," recalled John Wakeman. Moon, said Wakeman, emphatically rejected this passive approach:

Eric held that if someone came into his library for a piece of information, they should not be sent away hungry. So, if we couldn't squeeze an answer out of our own tired books, we'd telephone the central library or a specialist library elsewhere. Or the Polish Embassy, or ICI [Imperial Chemical Industries], or Lord's Cricket Ground, or whoever might supply a solution. When no one else could establish the exact date of the first production of Anouilh's play *Antigone*, I called Paris and got the answer from Anouilh's wife or secretary or whatever she was.

A similar incident involving another famous French writer exemplified the kind of heads-up reference service offered at North Finchley during Moon's time there. He vividly recalled Wakeman's quest to track down the meaning of an enigmatic reference in an André Malraux novel:

We had a policy that nobody could come into North Finchley with a question that we couldn't answer. One episode stands out. There was this lady with a novel by André Malraux that had a passage with an obscure context, and she wanted to know what it meant, what the author was referring to. Wakeman was on the desk and said we'll find out what it means. He made a photocopy of the page and called French literature experts at the University of London, British Museum, and hither and yon. He spent about a day on this but came up with nothing.

Eventually he sought me out in my office: "Eric, I think we're beaten. I've tried everything I know on this, but no luck. I can't get an answer." I said, "But you haven't tried everything. How about Malraux? Let's write to his publisher and see if we can get an answer." Within two weeks we had an answer — in Malraux's handwriting. We called the lady and apologized for taking so long but the only person who could answer the question was Malraux himself. She said, "I am impressed!" That woman lobbied for money for the Finchley Public Libraries from then on; she was a fantastic supporter. Now *that's* information retrieval.

A Yank at North Finchley

Hankering to see more of the world and expand his library horizons, Wakeman left Finchley and England near the end of 1953 for America, signing on with the Brooklyn Public Library as part of a one-year exchange program. In return, Stanley Crane, a young Brooklyn Public librarian, came to work for a year at North Finchley. Moon remembered that the personable Crane "spent most of his time at the enquiry desk, where he was quite a favorite with patrons. Stanley was probably the greatest Anglophile who ever lived. He had this vision that England and everything English was perfect. He arrived at Waterloo Station just as the city boys [financial types who work in the City of London] were arriving, and Stan looked at them and said, 'My God, this really is England.' There they were with furled umbrellas, striped trousers, and bowler hats." From Waterloo Station Crane proceeded up to Finchley via the Northern line to check in with John Reynolds. That, according to Moon, is when the American's disillusionment began:

Stan walked into the library and over to the desk and said, "I'd like to see Mr. Reynolds, please." Directed up the stairs, he came into an office with books everywhere, piled around the walls, all over the place, but no sign of anyone. So Stanley very politely coughed and a head appeared from above one of these piles of books, and there is a guy wearing an old checked shirt with sleeves rolled up and corduroy pants. Stan said, "Oh, I'm sorry, I was looking for Mr. Reynolds." And the man said, "I am he." Stanley was flabbergasted: "Here's the head librarian and he looks like a laborer, for Godsake."

After squaring away his work permit and other business with Reynolds, Crane was sent to North Finchley to meet Mr. Moon, his new supervisor. Moon was working in his office when Crane arrived: "Stan found me in my office where I'm sawing up boards for a display and I'm wearing an old checked shirt and corduroy pants. Stanley said, 'You're not Mr. Moon by any chance, are you?' And I said 'Yes.' He said, 'The librarians in this system do not look like Englishmen to me.' And I said, 'Well, goddamn it, you don't look like an American either. Where's your Marilyn Monroe tie?' That is how we started."

Stan Crane recalled he "expected a librarian in a formal frock coat and found — Eric. Informal to the *n*th degree." Not to worry, Crane and Moon hit it off like long lost brothers, working well together and often socializing after work. Crane remembers he and his wife Leila saw quite a lot of Moons, as well as Diana's parents. For his part, Moon enjoyed introducing the American librarian to things British:

> Stanley was interested in British beers, and once we went to a cricket match at Lord's. At one point Stan leapt up and shouted, "A goddamn homer!" Another time we were in London and happened to be going by the Houses of Parliament and there was a line, a queue longer than any theater queue, and Stan asked, "What the hell's that?" And I said, "I'll bet Churchill and Nye Bevan are debating today. It's the biggest show in town when they're on." Stan said, "Politicians?" I said, "Yeah, politicians." Stan could hardly believe that the people were so passionately interested in political debate.

Crane remembered these events differently: "I have never been to Lords. I think the story actually took place in a pub near the North Finchley library. The cataloger and Eric tried to 'explain' cricket to me and I found it impossible to understand, and never went to a match — ever! The Houses of Parliament story is another one. I always took politics very seriously."

By the time John Wakeman returned to Finchley and Stan Crane to Brooklyn at the end of 1954 Moon had moved on to the post of deputy chief at Brentford and Chiswick. Crane eventually became director of the Pequot Public Library in Southport, Connecticut, where he and his former boss at North Finchley crossed paths again ten years later when Moon, then editor of *Library Journal*, was shepherding around a group of visiting British librarians. As for Wakeman, after the Brooklyn Public, Finchley seemed dull, especially since Moon and his razzle-dazzle brand of librarianship had departed the scene. Soon thereafter he returned to the United States, working in the public relations department of the Brooklyn Public until 1959, when he became editor of the *Wilson Library Bulletin*, an appointment that would ultimately have a greater effect on Moon's career than his own.

Shortlist Tales

The next job, like the next pipe of St. Bruno's, was never far from Moon's mind during the nine years he worked as a professional in England. After a year or so at Hertfordshire he began contemplating his next move, and the same was true at Finchley. And he was not alone. Because the new library schools created after the war were turning out scores of qualified librarians every year, competition for professional positions at all levels in British libraries during the 1950s was much keener than it had ever been in the prewar years. Obviously, the further up the ladder one went, the tougher the climb became. "I was like everybody else in that postwar gang, applying for jobs all over the place," confessed Moon. "There was a gang of people, particularly around the London area, who were all equally qualified, who all had about the same experience, who all had come back about the same time after the war and had gone through library school, and who were all trying to move at about the same pace from the middle to the top of the profession."

To have any hope of securing that next position in the scramble to the top, the aspiring librarian had to make the shortlist — that is, become one of half a dozen or so finalists for the job. "There would be 200 to 300 candidates, but only five or six would be shortlisted," explained Moon. "Once you got on the shortlist, everything rode on how good was your ability to interview. It varied but interview committees normally had from six to 12 people, plus the librarian, who might or might not have real influence. The candidate would sit in front of the committee and each member would ask questions." Often the same men — rarely women — turned up on the shortlist, Moon usually among them. Soon, he remembered, "We began to think of ourselves as members of a club. We would go to one shortlist after another — it was like a reunion every three months." In addition to Moon, the London area shortlist regulars included Ron Surridge, Edward Dudley, Ken McColvin (Lionel McColvin's son), and Bill Smith, who was a London librarian and later well-known bookseller Moon got to know and become fast friends with through the AAL.

One of Moon's enduring memories of the shortlist circuit involved the time he competed with Norman Horrocks for the position of British Council librarian in Cyprus (the council being an organization that promotes cultural relations between Britain and other countries). Horrocks got the job in 1954 but the following year was wounded in an anti–British terrorist attack in the Greek Cypriot campaign for union with Greece. Horrocks's colleagues later referred to his injury with a certain jocularity, reporting that Norman returned from Cyprus with "a piece of hand grenade in his behind" (Dudley) or "his ass full of lead" (Moon). At the time, however, Horrocks did not find the experience amusing, spending months recovering in a London hospital. In retrospect, Moon had no regrets about not getting the job.

In another memorable instance he received a bit of shortlist advice that backfired. Eric Clough, an early mentor at the Southampton Public Library, suggested that during the interview it was advisable "to address yourself to the women on the committee, because in the final analysis the women are usually the ones who come up with the arguments that finally decide who gets hired and who doesn't." Moon took Clough's advice, which proved remarkably prescient but lost him the job:

While at Finchley I went to an interview for deputy librarian at Great Yarmouth in East Anglia. There were two women on the committee, and I directed my answers to them, as Clough had advised. But another guy got the job. I was disappointed because I thought I had done really well. At the next Library Association conference I ran into the director of the Great Yarmouth Library, who said, "Eric, you might be interested to know why you didn't get the job as deputy." I said, "Sure, I'm always interested in learning from my mistakes." "Well, what happened was that after your interview, one of the women said, 'That young man has a lot of talent but I don't think we ought to appoint him because if we do within a month he'll be found in the stationery cupboard with one of the young women on the staff.'"

Apparently Moon, the once and future amateur actor, had not yet mastered the distinction between winsome eye contact and the lecherous look.

In the case of the deputy chief position at Brentford and Chiswick, a job Moon did get, he and the others on the shortlist almost missed the interview — by a whisker.

Moon remembered the candidates "were told to wait on a bench over in city hall. I think it was Ted Dudley, who had just acquired his first electric razor, who brought the razor along with him so that he could get a last minute cleanup before the interview. All the candidates went to the men's room with Ted to try out his electric razor, and when the first candidate was called, we were all in the men's room!"

Sometimes a candidate who had just completed the interview would tell those waiting what sort of questions to expect from the committee. This is how Moon learned that one member of the Brentford and Chiswick interview panel was "hot" for the *TLS*— the *Times Literary Supplement*: "When he asked me about *TLS*, I said, 'Well, sir, I like it. It has the best and most job adverts for librarians of any publication in the country.' And the committee just broke up. I think I got the job because of that. It was a curious beginning to what was going to be a curious episode."

On to Brentford and Chiswick

Moon spent two and half years at Finchley, roughly the same amount of time he had been at Hertfordshire. A highly positive experience, Finchley allowed him to build on what he had learned at Hertfordshire, especially at Oxhey. By giving him the freedom to develop a reference service and to experiment as he wished with collection building and library promotion, John Reynolds gave Moon a taste of running his own show and, like a child greedy for sweets, he wanted more. It seemed only a matter of time before the ambitious North Finchley branch librarian, who had turned 30 in March 1953, would land one of the jobs for which he was shortlisted.

In the spring of 1954 Moon applied for the position of deputy chief librarian (or assistant director) at Brentford and Chiswick, a residential London borough nine miles west of the inner city and about equal distance southwest of Finchley. He made the shortlist, gave a bravura interview capped by his quip about the *TLS*, and got the job, starting that summer. (His successor at North Finchley, interestingly, was none other than his Loughborough mate, Ron Surridge, who was also climbing the career ladder in London libraries.) At that time the borough had a population of 60,000 and included the towns of Brentford, located on the Thames at the mouth of the Brent River, not far from Kew Gardens; Chiswick, also on the Thames and home in his later years to William Hogarth, the great 18th-century painter and engraver; and tiny Gunnersbury (population 5,600), which boasted a large public park.

The library also administered a local museum, and Moon's full title was, impressively, Deputy Chief Librarian and Curator, Brentford and Chiswick Public Libraries and Museum. In reality the buildings were antiquated and uninviting and, in Moon's opinion, the library system was "one of many metropolitan London libraries and not one with a very great reputation." He said he wanted the job "because it was that level up from where I had been. It was next to a chiefship, and you didn't really care at that stage what kind of library it was, because the competition was so heavy you had to take what you could get in order to climb the ladder."

His new chief was a chain-smoking 40-year-old woman named Florence Green, called Molly by most but Flo by Moon. Miss Green, who had become head librarian at Brentford and Chiswick nearly a decade earlier in 1946, was dedicated to her west London community (which became the borough of Hounslow as the result of a London governmental reorganization in 1965) and remained in the job until her retirement in 1977. Moon found her knowledgeable and supportive but eccentric: "Flo was an odd woman. She had a lady friend who was a little weird — into black leather and tights. She also had a habit of coming into the staff room and sitting up on the table, legs anywhere, and regaling us with stories about things that happened at conventions, and how the chairman of the board or someone had tried to make out with her. It was difficult to get the staff back to work."

Moon also remembered Green, who died at age 81 in 1995, as being well read — a "very literate woman" — and very political: "She was a big and well-known Labour Party supporter," who openly campaigned for Labour causes and candidates. Brentford and Chiswick, however, was a swing constituency and in the mid–1950s, following the national trend, it had a Conservative MP. Moon: "So the library committee was naturally heavily Conservative at the time, and Flo was in bad odor with the committee." Soon Moon, whose political radar had grown more sensitive as he progressed up the career ladder, was maneuvering cautiously behind the scenes on behalf of the library:

> I had to find ways to work with the committee that wouldn't be obvious or obviously undercut Flo, but at the same time getting things for the library she couldn't get because of the board's antipathy toward her. I never really made it known to anyone on the board that I was a very pro–Labour person, primarily because we were already in such difficulty because of her connections. Very quickly I decided that I'm not going to say anything about politics while I'm here or I'll be in the same boat as Flo. I would have drinks in the pub with members of the committee and managed to save some library programs this way.

If nothing else, the Brentford and Chiswick experience contributed to the maturation of Moon's thinking about politics in the workplace. He had come a long way since Bushey where, fancying himself a budding Nye Bevan, he wore his political convictions on his sleeve and made known his distaste for anyone or anything deemed Tory or bourgeois. He remained adamantly a man of the left, but Brentford and Chiswick presented an opportunity for him to play a more subtle or crafty political game, to temper his partisanship in the expectation of achieving a strategic goal. It was at Brentford and Chiswick that he began to see the wisdom, as he put it later, of keeping "party politics out of library business."

Headaches: A Flood, a Smelly Clerk, a Vindictive Janitor

The main library badly needed a face-lift when Moon arrived at Brentford and Chiswick in 1954. An "old, old" structure, it had a gloomy, forlorn appearance that turned off all but the most dedicated library users. Moon convinced Green to put him in charge of a refurbishing project: "I wanted to brighten the place up to attract young people, who didn't use the library heavily. We painted and I put in bright colors all over the place. I also tried to get Flo to move her office away from the staff room, and I eventually managed to swing that." Then calamity struck:

The tragedy was—after getting the library repainted, redecorated, and looking about a hundred years younger than when I got there—I'm called at home in the middle of the night by the police saying I've got to get back to the library because a huge water tank on the roof had burst and the whole library was totally flooded. I got there and our Chiswick Press collection—the finest collection of Chiswick Press publications in the world—was floating in water. Our great collection of Hogarths was floating in water. When I got there I stood and literally wept. It was the most horrible thing I had seen in a long, long time.

The flood and its aftermath preoccupied Moon for much of the remainder of his unhappy stint at Brentford and Chiswick, but he had other administrative headaches as well, not least of which was a seemingly endless string of personnel problems. A typical case was Michael, a junior assistant in the central lending library who had a bad case of body odor. Moon: "One day a delegation of half a dozen young women from the staff came to me and asked if I could do something about Michael." He wondered what the problem was: "'Michael seems a perfectly nice young man,' I said. 'He is,' they said, 'but he smells. Can you do something to get him to take a bath?' This was the first time I had had this sort of staff problem, so I had Michael in for a talk." It turned out that Michael claimed to own only one shirt, which he washed faithfully every two weeks. Moon solved the problem by offering to buy the stinky clerk a couple of extra shirts.

In another instance he had to deal with an overzealous Communist organizer on the staff, who was constantly importuning and upsetting people, readers and employees alike. But without question his most bizarre personnel problem involved the janitor at Chiswick, who, Moon believed, "had something" on the previous deputy librarian: "I think he had caught him screwing the chief cataloger or something like that." At any rate the janitor did pretty much as he pleased, spending most of his time while at work in the back alley taking his motorbike apart and putting it back together. It did not take Moon long to discover that "the janitorial work at Chiswick was going to hell. I talked to him and told him that he had to do his duties or he was going to go. I took the matter up with Flo and she decided to transfer him to a small branch, which was done."

A new janitor for Chiswick was subsequently hired, but he didn't last long: "One day shortly after the new janitor started," remembered Moon, "he was up on the ladder when he fell and broke both collarbones. We later found that the original janitor—in a vindictive move—had sawed the ropes of the ladder. It was a really strange crowd at Brentford and Chiswick."

On to Kensington

Moon admitted he "was dying to get out of Brentford and Chiswick because of all the problems we were having there," and by March 1956, less than two years after his appointment as deputy chief, he was gone, leaving for a newly created post with the Royal Borough of Kensington Public Libraries. Located in London's West End, the fashionable borough (today Kensington and Chelsea) had a population of approximately 175,000 and was a favorite destination of tourists, drawn by such attractions as the Royal Albert Hall, Kensington Gardens, Hyde Park, and Kensington Palace, a Crown property since the days of William III and birthplace of Queen Victoria. Edward VII granted Kensington its "Royal Borough" designation in 1901 in honor of his mother, who died that year.

When Moon arrived at Kensington Public the system consisted of a central library, which was quite old and terribly crowded with little space for new materials, and half a dozen branches. He had minimal contact with the chief librarian, a man named Massey who was near retirement, reporting instead to the deputy chief, Stan Holliday, a laid-back administrator whose duties included building Kensington's music record collection. "Because of space problems," recalled Moon, "the records were kept in Stan's office. Sometimes we used to play records all day in there. I had a seat in the corner of his office and it was here that I learned to appreciate Oscar Peterson and other of Stan's favorites." Holliday eventually became chief at Kensington and is best remembered for having written a little book called *The Reader and the Bookish Manner*, a humorous comment on the art of library administration.

Moon's position at Kensington had the official title of Head of Technical Services, though later in North America it became Head of Bibliographic Services on his résumé. To confuse matters more, he usually referred to himself as a "stock editor." Whatever his title, he was no longer a deputy chief. Had he gone down rather than up the career ladder? Had he taken a wise gamble — or stumbled — by leaving Brentford and Chiswick before landing a coveted chiefship? The question concerned him: "In a sense I was stepping down a level in the library hierarchy to a job that was number four at Kensington, behind the director, assistant director, and chief assistant," but on the other hand Kensington was a "much larger and more prestigious library system" than Brentford and Chiswick. Still, no matter how he rationalized the situation, the suspicion that he had lost a step on the competition in the race to the top of the British public library heap gnawed at him all the while he worked at Kensington. Still, in typical Moon fashion, he gave the job everything he had.

Before Moon, Kensington had not had the position of stock editor, nor had any other library in Britain, save one. The job came about when an independent group of government efficiency experts— not librarians— evaluated Kensington's library operation with an eye toward improving performance. According to Moon, the team's report was generally favorable with one exception: "They said, 'One thing we don't understand is why there's no one top person in the library whose responsibility is book stock. It seems to us that in a library this would be a paramount function.' So the team recommended that a new position at a top administrative level be created for a person whose sole responsibility would be, what we would call today, collection development." Kensington acted on this recommendation and in due course hired Moon. As far as is known, at the time there was only one other stock editor in England, that being Ken McColvin at Lambeth, another metropolitan London borough.

Fascinating Job

Whatever qualms Moon might have had about leaving Brentford and Chiswick for Kensington disappeared, at least for the nonce, when he rolled up his sleeves and began to do what he perceived to be the work of a stock editor:

It was perhaps the most fascinating library job I ever had. I was always more interested in the collection and its use and the relationship between it and readers than I was almost anything else. This was the most interesting job I ever had in libraries because it focused on the collection — and I loved doing it. Book selection and the use of books have always been at the center of my interest in librarianship. It's the most interesting part of the profession — and the most important.

All aspects of collection development — selection, acquisitions, cataloging and classification, allocation of materials (or stock) between the central library and the branches, and weeding — came under Moon's purview. He delegated day-to-day administration of the cataloging department to a subordinate, preferring to spend the bulk of his time selecting and acquiring books. He brought his "saturation buying" experience, field-tested at Finchley, to Kensington, and concurrently developed a plan for reducing multiple copies, or reserve stock, within the system. He assigned each Kensington library responsibility for collecting certain subjects and authors, which reduced the need for duplication among the system's libraries and thus created space for additional titles.

He also got to know the London book scene well, becoming familiar with all the major sellers and many of the independent shops, especially those on Charing Cross Road, which was only a hop, skip, and jump from Kensington. On occasion he bought entire private libraries and once a whole bookstore. Likewise, he developed a close working relationship with several area booksellers who specialized in supplying libraries. One of these was Harry Karnac, a savvy bookman who ran a small operation in south Kensington. Initially drawn to Karnac because he carried a large selection of American titles, Moon soon discovered the bookseller offered prompt, efficient service plus a substantial discount. Over time he gave Karnac a sizable share of Kensington Public's book business, a decision that later caused both him and Karnac some pain: "Someone in local government," growled Moon, "thought maybe there was something fishy about my giving so much business to Harry Karnac, but an investigation revealed no kickbacks or anything of that sort." Nonetheless, the allegation left a bad taste, and in a paper entitled "A Stock-Editor's Viewpoint" delivered at the North-Western Polytechnic School of Librarianship in March 1957, Moon aimed a barb or two at the bureaucrat who dared question his integrity:

This job cannot be done entirely by sitting at a desk and checking numerous lists which pour in from publishers and booksellers. It can only be done satisfactorily if the stock editor or book-buyer has the time and freedom to get out often and without restriction, so that he can discover resources for himself, and so that he can buy any book worth having wherever he may find it, without being hampered by petty rules about petty cash, booksellers on or off the licence, or the shadow of the audit department.

Moon delivered this paper on March 5, the day before his 34th birthday, hardly an occasion for celebration: he was approaching middle age, he was still not a chief, and time was slipping away.

Novel Reprints

During this time public libraries in the Greater London area had a "last copy" cooperative program for preserving books, both fiction and nonfiction. In the case of fiction, each cooperating library agreed to save the last copy of all novels within a particular span of the alphabet based on the author's surname. Kensington, for example, agreed to retain at least two copies of books by authors H through K. Moon remembered one particular title—*Blood and Sand*—very well. Written by Vicente Blasco Ibáñez and first published in 1908, *Blood and Sand* served as a catalyst for a much needed reprint service:

Kensington had the last two copies of *Blood and Sand* in all of London—for whatever reason it was filed under I, for Ibáñez, instead of B, for Blasco, which it should have been. Our copies were always out because the novel had been made into a movie with Tyrone Power as a bullfighter who falls for Rita Hayworth. For years after the movie came out everybody wanted that book. It was totally out of print and unavailable except at Kensington. Among the wholesalers I used to deal with in my job was Chivers, which also ran a big bindery. One day I happened to mentioned *Blood and Sand* to the Chivers rep I dealt with, and not long afterward Chivers started a fiction reprint scheme based on demand in Greater London public libraries, and of course *Blood and Sand* was the first novel reprinted.

Missing Shoes and Itchy Feet

One evening Moon was on duty at the Kensington central library when something peculiar happened:

I was in charge of the system because the deputy and chief assistant were away. About seven o'clock the reference librarian came scurrying downstairs to my office and said, "Eric, you better come upstairs, we've got a real problem. A borrower's shoes are missing!" We were all puzzled—the patron had kicked off her shoes while reading and now they were nowhere to be found. There seemed little to be done except to call the police and a cab for the patron, which I did.

The next night, the same thing happened to somebody else. This time the press got ahold of the story from the police, and pretty soon the *Daily Mirror* and reporters are there to cover the story: SHOE THEFT AT KENSINGTON LIBRARY. Eventually we learned that Radio Luxembourg set up the thefts. The offshore station had a program that was a predecessor to *Candid Camera*, and this skit involved stealing people's shoes and reporting their reactions.

The missing shoes incident perhaps subconsciously reminded Moon of his own predicament. His feet were itching to move on, to run, not walk, up the career ladder, to fulfill his destiny, whatever that might be. But at Kensington he was going nowhere. As interesting, even fascinating, as the job was, it was not enough: "You had to get a chiefship eventually," he knew, "or you could wind up stultifying somewhere forever." Time was beginning to turn against him: no longer "young" Mr. Moon, he would be 35 on March 6, 1958. He assessed his prospects and found them bleak: "While at Kensington I looked around the profession and did a very deliberate tabulation of the jobs that were left in the country that I would be interested in and that were financially attractive. I determined that there were about 80 jobs like that that would come open within a reasonable period of time in the whole country, and then I figured there would be 300 to 400 candidates. The odds weren't too good."

Moreover, Moon had enemies within the profession, especially among the old guard — prewar men who were viscerally predisposed against the new wave of librarians produced by the postwar library schools and who actively disliked disputatious smart-asses like Eric Moon, whom they knew or had heard of through the LA. Moon looked longingly toward North America, but ran into a formidable roadblock: "I was always interested in America. I thought, gee, that's a move I would like to make. I wondered how to do it, and I found that it was virtually impossible, because American libraries would not recognize British qualifications, especially since I had no university degree." But what about Canada, with its historic ties to Great Britain?

So I thought that might be a backdoor. I wrote and applied for several jobs in Canada and got negative responses. Again, I had no degree and they wouldn't recognize British qualifications. Then I wrote to the executive director of the Canadian Library Association and told her who I was and of my interest in getting a senior public library job in Canada. She wrote back and said unfortunately nothing much was available, although there was an assistant children's librarian position open that might be worth a shot. Here I was, a fairly prominent librarian in Britain by then — I was so pissed off with that response.

By the end of 1957 Moon had spent nearly two years at Kensington. He had mastered the job of stock editor and was anxious for the next challenge. But what? Where? When? How? Kensington was his wilderness. The waiting ate at him.

– 6 –

Ruffling Establishment Feathers

Domestic Life at Cricklewood

Moon worked in England as a chartered librarian from mid–1949 to mid–1958, and despite sometimes becoming frustrated or disheartened by what he considered slow progress on the career front, especially in the latter years while at Brentford and Chiswick and Kensington, he gave each job everything he had, often going well beyond what was required or expected. Most people would have been satisfied, and many exhausted, by the effort he put into his work; few would have felt the need or urge to do more. Not Moon. He could no more contemplate being *just* a librarian than he could voting for a Tory. For many reasons—an everpresent need to be in the limelight, a hunger for professional recognition, a relentless competitive drive, an intrinsic desire to lead, the attraction of being at the top — he was compelled, like a climber drawn to the mountain peak, to become a player at the highest levels of librarianship. He envisioned himself as both librarian and library leader, roles that, while interrelated, were distinct in his compartmentalized mind. As a consequence he spent his years as a professional in British libraries not only working extremely hard at his regular job but devoting untold hours to association activities, writing and editing, teaching, and union business.

The demands of such a schedule inevitably took a toll. "It was frightening," he conceded years later. "I never realized until the moment when I was leaving England and I had to resign from everything that I was involved in, just how many things I was doing. And I look at that today and I'm absolutely horrified. How the hell could I have done all that? What kind of life could I have had?" For one thing, he rarely got what most mortals consider a normal night's sleep. For another, his busy professional life left scant room for family. Moon acknowledged that he and Diana "had a hard time" during the 1950s in England: "My hours were unbelievable. I was writing, on committees, teaching, everything. Frequently I wouldn't be home before midnight or later most nights of the week."

During most of this time the Moons lived in rented quarters in Cricklewood, a small northwest London community not far from Wembley Stadium. When Eric left Hertfordshire for Finchley in the fall of 1951, Diana, pregnant and close to term, remained at their Langleybury flat in Hertfordshire while Eric commuted via motorcycle. But after a few weeks they gave up the flat, Diana going to her parents in Southampton for the delivery in November of their second child, Alan Richard, and Eric renting a room in Finchley, scouting the area in his free time for suitable housing for his growing family. "Eventually I found us a place to live near Finchley—a place called Cricklewood, which was not far from the library, and we lived there the rest of the time I worked in England." Cricklewood, which at the time had a population of just over 5,000, turned out to be well situated for Moon's various London jobs, being about five miles south of Finchley, six miles northeast of Brentford and Chiswick, and four miles northwest of Kensington.

At Cricklewood, as she had done at Langleybury, Diana stayed home, her time taken up with domestic and parental responsibilities, more demanding now that there were two children; Max was nearly four when they moved to Cricklewood and Alan a newborn. Diana's parents visited every so often, which was too often for Eric. Her father—a blustering, opinionated blue-collar type—wasn't exactly Eric's cuppa. Still, he remembered married life at the time as "pretty good on the whole." Diana occasionally attended AAL events, such as a big cricket match in Sheffield in 1954 between the Greater London Division, for which Eric and Ron Surridge played, and the Yorkshire AAL team. ("Ron was a good cricketer," Moon recalled, adding: "He was better than me.") The Moons spent annual vacations with the Surridges at one of the popular seaside camps operated by Billy Butlin, a well-known British showman and entrepreneur known as "Mr. Happiness." Butlin, who had several such camps in England, offered economical holidays for middle-income families, featuring celebrity guests, variety shows, hokey communal activities, and plenty of hearty food—food being an important draw because certain items remained in short supply in the UK as late as the mid–1950s. Eric dutifully spent a week at Butlin's each year, though he disparaged the camps as too lowbrow for his taste, calling them "terrible places." But the presence of Surridge made the experience palatable: the two men could talk shop and sports while their wives and children partook of Butlin's many amusements.

The Moons also visited Southampton periodically to see Diana's family as well as Eric's mother and brother Bryan and old friends like Bill Graham, now a fixture in the city library's reference department. During one weekend in Southampton Eric rashly agreed to act as master of ceremonies at a dog show organized by Bryan. The gig, which tested Moon's impromptu stage skills, turned out to be a notable farce, bringing back memories of the Eastern Brothers and his "showbiz" days in the RAF. Despite all the problems, Bryan had faith that big brother Eric would save the day:

I was then a student at the Southampton College of Art making ends meet by giving police dog demonstrations with my two German shepherds. Another chap joined up with me with his two dogs. Our foursome was extended by my girlfriend's dog, so we rented a town hall one weekend for an ambitious showing of "doggery." There was an admittance charge to see police dogs in action, my girlfriend's show dog, and an animal talent contest. However, on the day, I had to brief Eric, who was MC, on a few minor problems. First, the female police dog was in heat and unwilling to perform. This upset the male dogs who were close to being irrational. Then my girlfriend's dog developed gun-shock from training and would not appear. Finally, there were no entries for the talent contest. I recall Eric was a little taken aback and asked how he was supposed to talk the audience through a two-hour dog show under the circumstances. I think I said, "You'll think of something. I have faith in you!" Somehow we got through and, as brothers, it may have been our finest hour. To which Eric probably would say, "What's this OUR stuff?!"

But diversions such as Butlin's and dog shows were the exception. Moon's life was essentially his work, in and out of the library. He did not believe Diana resented his hectic schedule or felt "left out," notwithstanding the large amounts of time he spent away from home. "But it was clear, I suppose, in retrospect that we were moving somewhat apart. She really was not developing anything for herself, and I was spreading my wings everywhere." Were there other women? "Oh yes, there were, here and there, but only one was serious. I don't want to name names." Ron Surridge, his best friend in London, summed up Moon's domestic situation this way: "I've no reason to think that Eric had other than a happy marriage with first wife Diana and the two boys, Max and Alan. We both had our first born at Loughborough, our families socialized a great deal, and we went on holidays together. They were always happy and pleasurable occasions. I know of only one relatively brief and passionate love affair Eric had outside the bonds of marriage to Diana."

The Moons suffered a painful personal loss in the mid–1950s while at Cricklewood when Diana became pregnant again but this time miscarried. The infant, a female, was born dead. "Somewhere inside I always wanted a girl," said Moon. The miscarriage was especially sad because there were so few women in the Moon line: Eric had no sisters and he and brother Bryan produced only male offspring, who in turn have (thus far) produced only more males. (His father Ted, however, did have two sisters among seven siblings and Ted's Australian sons Michael and David each begat a daughter.) Presumably Diana shared his desire for a daughter, though he was unsure if she ever learned the sex of the dead child; apparently he never discussed it with her. In any event, the miscarriage did nothing to strengthen the couple's increasingly detached marriage.

Association Man

Even as a junior assistant starting out at Southampton Public Moon sensed the key role associations play in British librarianship. Later, after studying at Loughborough and qualifying as a librarian, he became actively involved in the two most prominent of these associations, the staid Library Association, which he sought to change, and the feisty Association of Assistant Librarians, which he used as a power base. Later still, after leaving England for North America, he had a major impact on the fortunes of the largest library organization in the world, the American Library Association. Throughout his career, no matter which country he was in, Moon never wavered in the belief that strong, effective library associations are central to a strong, effective library profession.

In Moon's day the LA had its headquarters at Chaucer House in London, a stone's throw from the British Museum. The association, founded in 1877, very much reflected the views of the British library Establishment — a professional culture that was instinctively autocratic, excessively cautious, politically conservative, socially elitist, and almost exclusively dominated by white males. To protect its prerogatives the association developed traditions and procedures that discouraged or muzzled dissenting voices. But after World War II the LA had an increasingly difficult time maintaining its old, clubby ways. The new library schools were turning out a new breed of practitioners: bright, articulate military veterans— Moon and Surridge were but two examples— who balked at playing by the old, clubby rules. These outspoken young librarians— dangerous radicals in the eyes of the Establishment — found much wrong with the LA and immediately began pressing for change.

A major sticking point concerned representatives of local library boards who, while not librarians, were able to participate in — and *vote on*— LA business, this owing to their standing as "institutional" members. What most angered librarians opposed to this practice was the disproportionate influence these lay members— Moon called them "parish pump politicians"— exercised in the affairs of the association, particularly at annual conferences. Resentful librarians wondered whose sodding association was it anyway? Even the president of the LA in those days was not always a librarian, but some pooh-bah from the titled ranks of British society whose Old Boy tie and accent were always spot on.

If the hidebound LA resisted change, the upstart AAL encouraged it. Established in 1895 as the Library Assistants' Association and renamed the Association of Assistant Librarians in 1922, the AAL was originally an autonomous organization dedicated to improving salaries and working conditions for library assistants and providing educational support for those who wished to study to become chartered librarians. In 1929 the AAL relinquished its independent status and became part of the LA, a move that created what one past president of the AAL, Arthur Jones, called "an uneasy stepmother, stepdaughter relationship."

When the AAL agreed to affiliate with the larger and more powerful LA it did so only on the condition that it would retain much of its original structure and autonomy. The agreement permitted the AAL to keep its name, its national council, its various regional divisions (such as the Greater London Division, to which Moon belonged), and its official journal, the *Assistant Librarian*. In addition, the AAL was granted a number of special privileges, including automatic representation on the LA Council and major committees. For its part the LA welcomed the AAL into its ranks with the tacit understanding — mistaken, it turned out — that the AAL would eventually amalgamate or merge with the LA and ultimately cease to exist as a separate entity. Hotly debated for a decade, the merger question came to a head at a raucous AAL meeting in Dagenham in June 1939. In the end, the membership emphatically rejected amalgamation. Instead, the AAL continued on as before — a conspicuous and often rebellious junior member of the LA family.

After 1929 any member of the LA could join the AAL, including chief librarians, though by unwritten rule chiefs did not attend meetings or stand for office, the fear being that they might take over and run the association to suit themselves, thus subverting its original purpose. Curiously, the custom of banning chiefs did not apply to deputy chiefs or other top library administrators, who over the years frequently held leadership positions in the AAL. According to Norman Horrocks, a keen student of library association governance, this situation "led to the obvious anomaly that deputy chiefs from large city libraries could participate in AAL whereas chiefs from very much smaller institutions did not do so. But British life was never known for its being logical."

Always the AAL

Conflict between the LA and AAL was put on hold during the war years but soon afterward tensions resumed. By the time Moon began his career as a librarian in 1949 the AAL was widely considered a "ginger group," or radical element, within the LA. Stan Crane, the American librarian who worked for Moon at North Finchley, put it more colorfully, describing the AAL as "a gadfly in the skin of the Library Association — the Establishment." In the 1950s Moon and a small band of cronies gained leadership positions in the AAL. They had two fundamental, interlocking goals: to make the AAL as strong as possible; and to use it as a vehicle to get the stick-in-the-mud LA moving.

Moon first joined the AAL shortly after starting at Southampton Public in 1939. He was specifically interested in the association's correspondence courses that helped assistants prepare for the LA's Elementary Exam. After qualifying and going to work at Hertfordshire he became active in the association's Greater London Division, first editing its newsletter and then becoming GLD chairman, which included a place on the AAL Council. In 1955, while at Brentford and Chiswick, he ran for and was elected national secretary of the AAL, a key position that entitled him to a seat on the LA Council, where he had the opportunity — which he exercised fully and boorishly — to beard the library Establishment in its den. Three years later AAL members voted him vice president/president-elect, and had he not left England for Canada in 1958, he would have assumed the AAL presidency in 1959.

Of all the library associations Moon belonged to over the course of his long career, the AAL was clearly his favorite. It was the association that influenced him earliest and most deeply; it was the one he benefited from and identified with most completely. Open and alive, fraternal in spirit, and largely free of the pomposity that infected the LA, the AAL embodied his core professional beliefs and desires with greater fidelity than any other library organization (the only possible exception being the ALA in the late 1960s and early 1970s when American librarianship got caught up in the spirit of revolution for one brief, glorious moment). Whereas Roy Stokes had introduced him to confrontation librarianship as an academic concept at library school, the AAL gave him his first opportunity to practice it in the real world. In many respects the AAL experience was a seamless continuation of his professional education begun at Loughborough.

Shortly after moving to New York and becoming editor of *Library Journal*, Moon described himself in a published letter to his former British colleagues as still "an AAL member at heart." Years later when he returned to his native country for a visit, an interviewer noted that, though Moon had of course been an active member of the LA when he had worked in England, he was "always Moon of the AAL."

The AAL contributed to his professional growth in several important ways. Most conspicuously, it provided him and his mates with a freewheeling forum to debate the important library questions of the day. Many an evening meeting or weekend session was devoted to discussing such issues as interlibrary loan policy; cooperative acquisition schemes; the merits of the new (in 1950) *British National Bibliography*; the need to modernize circulation procedures (the ubiquitous Browne system was widely regarded as antiquated but what to replace it with?); the need to expand and improve assistance to readers (reference service); the perennial problem of censorship; and — a constant underlying concern — how to push, or at least nudge, the LA into a more progressive stance? Change, observed Edward Dudley, a London librarian heavily involved in association politics, was the watchword: "Above all, there was a feeling that many of us had that things just had to change — but that they weren't changing quickly enough."

Meetings of the AAL in the 1950s tended to be intense, combative, often impassioned affairs, words and ideas flying like hot sparks, some bursting into flame, others fizzling immediately. An inclusive, egalitarian organization, the AAL encouraged all members to join in the debate, to have their say, to press their case to the fullest extent of their abilities. Though hardly conscious of it at the time, members were honing their leadership skills through extemporaneous public speaking, chairing meetings and committees, writing for publication, and the like. Ron Surridge, who served as president of both the AAL and the LA during his career, viewed participation in the AAL as "a marvelous training ground in the 'politics' of the LA and in the fields of debate, organizing conferences, and producing lively newsletters and a very effective journal." Arthur Jones credited the AAL (in his presidential address to the association in 1960) with improving his self-confidence and the ability to express himself effectively:

I can well remember being far too tongue-tied to stand up and make any contribution to the discussion in the early meetings I attended. That kind of nervousness never leaves some of us, but at least in the AAL we have plenty of opportunities for practice in controlling it. It doesn't matter very much if we say something which afterwards seems to have been ill- considered. We shall probably be put right on the spot anyway, and therein lies half the pleasure and half the profit in our discussions. Much the same can be said of our arguments in print, in the pages of our monthly journal. We are as much concerned with fashioning our own thoughts and opinions as with making any important contribution to the literature of librarianship.

Like Surridge and Jones, Moon believed the AAL experience helped him and others of his generation become more articulate, better prepared professionals — a point he vigorously pursued in a speech to the AAL membership at the LA Centenary Conference in London in 1977. At the time Moon was ALA president and in a perfect position to compare British and American styles of library leadership:

A little over a year ago, my wife and I were at a Canadian Library Association conference. We watched and listened as a comparatively young man handled a very thorny and potentially explosive meeting with complete aplomb, quiet skill and total authority. He clearly knew parliamentary procedure, and just as clearly had solid experience on the platform. His accent was unmistakable, even to an American, and my wife said: "How come all you British librarians are so good at this stuff?" I knew that British librarian, and knew where he had learned that "stuff." I said, simply, "He's an old AAL type."

I don't know how many hundred conferences, meetings, committees I've sat in on during my years in America, but I can tell you that I've seen dozens of meetings mangled, mired in confusion, suffused with boredom, flooded with anger, when that kind of competence in the chair, or even at the floor microphones, might have prevented any of these reactions. In general—and of course there are a good number of shining exceptions—American librarians do not handle such matters as well as you [the AAL audience] do, and I think the early training in the heat of the kitchen that younger librarians get through involvement in the AAL may really account for some of the difference.

The AAL in Greater London (and this was true elsewhere as well) also offered members a strong social component, the GLD serving as a companionable club for those actively involved in association business. During Moon's time, evening meetings were normally held in a London area library or at Chaucer House and almost always ended up in a favorite pub. Here the faithful repaired to continue the colloquy, including mapping strategy for upcoming battles. "Here the arguments and discussions would go on long after the meeting itself," recalled Dudley. "Most of those attending were people our age — early and mid-thirties— as well as younger ones, students in their twenties." The talk was spirited but rarely malevolent, the atmosphere usually comradely, familial, uninhibited. The regulars, who knew and made allowances each other's foibles, were relaxed in this wordy, cozy, earnest, beery company.

In addition to evening meetings during the work week the GLD crowd periodically attended AAL weekend sessions held around the country. These association-wide caucuses attracted large turnouts and customarily involved informal discussions rather than set speeches and structured programs. And they were ideal for trysts. Moon:

> The idea was to involve more people in the association, and also to develop AAL positions on issues that we could take back to the AAL Council and then proceed on to the LA with. We wanted to develop a cadre of people around the country who would work to strengthen the AAL's positions and proposals in their areas. These meetings were professional — and very social. We had a lot of boozing and a lot of screwing. Diana was not at these meeting, nor were most of the other wives. Some people were seen crawling through windows at 3 o'clock in the morning.

Moon's commitment to the AAL knew few bounds. He seemed prepared, like a Homeric warrior, to go anywhere and do anything to further the association's goals— that is, *his* goals for the association. In a famous instance, he and Bill Smith — dubbed "the terrible twins of the AAL" by Norman Horrocks— drove 200 miles from London to Wales on a motorcycle in a rainstorm to speak against a proposal they deemed dangerous. The proposal — to move the site of the AAL's annual conference away from the large cities to more remote spots in the UK — was put forth as a matter of fairness to members who lived and worked in nonurban areas. Moon and Smith, however, saw it as a threat to their control of the association and its agenda: "We wanted to keep the conference in London or Manchester or Liverpool," Moon explained, "so that we could always get a large body of people to oppose anything we didn't like."

Those who advocated moving the site of the conference set up a meeting to debate and vote on the issue in far away Llandudno, a town in northwest Wales. Moon instantly smelled a rat and sprang into action:

So Bill Smith, who was editor of the *Assistant,* and I held a protest meeting at Chaucer House and said somebody had to go to Llandudno to oppose this proposal — they were holding this meeting out there so there would be no opposition. So we took up a collection so we could go to Llandudno to lead the opposition to the proposal. Bill and I set off on Bill's motorcycle — he had got his license to drive this thing only the week before — and we drove all the way from London to North Wales on this motorcycle. It rained like hell half of the time, and we didn't have real rain gear, so we were soaked to the skin.

When we finally got there late in the evening, having gone through another great rainstorm, the meeting was in progress. We're dripping water all over, and people are saying, "They finally got here." We walked down the aisle dripping water everywhere. Then we went up to the microphones and made our great impassioned spiels. We're doing great — we thought we had the audience coming with us. And then some young woman about 18 or 19 got up at another microphone and talked about these radical librarians coming in from London trying to tell us what to do. She gave this beautiful speech — and defeated us absolutely. She killed us. So we went back to London with our tails between our legs. The moral was we knew who the enemies were — they were the big chief librarians who controlled the LA and that's who we wanted to do battle with. But we were defeated by this young girl.

In the crowd that evening was an eager, observant student from the Manchester School of Librarianship who would in time become one of Moon's closest professional confidants. That student, Norman Horrocks, remembered the meeting well: Moon and Smith "were forceful and eloquent and almost won the day when a fellow student of mine from Manchester — a rather wispy young lady named Miss Nicholson—came on the platform and gave a very emotional appeal. There were tears at the end, and she managed to turn the entire audience against Eric and Bill. So, dejected, they went back to London on their motorbike. This was the first time I met Eric Moon."

Sins of the Library Association

Moon used his position in the AAL adroitly as a base from which to attack the alleged sins of the LA and to fight for reforms. As a prominent figure in the AAL he automatically had the attention of those who governed the LA — some of whom, quite frankly, hated his guts. But even those who disliked him most acknowledged that Eric Moon, FLA, was not some scatterbrain or idle windbag: his obvious intelligence, his status as an AAL leader, and his strong commitment to the profession gave his words and actions legitimacy and real weight. Moreover, he was not completely an outsider, a man from Mars; though young, he was already a presence in the LA. From 1955 to mid–1958 (when he left for Canada) he sat on the LA Council and for two of those years he was an LA examiner, which entailed marking Registration Exams prepared by candidates (like himself a few years earlier) seeking to become chartered librarians. Also, while on the Council he served on the board of the LA's London and Home Counties Branch.

Yet, despite this high level of involvement, he refused to moderate his criticisms of the LA or to appease or toady up to Establishment muckety-mucks. Perhaps if he had been successful in securing a chiefship he would have responded differently, softening his opposition and making peace with the powers that be, eventually sliding into the role of elder statesman. No one, including Moon himself, could know for certain how he would have acted had he become a chief, though Harold Smith, who knew him well at the time, believed he would always have been a rebel, that Moon and the LA were simply a bad fit, as different as Labourite and Tory. "Despite all his work for the profession and the LA," observed Smith, "Eric was never accepted by the Establishment, nor would he have welcomed that. He was a kind of guerrilla fighter for causes and issues. Not all of them were worthwhile but they usually raised the temperature, which I suspect was all he wanted to do on many occasions." Smith continued, "Eric and I were always friendly, but on occasion our relationship was that of adversaries. I was more straightforwardly political whereas Eric was, as I have said, a guerrilla fighter."

Moon's specific complaints about the LA pertained mainly to issues of governance and how the association conducted its business, with the question of undue influence by politicians and local library board members—all nonlibrarians—topping the list. Arthur Jones described Moon's deep feelings about this issue:

The Library Association in the 1950s was dominated by two elements: former presidents of the association who had a permanent right to continue to participate in the LA Council's affairs; and representatives of local library authorities—politicians, not librarians—who exercised a similarly blatant and shameless domination of annual meetings of members. The contemporary views of professional librarians were therefore largely squeezed out of both the Council and the Annual General Meeting. This was the most obvious of the evils which Eric Moon set himself to eradicate, and the AAL was the instrument he used to achieve his end.

Moon disdained the LA's so-called "institutional" members who, he and his colleagues believed, had too much power in the LA, most of it undeserved. These members needed their "wings clipped," he argued, adding: "Perhaps 'wings' is inappropriate, and 'horns' would be more suitable." He was likewise critical of the undemocratic method the LA used to select its presidents, who in his day sometimes came from outside the ranks of librarianship, the logic being that a luminary as leader would afford the association increased prestige and political clout. For instance, Prince Philip, Duke of Edinburgh, was LA president in 1950 when Moon received his FLA and hence the Duke's signature graced his fellowship certificate. Duke or no Duke, Moon condemned the way LA presidents were chosen in no uncertain terms: "I find it hard to believe that there is general acceptance and equanimity about a procedure by which a small group of senior citizens of the association retires to a small, closed room, like some medieval Star Chamber, later to emerge and tell you who your next president will be." He urged bylaw changes calling for presidents to be elected by popular vote.

His most visceral unhappiness with the LA, however, concerned its general ideological bent, which he condemned as narrow-minded, imperious, uncaring, reactionary. The association's apparent lack of interest in and regard for the great social issues of the day and how they impacted on libraries and librarianship rankled him no end. Arthur Jones, part of the AAL inner circle at the time, characterized Moon and his allies (who often included Jones) as "impatient to improve the role, image, and management of the Library Association and hence of the library profession." Above all else, Moon wanted the LA to connect with the real world. Instead of ignoring social problems he wanted the association — and by extension, the profession itself — to recognize and deal with them. He wanted a librarianship that was "political in the broadest social sense," a librarianship that "related libraries to society and its problems," a librarianship committed to the idea that libraries and librarians "have a social purpose." He argued that AAL activists were simply "trying to humanize the profession, to get it to understand that it had a social role — and the LA was doing little or nothing to promote these goals."

That LA leaders resisted such calls for social and political activism as vigorously as AAL firebrands persisted in making them comes as no surprise. The LA was a chummy, clubby, conservative organization operated principally by and for Old Boys: staff bureaucrats, current and former presidents, glad-handing local politicians, and some "big chief" librarians. These pillars of the British library Establishment were not about to embrace some Fabian folderol spouted by callow, caterwauling AAL agitators, some of whom were surely — yes—communists! Occasionally the LA brass would make minor concessions to the mad dogs of the AAL, tossing them a bit of meatless gristle to quiet the barking for a time. But concerning the major bones of contention, those running the LA gave little real ground in the 1950s. Meaningful change would come, but not during Moon's time in the UK. That he was instrumental in helping lay the groundwork for reform is indisputable, but others would reap the benefits of his work.

Father-Son Chat

Moon's election as national secretary of the AAL in 1955 carried with it a seat on the LA Council. His first Council meeting got him noticed by none other than the great Lionel McColvin. Moon:

The meeting was held at LA headquarters at Chaucer House. I was trying to behave like a typical AAL type. I guess I was thoroughly objectionable. I spoke up on everything and criticized everybody, attacking most of the godly figures in the association. At the end of the meeting, Lionel McColvin came over and said, "I'm going up to the Marlborough for a beer. Would you like to join me for awhile? I'd like to have a talk with you." I thought, good heavens, here is God himself. I said, "Yes sir, I'd like to, Mr. McColvin."

This was the same Lionel McColvin Moon had rudely questioned at a library meeting in Nottingham while a student at Loughborough seven year earlier. McColvin, a hugely respected public librarian, was acclaimed for both his vision and plainspoken common sense. Once, when asked how he knew so quickly that a particular library was not up to speed, he replied, "You don't have to go far up a drain to find that it stinks." The two men walked the short distance to the Marlborough pub, ordered a couple of pints, and, according to Moon, settled in for a lengthy chat, McColvin doing most of the talking:

We drank for four hours, during which time he gave me more useful advice on how to deal with the LA Council than I could have ever acquired in any other way. He talked to me like a father for four hours. What impressed me most was that a man of McColvin's stature would bother with this noisy little trouble-making fart. Here he is, he sees a problem, and he takes the trouble to do something about it. I thought that was magnificent. Later I got to know Lionel better when I became good friends with his son, Ken, who was stock editor at Lambeth when I was at Kensington. Lionel McColvin was a marvelous man, probably the most important librarian in Britain in the 20th century.

Red and Pink Librarians

The AAL was not the only group of librarians dissatisfied with the LA in the 1950s. On the far left, dissident elements representing ideologues of a variety of political hues from bright red to pale pink, including Marxists, Stalinists, Trotskyites, crypto-communists, fellow travelers, and hard-line socialists, also labored, sometimes at cross-purposes, to change the direction and philosophy of the LA. Like the AAL, their efforts bore little immediate fruit; but unlike the AAL, which eventually did achieve much of its reformist agenda, the radical left's influence in British library circles ebbed to the point of nearly nil by the late 1950s after the Soviet invasion of Hungary and Khrushchev's destalinization speech undermined the appeal of communism in the west.

Perhaps the most visible doctrinaire leftists among London area librarians at the time were Ronald Benge, Douglas Foskett, and Edward Dudley, each of whom was a product of the English working class, served in World War II, and belonged to the Communist Party of Great Britain in the 1950s. Together they and a few followers formed a small group of smart, disciplined librarians interested in transforming the existing system. Benge, a noted library educator in Britain who later taught in the West Indies and Africa, recalled how their activities frightened LA bureaucrats at Chaucer House: "Our group was active in various LA committees, and at one time Bernard Palmer, the then education secretary, went about muttering dolefully that there was a communist conspiracy to take over the LA. Such improbable plotters, apart from myself, included Edward Dudley and Douglas Foskett, and indeed the three of us then were closely knit, as they say." But Benge dismissed the notion of a "plot" as fantasy: "Our ideological background, insofar as it could have professional implications, did influence our earlier publications (one critic said my first book, *Bibliography and the Provision of Books*, 'reeked of Marxism'), but in fact it was only the *method* that had influenced me. Needless to say we all left the Party at different times thereafter."

Dudley saw it much the same way, adding that only a small number of librarians were actually party members and that in retrospect they were not really much of a force in the profession. Still, the library Establishment at the time recoiled from even the whisper of a connection with "communists." This was, after all, the period of McCarthyism in America, and such paranoia was not unknown abroad.

David Gerard, a leftist librarian and Moon contemporary who spent his entire career outside of the London area, knew colleagues who paid a heavy price for their political beliefs during those dark days. Certainly organizations like the LA and AAL wanted no truck with communists or sympathizers. Gerard: "There's no doubt the official AAL would have been scared of any hint of such affiliation." Library boards around the UK also had the red menace on their mind. Gerard recalled being interviewed for the post of deputy city librarian at Chester in the early 1950s: "It was at the end of an exhausting interview with 12 city councillors around the table, the one nearest me a replica of Sidney Greenstreet [the rotund actor]. He had been silent all through, until the chairman asked if there were any further questions. Sidney grunted, 'Yes.' He turned to me and asked, 'Are you a communist?' I was sporting a red tie. It was during the era of the McCarthy hearings. My stuttered reply probably confirmed his worst fears."

As a rule, Benge, Foskett, Dudley, and others in their tight little group did not participate much, if at all, in the AAL. Not only were they a bit older than most AAL activists, they generally disapproved of Moon and his cohorts, considering them politically unsophisticated and overly concerned about their careers. Benge put it this way: "Possibly for ideological and generational reasons our lot was not involved with the AAL. We associated them [Moon, Surridge, Bill Smith, Arthur Jones, et al.] with certain attitudes which we deplored. They were, we thought, opportunistic careerists and incapable of higher thought. This alleged opportunism is important because it could help to explain Eric's ambition and his impatience with many English characteristics." Dudley placed Moon politically "well left-of-center," a member of the "unattached left," and Harold Smith came to the interesting conclusion that Moon was "a nihilist at heart."

Moon characterized himself as a mainstream socialist and supporter of the Labour Party during this period, nothing more and nothing less. True to his earliest influences, he viewed Labour as Britain's best hope for an egalitarian future. As a leader of the AAL his main concern at the time was finding ways to goose the LA into adopting a more liberal posture. He had no abiding interest in grand political ideology. He did, he admitted, "flirt" with the Communist Party as a young man, but quickly rejected it as fascistic:

I differentiate between Marxist theory and communism in practice, which becomes fascism. It's the implementation that makes communism such a lousy proposition. I've always been on the left, no question. When I was a teenager we used to have gatherings to get rid of Oswald Mosley, the fascist. My big hero was Nye Bevan, who was certainly well on the left. I think of myself as a British socialist. I've been on the left all my life and I've never found any reason to be anywhere else.

Early Journalistic Efforts

All during his career as a librarian in England Moon was constantly writing—not poems and stories as he had done as a youth before the war in Southampton, but articles, papers, reviews, meeting minutes, conference reports, and news items for professional publications. He discovered that he had a fluent and sometimes wicked pen. Likewise, he was critical, sometimes hypercritical, of the literature of librarianship, which he felt often lacked substance and verve as well as the elements of good style. Moon's bête noire was the *Library Association Record* (or *LAR*), the official journal of the LA, whose contents he once likened to "dead meat."

In 1956 he and sidekick Bill Smith (who also had a rascally pen) decided to do something about the deplorable state of library literature and particularly *LAR*. They proposed an ambitious new periodical that would furnish the British library community and other interested parties with current, informative, brightly written news features—something entirely lacking in the leaden *LAR*, which looked like, and usually read like, a learned journal. The new publication, to be called *Liaison*, would complement rather than compete with or replace *LAR*; it would have a newsletter format and, like *LAR*, appear monthly; Moon and Smith (naturally) would be the editors; and—here might be a problem—it would be published by the LA. The question became, Would the LA be willing to sponsor a publication produced by Moon and Smith, neither of whom was considered "sound" by the gray beards who governed the association? Fortunately, they received a boost from a former AAL rebel, Frank Gardner, who had since matured into a "big wheel" at the LA.

Moon first took the proposal to the AAL Council, hoping to get it speedily approved and sent on to the LA for consideration:

At an AAL Council meeting I put forward the case in a memo for something to be done about the *Library Association Record*—not just to improve library lit but because we felt that the LA did not speak to librarians across the country and not at all to the world outside librarianship. What we wanted was the LA to have a voice that could be heard not only by members of the organization but the world at large. This was the memo that led to my taking a lengthy proposal to the LA Council advocating the establishment of *Liaison*—a publication that would reach out, would use journalistic tactics, and would bring librarianship alive to the rest of the world, as well as to our own membership. We needed a publication that would use newspaper techniques.

It was a huge memorandum, and the LA Council passed it on to its executive committee, which was headed by Frank Gardner, who was one of the AAL terrors of the 1930s but who by then was one of the big wheels of the Library Association. [Gardner became president of the LA in 1964.] Frank suggested that I do a dummy issue of the publication. I said I wanted to work on it with Bill Smith, who was editor of the *Assistant Librarian*, and he said fine. Bill and I sat down in a pub one night and pasted up a dummy issue of what was to be *Liaison*, which contained all kinds of wild stories about things happening in libraries and the profession. I took the dummy to Gardner who presented it to the exec committee. Some of the elders on the committee were shocked: "Does the chair recognize who these two young men are? They are radicals and communists!" But somehow Gardner overcame their doubts, and the committee and LA Council approved the project.

The first issue of *Liaison* was published in January 1957. Originally the newsletter came out as a separate publication, but after a short time it became an insert in the center of *LAR* with its own logo, where it continued to appear for the next two decades. Moon and Smith formed an effective editorial team. Both men were highly motivated and had experience editing periodicals, Smith the *Assistant Librarian* and Moon the GLD newsletter. The two had met through the AAL and quickly became comrades in arms, sharing a passion for, in Moon's words, "library politics and books." Smith worked as a public librarian in the London area until around 1957, when he left the profession to edit the review journal *Books and Bookmen* and a couple of spin-off publications. Later he founded a small chain of retail bookstores in England, called Booksmith Bargain Bookshops, which specialized in selling remainder copies.

Moon had great affection for W.G. (Bill) Smith, though the two disagreed about many issues and frequently engaged in lengthy public debates, albeit without major or lasting animus. "Bill was one of the most dynamic speakers around," recalled Moon. "On the floor he could grab an audience — he was charismatic. Bill Smith at a microphone at AAL meetings was like Al Jolson getting down and singing *Mammy*. He was an independent cuss, and he loved to be a provocateur." When Moon returned to England in 1977 to speak to the AAL at the LA Centenary Conference he was not surprised that when he finished, "Bill Smith was the first one up in the audience to attack me. And everybody said, 'My God, it's like the old road show again!'"

Despite ruffling Establishment feathers on more than one occasion, *Liaison* proved a great success. The experience, Moon later declared, was "good training for the kind of rumpus that started when I got to *Library Journal*." As promised, he and Smith did bring "newspaper techniques" to the publication, including some borrowed from London's lively tabloid press — though no photos of curvaceous semi-naked ladies appeared in *Liaison*. In one memorable incident, Moon pounced, paparazzi-like, on several illustrious visiting American librarians, seeking an exclusive interview for *Liaison*. He described that "early exploit," which occurred in 1957, in his foreword to Lawrence Clark Powell's autobiographical *Life Goes On*:

I had heard that three famous figures of the American library world were to be present at the Library Association conference in Harrogate, Yorkshire that year, and was eager to pull off a scoop by interviewing all three for our fledgling publication.

Discovering them all together one evening, ensconced in armchairs around a large fireplace and sharing drinks and conversation with some of the greyer eminences of the Library Association, our enterprising but brash young reporter, armed with camera, pad, and pencil, charged upon the scene. The three Americans were LCP [Lawrence Clark Powell], Quincy Mumford, the Librarian of Congress, and Howard Haycraft, president of the H.W. Wilson Company and master analyst of detective fiction.

I have often wondered since what it was that made me choose Larry [Powell] as my first target — perhaps blind luck, or fate, if one is inclined to believe in that. At any rate I planted myself in front of him and said something like: "So you're Larry Powell. Why don't you come outside with me for a few minutes and tell me what makes you so great?" Amid dark frowns all around — bad British form and all that — like a burst of sunshine through the clouds there emerged the famous twinkle in the Powell eyes. "Sure, young man," he said, getting up out of the chair, "You have almost as much gall as I had at your age."

Another "scoop" was one of the first interviews with John Braine, an English librarian turned writer, after his blockbuster novel *Room at the Top* hit the bestseller charts in 1957. Braine, part of the Angry Young Men movement that exploded on the British scene in the mid–1950s, told the editors of *Liaison* that, notwithstanding his recent literary success, he would never, never, ever quit his librarian job. The next week Moon read in *The Times* words to the effect that "John Braine has quit being a librarian!" So much for *Liaison*'s exclusive — and the sheet's reputation for accuracy. Moon and Smith survived such reportorial setbacks with good humor, happy in the knowledge that their goals for the infant newsletter —"to bring life to librarianship" and to counteract the "determined dullness" of *LAR*— were being achieved, if imperfectly.

Moon's tenure as coeditor lasted about 18 months, from January 1957 until the summer of 1958, when he resigned to go to Canada. His experience with *Liaison*, though brief, was excellent training for what lay ahead when he became, out of the blue, editor of *Library Journal* a year and half later. Bill Smith continued with *Liaison* until Ron Surridge took it over at the end of 1958. Displaying both laudable journalistic skills and remarkable endurance, Surridge remained editor for nearly 20 years, until 1975, when *Liaison* merged with *LAR* and ceased to have a separate identity.

During the 1950s Moon also wrote numerous articles, reviews, and reports for various professional journals in the UK, a sampling of which are reprinted in his 1993 book *A Desire to Learn*. His publications appeared most frequently in the *Assistant Librarian* (and its predecessor, the *Library Assistant*) and were often controversial, eliciting strong reader response. Edward Dudley recalled Moon once reviewed a book by Lionel McColvin in the *Assistant*, which ended with the comment that it was a "damned good book." "The next issue," said Dudley, "carried letters protesting Eric's bad language!"

In another instance, Arthur Jones took Moon to task for the flippant tone of his AAL Council meeting minutes in the *Assistant* when he was national secretary. In a letter to the editor, Jones complained, "When dealing with serious matters the latest witticism of Mr. Surridge or Mr. Smith (W.G.) assumes more importance than the careful presentation and argument or the adequate explanation of the point under discussion. I think Mr. Moon has underestimated the intelligence of members.... Am I alone in finding these notes, like those sections of the popular press which they imitate, to be uninformative and pathetically anemic?" Moon shot back: "I want *assistants* to realize that the AAL is their association, and not an organization run by and for deputy librarians, chief assistants, and other weighty members of the APT [Administrative, Professional and Technical national salary scale]. I want the *Assistant* and council minutes read by all the young assistants who throw the *LA Record* and its dull reportage, which Mr. Jones applauds, straight into the wastepaper basket every month."

Moon wrote extensively too for *Books and Bookmen*, a general review magazine resembling the old *Saturday Review of Literature*. Bill Smith took over *Books and Bookmen* in 1957 and Moon immediately became a major contributor. In addition to book reviews he produced feature articles on authors, focusing on contemporary American writers like Henry Miller and William Faulkner. These articles were often done on short deadline; Moon remembered Smith once called him in the evening and said, "I need 2,500 to 3,000 words on Steinbeck by tomorrow morning"—and he got them. Moon also reviewed for two smaller magazines edited by Smith, *Bookguide* and *Technical Bookguide*. And at one point he wrote the script for a radio program entitled "I Want to Be a Librarian," which the British Broadcasting Corporation aired in 1955. Moon had a small reading part in the program but failed to recognize his own voice during the broadcast.

Professor Moon

While working at the North Finchley Branch, Moon tried his hand at teaching library science. Specifically, during the years 1952 through 1954, he taught an evening course—sometimes bibliography, sometimes reference—as a part-time lecturer (or adjunct) at the North-Western Polytechnic School of Librarianship in London. It was here that he first got to know Ronald Benge, then second in command at the school. Moon was not certain how the opportunity to teach at North-West Poly came about: "They must have asked me, because at that time I was getting pretty well known." In any event, he jumped at the chance to teach. Not only was he eager to share his growing fund of knowledge about library work with students studying for the LA Registration Exam, he liked the *idea* of teaching, which increased his professional stature, offered him an attentive and mostly admiring audience, fueled his considerable ego, and appealed to the actor in him.

Moon was determined to bring librarianship alive for his students. Sidney Gadsden, a former librarian who was in one of his classes at North-West Poly, described him as "a good teacher, though I doubt he thought much about technique and methodology. This was a part-time evening class; he worked full-time and so did his students. It was a case of impart the information as succinctly as possible and set the homework. But he was always entertaining and held his students' attention." Moon's pedagogic style tended to be loose, informal, and unpretentious. He disliked the typical classroom setting, considering it sterile and sleep-inducing. He preferred to meet his classes in a more conducive environment—like a pub. Unfortunately, the desire to be stimulating led to conflicts with educational authorities and finally his termination at the school.

"I always tried to get my students out of the classroom and into direct contact with the things I was talking about," explained Moon:

It was this philosophy that eventually got me into trouble at North-West Poly. These government inspectors would come around to the school periodically to see how things were going. One time the inspector came around and I wasn't in the classroom. Benge, who was the number two at the school, said they're all at a pub on Fleet Street called the Printer's Devil. Benge explained that this pub has one of the finest collections of examples of early printing and early printing equipment in London, and Moon likes to teach in that sort of congenial atmosphere because he believes students will learn more that way.

We got away with that one. But the next time the inspector came around, my classroom was empty again. So where is he this time? Benge said he's at the *Daily Worker*. The *Daily Worker*?! Yes, Moon heard they have the best printing equipment in London, and since he was dealing with printing at this time, he took his class over to see it. At which point the inspector recommended that maybe I ought to be canned. And I was.

Moon remembered, "Benge tried to save me but couldn't. He was not in good odor at the school because of his political leanings, and the head of the school was a very conservative man."

Teaching at North-West Poly had its rewards but Moon, as he remembered it, actually didn't mind being sacked: "I would have given it up anyway, because I found teaching too great a strain on my motor system. I've always been very nervous in front of a class or group." An acting career had been rejected earlier for similar reasons. But as time went on he learned to cope with his nervousness while speaking in public:

I was at a Library Association meeting where Sir Frank Soskice was speaking. He was a senior minister in the government, the British equivalent of the American attorney general. Sir Frank gave a brilliant speech. He was the most fluid, articulate speaker I had ever heard in my life, hardly used a note, so cool. I went up to him afterwards and said, "God, how did you do that? I do a lot of speaking and I'm always so nervous." And Sir Frank looked at me and said, in this very avuncular voice, "My boy, if you ever get over being nervous, you will be flat as a pancake."

So I ceased feeling bad about being nervous while speaking. And after many years I got fairly good at public speaking, being cool as if it were nothing. The only thing I can say is that I've learned to cover up. I'm still nervous as a kitten up there — the only thing that has improved is it doesn't show anymore.

Also while at Finchley he served an AAL correspondence course tutor for the Army Institute of Education in London. The course covered library fundamentals and was aimed at servicemen and women interested in learning how to use libraries and information resources more effectively.

Union Man

Along with all his other work-related activities in England in the 1950s Moon devoted a certain amount of effort to union business, which was normally conducted on his own time, not the library's. The union, the National Association of Local Government Officers (NALGO), represented the interests of various white-collar government employees in the UK, from town clerks and workers in local departments to teachers and public librarians. Over the years Moon sat on a number of NALGO committees and in 1955–56 was president of the Brentford and Chiswick local branch. Prior to leaving England in 1958 he served on the executive board of the Kensington local.

Moon, however, never developed a consuming interest in NALGO. He came to believe that the union, because of its huge and diverse membership, was not, and could not be, as effective a representative of librarians' interests as the LA, which was dedicated exclusively to library issues and therefore better positioned to understand and, if so inclined, fight for the rights and causes of librarians. By way of example, he pointed to the fact that the LA, not NALGO, once considered using—and for a short time actually did use—a blacklist as a means of trying to raise the salaries of public librarians. Moon: "The Library Association took rather strenuous action like running ads in the *Times Literary Supplement* opposing classified ads from certain local authorities which sought to hire librarians at despicably low salaries. In effect, the LA was imposing a blacklist on the job." He applauded this effort but conceded, "it didn't last long."

Plots and Ploys

Not all his colleagues in the UK liked Eric Moon as a person or approved of his ideas and tactics, but almost everyone respected him, if grudgingly, for his astonishing capacity for work and obvious devotion to the profession. Likewise, no one who knew him could deny his enormous energy, his steel-trap intelligence, his talent for public discourse, his sharp political instincts, and his natural appetite for leadership. Indeed, he stood out as a formidable figure among the younger generation of British librarians in the 1950s. Ron Surridge pointed to a confluence of intellect and drive as the key to Moon's success as a library leader: "The AAL did thrive under his secretaryship. It now had that rare combination in librarianship, a thinker and a doer with the personality, authority, and ability to get decisions through. With a very clear mind Eric knew what he wanted and how to get it."

Edward Dudley, who often disagreed with Moon about particular issues (such as how to improve library education), saw some of these same qualities in him:

Eric, who had a commanding personality, had a number of followers. There was a circle of librarians of his age and younger ones whom he influenced, particularly in pub discussions and other places too. I remember him as tall, slow-speaking, ironic, shading sometimes into sarcasm, but obviously enjoying not only the work of being a librarian but all of the politics of the professional association. He was a great, as we now say, change agent. The AAL never again quite had the zest and fire it had in the 1950s when Eric was there.

Arthur Jones recalled how impressed he was simply by Moon's presence the first time he saw him. It was at an evening meeting of the London and Home Counties Branch of the LA circa 1953:

With other latecomers I was obliged to stand at the side of the crowded hall, and soon became aware of a constant mumble of trenchant comments on the proceedings from somewhere behind me—not quite heckling, but rather more than whispered asides, welling up from time to time into more formal questions and interjections addressed to the platform. "Do you know," said my neighbor, "that that is Eric Moon?" When I glanced round, my first impression was that the person standing there did not look like a librarian at all. I suppose none of us do, but it was a more appropriate reaction to Eric Moon than to most of my other colleagues. It still surprises me that he should have found his way into librarianship, but we must all be grateful that he did.

Still, despite his many strengths, Moon annoyed or turned off more than a few potential allies due to a fondness for backroom machinations to get what he wanted when he wanted it. Early on he had shown signs of a manipulative personality, using exaggeration and guile to get his way or gain attention or get even or show how clever or special he was. It did not take long for this trait to show up in his professional dealings: foisting paintings by Gauguin on the branch at Bushey; tricking the deputy librarian at Finchley into believing six copies of *War and Peace* had flown off the shelves in a single morning; negotiating with the library committee behind Flo Green's back at Brentford and Chiswick. Such behavior no doubt got Moon what he wanted more often than not — and it generated amusing stories to share with admiring cronies. But it also offended some colleagues, who thought the less of him for it.

Moon's penchant for manipulation was often most transparent in his handling of association matters. Edward Dudley: "Whereas I shared their [Moon, Surridge, Bill Smith, et al.] desire to overturn the Establishment and get a bit of life — a bit of laughter too — into professional affairs, I did not always share their way of achieving it. I thought they were overconcerned with scheming to get the 'right' people on the right committees, subcommittees, working parties, and so on. In short, they tried to achieve power not only by the usual method of popular ballot, but also by plots, ploys, and stratagems." Harold Smith too was put off by Moon's games: "If I were to voice a criticism of Eric's activities in that period it would be not that he was irreverent, which he undoubtedly was — and what's wrong with that? — but that many of his machinations seemed to be mischievous, often for their own sake."

Dudley gleefully recalled one instance when a plot by Moon and company failed:

Bill Smith gave up the editorship of the *Assistant Librarian* around 1957 and I gathered — shall we say from an informant on the LA Council — that there was a Moon-Smith nominee to succeed Smith as editor. I remember saying, "Oh dear, there's the ploy and stratagem for their perpetuating the editorship of the journal." And my informant said, "Wouldn't you like to do a little counterplotting?" And I thought, here's some fun. But what to do? He said, "There are two candidates who will be put forward, the Moon-Smith nominee and another chap named Dean Harrison, who doesn't stand a chance to be elected. But if you [Dudley] stand, you'll split the vote. You won't be elected, but there's the chance Harrison, the non–Moon-Smith nominee, will get in." And that's exactly what happened. Harrison, who later became the county librarian of Kent, was elected. I took a small delight in foiling this particular Moon-Smith ploy.

Rude Rebel

There's no doubt Moon's affinity for manipulation irked certain people, but an even more widespread criticism concerned his general demeanor, which many outside his immediate circle found to be gratuitously arrogant, caustic, and condescending. He sometimes gave the impression that only he and a few chosen confidants had all the answers; everyone else's ideas were rubbish. His friend Surridge puts his abrasive style in the best light: "After Loughborough Eric became the rebel, challenging the orthodoxy of the day. In him there was one of the most confident, competent, best equipped librarians of his generation. Entering the lists of controversy as he did, not everybody loved him." The unkinder truth was that some of his colleagues actively disliked and even loathed him, especially senior members of the profession. Ken Stockham, who knew Moon only fleetingly, summed up the prevalent feeling about him at the time: "His reputation was as a rather rude rebel and the chiefs of that day did not like his blunt cockney approach." (Note that Moon was not a "cockney"—that is, a native of East London; Stockham used the word here in its broadest pejorative sense.)

Even Roy Stokes, who introduced Moon to confrontation librarianship at Loughborough, was taken aback by the way his former star pupil was conducting himself: "I do remember that Eric and the crowd of young turks who were gathered around him during those years did create a very great deal of interest, confusion, and, to a very real extent, some dismay in the minds of the elder members of the profession." The gentlemanly Stokes advocated confrontation—but only if tempered with civility. One of Moon's worst habits (or best, depending on your viewpoint) was a tendency to bait the famous and powerful. "It may have been a schoolboy characteristic," Harold Smith observed, "but he always liked ruffling the feathers of the great. This, of course, did not endear him to them."

A case in point involved publicly embarrassing Sir Frank Francis, then director of the British Museum (the national library). Moon, who was serving on the LA's Register and Examinations Executive Committee (REEC) at the time, described the incident:

> This committee decided on the final qualifications of all librarians in Britain. The only people who could serve on it were members of the LA Council who held the FLA, which I did, but which Sir Frank did not. So Sir Frank and a number of other dignitaries used to be waiting outside the chamber for the committee to finish so they could take their seats on the LA Council, which met after the committee. I used to wave to Sir Frank on the way into the REEC meeting, saying "Can't get in again, eh, Sir Frank?" This was very annoying to the director of the British Museum, coming from a young squirt like me.

An undercurrent of criticism regarding Moon's personal life was also palpable at the time. He was not averse, in the language of the street, to a bit of slap and tickle now and then, but neither was his behavior sexually profligate; he acknowledged only one serious affair while married in England. Still, there were whispered insinuations and tittle-tattle among library insiders, which possibly had a negative effect on his standing within the profession and might have harmed his chances for advancement. Harold Smith, for one, believed Moon may have been hurt by the gossip: "One of the things that his enemies, and they were many, held against him was his libertine lifestyle. Nothing ever said in public—you know, the British way."

All the while Moon was forging a career in libraries during the 1950s Great Britain was undergoing a series of unsettling political, economic, and cultural shocks. Like an old tree in a wild storm, the nation sometimes seemed ready to splinter under a barrage of postwar problems and disappointments. Labour's great victory in 1945 had promised a new era, one in which the common people, and not the privileged and high born, would finally govern. The nation's rigid class system, long a roadblock to progress, would wither away, and the socialist-inspired welfare state would usher in a period of true concern for the poor and sick and jobless, fostering a new bond between government and the people. Regrettably, it didn't happen that way.

True, Labour did accomplish some great deeds in its first few years. But for many the reforms did not happen as rapidly or smoothly or completely as desired. Euphoria slowly gave way to disillusionment as Labour's socialist revolution turned sour. In July 1945 Labour had crushed the Conservatives, but five years later after the next general election, Labour's parliamentary majority had shrunk to half a dozen seats, a tenuous hold on power. In January 1951 Nye Bevan, head of the National Health Service (and Moon's political hero), resigned from the government in a policy dispute, and in the election that followed in October Labour was soundly defeated, beaten by the Tories and Churchill, who returned to Downing Street for a last hurrah. During the remainder of the decade Labour's strength continued to wane. The revolution that began so resplendently at the end of the war had become, especially for the young, a macabre joke, ending with a return to the discredited policies of the past.

One manifestation of Labour's failed revolution was the literary phenomenon known as the Angry Young Men movement. Consisting of a motley group of rebellious young writers, including Kingsley Amis, Alan Sillitoe, John Braine, John Osborne, John Wain, and even a woman or two (Doris Lessing, for example), the Angry Young Men (or Angries or AYM) introduced a harsh new reality into British fiction and theater, first observable in the mid–1950s. In such popular novels and plays as *Lucky Jim* (Amis; 1954), *Look Back in Anger* (Osborne; 1956), *Room at the Top* (Braine; 1957), and *Saturday Night and Sunday Morning* (Sillitoe; 1958), the Angries expressed working-class bitterness at the rottenness of society in general and the Establishment in particular, which included Britain's smug middle classes. They attacked and condemned sacred cows from the Royal Family and House of Lords to elite public schools and the Church of England. They were incensed that class prejudice remained a virulent reality, that Britain remained essentially two countries, one of wealth and privilege and the other of dehumanizing factories, bad air, and resentful workers. Writing with great passion, they created memorable protagonists—brash, bad-mannered, sexually amoral antiheroes fed up with kowtowing to the past and their elders, who they argued had miserably failed the younger generation.

Not surprisingly, some saw Eric Moon in the pages of the Angries. Gawan Vesey, a Moon classmate at Loughborough and the librarian who succeeded him at Bushey-Oxhey in Hertfordshire, observed that "Eric had a rather abrasive personality and, indeed, was somewhat typical of the Angry Young Men featured in English novels and plays of the period." Other Moon contemporaries made similar observations. For his part, Moon denied that he or his AAL friends were unduly influenced by the AYM movement: "We were obstreperous but not necessarily angry," adding: "But we let them know we were not going to take a lot of shit anymore."

Perhaps the stories and characters created by the Angries did not directly provoke or encourage Moon's rude behavior in the 1950s. Still, in retrospect, it seems clear that at least some of the working-class resentments that fueled Amis, Osborne, and the others also infected Moon, contributing to his belligerent attitude toward the British library Establishment.

New World Beckons

Early in 1958, around the time of his 35th birthday, Moon received word that he had been appointed the top public librarian in Newfoundland, Canada. It took awhile for the news to sink in. He had been treading water at Kensington for the last year or so, calculating his chances of getting a chiefship in the UK, which seemed less auspicious with each passing day. Now Newfoundland — he could hardly believe it! — had come through. He was as excited as an explorer preparing to enter an uncharted land — a new challenge, a new country, a new continent!

Earlier he had applied for several library positions in Canada with no luck, being told in so many words that he lacked the necessary qualifications, namely a college or university degree. He had also written to the Canadian Library Association and got the brush off — only a children's position *might* be available. He was insulted. Then, toward the end of 1957, an advertisement appeared in the *TLS* for the provincial librarian of Newfoundland, and for the hell of it he sent off an application:

I thought, I'll make one more stab at Canada. I didn't realize at the time that this would turn out to be a great way to crack the qualifications system, because Newfoundland at heart was still more British than Canadian, even though it had joined the Canadian federation approximately ten years before as the country's tenth province. It was about half way out there in the Atlantic and sentimentally its ties to Britain were still very strong. And I got the job! I wrote a letter to Elizabeth Morton, executive director of the Canadian Library Association, and told her what she could do with her children's job: I was the new provincial librarian of Newfoundland and I would be seeing her around.

His starting salary was roughly double what he was making at Kensington but it was, he remembered, "pretty abysmal compared with equivalent jobs in Canada at the time." He and Diana quickly learned too that living in Newfoundland was expensive — everything had to be shipped in — and they found that they were "worse off than in England." Also, he soon discovered that few Canadian librarians had expressed interest in the Newfoundland post: "Most Canadians have such a jaundiced view of Newfoundland that they wouldn't go there."

But Moon had little knowledge of these disturbing facts in the spring of 1958 as he and his family prepared to leave England for Newfoundland and St. John's, the provincial capital. His last act as stock editor at Kensington was to buy a complete bookstore, which he left for his successor, Ron Surridge (who else?), to cope with. The bookstore, Moon recalled, "was in some trouble" and the owner "wanted to retire," so his whole stock was on the market:

I made the owner an offer for everything and he said, "Done!" I went back to the library and told my boss that I had just bought an entire bookstore and he said, "Jesus Christ!" I said, "It's a steal." Two-thirds of the stock was junk, but the other one-third contained many good things, and given the overall price for the collection, it *was* a steal. When I left, Ron Surridge was appointed in my place, and one of the first letters I got from Ron in Newfoundland complained about my leaving boxes upon boxes of books at Kensington, all of which had to be sorted and cataloged. That was my final buy.

Actually, Surridge was sorry to see Moon leave England, not because of the many boxes of books his old chum had left behind, but because the two men were comrades who, Surridge sensed correctly, would never work together again: "I was somewhat saddened. He, I, and Bill Smith had formed a little rebel triumvirate to try to change things. Bill went off to other journalism and to found a run of Booksmith Bookshops, and with Eric gone as well, some of the punch must have gone out of the attack." Harold Smith, on the other hand, saw Moon's leaving England as a logical move: "I think he left Britain at the right time for his career. He never reached a top job here and if he had done I feel that this country, with its slow moving nature and rigid institutions, would have frustrated him."

Beneath the surface excitement of celebrating the new job and preparing to go to North America, Moon knew that Newfoundland was a large gamble. Yes, he would finally be a chief, but a chief in a place no one much cared about, a place widely considered a cultural backwater. Where could he go from there? What would be the next rung on the ladder to the top? In fact, most of Moon's peers in England, friends and enemies alike, believed the Newfoundland move meant his career was effectively over or, if not that, at least it would be stymied for a good long time: "When I announced to everybody that I was leaving for Newfoundland, they all said that's the end of Eric Moon. That's death. But I thought if I could get that far, I could probably find my way into the States. I definitely saw Canada as a way into the States."

So it was cheerio to decaying Olde England and on to the bright, shining New World. Though unaware of it at the time, he was leaving the country of his birth for good, never to live there again. There he had come into the world, been raised, educated, and formed as a social and political being. There he had seen war up close, served in the military, married, had children, and found a career, which became a consuming passion. His contribution to librarianship in the UK ultimately left only a small mark, but for him it was a shaping experience. For now, however, it was just the four Moons—Eric, Diana, Max, and Alan—on a big ship sailing from Southampton to St. John's, Newfoundland, and a new life.

– 7 –

Rabble-Rousing in Canada

Journey into the Unknown

The Moon family set out from Southampton for St. John's, Newfoundland, in the middle of June 1958, crossing the North Atlantic by passenger ship in six days. The seas were choppy much of the way and the ship tossed from side to side ... up and down ... side to side ... up and down. Eric and Alan, an inquisitive youngster who would be seven in November, enjoyed the novelty of the journey, whereas Diana and Max, now ten, were ill most of the time. Alan remembered the experience vividly, especially the plight of his mother and brother:

My first significant memory of my father is when we were traveling by boat from England to Newfoundland. I was six at the time and the trip was a real adventure for me. The seas were fairly rough the whole way and the majority of the passengers, including my mother and brother, were seasick throughout the trip. On the other hand, my father and I were just fine. We spent lots of time strolling the decks. I would be constantly asking my father, "Why are all these people so sick, Daddy? We're not sick are we, Daddy?" My father kept telling me to keep my voice down as we passed passengers bent over the side of the ship. I didn't realize it at the time but now I know he actually thought my comments were very funny.

I was a very finicky eater as a lad. About the only thing I wanted to eat on the ship were sardines. As you can imagine, the sight of me eating raw fish was just about all it took to send my mother and brother running for the toilet. It would probably have bothered lots of other people too, but the dining room wasn't very crowded during most meals. The railings on the sides of the boat were another story.

The trip was a breeze for Moon, as easy as puffing on his favorite pipe filled with the rough-cut tobacco he preferred. The hard part would come once the ship docked: he had only the vaguest notion of what to expect when he and his family arrived in St. John's. It was, he later wrote, "virtually a voyage into the unknown." Of course he had consulted travel guides and gazetteers and encyclopedias for basic information about Newfoundland as well as talked with people in England he knew. Very few of the latter had firsthand knowledge of faraway Newfoundland, but still they had opinions. One friend told him, "You will surely die there," and his father-in-law, whom he tended to dismiss as a blowhard, said, "You are going to the land where they have nine months of winter and three months of cold weather." In point of fact, Newfoundland's weather came up quite often, both in casual conversation and the reference books he perused. Apparently the place had more than its share of cold, fog, wind, rain, ice, sleet, and snow.

Despite trepidations about the whole venture Moon did not look back once he accepted the job. There were literally thousands of large and small tasks that needed doing in a short time: "Having fought through the awkward preliminaries of getting a job by airmail, one fine spring day in London I announced my intended departure," he recalled. "There followed the plunge into the complicated rigmarole of resignations from accumulated commitments, of emigration formalities, of passports and vaccinations and the endless nightmare of form-filling." It was an outwardly relaxed but inwardly tense Eric Moon who gazed upon St. John's for the first time from the deck of his ship as it sailed into the city's sheltered harbor, known for its narrow entrance and waters deep enough to accommodate almost any seagoing vessel of the day. He relived the experience in an article, "The Province Nobody Knows," published in the *Atlantic Advocate* the following year:

Before us were what might have been the white cliffs of Dover, aged by a fiercer sea, browned, and greying at the temples. Then through the historic Narrows a shutter-eye view of a wooden town, strangely toylike to redbrick-accustomed English eyes, like a shanty town sleeping in the sun. Untidy and unkempt it looked, certainly, with the houses facing every and which way, but there was a happy absence of the town planner's iron glove, an assertive freedom about it all. Authority seemed to be vested in the twin spires of the Basilica standing ramrod straight, high on the hill like a pair of sergeant-majors on the parade ground, and beyond, the houses stretched on up the slopes as though reaching for the skies and the promise above of better things than were to be found on the typical Skid Row of the waterfront.

The above is poetry, reminiscent of Matthew Arnold's melancholy *Dover Beach*. But once the Moons reached terra firma the mood was anything but poetic. Recalling these events years later, Eric bluntly described arriving in St. John's as "the most serious culture shock I ever experienced." The disjuncture between London and St. John's never felt greater than on that first day:

It was like going back a century in time. It started immediately when we landed. We had all our possessions on board in big crates, which were sort of dumped on the dockside and the customs people there insisted on opening them all, and there was nothing we could do about it. Here was all our stuff all over the place on the docks and we had nowhere yet to take it. We didn't know where we were going. As I remember, some person from the library board came down and met us, and we were put up in what seemed like the attic of a house for awhile until we found a place to live.

When we got there Diana and I walked around the town — St. John's is all straight up and down from the waterfront, so climbing those hills in the warm weather was, well, it was pretty hot walking up and down the streets, so we walked into a bar, and the bartender said, "Out!" And I said, "What are you talking about? We just came in for a drink."

And the bartender said something I couldn't make out, then said "Out!" again. "But why?" I asked. "We don't serve *women*," was the reply.

It was not an auspicious beginning, and there was more of the same that evening:

On the way over on the ship I played quite a lot of bridge with people, including a young American who was going on to Boston. He came off the boat that evening for an evening on the town, and came up to where we were staying and said, "Eric, let's go out for a drink." I said, "I'm not going out — I'm not going to be thrown out again." But he persisted, so Diana stayed with the boys in our lodging and he and I went to the New-foundland Hotel, which was the only place in town licensed to sell liquor. You could get beer in other places, but this was the only place for harder stuff. I walked up to the bar and ordered a couple of Scotches, and the bartender says, "Out!" And I say, "What?! This is not for my wife, it's for this man, he's an American!" He said, "I don't know what you're talking about, buddy, but you're not wearing a tie — so, Out!" I said to my American friend at that point, "Gee, I wish we could get a ticket and come on to Boston with you. I've had enough of this place already." And that was just the first night.

Life in St. John's

The Moons quickly learned that they had relocated in one of the world's truly unique places — an island whose independent people, known as "Newfies," existed in a social and cultural time warp. Actually Newfoundland is two places, being at once Canada's tenth and newest province as well as a triangle-shaped island separated from Labrador and mainland Canada by the Strait of Belle Isle. The province consists of the island (about 41,000 square miles) plus the eastern coastal area of Labrador (102,000 square miles), which is part of the Canadian mainland. Though smaller geographi-cally than Labrador, Newfoundland island contains practically all of the province's population — roughly 450,000 in the late 1950s when the Moons were there and over 550,000 today. Jutting far out into the Atlantic, the province is the easternmost point in North America and, befitting its distinctive people, it has its own time zone, called Newfoundland Standard Time, which runs an hour and a half ahead of Eastern Stan-dard Time. The Province of Newfoundland, along with the three Maritime Provinces of Nova Scotia, New Brunswick, and Prince Edward Island, make up Canada's Atlantic Provinces.

Newfoundland island was discovered in 1497 by John Cabot (Giovanni Caboto), a Genoese explorer sailing in the service of the king of England. Newfoundland was referred to in historical records as "New Founde Launde" as early as 1502, though recent evidence confirms that the Vikings and Leif Ericsson visited the area at least 500 years before. In 1583 Sir Humphrey Gilbert established a settlement at St. John's (on the southeast coast) and claimed the Newfoundland territory for England. Not for-mally recognized as a crown colony until the early 19th century, the island finally became self-governing with its own parliament in 1855. But in 1934, as a result of the world economic collapse, Newfoundland went bankrupt and Britain, which assumed its debt, suspended home rule in favor of a government commission appointed in London.

Twice in the 19th century the people of Newfoundland rejected, by plebiscite, opportunities to join the Canadian federation. Many of those opposed wanted to maintain ties with Britain while others dreamed that one day Newfoundland would become an independent nation. Finally, on July 22, 1948, in a bitterly contested election, Newfoundlanders agreed (52 percent to 48) to became part of Canada; confederation was officially proclaimed on March 31, 1949. The drive for union with Canada was led by the Liberal Party leader, Joseph R. Smallwood, who became the province's first premier, a position he held for 23 years until ousted by the opposition in 1972.

Newfoundland has a strong Roman Catholic presence, which dates back to the 17th century when French settlers colonized the area; and in the 19th century Irish immigrants, fleeing poverty in their homeland, swelled the island's Catholic population. For centuries the chief industry was fishing, the famous Grand Banks southeast of Newfoundland in the Atlantic providing a seemingly inexhaustible supply of cod, haddock, herring, mackerel, salmon, etc. But by the time the Moons arrived in Newfoundland, overfishing had begun to take its toll, threatening the profitable salt cod trade, forcing limits on catches, and causing considerable economic hardship in the province.

Accustomed historically to social and geographical isolation, many Newfoundlanders have never really accepted being part of Canada, except as a political expediency. In like manner the rest of Canada often looks askance at the province, making jokes about Newfies and their customs and speech habits, which both baffle and amuse citified Canadians from Toronto and Montreal to Calgary and Vancouver. Almost all Newfies, for instance, speak English, but it can be a heavily accented strain dense with quaint phrases, similes, and local proverbs incomprehensible to outsiders— or, in the local patois, "come-from-aways." Food is another curiosity, usually somehow involving cod, as in fried cod tongues with scrunchions, a Newfoundland delicacy; the latter are similar to cracklins found in the American South and, yes, cod apparently do have tasty tongues. The Moons found the Newfie experience by turns frustrating, charming, vexing, edifying, stifling, and daunting.

The province's inhabited places are scattered around the island's rugged thousand-mile coastline, plus a few settlements up and down the Labrador coast. Most are small fishing villages, called outports, tucked away in coves and inlets often accessible only by boat. There's no significant human habitation in the interior of the island, a barren, roadless wilderness. Happily for the Moons, Eric's job was in St. John's, the provincial capital and long Newfoundland's most populous and culturally advanced community. Located on the island's Avalon peninsula off St. John's Bay facing the Atlantic Ocean, the city had a population of 75,000 in the late 1950s (now grown to nearly 100,000). St. John's had then (and still has) a college, a university, two cathedrals, and Newfoundland's largest public library, which served as Moon's headquarters during his 16 months as head of the province's library system. St. John's was also the only place in the province at the time that had paved roads. Still, the community had little to offer by way of big-city amenities like museums, concerts, theaters, nightlife, and upscale restaurants.

The Moons lived on the second floor of a boxy, four-family frame house about halfway up a very steep and narrow street in St. John's. The entire city sits on a hill-side rising up from the harbor, and navigating the streets, some as precipitous as those found in San Francisco, could be an adventure, especially for come-from-aways like the Moons, who were used to the relative flatness of London. The terrain made getting around a chore and sometimes impossible, particularly in wintertime. "During winter the whole town closed down for well over a week," Moon remembered. "Snow was up over parking meters on Water Street, the main street. In our driveway it had piled up so high that the car was totally buried. But the kids loved it, absolutely loved it."

In addition to foul weather and menacing slopes, two other aspects of daily life in St. John's annoyed the Moon family, namely the schools, which were not up to British standards, and the strict government regulation of the sale of alcoholic beverages, which threatened to crimp Eric's joie de vivre. Alan especially disliked his school: "The public schools were all full so my brother and I were enrolled in Catholic schools. I still have nightmares about that time." Both Diana and Eric had doubts about the quality of education their boys were receiving; they were concerned, for example, that Max's school taught American-English spelling while Alan's favored British-English. As for drink, Eric schemed to circumvent the regulations, which attempted to control how much alcohol each resident could purchase during a given period: "What one did, of course, was find teetotalers and use their name. It got to the point where I'd walk into the liquor store and the guy would say, 'Who are you today?'"

Moon Buys a Car

Prior to coming to Newfoundland Moon had never owned, much less driven, an automobile. He had learned to drive, after a fashion, on an abandoned Japanese signals wagon in Singapore at the end of the war, and he had operated motorcycles in England, but he had never actually been behind the wheel of a real motor car. Because public transportation was minimal in St. John's and a motorcycle out of the question because of treacherous road conditions most of the year, he concluded he had to buy a car:

When we got there it became apparent that I was going to have to have a car. There was no other way to get around. I had a driver's license from Britain for my motorcycle — it was bound in royal blue morocco with gilt covers, very impressive. So I went out and brought an old secondhand car, then went to the driver's license place where I presented my British license, and they accepted it right away. It looked so damned formal — so they gave me a Newfoundland driver's license. The car dealer had to give me some lessons up and down the road before I could drive it home, where I had to negotiate some pretty steep hills.

About a week later the library board decided to take me out to a little place called Pouch [pronounced *Pooch*] Cove to see what a typical outport library was like. I volunteered to drive Tony Ayre, the chairman of the board, in one car. I didn't know what I was getting into. The road to Pouch Cove was a narrow, unpaved dirt road going around cliffs, some that dropped down a 1,000 or 1,500 feet into the ocean. There were rocks down there and old cars that had gone over the edge. About half way there I revealed to Tony that I had just got my driver's license, and that I'd never driven a car before, and that I was absolutely petrified. He said, "Get out of there! I'll drive!!" Driving in Newfoundland was full of that kind of hilarity.

Alan remembered a singularly thrilling ride home from school with his father one glacial afternoon:

When winter arrived, all the side streets in St. John's became very icy. One day during our first winter, my father picked up my brother and me from school in the car. We got to the bottom of our street and started up, but it quickly became apparent that we were not going to be able to make it to the house. We kept sliding back and eventually all forward motion became impossible. My father decided to drive out of town, quite a ways I seem to remember, and circle around up to the top of the hill, so he could come down the street.

This decision turned into another one of my great adventures. As soon as the car started down the hill, it was apparent that my father was no longer in control. He yelled to us to get next to the doors and be ready to jump if necessary. I was alone in the back seat and too young to be scared. I was smiling and yelling as we slid down the hill. The house approached on the left and my father tried to turn and slide into the driveway. We almost made it. Luckily, a snowbank prevented any real serious damage to the car, and us. That was the only time my father tried that maneuver. My mother was pissed when I told her about it, but I think my father enjoyed it as much as I did. I've been on some of the best roller coasters in the country, but that will always be my favorite ride.

Ten years later Moon returned to Newfoundland to cover the 1969 annual conference of the Canadian Library Association for *Library Journal*, held that year in St. John's. John Berry, his *LJ* alter ego, was along for the ride, literally and figuratively. One evening during a night on the town Moon drove himself and Berry to a party at a motel on steep Signal Hill, a landmark in St. John's overlooking the harbor. He recalled racing "flat out up the hill and roaring into a huge parking area, which was all gravel — and very close to the edge of a cliff." Berry "panicked," said Moon, pleased as Mr. Toad of *Wind in the Willows* fame after one of his madcap motoring escapades: "John jumped out and shouted, 'Christ, Eric!' He got gravel burns all over his hands." Something in Newfoundland — was it the air, the water, the libation? — brought out the hellion in Moon.

Finally a Chief

Newfoundland was the first and only time in Moon's career that he was a chief, or head, librarian. The job — analogous to being a county librarian in the UK or state librarian in the U.S. — had been obtained without a traditional interview, either in person or by telephone. Rather, all negotiations had been carried out via correspondence with a member of the library board, an older man named W.C. Hudson. The position had an imposing title — Director of Public Library Services and Secretary-Treasurer of the Newfoundland Public Libraries Board — and commanded an annual salary of $6,500 (Canadian). Just as he knew little about Newfoundland prior to immigrating, he came to the job with only the vaguest knowledge of Canadian library practices and customs. This potential obstacle turned out not to be a serious problem: Moon had always been a quick study and, besides, the differences between library service in the UK and Newfoundland were relatively minor, due to the fact that at the time the province was more British than Canadian in orientation and attitude.

What did disconcert him from the beginning, however, was the parlous state of the library system itself. In the late 1950s Newfoundland Public Libraries claimed roughly 260,000 cataloged items, circulated some 750,000 books and other materials each year, and had an annual budget of approximately $145,000. The Gosling Memorial Library in St. John's, where Moon had his office, served as the system's headquarters library as well as the city's main library. Opened in 1936 with 8,000 books (2,000 donated by the widow of William Gilbert Gosling, a former mayor of St. John's and library namesake), the Gosling had grown steadily if slowly over the next two decades, until in 1958 its collection totaled 57,000 volumes. Unfortunately, the library, which was still in its original building, a small brownstone on Duckworth Street just off Water Street, the city's main commercial thoroughfare, had become horrendously overcrowded. In an article about the Gosling prepared for a history of Newfoundland, Moon lamented: "It would be overstating the case to suggest that the library is able to meet adequately all the actual or potential demand.... [T]he old brown stone building is no longer an adequate home. It has become a cramped cage which will soon prevent the library service from spreading its wings any further."

The library system also included some 50 small branches, almost all located in the outport communities that ringed the Newfoundland coast. These little libraries, which served approximately 400 of the more than 1,000 outports in the province, were staffed by nonprofessionals and volunteers. Actually, the system had only a few professionals, all based at the Gosling in St. John's. In addition to Moon, there was Jessie Mifflen, who oversaw the outport libraries; Mona Cram, reference librarian; Faith Mercer, cataloger; and Marjorie Mews, who managed the Gosling itself.

Among these hardworking maiden ladies, Jessie Mifflen stood out as an exceptional librarian. A native of Newfoundland with a library degree from the University of Toronto, she devoted her professional life to bringing library service to remote areas of the province. Moon remembered Mifflen, who died in 1994 at age 87, as "a real old Newfoundlander, full of marvelous stories, who had a great sense of humor and a lovely Newfoundland accent." Another member of the library staff, Grace Butt, a reference assistant at the Gosling, intrigued Moon because she wrote plays and had a vibrant personality. She was, he recalled, "probably the brightest, most scintillating member of the staff." Occasionally he and Diana socialized with Grace and her husband Bert, a prominent insurance executive in St. John's. Later, when Moon got into trouble with the law in St. John's, he turned to Bert Butt for help.

Moon's predecessor, Harold Newell, also remained on the library staff for a time in the rather amorphous role of "advisory director." Newell, a former schoolteacher without formal training in library science, had been in charge of public library service in Newfoundland since its inception in 1934 and, though he retired as director in 1958, he agreed to stay on through March 1959 to assist the new chief, almost surely at the urging of the library board, which knew that Moon had no experience with libraries in Canada or outside England. Moon, who knew nothing of this arrangement until he got to St. John's, understandably took an instant dislike to Newell, dismissing him as "a nervous little man who didn't know much about libraries" and who had left the Newfoundland system "in desperate shape."

Given staff, budget, and plant limitations, the province's public libraries normally provided only the most rudimentary services, such as circulating books, answering basic reference questions, and offering regular children's story hours and film shows. One area where the library did stand out was its extensive use of radio as a medium to bring the world of books and knowledge to the people of Newfoundland, no matter how small, distant, or secluded their community. Both Moon and Mifflen worked closely with the Canadian Broadcasting Corporation in Newfoundland, writing scripts and doing broadcasts on a wide range of library-related subjects. Programs included book talks, interviews, feature stories, and panel discussions. Moon used the medium to promote library service in St. John's and beyond:

> I tried to do some things that would broaden the use of the library in both St. John's and outside. I used the radio a lot. I started to do a regular library program. They had had one, but it was the sort of ordinary book talk program. I expanded the program to include people talking about how the library related to them and their lives. We discussed ideas. I got people who were well-known in the area and put them on a panel, threw controversial questions at them, and sat back to see how it would go.

Moon Tours Outport Libraries, Drinks Screech

Jessie Mifflen, who singlehandedly brought library service to the province's many outports, has rightly been called "Newfoundland's library missionary." Over the course of her 22-year career she gave countless talks, did numerous CBC radio shows, and wrote two books about her experiences, which included descriptions of travel by train, boat, coastal steamer, small plane, and dogsled to reach the most isolated destinations. A few months after Moon started as director, Mifflen suggested he should have a first-hand look at the outport operation, and in October 1958 the two librarians set off on a tour of Newfoundland's far-flung branch libraries, which would take them to hard-scrabble places with whimsical names like Come-by-Chance, Heart's Content, and Tickle Bay. Moon never forgot the trip:

> There was one little narrow-gauge railroad that went all the way around the north and down the west coast of Newfoundland. It was the only way we could go, other than by car, which would have been too hazardous. After a time the weather moved in — I hadn't realized that October was already winter in Newfoundland. Soon the tracks were snowed under and the train was in danger of being blown off the tracks. Jessie and I were dumped in one of the little outports in the north of the island. There were no hotels outside St. John's at that time, so we went knocking on doors around the outport to see if anyone could put us up for the night.
>
> Eventually somebody said yes, they could put us up. It was very, very cold, the wind was blowing and the snow was coming down. And so the family putting us up said they would

bring us something to warm us up, and they brought out these huge tumblers of rum filled right to the top—and it's straight! They called it Newfoundland screech. So we sat around the fireside drinking these great tumblers of screech. Jessie regarded all this as very normal but I'm thunderstruck. Next morning, the guy says, "You can't go out there without something to warm you up," so he gave us more screech! Eventually we got on our way. But I had learned an important lesson: if you're going to go around the outports, you had better do it earlier than October.

The new chief now had a hands-on sense of what the outport libraries were all about, what they looked like, and what problems they faced. But in reality he had little to do with them on a day-by-day basis—they were Jessie Mifflen's domain. Once, however, Moon did temporarily close a few of them to make a statement to the powers that be about the library's budgetary miseries.

Pressure to Buy Canadian

Most of Moon's time and energy at the Gosling was spent dealing with such matters as the budget, personnel, programming, and, of course, collection development, his forte. Throughout his career, books were paramount, whether he was reading them, selecting them, reviewing them, buying them, publishing them, or writing them. In Newfoundland he naturally undertook the job of improving the collection. While not neglecting best-sellers in heavy demand, he emphasized acquiring works of quality in an effort to elevate the reading public's taste, just as he had done in his various posts in England. Because every penny counted he ordered most stock directly from the United States and the UK, where the books were published and cost less than if he purchased them through Canadian vendors, who ordinarily tacked on a hefty surcharge of 30 to 40 percent. It did not take him long to learn that the practice of buying direct from foreign sources was viewed by many Canadians, including librarians, as unpatriotic, an act somewhere between besmirching the flag and treason. Moon:

At the time, the Canadian Library Association frowned on buying direct, a controversial practice called "buying around." Canadian librarians were supposed to support the Canadian book industry. So I and, I believe, the librarian at Vancouver, who also "bought around," were in bad odor with the CLA for awhile. But I came to understand the Canadians' feelings. Canadian culture was under the shadow of the giant to the south. Canadians wanted to retain a Canadian identity, and the Canadian publishing industry was a good example of how the giant down below dominated. At first I did not understand the intensity of this feeling on the part of Canadians, because I had just come into the country, and I did not really feel part of it because nearly everybody wrote Newfoundland off as some sort of weird appendage.

Budget Battles with Joey Smallwood

During Moon's brief tenure as Newfoundland's top public librarian he had a budget approaching $150,000 per annum (not reindeer feed in those days), a book collection in excess of a quarter of a million volumes, and an annual circulation of three quarters of a million. Sounds pretty good, eh? But looked at through Moon's professional eyes, the system was sadly understocked, underfunded, and underutilized: there was only *half a book* in the collection for each resident, only *one and a half books* circulated each year per resident, and the province spent only about *$0.30 each year per resident* on library service. Library facilities, moreover, were generally inadequate and the Gosling was strained almost to the breaking point. Not long after starting work in Newfoundland, Moon began a regular drumbeat of public and private complaint about the library system's many deficiencies: "The butter is spread more thinly all the time," he wrote at one point, "and those who run the service are always aware that they still reach only half the population, that seven or eight hundred [outport] communities remain without library service of any kind."

Little wonder then that Moon hit the roof when he found out the library board had endorsed a timid five-year plan prepared by his predecessor just before he arrived. Livid, he informed the board that a *new* five-year plan, with *new* budget projections, would be necessary. He was "horrified," he said, that the board had acted in such a furtive manner. Board members—all appointees of the province's powerful premier, Joseph Smallwood—were flummoxed. They feared Smallwood but sympathized with their new librarian's predicament. Eventually Moon gained the board's reluctant support for a new five-year plan, which he prepared and decided to present personally to Smallwood:

> When I got to St. John's I discovered that Harold Newell, the previous director, had drawn up a five-year plan for the library, and I was presented with this and found it horrifying. The budget for the library was already dismal, and Newell had recommended that it go up only $20,000 over the next five years. So I went to the first board meeting and aid I was horrified that they had agreed to something like this when I was about to be appointed. I couldn't accept this and I proposed a revised five-year plan at the next board meeting. My new plan recommended funding to go to $2 million in five years. They just fell off their chairs and said where did I think I was? At first the board rejected my plan but I talked them into OKing it and letting me try to sell it to Joe Smallwood.

The Honorable Joseph (Joey) R. Smallwood, Newfoundland's chief executive for a decade by the time Moon came on the scene, was a short, crafty, bespectacled politician who knew all the right buttons to push to stay in power. He sold the people of Newfoundland on confederation in 1948 by trumpeting the many economic benefits that would flow to the province upon becoming part of Canada—and flow they did. On the other side of the ledger, confederation saddled Newfoundland with a crushing monetary debt, but this was less talked about. Once Newfoundland was part of Canada, Smallwood was not above threatening the central government in Ottawa with pulling out of the union if he did not get his way: "I took them into confederation," he liked to say, "and I can take them out." Some called him a dictator, the Huey Long of Newfoundland; Moon preferred the Salazar of the North Atlantic, after the longtime strongman of Portugal. Whatever he was called, Joey Smallwood ruled the province with an iron hand.

But he was also a thoughtful leader who wanted the best life possible for his people, constantly warning them against insular thinking and wallowing in what he called "the old-time Maritime grievance psychology." Though Moon had his battles with Small-wood (who was in effect his boss), he grudgingly admired him, characterizing the premier as "a tough cookie with a magnetic personality who had created much of what the province was at that time." (For vivid portraits of Smallwood and his political career, see Wayne Johnston's fictional biography *The Colony of Unrequited Dreams* and memoir *Baltimore's Mansion*, both published by Doubleday.)

Unfortunately, the premier and the new librarian never clicked. Moon, because he lacked knowledge of Newfoundland's past political battles and feuds, apparently made an innocent mistake soon after arriving in St. John's that put him in the dog-house with Smallwood and his people. He got off on the wrong foot by inviting one of the premier's old political enemies to participate in a radio discussion program sponsored by the library. Moon described the incident:

One of the people I got on my show right at the beginning was a guy called Harold Hor-wood, who was a very prominent journalist with the *Evening Telegram*, the newspaper in St. John's. One of his buddies was the Canadian writer Farley Mowat. What I didn't know was that Horwood had been a member of Joey Smallwood's original cabinet, when Joey first came to power. And he was one of the first to leave the cabinet because of his vast disagreements with Joey. So after that move I was under some suspicion by the Smallwood clan — they thought I had done this to embarrass the administration.

Moon hoped the Horwood flap would not prejudice Smallwood against his revised five-year plan for dramatically upgrading Newfoundland's public libraries. No matter, he was prepared to fight — with AAL-style spunk and tactics if necessary — for the resources he knew he needed to bring the library system up to speed. He sent Small-wood a copy of his plan and new budget and waited for a response. And waited. And waited. Until he got tired of waiting:

A week went by, so I called and asked for a meeting with Joey. When I went into his office, he looked up and said, "Young man, you are stark, staring, raving mad." I said, "Well, that's a possibility, Mr. Smallwood, but could we get into specifics?" He said, "Specifics?? Look at this. You're advocating paying your senior librarians more than I pay my cabinet ministers!" And I said, "But of course." And he said, "Of course? What do you mean, of course??" And I said, "You can pick up cabinet ministers off Water Street down here. Where do you think I'm going to get professional librarians? I've got to get them from mainland Canada, the U.S., or Great Britain, and that's what they pay them there." "Get out," he said. And I was ushered from his office. Obviously, my plan was not going to be approved.

In due course, Moon, experienced in political infighting from his days in British libraries, got a bit of what he wanted, including a smidgen of revenge, when during the next election campaign he closed half a dozen outport libraries in places where the loss of library service might hurt Smallwood at the polls. The idea was to put heat on the premier — and it worked. "There was an absolute uproar about it," remembered Moon, pleased as a firebug at a conflagration. "Smallwood called me and asked why I had closed down these outport libraries, and I told him that we didn't have enough money to maintain them. So I got a check for a substantial amount right away. It seemed like this was the only way to work. I had to use awful tactics to get any response at all."

Lolita *in Newfoundland*

"Over the short period I was there, the differences kind of grew," Moon said of his stormy relationship with Joey Smallwood. One of those differences concerned censorship. When he arrived at the Gosling he found a room full of books "that had been complained about"— many of them books Moon had read and enjoyed, and he lost no time ordering all of them back on the shelves. He waited for a reaction, but nothing came of the matter.

Later, however, Vladimir Nabokov's pedophiliac novel *Lolita* threatened to bring the premier and his chief librarian into a knock-down-drag-out conflict. The novel, first published in France in 1955, created enormous controversy when it finally appeared in the United States and Canada in 1958. In Toronto, for example, the public library first refused to buy the book, using the excuse that the library could not afford enough copies to meet the demand so it would not buy the book at all. Then Pierre Berton, a popular Canadian writer, got into the act, going on television saying he would personally buy 100 copies and donate them to the Toronto Public. Berton's gesture was not accepted, but the library did finally relent and acquire the book, by then a cause célèbre. In Newfoundland, Moon ordered multiple copies of *Lolita* as soon as he learned about its publication in North America. Meanwhile, Smallwood decreed a ban on the book. Moon schemed to head off the premier:

Joe Smallwood issued a dictate that the book should not be allowed into the province, that the university library couldn't have it, that the bookstores couldn't sell it, and the public libraries couldn't stock it. I had already ordered 26 copies for the public library system, so I called Don Jameson, who was then the czar of Newfoundland television. Don used to have an interview segment every night in the middle of his news program — someone who was in the news would be interviewed for ten or 15 minutes. I called Don and said, "Do you want to do an interview tonight?" He said, "What have you done that's interesting?" I said, "I've just bought 26 copies of *Lolita*." He said, "Come on up!" I went up and did the interview. When I got back, the staff said you've had it now, you're dead. But I never heard a word. It was the old principle: attack first, go public first.

At the height of the *Lolita* controversy Moon visited his old friend and colleague from Bushey-Oxhey days, Al Bowron, who was now working at the Toronto Public as head of technical services. While at the library he dropped in to see Toronto's director, Harry Campbell. The two men had a pleasant chat, Moon remembered, until he mentioned *Lolita*, asking Campbell if he had had any difficulty with the book? "The next thing I knew it was as if the Berlin Wall had been built, and all conversation ceased and I was out of Harry's office." Moon claimed he was unaware at the time of the ruckus over the book in Toronto: "Harry thought I was giving him the needle." For his part, Campbell, who remained director at Toronto Public until 1978 and then became general manager of the Toronto-based Espial Productions, commented sardonically, "Nabokov got good value for the publicity."

Hopeless Situation

Moon had one other potentially serious censorship case while in Newfoundland. It involved a library board member who tried to have one of John O'Hara's novels removed from the system, but swift, firm action by the director quelled that bit of nonsense. Happily, in most matters, including attempts at book banning, Moon enjoyed the support of his board, though in reality its members had little authority, the real power residing with Smallwood, who controlled the money. One reason he had good relations with the board was that he got on well with the chairman, Anthony (Tony) Ayre, a man close to his own age and the scion of a well-known Newfoundland business family. Ayre, recalled Moon, "was a bit of a man about town — liked to drink, liked the ladies. So he and I got on rather well. We used to have a drink together periodically." He remembered that Ayre made him "feel a little better about the job but not much, because the situation just looked so hopeless — not much money, not much chance of development or change. It was the one time in my life that I really felt that this was a job that I couldn't do anything with."

In fact, Moon had been in Newfoundland for no more than seven or eight months when, troubled by various aspects of the job, he made an attempt to escape — not back to England but to the giant to the south. In early 1959 he spotted an ad for the position of assistant director of Cuyahoga County Public Libraries in Cleveland. He decided to try for it:

So just on spec I put in an application for it. I got a call from the chairman of the board, who said they had been fascinated by my application, but couldn't afford to pay expenses for the interview, except for the person who got the job. I said, "You know it's a helluva long way from St. John's to Cleveland, and I really can't afford to do that. But I'll make you an offer — if you're interested in interviewing me, I'll meet you half way. I'll meet the board in Montreal." He said, "Hey, that's a terrific idea." But he couldn't sell it and I was never interviewed. Given the subsequent history of Cuyahoga County Libraries, I think I was very lucky.

Association Man in Canada

One of Moon's first acts after arriving in St. John's and settling into his office at the Gosling was to join the Canadian Library Association. A confirmed believer in the power of professional associations he was eager to see how the CLA differed from the LA and AAL and how he might use it to advance the cause of public libraries in Newfoundland as well as his own career. At his first CLA conference (in Edmonton) he got appointed to a couple of committees (on federal aid and comparative library education) and began making contacts with other Canadian librarians. Later, he served briefly on CLA's pensions committee, but his stay in Canada was so fleeting and the general attitude toward Newfoundland so dismissive that the association had no discernible impact on him, nor he on it. He joined too the Atlantic Provinces Library Association, a regional organization serving Newfoundland and the three maritime provinces, but again the experience was perfunctory and uneventful.

One association-related issue Moon did pursue with some diligence while in Canada concerned how best to equate or reconcile British and North American library qualifications. Librarians in the United States and Canada had to possess both a baccalaureate and library science degree from accredited schools in order to achieve professional status whereas their counterparts in the UK were not required to have such degrees or, in fact, any set amount of formal education. Rather, British librarians qualified by passing examinations devised and administered by the LA. Such disparities in standards created credentialing problems when British librarians came to work in North America and vice versa. Indeed, some in Canada got quite emotional about the issue, denouncing immigrant British librarians as "scabs" who were willing to undermine efforts to raise the status and salaries of hardworking Canadian librarians.

D.A. Redmond, a Canadian librarian writing in the *APLA Bulletin* in 1959, used a picturesque metaphor to describe the dilemma: "The whole problem of library education in Great Britain, as well as the specific problem of British librarians fitting into the Canadian scheme, is as disturbed as a hollow tree full of bees, honey and bear paws."

Moon, of course, had run into this thicket when he originally tried to get a job in Canada, and questions about his qualifications rankled for the rest of his life: "I had great difficulty when I wanted to come over to this side. Nobody would recognize British qualifications because we did not have university degrees, although it's always been my firm opinion that the FLA is better than the MLS."

In the 1950s both ALA and CLA had committees considering the qualifications question, but Moon and two other British émigrés working as librarians in North America, Vincent Richards and T. Mark Hodges, decided a more activist approach was needed. In 1958 they started an organization called Fellows and Associates of the Library Association in North America (FALANA), which, according to Richards (who knew Moon, having worked for him in England at Brentford and Chiswick), would provide British librarians in the United States and Canada with "a medium for the exchange of information and ideas on library education and qualifications," mainly through a quarterly newsletter. To no one's surprise, FALANA lasted for only a short time, but it did serve to highlight a difficult problem — one that remained unresolved for the next forty years.

Moon was looked upon by some colleagues in North America as a trailblazer, one of the few British librarians able to overcome the qualifications obstacle. "I was delighted," observed Canadian-born Harry Campbell, "that some venturesome, capable member of the LA had broken the taboo. Canadians did not think UK library qualifications academically respectable. The utter insularity of North American librarianship was a barrier that needed to be broken, and Eric was one of the first really topflight people who 'came over.'" Mark Hodges, then a reference librarian at Hamilton College in Clinton, New York, who had also "come over" a few months before Moon, echoed these sentiments: "I was particularly pleased about Eric's Newfoundland appointment because he, like so many British librarians at the time, lacked a university degree. This was something that, in the eyes of some Canadian librarians, rendered them substandard."

Creative Outlets

The restless, seemingly limitless energy Moon expended in England on professional activities above and beyond his regular job had far fewer outlets in Newfoundland. His heart was not in the CLA or APLA, which seemed pallid in comparison with the LA and especially the spirited AAL; no teaching opportunities presented themselves; the country's few library publications did not interest or inspire him; there were no union functions (besides, he was now management). He felt stifled, confined, alienated, isolated, depressed, beaten down, defeated—by the job, the miserable weather, the treacherous roads, Joey Smallwood, the provincialism of St. John's, the high price of everything, and, most of all, the lack of a platform to showcase his talent, to show off how good he was. His library radio scripts and broadcasts for the CBC offered one avenue for self-expression but he needed much more of that sort of challenge to satisfy pent-up creative urges.

Happily, he discovered the *Atlantic Advocate*. A good-looking, carefully edited magazine featuring stories about Canada's Atlantic provinces, the *Advocate* first came to his attention at the Gosling, which naturally had a subscription. Then one day, he remembered, "I was browsing in our collection and figured that there were some great stories here, so I started writing again, with the *Advocate* in mind." During the short time he was in Newfoundland, he produced a series of substantial historical articles for the magazine, including "The Fighting Women of Foxtrap," "No Place for Ladies," "Air Race from Newfoundland," and the aforementioned "The Province Nobody Knows," an evocative account of his journey from England to Newfoundland.

Also, just before leaving St. John's for New York and *Library Journal*, he again tried his hand at acting, playing Otto Frank in a local production of *The Diary of Anne Frank*. He said he got involved partly because of frustration with his job and partly because there was nothing better to do in St. John's: "It was a cultural desert, and one had to find things to do to fill the time." His brief bio in the *Anne Frank* playbill offered only a slightly inflated description of his previous stage credits: "ERIC MOON. The role of Otto Frank is played by this incomparable Englishman from London, who counts as previous theatrical experience, barnstorming in 1940 with a 'rep' company and revue and comedy work in RAF shows. It is disappointing to lose Eric to New York, but it may well enable him to realize his ambition to retire at 37." He was 36 at the time.

Arrest for Drunk Driving

In the end, Newfoundland and St. John's simply did not offer enough professional and personal action for a man of Moon's talents, vitality, and appetites. Despite half-hearted efforts to fit in he never felt comfortable or at home in Newfoundland. Even an extramarital fling—which might at least have added spice—was out of the question in such a conservative milieu: "It was too tight a society," he explained. "Any indiscretion would have been known the next day." Later, after going to *LJ*, he did have a serious romance with a woman from the Scarborough (Ontario) Public Library whom he met at a conference, but during the 16 months he worked in Newfoundland he remained a faithful husband.

Boredom, lack of challenge, and feelings of acute dissatisfaction with the job and life in St. John's prompted him sometimes to drink too much. On one occasion alcohol led to trouble. Big legal trouble. Moon's "downfall" occurred early one cold March morning in 1959 on an icy road somewhere between the Newfoundland Hotel in downtown St. John's and his home:

Newfoundland was a very dangerous place to drive in. It was this that led to my downfall. I got into deep trouble. Canadian publishers and their representatives would come over to Newfoundland en bloc at a certain time of the year and party at the Newfoundland Hotel. I was there partying with them one night until very late and got drunk to the gills. They tried to persuade me to stay the night at the hotel, but I said no, I had to get back.

So I get into my car to drive across those hazardous roads in this state, and I'm doing like 70 going across this icy road and suddenly I realize there's something in front of me — and I smack right into the back of a parked cop car. So I'm thrown into the tank for the night; this place is way down in the dungeons; I felt like the Spanish Inquisition had got me. I came up the next morning, looking bedraggled and feeling awful. I had to go into court, and who's sitting on the bench but a member of my library board. Earlier I had called Grace Butt, a reference assistant at the library, and her husband Bert for advice about a lawyer to represent me. Bert, who knew everyone and was part of the power structure in St. John's, helped me get a big-wheel lawyer.

My lawyer came in and got the whole thing deferred. When we talked about it later he said, "Boy, you are really in a lot of trouble. I don't know if you know it but for drunk driving in Newfoundland it's automatic jail — for six months, or something like that." Our only hope was to keep getting the case deferred and eventually get the charge reduced to impaired driving, which had no jail time but a fine and loss of driver's license. The thing dragged on for months, but eventually my lawyer got me off on the impaired driving charge. But I lost my license and got fined several hundred dollars.

This Is Dan Melcher Calling

Moon's arrest for drunk driving and the drawn out adjudication process was, he remembered, "quite a scandal, you can imagine." Now at the nadir of his fortunes as Newfoundland's public library director, he was desperate to get out, to put the whole wretched mess behind him, to start afresh, preferably in the United States, a move that had been in the back of his mind since the first day he set foot in Canada. During his period of disgrace he considered leaving librarianship, possibly to work for the CBC, which made "some tentative offers" to hire him as a producer-scriptwriter. Were these offers serious or merely wishful thinking by a downhearted man? An unexpected telephone call rendered the question moot.

In early August, five months after the drunk driving incident, Moon was at home for lunch when his secretary at the Gosling received a phone call for him from New York City. The call sounded important, so she told the gentleman from New York that Mr. Moon could be reached at home and gave him the Moons' number. Moon meanwhile had finished his meal and was on his way back to work:

When I got back to the library my secretary told me about the call. Then Diana called and said, "Somebody from New York just called you." I thought what the hell's all these calls from New York. It was not every day that I got a call from New York. So in a little while New York calls back. The voice says, "Hi, my name is Dan Melcher. I'm with the R.R. Bowker Company in New York. We publish *Publishers Weekly* and *Library Journal.* How would you like to be editor of *Library Journal*?" I was stunned. I said, what's the gag? He said, no gag, would you interested in being editor of *Library Journal*?

I said I'd be very interested, but how come you're asking? So he told me that they had just recently interviewed some people for the job, including a young man named John Wakeman, who subsequently had written to them and said that he knew a guy named Eric Moon who would be ideal for the job, describing me as the leader of the avant-garde young revolutionary librarians in England—all kinds of crap like that. Dan said, "I was interested to hear that and I thought I would call you up and chat with you about it." And we talked for awhile, then he said, "I'll tell you what we'll do. I'll write you a long letter telling you all about Bowker and *Library Journal* and why don't you write me a long letter about yourself and we'll take it from there." I went and got together one of those typical grand British applications—about 17 foolscap pages—and dazzled him with that.

A few weeks later Moon received a follow-up call from Dan Melcher, who said, "I think you better come down and see us." Melcher indicated Bowker would pay his expenses and suggested he fly down and spend a weekend—would September 12–13 be agreeable?—in New Jersey with him and his father, Fred, who was chairman of the Bowker Company. Then on the following Monday, the 14th, Moon could visit the magazine's offices in New York City, at which time he would have an opportunity to look over the operation and talk with key people in the Bowker organization. Ecstatic, Moon readily agreed to all these arrangements.

He flew to New York on Friday, September 11, getting in quite late that evening. "I'm met at the airport by none other than John Wakeman, with whom I'm in touch again after this development. John drives me into Times Square to a place he says will do my old English heart good, a restaurant called Hector's. I still remember it because its window was full of the creamiest cakes you've ever seen in your life, and John knew that was the way to start out in New York. So we sat in Hector's and ate cream cakes my first evening in New York." On the way into the restaurant the visitor could not help noticing a huge tabloid headline at a newsstand: MOON SHOT, blared the paper, announcing the launch of the Soviet's Luna 2 moon probe. Was it an omen? Maybe he wouldn't get out of New York City alive? Or better, perhaps his career was finally ready to take off like a rocket?

The next morning Dan Melcher collected him in the city and they drove to Fred Melcher's home in Montclair, New Jersey, where Moon spent the weekend getting to know Fred and his wife Marguerite, Dan and his wife Peggy (the younger Melchers also lived in Montclair), and other members of the family, as well as most of the Bowker directors, who conveniently dropped by one by one, like judges at an art show. Frederic G. Melcher, then 80, was a courtly man who had spent a lifetime building the Bowker Company into a powerful player in the American book publishing industry, serving as president of the company from 1934 until early in 1959, when he became chairman of the board of directors. Both a savvy executive and dedicated bookman,

Fred Melcher was a legend in the publishing business. It was he, for instance, who originated the Newbery and Caldecott awards, the nation's most prestigious for children's books. Moon remembered talking literature with Bowker's grand old man:

I spent the weekend there sitting on their porch chatting with Fred and Dan. Various of the Bowker Company directors stopped by to talk with me over the weekend. I suppose by the end of the weekend I had met nearly all of them. And Sunday evening, Fred and I sat up nearly all night talking poets and poetry. He had a wonderful library and he would, for example, show me Stephen Vincent Benét, and I would say, "You know, he kind of reminds me of G.K. Chesterton," and I would find a volume of Chesterton and Fred would say, "Gee, I hadn't thought of that." By the end of the weekend, I thought if I haven't got this job nailed down now, it's not going to happen.

The previous evening Moon had dinner at the home of Richard Bye, a Bowker director who, then in his late thirties, was just a couple years older than Moon. Bye immediately liked Moon:

For my turn as interviewer, I invited Eric to my house for dinner. I think the only other guests were Arthur Wang of Hill & Wang and his wife, Mary Ellen. I had known Arthur since college and had, and still have, a high regard for his taste and integrity. We share social and political views that are somewhat left of comfortable liberalism. Stimulated by some preprandial drinks, the conversation, as I recall it, was animated and revealing. In short, we liked Eric because he seemed to hold many of those same views.

On Monday morning the Melchers and their guest set out early for Bowker headquarters in New York, then located at 62 West 45th Street. Moon recalled that day, September 14, 1959, as one of the most intense of his life:

We got in there just before 9:00 A.M. and Dan took me to the *Library Journal* editor's office and said, "There's Melvil Dewey's chair. Try it on for size." And I sat in it and said, "It's a bit tight, Dan." Then he left me in this office for the next seven hours. Over the course of the whole day they sent in everybody who was the head of every different kind of operation at Bowker. The production guy came in and talked to me about type and printing and paper; the promotion head came in and talked to me about promotion and advertising; Chandler Grannis of *Publishers Weekly* came in and talked to me about editorial stuff. I was grilled all day long, and I'm beginning to wilt. About 4:00 P.M. I finally got a call from Dan, who said, "Would you come up to my office?" I went up and he said, "OK, we've decided. Will you be our editor?" And I said, "God, I thought you'd never ask!"

Later Moon learned that Anne Richter, one of Dan Melcher's top lieutenants and a Bowker director, had spent a fair amount of time in London checking him out: "She went all around London asking librarians did they know Eric Moon and what did they think of him. She came in with a report that half of them said he's the cat's whiskers and the other half said they wouldn't go near him with a bargepole."

Library Journal had been rudderless for a long time, and the Melchers wanted to be as certain as humanly possible that they were getting the right person for the job. They scrutinized Moon's letter about himself and his credentials; they spent a relaxed weekend in his company, testing his intellectual and social acumen; they subjected him to an exhausting daylong interview at company headquarters; and they conducted an informal investigation into his background. At the end of this lengthy process the Melchers were reasonably convinced they had found someone who had what it would take to revitalize *Library Journal*. They reasoned that the magazine deserved the best editorial talent they could afford. After all, *LJ* had long been American librarianship's foremost periodical publication and its original editor, Melvil Dewey, the most famous librarian of them all.

Goodbye Newfoundland, Hello New York

A very happy Eric Moon returned to St. John's and immediately submitted his resignation as director of Newfoundland Public Libraries, effective the middle of October 1959. The plan was for him to take up his new responsibilities at *Library Journal* sometime in November, depending on how quickly he could wind up business and personal affairs in St. John's and get situated in the New York area. Leaving Newfoundland occasioned no tears, real or false. Moon relished the prospect of quitting the province as soon as possible, as did Diana and the boys. He knew too that others in St. John's felt the same way: "In some quarters there was a good deal of happiness about my resignation." He heard nothing from Joe Smallwood or any of his aides, though the premier was doubtless delighted to have fortuitously rid himself of such an irksome librarian. The faithful Harold Newell agreed to return to manage the library until a new director could be hired.

Some Canadian librarians, like Harry Campbell at Toronto Public, were sorry to see Moon go, but realized it was inevitable. "I was enthusiastic about Eric from the start," recalled Campbell, "but I could see he was overshadowing his Canadian colleagues. He needed a larger playing field." Others regarded Moon as an opportunist who had deserted Canada for the behemoth to the south as soon as he could. Pearce Penney, who served as Newfoundland's provincial librarian from 1972 until 1993, put it this way: "Eric Moon spent such a short period in Newfoundland that the records are thin — to say the least. Some would say it wasn't long enough to warm the spot he stood on. I would only say that Eric's stay in Newfoundland was so temporary it could almost be compared with the migratory birds that stop over briefly before going south."

Looking back, Moon regarded the Newfoundland experience as a strange interlude; it was "some kind of weird interval between a big-city boy going from London to New York." He was hugely pleased to be returning to a major metropolitan area. After moving to New York, people sometimes asked him if he didn't find the pace of the city a bit terrifying, and he would say, "No, the pace of New York seems pretty normal to me; it isn't that much different from London. It was the interval in between that was terrifying." Moon was quick to acknowledge that Dan Melcher's call not only radically changed his life but came at exactly the right moment: "That call came like a blessing. I had had it up to here with Newfoundland by that time." Likewise, he always acknowledged his debt to John Wakeman for bringing his name to the attention of the Melchers: "*LJ* was the dream come true. It enabled me to use all my professional experience, but it also allowed me to do the thing that I really wanted to do, which was write. I was just unbelievably lucky. The moral of the story is, be good to your staff, because if John Wakeman hadn't recommended me, Bowker would never have known about me."

Finally, the big day came and the four Moons flew down to New York, eager as the birds to escape the bitter cold, bringing with them only the clothes on their backs and a few necessities. Most of the family's possessions were coming by sea and would arrive much later. Once they were in the air, Newfoundland suddenly seemed far away, a surreal dream — or nightmare — that faded from memory in the wee hours. For Eric, the 16 months in the Canadian province had been largely a holding operation, a period of waiting for the next career opportunity to present itself. True, he had finally become a chief, but he had mishandled the situation so thoroughly that only good fortune saved him. Ultimately, Newfoundland served one — and only one — purpose for Moon: it got him and his family to North America. No matter how disagreeable or botched the experience, Newfoundland got him to the threshold of the land of opportunity, to the edge of the golden door. Then luck, or fate, coupled with a decade of rich professional experience, opened that shining door and he was off and running, soon to breathe new life into Melvil's venerable rag.

Metaphorically, the library profession resembles a three-ring circus, teeming with clowns, acrobats, magicians, jugglers, freaks, fire-eaters, dancers, trapeze artists, barkers, roustabouts, and lion tamers— all performing under the direction of a ringmaster. When Dan Melcher's call came, Eric Moon, a fire-eater, sensed his time had arrived, that his apprenticeship was over, that the life-shaping experiences lay behind him. He was ready for the big show. Eventually he would become ringmaster.

8

Reviving *Library Journal*

LJ *from Dewey to Moon*

Library Journal, the oldest English-language library periodical of any consequence, first appeared in 1876 under the imprint of Frederick Leypoldt, a New York publisher whose modest establishment founded a dozen years earlier subsequently became the R.R. Bowker Company, a publishing industry giant. Leypoldt, a German immigrant who started life in the United States as a bookseller in Philadelphia, recognized that the booming but undisciplined American book trade lacked the reference tools, bibliographic and otherwise, necessary to conduct business in the most efficient and profitable manner. Entrepreneurial to his fingertips, Leypoldt seized the opportunity and began developing bibliographies, directories, and journals intended to bring order and structure to the book business, thereby improving the lot of all concerned, including publishers, booksellers, librarians, writers, teachers, scholars, and the general reading public. He issued the first edition of his *Annual American Catalogue*, a list of in-print publications, in 1870; *Publishers Weekly*, a magazine featuring book trade news and announcements of new titles, made its debut in 1872; and a version of *Publishers Trade List Annual*, a collection of publishers' catalogs, was introduced the following year. In 1878 Leypoldt gained a partner when Richard Rogers Bowker, a bright young man with newspaper experience and a literary disposition, acquired *Publishers Weekly*.

Together, Leypoldt, who died in 1884, and Bowker, who lived into the 1930s, had a major impact on American publishing during its formative years, and their influence is still evident today. For instance, *Books in Print*, the Bowker Company's flagship publication and indispensable bibliographic database since its introduction in 1948, grew out of their early efforts. It has been said, with justification, that Leypoldt and Bowker "invented trade bibliography as we now know it." The two men also laid the groundwork for such standard reference sources as *Literary Market Place* and *Ulrich's International Periodicals Directory*, and they helped establish the American Booksellers Association and successfully argued for needed copyright legislation.

Both Leypoldt and Bowker viewed libraries as an integral and vital part of the book industry in North America. The public library movement, in its infancy in the early 19th century, accelerated rapidly between the 1830s and the Civil War, and by the time Leypoldt's small publishing company started up in 1864 many communities already had a tax-supported municipal library. Also, numerous public and private colleges and universities, including land-grant institutions, came into existence around this time, and each new school meant a new library. Concurrently, a new order of librarians—activists who believed they were, or should be, more than mere keepers of books—came to the fore, full of missionary zeal and a desire to change the old ways. In response to this ferment Leypoldt launched *Library Journal* (initially called the *American Library Journal*), the country's first magazine devoted to the profession of librarianship. The inaugural issue, dated September 30, 1876, was timed to appear just days before a much anticipated national conference of librarians. Held in early October in Philadelphia, this historic meeting culminated in the founding of the American Library Association, and for a generation, from 1876 to 1907, *LJ* served as the association's journal of record.

The magazine's founding editor, Melvil Dewey, stands out as the era's foremost representative of the progressive impulse in American librarianship. Rejecting the old image of the librarian as "a mouser in musty books," Dewey called for a new, revolutionary approach to library work, one in which "the librarian is in the highest sense a teacher." He enlarged on this theme in an article entitled "The Profession" in the first issue of *LJ*:

It is not now enough that the books are cared for properly, are well arranged, are never lost. It is not enough if the librarian can readily produce any book asked for. It is not enough that he can, when asked, give advice as to the best books in his collection on any given subject. All these things are indispensable, but all these are not enough for our ideal. He must see that his library contains, as far as possible, the best books on the best subjects, regarding carefully the wants of his special community. Then, having the best books, he must create among his people, his pupils, a desire to read these books. He must put every facility in the way of readers, so that they shall be led on from good to better. He must teach them how, after studying their own wants, they may themselves select their reading wisely. Such a librarian will find enough who are ready to put themselves under his influence and direction, and, if competent and enthusiastic, he may soon largely shape the reading, and through it the thought, of his whole community.

Throughout Dewey's editorship, *LJ* gave voice to the issues, ideas, and concerns engendered by the new professionalism he preached with such determined passion. "In a word," he wrote in his maiden editorial, "the *American Library Journal* hopes to collate for the librarian every view or fact which may be of use or interest in his work, to the saving of time, money, and effort for him, and, as a final aim, to the advancement of his honorable profession." In Dewey's mind *LJ* was always more than just a journal: it was a key component in his grand design to forge a modern library profession, one that would carry practitioners triumphantly into the next century, an American promised land where the unrelenting quest for progress would surely place books, knowledge, *and* libraries at the pinnacle of an increasingly powerful industrial society.

In addition to the journal, Dewey's blueprint for librarianship included a national association (he had an active hand in creating the American Library Association in 1876), a library school (he established the first such curriculum at Columbia College — later Columbia University — in 1887), and a library supply house (he founded the Library Bureau in 1882 and served as its president for 25 years). Whatever his failings, and he had some large ones, Melvil Dewey never lacked energy or vision or dedication when it came to library work, which he referred to as his "calling."

The early volumes of *LJ* listed some of the most celebrated names in 19th-century American librarianship as associate editors, among them Justin Winsor, Charles Cutter, William Poole, and Charles Evans. Still, despite the enlistment of such an impressive editorial roster, the magazine's existence in the early years was anything but assured. Among the most serious problems were a disappointingly small number of subscribers— only 300 by April 1877 — and not enough revenue to satisfy the editor's desire for adequate compensation or the publisher's for a fair return on his investment. At one point Dewey demanded more money, did not get it, and retaliated with a threat to withhold copy for the next issue. By the early months of 1880 the situation had become so grim that Leypoldt, on the advice of Bowker, announced the magazine would cease publication in June, with major features folded into the older and financially viable *Publishers Weekly*. Protests from the library community caused Leypoldt to reconsider and, after some soul-searching, publication was resumed in August. *LJ* finally began turning a small profit by the mid–1890s, but the magazine never became a real moneymaker for the Bowker Company until the 1960s when Eric Moon arrived.

Satisfied that *LJ* stood a reasonable chance of survival, Dewey quit the magazine in 1881 to start the Library Bureau and two years later he accepted the post of library director at Columbia. While his five-year tenure as *LJ*'s editor had not been smooth, he did succeed in, first, getting the fledging publication off the ground and, second, making it required reading for every serious librarian in North America. Moreover, while sometimes cavalier about details and deadlines, Dewey adhered to high journalistic standards and set an ambitious editorial course: "The plan of the *American Library Journal* is intended to cover the entire field of library and bibliographical interests. But its conductors mean to make it a medium of communication in the proper sense, rather than to impress views which can be identified as those of the *Journal* itself." This early receptivity to diverse points of view became the journal's sine qua non nearly a century later when Moon became editor.

The history of *LJ* from Dewey to Moon roughly mirrors that of the profession. Libraries of all types— public, academic, school, special — multiplied at a dizzying rate in North America from the 1870s through the 1960s, as did the number of librarians needed to minister in them. During this period Andrew Carnegie, the philanthropic steel baron, donated millions to build more than 1,500 public libraries in the United States alone, and after World War II the federal government began providing significant financial support for libraries, reaching unprecedented levels in the 1960s under Lyndon Johnson's Great Society programs. *Library Journal* became a permanent fixture in the library firmament well before the end of the 19th century, and its circulation climbed steadily as the profession prospered, reaching the 10,000 mark after World War II,

13,000 by 1955, and well over 30,000 by the time Moon stepped down as editor at the end of 1968. The magazine's publication frequency also reflected the times. Originally a monthly, *LJ* soon expanded to 22 issues per year, its frequency until 1984 when it was scaled back to 20 issues a year. As the profession grew, other journals catering to librarians' interests and needs appeared, many of them quite specialized. The closest competitors of *LJ*— the *Bulletin of the American Library Association* (later the *ALA Bulletin* and now *American Libraries*) and *Wilson Library Bulletin* (now defunct)— began publishing in 1907 and 1914 respectively.

Frederic G. Melcher, who joined the Bowker Company in 1918 as managing editor of *Publishers Weekly*, became president of the firm after the death of Richard Rogers Bowker in 1933, a position he held for a quarter of a century. As Bowker's head man, Melcher took a hands-on interest in both *PW* and *LJ*, constantly seeking ways to enhance their content and broaden their reach. In the case of *LJ* he supported the addition of a general book review section, reasoning that librarians involved in book selection would welcome brief, timely critiques of new titles written especially for them. The magazine's book review feature first appeared in 1940, with a grand total of 270 books reviewed that year. Under the strong editorial hand of Margaret Cooley, who joined *LJ* in 1946 (as Margaret Eliason), the review section, then called "New Books Appraised," became an essential part of the magazine, evaluating thousands of reference and trade books each year as well as generating satisfying amounts of advertising revenue. Cooley remained *LJ*'s book review editor for 23 years, until she and her husband, Lesley Cooley, Bowker's longtime advertising director, retired in 1969.

In 1943 Melcher recruited Karl Brown of the New York Public Library to edit *LJ*. Primarily a bibliographer and reference specialist, Brown brought considerable know-how to the job, having edited various NYPL publications, including the library's *Guide to Reference Collections*, as well as two editions of the *American Library Directory*, a standard work published by Bowker. Prior to his appointment he had also edited *LJ*'s "Current Library Literature" column. Brown proved to be a diligent but unimaginative editor, rarely venturing beyond the narrow confines of librarianship as perceived in the 1940s. When Brown left the magazine in 1951 to return to the New York Public (as head of the its publications program) he was replaced by Helen E. Wessells, a librarian with little previous editorial experience. Prior to coming to *LJ*, Wessells headed the U.S. State Department's Libraries Branch, an agency that managed the department's overseas libraries, and before that she worked for many years at the New York Public in the system's branches and circulation department.

Like Brown, Mrs. Wessells (as she preferred to be called) was a conscientious editor, dutifully cranking out 22 issues each and every year, but the magazine she produced offered readers little by way of professional vision or journalistic flair, and her management style tended to be heavy-handed. According to Bowker legend, on her first day on the job Mrs. Wessells stationed herself at the entrance to *LJ*'s offices with a stopwatch, checking to see who was— and who was not — on time. She remained editor for six years, leaving in early 1957, apparently for personal reasons: "There comes a time in everyone's life," she wrote cryptically in her farewell editorial, "when one listens to warnings and obeys them."

For the next two and half years, until Moon's arrival in early November 1959, the magazine drifted, essentially leaderless. Lee Ash, a bookish librarian best known as the compiler of *Subject Collections*, a Bowker reference publication, succeeded Wessells, his appointment announced in May 1957 though he did not actually start work until that fall. Karl Brown filled in as editor on a part-time basis during this period. Fred Melcher and his son Daniel, who had the title of publisher of *LJ*, were overjoyed to have found someone with Ash's credentials to take over the journal—"His friends know him as a rare mixture of scholar and extrovert, book collector and joiner," burbled Bowker's brass about their new hire—but the Ash editorship turned out to be anything but joyous. Within 18 months he was gone, his final issue dated March 15, 1959. After Ash's unannounced departure (allegedly due to unacceptable personal behavior in the workplace), Fred Melcher assumed the title of acting editor. At the same time he and son Dan embarked on an extensive search for the right person to guide *LJ* into the post–Eisenhower years.

The Melchers prevailed upon the amenable Karl Brown (then head of school and library services at St. Martin's Press as well as editor of the New York Library Association's *NYLA Bulletin*) to lend an occasional hand during this unexpected hiatus. But the day-to-day work of putting *LJ* together fell to Shirley Havens, a young woman who had joined the magazine as managing editor only a short time before Ash's abrupt exit. Though not trained as a librarian, Havens, a Phi Beta Kappa from Hunter College, had worked previously as an administrative assistant in the library at the Carnegie Endowment for International Peace. A tribute to Fred Melcher—F.G.M. to his colleagues—written by Lillian Gerhardt, former editor of *School Library Journal*, offers this glimpse into how Havens and *LJ* endured the trying period prior to the coming of Eric Moon:

One of my favorite stories of F.G.M. comes from Shirley E. Havens, senior editor on the staff of *Library Journal*. Shirley started work on *LJ* in the late 1950s and, within days, *LJ*'s chief editor [Ash] resigned unexpectedly to take another job. Shirley was *it* for *LJ*'s news and features section over the long months before Eric Moon arrived. She worked days, nights, and weekends. As a salaried employee, she was ineligible for overtime. As a new hire, she was ineligible for an immediate raise or bonus. But, every Monday morning she'd arrive at her desk to find a vase of flowers that F.G.M. cut in his own garden and carried by train from his home in New Jersey. He arranged the flowers himself so that she wouldn't have to stop to do it, and they were always accompanied by a handwritten note of thanks and praise for work well done.

Guy Fawkes Day 1959

The Melchers cast a wide net in their search for *LJ*'s new editor. Like careful detectives they followed up every plausible lead, no matter how remote, going so far as to check out an unknown English librarian working in, of all places, Newfoundland—a long shot by anyone's reckoning to edit the number one library magazine in North America and arguably the world. At one point they came close to hiring Harold Lancour, an affable library educator of some renown, but the deal fell through when Lancour reportedly wanted a thousand dollars more a year than the Melchers were willing to pay. They talked too with Robert D. Franklin, director of the Toledo (Ohio) Public Library and editor of its venerable house organ, *The Tee Pee*, but again no deal was struck. And they gave serious consideration to John Wakeman, Moon's former assistant at North Finchley, who was working at the Brooklyn Public Library as assistant director of public relations.

When the *LJ* position opened up, Wakeman, a skilled writer and ambitious fellow, applied. Simultaneously, he pursued the editorship of the *Wilson Library Bulletin*, which was also vacant at the time. Whether Wakeman was offered *LJ* is in dispute (he said yes, Moon said no), but there's no doubt about the fact that after his interview at Bowker — and after accepting the *WLB* job — he wrote a letter to Dan Melcher extolling Moon, then toiling away in obscurity in St. John's, Newfoundland, as an ideal candidate for the *LJ* job. His interest piqued, the younger Melcher contacted Moon, liked what he heard, and before long *LJ* had its new editor.

When Moon finally got the job, he could scarcely believe his astonishing good luck. Not only had he escaped the Newfoundland morass with his sanity and hide intact he had almost effortlessly landed one of the preeminent library positions in the United States of America, to him the most desirable, most exciting country in the world. What's more, Moon suddenly had, at least potentially, the power to influence people and events in the profession in ways that made his efforts in England and Canada seem as nugatory as a mosquito biting an elephant. He understood that he had a lot to learn: "Remember, I was not very experienced at these things. I had done editing on a small scale part-time in England, but here you're talking about a major publication that comes out twice a month with a worldwide circulation and is physically so big it required six bound volumes a year." On the other hand he felt fit and strong and confident, full of vim and vigor, and not at all intimidated, at least on the surface, by the challenge of being responsible for such a large, well-known, and important publication. To add to his euphoria, Moon's starting annual salary — $10,400 — was much, much more money than he had ever earned. Wasn't life bloody grand!

Outwardly little changed since starting his professional career as a branch librarian at Hertfordshire ten years earlier, Moon was a slim, agile man a bit above average height with slicked-back dark hair, pronounced nose, rakish mustache, and, in the words of John Wakeman, "wolfish grin" when he arrived in New York in late 1959 to take over the reins of *LJ*. He still smoked a pipe and his unstylish wardrobe bespoke his British working-class roots. Inwardly, however, he had grown since Hertfordshire. Now almost 37, he was young enough to possess the physical and mental stamina required to meet the demands of a taxing job like *LJ*, but old enough to have gained a soupçon of wisdom. No longer, for instance, would he be tempted to publicly embarrass a library leader of the stature of a Lawrence Clark Powell, as he had done just a few years earlier with the rude question, "So, what makes you so great?" But neither had he become a pussycat inclined to shrink from a fight, as his recent confrontations with Joey Smallwood in Newfoundland amply demonstrated. Only now the fight had to be over a cause important enough to justify the cost.

The Moon family landed in New York City in early November and immediately checked into a hotel in Times Square. "We had practically nothing with us when we arrived," Moon recalled. "Bowker put us up in a hotel in midtown, not too far from 42nd Street. It was one helluva place to leave a wife and two kids." As soon as he could manage it, he made his way to *LJ*'s offices at nearby 62 West 45th Street, eager to begin learning all he could about the magazine and the people and company he would be working with and for. His first day on the job, November 5th, a Thursday, was just another work day to his new American colleagues, but to the British-born Moon the date was full of significance. In England, November 5th is Guy Fawkes Day, a holiday observing the failed plot to blow up Parliament in 1605. Moon later came to see his starting date at *LJ* as a portent of things to come: "The British are very peculiar in celebrating something like Guy Fawkes Day because, after all, Guy Fawkes was the guy who tried to blow up Parliament. I'm not sure the Americans would have a day celebrating someone who tried to blow up the White House or Congress. But my arrival at *Library Journal* on Guy Fawkes Day was symbolic, because during the next few years all sorts of people thought I was trying to blow up the American library profession."

Moon and *LJ* would in fact soon be at the center of some of the most divisive issues to confront American librarianship in modern times. For the moment, however, he was content to keep his powder dry until he got his editorial bearings. The first issue of the magazine listing him as editor—December 1, 1959—covered new library buildings and carried an erudite, albeit soporific, editorial on the subject by Karl Brown who, with Shirley Havens, had cobbled the issue together. It would be some months before Moon's style began percolating through the pages of *LJ*, and roughly a year before he detonated his first big explosion.

Finchley Mystery

The Moons vacated Times Square as quickly as they could, moving to a residential hotel in Brooklyn Heights recommended by John Wakeman, who lived in the area; John's wife Hilary helped Diana set up temporary housekeeping, providing dishes, silverware, and the like. Wakeman by this time had left Brooklyn Public for the *Wilson Library Bulletin*, where he was working with the outgoing editor, Marie Loizeaux, learning the ropes and concentrating on preparing his first solo issue, set for January 1960. To celebrate their new jobs and good fortune, the two expatriate editors gave a party. Held at the Wakemans, guests included mainly New York area librarians John had come to know over the years. Moon remembered antagonizing the natives: "At the party in Brooklyn we put up a copy of each of the magazines on the mantlepiece with a little Union Jack, and the Americans were all pissed off with us."

Stan Crane, who had worked for Moon at North Finchley in the early 1950s when he and Wakeman exchanged jobs, viewed his British colleagues' new circumstances not with irritation or envy but wonderment: "The point that impressed me most was that the branch librarian and first assistant at North Finchley (Eric and John) went on to become the editors of two of the most popular American library periodicals. Finchley had many good points but nothing in the air or water there could easily explain this double transformation." To add to the mystery, Moon's old boss at Finchley, John

Reynolds, became editor of the *Library Association Record* around the same time, and Ron Surridge, another former Finchley staffer, served for many years as editor of *Liaison*, the newsletter Moon and Bill Smith founded in 1957. Perhaps there was something in the library paste at Finchley?

New Jersey Domicile

The Moons roughed it in Brooklyn Heights for a month, during which time various Bowker associates helped the newcomers search for permanent housing. Elizabeth Geiser, the company's marketing director, recalled she had the job of scouting out prospects in suburban New Jersey, where many Bowker executives lived, including both Melchers. In addition, Eric and Diana perused *The New York Times* classifieds for leads, and every weekend someone would drive them around the metropolitan area to check out the possibilities. "Joe Davis, a production manager, drove us out to Westchester once," Moon remembered, "and later Dan Melcher was driving us one day in Fanwood, New Jersey, and there was a brand-new house for rent. So we rented it."

Fanwood, a small town near the larger Jersey communities of Westfield and Plainfield, was about an hour to an hour and half commute into midtown Manhattan and Bowker headquarters. The Moons lived there for almost three years, before moving to Elizabeth, a blue-collar city nine miles northeast of Fanwood and just that much closer to midtown and Eric's office. From the start Moon wanted a car but because of a lack of a credit rating in the United States he couldn't afford one. Dan Melcher stepped in and solved the problem, giving Moon his old Austin, which filled the bill for a time. The Moons likewise tried to buy furniture at Macy's department store but again ran into the credit roadblock, and again Dan Melcher came to the rescue, this time with a cash loan.

As she had throughout her married life in England and then in Newfoundland, Diana did not work outside the home while at Fanwood, preferring to remain a full-time mother and housewife. Her most pressing problem was getting around town and the suburban area, which meant she finally had to learn to drive. Eric undertook to teach her: "She eventually made it, but it was a horrific experience." Credit hassles and driving lessons notwithstanding, the Moons' domestic life settled down considerably after they moved to Fanwood: the new furniture eventually arrived, the boys started school, routines were established, and certain American customs and expressions began to seem less strange. Eric — rarely ever fully engaged as husband or father (and certainly not at this point in his life) — airily recalled, "Everything was going along pretty smoothly at home at this time."

The Library Journal *Staff*

When he took over at *LJ*, Moon had an immediate staff of three: himself (editor), Shirley Havens (managing editor), and an office secretary. Havens and her new boss hit it off well from the start, promptly establishing a positive working relationship, one grounded in mutual need and respect. "The first years were a learning experience for both of us," Havens said years later. "Eric familiarized himself with American librarianship and I developed a more international outlook on the library scene. I also spent considerable time editing his Britishisms and British spelling!" As for Moon, Shirley Havens was little short of a godsend, particularly in the early going when so much — the job, the people, the country, the culture — was new to him. He quickly came to rely on her as a steady, clearheaded, hardworking, supportive colleague with a natural talent for editorial supervision:

When I arrived Shirley was really responsible for putting the magazine together. I was so busy trying to change the editorial content that the actual operation of the magazine was very heavily in her hands. For one thing, she had to proofread everything that I wrote for the first year or so to make sure that I didn't use English expressions that might be misunderstood or unclear here, and of course she had to correct my spelling. Throughout the period I was at *LJ*, Shirley was a stalwart of the magazine. She was the person that the senior editors went to if they weren't sure about something. Shirley was always the anchor. I couldn't have done without her.

Moon also oversaw *LJ*'s largely self-sufficient book review department, which then had an all-female staff of about half a dozen headed by Margaret Cooley and her assistant, Judith Serebnick. Moon at once recognized that the book reviews "were key to *LJ*'s success," that they "carried the magazine," owing to the large number of subscriptions and advertising dollars they brought in. And it did not take him long to discover that Cooley and her staff did "a pretty tremendous job," especially in light of the magnitude and complexity of the work:

Margaret ran an operation that was hell on wheels to run. It was physically an enormous operation. Not only did *Library Journal* review more books than anybody else in America, but we had all these forecasting issues with prepub listings by subject. The physical job of getting all that information and checking it was incredible. Remember, this was all pre-computer — it all had to be done by hand. Margaret worked hours you wouldn't believe — she and Judy Serebnick and others in the department worked 60–70 hours a week. I had a great admiration for the department. Some things I wanted to change, like the quality of some of the reviews and reviewers, but I did this gradually through conversations and diplomatic efforts with Margaret. But on the whole I had very little quarrel with the book review operation.

Serebnick, who was Cooley's assistant from 1957 to 1964 and, after getting her MLS and working as a librarian at Northwestern University, succeeded Cooley as book review editor in 1969, remembered Moon as being "extremely interested" in books and reviewing:

Eric was passionately concerned about book publishing and the content of books. He read a great deal. We considered him a first-rate reviewer, and I think Mrs. Cooley (who assigned the books for review) deeply appreciated his reviews and trusted him with many potentially controversial titles. He often recommended new reviewers, people he had met through professional contacts. I don't believe that Eric and Mrs. Cooley always saw eye to eye on policy issues, but they both were committed to the importance of *LJ* reviews for librarians, and Eric constantly supported our department.

One specific beef Moon had with *LJ*'s reviews was the tendency, on the part of staff and reviewers alike, to caution readers about controversial subject matter and naughty language: "I didn't like those warnings about certain books because of sex or whatever. I thought a good reviewer should be able to provide enough information so the reader could decide if the book was right for his or her library without resorting to such caveats." Moon himself reviewed some of the decade's major risqué novels for *LJ*, including the first American edition of the *Memoirs of a Woman of Pleasure* (aka *Fanny Hill*), published in 1963. To his chagrin he found it difficult to practice what he preached. In the case of *Fanny Hill*, he recommended the book for all academic libraries as well as public libraries "with substantial literature collections," but ended his review with a finger-wagging warning worthy of Mrs. Grundy: "But others had better be careful—a great many 20th-century puritans will find grossly offensive this elegant product of an elegant but licentious age."

Another aspect of the *LJ* operation that required Moon's oversight was *Junior Libraries*, a sister journal Bowker published each month for school and children's librarians. The magazine had originated years before as a section of *LJ* and, though it became a separate publication in 1954, it was reprinted as part of *LJ* on the fifteenth of each month all during Moon's editorship and for some years thereafter. When Moon arrived at Bowker, Margaret Saul was editor of *Junior Libraries*, though she shared the responsibility with *LJ*'s editor, who literally functioned as coeditor, reading copy, making suggestions for features, coordinating news stories with the parent journal, and so on. Saul, who became the second Mrs. Daniel Melcher in 1967 after the death of his first wife, left *Junior Libraries* in the fall of 1961, just after its name was changed to the now familiar *School Library Journal*. All during his nine years at *LJ*, Moon had a hand, or at least a pinkie, in the editorial affairs of *Junior Libraries/SLJ*, which then looked upon *LJ* as "our daddy."

Moon also worked closely with, but did not supervise, those responsible for *LJ*'s (and *SLJ*'s) advertising content. Leslie Cooley, the magazines' advertising director for many years, quietly planned and carried out ad campaigns from his office at company headquarters. Among his most successful efforts were issues of *LJ* targeting special categories of books ("Fall Paperbacks," for example), which prompted much additional advertising by publishers. Famous as "the man who would not cross a river," Cooley rarely traveled far from midtown where he worked or Greenwich Village where he lived with wife Margaret, preferring to conduct his life and business strictly on the terra firma of Manhattan Island, which seemed to have everything he ever needed or wanted. While Cooley functioned as the inside man, his energetic assistant, George Wieser, spent most of his time on the road, selling clients (publishers, book wholesalers, library supply houses and others) space ads in *LJ* and *SLJ*. Lastly, all the magazines' classified advertising was handled by a young woman named Maureen Rose.

Advertising revenues, along with circulation stats, tell the bottom-line story of any commercial periodical venture, from general magazines like *Time* to professional journals like *LJ*. Moon, while not directly involved in *LJ*'s business operation, naturally kept a watchful eye on these key indicators, aware that in the long run they, more than anything else, would determine his success or failure as editor. Happily, he had no problem working with the advertising staff, whom he came to hold in high regard: Les Cooley was, in his opinion, "a brilliant advertising man," George Wieser was "the best salesman in the business, no question," and Maureen Rose proved "very efficient" at her job. Moon believed that if both components of the magazine — editorial and business — respected each other's prerogatives and turf the whole enterprise would benefit:

> One of the good things that happened was that we worked together very well with a clear understanding that editorial was independent and was not going to be influenced by advertising. On the other hand I realized how important advertising was to us, so I would cooperate with Les and George when I could. I would go to lunch, for example, with this or that publisher and explain what the magazine was all about, who its readers were, and so on. I would do that and didn't see anything wrong with it at all. But if they said, would you run something that would appeal to or please a particular advertiser, I wouldn't do it.

"Redirect to Eric Moon"

Moon reported directly to Dan Melcher, who had been *LJ*'s publisher for a dozen years. Because both men shared a common goal — to make *LJ* the best *and* most profitable journal of its kind — they formed an effective team, despite striking dissimilarities in their backgrounds and personalities. Eleven years older than Moon, Melcher was born in 1912 into a world of upper middle-class affluence. Following his father's lead he entered the publishing business after college (Harvard '34), working (at his father's insistence) at a variety of companies to gain a breadth of experience, first abroad in London and Leipzig and then in New York City. During World War II he left the business to work in Washington, D.C., for the Treasury Department and later as staff director of the National Committee on Atomic Information, an organization devoted to limiting the spread of nuclear weapons. In 1947, at the behest of his father, he joined Bowker as the publisher of *LJ*, historically the weaker of the company's two major journals. In 1956 the junior Melcher added the role of company general manager to his duties and was elected to the Bowker board of directors. When father Fred retired as Bowker's president in 1959 to become chairman of the board, son Dan became vice president, and when Fred died in 1963, Dan moved up to president, a position he held until the Xerox Corporation acquired the company at the end of 1967.

Though primarily a businessman, Dan Melcher possessed a strong scientific bent and especially a gift for invention. For example, during his first wife's long illness (multiple sclerosis) he fashioned a type of revolving bed later used in some hospitals, and he held a patent on a gas metering system. More important from Bowker's point of view he devised an automated card sorting machine that helped pave the way for the computerized compilation of *Books in Print* and its various spin-offs. He also made significant technical contributions to the development of the belt press method of book production, widely used by Bowker and others in the industry after its introduction in the late 1960s. Anything mechanical fascinated Melcher, who occasionally wrote articles for *LJ* and *SLJ* about innovative products, such as interactive learning machines.

Because of his conservative dress, dark-rimmed glasses, and proneness to early balding, Dan Melcher in the 1960s impressed most people as a cautious, controlled, studious individual, which in many respects he was. But he was also a political liberal, active in the civil rights and peace movements, and when the situation called for it he could be a risk-taker. Hiring Moon to edit *LJ* represented the venturous side of his personality. What Melcher wanted was someone who would bring some spark and spunk to the magazine's bland pages, someone who would take a fresh look at American librarianship and, when appropriate, rattle some cages, perhaps even beat up on a few of the profession's prize fossils. Obviously no one could predict with certainty (remember Lee Ash) how this interesting but unproven Englishman might turn out, but after due consideration Melcher rolled the dice and conferred *LJ*'s editorship on Eric Moon.

Moon, of course, understood that his appointment represented a risk for Melcher, the magazine, and the company: "It was one helluva gamble on Bowker's part. This was one of the things I admired about Dan Melcher. He sensed from John Wakeman's letter that there was something controversial about me, something that might be dangerous about me. This didn't scare him away; rather, it interested him. So he decided to check me out. Dan's attitude, I was to learn, was very beneficial, because there was a lot of trouble coming."

Moon's main anxiety when he first landed at 62 West 45th Street was not Melcher's willingness to take risks or ominous thoughts of trouble down the road. Instead, what concerned him first and foremost was gaining editorial control of the magazine. Normally, such authority goes with the position, but in this instance *LJ*'s recent history had created a messy internal organizational structure that would have been tough for any new editor to cope with — and was especially difficult for Moon who came to the job as an almost totally unknown quantity. Because *LJ* had been headless for so long, practically everyone on the staff, Moon soon discovered, seemed to have a hand in running the magazine. During the leadership vacuum, key players had grown accustomed to making decisions and changes that ordinarily would have come from or been discussed with and approved by the editor.

At first, Moon, a complete stranger to the American library world, was viewed, in his words, "very warily" by most people involved with the magazine, particularly those who wanted to keep things operating much as they were. Among those most interested in maintaining the status quo: Margaret Cooley, who was used to running the book review department with little or no interference; Les Cooley, who knew the advertising game inside and out and hardly needed a rookie editor peering over his shoulder (together, the Cooleys were a formidable power bloc at *LJ* for many years); Fred Melcher, who, despite his advanced years, still enjoyed mucking around in editorial matters; and Karl Brown, the former editor who knew the *LJ* operation cold and continued to keep a toe in the door as a member of the magazine's board of editorial consultants.

As soon as he could, Moon moved to establish himself as *LJ*'s final authority over all things editorial. The key was Dan Melcher. Without Melcher's enthusiastic cooperation and support Moon knew he could not succeed:

When I took over it was quite clear that *LJ* was a pie in which there were a great many fingers. I said to Dan, "Look, the only way this magazine is going to work is if everybody understands very clearly that I'm running it — I'm the boss. My decisions are final. Otherwise, the magazine will come out looking like one of those horses designed by a committee. But I can only achieve this with your support." During my first few weeks all kinds of memos were flying to Daniel and Fred from various parts of *LJ* saying what about this and that and so and so. I said, "These communications have got to be redirected to me. As long as you guys are hanging on to these little advisory powers, I can't run this magazine."

So Dan said, fine. He was as good as his word, and anything henceforth directed to him, he would simply write on it, "Redirect to Eric Moon." And if people came to him, he referred them to me. It became clear after awhile that this was the way it was going to be, and it worked fine. Not long after my arrival we were all a very cooperative and happy working team.

Dan Melcher, Moon frequently declared, "was absolutely the best boss I ever had on any job," though he did, like most bosses, have blind spots and could be difficult: "Dan sometimes lacked social niceties and then didn't understand why people were upset. He was too narrowly focused at times." For example, at first he refused to close Bowker's offices the day President Kennedy was shot, taking the position that the assassination had nothing to with the company and its work. Others, including Moon, helped change his mind posthaste. Another time, after he had become Bowker's president and was no longer *LJ/SLJ* publisher, Melcher called Moon into his office and said, "How come nobody around this goddamn place can write an editorial except you?" Moon asked what was the problem. Melcher: "I just picked up the latest issue of *SLJ* and this woman can't write an editorial for beans." Moon replied that wasn't true and asked how many of her editorials he had read. Melcher confessed, "Just this one." Moon: "Don't you think that's a rather small sample to base a judgment on? I suggest you get the whole past year's issues of the magazine and read all her editorials, and then if you want to talk about it, we'll discuss it." Melcher: "Fine." Moon: "Later that morning Daniel called back and said, 'I apologize. She's pretty good. Let's have lunch.'" Melcher's ready willingness to admit a mistake impressed Moon, who usually had difficulty admitting he might be wrong about anything.

Dan Melcher deserved much credit for *LJ*'s great success in the 1960s. He had the intuitive intelligence to bring Moon, a nobody, to New York to edit the journal, and then the wisdom to give his new editor the authority he needed to do the job. Yes, Moon was the editorial genius who remade *LJ*, but without Melcher's backing it would not have been possible. Neither man would have made his unique contribution to *LJ*'s renaissance without the help, strength, and courage of the other.

Rivalry with Publishers Weekly

Quick to see the big picture, Moon felt almost from day one that within the Bowker organization *LJ* and *Junior Libraries* were considered small potatoes when compared with the company's two other publishing centers, namely *Publishers Weekly* and *Books in Print*. The latter, supervised by Anne Richter, a Bowker director and a strong woman who had come up through the ranks after starting out years earlier as a company secretary, included *BIP*'s basic author-title volumes plus a number of companion products, e.g., *Subject Guide to Books in Print* and *Paperbound Books in Print*. Richter's group also produced such standard Bowker reference items as *Ulrich's International Periodicals Directory*, *Literary Market Place*, and *Reader's Adviser*, along with an assortment of monographs on publishing and library science topics. The *BIP* series and other Bowker book publications had an established, predictable market base and were a consistent source of substantial profits for the company over the years.

Bowker's other moneymaker, *Publishers Weekly*, was an American publishing icon, the industry's premier trade journal ever since it debuted on January 18, 1872, as *The Publishers' and Stationers' Weekly Trade Circular*, the magazine's cumbersome title for the first few years. As Frederick Leypoldt and Richard Rogers Bowker's earliest and most successful creation, *PW* had long been the darling of the Bowker Company, doted on and indulged like a comely firstborn.

Moon had no strong feelings about Richter's fiefdom, but *PW*'s lordly place in the company irked him, activating a competitive compulsion that was never far from the surface. Everyone seemed to take it for granted that *PW*— the older, handsomer, sleeker, more profitable *PW*— had it all over the younger, plainer, bulkier, less well-off *LJ*. Even more galling, they seemed to believe that nothing could ever or would ever occur to change this immutable fact of Bowker corporate life. Moon soon discovered that *PW* "was a law unto itself," that it "had always been the Bowker kingpin," and that "the *PW* people had always looked at *LJ* as a weak sister." To confirm *PW*'s preeminent position in the company he had only to scan the composition of the Bowker board of directors. Chaired by Fred Melcher, who had been managing editor of *PW* for many years before acceding to the Bowker presidency, the eight-member board included Louis Greene, former *PW* advertising director and now board president; Richard Bye, *PW*'s current advertising director; and Mildred Smith and Chandler Grannis, the magazine's top editors. Conversely, *there was not a single representative from LJ*. "When I got there," recalled Moon, "the Bowker board was a *PW* powerhouse."

Library Journal's "weak sister" status annoyed him no end. Thoughts of engaging *PW* in a grand head-to-head rivalry stirred his imagination. Just as years before he had labored to transform the North Finchley branch from the worst to the best library in the Finchley system, he dreamed of making *LJ* the equal of *PW*— and then its better. And, truth be told, within a few years *LJ* did in fact challenge *PW* as the company's most lucrative magazine property. According to Elizabeth Geiser, a "natural feeling of competitiveness between the two magazines had always existed," but it intensified when "*Library Journal* began to pull its weight financially after Eric turned it around." Judy Serebnick noticed the same dynamic: "I think there was a strong rivalry between *LJ* and *PW* in terms of profits, circ, etc. I'm sure that Eric, Mr. Cooley, and others felt it, and we were all aware of the strong fiscal position Eric brought to *LJ*."

Still, Moon never felt entirely confident or satisfied about *LJ*'s position vis-à-vis its older rival, believing that *PW*'s editorial big guns failed to recognize — or even care about — his magazine's accomplishments: "Dick Bye and *PW*'s advertising people began to respect *LJ* more as it became commercially successful, but Chandler Grannis and Mildred Smith continued to ignore us. They really didn't pay us much attention because they were so convinced that *PW* was so superior to anything else that it was the only thing that mattered. It really didn't matter what *LJ* did, they still perceived us as a poor sister, although some of that began to change when I went on the Bowker board in 1965."

During his years at *LJ*, Moon never developed much more than a nodding relationship with anyone on *PW*'s editorial staff, except for Roger Smith, the magazine's chief reporter and nephew of editor Mildred Smith. Moon, George Wieser, and Roger Smith (described by Wieser as a "very open, friendly, sometimes caustic guy") got together every so often for drinks at the Absinthe House, a local watering hole a few blocks from the Bowker building, where Wieser recalled "heady discussions deeply steeped in alcohol." Their talk inevitably involved the *LJ-PW* rivalry and at one point they kicked around the idea of leaving Bowker and starting a new journal that would compete with *PW*—"We thought *PW* was full of shit," said Wieser — but nothing came of this or any other of their boozy schemes.

First Year

Moon: "The first year was a period of learning and getting into place what I wanted the magazine to do. One of the first things I did after taking over the job was to look around at the library literature. My feeling was that it was terribly boring, dull, ill. It seemed to me not to be looking at any issues of importance. It was cautious and had very little to do with reality, with real life." In one of his most influential and widely quoted articles, "The Library Press," Moon wrote that when he began his nine-year stint as *LJ*'s editor he was struck by the "flat conformity and dullness" and "lack of individuality and viewpoint" that pervaded library literature: "My reaction was a mental echo of Jimmy Porter's anguished cry in *Look Back in Anger*: 'How I long for a little ordinary human enthusiasm.'"

His assessment of *LJ* was equally candid. The magazine, he bluntly told Dan Melcher, who required little convincing, "looked tired and middle-aged and badly needed livening up." To improve *LJ*'s position in the competition for readers and influence within the library community as well as for those all-important advertising dollars, changes would be necessary, that much he knew. But how? What? When? Who? These familiar questions that journalists ask flashed in his mind like pulsating lights on a neon sign. How to breathe life into Melvil's limp rag? What issues merited his attention? When and how to tackle them? Who would help him and how to find them? More personally, how good were his chances of coming out of this editorship a winner? What if he failed?

After the question of editorial control had been resolved to his satisfaction Moon began casting around for ways to pump life into the magazine, to pep it up, to erase some of the tired lines so evident on so many pages. His initial strategy was simple, logical, and intuitive: he would introduce *controversy* into the magazine. Library literature, he decided, had too much of the Pollyanna in it. The negative, the unpleasant, the uncomfortable, the provocative, the irascible, the contentious— all were lacking in the publications he examined, including *Library Journal.* There was an unmistakable tendency on the part of the library press to avoid bad news and the rough-and-tumble of strong debate. Why not then, when appropriate, inject some controversial ideas and perspectives into the magazine? Perhaps no one would care. Then again, they might.

But to use controversy effectively as a device to liven up *LJ,* Moon needed, first, issues that mattered, not ones that were manufactured or in any way disingenuous; and, second, writers capable of treating such issues in a readable, intelligent, trenchant manner. He wanted writers whose ideas and prose hit the reader like a spitball in the face, ideas and prose that woke people up, that demanded to be read and discussed.

Some helpful suggestions about possible issues and writers came from a board of editorial consultants Dan Melcher put together to advise and assist Moon. The consultants, seven American library luminaries, included Luther Evans, a senior staffer at the Brookings Institution and former Librarian of Congress; Lawrence Clark Powell, dean of the library school at UCLA and the most famous librarian of his day; Ralph Shaw, dean of the library school at Rutgers, founder and head of Scarecrow Press, and a former ALA president; Robert D. Franklin, librarian at Toledo Public and editor of *The Tee Pee,* TPL's much admired in-house bulletin; and the peripatetic Karl Brown, former publications chief at NYPL, former *LJ* editor, and now the head of school and library services at St. Martin's Press. Melcher thought an advisory group necessary because of Moon's obvious lack of knowledge about American librarianship. Moon agreed, with a proviso:

None of the consultants had any policy role but some were helpful to me in finding talent or looking at particular problems. Before I started, Dan said, "Since you're coming into the country new with no experience in American libraries, with no contact with the profession here, don't you think it would be a good idea if you had a board of top-level people from the profession as advisers?" And I said, "Sure, providing they understand that they are advisers and not try to direct my activities." Luther Evans and Larry Powell and Bob Franklin were all very helpful; they gave me good ideas and contacts, but I don't remember the others doing much.

The first board served for two years, 1960–1961. A new board, appointed for 1962–1963, consisted of six members, including, at Moon's suggestion, several women, one of whom was black: Lillian Bradshaw, director of the Dallas Public Library; Marjorie Griffin, a special librarian with IBM in San Jose; Virginia Lacy Jones, dean of the library school at Atlanta University; Jerrold Orne, librarian at the University of North Carolina, Chapel Hill; Hannis Smith, head of libraries at the Minnesota State Department of Education; and Al Bowron, Moon's assistant at Hertfordshire, then in charge of technical services at the Toronto Public Library. After 1963 the board was disbanded; Moon was by that time thoroughly familiar with the American library scene and its key players.

During the first year at *LJ* Moon tried to meet as many librarians as he could. Not only did he have his antennae out for potential contributors to the magazine, he wanted to get a firsthand sense of what was happening around the country, what issues concerned ordinary practitioners working on the front line day in and day out. He told Dan Melcher and anyone else who would listen that he could not edit *LJ* from an office in Manhattan. He had to be on the road, talking with people, looking for new ideas and talent. And he was always in search of additional "ears":

One of the first things I did when I got to *LJ*, I said to Dan that it's clear that the magazine is not as in touch as it should be, therefore I've got to travel around the country to meet people. I told him that A) I have to find out things for myself, and B) I've got to start finding some people out there who will be my ears. I traveled nearly every month in the U.S. for years on end, visiting most of the states, trying to set up contacts—not stringers in a formal sense, but people who would help keep me informed. I would tell them that I can't edit the magazine from a chair in New York. You must help me keep in touch. If anything breaks in your area, all you have to do is call me collect, drop me a note, whatever, and I'll follow up. You don't have to do a lot of work, just give me a tip, an opening. In this way I found a lot of friends, the first of whom was Bill Eshelman in California.

Moon met William Eshelman, then librarian at Los Angeles State College and newly appointed editor of the *California Librarian* (the state association's journal), while at a California Library Association conference in Pasadena in October 1960. Eshelman described the encounter in his memoir, *No Silence!*: "Early in the conference I spotted a stranger, looking lonely. 'Who are you?' I began, 'I don't recall seeing you before.' 'I'm Eric Moon,' he replied, 'new editor of *Library Journal*.' 'I'm Bill Eshelman, new editor of the *California Librarian*. We should get to know each other. Why don't we duck out of here and go to my place for a drink?' That was an offer Eric would never refuse."

The two men met again the following summer in Cleveland at the Annual ALA conference where Eshelman's magazine received the H.W. Wilson Library Periodical Award, given annually to the outstanding state or regional journal in the field. Moon had been on the jury for the award that year, and after the awards program he and Eshelman ran into one another in Will Ready's hotel room. Ready—a library educator, short story writer, and genuine character—had been Eshelman's reference teacher in library school. Eshelman had promised to meet another colleague, Everett Moore, the person most responsible for his becoming editor of the *California Librarian*, for a drink after the presentation of the award, but he never made it. Feeling a pang of guilt about standing up his benefactor, Eshelman explained, "Eric liked Moore but found him stuffy and stodgy. So for me the appeal of drinking scotch with a literary man and another library editor won out over a get together in Everett Moore's room." This fortuitous meeting, lubricated by Ready's whisky, helped seal the budding Moon-Eshelman connection, which over the years blossomed into a lifelong friendship built on common professional interests and uncommon personal compatibility.

Other travels during Moon's first year included a trip to Chicago in January 1960 to attend the ALA Midwinter meeting, where he first met David Clift, ALA's executive director, and other association leaders; and a memorable journey to Montreal in

June, where the American and Canadian library associations held a joint conference. He remembered that crossing the border into Canada was a hassle:

Dan Melcher had the idea of getting a big car and driving up with all the stuff for the Bowker booth. So Dan, Marge Saul, the president of the Mexican Library Association, and I drove up to Montreal in this car, loaded to the gills with convention stuff. When we got to the border I was driving. The border guard said, "Is this your car?" and I said, "No, it's a hired car." Then he asked if we were all American citizens and I said, "No, we've got two Americans, one Englishman, and one Mexican." He asked about all the stuff in the car. Were we going to sell it? Then we were taken into his office and grilled and grilled. He seemed to think there was something very suspicious about this group altogether. It took us almost as much time to get through customs as it did to drive up from New York to it. Dan said, "That's the last time I'm going to drive over the border with you!"

Once in Montreal, Moon basked in his new fame as *LJ* editor. He worked the conference like a politician on the hustings, meeting and interacting with numerous people, including such stars of the profession as Roger McDonough, Harold Hacker, Katherine Laich, Robert Rohlf, and Harold Lancour. These prominent librarians and others like them were potential recruits for his "ears" network as well as possible *LJ* contributors. In most cases he filed the names away, making quick mental notes about the interests, views, and persona of each. After returning to New York he pounded out a long, detailed account of the conference, published in the July and August issues of *LJ*. In a style that would soon become familiar to the magazine's readers, the report offered informative, opinionated, and sometimes biting commentary on conference events and personages as seen through Moon's gimlet eye.

Toward a Stable of Writers

His first year at the magazine sped by faster than candidates John Kennedy and Richard Nixon, then locked in a tight race for the presidency, could say federal aid to libraries. By all accounts Moon impressed people he met during the early days as a sensible, intelligent, likable, industrious fellow strongly committed to *LJ* and the betterment of the profession. They saw him as a bright spirit from across the pond who, along with John Wakeman at *WLB*, brought a certain savoir-faire to the North American library scene. He was articulate in front of a microphone and handled himself with confidence in both small groups and one-on-one situations. He was a man people listened to; he had gravitas, and the British accent was a decided plus. Some kidded him about the accent — Luther Evans, for instance, an ebullient Texan, got big laughs at a meeting of the *LJ* editorial board by burlesquing Moon's "un–American" pronunciations, as in "the ConTROVersy over caPITalism"—while others were charmed, apparently mistaking his common Southampton intonations for those of the English upper class.

Incredibly busy, he worked 65–75 hours most weeks and sometimes more. The telephone went from being despised instrument to essential communications tool: "I had to be encouraged to use the phone at first," he confessed, "because I hated telephones. Dan Melcher gave me a lecture about it one time. He said, 'Don't write so many letters—telephone, it's much cheaper. Have you ever thought about what it costs for correspondence? It involves secretarial time, filing, stationery, and postage. It probably costs $4.50 every time you send someone paper. You can talk to a person for half an hour on the phone for that.'"

In addition to talking on the phone, Moon's workday was spent writing editorials, conference reports, and news items; traveling around the country, learning about libraries and librarianship American-style; meeting hundreds of librarians, educators, students, and publishers, all the time sowing seeds that he hoped might bear fruit in some future issue of the journal; and always, always, always keeping a watchful eye out for that gifted someone capable of bringing a bit of "ordinary human enthusiasm" to his magazine's vanilla pages. (Yes, at some point fairly early on, *LJ* became *his* magazine.)

Ironically, the first article Moon published that caused a real hubbub—an attack on the hallowed *Fiction Catalog*—came not as a result of his travels or through his ever expanding list of contacts. Rather, it came in over the transom from a young library science professor teaching at St. John's University, which was right in Bowker's backyard in the New York borough of Queens. The article, "Librarians and Literature," was written by Dorothy M. Broderick and appeared in the August 1960 issue of *LJ*. Broderick slammed *Fiction Catalog*, an influential standard list and library buying guide published by the H.W. Wilson Company in various editions since 1908, for including too many titles of less than surpassing quality while omitting others by such important contemporary novelists as Faulkner and Hemingway. "That mediocre value judgments should be perpetuated in standard tools," flared Broderick, who became well known to the library world for her fiery convictions and fierier pen, "is a disgrace. I have no quarrel with libraries buying a *limited* number of mysteries, westerns, science-fiction or light love novels. I do, however, proclaim loudly that these items have no right to inclusion in a selected buying guide."

Broderick's main complaint centered on the failure of librarians as "literature experts." After all, a group of librarians—not the Wilson Company—was responsible for the selections in *Fiction Catalog*. Toward the end of her article Broderick threw a haymaker, arguing that nothing less than the reputation of librarians as professional beings was at stake: "If we want status, if we want to be recognized as book experts, if we want to convince our public that it needs library school graduates running its libraries and that such librarians are worth high salaries, then we have got to begin to work toward earning that respect.... We have got to begin to read more widely, more wisely, and more critically."

In Broderick, Moon found a soulmate. Both believed unequivocally that knowledge of books constituted the librarian's central professional responsibility. As if to underscore this meeting of minds, Broderick began her article with a quote from one of Moon's earliest *LJ* editorials, "The Uninvited": "If librarians cannot claim, earn, deserve, or receive recognition as experts in their own field—books—they have no right to expect greater status."

Moon knew the Broderick article was hot:

Soon after I arrived at *LJ* I read in *The New York Times* about a speech by the president of St. John's University, which expressed a conservative point of view about censorship. A little while afterwards I got this article in the mail from Dorothy Broderick, which expressed absolutely the antithesis of the president's views. So I called her and said, "If I publish this you'll likely be in deep shit." She said, "I know but go ahead and publish the article. I'll probably get fired, but I want you to publish it." And I said, "OK, but I don't want to be responsible for getting you fired." She said, "Stop chickenshitting on me and publish the damn thing." I did and she got fired. That's the kind of courage the woman has.

According to Broderick, "Eric's memory of that occasion is flawed." St. John's, a conservative Catholic school, viewed her "as a corrupter of youth, like Socrates and Gide," and she had been warned by the dean of the library school, who had read her article in manuscript form, that its publication — anywhere — would lead to her immediate termination by the university. Broderick:

Eric was going to publish the article in March or April. I told him I'd been told I was through teaching the moment it saw print so I asked if we could delay it until the end of the semester. I did not want to leave my class with a new teacher halfway through the term. He agreed and published it in August. There was never any question of my resigning. I was done, washed up, terminated. It would have happened even if the article hadn't been published, since my defense of authors like Hemingway and Faulkner, at the time on the Condemned List, and the inherent assumption that libraries ought to buy gay novels receiving positive reviews, doomed me. Also, I never used the word "chickenshitting" in my entire life and never will. I did not learn to say an outloud curse word until the late 1960s or early 1970s. I still limit cussing to an occasional "oh shit" when I do something really stupid.

Accompanying Broderick's broadside were five pages of "Opinion" based on advance copies of the article Moon circulated "to a number of Lj readers because we felt that some of her comments merited further discussion." Respondents included Edwin Colburn of the H.W. Wilson Company and librarians Wen Chao Chen (Kalamazoo College in Michigan), Bill Katz (King County Public Library in Seattle), Jerome Cushman (Salina Public Library in Kansas), and Lawrence Clark Powell (UCLA), along with *LJ*'s own Margaret Cooley. Moon was disappointed by the initial lack of fireworks: "Frankly, we expected some difference of opinion. Comments received, however, were almost without exception favorable. All of our readers, apparently, are on the side of the angels." How discouraging — angels don't sell magazines.

He also devoted his editorial in the August issue to the Broderick article. Entitled "The Right to Write," the piece praised her willingness to put her job on the line for her beliefs while lambasting this and other instances of prior censorship. In a subsequent issue (October 15), Moon reported that "a barrage of correspondence" had been received concerning Broderick's critique of *Fiction Catalog*, and that "a selection of letters" was being published "as a general discussion forum of unusual interest." Finally, he had the response he had hoped for. The letters covered a multitude of issues, including what's wrong with library education ("I would suggest that the library schools come of age by offering more bread and fewer circuses," wrote Rosemary Neiswender, a librarian at the Rand Corporation); what's wrong with library literature ("What we librarians need is an avant-garde periodical devoted to letting the hot air out of the numerous stuffed shirts in the field," suggested Dennis Murphy of the Detroit Public Library); and what's wrong with Dorothy Broderick ("Apparently Miss Broderick has not come down from her ivory tower for some time," observed Dorothy Bennett of the Pasadena, California, Public Library).

Ah, now this was controversy! Early on he had been frustrated by the relative lack of reader response to edgy material in *LJ*, some of it, he thought, pretty strong stuff: "I thought, gee, I'm really losing my touch. I remember saying to Daniel [Melcher] at one point, 'I don't know if I'm doing a good job here or not. I feel I'm working in a void, that nothing is happening.'" The Broderick article changed that. Moon: "The article produced so much response we could have filled the next issue with nothing but letters. But that was rare; you really had to goad to get response. What I wanted was a healthy flow of a great variety of opinions coming into the magazine all the time. It was much harder to get that in the U.S. than it was in England, where argument seemed to be an actual way of life."

Moon adroitly kept the *Fiction Catalog* controversy alive for months by printing more needling letters— John Neufeld of the Michigan State Library, for instance, wrote, "Now that Dorothy Broderick has managed to question the *Fiction Catalog* without being struck dead, perhaps a detailed study of the Wilson catalogs can be made soon" (November 1, 1960); and the March 15, 1961, issue carried a review of a new (seventh) edition of *Fiction Catalog* by the intrepid Broderick, who surprised just about everyone by giving the revision high marks: "The changes can only be described as exciting and dramatic." Around the same time, Mary Lee Bundy, then a research consultant at the Illinois State Library, prepared a report called *Public Library Administrators View Their Professional Periodicals*, in which 115 recent articles from all types of library periodicals were rated. Among the nine articles deemed best, seven had been published by *LJ*, with Broderick's mentioned most frequently.

A youth services specialist with a doctorate from Columbia University's School of Library Service, Dorothy Broderick continued to write frequently and polemically for *LJ* (and *SLJ*) during and after Moon's editorship. From St. John's University she moved on to the New York State Library in Albany as a public library children's consultant. In 1962, with the blessing of Columbia's powerful Frances Henne, she returned to teaching, joining the faculty at the library school at Case Western Reserve in Cleveland, where she remained until 1969. Later, she taught at the library schools at the University of Wisconsin — Madison and Dalhousie University in Halifax, Nova Scotia. She capped her distinguished career by founding *VOYA* (*Voice of Youth Advocates*), a leading review journal. In 1997 she described herself as "physically but not mentally retired" from librarianship.

Broderick was not the only writer Moon nurtured in the 1960s. He encouraged — and published — dozens of mostly young or newly qualified librarians who showed particular promise. A case in point was Fay Blake. Like Broderick, Blake was a bright, mature woman just beginning her library career who had something to say and knew how to say it. She remembered her first article in *LJ* well. Called "Librarians and Labor," it appeared in the November 1, 1961, issue:

My first contact with Eric occurred while I was still in library school in 1960 or 1961. I had become quite exercised about the elaborate services public libraries offered to businesses, including whole separate branches (e.g., Oakland, California, and Newark, New Jersey), while services to labor were practically nonexistent. So I wrote an article documenting the situation and offering some proposals. Eric published the article together with comments from several eminent public librarians. Apparently they didn't realize I was a mere student, so their replies were properly respectful — but rationalizations, nonetheless.

Later Blake met Moon on one of his trips to California:

I actually met Eric for the first time when I was a brand-new librarian at UCLA and attending a California Library Association conference. The invited speaker was developing an involved metaphor calling librarians "eunuchs more interested in guarding books than distributing them" and urging librarians to become "lovers of books." In the discussion period I suggested to the speaker, "No amount of exhortation will turn a eunuch into a lover." There was an explosion of laughter, and Eric characteristically sought me out after the session and introduced himself. I found that gesture pretty enchanting.

Moon's goal was to build a stable of writers whose interests and style meshed with his vision of *LJ* as an informative, inviting, combative professional magazine. He wanted writers who would express "their ideas and convictions without equivocation." In return, he gave them the opportunity to invent themselves: "My gambit was never to ask them to write on assigned topics but to try to find out what moved them. I'd ask: 'What do you get excited or angry or impatient about? What do you really care about? What's your thing? That's what I want you to write about'." Talented writers like Broderick and Blake thrived in such an environment. Eventually Moon's stable came to include such diverse librarian-authors as Bill Katz, E.J. Josey, Wyman Jones, Dorothy Nyren, Daniel Gore, Gordon Stevenson, Murray Bob, Robert D. Franklin, John Pine, Ralph Ellsworth, Walter Brahm, Jerrold Orne, Paul Dunkin, Robert Downs, Jesse Shera, Rose Sellers, and John Weatherford.

Trouble Ahead

By the time Moon's first anniversary at Bowker rolled around on November 5, 1960, *LJ* was looking much better, like a patient on the mend after a long, debilitating illness. The man from England via Newfoundland appeared to be the tonic the magazine needed. Its articles tended to be more lively and diverse, and there was no doubt its editorials were more animated and probing. Even news stories seemed better written and often covered events that previously would have been ignored. A case in point: a May 1, 1960, story detailed a march on city hall in Boston by 50 women protesting the closing of two branches of the city's public library due to budget cuts. At one point the reader learned, deliciously, "Miss Evelyn Smart, a Roxbury resident and spokesman for the women, tossed 2½ pennies on Mayor Collins' desk and said, 'You have set the city back 100 years by closing the libraries.' Miss Smart, who had cut one penny in half, added that the 2½ cents was an advance on her share of the library deficit." Under Moon, *LJ* sharply increased its coverage of hard news in the 1960s, a policy that did not always please librarians and politicians on the receiving end of negative stories.

Moon's long hours and hard work were paying dividends. During his first year in the catbird seat he earned the confidence and respect of the Melchers and most other Bowker colleagues, demonstrating sound editorial instincts and proving that he could play in the library big leagues with the best of them. On November 8, 1960, almost exactly one year after Moon took over *LJ*, Americans elected John Kennedy their new president. Though Kennedy's margin of victory was thin, the country seemed ready psychologically for real social change after the relatively placid Eisenhower years. Moon, a legal alien, had no vote, but had he had one, there's no doubt that Kennedy — pro–library, pro–federal aid, pro–civil rights — would have received it.

Like many ordinary people across the nation, Moon responded favorably to the president's sense of urgency, his call to get the country "moving again." But in Moon's case the urgency was specific, it had a name. For months he had been carefully preparing a frontal attack on American librarianship's deepest shame: the profession's mute acceptance of, and complicity in, acts of blatant discrimination against black people, particularly in the South where most libraries and some library associations were racially segregated by law or custom. Moon's decision to take on the issue of racism did not hinge on who won the presidency in 1960, but Kennedy's election did signal, however tentatively, a readiness on the part of the country to move forward, finally, to try to find solutions to its deepest and most tragic social problem.

At the conclusion of a long news article entitled "The Danville Story" (November 1, 1960), which dealt with segregation at the Danville (Virginia) Public Library, Moon unobtrusively set the timer for a bomb that would explode six weeks later: "An article on segregation and libraries," he wrote, "will appear in the December 15 issue of Lj." That article, by Rice Estes, and Moon's accompanying editorial, would put the question of race front and center on the national library agenda, where it would remain until the stain of official segregation had been removed. To put it euphemistically, not everyone welcomed this initiative, and by the end of the fight neither Eric Moon nor *Library Journal* nor American librarianship would be quite the same again.

– 9 –

Exploding the Silent Subject

Libraries and Race in Postwar America

American society began coming to grips with de jure segregation after World War II, albeit slowly, fitfully, reluctantly, sullenly, sometimes violently. For decades prior to the war, racial discrimination in the United States was largely a silent subject, ignored by those in power, hidden away like a mad relative in the root cellar, except when an ugly eruption occurred, such as a riot or a lynching. After all, hadn't the race question been "settled" by the Civil War, Lincoln's Emancipation Proclamation, and Amendments 13, 14, and 15 to the U.S. Constitution? This mind-set was especially prevalent in the South where Jim Crow laws, enacted after Reconstruction and sanctified by the Supreme Court in *Plessy v. Ferguson* in 1896, institutionalized two cultures, one dominant (white), the other subservient (black). The rest of the country either knew little about the South's rigidly enforced system of apartheid or did not care and opted to look the other way. Moreover, the rest of the country, where de facto segregation was the rule, could hardly hold itself up as a bastion of racial enlightenment and freedom. But by the 1940s change was in the air: many restrictive American social conventions were being questioned, among them old racial codes and prejudices.

Franklin Roosevelt included black people in his New Deal coalition, the first time members of that race had participated in the American political mainstream in any significant way since post–Civil War days. Not only did FDR open up jobs in the federal government to Negroes but assembled an unofficial black cabinet (or brain trust) to advise him on racial matters. His wife Eleanor, an uncompromising advocate for human rights, raised eyebrows by inviting African Americans to the White House, visiting black schools and colleges, and championing talented black artists like singer Marian Anderson. Roosevelt's successor, Harry Truman, ordered the desegregation of the military and supported federal legislation aimed at eliminating Jim Crow laws in the South. In 1954 the Supreme Court issued its historic *Brown* decision, which overturned *Plessy* by ordering the integration of all public schools in every region of the country. A year and half later a modest black woman, Rosa Parks, refused to give her seat to a white man on a segregated bus in Montgomery, Alabama, an incident that sparked a famous bus boycott — and gave the nascent civil rights movement a new and powerful voice in the person of a 26-year-old black minister, Dr. Martin Luther King, Jr. In 1957 President Eisenhower sent troops to Little Rock, Arkansas, to enforce court-ordered integration of the city's Central High School.

Meanwhile, the American library profession seemed unaffected by — and curiously indifferent to — these portentous developments. Issues involving race relations of course had great personal meaning for many individual librarians, black and white, but the profession as a whole displayed almost no overt interest in such matters, as if acts of racial inequality and segregation were problems outside the purview of librarianship. Yet this was a time when library service to black citizens was pitifully inadequate in most places in the United States, and practically nonexistent in much of the South. One informed observer estimated that in the early 1950s, "two-thirds of the Negro population of 13 Southern States were entirely without library services," and by all accounts that situation remained unchanged for the next dozen or more years.

By the time Moon became editor of *LJ* at the end of 1959 the civil rights movement was underway but far from its peak; national attention was focused almost exclusively on Southern intransigence. In a key moment during the 1960 presidential campaign John Kennedy publicly criticized the jailing of Dr. King, who had been arrested leading a protest demonstration in Atlanta. Kennedy telephoned King's wife to express his concern, and his brother Robert contacted the judge in the case and arranged for King's release on bail. Richard Nixon, on the other hand, said and did nothing. This incident symbolized for voters how the two candidates truly felt about civil rights, and Kennedy's subsequent election was viewed as a victory for those determined to ratchet up the pressure on the South, both in the streets and in the Congress, to end de jure segregation once and for all.

Moon picked up on these currents at once:

As I began to move around the country in that first year on my new job it seemed to me that you didn't have to be particularly acute or understanding to see that something important was underway in America. A few years behind us already were the Montgomery, Alabama bus boycott and the Supreme Court decision in *Brown vs. the Board of Education of Topeka, Kansas*; sit-ins in restaurants and other public places were hitting the headlines with growing frequency, and the voice of Martin Luther King was being heard, and sometimes listened to, throughout the land. Even to this newcomer it was obvious that a social revolution was gathering steam. So what impact, I asked myself, was all this having on libraries?

I spent several weeks scouring through the library literature, going a long way back, to see what was on record about the condition of black people in our profession and to find out whether blacks had the same kind of difficulties in using libraries that they clearly had with other kinds of public institutions. The search was revealing: there was virtually nothing to indicate that any such problems had impinged on the serene world of libraryland. I said *virtually* nothing; there was one shining exception. Back in the thirties poet Stanley Kunitz, then editor of the *Wilson Library Bulletin*, wrote a marvelous editorial entitled "The Spectre at Richmond" which dealt with the shameful indignities that black librarians could expect to face at their own professional association meetings.

Kunitz Editorial

The Kunitz editorial — the first and only piece of its kind in the American library press until Moon came along — appeared in the May 1936 issue of *WLB*. It denounced the profession for subjecting Negro librarians to a "shockingly cruel and feudal policy" at that year's annual ALA conference, held in Richmond, Virginia, then very much a segregated Southern city. After quoting from a "semi-official" letter sent by an ALA representative prior to the conference to those librarians "whose skins are more highly pigmented" than their white colleagues, an angry Kunitz wrote:

> In brief, Negro librarians will be segregated thruout the conference; they will not be permitted to attend meetings where food is served.
>
> Unless you believe that Negroes are incapable of being insulted, you must agree with me that a minority group of the A.L.A. has been greatly offended. If you permit this organized insult to pass unchallenged, there is but one conclusion to be made: that American librarians do not, in their hearts, care for democracy or for the foundation principles of decent and enlightened institutions. No elegant platform phrases of devotion to the idea of a free and equal society or to the theory of liberty can be sufficient to obviate that conclusion.
>
> You may say, as assuredly will be said, in defence of the Negro policy at the conference, that it is merely conforming with the laws of Virginia. To this I reply that there is a higher law ... and that we have forty-eight States in the Union. Other organizations make a practice of convening only in communities where their own standards of eligibility and respectability are honored. An association of American professional men and women cannot go into convention part white and part black without doing violence to the best thought and the highest hope of our national life.

Kunitz provided a telling footnote to his editorial in the next issue of *WLB*: "Since there has been some curiosity as to whether my remarks last month on the segregation of Negroes at conferences of the American Library Association ('The Spectre at Richmond') represent the viewpoint of the publishers of the *Wilson Bulletin*, I have been asked to explain that my observations in this department of commentary on the contemporary scene are invariably founded on my personal views and that The H.W. Wilson Company, as a corporation, has no opinions whatever to express on this controversial matter." Another footnote: not long after the embarrassing Richmond meeting, ALA decided that future conferences would be held only in cities that provided integrated public services and accommodations for all its members. And one final footnote: in July 2000 Stanley Kunitz, 95, became the tenth poet laureate of the United States.

Moon Strategizes, Is Scooped

Moon began running news stories, at first cribbed from the national press, about segregated libraries in the South within months of taking over at *LJ*. Among the earliest was an item headlined "Faulkner Condemns Closing of Libraries in the South," in which Mississippi-born novelist William Faulkner spoke out against the tactics being used to keep some Southern libraries lily-white: "Books should be open to everyone. The ends the white man is trying to gain are not worth the means he's using to get them. In principle, I think everyone should not only have the right to look at everything printed, they should be compelled by law to do so." (Possibly the future Nobel laureate, whose comments followed a reading at the University of Virginia in Charlottesville, had had a tad too much libation when he proffered that last suggestion?) Subsequent *LJ* news items on the silent subject described segregation problems and protests at a number of public libraries, including those in Danville and Petersburg (Virginia), Greenville (South Carolina), Jackson (Mississippi), and Savannah (Georgia).

By the middle of 1960, convinced of the enormity of the problem and troubled by the library profession's impassivity in the face of it, Moon decided to launch a major journalistic strike against segregation in Southern libraries. "*Library Journal*, I felt, had to make a dent in that stolid wall of silence because, as I saw it, libraries had a simple choice: to be a significant thread in the social fabric, an active participant in social change, or to face an inevitable passage toward irrelevance, possible extinction, or a grey existence as some kind of historical relic." The only question was, as he put it, "how best to explode the bomb":

If I simply wrote another of those argumentative Moon editorials, which were already beginning to annoy a good many people in the profession, it might simply be written off as another of the excesses of that crazy limey, and what did he know about it anyway, having been in the country less than a year? A tactical sense is useful when you're going into battle, and I decided that what I needed was a statement by a person with impeccable credentials, a product of that white Southern magnolia world where segregation was practiced as a fine art.

By a stroke of good fortune he met Rice Estes around this time. Estes, then library director at Pratt Institute in Brooklyn, was a son of the South, a native South Carolinian whose first library job had been at the University of South Carolina. What made Estes special from Moon's point of view was that, in addition to being a Southerner, he was white, knew and detested Jim Crow racism, and was not afraid to say so publicly. One afternoon during a break at the ALA conference in Montreal in the summer of 1960 Moon casually suggested to Estes that he write an article on library segregation for *LJ*. Estes vividly remembered their conversation:

Eric appealed to me the minute I met him. He had brains, an acute analytic sense, and a fervent loyalty to librarianship. I immediately felt drawn to him. One day over coffee with John Wakeman, the editor of the *Wilson Library Bulletin*, Eric and I got into a discussion about segregation in libraries. I had always been a maverick Southerner and launched into an attack on how backward librarians were about doing anything to ease the problem. Eric said, "Why don't you write this down and I'll try to publish it." Well, I didn't give much thought to an article and put the idea away in the back of my head.

Moon hoped to deliver his anti-segregation blast that fall or, at the latest, by the end of the year. The subject was hot and getting hotter with each new report of a sit-in demonstration or federal court order involving a Southern library. In the meantime,

John Wakeman at *WLB* was planning his own treatment of the segregation problem. Like Moon, Wakeman wanted to shake his magazine out of its customary torpor, and libraries denying service to an entire group of people was a torpor-busting topic. Moon naturally remained grateful to Wakeman for bringing his name to the attention of Dan Melcher, a piece of luck without which he almost certainly would never have become editor of *LJ*, and the two men now got together on a fairly regular basis to bat around ideas, exchange information, and chew over old times. But despite the companionable socializing and warm personal history, they were also now journalistic competitors. Both men now edited one of the Big Three American library periodicals (the third being the *ALA Bulletin*); both were Brits trying to make their mark in a foreign land; and both were committed, each in his own way, to outdoing the other.

Moon — the ever competitive Eric Moon — therefore felt something less than elation when Wakeman beat him to the punch on the race issue by publishing an editorial entitled "Segregation and Censorship" in the September 1960 issue of *WLB*. The editorial began with a review of the situation in several Southern libraries, and then asked, "How has the American Library Association reacted to these developments?" Wakeman's answer appeared to give comfort to racial conservatives:

> Surely then, ALA's record is that of an organization opposed to segregation, and as effective against it as its structure permits. But there are obvious and inevitable limitations on its effectiveness in this area. It is evident that one of the things a national association based in Chicago should *not* attempt is intervention in local situations where the segregation of tax-supported public libraries is an issue. Such intervention would stiffen the resistence [sic] to library integration even of moderate Southerners. It would retard, if not end, such progress as is being achieved by Southern librarians themselves.
>
> For, it need hardly be said, many Southern librarians are opposed to segregation, and are working "with all deliberate speed" for an end to it. They can move only as rapidly as the temper of their communities permits. Impatient injunctions from Northern librarians with no conception of what that temper is must be very hard to bear.

Soon after Wakeman's editorial appeared, the two editors got together at a favorite New York bar. Moon said, "Jesus, John, that was a tame editorial." Wakeman responded (according to Moon), "Yeah, but it wasn't exactly what I wanted to write," the implication being that the Wilson Company — the stuffy, cautious, conservative Wilson Company — kept him on a short leash. Moon: "Well, I think I'll have to come out in *LJ* and attack it. I hope you realize I'm not attacking you." Wakeman: "You'll only make things [library segregation in the South] worse." Moon: "I don't have any options on this. I have to attack you."

Incendiary Package

If Wakeman's editorial irritated Moon, it infuriated Rice Estes: "Shortly after my discussion with Eric about segregation, there appeared an editorial in the *Wilson Library Bulletin*, obviously trying to scoop Eric's plan. The editorial was wild. It made me so mad that I sat down and wrote my article straight off, completing it the next night. I gave it to Eric as soon as possible, and he read it as we sat again over coffee. I'll never forget the look he gave me when he finished. It was a look of surprise, gratitude, and utter warmth." After receiving Estes' article, Moon announced that "An article on segregation and libraries will appear in the December 15 issue of Lj." In fact, the December 15, 1960, issue would contain not only Estes' condemnation of library segregation but a strongly worded editorial on the subject by Moon, plus a moving excerpt from Richard Wright's autobiographical *Black Boy*, in which the author as a young man had to scheme and lie simply to borrow a few books from the public library in Memphis, Tennessee, during the Jim Crow era.

It was an incendiary package intended to render the silent subject silent no more.

"Eric published my article without changing a word," Estes remembered. The piece, entitled "Segregated Libraries," was both closely reasoned and a roar from the gut, and Moon had enough editorial sense not to tinker with perfection. Estes first attacked ALA's logic, articulated by association president Benjamin Powell at the Montreal conference, that "the Association cannot and does not attempt to intrude upon local jurisdiction." Wrote Estes:

So far no library association seems willing to do anything about the most pressing domestic issue the nation faces today, the integration and education of our Negro citizens. Instead librarians are piously declaring that they will not become involved in local problems. The term "local" is never defined.

But when did librarians become shy of local problems? Was not the Intellectual Freedom Committee of ALA set up primarily to deal with local interference with reading? When a book is banned in the smallest hamlet, there is a vigorous protest — as indeed there should be — that the Library Bill of Rights is defamed and that reading privileges are being denied. Such a protest is usually supported by a majority of librarians. But when a city takes away the rights of citizens to read *every* book in the public library, we say nothing. The problem has suddenly become "local," a very good alternative for "untouchable."

Estes then described the pervasiveness of segregation in Southern libraries, which he had observed firsthand:

Many librarians are unaware of the fact that *most* public libraries below the Mason and Dixon Line are segregated. In the majority of towns and cities Negro readers are not only denied entrance to white branches, they are also denied entrance to the main central library where most of the books are housed. They are thus not only confined to a small branch or branches of their own but are deprived of access to the principal book collection in the locality.... In some localities there is no library service for Negro citizens at all. In one such place where I was a recent visitor, I asked one of the librarians how Negro readers were serviced. "Oh," she said, "they are not interested in reading." I wondered if she had ever read the poignant passage in Richard Wright's classic *Black Boy*, which recounts his experience of illicitly withdrawing books from the public library in Memphis.

Toward the end of his article Estes criticized ALA's do-nothing approach to the problem and took a swipe at Wakeman's editorial:

An editorial in the *Wilson Library Bulletin* of September 1960 states, in discussing this matter, that the American Library Association is as effective against segregation "as its structure permits." I challenge this statement. The American Library Association has been completely ineffective about the issue. It has never even passed a resolution on the subject. It has never commended the efforts of Negro readers and organizations who have tried to end library segregation by doing everything from making a mild request to staging library sit-ins. It has not attempted to bring a law suit or lent its name as *amicus curiae* to any group bringing a suit.

In Montreal we were told that ALA's attitude toward segregation was defined in the Library Bill of Rights, but if the principles of the bill are not implemented, of what value is the Bill of Rights to Negro readers — or for that matter, to anyone?

Following his reference to Wright's *Black Boy*, Estes mused, "If only this passage could be reprinted and sent to every trustee of every library in the South, surely fruit would be borne." Moon cleverly did the next best thing by reprinting the passage at the end of Estes' article. It included the 19-year-old Wright's heartbreaking forged note to a white librarian: "*Dear Madam: Will you please let this nigger boy—* I used the word 'nigger' to make the librarian feel that I could not possibly be the author of the note — *have some books by H.L. Mencken?*"

Rarely if ever had American librarians encountered such raw social reality in one of their professional journals. Moon and Estes sought to expose the crime of official segregation to every librarian, even the most sheltered and genteel of the breed, in every part of the country. Like it or not, they were saying, this is the way many libraries in the South are, and if the profession does not fight as hard as it can to end this evil, all of us are complicit.

The third and final blast in Moon's bombardment was his own editorial, appropriately called "The Silent Subject." Published almost exactly one year after he arrived at *LJ*, the editorial stands as one of his most consequential writings. "It is common knowledge in the library profession," he began, "that segregation is not something that happens only in schools and lunch-counters; that it happens in libraries too." Which goes to prove, he continued, "that word of mouth is a pretty effective medium of communication, for any librarian looking at our library periodicals over the past five or six years would find it difficult to divine that libraries were involved in such problems, or even that a 'segregation' problem existed."

After recounting his mostly futile search for published material on the subject Moon declared that the "years of vacuum" were at an end. No longer would the library press be silent about racial prejudice as long as he had anything to say about it. At the same time he attacked (as he promised he would) his pal Wakeman for being too timid in his treatment of the segregation issue:

It is encouraging to see at least two of our library periodicals [*LJ* and *WLB*] becoming aware that segregation is a social menace that inflicts itself upon libraries as well as other institutions. Even reporting without comment what has been happening recently in Danville, Petersburg, and other places is an improvement. Even the bland, benign and tentative discussion of segregation in the *Wilson Library Bulletin* is a big step forward. But something more is needed, and we welcome the forthright and honest statement by Rice Estes in this issue (see p. 4418). We hope that it will be the beginning of a much wider expression of opinion on a situation which is improving, if at all, desperately slowly, a situation of which the profession can hardly be proud.

Moon then questioned whether ALA was doing all it could to fight segregation: "With Mr. Estes we challenge the assumption of the editor of the *Wilson Library Bulletin* that 'ALA's record is that of an organization opposed to segregation, and *as effective against it as its structure permits*.'" If ALA's structure is such that it does not permit vigorous and forceful opposition to segregation, argued Moon, then that structure should be changed. He also assailed, as had Estes, ALA's position on "local jurisdiction," code words for acquiescence to Jim Crow. How long, he asked, does an injustice that "affects thousands of would-be library users in perhaps a third of the country" remain "local"?

Finally, Moon put forward two suggestions for action intended to hasten the end of library segregation in the South. First, and most urgent, he said, was "the need for the profession to find some way to give legal as well as moral support to librarians—and if need be, groups of citizens—who at present fight alone to keep libraries open and free." In this context he wondered, "How actively does the profession support other bodies involved in the struggle for civil liberties when libraries and library readers are involved? Is it considered unprofessional to associate with 'dangerous' bodies like ACLU or NAACP?" His other suggestion — to withhold federal funds from libraries "whose services are not available to *all* the people who wish to use them"— seemed radical in 1960. The mere thought of cutting off federal aid as a stick to force integration alarmed powerful library interests in the North as well as the South. Moon, however, proved to be ahead of his time, because eventually the U.S. government began using this tactic in the fight against segregation.

Readers Respond

Moon's offensive against racial bigotry had a startling effect on *LJ* readers and, by extension, the library community at large. Instantly the segregation issue jumped to the top of the national professional agenda, even for those librarians who remained in denial. Though few realized it at the time, American librarianship was changed irrevocably by the explosive words in the December 15, 1960, issue of *Library Journal*. Never before had an abhorrent social evil intruded so painfully, so starkly into the quiet, orderly realm of library work, where the 3 × 5 card signified a worldview. Unequivocal empirical evidence of flagrant racial discrimination in some of the nation's libraries had been prominently exhibited for all to see in a major professional publication. No longer could segregated library service be ignored or wished away or winked at by the profession's leaders, including ALA policymakers. Pandora's black box had been opened, the words had been spoken, and they could not be disavowed or discredited or disregarded. Moon later claimed that his attack "really launched publicly the battle that would be fought throughout most of the decade to integrate libraries and library associations." This might sound immodest (Moon was no stranger to immodesty), but the boast was true.

The "Readers' Voice" (or letters) section of the February 15, 1961, issue of the magazine was given over completely to the segregation question. The outpouring included comments from Dorothy Bendix, a high-profile professor at the library school at Drexel Institute of Technology in Philadelphia: "I would like to congratulate you for coming to grips with the issue of segregated libraries which the library profession has chosen to ignore for so many years in the vain hope that it would go away." Bendix concluded with action proposals: "ALA should create a 'defense' fund similar to that of the AAUP" (the American Association of University Professors), and "Funds should be sought for a study of: a) the current status of free access to knowledge in Southern public libraries; b) the factors responsible for the successful transition from segregated to integrated libraries in some Southern communities."

Others letter writers included Ruth W. Brown, who told her story of being fired years earlier as librarian at the Bartlesville (Oklahoma) public library, in part because of her enthusiastic support for integrated library service; Joseph Wheeler, former librarian at Enoch Pratt Free Library in Baltimore, who wrote, "What a fresh breeze blows through the December 15 issue. Thanks to Mr. Estes for bouncing on the white librarians who do nothing to break the segregationists"; Daniel W. Hagelin, reference librarian at the Lakewood (Ohio) Public Library, who praised "Rice Estes' clear summons to concrete action to end the shocking situation in which millions of Negroes are denied access to publicly owned books. The article left me with a very guilty feeling about my own individual failure to speak out against segregated libraries"; and Lee Ash, the former *LJ* editor then with Yale University Library, who declared, "It is embarrassing and humiliating to think of our allegedly progressive profession sitting on the side lines in agreeable politeness throughout this period of national shame since 1954."

John Wakeman also responded, defending his *WLB* editorial against the criticisms leveled by both Moon and Estes:

It is difficult to understand why you and Mr. Estes have devoted so much energy and space to opposing my position, which is so close to your own that you have between you echoed every proposal I advanced for improving the situation.

So far as I can see, the only real difference between Lj's position and the *Bulletin's* is in the matter of direct intervention by ALA in law suits precipitated by segregation struggles, or its intervention as *amicus curiae*. Mr. Estes, who is a southerner, believes that this would be desirable. On the admittedly shaky basis of observation, I must persist in disagreeing. The overt entry of a national professional association, based in the north, into situations where the segregation of local tax-supported libraries is at issue would in my view do more harm than good.

Pressure to Back Off

When Moon found an issue that generated exceptional reader interest, as in the case of Dorothy Broderick's attack on *Fiction Catalog*, he stayed with it doggedly until there was some satisfactory resolution or a natural petering out of interest. He became a master at extracting the last nugget of controversy from a contentious issue. In the case of racism in libraries he hit upon a mother lode — a sorrowful, virulent subject so deeply entwined in the American experience that it could be years (if ever) before the vein was exhausted, journalistically speaking. Beginning with his incendiary package in December 1960 and continuing well into the decade Moon kept blasting away at the issue, finding more and more layers of intolerance the deeper he delved.

At the outset almost everyone (or so it seemed) supported his basic position on segregated libraries. "All the correspondence we received, without exception," he reported in the March 15, 1961, issue, "called for stronger and more positive action and leadership by ALA in this area." But behind the scenes, off the record, old boy to old boy, Bowker executives soon began getting an earful about Moon's aggressive editorial style and particularly his utterances on race and libraries. Most disturbing to Moon was the fact that some of these complaints came from the highest levels of the profession, including top ALA officials. Privately, they warned Fred and Dan Melcher that Moon (as he remembered the words) "had to be stopped" because he "was destroying all relationships between the profession and the company." Moon's detractors also pointed out, ominously, that his crusading efforts could upset powerful Southern members of Congress who exercised considerable influence over library legislation and appropriations. As Moon put it, both he and Wakeman "were urged to cool it because too much noise about all that racial stuff was calculated to upset our southern sponsors in Congress and thus jeopardize all that lovely federal loot they were dealing out to libraries."

As the barrage of sub-rosa criticism intensified he began to think of himself "as much a public enemy as those gentlemen whose photographs adorn the walls of local post offices." Certainly Moon and Wakeman both knew by fall 1961 that they were on ALA's hit list. At first, association leaders had welcomed the British arrivistes, who seemed like such nice, polite — read compliant — young men. "When John and I went to our first Midwinter [in January 1960], we were feted by the ALA executive director [David Clift] and the Establishment," Moon remembered, "and we thought isn't this lovely." But within a year or so these same leaders were shunning the two editors, dismissing them as anti–American troublemakers. "We had become social lepers," continued Moon. "In fact, after one membership meeting, at which both John and I had spoken on the race subject, one very, very senior staff member of ALA [Grace Stevenson, the association's deputy executive director] came over to us and said, 'Why don't you two young bastards go back to England where you belong?'"

Moon acknowledged his critics in an editorial that summer but refused to back off:

A number of librarians have been dismayed in recent months by our handling of the issue of segregation in libraries and within the professional ranks. Lj, we have been told, has been unnecessarily harsh in its criticism of an association which has repeatedly made abundantly clear its position on this and other freedoms.

Let us say here — for the record — that we believe in ALA's sincerity in this matter and that we are enthusiastic members and supporters of an association which has done a great deal for libraries and librarians in this country and around the world. But pride and devotion do not imply that we should wear blinkers. We are convinced of the association's strength of conviction and moral purpose, but we are not alone in sometimes doubting whether ALA is clear about the ways in which these beliefs can be translated into the kind of leadership that is urgently required.

Fortunately for Moon the Bowker Company backed him and his editorial efforts fully. Led by Dan Melcher, who made no secret of his liberal leanings, the company refused to yield to pressure from the library Establishment to shut up its opinionated editor. Moon: "When the phone calls and letters from some of the 'names' in the profession started coming in, saying you've got to get rid of this guy, he's destroying relationships between the profession and the Bowker Company, it was Dan's wholehearted support that allowed me to keep going full blast." What the library barons failed to take into account or possibly did not understand was the Bowker Company's pride in its record as a socially enlightened enterprise. The company's progressive philosophy dated back to Richard Rogers Bowker himself who, in addition to being an important New York publisher in the late 19th and early 20th centuries, was an ardent political reformer and staunch opponent of ethnic and racial discrimination all his adult life.

Moon also had the bottom line on his side. Since he had taken over the magazine *LJ*'s circulation was way up, advertising was booming, and profits were at record levels. When the protests about his handling of the race issue reached fever pitch, Dan Melcher and the Bowker board met with him to review the situation. Moon recalled Melcher saying, "The magazine's clearly doing marvelously, but there's something we don't understand. We would have expected the deep South to be the place where you were doing least well, but your circulation is up by the highest percentage in Mississippi, second highest in Alabama, third highest in Louisiana. How do you explain it?" Always ready with a quick answer (even if it might be pure bull), Moon shot back,

"Haven't any of you read Mencken?" They kind of blinked and said what do you mean? I said, "Mencken said something to the effect that if you want people to read you, you have to get them to the point where they wonder what you're going to say about them next." Of course, I didn't know if Mencken ever said that, I made it up on the spot. But they were very impressed by it. Then they asked, "How do you account for Kansas? It's the only state where your circulation is not up." I said, "I hate Kansas," and that was the end of the interview.

Moon and Wakeman were not the only anti-segregationists in the library arena subjected to private abuse by bigots. After publication of his article in *LJ*, Rice Estes received a lot of mail, not all of it pleasant or printable: "The impact of my article astounded me," Estes revealed many years later. "You should have seen my fan mail. If words could have killed, I'd have been dead long ago back in 1960." Still, his daughter, Helena Estes, also a librarian, had positive memories of that time: "I was only 12 years old when my father and Eric Moon stirred up the library community in the United States, but I remember the underlying excitement in our home. I was always enormously proud of my father as a child and later in my adult years." Moon too was always quick to praise Rice Estes, who died in 1996, for his unique contribution to the cause of racial justice: "Rice's article might not look that exciting to you today, but it took courage for him to write it and he became a pariah in some circles where he thought he had friends. When the full story of the civil rights battle in librarianship is written, I hope the author will recognize that the name of Estes deserves a place of honor in it."

Other Library Journalists Respond

Despite obstructionist tactics by avowed segregationists and closet racists, the forces fighting for color-blind library service gained momentum and adherents in the early 1960s. Moon was especially encouraged when two editors of state library periodicals at opposite ends of the country began attacking Jim Crow, each from a different angle.

William Eshelman wrote in the January 1961 issue of the *California Librarian* that before reading Moon's "Silent Subject" editorial in *LJ* he had been "only vaguely aware of the existence of segregated libraries in the south" and afterward "was astounded at the *extent* of the problem. Once pointed out it does not seem surprising, but from this edge of the continent it is a situation all too easily overlooked." Eshelman called on ALA to "sponsor or conduct a survey of libraries in the south to define the problem: how many libraries have quietly integrated? How many remain segregated?" He concluded by echoing Moon's recommendation that federal funds available through the Library Services Act should be withheld from libraries practicing racial discrimination.

John N. Berry III, editor of the *Bay State Librarian*, the bulletin of the Massachusetts Library Association, entered the fray with a spirited editorial (April 1963) suggesting that a public library awards program sponsored by the Book-of-the-Month Club and endorsed by ALA had benefited segregated libraries in the South, which he proceeded to name. "We violently oppose any award to strengthen institutions which maintain a system of service that in any way separates one citizen from another in his use of books," thundered Berry. Moon later questioned Berry's methods and facts in a long editorial of his own, but he liked the spunk shown by the young man from Massachusetts so much that he hired him in 1964 to be *LJ*'s assistant editor.

Wilson Library Bulletin continued to pursue the segregation issue as long as John Wakeman remained editor. In May 1961, for instance, Wakeman published an informative symposium featuring the views of four well-known black librarians, including Virginia Lacy Jones, then the profession's most prominent black educator. Over time, Wakeman's position concerning the race problem in libraries became increasingly similar to Moon's, a point Moon confirmed in *LJ* in June 1961: "Some readers seem to have made much of the division between Lj and WLB on the subject of segregation of libraries. Let it be said now that, except in one or two matters of detail, there is no basic difference between us; in all the essentials we are absolutely in accord." Nevertheless, Wakeman felt constricted, lacking the same solid support at the Wilson Company that Moon enjoyed at Bowker: "John was trying hard to deal with segregation issues, as I was," recalled Moon, "but the leadership at Wilson was always very stuffy, and I know that some of his editorials were watered down." Toward the end of 1962

Wakeman gave up his editorship, returning to England after three eventful years at *WLB*'s helm; the fact that his wife disliked living in America also figured in the decision. (The Moons hosted a farewell party for the Wakemans, at which John, under the influence, insisted on singing "Moon River.") Wakeman's successor at *WLB*, Kathleen Molz, showed little interest in the silent subject, or most social issues for that matter. According to Moon, "Kathleen wasn't that kind of editor; she was a good editor but she wanted to turn the *Wilson Bulletin* into the *Atlantic Monthly*."

One major library periodical that disappointed — but did not surprise — the integrationist forces was the *ALA Bulletin*, the official journal of the American Library Association, which seemed timid and defensive about the race issue throughout the years of conflict and controversy. Editor Samray Smith's first editorial on the subject (in June 1961) dismissed those calling on ALA to more vigorously oppose library segregation as "a small but vocal element of the membership." Smith continued, "It is a necessary task to point out why the ALA is not doing and cannot now do some of the things demanded of it." Moon, who publicly bashed the editorial as "terribly negative," remembered Smith as an editor who made "limp excuses for everything. It was pathetic."

The Problem Metastasizes

The race problem in American libraries eventually proved to be more pervasive and bewildering than anyone could have foreseen when Moon and Wakeman first publicized it in 1960. The most obvious manifestation — officially segregated service in the South — soon grew to include allegations of de facto segregation in the North, a much muddier construct. Northern librarians tended to dismiss such charges as diversionary or stalling tactics by their Southern brethren, but outright refutation often proved difficult if not impossible. Why? Because such allegations usually contained at least a kernel of truth, de facto segregation being just as much a fact of life in the North as the de jure variety was in the South. Around the same time another ticklish question arose: should not libraries that discriminate on the basis of race be denied membership in the American Library Association?

Like a pernicious tumor, the race problem spread into yet another area of the library body politic when Virginia Lacy Jones, dean of the library school at Atlanta University (now Clark Atlanta), revealed to a national audience (in *WLB*, May 1961) that she was unable to join the Georgia Library Association because of the color of her skin. In an editorial entitled "Internal Integration," Moon put the issue in stark perspective: "Not only do we have segregated libraries— we have segregated library associations too. When the dean of a library school is refused membership in her own state library association, it is hard to believe that there can be any other reason than racial discrimination *within the profession*."

The profession — leaders and rank and file alike — spent much time and energy during the next half-dozen years or so grappling with and fighting over the twin dilemmas of segregated libraries and segregated library associations. Two principal battlegrounds emerged: the library press, with *LJ* leading the charge, aided and abetted by *WLB* while Wakeman was editor and on occasion Eshelman's *California Librarian* and Berry's *Bay State Librarian*; and the floor at ALA meetings, most notably membership meetings, which in Moon's words "came more and more to resemble a gladiator's arena" during numberless debates on the subject.

A large cast of characters interacted in these struggles, ranging from ALA bigwigs and bureaucrats to ordinary librarians from every corner of the country, all trying to come to grips one way or another with the reality of racial discrimination in their profession. At the center of it all, quite improbably, stood Eric Moon, a white English librarian of working-class ancestry and modest formal education who had come, unheralded, to live and work in the United States just a short time before. Not only was he the person most responsible for initiating the debate about segregation in American libraries and librarianship, he tenaciously pursued the subject for years as a crusading library journalist and outspoken member of ALA. Moon did not win every argument or battle, nor did he always get the particulars exactly right, but his contribution to the fight to integrate both libraries and library associations in the American South in the 1960s was immense. It was without doubt the defining experience of his career.

The Fight to Integrate Southern Libraries

Once the silent subject had been exploded, most librarians looked to ALA for leadership to correct or ameliorate what was clearly an unacceptable situation. Instead, their national association gave them equivocation and pretty words. After "considerable study for some time"— a damning public admission by Frances Lander Spain, ALA president for the year 1960-61— a Special ALA Committee on Civil Liberties finally succeeded in amending the Library Bill of Rights to read, "The rights of an individual to the use of a library should not be denied or abridged because of his race, religion, national origins, or political views." Moon and other liberals on the race question welcomed this long overdue declaration, but continued to fault ALA for failing to take specific action — action with teeth — to try to end library segregation in the South.

As criticism of ALA's tepid efforts mounted, association leaders became increasingly testy. Mrs. Spain vented her frustration in a letter to *LJ*: "I was amazed that members of the American Library Association, as indicated by the materials appearing in recent issues of Lj, are unaware of the position that the Association has taken repeatedly on freedom to read, access to libraries, and segregation. The Association is not a regulatory body, but it has unhesitatingly declared its stand in these matters." The president of ALA seemed to be saying that noble sentiments were all the association had to offer. Again, civil rights activists in the profession were pleased to know that ALA's heart was in the right place — but what about its head? The clamor for substantive action to deal with the problem continued.

At the association's 1961 annual conference, held that summer in Cleveland, the Intellectual Freedom Committee attempted to respond to such demands, offering two proposals that, if approved, would put real pressure on segregationists to change their behavior. The first would require ALA to take "every appropriate action" to determine if affiliated state associations (called chapters) were in compliance with ALA's new policy on racial discrimination as stated in the recently amended Library Bill of Rights. The second, and stronger, proposal would expel libraries practicing segregation from the association; libraries applying for ALA membership in the future would "be required to state in writing that no discrimination is practiced against users on the basis of race, religion or personal beliefs."

At the association's Midwinter meeting in early 1962 the Executive Board (ALA's management team and wielder of considerable behind-the-scenes power) advised the Council (the organization's representative policymaking body) to reject the IFC's proposals because such "drastic action" was "neither wise, helpful, nor possible of implementation at this time." A firestorm of criticism ensued. The Executive Board appeared to be more concerned about losing Southern members and financial support than it did finding ways to end segregation. Lawrence Clark Powell, a longtime supporter of civil rights, lambasted the board's written advisory as "a monstrously cynical statement, a confession of moral bankruptcy." Said Powell, "If we're a professional group, we have a moral responsibility to take a position of leadership, to say to our friends in the South and all over the world, this is what we stand for. If we don't, the status quo is likely to remain for another hundred years." Others accused the board of intellectual dishonesty and "weasel words." The Council, which normally went along with whatever the Executive Board wanted, demurred this time. Moon later noted, "Even the Council couldn't go along with this barren refusal to recognize the basic issues involved, and for once withheld its rubber stamp."

Revised versions of the IFC proposals were debated and eventually adopted by the Council at ALA's 1962 annual conference, held in warm Miami Beach. The new policy mandated that ALA "Urge libraries which are institutional members not to discriminate among users on the basis of race, religion, or personal belief, and if such discrimination now exists to bring it to an end as speedily as possible." This was a far cry from the original resolution, which called for the expulsion of member libraries that refused to integrate. Concerning state associations, the new policy required chapters to "certify" their compliance with all ALA policies, including those prohibiting racial discrimination. Segregated chapters "may request of the Council postponement of application of this provision for a period of time not to exceed three years. If they are unable to do so, or the Council is not satisfied that they are following the policies prescribed, such chapters shall be asked to withdraw until the provisions can be complied with."

Moon participated actively in the heated and frequently muddled deliberations resulting in the Miami Beach decrees, which were codified in a lengthy policy statement. He expressed satisfaction with the outcome: "What has finally emerged from this prolonged debate," he wrote in his report on the conference, "is, in our view, a document of conscience, firmer and more positive, at least in the section dealing with chapter status, than anything ALA has yet produced in this terribly sensitive and involved area of discrimination." Though he did not say so here, Moon was relieved that the IFC's original proposal to boot segregated libraries out of ALA had been defanged. He opposed *all* requirements for personal or institutional membership in ALA, save for payment of dues, contending that the association's strength would be diminished if it began excluding members, no matter how cogent the reason. The expulsion issue, however, was not dead; it would return several years later, bringing Moon into direct conflict with liberal allies and a wily opponent named Eli Oboler.

Access Study Debacle; or, Sandbagged by Conservatives

The policy on discrimination adopted at the 1962 Miami Beach conference also contained a provision requiring ALA to "Pursue with diligence the study of access to libraries so that factual data on this subject [racial discrimination] is collected." A study along these lines had been suggested earlier by Moon, Dorothy Bendix, and Bill Eshelman, among others. The idea was to obtain accurate, documented information about library segregation in the South so that future discussions and actions by association members would be based on fact rather than hearsay or anecdotal evidence. The profession needed to know "precisely," declared Moon in a March 1961 editorial, "which libraries are still segregated, which libraries claim to be [integrated] but still practice variations of discrimination, and which libraries have managed to integrate quietly in recent years." A few months later IFC chair Archie McNeal (library director at the University of Miami in Florida) announced that his committee had developed a plan for just such a survey, though its scope was broader than that envisioned by Moon, et al. The IFC study would encompass "freedom of access to materials in libraries throughout the United States."

This was the model for the "Access Study" (as it came to be known) that the Executive Board approved and Council ratified in Miami Beach. Functionaries at ALA proceeded with rare alacrity to implement the project, first securing funding from foundation and corporate sources, including the Bowker Company, and then hiring International Research Associates, Inc. (INRA), to undertake the actual work. This outside research firm, which agreed to do the study as expeditiously as possible, managed to complete the research phase in just six months, and by August 1963 — little more than a year after the Miami Beach conference — it had a 150-page report entitled *Access to Public Libraries* ready for distribution to ALA members. In addition, the study's project director, INRA's Robert W. Brown, agreed to present a prepublication summary of the study's findings in July at the association's annual conference.

Brown's presentation, Moon wrote in *LJ*, "electrified the conference with controversy." It turned out that *Access to Public Libraries* concentrated on de facto segregation in libraries in such places as Detroit, Philadelphia, and Washington, D.C., while glossing over or minimizing de jure segregation in Dixie. In a section of the report dealing with branch libraries in ten large cities around the country, for example, INRA researchers found that only San Francisco was "immune from 'de facto' racial discrimination in the location and resources of public library branches." Big city librarians in the North were hopping mad. In an acrimonious exchange with Brown, Ralph

Ulveling, Detroit's library director, disputed the report's conclusions, growling as he sat down, "This study will be of no help and no service to librarianship, believe me, sir." Emerson Greenaway, Philadelphia's chief, told Brown, "It seems that you need to get your glasses out again and I need to get my thinking cap on again."

Moon provided *LJ* readers with a detailed analysis of the full report after its publication in August. In a long editorial in the December 15, 1963, issue he disputed INRA's findings and methodology, while pointing out that "The fault lies not nearly entirely with INRA." Part of the problem with the Access Study, Moon concluded, was due to ALA's insistence that "access" be defined to include such nonracial "digressions" as restrictions on student use of libraries. He also criticized ALA's decision to include the whole country in the study instead of limiting it to the South, "where it was clear that direct discrimination was most prevalent and stringent." He continued:

The very term "access" was the beginning of the process of dilution (like so much that was to follow, and like the phraseology of the report of the Access Study, the term had many connotations): the real purpose, it seemed, had to be camouflaged in some kind of research neutralism and respectability. The proposal finally approved by the ALA Executive Board expressed concern "about the Negro and the restrictions still imposed on him in certain areas," but added, "the problem is not limited to one minority group or to one geographical area."

In a sense this was true, but it was also an avoidance of another truth, that the most acute and obvious problem was precisely the restrictions placed upon the Negro reader in particular, and particularly in one geographical area. Nevertheless, diplomacy quickly prevailed over common sense, and we found ourselves faced with a study involving all 50 states and bringing under the research umbrella a variety of digressions.

Moon then documented the study's biased methods and misleading inferences:

While rooting for malpractice in the North, determined to find it whether it is there or no, the surveyors have done their best to present the Southern situation in a kindly light. No one objects to sympathetic reporting of course, providing it is done within the bounds of reasonable accuracy. But is it?

In an appendix, the report provides a "List of Integrated Public Libraries," all located in "the eleven states of the Confederacy." Now admittedly, the report also defines its terms— in a footnote—as follows: "The term 'integrated' is used in this listing to indicate library systems in which the main library is accessible to members of all races. Many of these libraries, however, are not *fully* integrated in the sense that they provide more restricted services for one group of the population than for another."

The surveyors are not kidding! But they don't indicate in any way which of those libraries on the list impose some of the most unpleasant restrictions or perpetrate various indignities on their Negro readers. There in the appendix, proudly listed as "integrated," are Albany, Georgia, Montgomery, Alabama, and Danville, Virginia, where various forms of insidious maneuvering like so-called vertical or horizontal "integration" are still in force to remind Negro readers that they use these libraries on sufferance. Footnote or no, the use of the word "integrated" to describe these situations is laughable.

Access to Public Libraries was, observed Moon at the end of his lengthy critique, a "disaster." In the long run the flawed INRA study had no lasting historical consequence, though at the time it did temporarily slow down the fight to integrate libraries in the South by diverting the profession's attention away from the main problem area. Coincidentally, the study's skewed results frustrated and demoralized liberal librarians, who saw it as yet another successful rearguard action by segregationists and their friends at ALA.

In this case the conservatives who controlled ALA cleverly used the trappings of social science to outfox—perhaps sandbag is a better word—the profession's civil rights activists, including the usually politically savvy editor of *LJ*. The same people who tried to muzzle Moon or get him fired used the study as a means of sticking it to the integrationists. Moon knew from earlier experience in England that library associations customarily resist rather than embrace change. The Access Study debacle reinforced his growing sense that quite possibly the leaders of the American Library Association had an even more recalcitrant mind-set than those who ruled the Library Association in the UK. But in the 1950s in England he had had relatively little power to effect real change, whereas in the 1960s in the United States he had the resources of *LJ* and the R.R. Bowker Company on his side. Though the Access Study was a humbling defeat, its lessons were not lost on Moon.

Firm Allies

While some conspired to hide or ignore or blur the truth about racial bigotry in American libraries in the 1960s, Moon worked hard to provide *LJ* readers with a realistic picture of what was happening in the South, where Jim Crow had been a way of life for nearly a century and the worst indignities of segregation continued to occur, the Access Study notwithstanding. As soon as he decided to deal with the silent subject he began looking around for librarians—most particularly black librarians—who might be willing to help him, mainly by serving as *LJ*'s eyes and ears at the state and local levels. He wanted most urgently to expand the magazine's news coverage of racial problems, but to do so he needed people in the field to alert him about what was going on and to feed him the essential facts. At first he got nowhere with the black library community. Being white, foreign, and new to the American profession equaled zero credibility: black librarians could not help but wonder who this guy was and what his motives were. Could he be trusted? Would he soon be in bed with the white conservative Establishment? Maybe he was already?

But the explosive December 15, 1960, issue featuring Estes' exposé, the moving excerpt from Wright's *Black Boy*, and Moon's own unequivocal editorial calling for strong action against segregation left no doubt about where *LJ*'s editor stood on the matter of race and libraries or his understanding of the issues involved. Not long after that he met and developed a synergistic relationship with Elonnie (E.J.) Josey, an intelligent, sensitive, dynamic black librarian at Savannah State College in Georgia.

Josey, who would become the preeminent African American librarian of his generation, was roughly Moon's age (late thirties) when they met, and he had much the same competitive drive. Though they came from entirely different backgrounds and viewed the race problem through vastly different lenses, both men believed fervently and irrevocably that segregation had no place in the American system and, what's more, both were willing to—and did—put their careers on the line for that belief. Certainly after December 15, 1960, Josey had no qualms about embracing Moon as a brother in the fight against racial inequality. He looked upon Moon's "Silent Subject" editorial as manna from library heaven: "That editorial alone was worth a million dollars, if we were to give monetary value to the fight for equal opportunity and equal access for Black people to libraries." And when he first met Moon in the flesh (at ALA in 1961) Josey saw his white mirror image: "He seemed fearless. He seemed to speak honestly about the race question. I trusted him. We needed a man like Moon."

With Josey's active cooperation, Moon created an informal network of librarians and community leaders, mostly black, that over the years furnished him with much valuable grassroots information about the library scene in the South. "Certainly, my close connection with E.J. stemmed from the silent subject," said Moon. "That's when the E.J.-Moon alliance was established and from that point on we were in constant touch. He helped me get information about the state of segregation in the South. He put me in touch with people who otherwise surely would not have talked to me, a white journalist. We were frequently together on the floor of ALA fighting for the same issues, frequently seconding each other's motions, and so on. We became very firm allies."

As a result, *LJ* became the principal source for news, features, and editorial comment about civil rights issues in the profession in the 1960s. Moon also tapped his black contacts for opinions and ideas about various race-related developments, such as the Access Study controversy. The Josey-Moon collaboration, born out of self-interest on the part of both men, had a far-reaching impact on American librarianship, contributing enormously to enhancing the racial sensibilities of countless librarians and to the eventual demise of official library segregation in the South.

Fight to Integrate Southern Library Associations

In 1961 many American librarians were surprised to learn that an unspecified number of Southern state library associations accepted white members only; that the Georgia Library Association, for instance, refused to admit black librarians, including well-known leaders such as Virginia Lacy Jones and E.J. Josey. Writing in *WLB* in a symposium edited by John Wakeman entitled "Segregation in Libraries: Negro Librarians Give Their Views," Jones described the situation in crystal clear terms: "It is unfortunate that in some Southern states Negro librarians may not belong to state library associations. Last year my application for membership in the Georgia Library Association was turned down and my check for dues was returned with a letter stating that the Executive Board of the Association had tabled the matter of my holding membership. I wrote back to ask when a definite decision would be made and after a year I still have no answer."

In 1962, ALA took uncharacteristically strong action against affiliated associations, or chapters, that practiced segregation, informing them in so many words to shape up on the race issue or ship out of the national association. "War," said Moon, "had thus been officially declared on the library association front." By 1964 all chapters reported being in compliance with ALA's integration policy except Louisiana and Mississippi, which chose expulsion from the association rather than accept Negroes as members. Two other state associations, Alabama and Georgia, also remained segregated but were not ALA chapters.

The efforts by ALA to pressure state associations to integrate obviously had had some success but just as obviously had failed to move the most hard-core cases; and Alabama and Georgia, not being affiliated with ALA, appeared to be immune from any action the national association might take. By the time ALA's 1964 annual conference met (in St. Louis), it was clear to civil rights activists that, in Moon's words, "more heat had to be applied." The "heat" came at a membership meeting in the form of a motion by Josey, seconded by Moon, stipulating "That all ALA officers and ALA staff members should refrain from attending, in their official capacity or at the expense of ALA, the meetings of any state associations which are unable to meet fully the requirements of chapter status in ALA." Josey prefaced his motion by noting that the main speaker at a recent meeting of the Georgia Library Association — the *segregated* Georgia Library Association — had been a high ranking official of ALA. The intent of the motion was to prohibit segregated state associations from drawing on the resources of ALA for programs, workshops, training sessions, and the like, thus ostracizing said associations professionally and punishing them financially.

Josey, who had a reputation as a "hothead" and "troublemaker" among some white as well as some conservative black librarians, came to the St. Louis conference in a state of high emotion: President Johnson was set to sign the historic 1964 Civil Rights Act that same week. But as soon as he arrived at the conference he learned that ALA had apparently "honored" the Mississippi Library Association — the *segregated* Mississippi Library Association — with an award for its National Library Week activities. Josey: "I exploded! I was seething with anger, for I remembered that three civil rights workers — Andrew Goodman, James Chaney, and Michael Schwerner — had been murdered and lay dead and buried somewhere in Mississippi, their bodies not yet even discovered. I also remembered that the Mississippi Library Association had withdrawn from ALA rather than give membership to Negro librarians."

In this charged atmosphere Josey made his motion and then, in his words, "The shit hit the fan." Moon's conference report in *LJ* described the scene:

> The motion set off one of the longest and most interesting debates which this reporter has witnessed at an ALA conference. At microphones around the hall speakers were lined up for participation, and most were lined up behind Josey.
>
> The parade was too long to be recorded in full here, but the first real countermove came from Archie McNeal, retiring chairman of the Intellectual Freedom Committee, who felt Josey had "a sound point," but added, "The idea has just come up. I don't want to see the Association take precipitous action which might have detrimental effects." McNeal moved that the motion be referred to the Executive Committee [Board] or the Intellectual Freedom Committee at the next Midwinter Conference. Dorothy Bendix (Drexel) quickly pointed out that this would mean a whole year's delay before the membership could again vote on the matter.

But McNeal's amendment had found a seconder and the debate pursued the immediate question of "to delay or not to delay." Most dramas have a heroine as well as a hero, and if Josey was the male lead, the leading lady in this show came from Georgia too. Shortly after Lucile Nix of Georgia had supported delay because "Georgia is working on the problem" and "recent federal legislation may change the picture," there came to the microphone another lady from the Peach State.

That lady, the heroine of the debate, was Ruth Walling, a well regarded white librarian from Emory University in Atlanta who earlier in the week had received a major ALA award. Walling calmly but firmly declared her support for the Josey motion, pointing out that its adoption would "help all the states which have a similar problem." Walling's support turned the tide in favor of Josey's motion. "This quiet declaration of faith," reported Moon, "was so much in contrast to the other prophecies of doom from the South that the ultimate result of the debate never seemed in much doubt beyond this point." In due course McNeal's amendment to delay was defeated and motion passed "overwhelmingly." To top it off, Moon featured Josey and Walling on the cover of the August 1964 issue of *LJ*, depicting them as "Two Stars from Georgia."

But most dramas also have a villain, and at ALA's Midwinter meeting the following January the Executive Board and Council vied for the honor. Up to its old obstructionist tricks, the board weakened the Josey resolution by narrowing the definition of "all ALA officers" to include only the president, president-elect, second vice president, executive director, and treasurer — a questionable interpretation, but one unanimously endorsed by a docile Council. Moon, in high dudgeon, spoke for many when he wrote, "The membership of the American Library Association should mark down the date, January 27, 1965, as a gray day for democracy. This was the day on which its elected representatives, the ALA Council, refused (or to put it mildly, failed) to implement the declared wishes of the membership on a basic matter of principle."

But in the end this latest attempt by the ALA leadership to thwart the will of civil rights advocates mattered little. However much diehard segregationists did not want to face it, time had run out on Jim Crow in all areas of public intercourse in the South. The 1964 Civil Rights Act was now the law of the land, and the Voting Rights Act of 1965 followed within a matter of months. Soon schools, restaurants, drinking fountains, hotels and motels, restrooms, public transportation, swimming pools, theaters and movie houses, *and*, yes, libraries were desegregated, in most cases without incident, Jim Crow quietly disappearing like a snake down a hole. Integration of the renegade state library associations became only a matter of time, and by 1966 all four — Alabama, Georgia, Louisiana, and Mississippi — had bowed to the inevitable, agreeing to admit black members.

A heartwarming incident occurred toward the end of the bitter fight to integrate Southern library associations. At the 1965 ALA Midwinter meeting a Council member from Georgia announced from the floor that Mr. E.J. Josey had been accepted as the first black member of the Georgia Library Association. Josey, who had no advance warning of this, was stunned. According to Moon, the announcement was greeted with "thunderous applause." And in private — there were surely tears of joy and vindication.

Déjà Vu

The last big battle librarians fought over de jure segregation involved an old question: shouldn't libraries that discriminate on the basis of race be barred from membership in ALA? This deceptively simple idea first surfaced in 1961 at the Cleveland conference when the IFC proposed that segregated libraries be excluded from the association, a recommendation that ultimately got watered down to a toothless exhortation not to discriminate. Four years later at ALA's 1965 conference (in Detroit) the question came up again, raised by Eli Oboler, librarian at Idaho State University in Pocatello. Oboler, an energetic man with a voracious appetite for the limelight who made a name for himself in the 1960s and 1970s as a frequent commentator on hot-button issues confronting the profession, submitted a motion that would amend ALA's Constitution to read, "Any library or other organization interested in library service and librarianship which does not discriminate among users on the basis of race, religion, or personal belief may become a member upon payment of the dues provided for in the By-laws."

The Oboler motion, introduced at a membership meeting in Detroit's Cobo Hall, stimulated considerable discussion but no real opposition. In his report on the conference, Moon informed *LJ* readers, "It seemed clear that we have reached a point in ALA where no one will speak against a civil rights proposal, whether it be logical or not, defensible or not, possible to implement or not. The motion passed easily, without a dissenting vote." Whereupon the ALA Council immediately went into session and appointed a committee, chaired by the eminent Verner Clapp (longtime head of the Council on Library Resources), to review the amendment, the next step in the constitutional revision process. The committee was instructed to make its recommendation to the Executive Board reasonably quickly, so the amendment resolution could be voted on — and doubtless passed — by Council at its Midwinter meeting in early 1966. An emotional tide swept through the Detroit conference: suddenly everyone — including ALA's most conservative leaders — wanted on the integration bandwagon.

Moon had opposed ousting segregated libraries from the association in 1961 and he had not changed his mind since, though now he was going against the popular — and liberal — will. In a tortured editorial entitled "Discrimination at Detroit" he explained his position, acknowledging at the outset that some might think "that we [Moon] are no longer so hot on the integration issue as we once were." Essentially, Moon opposed the Oboler resolution because it "would actually *reverse* the association's long-standing open-door policy…. Now, for the first time, we are being asked to accept a revision of that bylaw to read 'any person, library, etc. *except…*.' Whenever you start talking about exceptions, it is wise to consider whether this does not open the door to other or future exceptions." Toward the end of the editorial Moon confessed to being torn:

This is not an easy editorial to write. All our emotions pull in the direction of the Detroit [Oboler] resolution, but our reason warns against acting without much thought of where actions lead, even by implication. Laws or regulations or policies which are sentimentally fine but which cannot be implemented undermine rather than strengthen the purpose of the body which passes them. "The law is an ass," Charles Dickens once said, and he surely had in mind the often insupportable 19th Century laws that the British authorities were charged to enforce. We should not like to see ALA's increasingly commendable position on civil rights and civil liberties weakened by asininities.

Oboler relished pen-to-pen combat and he responded to Moon's comments with a blistering attack, accusing *LJ*'s editor of "several errors," including faulty logic and introduction of "a malodorous red herring." He also charged that Moon "quite exaggeratedly" misconstrued a "rather well-known statement" in his zeal to prove a point:

Surely Mr. Moon is literateur enough to know that Charles Dickens never said "the law is an ass." It was Mr. Bumble, the sadistic, sneaky, thievish [here Moon inserted a "sic"] beadle of Oliver Twist's workhouse, who said this, and in reply to the statement that "the law supposes that your wife acts under your direction." Mr. Bumble replied: "If the law supposes that, the law is a (not "an" as Mr. Moon misquotes) ass, an idiot." How can this be quoted out of context to apply to "the often insupportable 19th Century laws that the British authorities were charged to enforce"?

At the 1966 Midwinter meeting the Clapp committee recommended that the Executive Board reject Oboler's amendment to ALA's Constitution, but the board instead rejected the committee's advice, voting 8 to 4 in support of the amendment. Council, however, had the final say and, after much debate, including a windy and mostly ineffectual presentation by the garrulous Oboler, the amendment to exclude segregated libraries from institutional membership in ALA was defeated, largely for the reasons advanced by Moon. One councilor who had a decisive impact on the debate was Albert (A.P) Marshall, library director at Lincoln University. Marshall, a black librarian, conceded that in the emotional atmosphere of the Detroit conference he had supported the Oboler motion, but "After time to reflect on what is good for ALA and for *all* members, I did not feel this proposal was right." To applause, he urged "repudiation" of the amendment.

Eli Oboler never forgot nor forgave Moon's opposition to his efforts to toss segregated libraries out of ALA, and it was fated that the two men would tangle again. Interestingly, years later, after Oboler was dead, Moon had a change of heart, explaining that he had come to believe segregated libraries *should have been expelled* from ALA in the 1960s: "Looking back, I think Eli was right and I was wrong. At the time I could not see suddenly saying, in an ALA that was open to anybody or any institution 'interested in libraries,' that if your library was not integrated you couldn't join. As I look back, it seems strange to me why I took that position, because I was absolute on the whole question of segregation. I spelled out my reasons then, but today they don't make much sense to me." This was one of few times this writer heard Moon admit that he might have been mistaken or wrong about something. It was a refreshing moment.

Southern Hospitality

His unrelenting advocacy of civil rights for black library users and librarians made Moon an anathema to white Southerners who believed in segregation yesterday, today, and tomorrow. Though never physically attacked, he received threats and endured numerous verbal assaults while serving as editor of *LJ*. For instance, Southern ire flared at the St. Louis conference after the vote on Josey's motion to prohibit ALA officers and staff from participating in programs at segregated state associations. Moon: "The fallout from this motion was dirty, noisy, and immediate. One friend of mine from one of the four affected state associations came over and cursed E.J. and me royally. 'You guys have just screwed up my entire Fall program,' she said. 'But that was the idea,' I replied. The remainder of the conversation is unprintable."

In another instance his mere presence caused a colleague, Mary Lee Bundy, to be mistreated. Moon and Bundy, a library science professor at the University of Maryland, were a cocktail party at an ALA conference happily minding their own business when a "brigade of Southern dragons" arrived. Moon:

> We walked in, got our drinks, and sat down on the couch. We were talking quietly when three or four lady battle-ax state librarians, all from the South, came marching into the room. Some of them became vitriolic every time they saw me. I would only have to appear at an ALA meeting and they would zoom in on me — it was sort of like being attacked by amazons. They saw me sitting with Mary Lee and zoomed right in and started their usual diatribe. Mary Lee listened to this for a little while and then said, "Eric, I'm going to get another drink and I'll see you later." And they just picked her up and literally threw her out in the hallway. She hadn't done a thing, but she was with me. This was the way it was.

For the record, Bundy remembered the set-to somewhat differently. In a footnote to an interview Frederick Stielow did with Moon (published in the book *Activism in American Librarianship, 1962–1973*), Stielow writes that Bundy (who is no longer alive) recalled "such epithets as 'dirty yellow journalist' being directed at Moon, but the assault was more of someone throwing a foreign object and hitting her."

Another time "Judge" Leander Perez, for many years the political boss of Plaquemines Parish in Louisiana and a truly benighted son of the South, threatened to have Moon put in a dungeon-like jail full of snakes if he continued making detrimental comments about Perez and his pronouncements on race. It seems the Judge — an unreconstructed segregationist — ordered the parish (or county) librarian not to buy any book by or about Franklin or Eleanor Roosevelt, any book published by or about the United Nations, any book by or about a Negro writer, or any book that portrayed the black race in a positive light. Moon publicly condemned this policy as "local totalitarianism at its most obvious, absurd, and repellent," thus earning himself a grim warning from Plaquemines Parish's top redneck. It sounds humorous today but at the time it wasn't funny.

In 1965, at the tail end of the battle over segregated state associations, Robert Severance, president of the Alabama Library Association, invited Moon to speak at the group's annual meeting, held that year in May in downtown Mobile at the Admiral Semmes Hotel. Severance, a progressive on race relations, wanted Moon to witness history — the association's first ever integrated conference. Moon recalled, "I went down there and when I checked into the hotel there was a note from Bob Severance inviting me to his suite after I got settled in. So I went up and hanging around the door to Bob's suite was a tough looking man. He said, 'My name is Luther Lee. I'm a segregationist.

What are you going to do about it?' I said, 'Not a thing. I don't have time to waste on fools' and went into the suite." Later that evening, after returning to his room, Moon received a threatening phone call, warning him, "You better get out of town or you may not live." Similar calls, Moon said, were repeated every hour on the hour during his stay in Mobile. "I didn't take them very seriously," he recalled, "but you do tend to start looking around…"

Moon Rewarded

In 1966 Moon received the Savannah State College Library Award, given annually for distinguished service to librarianship. The award, presented by his friend and ally E.J. Josey, cited Moon not only for his accomplishments as editor of *Library Journal* but for having "sensitized the library profession to many of its neglected obligations, including the democratization of the American Library Association" and for "pointing up many unexplored areas of librarianship that are not problems but golden opportunities."

While in Savannah to claim his award Moon was accused of being a "goddamn Yankee," which amused him mightily:

E.J. put me up in a lily-white hotel in Savannah. When I got there he told me he had arranged a television interview for me later that day with a guy who had an hour-long interview program — he wanted to interview me about censorship. So I went along to the TV station and did a rousing interview, being very controversial, criticizing the Georgia state censorship board and so on. Earlier, I had given a speech over at the college, to which all sorts of people came, including many of the area's white librarians who had never been to Savannah State College before. I criticized the white librarians for coming out when I was there but not other times when there were so many potential readers for them to reach that they had ignored for all these years. E.J. was delighted with this.

I went back to the hotel after all this to clean up and wait for E.J., who was coming by to pick me up to go to a party or dinner. I was sitting in the lobby waiting for E.J. when I saw this guy circling around. Finally he came over to me and said in this very Southern voice, "Didn't I see you on television earlier today? That was some pretty bad stuff you were saying." We got into a discussion about the program and eventually he asked where I was from, and I said New York. And he said, "A goddamn Yankee! I thought so." I broke into gales of laughter, and he said, "What's so funny?" and I said "I've never been called a goddamn Yankee before in my life." About that time E.J, the head of the Savannah NAACP, and two other black guys came through the door and up to me and said, "Eric, we're ready." The guy looked at me and said, "Now I understand."

Of all the honors Moon received during his remarkable career, the Savannah Award was the one that meant the most.

– 10 –

Remaking Library Journalism: Techniques

Revolutionary Decade

Historians like to sum up memorable decades in a single adjective, as in the "gay" nineties or "roaring" twenties. In the United States, no decade since World War II has had a more distinctive personality or lasting impact on the country's psyche than the "revolutionary" sixties—a traumatic, mutinous, intoxicating, wildly fecund time marked by the hippy phenomenon, the Kennedys, the civil rights movement, shocking political assassinations, frightening Cold War confrontations, wondrous space explorations culminating in humans going to the moon, the misbegotten presidency of LBJ, the War on Poverty, the war in Vietnam, student protests, the Yippies, urban riots, Dr. King, the Black Panthers, drugs/LSD, the sexual revolution, women's liberation, the Beatles, Woodstock, Janis, Jimi, love beads, bell-bottoms, and the bourgeoisification of previously taboo street language, including the once infamous f-word.

As the stodgy 1950s, personified by Dwight Eisenhower, an elderly military hero-cum-president who garbled his syntax in public and read westerns in private, gave way to the new decade and its earliest champion, the vigorous, articulate, boyishly magnetic John Kennedy, many Americans, especially the young, were ripe for change. Extreme, mind-blowing change. They became foot soldiers in the struggle for equality for black people, enlistees in the noble Peace Corps, flower children high on countercultural fantasies, swaggering cadre demonstrating and seizing buildings on college campuses. They were the precipitators of an inchoate rebellion against war, racism, material greed, political deceit, sexual repression, and autocratic authority everywhere. Women too began to rebel, challenging the male-dominated power structure, and homosexuals started the painful process of coming out and insisting on their rights. And the environmental movement and electronic information age had their first glimmerings in the 1960s, along with hundreds of other causes and creations, some great, some small, and some that were, frankly, weird.

Library Journal *Joins the Revolution*

Eric Moon, his luck and timing impeccable, arrived at *Library Journal* just as the decade was getting underway. Plunked down in New York City after a year and a half in Newfoundland, *LJ*'s new editor felt like a time-traveler in a science fiction novel who had just hurtled through the infinity of space at warp speed, going from dark to light, from dread to joy. Oh, how he welcomed the companionable beat of the big city! Not only were New York's people, customs, landscape, weather, and raison d'être profoundly different from Newfoundland's, the American city and its urban satellites radiated an energy, a spirit, a warmth, a freedom not found nor even possible in the frozen Canadian province, at least from Moon's perspective. Furthermore, as he settled in at *LJ*, his sociopolitical antennae fully extended, straining to comprehend and master his new world as rapidly as possible, he sensed that transforming changes were in the offing. Of course he had no idea in early 1960 — no one did — just what form these changes might take, but from the beginning he was there: listening, observing, seeking, questioning, pushing, probing, provoking, recording, analyzing, scheming, participating.

It is not an exaggeration to say that Moon was made for the mayhem of the 1960s. All of his significant life experience up to that point — the working-class childhood on Ocean Island and in Southampton; the grammar school education as a poor scholarship student at Taunton's; the stepfather who taught him to value knowledge and to fight back, with fists if necessary; the first job as a meanly paid junior assistant at the local library; the introduction to amateur theater and avant-garde literature as a member of the idealistic Group; the innate allegiance to the Fabian socialist politics of the British Labour Party; the firsthand exposure to the miseries and contingencies of war; the two years spent studying library science at Loughborough, said to be "a school for revolution"; the varied work experience in public libraries in and around London after the war; the incessant association battles as both an emerging leader of the feisty AAL and strident critic of the archconservative LA; the spirited early articles and reviews published in library and book trade journals; the founding and editing of the lively library news sheet, *Liaison*; the affinity for and (unwitting?) emulation of the bad-mannered antiheroes found in the fiction of the Angry Young Men, in vogue in Britain in the 1950s; the permissive attitude toward sex; and, finally, the bleak months in Newfoundland after alienating the big boss and being arrested for drunk driving — all of these experiences coalesced to produce in Moon a library journalist singularly equipped to thrive in a period of monumental change. He was, as the cliché goes, in his element.

From his earliest days in libraries, Moon was in constant and open revolt against the narrow, pinched 3 × 5 card mentality so prevalent in the profession before and after World War II. He wanted a librarianship that was both responsive to and immersed in the broad social and political life of the community, an expansive librarianship that touched people's lives in a fundamental way, much as medicine, law, government, and education did. Like Melvil Dewey before him, he wanted to be part of a profession that had a major role in shaping the thought, imagination, and character of the society in which he lived and worked. What he did *not* want — what he emphatically rejected and fought against — was a librarianship dominated by smug conformists and sad milquetoasts seeking a comfortable refuge from the demands of the real world. It comes as no surprise, then, that when he got to *LJ* he soon began using the magazine to promote his own capacious vision of the profession.

Moon's philosophy of librarianship neatly dovetailed with his ideas about library journalism:

It is the job of the library journalist to explore any cause or phenomenon that affects or involves libraries. I believe that libraries are involved in society per se, and that actions such as Vietnam involved libraries. I believe that war affects libraries. I believe that racism affects libraries. Therefore the journalist has the responsibility to look at such things in terms of their impact on our profession, on library service, and deal with them. To me, it was disgraceful that for so many years the library press failed to express even an awareness that, in the case of race, there was a problem.

I wanted *Library Journal* to make more people realize that we had to think and act politically if librarianship was going to have a larger voice and better support. Certainly *LJ* was the first journal of its kind ever to be politically active to such an extent. For instance, we endorsed Johnson in 1964; we ran Kennedy and Johnson and Goldwater on the cover. No one had ever done stuff like this before.

After a brief period devoted to getting his bearings and gaining control of *LJ*'s editorial operation, Moon began putting his stamp on the magazine's contents. Before long, alert readers noticed that *LJ* was venturing into new territory, or when covering old ground, doing it in ways that were fresh and innovative. The journal, in the doldrums prior to Moon's appointment, started to take on a new luster, a new cogency. The worthy old mag was soon brimming with interesting ideas and strong convictions, some of which clashed with prevailing opinion and consequently irritated the profession's more conservative members, who began to wonder who this fellow Moon was and what he was up to. Dorothy Broderick's slashing attack on *Fiction Catalog* (a holy of holies) in the summer of 1960 served as a marker for *LJ*'s new direction.

Encouraged by the response to Broderick's article Moon moved on to other controversies, the most volatile and difficult being racism in libraries and the profession. The long, bitter, circuitous but ultimately successful fight against segregation in Southern libraries and library associations validated Moon's belief that library journalists had both a right and a responsibility to deal with human problems affecting the profession. This was essentially a new way of viewing the role of the library press. Until Moon took on the silent subject, no library periodical had ever presented sustained, aggressive reporting on a crucial social issue. Coincidentally, the fact that so many librarians from every part of the country responded with so much fervor (positive and negative) to *LJ*'s coverage of the civil rights struggle suggested that Moon's approach was not only good journalism but good business. As more and more readers were attracted to his brand of hard-hitting, socially aware reportage, *LJ*'s circulation and advertising revenues soared.

What Moon in fact discovered during his early years at *LJ* was that there were countless librarians out there who hungered for social and political relevance in their professional publications. These librarians disdained the repetitive fluff or "kettle of mush" (as one wag put it) that so often passed for library literature. They were tired of sunny how-I-run-my-library-good articles and sappy features about those doggone hilarious reference questions our staff received last year; they were turned off by puff pieces singing the praises of public relations exercises like National Library Week and ALA events that did nothing for ordinary librarians, the people who did the real work of the profession day in and day out. But now with Moon ensconced as editor of the oldest and best-known journal in the field, librarians inclined toward activism suddenly had a friend in high places. Not only was the new man at *LJ* ready, willing, and able to give them ink, he was eager to lead the charge. Though no one had the slightest suspicion at the time, library journalism was in for a radical remake the day Eric Moon first walked through the door at *LJ*.

Moon Versus the Censor

Over the course of his nine-year editorship Moon produced exactly 200 issues of *LJ* totaling more than 40,000 pages of magazine text. Among all that printed matter were memorable articles, symposia, editorials, conference reports, surveys, columns, and reviews on all sorts of topics, major and minor. In addition to the race problem a constant subject was censorship, which often focused on material of a sexual nature that someone found objectionable. Sex went public in the United States in the 1960s in a bold way. The pill, illicit drugs, rock music, miniskirts, increasingly risqué films and television programs, a thriving alternative press gleefully dedicated to offending middle-class rectitude, adult arrangements like wife swapping and open marriage, the nascent feminist movement — these and a hundred other cultural threads conspired to lubricate the American libido. In no time, Moon, who seemed at ease in this orgasmic atmosphere, had *LJ* in the thick of it.

The new sexual daring prompted countless battles between intellectual freedom advocates and opponents of obscenity and pornography, including celebrated court cases involving such blue classics as *Lady Chatterley's Lover*, *Tropic of Cancer*, and *Memoirs of a Woman of Pleasure* (*Fanny Hill*) — novels that by the end of the decade were finally able to be published and sold openly in North America after years of suppression. Moon read and admired these and similar books and was incensed that anyone would want to censor them. When British librarian David Gerard visited Moon at his home in New Jersey in 1967, he recalled, "How struck I was by Eric's current interest in censorship. I seem to remember he had quite a collection of material on that score — yes? Did this conceal a healthy appetite for scatology, I asked myself?" No doubt Moon had a taste for the scatological, but his chief interest in such publications was as works of literature that had suffered at the hands of censors.

Moon opposed censorship in all its guises: legal, extralegal, and self-imposed. He believed that, with a few well-established exceptions (such as defamation and military secrecy in wartime), any constraints on expression, no matter how distasteful or outrageous that expression might be, were detrimental to free and open debate, the lifeblood of the democratic process. What could be more inimical to the people's welfare — as well as the librarian's mission — than to deny the public access to certain information and ideas because some paternalistic authority (government, church, pressure group) deemed them immoral, sacrilegious, subversive, or in some other way dangerous or offensive? For Moon the operative word was access. "*Access*," he observed in a speech to the Westchester (New York) Library Association in May 1963, "lies not only at the heart of democracy. It is also the crux of librarianship — or rather, of library *service*. And it is in relation to access that censorship should be considered and defined. Censorship, then, becomes a matter of intent, the intention being to restrict unnecessarily access to a book, or a movie, or a magazine, or any of the other communication media."

Moon showed his colors immediately in *LJ*, reprinting two newspaper commentaries on censorship in his second issue (December 15, 1959) under the banner BOOKS ARE CENSORED BY TIMID LIBRARIANS. These blunt words left no doubt about where *LJ*'s new editor stood on the question. From that time on *LJ* almost always had some sort of censorship controversy boiling or brewing. The December 15, 1960, issue, for instance, carried a favorable review of *The First Freedom*, a collection of articles edited by Robert Downs and published by ALA that espoused the liberal position on intellectual freedom. The review brought a prickly response from the Rev. Charles Dollen, library director at the University of San Diego:

> Maybe the "censors" have some arguments that should be heard; maybe their right to freedom of speech is being abrogated. I have never seen their side given a fair or ample treatment in a library periodical.... Committees for decent literature need not propose censorship. They ask only for a refined and highly important degree of selectivity, plus punishment for those who traffic in the obscene. This trash certainly does more harm to young minds than narcotics do to bodies. Is it so wrong for parents and educators to be more concerned, therefore, about this crisis?

The Rev. Dollen's comments, which Moon published as a "Viewpoint" column, begat letters, some measured, some intemperate. Lloyd W. Griffin, who had written the review of *The First Freedom* that set Dollen off, replied with words exuding fairness and reason: "I am sure Lj has censored neither Father Dollen nor me; I hope he continues to enjoy the freedom to protest; and I trust that those who attempt to impose censorship — or whatever term they choose to call it — on the public without resort to judicial ruling will be combatted by librarians everywhere." On the other hand, Richard K. Burns, a public librarian in Virginia, weighed in with a delightful bit of casuistic invective: "The lopsided rationale intended to vindicate sophisticated censorship put forward by Rev. Dollen in your 'Viewpoint' feature is so inane and absurd as not to deserve rebuttal. I do hope, however, that the good man has received assurance of the sanctity of his 'first' freedom. Like all others, he has the further freedom to be wrong. No man, however, has the freedom to willfully inflict his stupidity upon the privilege and will of others."

Outbursts like these from Dollen and Burns were ambrosia to Moon. He knew that when people get riled they often impulsively say things that are impolitic or indiscreet or come across as pompous or harebrained. Such commentary stirs up other readers, who respond in kind, which stirs up more readers, which elicits more response, and on and on, until the debate plays itself out or, as sometimes happens, veers off in a new direction, possibly igniting (Moon hoped) another brouhaha, thus starting the process all over again. All during his years at *LJ* Moon deliberately — and adroitly — used controversial articles, reviews, letters, editorials, photos, etc. to stimulate reader interest and provoke response. Indeed, "response" became a yardstick he used to measure his effectiveness as editor:

If you get people annoyed they frequently will say things that they wouldn't say otherwise. If you write an editorial that doesn't put in all the ifs, ands, and buts, you leave room for response, which is what journalism ought to be about and what I wanted to do at *Library Journal*. I don't see the point of writing editorials that say, well on the one hand there's this, on the other hand there's that, and on the third hand, there's this. By the time you finish an editorial like that, everybody says, "Well, so what?" But if you write an editorial that says this is what I think and it doesn't give any other point of view — or admission that there might be any other point of view — then you get response.

Moon's objective was always to keep the editorial pot hot. A magazine bubbling with controversy did wonders for response, as well as the bottom line, a set of statistics never far from his mind. Yes, he recognized that indiscriminate or reckless use of controversy had dangers, such as unfairly sensationalizing or falsely polarizing, and thus distorting, an issue. But in the right editorial hands controversy — or *advocacy*— had the potential, he believed, to be a powerful journalistic tool for fostering honest debate, enhanced comprehension, and heightened sensibilities among serious readers. On a more visceral level he believed that keeping the pot hot rendered *LJ* a stronger force for the continuing education of librarians (an implicit objective of the magazine under Moon) than if he had ignored or downplayed polemical issues, as most of his counterparts did. Controversy, no matter what the subject, induced readers to peruse the pages of *LJ* with an interest and intensity they did not normally bring to other professional journals. Those caught up in *LJ*'s dialectics could not help but become better informed about the many concerns facing the profession and hence more knowledgeable, more articulate, and ultimately more successful librarians.

Moon, who had a deep-seated desire to convince everyone of the correctness of his position on everything, was at bottom an educator, and in the 1960s *LJ* was his classroom, his college. Figuratively, he assumed the role of master, or head tutor, a sort of Stokesian don whose duty it was to steer his students (i.e., readers) through the library thicket and on to the path of professional enlightenment. Underlying all his efforts was the desire to create a more dynamic profession, one in which librarians would take their rightful place among society's most influential people. Here's how Melvil Dewey, Moon's historical alter ego, expressed the same sentiment a century earlier: "The time *was* when a library was very like a museum, and a librarian was a mouser in musty books, and visitors looked with curious eyes at ancient tomes and manuscripts. The time *is* when a library is a school, and the librarian is in the highest sense a teacher, and the visitor is a reader among the books as a workman among his tools. Will any man deny to the high calling of such a librarianship the title of profession?"

Moon, in short, conducted his editorship as if he were the profession's guru at large. For nearly all of the 1960s—by any measure one of the most remarkable periods in American library history—he presided over a freewheeling dialogue in the pages of *LJ* in which the many difficulties, complexities, and challenges facing librarians in the postwar period were thoroughly aired. "Most of the crucial problems remain," he wrote in his farewell editorial (*LJ*, December 15, 1968), "but one aspect of change is that they have been brought out in the open for examination and discussion. And they are discussed with an urgency and passion that seemed to me, nine years ago, to be unhealthily and almost totally absent."

To keep censorship on the front burner after the Downs-Dollen rumpus had cooled, he published an article by the same Robert Downs, a distinguished academic librarian and intellectual freedom savant, that offered a candid assessment of a new book, *The Smut Peddlers* by James J. Kilpatrick, then editor of the Richmond *News Leader* and an increasingly visible national spokesman for conservative causes. Downs' lengthy critique, "Apologist for Censorship," appeared in *LJ* in June 1961 and, as expected, savaged Kilpatrick's book. Moon of course invited the aggrieved Kilpatrick to respond, an offer eagerly accepted. This produced a headline event—CENSORSHIP DEBATE—in the August issue in which the two men had at each other, no-holds-barred. Kilpatrick, a natural brawler who once used Shana Alexander as a sparring partner on network TV, won the bout on semantic points, aided by a low blow or two. Readers loved it. Roared Kilpatrick:

> For whatever it may be worth, now that your hatchet-man Downs has done his dirty work on my book, I would like to register my strong and emphatic protest against the total misrepresentation embodied in his article ["Apologist for Censorship"]. I am no longer astonished at the irrational and hysterical outcries of the professional liberal on the hustings, but I am amazed that so respected a magazine as *Library Journal* should have participated in publication of an article that resorts to every contemptible trick of the polemicist at work—guilt by association, exaggeration, misstatement of fact, and the use, ad nauseam, of ad hominem statements.
>
> Mr. Downs says that I emerged from research on my book, *The Smut Peddlers*, "embracing and condoning" various censorship groups "and advocating stringent repressive legislation." He lies. Nowhere in my book do I embrace these various groups.... Mr. Downs then goes on to make the flat and unqualified statement that in my book I "urge these busy bodies, soul savers, and do-gooders on to bigger and better censorship activities, along with more authority for the Postmaster General to dictate the nation's taste, and more laws to clutter up the statute books." This is an absolute falsehood. I do no such thing.... Is it your custom to permit your contributors to fling these reckless and wholly unfounded charges against an author in no position to defend himself?

Downs counterpunched ably, feigning "some feeling of sympathy" for the poor, muddled Kilpatrick who, he charged, supported the First Amendment as a newspaperman but as a political conservative was ready to jettison it in the fight to do away with smut. "He is simply confused," concluded Downs, "suffering from a split personality on the question of censorship." The debate naturally drew much response while at the same time, Moon had to believe, it promoted a better understanding of intellectual freedom principles on the part of *LJ*'s readers.

Early pieces like the Downs-Kilpatrick debate — bare-knuckled commentaries by recognized authorities presented without editorial interference — established *LJ* as the leading library publication for coverage of censorship issues in the 1960s. In addition to Downs, contributors on the subject during the Moon years included such librarian-authors as Ervin Gaines, Everett T. Moore, Dorothy Broderick, Henry Miller Madden, John Pine, Edwin Castagna, Stuart Sherman, Leonard Archer, Ray Smith, Jerome Cushman, and David K. Berninghausen, an impressive roster by any standard. Moon also published a goodly number of articles on censorship by notables outside the profession, among them Irving Wallace (novelist), William J. Brennan (Supreme Court justice), Edward de Grazia (attorney), Jack Nelson (political journalist), Jake Zeitlin (bookseller), and the aforementioned Kilpatrick.

Book Selection Surveys

Book selection (now called collection development) was another of Moon's pet concerns. He read books, he loved books, and he had an unshakable belief that knowledge of books was essential to the work of librarians at all levels, including administrators. He stated this conviction in one of his earliest *LJ* editorials, "The Uninvited": "There has been much ado in the library profession in recent years about status. Perhaps too much thought and time, and too many words, have been devoted to mumbo-jumbo about certification, salaries, punched cards, and public relations techniques. If librarians cannot claim, earn, deserve, or receive recognition as experts in their own field — books — they have no right to expect greater status." This steely declaration struck a nerve with more than one librarian. Dorothy Broderick, for instance, began her famous reaming of *Fiction Catalog* by quoting from it, after which she wrote, "Reading this [Moon's declaration] in the privacy of my own living room, I shouted aloud, 'Three cheers!' It is a statement that needs repeating over and over again until no one calling himself a librarian will not have heard the call and answered it."

Every aspect of books and their selection interested Moon, but none more than how librarians handled controversial, or "problem," titles. He maintained that the works of such 20th century writers as D.H. Lawrence, Henry Miller, Lawrence Durrell, William Burroughs, Alberto Moravia, John Steinbeck, John O'Hara, Irving Wallace, Elia Kazan, Erskine Caldwell, Norman Mailer, and Vladimir Nabokov — all of whom had run afoul of the censor — belonged in libraries, no ifs, ands, or buts. More than that, librarians had an obligation to make these authors and their books available *for no other reason than that they were polemical*. In his Westchester speech he said, "I agree with Harold Tucker, librarian of Queens, who answered one complaint about the presence of *Tropic of Cancer* in his library with the comment that it was precisely because the book *was* controversial that the library should have it."

To discover more about how American librarians actually dealt with controversial books he instigated a number of "quick and dirty" surveys over the years, some conducted by himself with assistance from the *LJ* staff and some commissioned or inspired by him. (In England, Moon had dabbled in reader surveys while editing *Liaison*. In one instance he and coeditor Bill Smith "rode the London tube during a newspaper strike to make a sort of on-the-spot survey of what people were reading.") He got the idea for the *LJ* surveys from a scholarly investigation of book selection practices in California by a sociologist, Marjorie Fiske. Sponsored by the Fund for the Republic and published in 1959 by the University of California Press, Fiske's monograph, *Book Selection and Censorship: A Study of School and Public Libraries in California*, caused a considerable stir at the time and continues to be cited today. Usually referenced simply as the *Fiske Report*, the study's key finding revealed a strong propensity among librarians for self-censorship: "When it comes to actual practice, nearly two-thirds of all librarians who have a say in book selection reported instances where the controversiality of a book or author resulted in a decision not to buy." Likewise, about a fifth of the respondents acknowledged they avoided publications known to be controversial; even more disturbing, these librarians reported not buying items they thought "might become controversial."

Moon the educator was horrified by these revelations. Not only did Fiske's findings fly in the face of everything he believed about the centrality of intellectual freedom in the library profession, her report presented a troubling picture of librarians as weak, mousy people unequal to the status as professionals accorded doctors, lawyers, professors, and others. In fact the *Fiske Report* concluded that librarians themselves tended to share "the public's allegedly low opinion of the profession." Moon the journalist, however, viewed Fiske's findings as more an opportunity than an embarrassment. How widespread was self-censorship among librarians, he wondered? How universal were Fiske's conclusions? Were they valid for other parts of the country, or was California unique, an aberration? In his Westchester speech he suggested more *Fiske Reports* were needed:

I suppose it was Marjorie Fiske who first really threw wide the doors of the closet in which this skeleton of the library family had been hidden for years. Even when the doors were open there was still a good deal of covering up. Oh well, everyone said, that's California — anything can happen there…. Since the evidence, however, is still spotty, I would like to see a Fiske study undertaken in every state. It's difficult to suggest cures until we know just how sick we are, but certainly there are enough symptoms of ill-health to warrant a thorough checkup. Some of the funds of the Council on Library Resources and other foundations which ALA manages to acquire to build better newspaper sticks and the like might be diverted to such a purpose.

By this time (1963) Moon knew full well the American library Establishment was not likely to "divert" real money for something as potentially negative and even mortifying as more book selection surveys à la Fiske. At the time, ALA was more concerned with papering over problems than exploring or solving them. Besides, a year earlier Moon had begun his own modest, albeit attention-getting, efforts along these lines in *LJ* with an article called "'Problem' Fiction." Published in the February 1, 1962, issue, the 12-page feature detailed the results of a questionnaire survey he and the *LJ* staff had constructed that showed how more than a hundred public libraries located throughout the United States dealt with 20 novels considered "hot" for one reason or another. This teaser, printed in bold type just below the survey's title, introduced the piece:

How many libraries provide homes for unorthodox ladies like "Lolita" or "Lady Chatterley"? Is the "Tropic of Cancer" too hot to handle? Will you find "The Carpet-baggers" or the sex- surveyors of "The Chapman Report" on the open shelves, under the counter or in the stacks? A recent Lj survey, which queried public libraries on their book selection in the area of contemporary controversial fiction, provides some of the answers.

The survey, which included revealing quotes from participating librarians about specific books and authors, found that roughly half the libraries canvassed followed "practices and principles which allow little scope for charges of censorship," while the other half ran the gamut "from weather-vane vacillation to rigidly restrictive or pro-tective practices." The February 1 issue also carried several other articles dealing with the selection of fiction, including John Pine's "Minor Masterpieces and Ghastly Mis-takes" on reviewing the genre, Ray Smith's "Legislators or Homogenizers" on the uses and abuses of standard lists, and a satirical editorial by Moon on the uncertain future of the novel.

The February 1 issue generated much mail, most applauding the magazine and its editor for addressing an area of vital concern for librarians engaged in book selec-tion. Robert B. Jackson, adult services coordinator at the East Orange Public Library in New Jersey, wrote, "While I have been most encouraged by *Library Journal*'s increas-ing attention to the significant problems of librarianship, the February 1 articles about public library fiction selection deserve special commendation." Jackson went on to note that certain categories of *non*fiction — health, nutrition, and parapsychology, for example — posed equally difficult selection problems for librarians. Moon, always on the prowl for new feature ideas, stored this nugget away for future use. Virginia Ross, director of the Mateo (California) County Library, wrote, "The report of the survey on 'problem' fiction is particularly interesting, and should be read and pondered by all public librarians, and should lead them to take a new look at their library's book selection policy as it is actually being applied. It has certainly caused me to do so." And Dorothy Sampson, head of the Sacramento City Library, emoted, "Too often we spend our money on the innocuous book that pleases the undiscriminating by offend-ing no one (and stimulating and enlightening no one either). And we will be leaving posterity a legacy of pablum which will imply that we lived mental lives of complete blankness — sans ideas, sans conflict, sans everything!"

These were Moon's sort of librarians — articulate, thoughtful, conscientious, open-minded professionals not afraid of change. It didn't hurt too that they agreed with him, that they were ready to march with him. But as a coldhearted journalist he also wanted reader feedback that pricked his favorite assumptions. Compliments were nice, but it was argumentation that added spark to the magazine, that churned the dialectic, that helped attract the subscriptions and space ads that paid the bills and goosed the profits. So he was delighted when a couple of heavyweight public library directors — Emerson Greenaway (Philadelphia) and Meredith Bloss (New Haven) — wrote to beg to differ. Greenaway: "That every public library, large or small, should buy even all the accept-able titles on your list is, of course, nonsense." Bloss: "The fact is, the librarian is not a literary critic, nor should he be. A critical evaluation of a novel, for example, by a fiction specialist of recognized stature is worth more on the face of it, it seems to me, than one by a librarian, any librarian."

Lovely stuff this, he thought, while considering how to keep the debate flowing. Toward that end he published a symposium entitled "Book Rejection: Is It Censorship?" in the June 15 (1962) issue featuring the opinions of eight prominent librarians, while holding out the possibility of more to come. His technique—quintessential Moon—becomes readily apparent in the introduction to the symposium:

> The February 1 issue of Lj was concerned mainly with book selection and censorship. As a result, we received a large number of letters. Among them, one raised a very interesting point that we thought worth pursuing further. Lelia B. Saunders, assistant director of the Arlington (Virginia) County Libraries, said the February 1 articles were helpful, but "I personally feel on much stronger ground defending the *inclusion* of a book than I do defending the exclusion of a book from a public library collection." Wouldn't Lj, she asked, consider doing something "on the obverse of the coin—how and when to reject a book"?
>
> How, in short, does a librarian reject a book, particularly a controversial book, without incurring charges of censorship? We sent Miss Saunders' comments and some of these questions to a number of librarians who have been much concerned with problems of book selection and censorship.... Below we present the views of some of those who responded. Several, in covering letters, admitted that the problem raised was an exceptionally difficult one, and one or two said they were not satisfied that they had come to grips with it. Lj hopes that these will be considered merely as opening shots in this discussion, and that more readers will want to contribute views.

Next, drawing on Robert Jackson's suggestion, he commissioned a companion to "'Problem' Fiction." Prepared by Dorothy Broderick, who used the same methodology as Moon's earlier survey, the article, logically titled "'Problem' Nonfiction," appeared in the October 1, 1962, issue and reported on whether participating libraries had purchased 24 selected titles dealing with such divisive subjects as race, sex, and Communism. Like the fiction survey, Broderick's was informative and readable, and it prompted a gratifying amount of response. Moon especially savored Broderick's words concluding the piece: "To lead or to follow is the only choice we have." No question, Eric and Dorothy were intellectual soulmates; as she once observed, "Eric and I bonded by being outcasts together."

In early 1964 Moon returned to an old interest from his days as a public librarian in England—saturation buying. To get a sense of how American libraries fared on this score, he conducted a survey of eight public libraries in the New York City–New Jersey metropolitan area to determine the on-shelf availability of 20 fiction and 20 nonfiction classics, old and new. Published as "The View from the Front," the survey produced no startling conclusions: "It was no more than an exercise in inquiry, a lightning foray prompted by curiosity and an old hobby-horse interest," he explained to readers, downplaying expectations. Still, the results were fascinating: "While seven out of eight [of the libraries surveyed] could produce *Sister Carrie*, only four had *Vanity Fair* on the shelf, and none could supply *Lord of the Flies*—and three didn't have a Milton in sight!"

Moon had made his point, suggesting yet another pertinent criterion for librarians to take into account when going about the business of building book collections, work he considered "the most important, most interesting and most difficult of the professional librarian's responsibilities."

In the course of preparing the saturation buying article he caused a bit of consternation at the East Orange Public Library, one of the New Jersey libraries surveyed. Always happy to escape the four walls of his office in Manhattan, he did most of the legwork for the survey himself, and one afternoon while unobtrusively checking the shelves at East Orange (the city was not far from Elizabeth where he lived), he was startled when the library's director, Harold Roth, came charging out of his office: "What the hell are you doing nosing around my library, Moon?" hissed Roth, his voice loaded with suspicion. A few years earlier the East Orange police, at Roth's behest, had carried out raids on citizens who repeatedly ignored notices to return overdue books. Delinquent patrons were arrested, taken to police headquarters late at night, and, if unable to post bail, jailed. The city's draconian overdues policy made national headlines—both *The New York Times* and *Herald Tribune* ran front-page articles—and naturally Moon gave the story lots of ink in *LJ*. Particularly funny—but cutting to Roth—was the headline of *LJ*'s original news item (March 1, 1961): AN ORANGE NIGHTMARE, OR THE HEADY GRAPES OF ROTH. Understandably, the East Orange librarian, who never did completely live down the notorious raids, was anything but pleased to find *LJ*'s smart-assed editor snooping around his library. Moon tried to calm him: "I'm just checking to see if you have these books on the shelves. I'm trying to find out if these books are accessible...." Yeah, sure, muttered Roth, as he stalked back to his office, wondering what Moon, the wisenheimer, was *really* up to?

Other book selection surveys published in *LJ* during Moon's editorship included Raymond Agler's "'Problem' Books Revisited" in the May 15, 1964, issue, which examined library selection practices in the Philadelphia area; "They Play It Safe" (June 1, 1965) by Eldon Tamblyn, a similar look at North Carolina public libraries; and "Statistical Wailing Wall: A Nationwide Survey" (June 1, 1968) by Bill Katz, which reported on poetry holdings in 149 libraries in the country.

The final survey undertaken by Moon, "In, Out, or Neglected?" appeared in two parts in the January 1 and February 1, 1966, issues. In the first part, he asked 60 librarians to pick one book published in 1965 that "should be on the shelves of virtually every public library, whatever its budget or size"; another that "should not be on the shelves of any public library"; and finally one that "has considerable merit" but is "likely to be neglected or purchased less widely by public libraries than it deserves to be." Part two involved checking all titles mentioned in the survey in 200 public libraries around the country to "see how the theories and guesses about 'in' books, 'out' books, or 'neglected' books match up against the actual selection and buying practices" of American librarians.

It was inventive, informative, captivating features like "Problem Fiction," "Problem Nonfiction," "The View from the Front," "Statistical Wailing Wall," and "In, Out, or Neglected?" that helped make *LJ* the most exciting, most talked about, most influential library publication of the 1960s.

Other Issues, Pressing and Mundane

Moon of course wanted his magazine read and discussed by as many people as possible, even those only incidentally interested in or connected to the world of libraries. To bring as many readers as he could into the tent he not only cast librarianship in the broadest possible terms but used every available journalistic device short of tabloid sleaze to stimulate interest. (Occasional photos of librarians in bathing suits and miniskirts, which predictably annoyed some prudish readers, were the closest he came to titillation.) *LJ* in the 1960s featured gutsy, outspoken articles, editorials, reviews, and columns; timely, innovative surveys, symposia, news stories, and conference reports; a large, brassy "Readers' Voice" (or letters) section; and enticing titles and headlines. Who, for instance, could resist an article called "Minor Masterpieces and Ghastly Mistakes" or an editorial called "Tiparillos and Hacksaws" (which dealt with the librarian image)? Moon once advised, "The title should be a sort of advertisement for the article. Like a low-cut dress it should make you interested in exploring what's underneath." Even covers, normally a sedate component of most professional journals, were used to make to editorial statements and hype reader interest. Moon strived to make every column inch of *LJ* contribute to the overall success of the magazine.

He tried hard too, within limits dictated by time, staff, and space, to deal with all relevant aspects of the profession. True, coverage of the race problem, along with censorship and book selection, tended to dominate the pages of *LJ* in the Moon years, but they were hardly the only pressing issues covered. Other major concerns receiving substantial attention included federal aid to libraries (legislation, funding, and programs), which expanded enormously during the decade with Lyndon Johnson's Great Society initiatives; the Vietnam War, an increasingly costly conflict that threatened to undermine Johnson's social programs at home, including assistance to libraries; professional status and image problems, topics always on the minds of insecure librarians, of which there seemed to be a limitless supply; labor unions, which at one point appeared destined to challenge professional associations for dominance in representing the interests of organized librarians; alleged Communist influence in American libraries, a holdover from the McCarthy hysteria of the 1950s that found the Red Menace lurking everywhere, even betwixt the covers of the Great Books; ALA governance, a hotly contested matter among those (like Moon) who believed the national association was crucial to the profession's advancement; student use of public libraries, which sparked debates about whom libraries should serve and how; library cooperation, a progressive concept that gained real momentum in the postwar period but was often resisted by parochial elements at the local level; and discrimination against women in the profession, a disgrace (like racial segregation) that was largely ignored until the 1960s.

That Moon's heart beat just a little faster when dealing with socially and politically charged issues like race and censorship and federal aid and Vietnam and unionization and ALA politics was apparent to any halfway alert reader of *LJ* in the 1960s. These were the issues he felt most passionate about, the ones he was prepared metaphorically to spill blood over. On the other hand he did not ignore or neglect the more pedestrian aspects of librarianship. Actually, a surprisingly high number of the thousands of pages of content published during his editorship concerned what he thought of as "mundane professional matters"—that is, the practical, nuts-and-bolts stuff of library work, such as reference and information sources and services; acquisitions, cataloging, and classification; circulation and security systems; publications other than hardcover books (paperbacks, periodicals, maps, government documents, reprints, microforms, films, and so on) that pose special problems for librarians in terms of acquisition, processing, storage, and circulation; and library architecture, buildings, equipment, furniture, carpeting, shelving, annual reports, and public relations. While Moon's *LJ* naturally concentrated on librarianship as practiced in North America, developments abroad received a fair amount of attention, though looking back he was not pleased with the scope or depth of coverage. Years later he confessed that if he had it to do all over again he would have tried to do something "real" in the area of international librarianship.

Moon understood that *LJ* had an obligation to cover the so-called mundane concerns, no matter how he might feel about them personally. This did not mean, however, that such concerns had to be treated in a mundane manner. Rather, he saw covering them as a journalistic challenge: how, he asked himself, can I bring some life to the routine, everyday business of librarianship? The goal became to make commonplace subjects interesting to readers who ordinarily wouldn't give a fig. How, for instance, to interest reference librarians in a critique of the latest edition of the *Dewey Decimal Classification*? Or get catalogers excited about a piece on how best to teach the art of reference work. "We didn't ignore the more mundane professional matters," he explained. "We got involved in battles here too, involving the top people in the field. So we didn't ignore those things—but they weren't at the center of my every heartbeat."

Typical of *LJ*'s treatment of less-than-scintillating matters was a cover story about the Library of Congress, which focused on whether LC should more aggressively take on the responsibilities of a national library. The library's role had expanded gradually since its founding in 1800 to serve the needs of the U.S. Congress, and in 1962 Douglas Bryant, a top librarian at Harvard University, proposed in a memorandum subsequently published in the *Congressional Record* that the time had come—indeed was long overdue—for LC to function as the nation's "National Library." In due course, L. Quincy Mumford, then Librarian of Congress, answered Bryant's memo—his cautious, rather defensive reply also appearing in the *Congressional Record*. Moon moved quickly to cover the story, but not in the conventional way. Instead of a dry recitation of the facts, which would have bored the knickers off most readers, he published (in the January 1, 1963, issue) a delightfully fey albeit perceptive analysis of the situation by Paul Dunkin, a well-known cataloging professor at the library school at Rutgers University. The title of Dunkin's piece, "Pyramid or Volcano?" appeared prominently on the magazine's cover along with facing photos of Bryant and Mumford, captioned THE GREAT DEBATE. Even *LJ* readers with little or no interest in the rather arcane question of LC's ultimate role found it difficult to resist Dunkin's article and the Bryant-Mumford face-off.

Moon employed a similar but more elaborate dialectic when dealing with the long and involved effort to revamp the ALA cataloging code after World War II. The story, a yawner for most librarians (including Moon), gained momentum in the early 1960s with the publication of a draft revision of the code by Seymour Lubetzky, a much admired professor at UCLA's library school who as head of ALA's Catalog Code Revision Committee had labored over the document since the late 1940s. *Library Journal's* coverage began with the May 1, 1961, issue, which carried two solid articles criticizing the draft revision—"The Grand Illusion" by Johannes Dewton and "A Reference Librarian's View of the Draft Cataloging Code" by David Watkins—plus a table-setting editorial by Moon titled "Who Cares About the Code?" The editorial, which attempted to hook all librarians into the debate, began with a personal admission most readers could identify with:

We [Moon] may as well confess at the outset—be it heresy or no—that we find it difficult to get very passionate or excited about cataloging theory. We have worked in, and organized, cataloging departments, but these interludes do not remain in our memory as among the creative highspots of library life.

This confession of weakness is made because we suspect that there are many noncataloger librarians whose disinterest has enabled them to remain blissfully unaware of the smoke signals arising from the inner conclaves of catalogers heatedly discussing ALA's draft catalog code. This draft represents more than ten years' work by Seymour Lubetzky, more than the thousands of words in print and across the conference tables—it portends a potential upheaval of mammoth proportions in the years ahead.

Four months later, in the September 1 issue, *LJ* featured three articles defending the draft revision, including one, "Smoke Over Revision," by the great Lubetzky himself. Using a legal metaphor, Moon's prologue to these articles cast the issue in adversarial terms: "The case for the prosecution having been introduced [in the May 1 issue], the defense now takes over. In the pages that follow are rebuttals from the three authors above [Lubetzky, Paul Dunkin, and C. Sumner Spalding], all of whom have played a prominent part in the revision of the rules." The September 1 issue also carried a reply from Johannes Dewton (an administrator in LC's Union Catalog division) followed by a "P.S. to Dewton's Reply" from Lubetzky, who seemed to enjoy all the *LJ* razzmatazz, which represented a decided change from the rarefied treatment of the code controversy in the technical services journals where his writings normally appeared. The debate over the code prompted much feedback, including letters, additional articles, and even a "Viewpoint" column in praise of cataloging: Skidmore College librarian Mary Hickey informed all noncatalogers, "If you are laboring under the delusion that cataloging appeals only to withered old ladies and immigrants fluent in exotic languages, I have news for you. Cataloging is fun!"

Moon came to admire and take delight in librarians like Paul Dunkin and Seymour Lubetzky, though they were never part of his inner circle. He appreciated their intelligence and expertise, recognizing them as the best and brightest in their areas of specialization, and accordingly he wanted them as contributors to *LJ*. Dunkin, for instance, wrote a regular column for the magazine in 1967, and Moon cherished him as "an absolutely delicious writer; he had a lovely sense of humor and sense of fun,

but he could deliver a serious and penetrating message. He was my favorite columnist." No matter how dry the subject, *LJ*'s editor was determined to publish writers
who knew what they were talking about and knew how to say it in a clear and compelling way. This approach to library journalism, while starkly logical, seemed almost
radical in the 1960s because no one else was doing it, at least with any consistency.

Sacred Cows

Another trademark of Moon's journalistic style was a willingness to tackle subjects other editors avoided. "I suppose," he said reflecting on the *LJ* years, "that I was
more willing to take a chance than most editors who had been around the library press
for a long time. And that was why I was able to make such an impact. I raised questions and hammered away at subjects that formerly had been totally ignored or buried."
A prime example was *LJ*'s coverage of the civil rights struggle, which led to blunt confrontations with entrenched library interests in both the South and the North, as well
as at the highest levels of ALA.

Moon had no qualms about taking on the library Establishment when he thought
the point at issue warranted it. All his life he had chafed at authority. Growing up
working-class, he carried the hurts and suspicions of the breed into adulthood, including an intuitive distrust of those who ran things, those in control. Too often in Britain
these people were elites dedicated to maintaining the status quo while enjoying a cozy
sinecure at the expense of those who, like himself and his family and friends, were less
wellborn and lacked a network of high-powered social contacts and grand educational
and cultural opportunities. A fighter, the young Moon had lashed out forcefully and
often abrasively when his interests and ideas conflicted with the powers that be, and
he naturally continued in this mode when he got to *LJ*, though by this time — he would
soon be 40 — he had learned to choose his spots.

No matter how successful or prominent or materially well off Eric Moon became
in America, he would always psychologically be a poor boy from the British working
class. That said, subtle but important changes did occur in him when he came to the
States and entered the Bowker milieu. He had obviously matured personally and professionally over the ten-year period between leaving library school in the summer of
1949 and assuming the editorship of *LJ* in November 1959. By the time he arrived at
Bowker, age and experience colluded to smooth the sharpest edges off his personality.
His propensity for manipulation became more sophisticated, less blatant, and he no
longer felt a compulsion to bait people in high places just for the petty pleasure of punc-
turing their distended egos or showing off his impressive verbal skills or proving that
Old Boys shit and use bumf just like the less privileged lads.

What the American experience gave him was a sense of attainment and self-
definition he had not previously known. Becoming editor of *LJ*, a journal of considerable prestige in the world of libraries and books in the most powerful country on
planet Earth, satisfied his appetite for professional recognition and fulfillment — needs
never entirely met in England or Newfoundland. As *LJ*'s editor he no longer had to

fight his way to the top: *he was at the top*. He sensed soon after coming to New York that the old role of *enfant terrible* (last exhibited in Newfoundland) was, like a grown woman in pigtails, no longer appropriate. Accordingly, he adopted a less strident demeanor, modulating his behavior to fit his new circumstances. No, he did not sell his soul to the corporation nor did he succumb to some shallow rendering of the American Dream. Never as editor of *LJ* did he compromise on fundamental principle. Rather, once he got the job, he was able, because he was now at the top, to make small concessions that a short time before would have been anathema to him.

Essentially, Moon made an effort to control his conduct and tongue after becoming part of the Bowker family. The fact that he was an experienced amateur actor and well versed in the Machiavellian arts—one American colleague, Robbie Franklin, who later worked closely with him for nine years, described Moon as "a great artificer"—helped him camouflage or sublimate his true feelings when necessary and keep his worst self-destructive impulses in check. Still, he never became a conformist or a button-down man. As Elizabeth Geiser, who had ample opportunity to observe him at work during the 1960s, put it, "Eric was a maverick at Bowker." One of the ways he exhibited his independent streak was through attacks in *LJ* on cherished library shibboleths and sacred cows. He had an uncanny feel for just how far he could go without overplaying his hand.

"It seemed to me essential to establish at least one outlet in our professional press," Moon wrote after he had left *LJ*, "where any established virtue could be questioned, where no cow was so sacred that its tail could not be pulled in public, where criticism was more welcome than self-congratulation." An early instance of yanking the cow's tail involved an assault on National Library Week, a much ballyhooed and well-heeled publicity campaign underwritten largely by major American publishers—and an event, it turned out, close to the heart of Fred Melcher, Bowker's octogenarian board chairman and technically Moon's boss. National Library Week had never received an unfavorable comment in the library press prior to Moon's attack in the April 1, 1961, issue of *LJ*; previously everyone had publicly lauded it as the greatest thing to happen to libraries since Andrew Carnegie got the building bug. Moon, however, had picked up on grumbles about NLW through his informal channels (e.g., bull sessions at library conferences) and decided to open up the subject. As with the race issue, there was an explosion when he did, though it was a smaller one, more like the detonation of a grenade than an atom bomb. Moon:

I did an informal survey of librarians regarding National Library Week, which I thought was a really piss-poor operation. I could see some virtue to NLW if it were a hard marketing operation, but at the time it wasn't at all. It was a tea and cookies kind of effort, and a lot of people thought it was a waste of time and energy—a bunch of garbage. So I published an article ["End National Library Week—A Librarian's Minority Opinion" by Allan Angoff, assistant director of the Fair Lawn, N.J., Public Library] and wrote an editorial ["Whose Opinion?"] attacking NLW.

Before we went to press with this I had one director of the company after another in my office, saying "You can't do this. Why are you being beastly to Fred Melcher?" I said, "I like Fred Melcher. What are you talking about?" They said didn't I understand that Fred was one of the founders of National Library Week? I said I didn't know that, but it didn't make any difference: "I'm not attacking Fred, I'm attacking National Library Week." They said I couldn't do this in his own magazine, and I said, "I think I can and I think I must."

Eventually I called Daniel [Melcher] and said, "I've got half the directors of the company on my back about this editorial. I told you at the outset that I was going to publish what I thought I should publish and that anytime you didn't like it you could can me, but don't ever try to stop me from doing what I think the magazine needs to do." He said, "You're perfectly right. Go ahead." I learned a lesson from this: not to let anybody in the company, not even the directors, see any of the magazine before it went to press.

Moon's "Whose Opinion?" editorial seemed directed as much at his critics within the company as at *LJ* readers:

We have been as strong in support of NLW as any other library periodical ever since the annual event was born. We have published articles, news stories, pictures galore—*all* in favor of NLW. We know, however, that every March or April, there are librarians who grow irate at the flamboyance of NLW publicity methods and mumble into their beards: "Why don't they stop all this nonsense?" Now one of them [Angoff] is out in the open, and we would like to know how many agree with him, *and* how many will feel impelled to rush to ardent defense of the book and library world's big annual occasion.

Predictably, *LJ* received a flood of mail commenting on NLW and particularly Angoff's article, which minced no words about the author's distaste for the event: "There is little genuine library atmosphere in NLW because it is basically a stunt, in a familiar, commercial, advertising tradition, for selling books and magazines." A selection of the letters, about equally divided between those for and against NLW, appeared in the May 15 issue. Over the years Moon milked a number of other sacred cows in similar fashion.

Tomfoolery

Moon's *LJ* normally contained serious fare, though every now and then he slipped in some funny stuff—a facetious essay or irreverent send-up here, a witty poem or droll news item there. Levity served as a welcome counterpoint to the journal's customary earnestness, and many readers appreciated the occasional piece showing the lighter side of librarianship, a profession often perceived as uptight and humorless. Moon, a crossword puzzle enthusiast and lover of wordplay (his journalist friend Ben Bagdikian considered him "a demon punster"), took particular pride in having a good sense of humor, which often manifested itself in the telling—and retelling—of breezy stories he had amassed and polished over the years. Actually, the ever-competitive Moon tended to use his stories as a means of gaining attention and controlling social situations: his wolfish grin announced, watch out, he was about to knock the assembled company dead with a merry tale or wicked bon mot. Not everyone laughed. Gerry Shields, for instance, who knew him well through ALA and as a fellow editor, once observed, "Notice that Eric does not have a real sense of humor."

Wherever the merits of his funny bone, Moon did publish some comic stuff in *LJ*, usually of a satiric variety. Some examples:

- A biting article with the ironic title "I Love Librarians!" appeared in the January 1, 1962, issue. Written by "A Reader," the anonymous author, identified only as "an assistant professor of history at one of our most respected universities," took librarians to task, albeit in a decorous manner, for what he or she deemed self-inflicted impediments to good library service. The author wondered, for instance, why catalogers do some of the things they do? "I would list the sins of catalogers as: cataloging for their own sake, nonsensical listings due largely to lack of contact with users (i.e. a biography of Charles Darwin placed in entomology, a history of wooden naval ships in forestry, etc.), and the twisted logic under which institutes and the like are hidden. Moreover, I regret to say that it usually takes ten times as much time and effort to explain why not to insert a cross-reference as to make one."

- The February 1, 1963, issue offered a ditty entitled *The Bookworm*:

> She will not wear glasses, because
>   she doesn't want to look schoolmarmish.
> She is a librarian.
> She reads omnivorously
>   with practically no results.
> She is deeply devoted to her profession and
>   is never at a loss in this special field.
> She files books on nudism under
>   "Costumes."

- The December 15, 1964, issue carried a full-page spoof on the practice of publishing costly collections of scholarly esoterica on microform (microfiche, microfilm, microcards), which became popular in the 1960s due to the large amounts of grant money available at the time for library development. Moon introduced the piece, headlined "We Represent the Library's Interest," this way:

> The above is the slogan of the Tom Fool Publishing Company of Allagash, Maine. We are grateful to George Spavin, librarian of the Dewey State Teachers' College, Allagash, Maine, for sending us the following announcement from the T.F. Publishing Company about a notable new publishing project which has not received the publicity it deserves. Lj is pleased, therefore, to be able to draw it to the attention of all interested libraries. We reproduce the company's circular exactly as issued.

The "circular" noted that Tom Fool planned "to issue on microfiche a very large collection of the fiction published in North American and Great Britain during the nineteenth century," using Allbone Penny's *A History of English Fiction, 1660–1900* as its chief bibliographic source. The flyer continued:

> but, like the two similarly titled publishing projects recently announced by two other publishers, we do not propose either to limit our selection to fiction listed in this work or necessarily to include all that it does list. Our project will inevitably duplicate most of the fiction in those two other projects, but until they have announced precisely what fiction they intend to publish or where they intend to

stop, we can assure our own customers of nothing more definite on this point. You may be assured, however, that we will keep finding fiction to publish as long as the subscriptions continue (there are other centuries, too, remember)....

We cannot overemphasize how important it is for libraries, particularly those of small colleges without, as yet, Ph.D. programs in English literature, to add this collection of mostly minor fiction to their resources. Major research libraries with unspent funds toward the end of the fiscal year will, of course, not think even twice about it.

The flyer contained this postscript:

P.S. As a final note, we are glad to be able to say that a high school physics teacher in our neighborhood, using only commercially available parts from discontinued slide projectors and the help of our local tinsmith, has perfected a new multi-purpose microform reader. His first model naturally does not make microprint or Microcards quite as legible as microfiche or microfilm, but he expects to solve this minor difficulty during his summer vacation. We will give one of these very high quality "See-All" readers to every library whose subscription to our projects amounts to $635 or more.

- A letter from Nigel Molesworth, librarian and archivist at the Molesworth Institute in New Brunswick, N.J., appeared in the March 1, 1967, issue, complaining that a review of *Who's Who in Library Service* (in the January 1 issue) failed to note "the large number of fraudulent statements and entries" in the book. For instance, the reviewer—Jesse Shera, dean of the library school at Western Reserve University—overlooked errors in the entry for Dr. Norman D. Stevens, such as the claim that Stevens had received "a Litt.D. degree from St. Custard's in 1965." Molesworth explained that Stevens "was under consideration to receive such a degree but the special Old Boys Committee on Honorary Degrees had recommended delaying the granting of it for several years. By his fraudulent claim, however, Dr. Stevens has forfeited any chance of receiving that great honor."

Of course those in the know recognized Molesworth and the Molesworth Institute as inventions of none other than Dr. Norman Stevens, the preeminent library humorist of his time (and arguably of all time). Not only had Stevens included some phony baloney in his own biography in the who's who directory but submitted a bio for the fictitious Molesworth as well. Shera, an owlish-looking fellow who wore thick glasses and liked a joke as well as the next old bird, responded:

Nigel Molesworth was quite right in taking us to task for our failure to examine more thoroughly the latest edition of *Who's Who in Library Service*.... However, the truth of the matter is that by the time we had checked on the biographies of all our friends, we were as blind as moles and it wasn't worth the effort to go further. Anyway, we were checking on the biographies of our *friends*, and Norman Stevens is no friend of ours. In fact, we don't even know Norm, and couldn't tell whether he got his honorary Litt.D. from St. Custard's or St. Meringue's.

Like Shera, *LJ*'s editor thoroughly enjoyed Stevens and his pointed whimsy: "I always cherished Norman for his sense of humor," said Moon, adding: "I always looked forward to receiving anything from him, because it would be alive. It didn't come across the desk like a dead fish, which was how much of the stuff smelled." Interestingly, Jean Peters, longtime Bowker Company librarian, kept an *LJ* file labeled "Humor" during the Moon years, but discontinued it after he gave up the editorship. Reported Peters, "Humor in the journal virtually disappeared after Eric left."

Moon's Critics

Not all *LJ* readers approved of Moon's editorial methods and priorities, and some disapproved adamantly and vociferously. Some, for instance, objected to the humor he occasionally published. The Tom Fool "circular" elicited this letter from an obviously irritated Vernon D. Tate, librarian at the United States Naval Academy in Annapolis:

> How long has the *Library Journal* published anonymous fiction in the section presumably reserved for professional papers and discussions by presumably real people? Reference is made to page 4871 (in the December 15 issue) "We Represent the Library's Interest." Who is "We"? According to the *ALA Membership Directory 1964* there is no George Spavin within the membership. According to the *American Library Directory*, a Bowker publication where fictionalization may not have penetrated, there is no Dewey State Teacher's College, Allagash, Maine. So far as a preliminary study has revealed there is no Tom Fool Publishing Company, though I will grant that there are Tom Fools publishing. I, at least, have not seen the circular to which you refer with such pleasure.
>
> I repeat, how long has Lj published anonymous fiction? May I suggest that if you intend to embark on this kind of Library Journalism, that in future you identify it as fiction even though the author understandably prefers to remain anonymous. There is a convenient way to achieve this objective quietly and in good taste, namely to use colored paper for articles of this type... I propose yellow.

Others did not like the authors Moon published or his sometimes caustic editorial pen or the fact that he both reported on and participated in ALA business, which some deemed a conflict of interest. Mostly, however, they objected to the adversarial tone he brought to the publication and to his coverage of subjects they considered outside the purview of a professional journal. They called him a biased journalist, a goddamn bastard, and much more. But he never gave in, never said the hell with it, never lost the Stokesian desire to educate through debate and the dialectic process. In a candid speech to the Texas Library Association in Houston in March 1969 several months after he had left *LJ*, Moon discussed his critics:

> I never too much minded the correspondents who suggested I was an idiot, or ignorant, or insane, or just plain wrong. In such cases I used that classic stopper devised by H.L. Mencken for dealing with the irate correspondent, a brief letter that read: "Dear Sir, or Madam, as the case may be: You may very well be right. Yours sincerely..." The ones who bothered me were the people who were constantly insisting that it wasn't *proper* for a professional magazine to do this thing or that. I am prepared to admit that my view of the boundaries of professional propriety and legitimacy may be fairly broad, but I cannot help regarding some of the prodigiously varied taboos erected by some *LJ* readers a little short of quaint.

To give you a few samples: It is not, apparently, even in the nudie sixties, permissible to publish, in a "professional" magazine, a picture of a librarian, male or female, in a bathing suit. Nor, to take a different kind of example, is it enough to review the substance and style of a book; one must include specifics about the word on page 213 or the sentence on page 164 so that the "professional" will, without reading or glancing at the book, be fully prepared to deal with the certain convulsions of the local Mrs. Grundy. Further, it is a severe breach of professional etiquette to tell the truth about an unpleasant or difficult situation, especially when such truth reveals a librarian or library in a poor light (leave that to the newspapers and scandal sheets, we only want to hear good of ourselves). Similarly, it is OK to report pure fiction in the form of rosy predictions for some yet untested and unlaunched library project, system, or development, but it is very bad form to report the often poor results, and sometimes failures, from which, incidentally, we might learn much more than from those inspiring but unfounded advance trumpetings. And worst crime of all, no decent professional publication ever discusses, let alone advocates (horrors!), a political position or a public stance on a major social issue. (My editorials on Goldwater and, later, Vietnam, incited more angry letters, I believe, than maybe all of our library periodicals have received about everything they have published in a decade.)

Among his severest critics was Major James M. Hillard, librarian at The Citadel in Charleston, South Carolina. Hillard, a self-proclaimed "spokesperson for the Right," detested the "notorious liberal sentiments" he discerned in *LJ*'s editor. "Major Hillard was one of my deadly enemies," recalled Moon. "Every time I wrote anything we'd get a letter from the Major attacking me. I usually responded; certain people had to be responded to — and he was one." In a typical letter to the editor Hillard attacked Moon for publishing an article by John Sherman called "The Ninety-Four Hour Week" (*LJ*, March 15, 1964), which suggested American academic libraries should hire British and Asian librarians at low salaries to cover public service desks during weekends, holidays, and evenings — times when senior staff did not relish working. "It will be hard for you to believe," wrote Hillard,

but I am not one given to the writing of letters indiscriminately and I do not go through *Library Journal* looking for things with which to disagree, but I feel compelled to write another letter.... I am surprised that an editor of such notorious liberal sentiments* as you generally show would publish an article advocating literal peonage. Granting staffing a college library is a problem, let's not try to solve it by importing new problems.

Moon responded this way:

Ed. Note — It is precisely because of these "notorious liberal sentiments" that we publish articles reflecting a variety of points of view, including many with which we disagree. Although libraries are also supposed to be places where contrasting views may be represented and found, a number of our readers appear to find the practice hard to accept.

Objectivity: "The Death Knell of Journalism"

Another recurrent criticism of Moon's journalistic style centered on the question of objectivity. Shouldn't a professional journal like *LJ*, asked his critics rhetorically, strive to be as evenhanded and impartial as possible? Yet by their reckoning, the journal and its editor consistently flouted this time-honored editorial standard. By their lights, *LJ* was neither objective nor unbiased nor neutral nor fair. And, like Major Hillard, many of those who disapproved of Moon's techniques believed that he consciously — read insidiously — used *LJ* as a vehicle for the promotion of left-wing ideology, causes, and solutions. In short, he practiced the journalism of political partisanship. Here's how Marietta Daniels Shepard, a conservative librarian at the Pan American Union in Washington, D.C., explained the issue in a letter to *LJ* about the war in Vietnam:

> ... let me render my objection to the usurpation of a professional journal to express the political opinions of its editor. Who determines the editorial policy of *LJ*, and where is it determined? Would the makers of that policy prefer to support policies destined to bring about the downfall of Vietnam, the sacrifice of yet another country to communist perfidy, military take-over, and domination.... [W]e must demand that *LJ*, as well as other professional journals, stick to the purpose for which they are being purchased, and for which I assume the editors are being paid.

Moon rebutted such criticism by arguing that, as *LJ*'s editor, he had no obligation to be apolitical or politically neutral, and that moreover he often ran pieces in the magazine with which he disagreed. Many instances could be cited, including the Rev. Dollen's attack on "indecent" literature, James J. Kilpatrick's defense of *The Smut Peddlers*, and John Sherman's "The Ninety-Four Hour Week," but perhaps the most dramatic example involved a dispute in 1964 at the height of the civil rights movement over whether ALA officers and staffers should be allowed to attend or present programs at segregated state library associations. Moon wrote an editorial (*LJ*, August 1964) voicing strong support for prohibiting ALA officials from participating in "meetings of those state associations whose racial policies do not conform with those of the national body," a policy adopted by ALA at its annual conference that year. On the page opposite Moon's editorial was an "On the Grindstone" column by Wyman Jones of the Dallas Public Library, espousing a position diametrically opposed to Moon's. In a boxed note accompanying his editorial, Moon informed readers:

> *Wyman Jones's column, opposite, arrived after our editorial had been set in type. It deals with the same topic but its opinions are 180 degrees removed from ours. We have no hesitation in presenting opposing points of view, but in case some readers find us schizophrenic, we should explain that the editorial page reflects Lj's position, while guest columns reflect the opinions of our contributors, which we like to have but with which we do not have to agree.— Ed.*

Jones, it should be noted, was not happy that his column ran essentially as an op ed piece, considering it a "poor decision" and possible "treachery" on Moon's part. As a representative of the Dallas Public he felt particularly sensitive about racial issues since many people, including some ALA members, regarded Texas and Dallas as part of the South and hence part of the problem. Jones could not help but wonder if he had been set up by Moon?

Be that as it may, there's no question that *LJ*'s editor willingly, even eagerly, published items expressing ideas he did not agree with or support. But did this make the journal an objective, nonpartisan publication? Not on your nelly, said his critics, and (to their astonishment, had they known) Moon agreed: "People used to say that hardly anything in *Library Journal* was objective. And I said, exactly. I didn't want objectivity here — it's the death knell of journalism. I always thought objectivity was the road to dullness and futility." In a 1984 interview with Frederick J. Stielow on the library press, Moon added this about journalistic objectivity:

> I never believed that objectivity is very good journalism. I think you have to report facts objectively, but for the rest of the *Journal* I didn't feel a need to be objective at all. The rest of the *Journal*, in my mind, was a way to open up discussion for the profession, a way to open up thinking.... It's hard to separate issues and views and commentary from facts, and I'm not so sure we were always totally successful at that. But we tried in the straight news columns to be factual. In the rest of the *Journal* we weren't trying to be objective.

Moon does not exaggerate here. Apart from news stories (and even they sometimes contained sly editorial comments and partisan gibes), almost everything that appeared in *LJ* during the Moon years was subjective in one way or another. Articles, columns, reviews, and letters naturally reflected the views of their authors, as did comments of participants in *LJ*'s numerous symposia and surveys. And the magazine's editorials — written mostly by Moon (signed "EM" from July 1960 on; previous *LJ* editorials had been unsigned) though in later years John Berry, Karl Nyren, and Shirley Havens also contributed some — were strictly opinion pieces intended to instruct or persuade or fire up readers. Moon believed the editorial page "alone speaks *for* the magazine; it is the magazine's voice, its identity." Zoia Horn, the intellectual freedom advocate, was typical of many liberal librarians in the 1960s who drew strength from Moon's editorials, valuing them as incitements to change: "I remember feeling that his editorials sent arrows way ahead, sometimes outrageously beyond the then current views of the profession. He seemed to be egging on, cajoling, urging his readers to step out of the narrow traditions of the time."

Columns and Columnists

Moon encouraged his columnists to be as opinionated and controversial as they wanted to or felt they could be. He regarded columns mainly as a means of getting fresh perspectives into the magazine. "Viewpoint," the first regular column created during his editorship, billed itself as "a platform for those with an idea or a grouse to air, a stable for hobby-horses, a place where questions may be asked without obligation upon the author to have done years of research to find the answers." Other columns included the staff-written "Publishing Scene," which served mainly as a forum for Dan Melcher, and "The Consultants' Column," a place for commentary by members of *LJ*'s board of editorial consultants, the small group of distinguished librarians appointed to advise Moon when he joined the magazine in late 1959. When the board ceased to exist at the end of 1963 the column was replaced by one covering the emerging field of computer applications to library work; written by Allen Kent of the University of Pittsburgh, it ran under the punning title "From the Documentation Pitt."

Moon's pet column, "On the Grindstone," debuted in January 1962. Appearing once a month and written by the same person for a year (hence the grindstone metaphor), the column was named and inaugurated by the redoubtable Lawrence Clark Powell, bookman par excellence, celebrated university librarian, and founding dean of the then new (1960) library school at the University of California at Los Angeles. Roy Stokes, Moon's mentor at Loughborough, followed Powell, writing the column in 1963; Stokes later observed, "I think it gave Eric some measure of satisfaction in being able to mark and evaluate my literary compositions as some years earlier I had done with his." Wyman Jones assumed the "Grindstone" position in 1964, followed by Walter Brahm (Connecticut state librarian) in 1965 and John Weatherford (library director at Miami University in Ohio) in 1966, after which the column was discontinued as part of a general revamping of the magazine in 1967. "On the Grindstone" was replaced by an old Moon standby, "Viewpoint," with Paul Dunkin writing the column in 1967 and Leonard Freiser (librarian of the Toronto Board of Education) doing the honors in 1968, Moon's final year as editor.

Inasmuch as provocative and stimulating content was central to the success of *LJ*, Moon selected his columnists with care, wanting to be reasonably certain at the outset that they could and would generate some sparks. Few who were invited to be an *LJ* columnist in those years refused, so great was the distinction — it was like being tapped for Skull and Bones. In one instance, however, he had to use wily tactics to land the person he wanted for "On the Grindstone." This is how Moon maneuvered Wyman Jones into being an *LJ* columnist:

I met Wyman for the first time early in the 1960s at a conference in El Paso in Texas. One memory of this conference is of Lillian Bradshaw of the Dallas Public, already a great figure in librarianship. I was coming down a staircase and this rather attractive woman was coming up the other way and she threw her arms around me and said, "You're Eric Moon! Welcome to Texas, honey." I had never met Lillian before. Shortly afterward, I'm wandering along a corridor in my hotel and this tall young guy comes up to me and says, "You're Eric Moon from *Library Journal*?" I said, "Yeah." He said, "Well, you're doing a good job, but there's a helluva lot of things you ought to be doing that you're not."

He was Wyman Jones of the Dallas Public Library. I said to him, fine, come up to the room and you can tell me about it, and we drank for a couple of hours— he must have thrown about a hundred ideas at me. I said, "Wyman, I'm really grateful for all your ideas, but you must realize that I'm only one person and can't do everything and I need help. The best thing we can do about this is for you to help me. So I'm going to make you a columnist for *LJ*. He said, "No way, man. Writing's hard work, I've done that and I don't want to do anymore." I said, "Wyman, you can't just throw that load at me and then duck out." He said, "I'm not going to be no columnist."

So when I got back to New York, I wrote to Lillian Bradshaw and said it would be in the interest of DPL to have one of its bright young men as a national columnist for *LJ*. She responded it certainly would, and about two days later I got a call from Wyman saying, "You sonofabitch!" That's how I got Wyman as a columnist.

Library Journal columnists were theoretically free to write whatever they wished on any subject that moved them. But once in a while Moon exercised his editorial discretion and rejected or asked for changes in a particular piece. Once Wyman Jones submitted a column celebrating librarianship in closed couplets à la Alexander Pope; Moon apparently found the effort sappy and return it, saying, according to Jones, "I don't print anything that doesn't fit on a square page." Jones turned around and sent the poem to Kathleen Molz at *Wilson Library Bulletin*, who "loved it." Another time Moon's testy reaction to a column caused a major flap with a big-name contributor: Lawrence Clark Powell was not a person used to being bullied by any editor, and to the surprise of neither man, the incident ended with Moon in retreat. Moon's nuanced version of what happened appeared much later in his foreword to Powell's autobiographical *Life Goes On*:

I asked Larry to become a columnist for *LJ*, and for a year (all he would agree to), among his myriad other activities he ground out his "On the Grindstone" column, always coming in — a real rarity among columnists — ahead of deadline. It was over this column, though, that we had our first major disagreements, though not confrontations, as you shall hear. I wanted Larry to bring to bear his power and influence upon some of the critical issues with which *LJ* and I were so deeply involved in the sixties, but I couldn't budge him from his "Passion for Books" message, although he claims to have been "magnificently diverse" and to have tackled what he saw as the issues: they just weren't *my* issues. One tough day when things had not been going well, another of these bibliographic sermons dropped onto my desk. I read it with impatient fury and promptly dashed off a long, angry letter accusing Larry of avoidance of responsibility.... Larry's delightfully unfazed and coy response came by return mail: "You didn't *like* my column?" How can you stay mad at a man like that?

Powell's recollection of the incident, recorded in 1991 (he died in 2001), agreed substantially with Moon's, though his tone was much more direct, even blunt:

Eric wrote asking me to contribute a column to *LJ*. We met in New York and talked about it. He offered me complete freedom of subject, but it soon became clear that he wanted me to deal with issues uppermost to him. I flatly refused and went ahead on my own under the title I gave the monthly column: "On the Grindstone." He balked only once when my column was my farewell address to the graduates of that year's class in my new school [UCLA]. I insisted he keep his promise to leave choices to me and I told him I was through if he didn't. That was that!

Letters to the Editor

Of course, no one, not even Moon's sternest critics, expected the letters to the editor (or "Readers' Voice") section of *LJ* to be objective or neutral. People who write letters to the editor are typically exercised about something and state their complaints or concerns in the strongest possible terms. In Moon's case the more sassy or defiant or passionate the letter, the more likely he was to publish it; such letters helped keep the pot sizzling, the hackles raised, the dander up.

He also used letters to the editor as a means of gauging *LJ*'s impact. When he took over the listless magazine in late 1959 he found the letters file "virtually empty," which suggested something was wrong: "This is a good test; if this file does not consistently contain more letters than can be used, it is a fair bet that the magazine is not getting through to its readers." John Berry, who worked with Moon at *LJ* for five years before taking over as editor in 1969, made much the same point when he described unsolicited letters as "the great gratification" editors receive for their work: "It doesn't matter if they're for you or against you, as long as you get them. That's a true measure. And if you get a rabid redneck letter, that's gold. To run that is a joyous moment." Over the years Moon published hundreds of letters, many of them critical of *LJ*, himself, and his most cherished assumptions. Certain correspondents— Eli Oboler, Marietta Daniels Shepard, and James Hillard, to name several of his most persistent antagonists— usually received an "editor's note" at the end of their letters, which gave Moon the last word, which (he knew) made them all the more furious.

Visual Aids

Still another area of *LJ* where Moon eschewed traditional notions of journalistic objectivity was in the choice of pictures, photos, and the like that accompanied the printed text or appeared on covers. Early on he ran a brief appeal under the headline "The Paucity of Pictures"; it said, "Ninety per cent of our photographs seem to be of children or bookmobiles. There must be other areas of library work which can produce illustrations which interest, excite, arouse. We would like to see them." One type of picture that particularly interested *LJ*'s editor featured pretty women. For instance, after Frederick Wagman of the University of Michigan was elected to high office in ALA, Moon noticed that "Wagman also had a gorgeous wife, who was very photogenic. I put a picture of her in nearly every conference issue." In another instance Moon ran a photo (March 15, 1968) of a comely young lady showing lots of thigh with this cutline:

> Banned in Chicago: Miniskirts and modern art were thrown for a loss by the Chicago Public Library on February 15, when Susan Mero, 23, was fired after three months as the library's art director. Acting Director Alex Ladenson criticized her ability ("a rank amateur … with no ability to draw"); her clothes ("garish and extreme for public employment"); and her "frequent disagreements with department heads." Miss Mero, a graduate of the Chicago Art Institute, fired back, "there is just no room for young persons or young ideas" at the library.

The first of Moon's controversial covers (February 1, 1960) featured a photo of Senator John F. Kennedy seeking the Democratic presidential nomination. Moon included this note of explanation about the cover: "Not an announcement of Lj's sympathies in the battle for [the] Presidential nomination, but a newsworthy picture of one of the many eminent Americans taking part in the new television series, 'Reading Out Loud.' Here Senator John Kennedy, Pulitzer Prize winner as well as Presidential possibility, reads selections from Allan Nevins' work, 'The Emergence of Lincoln.' See news story on p. 509." Not unexpectedly, the cover drew some squawks from readers offended by what they saw as calculated political bias. Edith W. Taylor, librarian of the Smiley Public Library in Redlands, California, wrote: "I have just read your specious reasoning for having Senator Kennedy's picture on the cover of the February 1, 1960, issue of the *Library Journal*. Was he the only eminent and newsworthy member of that particular panel? I trust that you will include pictures of other potential candidates on future covers between now and June." Moon responded in an editor's note at the end of Taylor's letter: "We cannot guarantee to run pictures of other candidates between now and June [the Democratic Convention], because we have some doubts about the possibility of their being found 'reading out loud' in public."

Other *LJ* covers that drew fire in the 1960s included one sporting Lyndon Johnson's visage (January 1, 1967). "This was the first issue of the new format," recalled Moon, "and I wanted to have a startling cover." Another pictured a group of high school students at a "study-in" demonstration against censorship in their Farmingdale (Long Island) public library (October 1, 1967); the students were seated around a table in the library, showing off books that had been the object of the censor's wrath at one time or another. Mrs. M.D. Johnson of Wauwatosa, Wisconsin, wrote: "I am a librarian, and while I don't believe in censorship, I do believe in good taste! The cover on the October 1 *Library Journal*, showing students holding up the book entitled *Dirty Helen* while another student at the same table is holding up the *Holy Bible*, is surely a violation of good taste. I would expect *LJ* to be more selective in cover illustrations, even in this age of deteriorating morals."

Moon viewed covers as part of the magazine's editorial voice: "We did another cover during the period when library unions were just beginning to come to the fore, with several librarians in hard hats, which focused attention in that issue [November 1, 1968] on coverage of the growth of unions in libraries. That's what I wanted to do with covers. I wanted to have covers make a statement, primarily about what was in the magazine but also about the magazine's point of view. The cover was an extension of the editorial many times."

His most famous cover (October 15, 1964) dealt with the presidential election contest between Lyndon Johnson and Barry Goldwater. The cover, an example of cunning journalistic gamesmanship, consisted of Goldwater's portrait, suffused with a gold hue, accompanied by the intriguing caption, "Is it possible to be '...both a Goldwater Republican and a friend of the library'?— see page 3926." Readers turning to page 3926 found a Moon editorial ("A Clear Choice") that scrutinized the records of both candidates and ended with a ringing endorsement of Johnson. Librarianship had never seen anything like this before: "Magazines of many other professions have taken political positions at election time," noted Moon in the editorial, "but no library periodical, to our knowledge, has done so. We propose to make a dent in what we regard as a lamentable record of unnecessary neutrality."

Moon loved to tell the story of how the "epic" Goldwater issue came about:

The reason we put Goldwater on the cover was that, having made the decision to do something that had never been done before in library periodical history — that is, to make a declaration in a political election — we decided that it was so important that it had to have cover treatment. I wanted cover treatment that would ensure readers would turn to the editorial page first before they looked at any other part of the magazine. John [Berry] and I had gone over to the New York Public Library and had researched everything we could find regarding the candidates' voting records in the areas of education and libraries, and the results were devastating: the Johnson-Humphrey ticket was much more in sympathy with libraries than Goldwater-Miller.

So we ran this gold cover with Goldwater's picture with a little quote from the editorial at the bottom, which gave the page number. The New York Library Association conference was in New York City just at the time the issue was coming off the press. So I had a bundle of them delivered straight to the convention hall and put them on a table in front of the Bowker booth. I stood down at the end of the aisle, because I wanted to see what the reactions were. I could see people walking down the aisle and passing the booth casually looking around and they would get about two yards past the booth and do a gigantic double take and go back and grab a copy. It was working! They would look at this cover and then hurriedly turn to that page to see if I had gone crazy and endorsed Goldwater. So it worked!

Library Journal received a record amount of mail in response to the Goldwater cover and editorial — enough, according to Moon, to completely fill several issues. Some praised *LJ*'s editor for boldly advocating improved library service through active participation in the political process; others blasted him for bringing the unwelcome odor of raw politics into the vestal temple of librarianship. One letter accused him of attempting "to brainwash some idiots, such as you are one of…." Perhaps the strangest reaction to the controversy occurred when a longtime Moon antagonist, Maurice E. Walsh, Jr. (a reference librarian at the Jefferson Parish Public Library in Gretna, Louisiana), introduced a resolution at the 1964 Southwestern Library Association conference calling for the censure of the Bowker Company because its publication, *Library Journal*, had endorsed a presidential candidate. Walsh argued that, since *LJ* was a professional journal and "primarily a book review medium" that carried paid advertising, it had no right to express political opinions. The censure motion came to nothing, losing decisively on a voice vote to table after a librarian from Arizona, Goldwater's home state, reminded conferees of something called freedom of the press.

Moon, who never wavered about the rightness of his decision to endorse Johnson and put Goldwater on the cover, took full responsibility for the gambit: "There were some misgivings about it, even on the staff. Putting Goldwater on the cover rather than Johnson was my idea, and I wrote the editorial. It seemed to me if anybody was going to get into trouble it ought to be me." In the end *LJ*'s excursion into presidential politics, including the cover treatment, was deemed a great success: "Putting Barry Goldwater on the cover got people to read the editorial," said Moon proudly, "which is what I wanted."

Advocacy Journalism

At the time, no one, including Moon, thought much about what to call the subjective journalism that came to be so closely identified with *LJ* in the 1960s. Most people who read the magazine during those tempestuous years recognized, or had a strong suspicion, that something special was happening within its pages, but the exact name for it had yet to be coined. Moon's detractors tended to fall back on knee-jerk opprobrium, calling him a yellow journalist, a mudslinger, a scandalmonger, an idiot, and the like. Others viewed him as an early exemplar of "contrarian" or "investigative" journalism or a trailblazing representative of the so-called "new" journalism, but none of these terms quite captured what Moon and his magazine were about.

He, on the other hand, saw himself and his journalistic methods as very much in the tradition of the American muckrakers—gritty writers like Upton Sinclair, Lincoln Steffens, Ida Tarbell, and Ray Stannard Baker who investigated and exposed a host of social and political evils in the reform-minded progressive era circa the early 1900s. Interestingly, these writers owed a considerable debt to a British muckraker, William Stead, whose sensational articles in the *Pall Mall Gazette* in 1885 detailing sexual exploitation of disadvantaged women and children by upper-class men resulted in legislation outlawing white slavery (as it was then known). H.L. Mencken, Edward R. Murrow, and Kingsley Martin (longtime editor of the *New Statesman*, an influential socialist weekly in Britain) were Moon heroes too.

All of these journalists strived to discover and publish the truth as they saw it. Moon sought to emulated them: "I looked at Mencken and Upton Sinclair and the rest and said to myself, why don't more people write like this, question like this, and hammer away at our frailties so we can become aware of them?" He used *LJ* to raise questions, analyze problems, advocate solutions, but most of all to search for the truth. His enemies hated him for what he did to the library profession, while his supporters were full of admiration. John Wakeman, Moon's friend, colleague, and erstwhile rival, summed it up this way: "Muckraking energetically, naming names and places, *LJ* in the 1960s became essential reading for enlightened librarians everywhere."

Not long after Moon left *Library Journal* at the end of 1968 the term "advocacy journalism" entered the language. Merriam-Webster, the dictionary-maker and etymological authority, reports the coinage first appeared in 1970 and is defined as "journalism that advocates a cause or expresses a viewpoint." Later Moon himself used the term, acknowledging it as a fair description of his modus operandi at *LJ*. Certainly, *advocacy* embodies all the essential techniques he used in the course of remaking library journalism.

11

Remaking Library
Journalism: Triumphs

1963

Writers who specialize in the postwar period regard 1963 as a pivotal year in the American experience, some asserting that it marked the true end of the comparatively naive 1950s. Most horrendously, the murder of John F. Kennedy, a crime that continues to haunt, occurred on November 22. It was also the year the civil rights movement came of age. In June, before his death, President Kennedy proposed sweeping federal legislation that would eventually end de jure segregation in public accommodation, employment, and education in all sections of the country. In August Martin Luther King, Jr., delivered his historic "I Have a Dream" speech to a huge assembly gathered at the Lincoln Memorial in the nation's capital, and the following month the Ku Klux Klan bombed a black church in Birmingham, Alabama, killing four innocent young girls and further roiling the national conscience. In quite a different arena, 1963 was the year the United States first became involved militarily in the Vietnam conflict in any significant way. Bob Dylan, balladeer of the 1960s, wrote and sang the year's anthem: *The Times They Are A-Changin'*.

The year was pivotal for Eric Moon too. On March 6 he turned 40 — this at a time when the catchphrase "Trust no one over 30" was about to enter the American lexicon. But age hardly concerned him at this point: he was healthy, vigorous, strong, confident, totally involved in his job, on top of the world professionally, and busier than a ringmaster at a crowded circus. He had mastered the ins and outs of library journalism in double-quick time, as if born with printing ink in his veins and a clacking typewriter in the brain. In a few short years he had imbued *LJ* with a distinctive style and spirit, infusing the formerly leaden magazine with the energy, intensity, and conviction of a crusader while measurably improving its profitability. The last put a smile on the collective countenance of the Bowker brass.

In the fall of 1963, after nearly four years at the helm, Moon felt secure enough to respond publicly to a conservative critic who wondered when he might be vacating his editorship and returning to England: "It seems years since we were promised the departure of Eric Moon to the foggy confines of the British Isles," wrote Major James Hillard in one of his many churlish letters to *LJ*, "but each month his name continues to appear on the masthead as editor. Has the happy thought of his departure disappeared from the scene or what is the exact status of the editor of Lj?" Moon replied in an editor's note: *"We don't know who has been making promises to the Major, but his sources appear to be somewhat unreliable. Without attempting to define 'the exact status' of the editor of Lj, we are pleased to 'notify' Major Hillard that the person behind the name on the masthead is still here—and has hopes of remaining."* A tangible affirmation of Moon's success came toward the end of the year when Dan Melcher agreed that the magazine's board of editorial consultants—created to advise Moon the foreigner when he first came to *LJ*—was no longer necessary. By 1963, though still officially an alien in America, Moon was definitely *not* a foreigner.

The Bowker Company also experienced several important internal changes in 1963 that directly affected *LJ* and its chief editor. On March 9, only a few days after Moon had celebrated his birthday, Frederic G. Melcher, the company's elderly chairman, died. A publishing icon and the person most responsible for shaping the dimensions of Bowker in the 20th century, the senior Melcher was active almost until the end. His death naturally caused a shuffle in the Bowker boardroom: Louis Greene, who had been president, moved up to chairman of the board; Fred's son Daniel, vice president and publisher of *LJ* and *SLJ* while his father was alive, succeeded Greene as president; and Richard Bye, a rising Bowker star, was elevated to vice president. (Bye joked that he was "the youngest living member" of the company's board of directors.)

Moon got on well with all of these men. He had always had a warm spot for Fred Melcher, a true bookman, and he admired and respected the Harvard-educated, technically gifted Dan Melcher, whom he considered something of a genius as well as the best boss he had ever had. He knew—and readily acknowledged—that he could not have succeeded at *LJ* without Dan Melcher's unambiguous backing, a fact corroborated by Dick Bye: "Dan was as good as his word about giving Eric complete editorial freedom, and he supported him whenever he stirred up controversy, which was not infrequent." Though Moon had little in common with Greene, who had headed Bowker advertising for many years, he liked "Louie" well enough, remembering him as "a bit of a character." Once he went on a golf weekend with Greene, which said Moon, "amazed everybody, because they couldn't see that we would get along at all."

But they did. One of Moon's singular strengths as he matured, particularly after coming to North America, was his ability to work and bond with people very different from himself, people as diverse as Jessie Mifflen in Newfoundland, Dan Melcher and Louie Greene at Bowker, and later Al Daub and Ted Waller at Scarecrow Press and Miriam Hornback, Clara Jones, and Bob Wedgeworth at ALA. Moon's sensibilities became more urbane with age and experience, but it was more than that: his natural capacity for growth, both intellectually and socially, thrived in the freewheeling American environment, taking off in directions inconceivable had he remained in England, a much more stratified, less elastic society.

He and Dick Bye, a Greene protégé, connected right off the bat. Bye, roughly Moon's age, recalled, "From the beginning, Eric and I hit it off well and became personal friends as well as colleagues." The two men became especially close after Moon joined the Bowker board in 1965. Bye: "I have to confess that at times we were even somewhat conspiratorial about affairs, both business and personal, at Bowker. We were both shortly to go through marital breakups." For his part, Moon valued Bye as an astute colleague and agreeable companion:

Dick and I used to play hooky on occasion and go down to the Players Club in lower Manhattan, where he was a member, and play pool and have a drink at lunchtime, stuff like that. The club was always full of actors. One night before Max [Moon's older son] went overseas [while serving in the U.S. military during the Vietnam conflict], Dick and I took him on a night on the town and wound up very late at the Players. The club has two or three bedrooms on the top floor, one of which was Edwin Booth's bedroom. So we arranged for Max to sleep in Edwin Booth's bedroom on the night before he went overseas.

On April 5, less than a month after Fred Melcher's death, Bowker relocated its headquarters in midtown Manhattan from 62 West 45th Street to a brand-new, 22-story structure at 1180 Avenue of the Americas, a project that had been in the works for several years. The gleaming modern office building, not entirely finished inside at the time of the move, occupied the corner of West 46th Street and the Avenue of the Americas (the old Sixth Avenue), one block north of Bowker's former location. The company's magazines (*PW, LJ, SLJ*) were centralized on the 16th floor, while *BIP* and other book editorial functions found a home on the 15th floor. A photo in the April 15 issue of *LJ* showed Moon's spacious new office a month before the move in a state of raw construction: "Will it make the deadline?" asked the caption. Bowker's new quarters showcased the firm's prosperity and confident outlook in the early 1960s, an optimism enhanced by the resurgence of *LJ* as both a leading voice in the world of libraries and a moneymaker for shareholders. The company's new digs also provided space for additional staff, a point not lost on Moon, who for sometime had wanted to add a senior editor to the magazine.

Moon as Role Model

In October 1963, *LJ*'s editor took on the pleasant task of guiding a group of 137 British librarians on a two-week study tour of U.S. libraries in the Boston, Washington and New York areas. Moon knew most of the visitors, all members of the Association of Assistant Librarians. Among them were Ron Surridge, AAL president that year and the group's leader; Bill Tynemouth of Newcastle and long a power in the AAL; Jim Davey, a crony from London days; and Bill Graham, his friend from hometown Southampton, whom he was pleased to find in good nick.

Working in conjunction with Jack Dalton, dean of the library school at Columbia University, and Bill Woods, executive secretary of the Special Libraries Association, Moon took care of the arrangements for the tour on the American side, which included mapping the itinerary, securing transportation, and, aided by a committee of librarians in each city, scheduling library visits and social activities and finding accommodations for the visitors in the homes of American librarians. He met the group at Logan Airport and accompanied them on their rounds in Boston and then Washington. When they hit New York Moon "went back to work for a bit, leaving some of the hosting to Dalton and Woods, though I did join the group on a few social occasions." He relished his role as impresario, and it was with a swagger in his step that he guided the Brits on their tour, enjoying the opportunity to natter with—and impress—his former colleagues and meet some new ones.

By all accounts the AAL librarians had a most merry and informative time in the U.S. Surridge remembered it as "some party" and Jim Davey in a letter to Moon years later wrote, "I recall with pleasure our last meeting in Boston, Washington and New York when the AAL invaded the USA in 1963. I recall a bedroom scene when there were present Tom Featherstone, Tony Coles, Ron Surridge, yourself and myself, together with one or two young ladies, when we were planning the rest of the tour and on which occasion several calls were made to the reception for replacement bottles of whisky." Apparently the only sour note occurred in Boston where Surridge and Tynemouth, the most prominent AALers on the trip, got roped into being houseguests of Milton Lord, the august director of the Boston Public Library who sometimes confused his name with the genuine article. Lord crimped the style of the two Englishmen—both adventurous chaps—by insisting on picking them up each day at five o'clock in his chauffer-driven limousine and "entertaining" them at tea when they really wanted to be on their own seeing a bit of Boston.

Toward the end of the tour, after the group had arrived in New York, Moon, Surridge, and Graham cut out from the others to visit Stanley Crane in Connecticut. Crane, a Yank who had worked for Moon for a year at North Finchley, was now director of a small public library called the Pequot in the historic village of Southport on Long Island Sound. Stan and his wife, Leila, showed Eric and his friends around the library and then treated them to a meal of boeuf bourguignon. Crane gleefully remembered the main course had "so much wine in it that we poured the sauce into our glasses to ensure that none escaped!" Everyone got positively squiffy that night.

The AAL tour came at an opportune time for Moon. By the fall of 1963 he had been away from England for more than five years and he thoroughly enjoyed the opportunity to see his old mates again. They made him nostalgic for England, recalling a people and culture he instinctively knew and understood. Mark Hodges, an observant British librarian-émigré who had made his way to North America about the same time as Moon, attended one of the group's final meetings, held at the New York Library Club. Hodges, then on the staff of the Brooklyn Public Library, noted, "At the meeting Eric Moon and some of the visitors gave their impressions of American libraries. Eric, as I recall, was the moderator at that session. He was still very much a British librarian at heart at that time." This was doubtless true. In 1963 Moon was still viscerally British in demeanor. On certain levels he remained British all of his life. Nevertheless, by this time he had been in North America long enough to know in his head and heart that the decision to leave England had not only been right but was now irrevocable. Much as he enjoyed the camaraderie of his former English colleagues and reminiscing about the country of his youth, he knew by that time that he would never return to England, except as a sojourner.

The AAL tour provided an occasion not only for nostalgia but reflection on his current situation and all that he had accomplished and learned (not "learnt") since coming to America. He basked in his current prominence, happy to be a library VIP in the richest, mightiest country in the world. He remembered that many of his fellow librarians in the UK had consigned him to the professional dustheap when he departed for Newfoundland in 1958 — that's the end of Eric Moon, they said, as if writing his obituary. That had rankled him, piqued his ego, hurt his pride. But now here he was five years later, showing everyone that he had made it, that he had overcome the onerous qualifications obstacle, that he was a great success and personage in New York City of all places, the world's toughest town to crack.

He saw himself as a role model for other British librarians who dreamed of coming to America and making it too. He actively encouraged his AAL buddies to look for jobs in the States, and later he wrote an *LJ* editorial enumerating how many members of the tour had landed such positions: "Two of the group found jobs in Massachusetts public libraries, one is coming back to work in New York, and one gained a research fellowship at the Folger Library in Washington, D.C. Others took back application forms in their baggage, and still others voiced their intentions of finding exchanges or internships which would given [sic] them an opportunity to return, to see — and learn — more. Recruiters, take note."

An Epic Interview

Shortly after the British librarians' visit Moon returned to Boston to take care of some important *LJ* business: the recruitment of an assistant editor. The story, which begins well before the end of 1963, involves not only the earliest colloquy between the two men — Eric Moon and John Berry — who dominated American library journalism for the last 40 years of the 20th century, but what must be one of the most unconventional interviews in the annals of librarianship.

By the summer of 1963 Moon had convinced Dan Melcher that he needed an assistant editor to help him maintain *LJ*'s competitive advantage and take the magazine to the next level of journalistic achievement. To remain on the cutting edge, Moon argued, he needed someone who would share the editorial burden on a daily basis. He wanted a person as concerned and passionate about the social and political issues impacting librarianship as he was, a person who would work his ass off to assist him in making *LJ* the best professional magazine anywhere. Shirley Havens was Moon's right arm, but as managing editor she had all she could handle and then some. What Moon wanted and needed was an aggressive senior editor who would work directly with him, an editor whose job it would be to whip out spiky editorials and travel the length and breadth of the profession reporting on major happenings and trends in the field; an editor with the smarts and know-how to plan and produce entire issues of the magazine, so that he, Moon, might on occasion be freed from the semimonthly deadline grind to work on major features and related projects.

Moreover, Moon wanted — needed — a sidekick. He had always had a close male crony in England, a Bill Graham, a Ron Surridge, a Bill Smith, an Al Bowron, a John Wakeman — someone ready to share the load, someone to drink with, plot with, argue with, compete with. He missed not having such a relationship at *LJ*. For all sorts of reasons none of his colleagues at Bowker could fill this void. The closest he came was George Wieser, *LJ*'s crack advertising man, but George was on the road much of the time and besides their jobs were completely different. So when he came to recruit someone for the newly created position of assistant editor, he took into consideration not only the obvious qualifications but a variety of intangible attributes the candidate ideally ought to have, such as the ability to drink but remain in control; to bullshit and sound good doing it; to keep horrendous hours yet get up bright-eyed and bushy-tailed the next morning; to compete hard (for stories, attention, success, women, whatever) and usually win, though losing to Moon would be no crime; and to challenge anyone anywhere at anytime concerning the validity of any of the library profession's hoary verities.

For more than a year he had had his eye on a librarian in Massachusetts named John N. Berry III, who gave off a strong whiff of the stuff he was looking for. A bright, ambitious, articulate young fellow with seemingly the right stance on the issues, Berry was then the assistant director of the Simmons College Library in Boston as well as an adjunct professor at the college's library school — at the time the only ALA-accredited library education program in New England. Berry himself had earned an MLS at the school in 1960. But it was his editorship of the *Bay State Librarian*, the quarterly bulletin of the Massachusetts Library Association, that drew Moon's attention. Berry had taken over the magazine in 1962 and immediately produced several sparkling issues, a rarity among state library periodicals, which normally offer little more than fluff and leftovers.

Ever on the alert to encourage fresh talent Moon applauded Berry's good work with the *BSL* in an *LJ* editorial titled "A Rebirth" (September 1, 1962): "We have been tempted several times during the past few months to comment on this rebirth of a library periodical, but we resisted hasty judgments. We wondered if the new editor, John N. Berry, III, of Simmons College Library could keep it up. It is relatively easy to produce one, or even two, fresh and lively issues of a periodical, but to do it with consistency takes effort and imagination. Mr. Berry seems up to the challenge." Articles by Lester Asheim and Dan Lacy, both big-name contributors, and one by Charles Copeland, city librarian of Salem (Massachusetts), particularly impressed *LJ*'s editor. Regarding the Copeland piece, which attacked state aid for libraries and was sarcastically titled "Pennies from Heaven," Moon wrote, "…in dealing with this truly sacred cow, the editor [Berry] even had the temerity to present one contributor who was distinctly 'agin.'" Moon also heaped praise on a "hard hitting" article Berry ran by Truman Nelson, a minor leftwing novelist, that called into question public library book selection practices. Concluded Moon, "If you think *all* library periodicals at the state level are as compulsively dull as yours probably is, take a look at the new *Bay State Librarian*. And ask your editor to do likewise."

Moon nominated the *BSL* for the H.W. Wilson Library Periodical Award, which annually recognized a local, state, or regional magazine for its contribution to the profession. Just as Bill Eshelman's *California Librarian* won the 1960 award with Moon's backing, Berry's bulletin took the prize for the year 1962. Thrilled, Berry went to the ALA conference in Chicago the following summer to receive the award, and there he met Moon for the first time:

I won the H.W. Wilson Award and it was all Eric's doing. I couldn't afford to go to the conference, but Galvin [Thomas J. Galvin, a colleague and mentor of Berry's at Simmons], to his credit, stepped into the breach and said I'll ask for money so you can go out to Chicago to accept the award. So I went out with Shaffer [Kenneth Shaffer, Berry's boss at Simmons] on the plane. He went along to show me the ropes. I got there and met Eric and I sort of went off with him. Shaffer didn't like that much. I felt bad about it afterwards but at the time I was so damned excited. Eric introduced me to all his cronies and we had a great time. That was when I first met him and got to know him. I really liked him; we played poker and discussed issues constantly. People were constantly attacking me. It was terrific.

Berry attracted attention at the conference not only because of his award but a controversial editorial about libraries and race he had written in the April 1963 issue of the *BSL*. Called "A Question," Berry's editorial implied that a prestigious national grants program for small public libraries—the Dorothy Canfield Fisher Library Awards, administered by the Book-of-the-Month Club with the advice and cooperation of the American Library Association—had given cash awards to nearly a dozen libraries, most in the deep South, *that apparently were racially segregated*. In 1963, with ALA in the midst of a battle royal over the segregation question, this was an explosive charge. Unfortunately, the *BSL*'s neophyte editor had not thoroughly checked his facts, a point Moon drove home in a counter editorial, "Questioning a Question—And Some of the Answers," in the July issue of *LJ*: "Is it responsible editorial practice to ask a question, loaded with dynamite as this one is, without first making an attempt to check the facts with the individual libraries involved, with the state library agencies or with ALA?" Moon's four-page editorial went on to present solid evidence, including statements from some aggrieved librarians, that young Mr. Berry had indeed got it wrong in all but one of the cases.

Moon recalled that "John was terribly wounded" by the criticisms leveled in his *LJ* editorial. Berry, who later pleaded "naive audacity" concerning the Canfield Fisher Awards flap, remembered, "I never had anything blow up into a firestorm quicker than this. I got letters from all the libraries I had named, and then Eric's editorial appeared in *LJ*." Prior to publishing his lengthy commentary, Moon invited Berry to defend his position, which he did at length. Part of Berry's defense appeared in Moon's editorial:

It is my contention that any such award, involving as it does the American Library Association, must expect the scrutiny of the profession, and its recipients should respond as freely to inquiries as several have done in this case. The truth, in print, will provide a unique and gratifying statement opposing segregation....

The question was asked editorially with the full intention that it would be answered editorially, regardless of the results. It is my conviction that asking libraries, many in the deep south, to respond to this question will serve one of two purposes. If they respond with the resounding "No!" to segregation that the editorial expects and desires, then we have an impressive collection of documentary evidence from southern libraries, to publicize a fact in which the profession should take pride.... On the other hand, if there are among the eleven libraries, some which do segregate, then we have forced the exposition of this practice, and at the same time discovered a flaw in the selection of recipients for the award.

Moon faulted Berry for poor judgment and for not doing his homework, but he admired Berry's gumption for raising the issue and for his composure under fire. When Moon finally met Berry in Chicago, he liked the kid, whose blond hair, good looks, restless eyes, lopsided smile, and facile tongue rendered him an agreeable companion. Moon was especially struck by Berry's natural enthusiasm for argumentation. So it was that soon after the AAL tour group returned home, Moon contacted Berry to set up a meeting in Boston to further observe the young man and assess his potential for the assistant editor position at *LJ*. Moon's interview technique was unorthodox:

I called John and said I was coming up to Boston and would like to get together with him for a drink. And we went on an enormous drunk through all kinds of seedy pubs, and I was trying to create problems wherever we went. We'd go into an Irish bar and I would declare at the top of my voice that "THIS IRISH BEER IS PISS, ISN'T IT!" It went on like that for about a day and half. At the end of the time I said to John I wanted to see how you could drink and how you would stand up to a little pressure. And now I'd like to invite you to become assistant editor of *Library Journal*. And he said, "Man, you're the craziest guy I've ever met in my life! First you absolutely assassinate me in print, then you come up here and get me drunk, and then you offer me a job!" Of course I had to clear John's appointment with Dan and the board, but there was no question that it was my choice.

Moon's offer came at a time Berry was at a turning point in his life. Though the idea of living in New York did not appeal to him, by the end of 1963 he was ready to leave Simmons. Early on he had been acclaimed a wunderkind at the college, sailing through library school with straight "A" grades while working full-time at the Reading (Massachusetts) Public Library. Politically conservative (he had worked for Nixon's election in 1960) and socially amenable (he was fair-haired and deferential), Berry became a protégé of Ken Shaffer (dean of the library school and director of the college library) and Tom Galvin (Shaffer's second in command), both of whom were eager for acolytes to assist them in making Simmons a powerhouse in the competitive world of American library education. After receiving his MLS, Berry joined the college library staff as reference librarian and he was invited to teach part-time at the library school.

Shortly thereafter Berry began to undergo profound personal changes. He had come to know and be influenced by an old-line trade union radical and fiery writer, Truman Nelson, a neighbor in suburban Boston. In the fall of 1962 Berry actively participated in a campaign to elect H. Stuart Hughes, an ultraliberal Harvard professor, to the United States Senate from Massachusetts. Around the same time he started making the coffeehouse scene and learning protest songs; *Big Bulls in Boston*, which told the story of a local black folksinger's encounter with police brutality, was a favorite. Meanwhile he was increasingly in the soup with his mentors, who were taken aback by his new attitudes and behaviors. Shaffer and Galvin, 1950s-style organization men who distrusted the liberal impulse in all but its most superficial manifestations, began to distance themselves from him, worried that he had gone off the rails or, worse, over to the enemy. And the powers that be at the Massachusetts Library Association, nervous about the direction he was taking their magazine, added to Berry's problems by imposing an editorial advisory committee on him. Finally, his marriage was in deep trouble.

When Moon called in late 1963 and said he was coming up to Boston and might the two of them get together for a drink, Berry was elated. He had enjoyed meeting and kibitzing with Moon that summer in Chicago and, despite the critical *LJ* editorial, he regarded Moon as a hero, someone to idolize and emulate. Berry said he had no idea Moon was considering him for a position at *LJ*, though this did not stop him from fantasizing. His version of the night on the town with *LJ*'s charismatic editor conveys the confusion of a young man at a crossroads:

So Eric and I had this night in Boston. And right away we began to get into an argument. He was contentious and competitive, and I was—I don't know—my attitude toward Simmons was ambivalent; I was feeling fairly empty about it all. So I was very receptive to Eric's seductions. At the same time we got very drunk. I took him to my favorite haunts, because I didn't know what else to do. I didn't want to do a Shaffer on him [i.e., PR on him], because he wasn't that way and I wasn't that way.

I used to frequent a bar down on Charles Street, called the Sevens—77 Charles Street—which was a beat hangout of that era. So I took Eric there. Then we went to Durgin Park [an informal restaurant in the Faneuil Hall area]. He liked that whole style—the women who would throw the food at you and yell at you. He got right into the spirit of the place, yelling back at the waitresses. One of his great attributes was that wherever he went he got right into whatever was going on. And there were some Irishmen at the other end of the table and he got into a big British-Irish thing; we nearly got into a riot right there. Then we went on drinking into the night. That's how I really got to know and like him. But all the time I had no idea I was being interviewed for a job. I would have been much more guarded if I had known.

The Boston phase of Berry's "interview" finally ended sometime in the small hours, leaving both men hungover but pleased that their encounter had gone so well. Moon, certainly, was satisfied enough with Berry's performance to offer him a key position at *LJ*, and Berry now had a face-saving way out of his difficulties. In due course Berry came to New York to meet the top Bowker people and have lunch with the board of directors at an upscale Manhattan eatery, The Lobster.

Among those who strongly favored hiring Berry was Anne Richter, the grande dame of Bowker's book publishing operation—and an old friend of the Berry family dating back to the 1930s. Eventually it was agreed that John would work principally for *LJ* but would also spend a portion of his time in Richter's bailiwick, getting to know something about the book side of the business too. Relieved to have escaped gracefully, even triumphantly, from Simmons and the Shaffer-Galvin axis, Berry "saw Bowker as a deliverance from a lot of things." He even started having good vibes about New York City, feeling "absolutely gaga" after his expensive luncheon with the Bowker biggies.

A Complex Relationship

Berry began his career at Bowker on Monday, May 25, 1964, and liked it so much he has stayed into the next century. He quickly learned the ropes at *LJ* while establishing an effective working partnership with Moon. The two men genuinely liked and respected each other, and their philosophies of librarianship, while not precisely the same, were reasonably close, as were their political convictions—though Berry's were still evolving in the mid–1960s. Both men were highly competitive, verbal, and argumentative, and they sometimes disagreed with each other simply for the sheer hell of provoking a response, much as Moon and Bill Smith had enjoyed skewering one another in public debates back in the 1950s in England. Berry's chief complaint in the early days concerned his office, which was not much bigger than the proverbial breadbox.

It did not take Moon long, however, to discover that Berry still had quite a bit to learn about the rudiments of journalism. His new assistant editor exhibited impressive raw talent but it needed shaping and direction. From the beginning Moon viewed Berry very much as his pupil, his apprentice, his junior. For his part Berry—though he had a wild and rebellious streak—readily acknowledged Moon as his leader, his mentor, his master.

Some observers have suggested that Moon and Berry formed a classic father-son relationship. Despite only ten years' difference in their ages—in 1964 Moon was 41 and Berry 31—there's considerable anecdotal evidence that the two men psychologically assumed the roles of parent and child during the four and a half years they worked together at *LJ* and that this continued even after Berry took over the magazine in 1969. Moon, for instance, often adopted a chilly patriarchal manner when Berry disappointed or failed him, which occurred more frequently than either man would have liked. Conversely, Berry looked for approval from Moon and was often hurt or angry when he didn't receive it. Moon was the stern, mature, disciplined taskmaster and Berry, the self-indulgent, undisciplined moppet.

It is clear that Berry did have some weaknesses as a journalist and editor when he arrived at *LJ*, and that Moon did work hard to shape him up, providing much valuable guidance via both word and example. According to Moon, Berry's major failings included his "never having learned to proofread" and his "lack of an eye for detail," which often caused him to miss typos and errors of fact. Even more egregiously, he sometimes failed to pursue factual accuracy with sufficient diligence. "The editor," Moon said years later, "must be responsible for every single thing in the magazine from cover to back page. I think it was apparent that when John took over, the number of errors in *Library Journal* increased considerably." Berry also had a problem with deadlines and procrastination, the twin bugaboos of many writers. Moon: "John was always struggling with deadlines. One of the things he used to get a bit annoyed about with me was conference coverage. We would be running the *LJ* suite around the clock for a week [during the conference] and then come back home. I would frequently type right through the weekend, and when we got back to the office on Monday morning I'd say, 'OK, I've got my conference report done, where's yours?' That really pissed off Berry."

Moon taught his new sidekick a few things about the art of writing as well: "John always claims I edited him rather cruelly, but like many people he was always a little florid at the beginning and inconclusive at the end, so I used to chop off his first and last paragraphs. This used to upset him." Moon remembered Berry once exploded, "You've got this fucking fetish about first and last paragraphs. You've just got to knock them out, don't you!" Berry confessed that he once angrily told Moon, "Your whole career has been devoted to killing my best writing." But over time, albeit reluctantly, Berry came to see the wisdom of much of Moon's advice: "John has said that he benefited from what I did to him in the early days, much as he resented it. He realized that he became a better writer as a result of it." The truth of this observation becomes apparent to anyone who compares Berry's first published efforts after joining *LJ* with those he produced just a year or so later. His style, at first stiff and dense, became increasingly fluid, idiomatic, and readable. Today Berry is universally regarded as the foremost editorial stylist in the library field.

Politically, Moon and Berry clicked from the outset, both being well to the left of the American mainstream in the mid–1960s. Berry got a boot out of showing off his relatively new radical habiliments to Moon: "Eric and I had immediate compatibility when I started dropping the old words and names— Progressive, Young Communist League, Wobblies. When I would break into the old revolutionary songs, he understood where they came from." But Moon's views were solid and settled, rooted in a lifetime of adherence to British Labour Party and Fabian Society ideology, whereas Berry's were very much a work in progress.

Soon after coming to New York Berry's marriage (in his words) "quickly deteriorated" and he began living with a woman whose father "was a New York Communist Party leader." This woman, said Berry, "taught me everything I needed to know for the rest of my life. I was a dumb, redneck WASP about sex, about politics, about everything. She gave me liberation for the rest of my life." John N. Berry III, who had been "raised Republican in the era of FDR" and had worked actively for the election of the Republican presidential candidate as recently as 1960, underwent a series of political shock treatments just before and soon after coming to *LJ*. By mid-decade, he had been slam-bang radicalized from head to groin.

It was not long until the competitive Berry, full of his new truths, began to see himself as a bigger lefty than Moon: "I began to press Eric. At this point in my life I was more radical than he was." By way of example, Berry cites the famous Goldwater cover issue of *LJ* (October 15, 1964), suggesting that he, not Moon, was the motivating force behind it. "To this day Eric takes total credit for the Goldwater cover. But I goaded him into it," recalled Berry, adding: "Now you mustn't say that — I think you should let him take credit for that." Which is what a dutiful son would say, isn't it?

Shoeleather Journalists

Moon always maintained he could not properly edit *LJ* from a chair in New York City. He believed the only way to find out how cows become steaks is to tour the slaughterhouse. To find out what was going on in the library field, to understand the American profession in all its guises and dichotomies, he made it a point to travel around the country and meet the players. His earliest outings took him to national and state conferences in Chicago, Montreal, Cleveland, Miami Beach, California, and Maine, among other places. He also abandoned the office as often as he could to attend or speak at meetings and symposia devoted to professional issues of the day, and occasionally he found time for small projects that took him into the trenches, such as his saturation buying survey of public libraries in the New York–New Jersey area.

Likewise, he eagerly accepted invitations to speak at library schools around the country. Not only did such engagements get him out of the office, they allowed him to size up the next generation of librarians. Who knew, tomorrow's "Eric Moon" might be sitting in the very classroom he was addressing. Bob Croneberger, for many years director of the Carnegie Library of Pittsburgh, remembered first meeting Moon "in 1962 in a materials selection class taught by Dorothy Bendix at Drexel. Eric was caustic, provocative, stimulating and irritating as hell." Like so many other students who heard Moon's dissident song in those days, Croneberger became an instant admirer of the outspoken *LJ* editor. For his part Moon truly wanted to find out what was on the minds of students: "When I went to talk at library schools I usually stayed overnight because I found that students who wouldn't say much in the classroom in the presence of faculty members would rap for hours in a late night party atmosphere."

Among the library schools Moon visited frequently was the University of Pittsburgh, where two British expatriates he knew and was fond of—J. Clement (Clem) Harrison and Norman Horrocks—had landed in the early 1960s. Moon's trips to Pitt provided an endless stream of amusing stories, the kind he loved telling. Most of the stories revolved around the dean of the school, Harold Lancour, the man who almost got the *LJ* editorship in 1959 after Lee Ash's sudden departure. Moon found Lancour to be an affable and sociable man, though one time he got the dean's dander up: "Harold loved to have little gatherings, breakfasts, and so on. I kind of liked him. One time at one of his gatherings I had been invited to be the guest speaker, and the program went on all evening. I don't remember what was dragging it out, but I finally got up to speak at about 11 o'clock at night and I said, 'Welcome to the Late, Late Show,' and Harold got incensed about this sort of levity." Another typical Pitt story involved excessive partying and esoteric poetry. Moon: "I was staying with Norman, and Harold had one of his Sunday breakfasts. We had all been drinking into the wee hours the night before and the next morning the telephone rang and Lancour said, 'Where are you all?' We all had to scramble out of bed and go over to his place for breakfast—I think I drank two jugs of Bloody Marys before we started breakfast. Nassar Sharify [a faculty member at the school] entertained us by reading Persian poetry in the original. We were dying."

The addition of John Berry to the *LJ* staff in May 1964 took some of the incessant deadline pressure off Moon. Immediately after the new assistant editor arrived Moon traveled to London on assignment for *Publishers Weekly*, where he covered a major international book fair. His report—"London's First World Book Fair: Trade Show or Public Fair?"—appeared in the July 24, 1964, issue of *PW*. (For reasons not clear this was the only work Moon ever did for *PW*; doubtless internal rivalry had something to do with it.) The coming of Berry also increased the opportunity for *LJ*'s editors to do more investigative reporting than had been possible previously. For instance, Moon launched an ambitious new feature called "A Day at (or in)…" in the fall of 1964. Published on an occasional basis, "A Day at…" offered readers substantial reports by staff on a variety of trendsetting library developments and worthy institutions.

Moon kicked off the new series with "A Day in Bedford Stuyvesant," published in the October 1, 1964, issue. The article provided a fascinating firsthand account of Hardy Franklin's pioneering work as a community coordinator with the Brooklyn Public Library in a desperately poor, heavily African American area of the city sometimes called the Brooklyn Harlem but known to everyone simply as Bed-Stuy, code for the worst kind of American ghetto. In the end Moon spent considerably longer than a day with Franklin:

I had heard about Hardy and decided to go over to Brooklyn and spend a day with him. He was the first street librarian in America. Actually, I was there for two or three days in the heart of Bedford Stuyvesant. We wandered around many places where I'm sure if I had been on my own I would have been wiped out. But Hardy knew everybody. His job as community coordinator was to help bridge the gap between the street and the library; it had to be done on the human level. He had many frustrations because of poverty and illiteracy — and because of library bureaucracy.

Over the years Moon contributed a number of other pieces to the popular "A Day at…" series, including one in 1968 on High John, an experimental — and controversial — program developed by Paul Wasserman and Mary Lee Bundy at the University of Maryland library school to study and improve public library service to disadvantaged youth. Shirley Havens did several articles in the series too, reporting on her visit (with Moon) to the Library/USA project at the 1964 New York World's Fair and solo trips to the library at the Pentagon in Arlington (Virginia) and the Library for the Blind in Philadelphia.

But it was Berry, *LJ*'s designated legman (don't snicker, it's an old and honorable journalistic term), who researched and wrote most of the "A Day at…" features. His first effort, published in the November 15, 1964, issue, involved a day-long session at the United Nations where he interviewed the director of the Dag Hammarskjold Library, a Russian named Lev Vladimirov who beamed with pride when he informed the *LJ* editor that the Soviet government, just like the American government, recognized libraries as a vital "part of the machinery for social change." Berry remembered that Moon "loved" this quote. He also did "A Day at Library School" (January 1, 1965), which probed the inner workings of the Graduate School of Library Service at Rutgers University, then headed by the dynamic Ralph Shaw, a polymath who had more irons in the fire than any librarian since Melvil Dewey. Moon warned Berry that interviewing Ralph Shaw in the morning was "like having six martinis for breakfast," a perfect metaphor that found its way into Berry's article.

Another memorable "A Day at…" piece by Berry, published in the April 1, 1965, issue under the title "To Catch a Thief," entailed traveling to Michigan to test new electronic anti-theft devices recently installed at public libraries in Flint and Grand

Rapids. Part of Berry's assignment called for him to try to smuggle books out of the libraries without activating the system. Moon advised him not to worry if he got caught:

Dan Melcher, who had a strong technical aptitude, spent a whole day showing John how to the beat the system before he went out to Michigan. We told him to go and break the system, to steal 20 books, and then go back and interview the chief librarian, asking what good is the system when I can break it so easily? And John says, "But what if they catch me and put me in jail?" I said, "That's an even better story." Anyway, he went out and did the story and it was very good. He was marvelous at doing the outside stuff, the "Day at…" kind of stuff.

Moon's Shop

While Berry's easy assimilation into the workings of the magazine resulted in a spate of excellent staff-written features and reports that clearly enhanced its substance and readability, *LJ* continued as before to reflect the style, passions, and vision of its chief editor. Throughout his nine-year reign at *LJ* Moon exercised tight control over both the quality and direction of the magazine. With an uncanny ability to focus on the big picture while keeping requisite details securely in mind, he initiated or approved practically everything that went into the journal, and any differences of opinion with staff were almost always resolved quickly and amiably. Moon had near perfect pitch for what would work in the magazine and what would not, an intuitive journalistic sense that inspired — and sometimes intimidated — his colleagues at *LJ* as well as editors at rival publications.

Though very much in control, he developed a managerial style that placed a premium on informality and open communication. His preference was to lead by calculated example and reliance on employee self-motivation:

I never really regarded myself as an administrative type. I think I operated very loosely and informally. I said to people, this is your job, get on with it. And while I would check on it, I didn't tell people in detail how to do their jobs. As I recall, we didn't have terribly formal meetings, but anytime anybody wanted to talk, we just sat down and talked. My door was always open and we would get together whenever we felt like it. We'd go out to lunch together and drink together, go to publishers' parties or whatever. We operated pretty much off the cuff. As far as I know it was a very happy outfit.

In 1966 Moon invited Bill Katz, a well-known library science prof (SUNY Albany) and experienced periodical editor (*RQ* and the *Journal of Education for Librarianship*), to come to New York and give *LJ* the "Day at…" treatment. Katz's article included a admirably textured description of Moon as he appeared at that time. At first glance, wrote Katz, "Moon is a disappointment," his physical presence not imposing:

He roars in print, but no one would pick him out of a line-up as the library world's answer to James Bond. Slight, the year around 40, faint moustache, conservative dress— sports coat and matching slacks, usually — pipe smoker, quick to laugh but generally slow and precise when talking, etc. It might be the man next door, possibly even the local librarian. Only his eyes betray the lively, inquisitive, sometimes almost frightening drive.

He's not an easy man to understand, and a visitor has the feeling that's just the way he wants it.

Everyone at Bowker in the 1960s, including Dan Melcher, understood that *LJ* was Eric Moon's domain, his baby. During those years Moon devoted the better part of his life to the magazine, putting in unbelievable hours and dealing with more paper in his shop in a week than most library editors handled in a year. His work habits stressed efficient organization and judicious use of time. Shirley Havens observed and esteemed these qualities: "Of all the editors I worked with on *LJ*, Eric was the only one who was not a deadline pusher. So well organized was he that articles were edited and editorials written in advance, letters were answered promptly, and his desk was clear by the end of each day. His cleared-desk habit was an admirable if infuriating trait, especially for those editors who could hardly be found behind the mounds of paper and galleys on their desks." Katz, in his "Day at Lj" account, also noticed Moon's orderly approach to work: "It was past 10 A.M. and from time to time someone would break in with a question or a phone call. A pile of papers, neatly stacked on Moon's desk, slowly disappeared. Swinging around in his chair, he placed some on the table behind him. Others he penciled rapidly, still others hit the wastebasket."

Every bone in Moon's body abhorred procrastination: "I've always liked to get things done immediately; I figure if I delay them, they might never get done. It was part of my habit to answer every letter the same day it was received. Every manuscript was dealt with one way or another within three days at the outside. Berry learned this lesson — ha ha." Similarly, deadlines were sacrosanct. Moon prided himself on never missing a deadline or coming up against one he couldn't lick: "I got so good at deadline writing in fact that the staff knew they could come to me ten minutes before deadline and say, Eric, we're got a 50-line gap here. Write something. I'd sit down and type up 50 lines and give it to them. When you're doing it all the time you can get that good. I couldn't do that now but at that time I could. I could tear off 20 pages on a conference in a day with no problem."

Though he did not like the instrument, Moon learned to use the telephone extensively as a means of saving time and cutting down on paperwork and clerical costs. On the other hand he rarely used a tape recorder, finding it cumbersome and inefficient: "I was a pretty good notetaker and I had a phenomenal memory at the time (which I don't anymore). I didn't like hauling the machine around and found the business of transcribing the tapes just awful. I also found that when I had a tape recorder with me, I didn't get nearly as good an interview than if I just sat down with a couple of glasses of gin and started talking."

Over the years Moon worked most closely at *LJ* with editors Shirley Havens, John Berry, Karl Nyren (who joined the magazine in the fall of 1966), and Margaret Cooley. Havens, who retired as *LJ*'s executive editor in 1987 (and who died in February 2000), noted that Moon challenged his colleagues to stretch themselves as editors and writers: "Eric encouraged staff to develop their sometimes 'latent' potential and perform to the best of their abilities, and even beyond their perceived capabilities. He involved senior staff in decision-making regarding 'questionable' articles, and encouraged staff to write articles and editorials (much to the dismay of some of the more timid of us)." Along the same lines Judy Serebnick, Margaret Cooley's assistant, recalled, "Eric consulted us in Mrs. Cooley's book review department when he was researching and writing about librarians' responses to controversial and/or neglected books. I recall that I was particularly interested in his article 'Problem Fiction.' I think I suggested a couple of the less well-known titles that became part of the final list of books he used for the survey."

He also took an avuncular interest in the careers of promising younger staff. In the case of Serebnick, Moon encouraged her to go to library school and get an MLS: "Judy, who was Margaret Cooley's number two and a smart young woman, got very interested in what we were doing at the magazine generally and this led her to become a librarian. I recommended she go to UCLA and wrote to Larry [Powell, the school's dean] and she got in and has since had a very successful career teaching at Indiana." Serebnick went on to get her doctorate and teach at the library school at Indiana University for 17 years before retiring in 1994.

As *LJ*'s reputation as a major influence in the library profession grew in the 1960s, Moon's shop on the 16th floor of the modernistic building at 1180 Avenue of the Americas in midtown Manhattan became a mecca for out-of-town and foreign librarians visiting New York City. Moon welcomed their interest and took pleasure in playing a knowing host. One time a prominent New Zealand librarian called on him and they discussed, among other things, which New York area public library system most likely had the best collections of English-language fiction from countries other than the United States and United Kingdom. Moon ventured that Brooklyn would be number one, Queens two, and the vaunted New York Public, the logical first choice, "dismally" last. The visiting librarian went off and did a quick-and-dirty survey and a week later called Moon to say, "You were right!"

Librarians dropping by *LJ* also served as a convenient way for him to develop new contacts and solidify old ones. Moon was always on the lookout for good people who might help him make *LJ* a better journal, and in due course he developed an extensive coterie of loyal writers, correspondents, and news sources. In one instance, however, his efforts to accommodate a star author almost caused a staff revolt. Daniel Gore was an academic librarian who had created a great uproar by publishing an article widely perceived as traitorous to the profession. Entitled "The Mismanagement of College Libraries," it appeared in the March 1966 issue of the *AAUP Bulletin*, a publication widely read by college administrators and faculty. This of course did not endear Gore to the academic library community. Around the same time Moon ran similarly controversial pieces by Gore in *LJ*. "In Praise of Error," for instance, dealt with cataloging and generated much heated response from offended catalogers, which only increased Moon's desire for more articles from the contentious Gore. So when Gore asked if he could have space at *LJ* to work on a project while on a visit to New York, Moon said sure:

Some people thought Daniel Gore was a creature of *Library Journal* but, no, I think I discovered him through an article he had written elsewhere, and I thought here's a guy who can write. I invited him to write for *LJ* and he did several things. What I do remember most vividly is that once he descended on *LJ* and said he was in New York for a period of time and could we give him an office where he could work while he was in town. And I said I'd find him a space somewhere, which I did. I remember that he smoked huge black stinky cigars and within about two days the staff said, "This guy has got to go!"

Moon Becomes Bowker Director, U.S. Citizen

By the mid–1960s *Library Journal* was doing very well indeed. The quality of the reportage, feature articles, editorials, columns, and graphics, including the covers, had improved dramatically since the dim days of November 1959 when the Melchers imported a totally unknown British librarian named Eric Moon from where?— Newfoundland!— to edit the magazine. By the middle of the decade *LJ* had helped spark large and small transformations in American librarianship, becoming *the* voice for advocates everywhere of progressive change and reasoned dissent in the profession. Not since Melvil Dewey launched the *American Library Journal* (shortly thereafter the *Library Journal*) almost a century earlier had a periodical publication had such a telling impact on the library world. The magazine now consistently offered the most informative, most penetrating, most inventive, and most inclusive coverage of the profession found anywhere in North America and quite likely the English-speaking world. Moon's efforts and those of his staff were driven by an energy and a spirit found only among those passionately committed to their work.

Outside confirmation of *LJ*'s new prominence came from many sources. The journal won the Edpress Award "for excellence in Educational Journalism" in both 1964 and 1966. A reader study conducted by the journal *College & University Business* in 1966 found that top U.S. academic library administrators read *LJ* on a regular basis more than any other periodical in the field, including those devoted wholly to academic libraries. In addition, *LJ* frequently received unsolicited praise from library leaders, sometimes even from those who normally opposed Moon's activist approach. For instance, Edward Holley, then director of libraries at the University of Houston and most certainly not a wild-eyed liberal, sent *LJ* the following letter, which appeared in the July 1965 issue:

> For some time I have been meaning to write a word of congratulations for the superb articles appearing in *Library Journal* during the past year. In a time when our profession is undergoing significant changes, Lj has provided stimulating articles on these controversial developments. I have not always agreed with Lj editorially, nor do I always agree with the authors. However, the quality of the writing has been excellent and the content thought-provoking…. I personally find the recent articles in Lj heartening evidence that the challenges and opportunities which are in the offing will be successfully met.

By the middle of the decade *LJ* was going great guns on the business side too. According to an article in the *Encyclopedia of Library and Information Science*, the magazine under Moon "began, for the first time in its history, to flourish fiscally as well as editorially." Subscriptions were way up and advertising revenues were rising as fast as liberal expectations during the early years of Lyndon Johnson's presidency. Major federal library legislation enacted in 1964-65 — the Library Services and Construction Act, the Higher Education Act, the Elementary and Secondary School Education Act, and an expansion of the National Defense Education Art — poured hundreds of millions of dollars into improving the nation's libraries at all levels. These were, in Moon's words, "fat, golden years for libraries," and a goodly amount of that largesse ended up in Bowker's coffers in the form of income derived from space advertising sold to promote new books, magazines, reprints, videos, filmstrips, microforms, and various services for the nation's libraries.

And why did *LJ*— along with sister publication *SLJ*— garner such a large share of the library advertising dollar in the 1960s? Because publishers, producers, suppliers, and booksellers knew that *LJ* and *SLJ* were the most extensively and intensely read journals in the field and that by placing their ads in these magazines they had the best shot at reaching their potential customers— librarians. George Wieser, *LJ*'s advertising sales wizard during those years, observed that Moon's editorial policies made his job a piece of cake: "All I needed to do my thing was for *LJ* to be *the* magazine for librarians— and Eric made it just that."

Moon's main reward for his success came on January 21, 1965, when he became a member of the Bowker board of directors. Five years of extraordinary effort and unconditional hard work had paid off: Moon was experiencing the American dream, or at least a felicitous version of it, and it was all due, he believed, to the R.R. Bowker Company:

I very quickly became a Bowker stockholder — and pretty quickly a director of the company, which was something that amazed me. This was one of the very positive differences I saw between the United States and Britain. I was impressed that I could come to a country as an unknown and in a relatively short time become a director of the company and a stockholder. This was a refreshing difference from the way it was in Britain — this willingness to recognize and reward ability. In Britain, you had to hope your tie was the right color when you went for an interview. What I did not know then was that Bowker was atypical, that it was not like this all over the U.S. Bowker was very much a socialist company, because it made stock available to employees throughout the company, down to the shipping room boys. And Bowker management had a marvelous ability to recognize when somebody had it, and then push that person into a position of greater responsibility.

Moon's elevation to the board was also an acknowledgment by the Bowker chiefs that *Library Journal* was no longer a pip-squeak among the company's products, that it was now in the same league as *Publishers Weekly*, long Bowker's most adored magazine product. Moon:

Daniel [Melcher] wanted to see some younger members coming on the board to develop as the future leadership of Bowker. Liz Geiser and I were the two who were picked — both of us had been very successful at what we were doing. Liz was in promotion and marketing at the time, which I didn't have a lot of connection with, but she was very good at it. Clearly, it was recognition of what we had contributed. But I also saw it as long needed recognition of *Library Journal*. This was a breakthrough for *LJ*, recognition that *LJ* ought to have a powerful voice in the company. It had had that to some extent with Daniel [who was *LJ/SLJ* publisher], but that was kind of indirect. It needed somebody who was totally identified with *LJ*, and that was me. The impact of this on the *LJ* staff—my appointment to the board—was considerable. They really felt it was a recognition for all of us.

That same year, 1965, Moon became a citizen of the United States, though the proceedings resurrected a painful ghost from the past: "During the citizenship business, they asked if I had ever been convicted of anything. In one of the early interviews I said no, but in the final interview they went over each question again and asked if I wanted to revise anything I had said earlier. I began to smell a rat, so I revealed that I had been involved in a drunk driving incident in Canada—and they knew it all along." Some years later Moon sponsored his brother Bryan for U.S. citizenship. Recalled Bryan, "Eric emigrated to the States and kept telling me to do the same. Some years later I decided he was right but entry to the States could be expedited by a sponsor. By then, big brother was an American citizen and he became my sponsor."

A New Assistant Editor

John Berry held the position of *LJ* assistant editor from May 1964 until the fall of 1966, when he was transferred to the Bowker book editorial department under Anne Richter, though he continued to work for *LJ* part-time as "a contributing editor on special assignments." As a consequence, Moon had to recruit a new assistant editor. His first choice, Arthur Plotnik, declined the offer. Art Plotnik, then in his late twenties, was in the midst of winding up an MLS at Columbia University, but he was no greenhorn, having worked as a newspaper reporter prior to entering library school. Moreover, he possessed a degree from a first-rate writers' program (Iowa) and was the pseudonymous author of a number of erotic paperback novels. Early in 1966, around the time Berry's transfer to book editorial had been decided, Plotnik sent Moon two smartly crafted articles for possible publication in *LJ*, marking the first contact between the two men. Moon liked Plotnik's style and originality and he was equally impressed by the young man's bona fides. After some minor revisions, Moon accepted both articles, the first published in the May 15, 1966, issue. A short while later he offered Plotnik the assistant editor position.

"It was flattering," Plotnik remembered, "but I wanted to taste library work itself; I was on my way to the Library of Congress as a Special Recruit." After Plotnik's rejection, Moon turned again to Massachusetts (from which he had plucked Berry earlier), inviting Karl Nyren, director of the Cary Memorial Library in the historic town of Lexington, to consider the job. Moon had admired Nyren's work for several years. Especially noteworthy was a 1963 film called *The Fifth Freedom* that Nyren wrote and narrated to promote National Library Week in Massachusetts. At the time Moon devoted an editorial to the film, singling out for praise the young female lead (Nyren's daughter), the script, and the narration—"delivered so well and so richly that Mr. Nyren bids fair to be the profession's Ed Murrow." Nyren did a similar film in 1964, and the following year he wrote a much discussed article, "Trustees in the Age of Consensus," that Moon published in *LJ* (September 15, 1965). Happily, Nyren accepted Moon's offer and began work at the magazine in September 1966.

Moon did not use the same interview technique on Nyren as he had on Berry. Why not? "I needed someone quickly and I was convinced that Karl had the horses— he seemed to me to have all the horses." Furthermore, Nyren, who had a fine arts background and wrote poetry, was much quieter and more reserved than Berry. And he was older — in fact he was almost two years older than Moon. Like Moon, Nyren had served in World War II, but unlike Moon he had seen action, had been wounded, and had received the Silver Star for bravery in the Pacific. Consequently, Nyren never became Moon's sidekick in the same way Berry had. Still, the two men got on well, working together until Moon left *LJ* at the end of 1968. "I liked Karl," said Moon, looking back, "but he was much harder to get to know on a personal level than Berry. He was a much quieter operator. But we were very good friends."

Just as Berry had done, Nyren had no difficulty adjusting to the *LJ* routine. He was soon contributing polished editorials and feature articles, plus perceptive reports from the field. He also wrote many of the news items that appeared in *LJ* beginning in late 1966, and in 1972 (well after Moon's departure from the magazine) Nyren founded a new Bowker publication called *Library Hotline*, a weekly supplement to *LJ* dedicated to breaking news stories. Nyren's only flaw, according to Moon, was his propensity for factual errors: "The only problem with Karl was that he tended not to double-check things, so he would make a lot of errors." Moon's friend Bill Eshelman was much more caustic: "Karl was always kind of laid back, and never got his facts straight. He misspelled names, et cetera. He just made the sort of errors you shouldn't make. I'm sure Eric liked Karl. He kept him on, although some wondered why."

Perhaps Moon kept Nyren on because he could write rings around most other library journalists, including Eshelman. Nyren's editorials often had a poetic quality, and during the 1970s he created a mini stir in libraryland with a series of creative pieces in *LJ* featuring the doings of an imaginary librarian named Hooper and his staff, including Sylvia, the Cataloger of Unbearable Beauty, who worked in the fictitious town of New Mills, USA. Nyren continued to edit *Hotline* right up until his death (of cancer) in 1988 at age 66. In a tribute, Berry summed up Nyren: "He was a fine writer, an honest journalist, unmoved by fear or favoritism, commercial or political pressure. As we once said, he really invented *LJ*'s style of reporting, gave it to a library world once starved for reports that told all, straight, direct, sometimes even brutal. He taught us all a lot."

The Library Journal *Format Changes*

In August 1961, after almost two years as editor, Moon initiated some modest changes in *LJ*'s format, switching the body (or text) type from Caledonia to Times Roman and moving a couple of regular features from here to there. At the same time he announced more changes would be forthcoming: "We shall go on making them," he promised readers, "in the belief, tinged ever so slightly with skepticism, that Spenser was right when he said: 'All that moveth does in Change delight.'" Small modifications did occur off and on over the next five and a half years, but it was not until January 1, 1967, that readers got a truly revamped magazine.

The most obvious change involved the magazine's page size, which increased from 6¼ by 9¼ inches to 8½ by 11 inches. In an editorial announcing the new format (in the December 15, 1966, issue), Moon suggested *LJ* should have the same size page as the "big boys":

Lj's last redesign of any consequence was in 1958; its last major format change in 1920. We have concentrated for several years now on improving the magazine's content, but it has been apparent that a face-lifting was overdue. When, at last, we decided to do something about Lj's appearance, we could see no good reason why the change should not be a drastic one. Nor could we see why Lj should not adopt the standard size of the major general periodicals such as *Newsweek, Time, Harper's, The Atlantic, Saturday Review, The New Yorker*. Although we were not in a circulation league with these big boys, we had, with a current circulation for Lj and SLJ of over 50,000, passed many respected magazines from general, literary, or political fields, such as *Encounter, The American Scholar*, or *Commentary*. We stood in fact, just about midway (in circulation) between *The Nation* and *The National Review*.

He went on to point out that in recent years *LJ* had experienced "awesome" growth and most likely would continue to do so, a happy development—though it created one big problem:

Lj, uniquely among the periodicals of the library profession, had a weight problem — and when a man grows out of his suit (let us not even suggest that ladies ever do), he buys a new one. We knew some of the reasons for our bulk problem: that we continue to combine professional coverage with major book information and reviewing services; that we refuse to be content with some selected corner of the library field but regard the whole of librarianship as our editorial beat; and that with the awesome growth of library activity in recent years, we must grow with it. The result is that our own growth has been awesome, too. Lj's total page count for 1966 (6,226) is 674 higher than just last year, and 1,750 higher than five years ago.

Only two options for dealing with the magazine's bulk problem were realistic, said Moon: "…move to a considerably larger page, or reduce or fragment Lj's editorial coverage. When reduced to this simplicity, the alternatives did not really constitute a choice." Only the larger format, allowing for more information per page, made sense. Some concerns were voiced at Bowker that such a change might adversely affect advertising sales and revenue, since most library and book trade clients at that time produced ad copy geared to the smaller page size, then the standard not only at *LJ* but *PW, SLJ, WLB*, and the *ALA Bulletin* (forerunner of *American Libraries*). Might not *LJ* lose space advertising and the dollars it generated if the journal went to a larger page? No, argued Moon, because "*LJ* was so strong, the others, including *PW*, would have to follow us." And that is largely what happened: "They nearly all changed within a short time to the *LJ* format size," said Moon. Little pleased the highly competitive Moon more than forcing two rivals—the *ALA Bulletin* and the haughty *PW*—to follow his lead. The *Wilson Library Bulletin*, which, according to Moon, "made little effort to sell advertising," did not switch to the larger format until 1984.

Library Journal's new look featured not only a bigger page size but new type faces, including the handsome, contemporary Optima. Coincidentally, Moon met the designer of Optima on one of his trips to the library school at the University of Pittsburgh. He was elated:

Harold Lancour suggested I stay over for an extra day because the next day the famous type designer Hermann Zapf was speaking at the library school. He was in Pittsburgh in connection with a limited edition book he had designed the type for. The Hunt Botanical Library wanted its own type for its books and Zapf did the design. We had lunch, and I told him I had just had *LJ* completely redesigned and one of the things I insisted on was the use of Optima for all the headlines throughout the magazine, and here I was meeting the man who designed this type I loved so much. And Zapf gave me a signed copy of one of only six copies he had that showed how the type had been designed, including drawings at various stages, which absolutely made my year let alone my day.

The January 1, 1967, issue also introduced some significant content changes. The "On the Grindstone" column was ended, replaced by a quite similar "Viewpoint." Bill Katz inaugurated his valuable "Magazines" column, which continues to this day (though Katz no longer does it). Eli Oboler, one of Moon's most memorable adversaries, was invited to do an occasional series offering profound thoughts under the heading "Oboler Dicta"; an example: "Before every national library conference the impossible is expected; after every national library conference the incredible is taken for granted. Between conferences library leaders plan for the acceptable." A profile of public library developments in Illinois kicked off an ambitious but never completed 50-part series called "Progress Reports from the States." And Karl Nyren upgraded the library news section, which in the redesigned *LJ* consumed a dozen or more pages covering everything from stories about new libraries ("LBJ Library Model Unveiled in Texas") to unsettling reports from the field ("Cleveland Librarian Slain; On the Way to Choral Practice").

In addition, the expanded news section gave increased attention to personnel problems at major libraries. The August 1967 issue, for instance, carried a story ("New Orleans Librarian Reinstated, But Penalized") describing in detail how Ruth K. Robbins, a senior librarian at the New Orleans Public, was disciplined for calling the head of technical services, Marvin A. Mounce, a "scared pup" and a "squirt." In the revamped *LJ*, Moon moved the news from the middle to the front of the magazine, an indication of the importance he attached to current issues.

The new format met with favor in just about every corner of the profession. John Lorenz at the Library of Congress offered his congratulations, adding "It makes the prospects for library service in the last third of the 20th Century look even brighter." Lillian Bradshaw, head of the Dallas Public Library, thought the new design was "magnificent." Ellsworth Mason, director of libraries at Hofstra University, chipped in, "I like the new *LJ* format, and the January 1 issue was very impressive in its contents…. There are very few professional fields as well served journalistically as librarianship is with *LJ*." Moon appreciated the bravos, especially from prominent practitioners like Lorenz, Bradshaw, and Mason. But by the time they had come in, he was off and running after new challenges. No matter what one thought of Moon — whether you loved him or hated him — no one ever accused him of resting on his oars.

Battles with the American Library Association

One of Moon's perpetual challenges—and frustrations—was the American Library Association. He wanted this behemoth of an organization, which he believed had great potential for helping librarianship become a central force in American society, to confront a wide range of divisive social and political issues—racial segregation, poverty, gender discrimination, invasion of privacy, government secrecy, and war were obvious examples—that impacted on both the society and the profession. Moon argued that for the association — the largest library organization in the world — to ignore these and similar problems was tantamount to operating in a moral and intellectual vacuum. But it did not take him long to discover that the ALA power structure cared little about such concerns and, ostrich-like, preferred to ignore them.

One of Moon's top priorities after arriving at *LJ* was to learn as much about ALA as quickly as he could and to begin attending its meetings straightaway. To understand ALA he needed to know how it was organized, what its rules of governance were, and who actually ran the show. What he found in those early days was an organization comprised of thousands of disparate members, both personal and institutional (including publishers, booksellers, and other commercial types), that were pigeonholed into dozens upon dozens of divisions, committees, and sundry other interest groups and subgroups, all serviced by a paid and heavily bureaucratized headquarters staff presided over by an entrenched executive, David Clift, who in 1960 had been in his job for a decade and would remain there for another dozen years before finally retiring in 1972.

On paper, ALA's governing authority rested with a large representative Council elected by the membership (the ultimate authority), while a much smaller Executive Board managed the affairs of the association, including the headquarters operation. But the real power in ALA had long since been ceded to the paid staff and a few gray eminences who influenced events behind the scenes. In the 1950s in the UK, Moon had battled the mossbacks of the Library Association in an effort to force recognition that libraries are part of society and therefore librarians must deal with its concerns. In the 1960s he encountered a similar situation in the United States, where ALA seemed every bit as obdurate as its British counterpart, sometimes more so.

It did not take Moon long to annoy the people who ran ALA. In what was deemed unseemly or uncivil behavior, he openly criticized ALA policies, actions, and inactions in needling editorials and conference accounts—the two were sometimes indistinguishable: a critic once observed that one of Moon's conference reports was the longest editorial ever to appear in *LJ*. His frontal attack on segregated libraries and library associations in the South and condemnation of ALA's tacit complicity in this shameful business earned him the enmity of many ALA movers and shakers. To put it in the vernacular, he ended up on the association's shitlist. Grace Stevenson, deputy executive director of the association at the time, told people, "*We* do not speak to Mr. Moon," and David Clift, the executive director, pointedly snubbed him.

Moon remembered one occasion, however, when Clift could not avoid shaking his hand:

David held some big ALA reception to which everybody who was anybody was invited. I was standing outside with George Wieser and some other guys chatting when Fanny Cheney [Frances Neel Cheney, the most famous reference authority of her day] arrived in all her finery, walking down the stairs with her usual flair, and she said, "Eric, what in the hell are you doing out here? You should be in there." I said, "Fanny, they won't let me in." And she said, "The hell they won't! Take my arm, boy." So we went down the receiving line and the last one we got to was David Clift. She said, "David, you are an idiot. This man is one of the most important men in this profession and he ought to be at this party, and shame on you for not inviting him." And we walked off together into the party.

Moon believed Clift and his minions misunderstood him, jumping too quickly to the conclusion that he was anti–ALA:

In reality, I was very pro ALA, but I wanted it to do things it wasn't doing and that it ought to be doing. In speeches all over the country I always said to people you ought to belong to ALA. If you want to do anything about this profession you have to belong to ALA because it's all we've got, and you can only change it from inside, not outside. If that doesn't sound like support for ALA I don't know what is. But I was perceived as an enemy, as were E.J. [Josey], John [Wakeman], and others. Clift and his people were very sensitive to criticism and usually overreacted to it.

Nevertheless, Moon found himself persona non grata with the ALA Establishment. More concerned about not offending powerful Southern interests than ending racial discrimination, the ALA barons could not forgive Moon for *LJ*'s exposure and relentless coverage of the race issue, which became uglier and uglier as it dragged on and on. He further antagonized the Establishment by leading a campaign to democratize ALA, an organization that in the early 1960s had more in common with benevolent despotism than democracy. A major aspect of Moon's campaign involved persistent efforts, assisted by John Berry and Bill Eshelman, to open up meetings of ALA committees and other bodies traditionally closed to rank and file members and the press.

Eventually Moon and his brother journalists succeeded in opening up practically all ALA meetings, including those of the powerful Executive Board, which had a history of secretive backroom dealings. In a speech delivered at the centenary conference of the Library Association in London in 1977, he looked back on those hectic days in the 1960s with a sense of pride and accomplishment:

As editor of *LJ* I wanted no strings on what I could report and I used to "crash" closed meetings regularly. I got very promptly marched out of quite a few. But the message got across and others began to understand the perils of privacy, and began to insist that the doors be opened. Today, it is a requirement that *all* ALA meetings be open to members, and to the press. You have to have a very solid reason for an executive (that is, a private) session — for example, a meeting at which individuals may be being considered for some appointment — and even then, the results must be reported in open session.

One library organization that adamantly refused to open its proceedings to any outsiders in the 1960s was the Association of Research Libraries, and naturally Moon made it a priority to breach that wall of secrecy. Ralph Ellsworth, a prominent ARL member who became one of Moon's "great favorites," gave him some advice—bad advice actually—about how to get past the ARL palace guard. Moon told this revealing story:

I got to know Ralph around the time I was trying to open up ALA meetings. For several years I kept going to what were described as closed meetings and getting marched out, and I kept doing it and doing it and then reporting on it in *LJ*, until ALA got to the point that almost all meetings were open to all members, not just those on whatever committee or division it happened to be. When we had virtually achieved this at ALA I said to Ellsworth, I think I'll have a crack at ARL. He said it won't work the way you're doing it. But I wanted to try anyway.

So I walked into ARL's next annual meeting, which of course was closed, and I was frog-marched out by three members of the association and told this is a private meeting and I was not welcome. Ralph said to me, "Eric, will you stop being a hardnose and try it my way? I have a couple of card games—poker—with the ARL leaders. Why don't you join us and let these people get to know you as a person and not this ogre everybody thinks you are? Maybe then we can sneak you in." So I said OK. But, he says, don't take all their money. So I said OK, Ralph, I'll play to lose and charge it off to taxes or something. And we played a few times and they were very dull players. At the next ARL meeting I walked in and I was frog-marched out again. I said, "Fuck you, Ellsworth, this is not working and I'm not going to pay for this privilege again."

Moon also irked the Establishment when he ran for and was elected to the ALA Council in 1965, serving until 1972. (He would return to Council twice more during his protean career, in 1976–79 and 1982–86.) From the beginning of his *LJ* editorship Moon actively participated in ALA floor debates while concurrently covering association deliberations in the magazine. No one thought much about this, but when he got elected to Council his detractors (and more than a few of his friends) questioned whether the editor of a leading library publication that reports on the profession should also be sitting on the governing body of the national association. Wasn't this an obvious case of conflict of interest?

Moon pooh-poohed their concerns: "A number of people wanted to have a new bylaw passed that would exclude members of the library press from running for Council. We defeated that, of course, but there was a lot of criticism from that point of view. My reaction to it was that it made no difference to me whether I was on Council or off Council. I was going to report the same way, so why shouldn't I be there—at least that way I could get all the facts and documents." Message to his opponents: don't argue with a pro. Still, even as close a colleague as John Berry had difficulty squaring Moon's position: "I do not have to give up my role as a member [of ALA] because I edit a magazine. But yes, I do think it would be inappropriate to run for office—although there are circumstances under which I might."

Vietnam

Toward the end of his editorship Moon found himself and *LJ* caught up in a much larger and more wrenching controversy—the war in Vietnam. In many ways the war went to the heart of his unhappiness with the ALA Establishment and its refusal to connect the dots between librarianship and major social and political concerns. By the late 1960s the United States had become mired in a seemingly intractable military conflict in Vietnam, a politically divided and partitioned country in southeast Asia. American troops in Vietnam, first a handful of "advisers," ultimately became an army numbering more than half a million troops. Television brought the fighting and its horrors into American living rooms, sharply dividing the country into hawks and doves. By 1968 bitter protests against the war had crippled and then brought down the Lyndon Johnson presidency.

The war had a profound impact on nearly every aspect of American life, and librarianship was no exception. Specifically, Vietnam affected the profession in two quite distinct ways. First, it helped radicalize a corps of young librarians and library students, who viewed the conflict not only as evil *qua* evil but symptomatic of all that was wrong with American society, including their chosen field. For them, the war exposed the country's institutions—political, military, economic, educational—as anti-democratic, hypocritical, inflexible, racist, and on and on. Encouraged by the pervasive climate of protest and riot on the homefront, these young people spearheaded a library revolution that first showed its colors at the 1968 ALA conference in Kansas City and then exploded the following year in Atlantic City.

In addition, the war had a chilling economic impact on American libraries. Johnson's Great Society legislation, enacted in the glory years of 1964 to 1966, addressed a broad range of pent-up societal needs in the country, among them improved schools and libraries. But soon the war started draining away dollars needed to fund Johnson's social programs, and by 1969 the country had a new president, the Republican Richard Nixon, who immediately began dismantling as much of the Great Society as he could. Nixon's first budget, for instance, drastically cut federal aid to libraries.

Much as Moon admired Lyndon Johnson for his domestic policies—"He was probably the best president this country has ever had domestically; he was fantastic for libraries, and he was right on the racial issues"—*LJ*'s editor became a critic of the war in Vietnam, considering it "pointless and evil" as well as a disaster for his profession. He agreed completely with Karl Nyren's poignant summary in a June 1969 editorial describing what Vietnam had cost American libraries: "…it looks as though we've spent our book money on the most expensive of all nonprint learning materials, the Vietnam war. The only consolation is that it will certainly teach the young a lot. About us."

Moon's major contribution to the war literature—an editorial "Voices on Vietnam?" (*LJ*, October 15, 1967)—challenged librarians to speak out against the conflict, to take a stand. It urged librarians to join publishers in signing and helping finance a full-page antiwar ad in *The New York Times*, a protest organized by Bowker's Dick Bye. The editorial was signature Moon:

We have noticed before when public protests have been made—even in areas closely related to library interests, such as censorship—that while the names of writers, publishers, editors, illustrators, and photographers can be counted on to appear in support of such statements, the names of librarians have stood out only because of their rarity. Among the possible reasons for this phenomenon are:

First, that because librarians properly assert that the library is neutral ground in that it represents (or should represent) *all* sides of public issues—the conclusion has been drawn that librarians themselves are all neutral, and they are therefore rarely asked to participate in public protest.

Second, that librarians really do *not* care, that their concern with social, political, and international issues is less than that of other members of society or members of other professions.

We are not prepared to accept the latter grim conclusion, nor to believe—if the first of the assumptions above has any validity—that the anonymity of librarians among the voices of dissent need continue.

In a clever journalistic move Moon published only letters *opposed* to his editorial, and there were many, representing every strain of conservative thought on the subject. Years later, in 1992, "Voices on Vietnam?" was reprinted in *LJ* as part of an "LJ Classics" series sponsored by Gale Research, and again the editorial drew fire from the right: "Thank you for reprinting Moon's misguided 1967 proposal for a response by librarians to the Vietnam War," wrote Patrick Tweedy, a librarian at the University of California. "I have become curious as to how and when the library profession came to be the leftist advocacy group that it is today, and Moon's editorial is a fascinating link in that devolution."

The Vietnam conflict touched Moon personally too. Both his sons served in the military during that time, and in the case of Max the war caused tensions between father and son. Reflecting on the situation 25 years later, Moon recalled "no harsh debate" with Max over the pros and cons of the war, only muted disagreement and repressed anger:

Max tends to clam up rather than argue when he is upset. But it was fairly clear that he, like other Vietnam vets, thought those of us who opposed the war were wrong and unappreciative of what they were going through. That was not my position, however; I was sorry to see him there and afraid his life might be terminated in a war I saw as both pointless and evil. It may be that the impetus for this was our disagreement over the college he should attend. We had visited a number and I wanted him to go to either North Carolina or Duke, either of which was prepared to accept him. But he wanted to go to Miami [in Florida], which I saw as Playboy University. I think it may have been the stalemate on this matter that provoked him into not going to university at all but enlisting. I think the resentment over this lasted a long time—indeed may still simmer.

The Moon Mafia Forms

When Eric Moon came to New York in the late autumn of 1959 to take up his duties as editor of *Library Journal*, very few American librarians knew anything about him, let alone had heard of him. That quickly changed. In a relatively short time Moon's name, style, and progressive positions on key issues became well known not only to readers of *LJ* but practically all American librarians with an ounce of interest in the profession beyond the confines of their specific job. By the mid–1960s a librarian would have had to have been close to comatose not to know who Eric Moon was and at least vaguely what he stood for.

From the outset Moon made it his business to meet as many of his new American colleagues as he could. He prided himself on being a shoeleather journalist out in the field rather than a button-down editor surveying the profession from his lofty chair — his famous chair — high in a tall building in midtown Manhattan. He wanted people to know him, and he wanted to know them. Not only was he curious about what made American librarians think and act as they did, but he was eager to discover which ones might in some way or other be useful to him and his magazine, either now or in the future. It did not take him long to meet the library lions, who were always on parade at ALA meetings. His friend and colleague Norman Horrocks remembered "attaching myself to Eric for a week and meeting all the movers and shakers at my first ALA meeting" in 1963 soon after he arrived in the States to teach library science at the University of Pittsburgh.

Moon had his eye out too for young, lesser known talent — librarians who would be the *LJ* mainstays and association leaders of tomorrow. Arthur Curley, who became a Moon protégé and eventually president of ALA, was a prime example. Curley, who died prematurely at 60 in 1998, left this evocative memory of the first time he met *LJ*'s famous editor. It was at a conference in Milwaukee circa 1965:

Eric had taken over *LJ* at about the time I came into the field. After working for a couple of years at the BPL [Boston Public Library], all of a sudden I was the director of a small library in Massachusetts at age 23, building a collection and engaging in all the great social issues. I was certainly a young, impressionable, idealistic kid — and Eric in every issue of *LJ* was saying what libraries should be, things that I could only struggle toward. I actually first met him after I left that little library and went to Palatine, Illinois, a suburb of Chicago. I was then only 25 years old. I was there no more than a couple of months when there was a big regional library conference in Milwaukee. It turned out to be the best conference I ever attended. It had everyone who was a name, like Lowell Martin and Ervin Gaines, but Eric was the star. The first night Eric held court in the bar. I was just a young kid wandering in, but I had been reviewing books for *LJ*, and Eric said to me, "Come on over."

The next day after a program — I would say it was about 3 o'clock in the afternoon — we all headed for the bar in this hotel squeezed between two breweries, and Eric again held court. He was this presence; he just exuded excitement, and idealism, and wit and charm. There must have been 60 people all trying to gather in a circle of tables around him. It got to be later and later and later — finally it got to be 3 o'clock in the morning, and we're down to about six or seven people still there, and we're all ready to cave in, and Eric says, "Well, I think we better close this place down." We figured that means let's call it a night. We find a cab and Eric hands the guy a bill and says, "Find us something that's open at this time of night," and, Jesus, we're off doing up the city! We come staggering back to the hotel at about 6 o'clock in the morning, dragging in from this all-nighter.

He had a 9 A.M. speech to give at the conference that morning. After having breakfast, it's about 8:30 in the morning. Eric simply goes up to his room, splashes water on his face, comes back down, and while I am having to tape my eyelids open, he gives, as somehow you knew he would, an absolutely stunning, relaxed, inspiring, everybody-on-the-edge-of-his-seat presentation. When the thing is over, Eric comes down off the stage and comes over to me and says, "Arthur, let's go get a hair of the dog that bit us," and he takes me out for a Bloody Mary.

Art Plotnik, another up-and-coming recruit to the profession, recalled encountering Moon at the Palmer House hotel at an ALA Midwinter meeting in Chicago in the late 1960s:

> Eric was holding court—how well he could always do that!—in a cocktail terrace that jutted out into the Palmer House lobby. He was surrounded by library royalty, and seemed to delight in making newcomers feel comfortable in this heady setting. Eric was a knockout at conference bars and restaurants. He acted like a winner, taking crowds to joints with potted palms and atriums, picking up enormous tabs, not giving a damn. This in an environment where others were counting every penny, splitting tabs down to the number of coffees ordered. It was awesome to a newcomer. What a stereotype-buster!

As the split between liberals and conservatives in the profession became more pronounced in the latter years of the decade, Moon emerged as the principal leader of a group of mostly younger librarians who wanted a more socially responsible librarianship—that is, a librarianship that was part of, and not dissociated from, society and its needs, problems, and concerns. The librarians clustered around Moon had no formal name, membership roster, or organizational structure, only a common perspective on the profession and its mission. Moon assumed a leadership role because, one, he controlled an influential publication that served the profession; two, he articulated the philosophy of social responsibility in words and deeds that adherents understood and admired; and, three, he was, quite naturally and irrepressibly, a leader.

One member of this progressive group of librarians, the late Elizabeth Futas, caught the flavor of those times in this 1994 recollection, published as part of a review of Moon's last book, *A Desire to Learn*:

> I met Eric Moon in June 1968. I had been invited by a colleague to attend a meeting of the Social Responsibilities Roundtable [ALA's Social Responsibilities Round Table, or SRRT, did not come into existence officially until early 1969]. The group met at the Jefferson Market branch of the New York Public Library and consisted of such "young Turks" as Arthur Curley, E.J. Josey, Patricia Schuman, Ellen Gay Detlefsen, John Berry, Dorothy Broderick, Betty-Carol Sellen, and Joan Marshall, to name just a few. About thirty in all, as I recall, met that night. The meeting was a planning session for the annual conference [in Kansas City] later that month of the ALA. The ideas, the causes, and the people I met that evening changed my life, and I owe (and blame) Eric Moon for filling the next twenty-five years of my professional life with challenges, causes, meaning, principles, and values in a manner I never dreamed possible.

At some point in the latter 1960s people began referring to the activists gathered around Moon as the "Moon Mafia," a label originally attributed to Thomas Galvin, a Moon antagonist who used the term in a deprecatory sense, though others found it catchy or sexy and soon it became part of ALA insider lingo. (Keyes Metcalf, a library eminence of the previous generation, was said to have had a "mafia" long before Moon, which he used to place disciples in key positions and increase his influence within the profession.) The Moon set was also jocularly referred to as the "Moonies" by some, and Bill Eshelman, who was there at the creation, suggests yet another name for the group—the "Moon Bunch"—in his memoir *No Silence!*

Moon himself always called his closest friends and allies in the profession just "The Gang." He explained who was involved and how they operated:

The Gang was an inner core of friends who spent a lot of social time together as well as politically active time. It included Pat Schuman, Arthur Curley, E.J. Josey, John Berry, Bill Eshelman, Pat Rom — all close friends — and of course Ilse [his second wife]. We spent a lot of time together; we were always seen together. But I don't think there ever was a Moon Mafia. It was a figment of the imagination of people like Tom Galvin.

There certainly was a group of people with whom I was identified over the years — people who argued for liberalization and social progress in ALA. Josey, Curley, Schuman, Berry — there were many others, but these are the kinds of people we're talking about. The group did not operate in any formal or coordinated way, but sometimes when an issue came up, somebody would come to me and say, "What do you think we should do about this?" At that point somebody would say, "We've got to get organized about this." It was a very informal network. There were people who were identified as part of the Moon group with whom I disagreed enormously and frequently — Dorothy [Broderick] and Zoia [Horn] are examples. Sometimes we fought together, sometimes we fought each other. But there was no machine or mafia.

Pat Schuman, like Arthur Curley a past president of ALA and Moon protégée, confirmed that "Eric and his inner circle often disagreed with each other," but, she added: "There was mutual trust; the group was held together by mutual trust." Another view of the Moon tribe comes from an observer outside the circle. Ernest DiMattia, long an active member of ALA and successful public library administrator, frequently interacted with Moon and his followers but remained apart from it:

Unless you were part of the Moon camp or a Moonie, Eric was difficult to know; he had a negative facade. I'm sure that Eric had some good friends but I'm not sure he had a whole host of good friends. I think he chose his friends very carefully. There was a clique — a group — and it was difficult to break into it because most of the people in the clique were of a similar ilk as Eric — people like Norman Horrocks, Arthur Curley, and E.J. [Josey]. They were difficult to get to know, a bit standoffish. I think Eric surrounded himself with people who were like himself, who were self-confident, who were determined to have an impact, who wanted to influence the direction of ALA. I've always felt that Eric, while not a loner, didn't have a lot of real friends.

The Library Journal *Suite*

Every group, no matter how casual or loosely structured, needs a home base, a place where members can relax and enjoy their fellows, a place where they can bounce ideas around, plan new ventures, relive old battles, a place to let their hair down and be themselves. For much of the 1960s and into the 1970s that place for the Moon Mafia and their friends, and friends of their friends, was the *LJ* suite at the conference hotel in whatever city ALA happened to be meeting. It was here the profession's activists came to rap, to plot, to gossip, to party, to connect. The *LJ* suite was where it was happening, man: talk, music, sex, booze, revolution.

But the suite was not just a gathering place for library rebels, especially at first. Moon:

In the early years of the 1960s, particularly, many of the big names came by regularly. (Those were the years when I was trying to broaden *LJ*'s contacts and influence.) Among frequent visitors were such as Harold Hacker, Harold Tucker, Lillian Bradshaw, Keith Doms, and many, many more who could under no circumstances be thought of as members of the Moon gang, group, bunch, mafia, whatever.

Later in the decade the suite certainly became more a regular haunt of the activists (there were not many around in the early years), but it was still not that only, or perhaps even primarily. One of its major purposes, always, was the broadening of contacts, the gathering of information. And we wanted to demonstrate that this was one place in ALA that was always open — to anyone. So, because we were so wide open (and informal, unlike Wilson or World Book parties, for example), just about everyone tended to come by at some time or other, even some of our adversaries (like Tom Galvin), perhaps because other parties had closed and they had nowhere else to go, or perhaps to whet their curiosity and see what "those people" were up to.

Moon remembered the suite — the generic suite — as almost a mythic place:

For ten solid years the *Library Journal* suite was a virtual center of activity of all kinds. It was the place that you could be sure anybody who was involved [politically active] would show up sometime during the week of the conference. The suite was open around the clock. It was a place where there was always entertainment. Dick Brown and George Wieser [Bowker admen] used to play their guitars and sing. It was the place that guys used to go to find girls. It was the place where booze flowed endlessly. So there were a million and one things that happened there.

Library Journal's male staffers — Moon, Berry, Nyren, Wieser — normally kipped at the suite, which always had at least two bedrooms, a fully stocked bar, and large and small areas for socializing. When they were at the suite and the mood struck them, the *LJ* guys played host, but more often than not they acted like guests at their own party. Among the regular visitors were Moon Mafia insiders Curley, Schuman, Eshelman, Josey, Horrocks, and, beginning in 1968, Ilse Webb, who became the new Mrs. Moon in 1971. Surrounding the inner circle was an astounding mix of politically engaged idealists, reformers, radicals, nonconformists, and eccentrics, all part of the extended Moon family at one time or another.

Who were these people? Think of them in no particular order or status — at the time most considered themselves levelers of some sort who abjured social hierarchies — but as an animated assembly of intelligent, intense, largely left-leaning individuals who for a variety of reasons were drawn to the suite at various times where they commingled, conversed, sometimes quarreled, sometimes laughed, but most often conspired and pontificated, frequently gesticulating with drink or cigarette or both in hand. They radiated an allure, a vitality, that spread outward in concentric waves.

They included Dorothy Bendix, Ken Duchac, Andy Armitage, Jim Welbourne, Bob Haro, John and Carolyn Forsman, Peter Doiron, Mary Lee Bundy, Binnie Tate, Boyd Rayward, Gordon Burke, Ellen Gay Detlefsen, Dorothy Nyren, Bill De John, Bernadine Hoduski, Fay Blake, Zoia Horn, Renee Feinberg, Michael Malinconico, Jana Varlejs, Bill Hinchliff, Jackie Eubanks, Joan Marshall, Mitch Freedman, Bob Croneberger, Ella Yates, Liz Futas, Betty-Carol Sellen, Gerry Shields, Dick Burns, Marty Martelle,

Joan Goddard, Roger McDonough, John Carter, Marva DeLoach, Dick Moses, Martha Boaz, Jean Coleman, Bob Wedgeworth, Peggy Barber, Seoud Matta, Gordon McShean, Wyman Jones, Oliver Kirkpatrick, Dorothy Broderick, Eldred Smith, Agnes Griffin, Fred Glazer, Art Plotnik, Ed Beckerman, Don Roberts, Miriam Crawford, Hardy Franklin… Of course there were more — many more — who wandered in and out from time to time, making brief appearances and then fading back into the pother of the conference. The suite was a magnet, pulling in library activists and militants from every corner of the profession.

Much of what occurred in the *LJ* suite during those wild years had the air of a guerrilla campaign fomented to challenge or annoy or undermine the library Establishment, especially toward the end of the 1960s when the movement to democratize ALA and make the profession more responsive to societal needs and problems came to a head. Johnnie Givens (now Barnes), then director of the college library at Austin Peay in Tennessee, was not an activist or rebel but she did sometimes drop by the suite, where she remembered "the Moonies were more or less plotting to get ALA." Gerry Shields, who got to know Moon upon becoming editor of the *ALA Bulletin* in 1968, described the suite in those years as a "crash pad that allowed the younger agitators for social change to plan and bolster each other's courage."

For his part Moon acted as chief adviser to the agitators, offering guidance on strategy and encouragement to take the fight to the enemy. Suite regulars referred to these coaching sessions as Moon doing his "guru bit," though he saw himself not so much as a seer but a tutor instructing young Americans in the doughty art of British-style confrontation librarianship. Moon:

I usually wound up in the middle of discussions about tactics—who was the person to watch on this or listen to on that. Frequently when people came into the suite, I would be sitting there in the middle of the floor surrounded by a bunch of people and expounding on one thing or the other, and everyone would say I was "doing the guru bit." Literally, the first time Ilse met me [1968 at the Muelhbach Hotel in Kansas City] I was sitting on the floor with beads and long hair surrounded by these young librarians listening to the word. I wasn't consciously trying to be a guru: what I was doing was trying to train some of these kids to be troublemakers. I wanted them to be prepared to get in there and attack just as Roy Stokes at Loughborough had trained me and others at the school to do. I wanted them not to swallow the word from above always. Some of that took and some of it didn't.

Fay Blake, a tough-minded admirer of Moon and his work at *Library Journal*, and a suite regular during the 1960s, viewed his penchant for playing the guru through a different lens:

I thought Eric had a real knack for building coalitions and for expanding political horizons. For my taste, he was a bit too prone to make use of cliques and behind-the-scenes maneuvers, but I'd be willing to concede that that's the way of the world, the world of organizations and associations. The one weak spot I detected in him was a bit of personal vanity. Eric liked being a guru and having adoring fans around him, but I don't know how that can be avoided by a personable, energetic leader, especially a man in a profession which is predominantly female.

Moon used the suite not only for political purposes but as a hub for *LJ*'s conference news gathering effort. "If you didn't come by the *Library Journal* suite now and then," he observed, "you weren't likely to be much involved in the action. It [the suite] was a good thing, editorially, as well as from the point of view of involvement. I knew a hell of a lot more about what was happening because so many people were coming by all the time." Certainly, when going full tilt, the suite buzzed with all sorts of knowledge, from hard information to tantalizing rumor — a cornucopia of source material that helped make *LJ* the hands-down leader in library conference coverage during the Moon era.

The suite was also the place to get or test an argument, a Moon specialty. Sometimes he and Berry got into it hot and heavy, and sometimes the two of them ganged up on a visitor, showing no mercy, like a couple of starving wolves ripping into a lamb. Once, Moon recalled, he and Berry were "blasting" Martha Boaz, head of the library school at the University of Southern California, "about something or other, I don't remember what, and she broke down in tears. We felt awful — here's the dean of a library school breaking down in tears because she's being attacked on some issue or other." Only at the *LJ* suite might one dine on rack of library dean.

Booze informed much of the activity at the suite. Proud of his reputation as a "hollow-leg man," Moon consumed generous quantities of alcohol while at conferences but he knew how to hold it, a necessity, he cautioned, for any successful library journalist: "The journalist has got to be able to drink and still keep a clear head, because one of the places you get the most inside information is at parties — and if you can't drink better than the other people you're not going to be aware enough to pick it up. Some might think that's very cynical, but it's very true." John Berry agreed: "The drinking, the grass, that was all part of the job. I really believe that. Drinking particularly has always been a staple of ALA conventions. It lubricates the wheels of interaction and discourse."

Moon remembered one famous night when the suite denizens were especially well lubricated:

We always had a suite with at least two bedrooms and a large parlor. We had never had any of the women editors stay in the suite, only the men. But one year Evelyn Geller [editor of *SLJ*, 1964–1971] thought it would be helpful if the editors of *LJ* and *SLJ* stayed in the suite. So I said fine. So we put Evelyn and another female editor in one room. One night we had a really drunken gathering and a number of the guys stayed over, sleeping in the parlor on couches, on the floor, wherever. We were up very early in the morning — I had to be at a meeting by 7:30 or 8:00 o'clock that morning — and we devised this incredible recovery technique.

We had this huge tub full of ice from the bar, and we had these guys going through this recovery technique. We opened bottles of ginger ale, which is very bubbly, and you would apply this to the eyeballs and then you would jump into this tub of ice and leap out again. All the guys were stark naked leaping around the suite. And Evelyn Geller opened her door and came out into the parlor! We never could quite explain this to Evelyn — why these naked guys were all leaping in and out of this great tub of ice with ginger ale on their eyeballs. We told her what we were doing was medicinal, but she never stayed at the suite again.

If alcohol was the suite's lubricant, sex was its lure. For many Americans, men and women, the revolutionary 1960s meant liberation from old, repressive sexual codes and attitudes, and librarians—frequently more concupiscent than their public image might suggest—were no exception. The suite became the place to find or be seen with new partners: "Some of the young guys, often at their first conference, would wait for me at the end of the corridor," Moon recalled, flashing a wolfish grin, "and say, 'Can we come to your suite? We understand you have a lot of women there.'" Many memorable bawdy antics took place in the suite. George Wieser, once described by Bill Katz as looking "remarkably like a wiser Dean Martin," remembered the time his penis served a new purpose. He had drunk too much and was sleeping it off in one of the bedrooms in the suite "when Eric, who was sharing the room with me, brought some women in, and they decided to throw hoops at my penis, which was standing straight up." Don't ask where the hoops came from.

Moon approached conference sex much as he did alcohol: he partook but insisted on remaining in control. During his stint as editor of *Wilson Library Bulletin*, Moon's friend John Wakeman remembered once being snowed in for five days at an ALA midwinter meeting held at the old Edgewater Beach Hotel in Chicago. Moon was there too of course, and Wakeman noted, tongue-in-cheek, "If Eric's behavior that week ever fell short of Old Testament standards of morality, I don't remember it (or anything else)." Gerry Shields was more direct: "Eric was known in certain circles for his ability to appear at a conference or a library school lecture and immediately zero in on an impressionable young lady for what was assumed to be the modern day version of a dalliance."

In the 1960s Moon indulged himself sexually with more different women than at any time in his life, before or since. In England and during his years in the RAF there were sexual encounters, including one serious adulterous affair in the 1950s, but once he got to the United States Eros's floodgates opened wide, and Moon took full advantage of the decade's swinging morals (or lack thereof) to satisfy a strong libidinous appetite. But he was never leering, louche, or indiscriminate about sex, nor did he seduce women, or try to seduce them, simply for the sake of scoring another notch on the belt. That was not his style. Jana Varlejs, Arthur Curley's soul mate for many years, knew Moon well from the late 1960s onward and was impressed by the fact that "You could be good friends with Eric without worrying about sexual games." He had, continued Varlejs, "remarkably equal relationships with women, free from sexual overtures. You could be open with Eric—he did not flirt. In fact, he would not tolerate women who were flirts when engaged in serious conversation."

Soon after coming to *LJ*, Moon found that he, in his words, "was something of a celebrity," and that there were any number of nubile librarians at conferences eager to get close to anyone who was someone, if only for a night or two. Moon called them "celebrity fuckers." One lady librarian who was there put it more gently: "Some women at these conferences were 'on the make.' After spending 50 weeks a year at home as sedate librarians, they came to the ALA conference to have as much fun and adventure as they could." Sometimes, said Moon, just scheduling assignations became a problem: "There was one evening I was supposed to meet a particular young woman at the suite. I told the staff that when she arrived to tell her that I was hung up, that I had to go to a late meeting that I had to cover, but that I would be back about 10:30 or 11:00 and ask if she would wait. Well, the staff told about nine women to wait in the suite and when I got back about 11:00 I was in more trouble than you can imagine."

Moon and Berry were competitive about practically everything, and this included women. Early on, Moon let Berry know he was playing with a master:

When John was first appointed and he came to his first convention with *LJ*, he found that by then I was something of a celebrity. One thing about ALA conferences is that they are heavily populated with celebrity fuckers. So John was sort of amazed to find out how many women were looking for me. He could not really understand that, when there was a charming guy like himself available, why anyone would be interested in this old fart. So he would start moving in on anyone who expressed the faintest interest in me.

I decided that he ought to be taught a lesson right at the beginning. So I pretended that my most passionate interest on the ALA scene at the time was Mary Lee Bundy from Maryland, and John promptly moved in heavily on Mary Lee and got involved rather deeply. Mary Lee was not one of your babes that you could pick up and throw away — she was a tough cookie. I remember John coming to me a few days later saying, "Hey, I'm really in trouble here. I can't shake this one." I said, "Don't come to me about it. You got yourself into it, you get yourself out of it."

There are questions about the literal truth of many of the tales of sexual shenanigans associated with the *LJ* suite during the Moon era. Moon especially has been known to exaggerate his exploits, not by outright fabrication (again, not his style) but through the use of wink-wink, nudge-nudge innuendo where more is implied than actually stated. In one instance, however, someone is telling a fib. In a "he said, she said" case, a comely librarian whom Moon named (strictly off the record) as a "celebrity fucker" he slept with back in the 1960s adamantly denied to this writer that she ever had a sexual relationship with him. Dick Bye wondered too how much of the suite action was real and how much braggadocio:

I used to look with rather stuffy disapproval at what I then regarded as sophomoric carousals by the triumvirate, Eric, John, and George. They seemed to take pride in being able to stay up all night partying, then still report for work the next morning and cover the essential news of meetings. I often thought they were making it all up. Some of this macho activity must have been taking place during the time when Eric's marriage to Diana was deteriorating, and perhaps the reports of conquests of females were mere fiction. I wasn't there, so I can't testify.

Karl Nyren, the other main *LJ* man during this time, is oddly missing from these recollections, not because he wasn't there but because, in Berry's words, "Karl took a sort of distant, watchful view of the proceedings." Moon remembered Nyren as someone, "alone among the *LJ* editors, who was not really, fully into the 1960s thing." Moon related this story by way of example:

Once we had a gang in the *LJ* suite, as usual, right before the ALA conference banquet — the banquet was a very big affair in those days, much more so than it is today. The usual gang of young rebels was there, including Binnie Tate [a children's librarian and Moon lady friend in the late 1960s], and I was wearing the typical sixties garb, not very dressed up at all — old sweater, very casual. And Karl comes in and he's in the full regalia — tux, the works. *LJ* had a press table right up front at the banquet and when Karl and I came in people said, Jesus, they look like the odd couple.

A private, rather solemn person, Nyren was nevertheless often involved in small dramas in the suite, most poignantly when his former wife, Dorothy (also a librarian), came by. After the Nyrens divorced, Dorothy entered a relationship with Arthur Curley, and the three of them — Karl, Dorothy, and Arthur — sometimes found themselves together at the suite. One evening Berry remembered, "Arthur got roaring drunk" and Karl and Dorothy, the sundered couple, "together put Arthur down for the night."

New York Publishing Scene

Back home after the rigors of an American Library Association conference, Moon would dash off his report on what had happened at the conclave and then take care of any outstanding *LJ* business generated during the days he was away. After that he would resume work on upcoming issues of the magazine, which entailed everything from writing editorials to evaluating unsolicited manuscripts to contacting possible contributors for a feature on this or that hot-button topic. In addition to the daily routines of writing and editing, he spent a certain amount of time outside the office attending meetings of various local professional organizations he belonged to, such as the New York Library Club, the Archons of Colophon, and the New York–based Library Public Relations Council.

He also attended publishers' parties, glitzy events typically connected with the launch of a big new spring or fall book. It was at such parties that he got to rub shoulders with authors, editors, and executives from the world of New York trade publishing. These gatherings often took place in a smart midtown hotel (the Algonquin, the Pierre, the Plaza) but sometimes the venues were more exotic. He remembered going to one publisher's party at the top of the Empire State Building and another at a Harlem nightclub; yet another was held partially in a New York steam bath. One party Moon never forgot was at George Plimpton's "pad" on the East Side:

What I remember vividly about that party was that Plimpton had this circular iron staircase that went up from one level to another almost straight over the living room. This party was like so many others during that time — it was full of gorgeous young women, all of whom wore skirts up to there [mid-thigh], and they kept parading up and down this circular staircase. I never heard a sentence finished in any conversation. Somebody would say something and the next thing everybody would be looking up and the sentence would be left unfinished. It was the most hilarious party because nobody ever made much sense.

Moon became something of a fixture at Grove Press parties in the 1960s. After reviewing the risqué *Memoirs of a Woman of Pleasure* (a.k.a. *Fanny Hill*) for *LJ* in 1963, he became, as he put it, the journal's "principal erotica book reviewer," and because Grove specialized in that kind of literature, he reviewed many of the publisher's titles. "I was greatly valued by Barney Rosset and the people at Grove Press," said Moon. "I became a sort of Grove Press hero, and they used to invite me to all their parties, which were nearly always held somewhere in the Village [Greenwich Village in lower Manhattan]. This is where I met so many of the famous literary people: Norman Mailer, Allen Ginsberg, LeRoi Jones [later Amiri Baraka], and others." Meeting Mailer for the first time was memorable: "It was right after Mailer had challenged Sonny Liston [the heavyweight boxer] to a fight. I looked at him and said, 'God, you've got some balls, challenging Sonny Liston.' And he said, 'Take off your jacket,' and we started sparring, just kidding around. I have this long left and he said, 'OK, that's enough — you have too much reach advantage.' So I became quite good friends with him, meeting him subsequently on a number of occasions."

Before long, Moon was cutting a small dash in New York's chummy publishing society. His position as editor of *Library Journal*, a respected and closely watched publication in the U.S. book world, gave him a certain cachet, and he almost always impressed people he met as an affable, knowledgeable, quick-witted guy who could talk a good line on just about any subject of interest to a crowd of literati. He was invited to sign petitions that the publishing community sponsored (against the war in Vietnam, for instance, and another in support of Ralph Ginzburg, a publisher convicted, fined, and sent to jail in the 1960s, incredibly, for sending soft-core pornography via the mails). He became so well known that in 1978 he served as a juror for the National Medal for Literature, awarded by the American Academy of Arts and Letters; he argued for Lillian Hellman but got his second choice, Archibald MacLeish.

Through these and similar activities Moon developed contacts that led to articles in *LJ* by celebrated people like novelist Irving Wallace and attorney Edward de Grazia, contributors who not only brought a prominent name to the journal but a different perspective. His participation in the New York publishing scene also led to some interesting opportunities. A casual conversation at a publisher's party, for instance, resulted in his reviewing books for *Saturday Review*, a widely read literary weekly in those days. Moon:

I began as a reviewer for *Saturday Review* after meeting Norman Cousins [the magazine's longtime editor] at a publishing party (they occurred several times a week in those days). Somehow we got to talking about the forthcoming volume of Miller/Durrell [Henry Miller and Lawrence Durrell] correspondence. When Cousins found that I had read just about everything by both authors and also knew Larry Powell and the English bookseller Alan Thomas, who had preserved most of the letters, he asked if I would be interested in reviewing the volume. He explained, carefully — and as *LJ* editor I well understood — that he first had to check out the possibility with his Book Review Editor. Editors-in-chief do not mess with their Book Review Editors!

Marriage Kaput

When the Moons first came to the United States they rented a single-family home in suburban Fanwood, New Jersey, where they lived until the summer of 1962 when they moved to a three-bedroom apartment in Elizabeth, an old rust-belt Jersey city of more than 100,000. John Berry painted this colorful picture of Moon at the time:

Eric hated the suburbs. At first he had this little house with Diana and the kids out in Fanwood, but he got fed up with mowing the lawn and all that stuff, so they took this apartment in the depths of Elizabeth, New Jersey, this grimy, fucked over industrial town — it was outrageous. And he loved it! It was his working-class home. His taste was working-class. I always thought he was an atrocious dresser — he's better now. He wore ugly stuff in those days. I was always put off by his attire: I saw him as the double-knit king.

The family remained in Elizabeth until October 1969 when Eric moved out and set up bachelor quarters in a tiny apartment in East Orange (also in New Jersey), effectively ending his union with Diana, though their marriage was not officially terminated for many months.

For most of the 1960s the Moons' domestic life had gone along matter-of-factly without major incident, though a devastating flood in 1966 ruined two of the family's automobiles, including Max's first set of wheels. Diana did not work outside the home until 1967, when Eric helped her get a job at Bowker in the book editorial department where she worked on *Ulrich's*, the periodical directory. During this period the Moon boys became young men. By 1964 both Max and Alan were teenagers, and by the time Eric left Diana they were 21 and 18 respectively. By all accounts the boys had a normal adolescence and young adulthood, both graduating from high school and serving in the military during the Vietnam conflict. Alan went to college and Max straight into the business world after returning from the service.

Alan — like his father, a natural storyteller — had numerous recollections of growing up in New Jersey, many revealing much about Eric and the Moon family dynamic. Alan recalled, for instance, his father's strong competitive instincts in the face of onsetting middle age:

My father was, and is, very competitive. Fair but competitive. He always used to say, "The way to improve is to play someone better than you." I was always trying to beat him at bowling and chess. When I finally did win, it seemed like quite an achievement. I can even remember him trying to keep up with me when playing soccer in the park one day. He was in poor aerobic shape — he'd been a smoker for most of his life, so it didn't take long until he was breathing pretty hard, but he didn't give up easily. He'd been quite an athlete as a young man, in tennis, soccer, cricket, and table tennis, and I think that day in the park was one of the first times he realized he'd gotten older. The skill was still apparent, the body just couldn't keep up.

Alan's favorite memory of his father occurred in 1965 when he was a student at Alexander Hamilton Junior High School in Elizabeth:

The vice principal decided one day that he wanted to stop students from loitering in the halls between classes, and to accomplish this goal, he instituted several unusual policies. The strangest of all was that no one was allowed to drink from the water fountains between classes. I don't remember why I took a drink that day, be it total disregard for authority, an undying thirst, or just forgetfulness, but no matter what the reason, I got caught. The vice principal said I had to bring a note from my parents to school the next day.

I was quite surprised by my father's reaction when I confessed that night. He decided a note just wouldn't do. Instead, he took the morning off from work and accompanied me to school. Sitting outside the vice principal's office that morning, I listened as my father told him exactly what he thought of his new rules. "Stupid rules are made to be broken," and "Don't you have anything better to do than this?" are specific lines I remember. I sat there proud and smiling. What continues to impress me about this incident, so many years later, is the way my father spoke throughout. He didn't curse or raise his voice. His words must have been just as effective as any knife though, because when my father came out, I got a quick look at the vice principal: he looked like he'd just been to see the vice principal.

Alan recalled too a trip the Moon family took in the summer of 1965, driving from New Jersey to the Florida Keys and back. The main purpose of the trip was to scout out potential colleges for Max (who never did go to college), but for Alan, a confessed "giggler," the laughs were what he remembered. Anyone observing the four Moons at the time would have sworn they were the happiest family in the world:

My second best memory happened on one of two long summer car trips in the South. When I was a kid, I was a real giggler. My father was the instigator. Many times he'd say something just trying to make me laugh and then try to keep me going as long as possible. My brother, who was always trying to be more mature (hah), tried desperately not to get caught up in this most of the time, but my father was often able to get both of us going and the three of us would laugh uncontrollably for long periods of time. If we were at home, my mother would join in restrainedly. If we were out somewhere, she would turn beet red and try to get my father to stop egging me on. Of course that only made him try harder.

The particular incident of note happened in a restaurant in North or South Carolina one evening after many hours in the car. I don't remember what got me started, but pretty soon I was completely into one of my giggling fits. My brother joined in early and my father a little later. But it didn't end there. When our waitress came over to the table, she was laughing too. And looking around, it suddenly became obvious that most of the people at the other tables had caught the bug. Just about everyone in the restaurant was laughing. Thinking about it now, it seems like a scene from a movie, but it really happened.

So what happened that made Eric and Diana's marriage go kaput? He was a good provider and attentive husband and father — when he was around. Certainly Diana — super good-looking, agreeable, responsible, domestic, shy, a woman who turned "beet red" over the least public display — was a good mother and dutiful wife. All of Eric's friends and colleagues liked her, and more than a few were taken aback when he left her. Norman Horrocks described Diana in the 1960s as "slim, attractive, very pleasant, easy company," and John Berry remembered her as "this wonderful pert little blond," adding: "I liked her a lot." What some found difficult to believe was that Diana presumably had no sense the marriage was in trouble until it was too late. According to Eric, "There wasn't anything happening [i.e., Diana was blissfully ignorant] until she discovered that something was going on with Ilse."

Before Ilse Webb entered his life in 1968 Moon stated he had "no serious relationships" with other women, though there were "quite a lot of casual ones." Yet his wife had no knowledge of his chronic infidelities — or if so she chose, like many women of her generation, to ignore them. What Diana almost surely did not know at the time was that Eric had long been planning to end their marriage as soon as the boys were grown and on their own. Why he wanted out of the marriage was not clear then, nor was he able to explain it clearly later. According to Ilse Moon, Eric never was forthcoming regarding his private, innermost self:

Eric had apparently been planning for years to leave Diana. One of the things that shocked me about Eric — I never really got over it — is that Diana had no idea that there was anything wrong with their marriage. How he hid that from her, and why he hid it from her, is something I've never quite come to terms with. Eric doesn't talk much about his personal life. He has a capacity for dividing things in his mind. It frightened me about Eric that he could continue in a marriage that was clearly not satisfactory to him and that she had no idea, no inkling, that was the case. He had managed to pretend so well that everything was fine that she never knew.

Xerox Acquires Bowker

Sometime before Moon's marriage began unraveling, Bowker employees received the jolting news that their company had been acquired by the Xerox Corporation in a merger deal. Specifically, on January 1, 1968, the R.R. Bowker Company became an operating unit of Xerox's Education Division. No longer was Bowker the small, autonomous, close-knit, family oriented enterprise Moon admired so much. Though it retained the Bowker name (which was coin in the library market), the company relinquished its independence — some would say its soul — to a megabucks corporation.

But there was an upside to the merger too. What drove the deal from Bowker management's point of view was the desire to position the company to compete in the computer age, which by the late 1960s had become a necessity for any publisher dealing with large quantities of raw data, as Bowker did with its *Books in Print* operation and other bibliographic and directory publications. Dan Melcher, president of the company, wanted to assure Bowker's future by hitching the company's star to a large corporation that had the resources, financial and otherwise, to do what Bowker could not do alone. Moon, who was actively involved in the preliminary discussions with Xerox and supported the merger, explained the situation:

Toward the end of the 1960s Daniel [Melcher] had just gotten us going on building huge computerized databases for *BIP* and all the other Bowker bibliographic apparatus. You must remember that Bowker was the central repository of publishing information in this country; we got the basic information before anybody else and we got more of it than anybody else — more than the Library of Congress and Wilson. Dan had suddenly begun to move heavily into computerization — and there were lots of early costly snafus. At any rate, we required capital for this investment, and Dan said if we could find the right kind of company that respected editorial prerogatives and freedoms and wouldn't mess with us the way some other companies had experienced, it might be beneficial to have a large corporation with lots of capital that would allow us to move much more quickly into areas where we were obviously going to move in any event.

Central to any deal as far as Moon was concerned was the question of "editorial prerogatives and freedoms." The last thing he wanted was a Bowker sugar daddy telling him how to run *LJ* and what he could and could not write or publish. When he first heard, by happenstance, that Xerox might be interested in acquiring Bowker, he checked out the giant corporation's record on social issues and found that it had a reputation as an enlightened corporate citizen. Moon:

Toward the end of the 1960s we were getting overtures from a lot of big companies— Dun & Bradstreet and Dow Jones were two—and we mostly gave them a glance and no more. Then I was at a conference and met up with Dick Drysdale, whom I had met earlier when he was with Brodart. He was now with Professional Library Service in Santa Ana, California, which had been bought by Xerox. We were having a drink and he throws out a feeler about Xerox acquiring Bowker, wondering if Bowker might be interested. I said I didn't know but I could find out.

I tossed this around in my mind for days and did some informal checking and found that Xerox was a socially responsible company that sponsored cultural events and its top people were involved in civil rights; its top guy—Sol Linowitz, a liberal—chaired a civil rights committee for President Johnson. So I thought maybe this is the kind of company we should get involved with. I went back to Bowker and said I think Xerox might be interested in us. Xerox looked better than anyone else, so we started to explore it. Daniel was the one mostly involved in the negotiations.

Discussions between Xerox and Bowker heated up in the summer of 1967. Around that time Dan Melcher came to Moon, saying "We've got three or four of Xerox's top people coming here tomorrow, and I want you to sit down with them and try to ascertain whether they really understand editorial freedom. If they don't, the deal's off." Moon said he'd be more than happy do this:

I picked out the most controversial editorials in *Library Journal* I could find published during the 1960s and a few from *PW*. In one case there were absolutely opposing editorials in *LJ* and *PW*. The next morning I went into this room and here were several of the really big guns of Xerox, and they all greeted me magnanimously. I asked them to read copies of the editorials—I said, "I want you to read these and then we'll talk." And I sat and watched them — it was a fascinating experience watching big executives reading these editorials.

Afterwards they said, "Aren't *PW* and *LJ* in the same company? How can they be on totally opposed sides on a major issue like copyright?" I explained that this is understandable, that there are different interests involved, libraries versus the book trade. And they asked, "But what about your company's interest?" And I said, the company's interest is in editorial freedom and freedom of expression, and that's what this meeting is about. If you can't deal with that, you don't want us. If this is something you can't comprehend or deal with, we are not in a position to discuss merger with you. In the end they professed to see the point. With some difficulty, they seemed to agree there was not an insuperable problem here.

Eventually the Bowker board approved the Xerox merger, though individual directors had different reasons for voting yea, as Dick Bye revealed in this recollection:

In the year or so before the Xerox takeover there were active debates in the Bowker boardroom about whether it was desirable to sell to a conglomerate. Dan seemed concerned, almost to the point of paranoia, about competition and lack of capital for expansion, particularly to computerize *Books in Print*. It was the beginning of the computer explosion. Eric and I began to look favorably on the Xerox deal primarily, I think, because we saw it as a way to retire the older directors, especially Mildred Smith (editor of *PW*) and Louis Greene, who held the largest amounts of stock and were drawing the largest salaries and bonuses but were almost totally noncontributing to the daily management. Of the companies that had romanced Bowker, Xerox seemed the most desirable because of its business strength then and because it seemed to have a sense of social responsibility that we liked.

After the merger, big changes naturally occurred at Bowker. Louie Greene and Mildred Smith did indeed retire, and Dan Melcher was "promoted" to the position of Bowker Company chairman, basically an empty job from which he resigned in early 1969, leaving for good the company he and his father had been associated with for half a century. (Melcher died in 1985 just after his 73rd birthday at his home in Charlottesville, Virginia.) George McCorkle, who had joined the firm in 1967 as a vice president and president of Jacques Cattell Press, a Bowker subsidiary, became the new Bowker president and chief executive officer. Dick Bye, vice president and director of advertising, took on the additional responsibility of publisher of all three major Bowker journals, *PW*, *LJ*, and *SLJ*. In the process he became Moon's boss, though Bye quickly conceded, "there was very little bossing on my part."

Xerox's acquisition of Bowker in the late 1960s made some people millionaires and gave others, like Moon, a huge boost in their economic well-being. "I made quite a bit at the time of the Xerox acquisition," said Moon, "because I had bought stock in Bowker as a member of the board, which Dan Melcher had encouraged. The stock multiplied several times at the time of the merger, so suddenly for the first time in my life I had some money." Elizabeth Geiser remembered that "the economic benefits of the merger were *very* important to Eric," and Moon admitted, "I would be lying if I said that I wasn't sure that I would gain from the merger," but money "was not my chief motive" for supporting the Xerox deal. In retrospect, almost everyone agreed, "It was not a happy merger."

Years later, John Berry summed up the whole business this way: "Despite the high hopes of Melcher and the rest of the Bowker management to the contrary, when you sell a company, you lose control of it."

Goodbye to LJ

At the end of December 1968, exactly one year after the Xerox acquisition, Moon quit the editorship of *Library Journal*, a move that surprised the magazine's readers as much as it did most of his Bowker colleagues. The decision to leave *LJ*, he maintained, was entirely his own. He was not pushed, nor did he leave because of unhappiness with Xerox management, nor did it have anything to do with his age (45) or his affair with Ilse Webb (which had only begun that summer and had yet to heat up) or the deteriorating state of his marriage:

I think I left when I did because I began to feel that if I stayed much longer I would start repeating myself, and I didn't want to do that. It was time for a fresh voice to take over, and there was no way for that to happen while I was on the magazine, so I had to get off the magazine. I talked to Dan [Melcher] about my leaving and eventually took another job at Bowker, director of editorial development, which turned out to be a dead-end job, and John Berry took over the magazine. It certainly wasn't that I was tired of *LJ*—I loved the job. But it was time for rejuvenation. I had given it all I had and now it time for someone else.

Actually, leaving *LJ* when he did conformed with Moon's approach to work throughout his career. The longest he ever stayed in any position was nine and a half years (Scarecrow Press), and by the time he left *LJ* he had been editor for nine years and two months. Not a person to settle into a comfy niche and wing it on automatic pilot, he was itching to try something new, to test himself in a different arena. His final editorial, "A Decade Minus One" (*LJ*, December 15, 1968), conveyed a sense of mission accomplished as a library journalist. The 1960s had been, Moon wrote,

an ideal time to be editing a library periodical. When the scene is alive and turbulent, good copy flows; it does not have to be ground out painfully from inconsequentials. Old Melvil was in at the beginning of *LJ* and of librarianship as an organized profession, with the birth of ALA and the British Library Association. But no *LJ* editor since, perhaps, has had so much library activity to record and comment upon. I have been lucky in occupying this seat during what seems to me the greatest revival period in American librarianship in this century.

Concerning his successor, Moon told Dan Melcher and the Bowker board "that, after nearly a decade at *LJ*, I knew what editorial talent was out there and it seemed to me we had two people on board, John Berry and Karl Nyren, who were far better than anybody they could find outside." Moon emphatically refused to choose between Berry and Nyren, despite efforts by the board to have him do so: "They said, what do you think, Berry or Nyren? The terrible thing is that we didn't at the time consider Lillian Gerhardt [then *SLJ* book review editor and later editor-in-chief for more than 25 years], who I think might have been ultimately better than either Berry or Nyren." Why wasn't Gerhardt considered? "At the time *LJ* and *SLJ* were thought of as very different entities"; moreover, Gerhardt was perceived as "a lone wolf."

"At any rate," continued Moon, "it came down to Berry or Nyren, and the board wanted me to decide, and I said, I don't want to decide, I wanted them to decide. I'm not sure if they didn't assume I wanted Berry for the job — but anyway he got it." Berry recalled that he went into the interview and told the board in no uncertain terms he was the right person for the job, whereas Nyren apparently went in and said, well, I'm good but Berry has a lot of strengths too. Moon: "That sounds likely, knowing the two. Karl was the more deliberate type, who would weigh things, whereas John would say 'I want it and I'm going to get it.' More single-minded, John saw less of the gray."

Moon left *LJ* at the zenith of the magazine's professional influence. During his editorship, circulation more than doubled and advertising revenues increased at a spectacular rate, making the journal consistently profitable for the first time in its history. Reading *LJ* became *de rigueur* for anyone seriously interested in libraries and the library profession. Unlike other mainstream periodicals in the field, *LJ* stood out as a vigorous and uncompromising voice for progressive principles and activist positions. Berry — molded as a journalist by Moon — continued to edit the magazine as an advocacy publication: "I followed Moon and tried to emulate him," Berry said. "Ultimately, I became Moon. I never tried to separate myself from that identity. I always felt that was a worthy thing. Don't misunderstand, I had some changes I wanted to make in the magazine; I had my own program in mind. But it was never to get away from what Moon had done."

Moon — lucky Eric — left *LJ* at the optimum moment, just as federal funding for libraries, a key to the magazine's financial success in the 1960s, was about to be severely curtailed. A month before Moon stepped down in December 1968, Richard Nixon was elected US president, and shortly thereafter the cutbacks began, a process that would last, give or take some zigs and zags, through the 1980s. Berry, in a sense, was left holding the proverbial bag. But he didn't pout or whine. Like a good advocacy journalist he took up his pen and fought back. In a black-bordered editorial titled "NATIONAL LIBRARY WAKE" (*LJ*, May 15, 1969), the son of Moon lambasted Nixon: "President Nixon opened National Library Week with the message that 'Libraries are the banks of our educational system.' His administration is about to take the first step toward a great educational depression.... Let us pray that Congress will not allow the Nixon administration to be remembered for replacing the 'banks' of education with the banks of ABM's [missiles]."

Upon leaving *LJ*, Moon became Bowker's director of editorial development, a newly created position charged with expanding the company's periodical and book publishing products for the library market. He still worked at 1180 Avenue of the Americas, though on a different floor than *LJ*, reporting directly to new company president George McCorkle. However, he never really enjoyed or got into the job, and within six months he was gone, leaving Bowker and Xerox for Scarecrow Press, a small publisher then located in Metuchen, New Jersey. Moon:

> For the last little while at Bowker I was director of editorial development, which has the acronyn DED — pronounced "dead." I really became a very high paid paper-pusher, doing reports to Xerox for the president of Bowker and examining various editorial possibilities. One was the development of a magazine [*Previews*] that reviewed audiovisual materials. I recommended against the magazine but they went ahead with it anyway and it failed. This was what was happening with me — I was doing what they asked me to do, giving them advice, and it was being ignored. So eventually I started looking and up comes the Scarecrow possibility. At that time most of the former Bowker directors were leaving. We had become disenchanted with Xerox.

In addition to the *Previews* project, where his advice had been rejected (and his ego hurt), Moon worked on several book publications during his interval as editorial director, including two collections he edited drawn from *LJ*: *Book Selection and Censorship in the Sixties* (Bowker, 1969) and *Library Issues: The Sixties* (Bowker, 1970), the latter coedited with Karl Nyren. Also during this period, in a bit of nostalgia uncharacteristic of Moon, he returned to Newfoundland to cover the 1969 annual conference of the Canadian Library Association for *LJ*. It was the first time CLA had ever met in the craggy province, and he used the opportunity to show Berry, who tagged along like Sancho Panza, the local landmarks, with emphasis on watering holes. Moon's report — "Newfoundland Revisited" (*LJ*, July 1969), as marvelous to read today as when as when it first appeared — was just one small example of why he and his pen would be sorely missed at *LJ*.

Moon's Journalistic Legacy

Eric Moon did not arrive at *Library Journal* tabula rasa. He had had substantial experience writing and editing in the UK and Canada prior to coming to the States, but *LJ* was where he blossomed. And what a great blossoming it was. Karl Nyren said it best in the introduction to *Library Issues: The Sixies*: "Looking back over *Library Journal* for this decade, the first and most notable fact is that journalistically it was the decade of Eric Moon. Under his skillful and impatient direction, *LJ* abandoned the echoing of platitudes which too often passes for editorial comment and took on the role of an advance guard, searching out and tangling with issues— often long before the main body of librarians were ready to start thinking about them."

Bill Katz, no slouch himself as a journalist, added, "At the professional level Eric may have been the best editor about. He ran the *Library Journal* with a firm, fair hand while digging for stories few would print. Those points of view won him many friends and admirers. The actual editing of copy submitted by others was done in such a way to improve it— vastly. I speak from experience. At the same time he left the writer thinking the revisions were not only good, but the writer's own. A rare quality, indeed."

Moon was fortunate to be the editor of a major library periodical like *LJ* in the 1960s, a decade as thrilling and ripe with possibilities as any in the century. He used the power of the press to influence the profession's agenda in ways not seen since Melvil Dewey set forth some first principles in the fledging *American Library Journal* in 1876. Beginning with trenchant coverage of the civil rights struggle and extending into other contentious areas of public policy, including freedom of speech, federal aid, presidential politics, and the Vietnam War, Moon took *LJ* and its readers into a place no other library periodical had ever been. Along the way he enlarged the sensibilities of a generation of librarians.

Moon's journalistic testament can be found in both his own writings and those of others who contributed to the magazine during his editorship. He had a knack for ferreting out people with strong opinions and the wherewithal to express them clearly and forcefully, criteria he demanded of his contributors and himself. He also had a fine eye for editorial talent. John Berry, Bill Eshelman, Art Plotnik, Shirley Havens, Evelyn Geller, Robbie Franklin, and Karl Nyren are just some of the accomplished editors he discovered, nurtured, or championed over the years. Berry, who was closest to Moon the journalist, added this: "Not only did he work individually with a generation of editors, all of whom later occupied leading positions in the library press, he also provided a model for open professional discourse that changed the fundamental character of that discourse, both in print and in professional debates."

Any assessment of the Moon legacy as editor and journalist inevitably recalls *LJ*'s trademark contents in the 1960s: stinging editorials, controversial articles and columns, brutally honest news stories, witty and colorful conference reports, imaginative titles and headlines, passionate letters to the editor, literate reviews, informative symposia, intriguing covers. Moreover, Moon's accomplishments included the fact that under his direction the journal thrived financially, regularly turning a profit for the first time in its nearly 100-year history. Moon understood and respected the traditional separation between editors and reporters on the one hand and business and advertising people on the other. But he also knew that if he had not made money for Bowker, he would not have made his mark journalistically: "Someone once asked me what is the most important attribute of an editor? I said, 'Making money.' Making money allows you the freedom to do whatever you want to do. That freedom is the greatest thing an editor can have."

He remembered his nine years at *LJ* as "the central point of my career and perhaps the real turning point in my personal life. Certainly the *LJ* period was the most exciting in my professional life, no question." His zest for the work was apparent to all, even those who reviled him. Like his illustrious predecessor, Melvil Dewey, Moon was not, for all his talents, a perfect editor or journalist. Dewey, for instance, had trouble with deadlines, and Moon, while compiling an impeccable record on punctuality, now and then allowed opinion to masquerade as fact. But his failings were insignificant compared with the triumphs. "Melvil Dewey may be considered the first distinguished editor of *Library Journal*," noted E.J. Josey, "but it was Eric Moon who made this journal the most widely read and most often quoted library periodical in the world."

Moon's influence on library journalism continues today. He brought toughness, realpolitik, and an advocate's perspective to library literature, flashes of which can still be seen in *LJ* and its competitors. Every time, for example, a library publication reports negative or unpleasant facts about an individual library or librarian or library project, credit Eric Moon; before him, publishing bad news about any aspect of the profession was widely considered a breach of professional etiquette. In the same vein, before Moon, library journalists shied away from the larger social and political issues that affect librarianship directly or indirectly; today there is no such taboo or reluctance.

No one was better positioned to assess Moon's journalistic legacy than John Berry, his successor at *LJ* who edited the magazine for more than 35 years: "In the pantheon of library journalists there's absolutely no doubt that Eric's the best of them. I think these things are always modified by the time in which they take place, but he outranks everyone. He created what we know as library journalism — to the extent there is such a thing as 'library journalism.' It's his creation, I believe that very strongly. Eric invented library journalism as we know it today."

– 12 –

Capturing Ilse's Heart

Ilse Bloch

Before she was Ilse Moon she was Ilse Webb but first she was Ilse Bloch. She was born on October 7, 1932, to German Jewish parents in Nuremberg, one of Germany's most historic communities and second largest city in the southern state of Bavaria. Her father, Fritz Jacob Bloch (pronounced Block), was an eye doctor; her mother, Kaethe (Americanized as Kate), a hausfrau. She was named Ilse (pronounced ILL-sa) because, she said, at the time it was the most common female name in Germany except for Mary: "My parents didn't think Mary was appropriate for a little Jewish girl. Their thinking was that Ilse was so common that no one would ever misspell or mispronounce it. Little did they know!"

Being Jewish in Germany in the 1930s spelled danger, and this was especially true in Nuremberg, a center of Nazi activity and anti–Semitic propaganda from the beginning of the rise of Hitler to the demise of the Third Reich in 1945. In 1933 the National Socialists, Hitler's political party, began holding annual rallies in the Nuremberg area. Around this time Fritz Bloch received a sinister warning of things to come — an event so menacing that it prompted him and his wife and small daughter to flee their homeland in 1934. Ilse heard the story as a girl growing up in America:

Apparently my parents left Nuremberg in the middle of the night when I was two years old. My mother saw the danger most clearly and said it was time to get out of here. Jews could still leave and take things with them, but it wasn't that easy. My father was an ophthalmologist and he had a lot of friends among union people because he had done work in the city's factories, and his friends the workers warned him about the Nazis. They called him up one day and said, "Dr. Bloch, you ought to take your family on a vacation this weekend." When we came back we found that all the Jewish men had been rounded up on Saturday and Sunday by a bunch of thugs — the Brownshirts or whoever they were. The men were taken to a field at gun point and handed shovels and told to dig their graves. When they did, the thugs laughed and said ha ha it's a joke, go home. The men were let go. But this was an ominous portent of things to come. Anyway, my father said, yes, let's get out of here.

253

Leaving home, friends, work, and native land was a painful decision for Ilse's parents, but history proved them right, many German Jews temporizing until it was too late. In 1935 the Nazis issued the so-called Nuremberg Laws, denying German citizenship to Jews and prohibiting marriage or sexual relations between "Aryans" and Jews. As all the world now knows, these racist decrees were the beginning of what became the Holocaust, the largest, most efficient mass murder in human history. Fortunately, Fritz Bloch's only brother (Ilse's Uncle John) had left Germany for the United States some years before, settling in New York City, and in 1934 Dr. Bloch took the same route, bringing wife and child to live in Brooklyn, where they remained for a time, adjusting to life in America as best they could like millions of immigrants before them.

An unexpected rebellion by little Ilse prompted the Blochs to leave Brooklyn. She started school in the borough but hated it: "I was a rather docile child. I did what I was told. I started school in 1937 in Brooklyn in the Depression. I remember the school was on double session, and I had to stand in long lines and be quiet and wait for the first session to finish. One day I came home and said I wouldn't go back — I just wouldn't go back. It was the first time I had shown any defiance. So my parents decided they had better move if I was going to get any schooling."

The Bloch family moved to Mount Vernon, New York, a small city north of the Bronx in suburban Westchester County about 20 miles from their old home in Brooklyn and 15 miles from the heart of Manhattan or, Ilse remembered, 26 minutes by train to Grand Central Station. Here Ilse grew up, a self-confessed "timid, very shy girl" who did well academically at the local public schools, graduating from high school at 16 in 1949. She had a younger brother, born in 1936, who died of polio at age five, and later a much younger sister whom she hardly knew while living in Mount Vernon. "My parents were terribly German," she explained. "They felt it was their duty to replace themselves with two children, so after my brother died they had my sister Susan — Sue — who is 12 years younger than I am. Today we're close, but in those early years Sue was more like a niece to me than a sister."

Dr. Bloch established a successful practice in Mount Vernon, his office located on the first floor of the Blochs' home. Neither parent was religious, at least in a formal sense. Ilse recalled, "They were both Germans and both Jews, but Jews only after a fashion. They were Jewish ethnically, but we came from a long line of rather determined atheists. They did not press traditional Jewish values on me or my sister." Her father spoke English with a heavy German accent, which, according to Ilse, he cultivated in America because his patients thought it was "cute"; her mother, on the other hand, "took some care to get rid of her accent." Though avuncular at work, at home Fritz Bloch was very much an authoritarian figure, an Old World paterfamilias who ruled his small roost with a firm hand. Ilse remembered her father — she usually called him Papa and sometimes Daddy — with a mixture of love, respect, and resentment:

Patients used our bathroom upstairs. My mother wanted to add a bathroom downstairs for the patients, but Papa wouldn't do it. He did this because he was occasionally mean in small ways to Mother, and because he was sometimes stingy. God, I hated living in that house. I adored my father, but I was glad to leave home after high school. He would not allow the temperature in the house to be more than 68 degrees, and I froze all my life in that house. He was too stingy to turn up the heat. I remember at the dinner table — dinner was family time and we all had to be there — I would ask why I couldn't do this or that thing he had done, and he would say no, without explanation, and I would say why not. And he would say, in Latin, "What's allowed to the Gods is not allowed to the asses."

Ilse remembered Wednesdays at home with particular distaste:

My father was a real intellectual. Wednesday afternoons he did not work, shutting the office at noon. That afternoon his German cronies would come to the house and talk about literature and political and social issues. But they only talked in German. I was allowed to sit in on this after school, but I wasn't allowed to speak English. In fact, on Wednesdays no English was allowed in our house. God, I hated Wednesdays. Remember, this was during World War II and German was not a very popular language. On the dreaded Wednesdays we read Goethe, Heine, and Schiller — in German, of course — and listened to Beethoven and the other great composers. I think they never could understand how a culture that produced these giants could also support Hitler.

She had memories too of feeling different because of her Jewish heritage and the shadowy specter of anti–Semitism:

My mother, who was a very social person, was always anxious. There was a good deal of prejudice at the time against Germans and against Jews. There were places we couldn't go. We would go on holidays to Montauk [on Long Island] in the summers and there was a famous hotel there that's since become a spa or something that didn't take Jews. And there were places in Connecticut that didn't take Jews. It didn't affect us very much — nobody burned crosses on our lawn or did anything to us, but it was there, it was certainly there. We didn't celebrate Hanukkah, we celebrated Christmas. But when I wanted a Christmas tree my parents said this was not appropriate for Jewish families, that it would be resented by Daddy's Christian patients. So there were things we didn't do in order to maintain a low profile.

As a teenager Ilse became aware of Zionism, much in the air after the war. At one point she wanted to go to Palestine and work on a kibbutz to contribute to the new Jewish state of Israel, then just coming into existence. Ilse's Zionist phase began when her parents sent her to temple Sunday school, not for religious instruction but to improve her social prospects:

At about 14 or 15 I was sent to the temple Sunday school because my mother wanted me to have appropriate friends. She knew that the gentile neighbors in high school, particularly those in the sororities, were segregated by religion, and if I didn't have Jewish friends I wasn't going to have any friends — there was no group of atheists to join. I was forced to go to this Sunday school so I could meet some good Jewish boys and develop a social life.

I did make some friends and somehow we got interested in Zionism, and we became rabid Zionists. There was a summer camp, Hechalutz Farm, up in Wappingers Falls [near Poughkeepsie, New York], where they trained kids to go work on the kibbutzim in Israel. People were going over and establishing these pioneer farms, mostly Jews from America. I hoed a lot of tomatoes during those summers. We sang folksongs and danced Israeli dances — it was like going to camp. Many of the kids were from the lower part of New York City, and some were dedicated Communists. We were all pretty socialistically oriented — after all, the kibbutz is a socialist organization of the most basic sort.

We used to ride in the back of trucks from Hechalutz into New York to the docks and see off small boatloads of friends who were going to start farms or work on them. A number of them got caught by the British — you weren't allowed to do that [prior to the establishment of the Israeli state in May 1948]. The British stopped them before they got to Palestine and interned them on Cyprus. This was very unpleasant. I don't know if people remember that the British established concentration camps for Jews on Cyprus at that time. I wanted to go, I was prepared to go. But my mother discouraged me, arguing that I should go to college to learn a practical skill that would be useful to my new country. So I went to college.

Ilse's mother wanted her to go to Barnard College in nearby New York City, where she would be a commuting student and live at home, but her father ruled she should attend a school away from home as part of learning to be independent. He chose Antioch College, a highly regarded private coeducational liberal arts school in Yellow Springs, Ohio. Young Ilse, who started classes in September 1949, found Antioch a good fit. The college not only stressed academics but development of the student's whole personality, including social conscience. Antioch also promoted liberal principles and educational experimentation and it had a much admired work-study program, a central feature of the curriculum. Ilse's work-study, or co-op, job mostly involved statistical calculation — numbers crunching in today's parlance. In addition, the college, which had roughly the same number of students as Ilse's high school, was small enough not to overwhelm or intimidate her. In 1949 she was still a shy, compliant teenager used to having decisions made for her.

Initially she took courses in the general area of conservation (or ecology), learning about agronomy, strip mining, and other aspects of land use, believing this sort of knowledge would be most useful when she moved to Israel after college. She also took some courses in rural sociology, which eventually changed her mind about going to Israel: "I learned I didn't need to go to Israel to be a pioneer; there was plenty to be done in this country." As she progressed as a student at Antioch, nourished by the college's intellectually stimulating atmosphere and liberated from the day-to-day domination of her parents, Ilse became more confident, more outgoing, more her own person. There were, she admitted, "some painful experiences at the time but on the whole Antioch was a wonderful place to get an education." She especially appreciated the freedom the school gave students to pursue diverse interests; for instance, she "learned to love pottery at Antioch." The college also exposed her to America's festering race problem as few other colleges could or would have done at the time. Long before the U.S. Supreme Court's landmark *Brown* decision on school desegregation and the subsequent civil rights movement, Antioch was a bastion of racial tolerance and enlightenment. When Ilse was a freshman, Coretta Scott — later Coretta Scott King, wife of Martin Luther King, Jr. — was a senior at the school. The fact that Coretta Scott could not do her student teaching locally in the town of Yellow Springs because of the color of her skin had a lasting effect on Ilse's understanding of the depths of racial bigotry in the United States. Yellow Springs — as conservative as Antioch was liberal — also had a barbershop at the time that refused to cut black people's hair, which prompted demonstrations and pickets by Antioch students.

Ilse Webb

Ilse left Antioch in June 1953 with an A.B. degree in sociology and a new surname. During her senior year she married a fellow student, Kenneth Webb, her first serious boyfriend. A biology major, Ken Webb was, in Ilse's estimation, "very bright" but also an introverted person, "a loner who was a social misfit outside his own circle." She met him soon after arriving at Antioch and each year the relationship deepened:

We started going out my first year and the second year it became serious. By my third year we really wanted to get married, but my parents would have none of it. They did not like him—not at all. He was a farm boy, the first person in his family to graduate from high school. He was far from sophisticated. Rather, he was a northern Ohio country boy from a Christian fundamentalist family. My mother especially was not happy—gentiles kill Jews; or if not that, they were nasty to them. She wanted none of this country bumpkin whose father was a hellfire Baptist. Ken and his sister were not even allowed to go to the movies as youngsters—movies were the devil's work.

But Ilse—no longer the timid, self-effacing girl she had been when she left Mount Vernon for Antioch—married Ken Webb despite her parents' objections:

My parents wanted to send me around the world after my junior year, but I stood up to them and Ken and I married during my senior year. My parents finally relented but insisted I finish college; that was no problem, I certainly wanted to finish too. They paid my tuition and put money in the bank for my room and board at college, plus expenses— not really a great amount—and said, "This is it. Live on it or starve." We got married in Mount Vernon in front of the fireplace at home with my parents barely speaking to Ken. Then we went back to school and lived on my small allowance. My mother tried to undermine the marriage in little snippy ways, and that didn't do the marriage any good. I probably stuck with it much longer than I would have because of that. I was going to show them; I have a stubborn streak.

After Antioch the couple moved to Columbus, Ohio, where Ken continued his studies as a graduate student at Ohio State and Ilse found full-time employment as a statistician in an aviation psychology laboratory, work similar to her Antioch co-op job. The Webbs remained in Columbus for seven years, during which time Ken earned advanced degrees in plant physiology, concluding with a year of post-doctoral work devoted to biochemical reactions in plants. While in Columbus the Webbs' marriage lost its sheen: "I didn't expect marriage to be all flowers and romance," confided Ilse, "and it wasn't. It wasn't great but we were getting along, though Ken got involved with at least two other women. These relationships didn't come to sexual fruition but nearly to that, and I had similar relationships—again not real affairs, but verging."

Finally the time came for Ken to leave the academic cocoon and find a job, which proved difficult. He did not want to teach, preferring research in the laboratory, but there were few such opportunities available in his specialization. Then in 1960 fortune smiled and he found what seemed an ideal position at a marine institute in Georgia devoted to research on salt marshes and the flora found there. The institute, operated as an adjunct of the University of Georgia in Athens, was located on Sapelo Island, one of the barrier islands south of Savannah that dot the Georgia coast, the largest being St. Simons. At the time Sapelo Island was mostly owned by Richard J. Reynolds, Jr., head of the giant R.J. Reynolds tobacco company, who bankrolled the marine institute through a private foundation, alleged by some to be a tax dodge. Today, the state of Georgia owns and maintains all but a small portion of the island as a natural preserve, and the institute, now funded by the state, continues to function as a research facility in the university system.

Life on Sapelo Island was a completely new experience for both Ilse and Ken. Hauntingly beautiful with pristine beaches, the island offered all sorts of simple pleasures from birdwatching to fishing in the ocean for one's dinner. On the other hand, it was isolated, a ferryboat operated by R.J. Reynolds being the only means to get to and from the island. Sapelo's remoteness appealed to Ken's personality, but Ilse soon found the daily routine "pretty boring and quite confining. There was no store, no nothing." The closest place to buy groceries and other supplies was Darien, a town on the Georgia mainland 30 minutes away by ferry. Because Reynolds did not allow automobiles or vans on the island, the Webbs and other institute staffers parked their vehicles at a dock near Darien.

Sapelo's inhabitants in the 1960s consisted of a small colony of Gullahs—black descendants of slaves—who lived secluded in a swampy enclave called Hog Hammock, and a number of Reynolds employees, including marine institute personnel and their families. Not large, the institute ordinarily had five or six resident scientists at any given time, plus a small support staff. It also hosted visiting researchers and graduate students who came for short periods, did their experiments or field work, and left. Among the regular visitors was the famous University of Georgia ecologist Dr. Eugene Odum. During their five years at the institute the Webbs were the only couple among the full-timers without children, and naturally Ilse looked for something meaningful to occupy her days. It did not take her long to make herself useful. She became Sapelo's substitute postmistress, which entailed assisting the ferryboat captain's wife with sorting and distributing the island's mail, work that normally took only a couple of hours a day; and, fortuitously, she began "tending" the institute's one-room library.

The latter job changed Ilse's life, but at the beginning it was merely something to do to pass the time and incidentally earn a few extra shekels. At first the work frustrated her no end. Like a neophyte swimmer caught in a strong current, she found herself floundering in a sea of 3 × 5 cards and cryptic procedures and terminology. Since there was no one on the scene she could consult, she turned to the university library in Athens for help:

Because I was the only one without children and needed a job, I got to tend the marine library. I didn't know a thing about it but I learned by the seat of my pants. The University of Georgia sent books, periodicals, and copies of articles to the institute that had been requested by the scientists. The books came with LC cards. Before I arrived someone had filed the author cards, but the rest were left in a big pile. The first thing I had to deal with was this stack of cards. So I called up the university librarians in Athens and said, "I understand the title, author, and subject cards but here's this other stack of plain cards without any headings on them. What are they?" The response was something like, "That's your shelflist, dummy. Of course you wouldn't know that because you're not a professional." So I swallowed hard and asked what a shelflist was, and they explained it to me. So I made a shelflist.

Among the institute's regular summer visitors was the captain of a research vessel from another marine facility. Happily, the captain brought his wife along, a retired librarian, and Ilse was able to pick her brain about library matters. This generous lady gave Ilse books on cataloging by Margaret Mann and reference work by Margaret Hutchins; she also suggested other basic library science titles, which Ilse acquired and read. She found she had a natural talent for the work:

Eventually I was doing all sorts of nice things. I had an early SDI [Selective Dissemination of Information] system — I didn't know what it was called then. I knew the scientists and their interests, so when the journals came in I would scan them and, if I found something that would interest one of them, I sent a note or the journal saying this might interest you. So I started being a real librarian. Also, I started ordering some books direct instead of going through the university, because the scientists got pissed off about how long it took to get books from the university. So I began doing more and more. I would order the books, do the cataloging, order the LC cards, do the labeling, et cetera. I also did a lot of ordering of reprints of articles for members of the staff. Eventually I put together a collection of reprints of articles by the institute's scientists and exchanged them for reprints from similar institutes around the country and the world. I was running a one-person special library.

The Webbs left Sapelo in 1965, a move prompted mainly by Ken's involvement in a messy bit of hanky-panky. According to Ilse, life at the institute in the liberated 1960s was rife with extracurricular sex:

There wasn't much to do socially except screw around, and that's what we did. Ken started having real affairs with a number of women. He started fooling around with a lab assistant and later the wife of one of the scientists, a biologist. There were graduate students there over the summer, and there was one in particular who was bored and started spreading rumors that Ken Webb was having an affair with this particularly pretty woman. I didn't believe it was true but the woman's husband made a big fuss about it, and in the end Ken was pretty much forced out because of this scandal.

By this time I was having my little affairs too. This was an open sort of marriage. We weren't having severe problems with this, except as it affected Ken's work. It wasn't the affairs that were the problem. I somehow managed that. It was a very open sort of thing — we talked with each other about it. I was no longer the little shy girl — I was now in my thirties. Ken was an interesting guy, but by this time we really weren't getting along at all.

From Sapelo, Ken Webb joined the faculty at the Virginia Institute of Marine Science in Gloucester Point, a research center and graduate school administered by the College of William and Mary in nearby Williamsburg, Virginia. The Webbs soon bought a house in tiny Gloucester Point financed with a loan from Ilse's parents, but initially she did not live there. Instead, she applied for and was accepted as a full-time graduate student at the library school at Columbia University in New York City. During the year she spent at Columbia, Ilse lived with her parents in Mount Vernon,

driving daily into the city. She remembered the drill vividly: "I didn't take the train —
I had a car. I drove to the Bronx and parked my car at a gas station for $10 a month at
the elevated subway at 235th Street and then took it down to 114th Street and Broad-
way [the university stop]. I did this practically every day for a year."

Ilse completed her MLS in two semesters and a summer, beginning in the fall of
1965 and finishing the following August. Because of her husband's career and personality, she assumed she might at anytime find herself running a one-person library in
a remote place similar to Sapelo Island, and she was determined — obsessively so— to
learn all she possibly could about libraries and library work during her year at Columbia:

I enrolled as a full-time student, and I mean full-time — I was a workaholic then as now.
I was at the school early in the morning and stayed and studied in the library till late in
the evening. At the time I assumed I would be stuck on some sand-spit forever running a
little special library all by myself. That was my intention from the beginning, so I had better get whatever I could out of the library school while the getting was good, because who
knew when I was going to be in a city again. I studied very hard. But I almost quit after
the first semester — I was tired and I was disgusted.

Like many before her, Ilse became disillusioned with library school because of the
"Mickey Mouse" quality of some of the course work. One particular incident soured
her big-time:

In the history of libraries course the teacher didn't like a paper I had spent hours on. I
had done a really meticulous paper. It was on bibliographic centers involving cooperative
collection development and reference service. God, I read everything available, did a lot of
research, did a lot of work putting all this together, and it was really a pretty good history
of these centers— and the teacher gave me a "B" because it "wasn't fun to read." Boy, was I
pissed off! I didn't think the assignment was to write something that was "fun to read."
This was during the civil rights marches and somebody in the class who went to Selma,
Alabama, on a march with her husband got a really good grade on her paper on the march.
She got an "A+" and I had spent the whole damn semester working on this paper and got a
"B."

Ilse credited Russell Shank, a professor at the school and her adviser, with helping her through this crisis: "I walked into Shank's office one day and said, 'I can't stand
it. Give me one good reason why I shouldn't quit.' He talked me into staying. I always
tell him today that he's responsible for me being a librarian. And he is." (In one of
library history's tiny ironies, ten years later Russell Shank ran for, and lost, the ALA
presidency to Eric Moon, who by then was married to the former Ilse Webb, whose
support helped Moon win the election. Might history have been changed if Dr. Shank
had not convinced the disgruntled Mrs. Webb to continue her library school studies?)
But despite almost quitting Columbia after the first semester, Ilse enjoyed and profited
from most of her courses, particularly those taught by Maurice Tauber (cataloging),
Winifred Linderman (advanced reference), and the aforementioned Russell Shank (science reference and bibliography). She benefited too from being in a class that included
a number of future library stars, among them Art Plotnik, Pat Schuman, Ann Randall, and Robbie Franklin.

In September 1966, MLS securely in hand, Ilse moved back to Virginia, joining Ken in the Gloucester Point house they had acquired the year before, determined to make the best of what was now a strained marriage. She looked for a job in the area and quickly accepted an entry-level cataloging position in the library at the College of William and Mary. Some months later the library hired another junior cataloger, Mary Louise Cobb, who became a key figure in Ilse's life at this point. Approximately the same age, both faculty wives, and both united in their dislike of the head cataloger, Ilse and Mary Lou struck up a sororal friendship, with Mary Lou clearly the big sister.

Mary Louise Cobb (now Cobb-Corbett) opened Ilse's eyes to possibilities beyond the library at William and Mary and domesticity in Gloucester Point. She encouraged Ilse to join and become active in ALA and the Virginia Library Association, pointing out that librarians have a responsibility to serve the profession through participation in their various associations. What's more, attending library association meetings and conferences was a convenient way of escaping the humdrum of everyday life, including husbands, a few times each year. Soon the two women became heavily involved in VLA business and, in Ilse's colorful phrase, they started "racketing around" together at ALA conferences.

Now in her mid-thirties, Ilse was ripe for this sort of experience. During the years in Ohio and on Sapelo Island she had matured into womanhood and coincidentally stumbled into a compatible profession, but it was not until Virginia that the adult Ilse — a strong, plucky woman with sharp political instincts, an aggressive sociality, and a fundamental belief in the liberal ethos — fully emerged. Previously she had been first and foremost Ken Webb's wife, a subordinate figure, an appendage to the striving Arrowsmith. But now, armed with an MLS and bolstered by her friendship with the more worldly Mary Lou Cobb, she became her own person, free to call her own shots.

Enter Eric

Ilse's first experience with ALA occurred in January 1968, a Midwinter meeting held in Washington, D.C. She and Mary Lou drove up from Williamsburg, about a three-hour trip by car. They shared a room, went to meetings, did the exhibits, and met and interacted with other librarians from Virginia and around the country. Agog, Ilse took to the proceedings like a child at the circus, delighting in the people, the bustle, the buzz, the glamour, the colorful antics, the serious acts. American involvement in Vietnam and protests against the war dominated the national agenda at the time, and the 1968 presidential campaign was just getting revved up. Two months later, at the end of March, President Johnson would quit the race, and shortly thereafter both Dr. King and Robert Kennedy would be assassinated. A growing number of librarians were urging ALA to take a stand on Vietnam and related issues, but those who controlled the organization — the "Establishment" — resisted, insisting such concerns were not within ALA's purview. The volatile atmosphere at the meeting appealed to Ilse's innate interest in people and politics, and during the next 30 years she rarely if ever missed an ALA midwinter or annual conference.

In late June she and Mary Lou flew to Kansas City (Missouri) for the 1968 conference. After Washington, Ilse was no longer an ALA rookie, though she knew — Mary Lou had warned her — that the summer conference was always a much larger and more frenetic affair than Midwinter. Accordingly, she went to Kansas City prepared to meet lots of new people, keep her eyes and ears open, learn as much as she could, and have some fun in the bargain: "This was only my second ALA. Mary Lou and I went to meetings and so on. We racketed around, more or less behaving ourselves, just having a good time. I remember we went out to dinner with a group of academic librarians — friends of Mary Lou's — and got lost, ending up in Kansas City, Kansas, instead of Kansas City, Missouri. And we had some other dinner dates and party kind of stuff."

Ilse spent a certain amount of time in Kansas City with another Virginia colleague, Richard K. Burns, director of the upscale Falls Church Public Library and a nationally prominent figure in the field in the 1960s. She and Dick Burns had met and become friendly a year or so earlier at a VLA event. Toward the end of the week Burns suggested they make the *LJ* suite scene where he would introduce her to the famous Eric Moon, whom he had known for some years. Ilse, game for any new ALA experience, said sure, let's go, but recalled, "I wasn't dying to meet Eric Moon. I knew of him, of course, and read his editorials in *LJ*, but I was rather shy about meeting socalled celebrities. I tended not to do that. I tended to turn away in the face of celebrities. I didn't go out of my way to meet them usually, and still don't."

On Thursday evening, June 27, 1968, Dick Burns and Ilse Webb made their way to the *LJ* suite, located that summer in the upper reaches of the old Muelhbach Hotel, then a Kansas City landmark. The suite astonished Ilse:

It was really something. Here was this spectacular, enormous suite. I think it had three bars and three television sets. It was so large and luxurious — I think it was the suite where Harry Truman stayed when he was at the Muelhbach. It was like walking into a movie set; it was really kind of a stunner. And there were lots of things going on. Eric was with a group of people but there was also a regular party going on all over the rest of suite. Eric was sitting in the middle of the floor on a hassock wearing peace beads that Carolyn Forsman had made for him. And sitting around him were all these librarians, mostly men: Eldred Smith, John Forsman, Bob Haro, Jim Welbourne, Binnie Tate, and a lot of others, all progressive young librarians. Eric was teaching them how to do the revolution and the kinds of things they needed to know about the ALA political structure.

Dick Burns introduced her to Eric, who said hello, nice to see you, et cetera, and returned to doing his "guru bit," as insiders called his impromptu sessions on revolutionary tactics. Meanwhile, Dick and Ilse circulated, joining the larger party in progress, and at some point in the evening she met up with Karl Nyren. It was an ugly, upsetting encounter. Ilse remembered behaving badly:

I somehow got introduced to Karl, who was not with Eric's group. We had talked for maybe a minute and something started to irritate me. I suppose part of it was having been mostly a wallflower all my life — shy, not popular. Here was this goodlooking man — Karl was so handsome, one of the most handsome men I ever met. Here was this extraordinarily handsome man — he was athletic, well-built, gorgeous — and he kind of came on to me a little bit, which I think was just the way he was. I found out later that Karl was the sweetest, kindest, gentlest person in the world. But for somebody like me having this guy come on to them a little bit — I thought, shit, this is the kind of guy who looks at his watch and says to himself, well, it will take me 57 seconds to make this one.

And I was terrible! I don't remember exactly what I did, but I decided I was going to play with this situation. I met him and I decided to be angry with him, for some reason. I was going to flirt with him and then be really impossible with him — I wasn't going to be a 57-second conquest! The evening went on and apparently we behaved extremely badly — or *I* behaved extremely badly. I remember I baited him outrageously and he bit and we had this thing and it became obvious and terrible. This was very public — there were hundreds of people there. It was an encounter that was inappropriate, and I suppose all of us had had a little more to drink than was wise, as one tends to do at those things.

Later that evening Ilse had a tête-à-tête with Eric. She recalled they "were clearly attracted to each other," and she accepted an invitation to accompany him to a big do — the inaugural party for incoming ALA president Roger McDonough — two nights hence. The next day (Friday), Nyren sought out Ilse and told her, "You behaved badly and I'm in real trouble," adding that Eric had almost fired him over the brouhaha the night before. Ilse, aware of her culpability, was genuinely apologetic, but deep down she also felt a certain satisfaction, knowing that the incident had helped her catch the eye of Eric Moon who, despite his celebrity, turned out to be a very appealing man. For his part, Moon found this lively newcomer to the suite, this headstrong Ilse Webb, both articulate and attractive, and her spirited performance only heightened his interest.

So it was that on Saturday evening, June 29, the last night of the 1968 conference, the famous Eric Moon took a charming Ilse Webb (she was now on her best behavior) to Roger McDonough's party in the presidential suite at the Muelhbach where, according to Eric, she "met all the pooh-bahs of the association. That's how it started." Ilse, on the other hand, didn't remember much about the party, only afterward when "I spent a fair part of the night with him. That was our first time."

In almost every respect the Kansas City conference was a harbinger of trouble ahead for ALA. Most significantly, the conference blew open the generational fault line that had developed in recent years between the conservative ALA Establishment and the organization's younger, more liberal or radical members, who by 1968 had coalesced into a loosely structured movement dedicated to institutional reform or, in some cases, revolution. Likewise, the conference saw the beginning of a serious, organized effort on the part of the ALA membership *as a collective entity* to challenge the authority of the Establishment, which throughout the association's 90-year history had done pretty much as it pleased, functioning largely as an oligarchy. Among those advocating power to the membership, none was more determined or persuasive than Eric Moon.

The most heated debates in Kansas City involved a move by the membership to establish a roundtable "on the Social Responsibility of Libraries" that would be empowered "to propose action programs to the Association" concerning such controversial issues as war and peace, race relations, gender discrimination, and sexual orientation. Ken Duchac (then head of the Suburban Maryland Library Project) and Dorothy Bendix (an outspoken left-wing library science professor at Drexel Institute) presented the roundtable proposal, while Moon worked tirelessly on strategy to get it adopted by Council. By the end of the conference, however, the matter remained unresolved. Another shock wave that rippled through the Kansas City assembly was a blistering attack on the association by its retiring treasurer, Ralph Blasingame, who publicly excoriated ALA as an out-of-touch bureaucracy "controlled by old people." By the end of the week, outgoing president Foster Mohrhardt (himself an old-timer) was heard to mutter, "Forty years ago, when I went to my first ALA, I thought this was a moribund profession. I've changed my mind." Though Kansas City settled little, it placed a number of big, undecided issues squarely on the table — issues that would erupt at the next annual conference, scheduled to be held in Atlantic City.

The Kansas City conference also foreshadowed momentous changes in the personal lives of Eric Moon and Ilse Webb, though neither at the time had a clue as to what lay ahead. When Eric left the conference — his last as editor of *LJ*— he had no idea that the fetching Mrs. Webb, whom he had so casually slept with after the McDonough party, would shortly become the love of his life. Similarly, Ilse, who flew back to Virginia with Mary Lou on Sunday, June 30, had not the slightest notion that in just 18 months she would be living with the celebrated Eric Moon and married to him a year or so later. In fact, after Eric and Ilse departed Kansas City, their relationship (if it could be called that) nearly died a natural death. Ilse had expected to hear *something* from him after she got home, but the days and weeks passed and there was only silence. It gnawed at her:

At the end of the conference I went home to Virginia. That was it. Nothing. Over the summer I guess I was pretty restless about this whole thing. Anyway, about a month or so later I wrote Eric a letter, wondering if he would remember me. I assumed he had millions of women at these conferences— not millions but more than several. He's a very exciting man, and an interesting man. Eric calls these women celebrity fuckers. I don't think I was one of those, but it certainly is true that many women who aren't interested in money, or celebrity, which I wasn't, are interested in interesting and powerful men. Anyway, I wrote him a letter — a sappy letter, written just to see if he would respond and how. And after awhile I got an answer, and I was really put down by it.

The disappointing reply, typed on *LJ* letterhead and dated September 9, 1968, read as follows:

Dear Ilse:
   How nice to hear from you. I guess many of us are in mourning, not only over Chicago but Miami Beach, too. It wouldn't be too difficult to get defeatist about the sheer hopelessness of the political process. But it's the numbers game, and maybe— just maybe—the balance of those numbers will change enough in the next few years to prevent another debacle like this one.
   I'll be at Midwinter and hope to see the ALA revolution continue—or even pick up the pace. I hope you'll be there to man the barricades.
                                         Best wishes,
                                         Eric Moon
   Editor
   EM: rdg

Apparently, surmised Ilse, she was just another Conference Connie: "I thought, Christ, the letter was a few lines dictated to his secretary. This is apparently what he writes to everybody. I was hurt by it." Still, she wrote back, saying she would try to see him at the Midwinter meeting in Washington in January 1969, which she did, tracking him down at the Shoreham, the conference hotel. Ilse recalled, "I went to the Shoreham where Eric always had a table in the front of the lobby bar — it was his Midwinter hangout. I found him there, and we took up the relationship. We saw a lot of each other after that, spending our nights together."

This time after they parted, their correspondence was frequent, intimate, and sometimes even mushy. At one point, according to Ilse, Eric wrote, "Even though I'm a cynical journalist, I feel like a kid in love." He sent his letters to her at William and Mary, and she remembered keeping a careful watch for them in the incoming mail: "Talk about lovesick calves! I think we both were. I remember, like a teenager, looking for that distinctive blue Bowker logo on any mail. Of course the Bowker Company sent a lot of mail to the library at William and Mary, so those letters weren't always for me. But I remember going in and snatching them out of the mail — and adoring whatever he wrote to me."

The lovers looked forward eagerly to meeting again that summer in Atlantic City. During this period Moon's career took a new turn. After stepping down in December 1968 as *LJ* editor, he became director of editorial development at Bowker, a job he quickly grew bored and disenchanted with. He shared his dissatisfactions about the job in his letters to Ilse, which gave further dimension to their affair. Ilse meanwhile had been promoted to head cataloger at William and Mary. She was also increasingly active in VLA, becoming assistant editor of the *Virginia Librarian*, VLA's periodical publication, in 1969; her friend Dick Burns was the magazine's editor. She also helped establish a Junior Members Round Table of ALA in Virginia:

I got involved with some people — political types — I met through the Virginia Library Association, in which I became very active. I was one of a group of people with Fred Glazer, Bill Roberts, and Ellis Hodgin [all public library directors in Virginia] who started the Junior Members Round Table in Virginia. We wanted to start a Social Responsibilities Round Table, but we knew we couldn't do it. Virginia was a really conservative state, so we decided to start a JMRT. I guess this was really the beginning of the development of my political skills, with a lot of help from Mary Lou Cobb, who was very good at this sort of thing.

Warriors in Atlantic City

The skirmishes between the militants and the ALA leadership in Kansas City in 1968 set the stage for the Atlantic City conference the following year, which turned out to be a raucous affair with the forces for change plainly on the offensive. Kansas City, observed Moon, had been "like the Olympic trials" for Atlantic City, a gathering he and many others later came to view as not only the climactic library event of the revolutionary 1960s but the preeminent library conference of the 20th century. In Olympic terms, Atlantic City was library Gold.

No sooner had the Kansas City conference concluded than anti–Establishment elements began ginning up for Atlantic City. Eldred Smith, one of the profession's most
visible "young Turks" and a Moon consigliere, issued this call to the colors in a letter
published in the October 1, 1968, issue of *LJ*:

[E]very effort should be made to attend the Atlantic City Conference. Pressure can be
exerted on libraries to send the maximum number of librarians, including younger, non-
administrative staff members. Where the libraries won't or can't bear the burden, staff
members can pool resources and send some spokesmen.

For years, I've heard complaints about ALA and how little it means to most of us. Complaints are no longer enough. Too much is going on in the profession for us to continue to
stand aloof. The Atlantic City Conference can be a very exciting meeting and a lot can be
accomplished there, but it will mean a serious commitment on the part of all librarians
who want to see their association play a more significant role in society and the future of
information management.

The question of the profession's role in society that Smith referred to dominated
the debate on the road to Atlantic City. Soon after Kansas City, for example, the California Library Association stole a march on the national association and created a
permanent Standing Committee on Social Responsibility. And *LJ* kept the issue on the
front burner, Moon and Nyren espousing the activist position while "Viewpoint"
columnist Leonard Freiser argued the other side in a piece archly titled "The Bendix-
Duchac Establishment." Wrote Freiser: "This group wants to discuss social issues.
They are too late, we've already had them. It's fun, it's easy and it allows us to avoid
tackling the difficult and pressing business of library issues. Looting, student hostility, military adventures—all heady stuff but what specific action can libraries take in
terms of information and education which will affect the conditions which give rise to
these problems?"

On Saturday, September 21, 1968, some 30 supporters of the proposed ALA social
responsibility roundtable, including sponsors Bendix and Duchac, met at Drexel Institute in Philadelphia for a planning and strategy session. Roger McDonough, New Jersey state librarian and incoming ALA president, attended and told the group, "I'll back
you in every way I can," adding cautiously that he hoped "we don't run into some
damned constitutional roadblock." Moon was at the Drexel confab too. In retrospect,
the most important development to come out of it for him was meeting a young librarian named Patricia Glass Schuman, who in due course would become an ALA notable
and key member of the Moon inner circle. Schuman recalled, "Eric and I hated each
other on sight. I thought he was an old lefty trying to tell young people what to do,
and he thought I was an insipid young kid after power. Later we had occasion to have
a drink together and found that we liked each other."

At ALA's Midwinter meeting in January 1969 in Washington (the same meeting
at which Eric and Ilse renewed their relationship), the Council bowed to the inevitable
and voted unanimously to establish an ALA Social Responsibilities Round Table, while
at the same time warning that the new roundtable could be discontinued at anytime.
Bill De John, a cool, bespectacled, under-thirty type from the Missouri State Library,
became the group's first chairperson. In March, John Berry, who had taken over *LJ*'s

editorial reins from Moon just a few months earlier, wrote of SRRT (pronounced "cert"): "Its activists are young, critical, and unafraid to question every phase of librarianship and its organizations…. By the time we get to Atlantic City one can be sure the voices of social responsibility will be heard."

A few days prior to the convening of the Atlantic City conference in June a hundred or so militant librarians and library school students—most of them young and many of them SRRT cadre—met at the "less than splendid" Manger-Annapolis Hotel in downtown Washington for what amounted to a rap session-cum-war council in preparation for Atlantic City. Organized by Jim Welbourne (student association president, University of Maryland library school) and calling themselves the Congress for Change, these people came together determined to challenge ALA's old guard in a major effort to humanize and democratize and perhaps even radicalize the organization. They were of course a naive lot, but they were full of themselves and the righteousness of their cause, pumped up by the general climate of protest on U.S. campuses and visceral distrust of authority in any guise. Hour after hour for more than two days at the seedy Manger-Annapolis, CFC participants debated and hammered out consensus positions on the issues they intended to fight for at the Atlantic City conference. High on their agenda was ALA policy on the Vietnam War, poverty, racial discrimination, and community control of libraries, and what CFCers saw as an urgent need to reform both ALA and library education, neither of which, according to critics, was sufficiently hospitable or responsive to new ideas.

The week-long Atlantic City conference opened on Sunday, June 22, with those in charge worried that radical elements might create havoc similar to that which occurred at the Democratic National Convention in Chicago the year before. No ALA official wanted to end up looking like Mayor Daley and his storm troopers. Conference security was extremely tight. Berry reported in *LJ*:

> For an entire year, and especially during the six months preceding the ALA Conference, the U.S. library field was rife with rumors that dissidents had plans to disrupt the convention, confront older librarians, and generally raise hell at ALA. They were labelled as "new left," the youth, or simply a radical or minority fringe. Nevertheless, the prospect of trouble seemed to haunt the library establishment and its preparations for the Conference were replete with an abundance of badge checkers, rent-a-cops, and monitors of one sort or another.

The conference—attended by 10,250 ALA members and an unknown number of nonregistrants—never got out of control, but numerous large and small confrontations between Establishment figures and activist rebels did occur. One conferee with a gift for metaphor suggested it was like "a hoop-skirted old maid trying to deal with a 'turned-on' 15-year-old." At one point during a Council debate on raising ALA dues (an unfortunate agenda item for such a contentious conference), a youthful dissenter declared he opposed paying more dues "to fatten the cats at 50 East Huron Street"—50 East Huron being the address of ALA headquarters in Chicago and symbolic home of the American library Establishment. In another instance John Berry was punched by an irate student. He explained: "Yeah, Ellen Altman [a library science doctoral student at Rutgers University] slugged me because I was questioning whether there ought to be a Ph.D. program at all. She just saw me as some kind of asshole who was questioning everything." Moon added these details:

John and I put on a party for doctoral students at all the library schools. We asked Hardy Franklin who was at Rutgers along with Bob Wedgeworth, Bill Summers, and a few others to organize it. On the night of this party I had to be elsewhere but walking back on the Boardwalk with Ilse I ran into Hardy. I asked him why he wasn't at the party. He said he had been at the party but it got kind of explosive and he left. He said John Berry is in a terrific fight with the doctoral students. I waltzed into this argument and tried to moderate but soon was on Berry's side. Eventually this woman hauled off and socked John in the stomach. He went down as if he had been poleaxed.

This belligerent us-versus-them attitude persisted throughout the conference, though leaders on both sides made frequent attempts to soften the rhetoric and search for compromise solutions. Much of the fiercest action took place in a marathon membership meeting that required several sessions stretching over a three-day period, finally ending on Friday the 27th with a 345-to-131 vote against the war in Vietnam. Pro-war librarian Marietta Daniels Shepard was hissed when she requested the record show that fewer than 500 of the association's 40,000 members participated in the vote.

Berry had attended the Congress for Change meeting in Washington as a reporter, and when the CFCers moved on to Atlantic City he offered them the *LJ* suite as a crash pad. Located in the Traymore Hotel (now long gone, a victim of the wrecking ball), the commodious suite opened via French doors onto a large veranda or balcony that ran the length of the front of the third floor of the building and overlooked the ocean, beach, and famed Boardwalk. Blessed with all this space, Berry also allowed Bill De John and approximately 250 SRRT activists to use the suite and adjoining veranda as a place to caucus the first night of the conference. To no one's surprise, the SRRT contingent made the *LJ* suite its home for the whole week. "They ended up staying throughout the entire conference," recalled Berry. "I mean sleeping there, playing there, fucking there, drinking there. They drank our bar dry eight times. It was an extended politically oriented orgy."

No one looked forward to the Atlantic City conference with greater anticipation than Eric Moon, who had sensed a revolution struggling to be born the previous year in Kansas City. Watching the momentum build during the months following Kansas City, he came to Atlantic City with high hopes, prepared to play a central role in the efforts to democratize the inner workings of ALA. Though no longer editor of *LJ* he continued to be an influential force in the profession, well-known as an advocate for reforming the national association and making social issues "a legitimate and unavoidable part of the professional agenda."

Moon aggressively pursued these goals in Atlantic City as a vocal member of the ALA Council, where he was very much a minority voice, and as a frequent participant in floor debates at the lengthy and highly charged series of membership meetings. But probably his greatest influence occurred offstage in the *LJ* suite where he acted as adviser and mentor to the young dissidents, who saw him not as an old geezer of 46, and hence someone to be scorned, but as a comrade who instinctively understood their desire to be heard, to be taken seriously, to effect real change. Gerry Shields, editor of the *ALA Bulletin* at the time, remembered how the Establishment feared Moon: "Many the time as an employee of ALA I was privy to staff meetings where speculation ran rife as to just what Eric Moon was either 'up to' or 'going to do,' particularly after the Kansas City conference. He was given credit for much of the agitating that upset the ALA status quo leading up to and immediately following the Atlantic City conference."

In an interview years later Moon reprised the Atlantic City conference and his part in it:

Atlantic City was probably the greatest library convention in library history anywhere, any time. Anybody who was not there can't have any idea how different it was from anything that ever happened before (or since, I might add). The *Library Journal* suite was a sort of revolutionary and tactical headquarters. We had one of the largest suites in Atlantic City, and the Congress for Change people, mostly students and mostly broke, had been at a meeting in Washington previously to get organized. And they came down to Atlantic City with lots of fervor but not much money. I don't know how many of them we had sleeping on the floor, all over the *Library Journal* suite. We had sessions there at which people reported, and great tactical discussions on how were we going to go about this, what should we do about that. It went on for days and days and days. I don't know how long the membership meeting lasted, but it must have been some two and a half days. I found it particularly fascinating because I was in a role that I'd never been in before. I was sitting with the Congress for Change people, but I was the only one who knew most of the guys sitting up at the top table. And periodically the Congress for Change youngsters would say to me: "Well what do they want?" Then the president or someone would call me up to the platform and ask: "What do they want?" So I was sort of translating and mediating between the two groups. It was an entirely unfamiliar role.

Later in his career, especially after becoming ALA president, Moon would often find himself in the position of mediator or bridge between opposing forces in the association. It was a position he said he "never consciously sought or cultivated. I was there when some things were needed and I was probably the right person to do what had to be done." But in 1969, at the rowdy Atlantic City conference, he savored the unaccustomed role of negotiator, enjoying the bargaining process as well as the sense of power and importance it conferred on him. John Berry witnessed Moon in action and verified his unique contribution: "Eric did a lot of the negotiating with the ALA leadership because he could get to them. He knew both sides. He knew Roger McDonough and Bill Dix, who were the leaders of ALA at that time. And he was able to get them to make some concessions. He banged away on the issues. Eric was right there at this fight, doing what no one else could do."

Ultimately, Moon saw Atlantic City as the dawning of the library revolution he had labored so long and hard to bring about:

The Atlantic City conference was really the culmination of efforts that began in the early 1960s with the integration battles, and that led to the formation of SRRT in Kansas City in 1968. Now, here in 1969, was the birth of the revolution that had been coming all through the 1960s. The fact that it almost died in one year is sad, but it was exhilarating to see. There were a lot of people who thought Atlantic City was a terrible waste of time, but I believe it led to some significant changes in ALA thinking. Forevermore it was much more difficult for anybody on the platform to say that we cannot discuss this because it's not a professional issue. What we made clear was that librarians are part of society and that social issues are professional issues. That may have been the single most important contribution of the conference. It was a unique conference. There's no question that there has never been another library conference anything like it. It was a watershed event.

Lovers in Atlantic City

Amid all the clamor and demands of the conference, Eric and Ilse resumed their love affair, picking up where they had left off in Washington in January, making the most of their short time together in Atlantic City like two randy kids on prom night. Still, not all went swimmingly for the couple, proving once again the wisdom of Shakespeare's admonition about the course of true love never running smooth. Fortunately, no tragedy befell the lovers, their tribulations at the conference more on the order of bedroom farce than gripping drama, complete with a slapstick entrance and exit by a supporting player and the sudden appearance of — who else? — the suspicious spouse.

Sleeping arrangements at the *LJ* suite practically guaranteed contretemps. Eric explained:

There were two bedrooms, one of which John and I were sharing. Our usual arrangement was to alternate nights and on the nights Ilse and I didn't have the room we had to look for other accommodation. [Ilse was sharing a room with her friend Mary Lou Cobb.] One night Dick and Nancy Bye helped us out — they had two rooms at another hotel and they were only using one. Dick and Nancy were just beginning their relationship too. Another night we got a room from a young guy from the *LJ* Card Service named Bob someone. It was his first ALA and he wasn't very tuned in. He was at the suite one night and said he'd switch rooms with me that night, so he gave me his key and I didn't tell him he wasn't going to be able to get into my room since it was Berry's turn, so he ended up sleeping in the suite with all these hundreds of SRRT and Congress for Change people. He didn't get any sleep of course and was royally pissed off the next morning when I came back. He said, "That's the last time I'll ever switch rooms with you!"

Another evening Eric and Ilse had the room at the Traymore, when Berry, in his cups, broke in and found them in bed. Eric recalled John's embarrassed retreat:

On this particular night we had our usual wild party at the suite going into the wee hours. Ilse and I were tired and went to bed. John, who was pretty smashed, had forgotten that it wasn't his night and he couldn't get into the room, so he wandered around this enormous balcony outside, found the window to the room, raised it and climbed in, camera over his shoulder. And there we were — in bed. Suddenly John came to his senses. He tried to back out the window, holding his camera and looking the other way and pulling the window down and almost falling off the balcony. Ilse was falling over the bed laughing.

Berry's version of the story went like this:

Eric and I shared this room and it was always a battle as to who would have privacy in the room and what night. It was always complicated and always mixed up. We would schedule the room at the beginning of the conference but the schedule was never followed.

On this famous, fateful night, it was his night in the room I guess, and I needed something that was in there, probably my stash, although I don't really remember. But it was something vital; I knew I had to get in. I tried the door and I knocked and of course there was no response. I knew right away I shouldn't do it but I was drunk enough not to care, so I went around to the patio [balcony] and opened the window to the room. I lurched into the room and there they were, *in flagrante delicto*—totally and very much so. I was really shocked. So I spun around and went back out the window, pulling the window and the shade down as I went. He says the last thing he saw was my arm pulling the shade down.

"The next morning at breakfast," confided Ilse, "John didn't know what to do—apologize or try to avoid us. We were more amused and he more embarrassed, I think, by the whole incident. Over the years we've teased him unmercifully about it."

Eric's wife Diana — by this time aware that something serious might be going on between her husband and another woman — drove down to Atlantic City toward the end of week to check out the situation for herself. Moon remembered trying to throw Diana off the track:

Diana went to the hotel and I was not there, then she came down to the convention hall where I was at the membership meeting. The meeting was endless that week, because the revolution was in full swing. I was sitting in the front row of the rebel group with one arm around Ilse and one around Madeline Miele [a comely Bowker staffer], and she walked in! Later there was a problem with my raincoat, which I had left in Ilse's room. Esh [Bill Eshelman] rescued it and got it up to his room, and he called me to tell me it was there. I told Diana I was going up to Esh's room to get my raincoat, and she wanted to know what my coat was doing in Esh's room, so I told her a cock-and-bull story about using the raincoat to hide bottles of booze to take to parties. It was a difficult situation.

All of this madcap activity ran counter to a riveting presentation on the personality and sexual habits of librarians offered by a psychiatrist from Philadelphia at a well-attended conference program on Thursday morning. Dr. Maurice Linden, who revealed he had more than a few librarians as patients, posited that people attracted to the library profession are typically introspective, passive, narcissistic, and sexually "timid, frugal, and clandestine." According to one published account of the meeting, Dr. Linden's remarks "were simply not accepted.... [A] number of librarians refuted the composite so masterfully on the basis of the action of this convention, that Dr. Linden himself was forced to back off and confess, 'Maybe I was wrong!'" Certainly Eric and Ilse's romance ran counter to the doctor's analysis.

A Party for Moon

Moon's schedule in Atlantic City was nothing if not hectic. In addition to helping birth a revolution and conducting a red-hot love affair, he was in the midst of changing jobs—and employers. He had quickly soured on the position of Bowker's director of editorial development, so when Theodore Waller of the Grolier Corporation approached him about the possibility of becoming head man at Scarecrow Press (a newly-acquired Grolier subsidiary in Metuchen, New Jersey), Moon seized the opportunity. He was slated to start the new job on July 1, right after the Atlantic City conference wrapped up.

Ted Waller, Moon's new boss, enjoyed playing publishing tycoon, and it was altogether in character that he should throw a grand party to introduce his new man at Scarecrow. Waller, excessively pleased to have snagged someone of Moon's stature in the library community to head the press, wanted to show off his prize. His party, however, did not go exactly as he had hoped. Moon gave this account of the early going:

> In the middle of all else that was happening in Atlantic City, I am changing from Bowker to Scarecrow. In the middle of the conference Theodore arranges one of his stuffy parties to introduce me as the new executive officer of the Scarecrow Press. And he invites all the leading dignitaries— Sir Frank Francis, Ralph Ulveling, Russ Shank, Lowell Martin, Verner Clapp, Archie McNeal, among others. Theodore said to me once, "We'll be a great team: you know all the radicals and I know all the important people."
>
> Anyway, I get to this party. I'm of course coming from various meetings, some quite wild, and I'm dressed typically late 1960s peacenik-style, including peace beads, and I wind up with this woman on my arm who Keith Doms has asked me to get out of some meeting because she's becoming a problem — she's threatened to disrobe at any moment — she's wearing only a tablecloth — and she's stoned to the gills. So I wind up with her and I can't do anything else so I take her with me to this party. We had been there about five minutes and she says to me, "Eric, is anything going to happen at this party? I'm really getting very teed off— I may have to strip!" I said something like don't do that, it would be very difficult for me.
>
> At that point I wandered over to the bar and ran into Sir Frank Francis [former director and principal librarian of the British Museum, whom Moon knew from his days in British libraries in the 1950s]. Sir Frank looks at me and says: "Moon!" I say, "Francis!" And he says, "What is that *thing* you're wearing around your neck?" I said, "Frank, you can't be that out of touch — it's a peace symbol." And he says, "A peace symbol?! I've never known a less peaceable young bastard in my life than you."

Moon recalled, "That was the beginning of my Scarecrow Press experience. Theodore was quite horrified that I turned up looking so sloppy and particularly with this wild woman on my arm." And Waller wasn't the only person taken aback by Moon's behavior. Al Daub, who ran the business end of Scarecrow, remembered "being shocked by Eric's dress— jeans and a peace medal — and the woman he brought. I've forgotten her name but she was a very, very outspoken young woman who had nothing on but a tablecloth with a hole in it." Daub and his wife Marty —"both conservative people"— viewed Moon "as a wild-eyed liberal." It was an unorthodox start to a new venture, but it typified the general spirit of the 1969 Atlantic City conference.

Atlantic City Aftermath

Many conferees— young and old, male and female, liberal and conservative — left Atlantic City feeling reasonably good about what had transpired. The militants had come prepared to stick it to the Establishment, which they did, and in the process they discovered that most ALA leaders were not ogres but sincere, dedicated, albeit often misguided elders who were—and this was the biggest surprise—willing to accommodate some of their demands. In fact, both Roger McDonough and William Dix, who succeeded McDonough as ALA president in Atlantic City, won plaudits from practically every quarter for their sensitive handling of a potentially explosive convention. As Berry observed in his report on the conference, "The old order, represented by McDonough, [Archie] McNeal, [David] Clift, and Dix, kept the Conference open to the new constituency. For this they deserve our respect. It was tough going, the pressure was never off, and outright hostility never far from the surface."

Incoming president Dix—for many years university librarian at Princeton and a political liberal—proposed and got a diverse committee charged with sorting out and, if possible, resolving the many criticisms of the association that had been raised in Atlantic City. The 12-member committee—officially the Activities Committee on New Directions for ALA but quickly dubbed the "Dix Mix"—included representatives from both the Establishment and dissident camps. In the coming months and years not every dispute got settled, nor were all members completely happy with every decision the committee made, nor did ALA's critics suddenly proclaim the association had become a rose garden. Still, Atlantic City and its aftermath represented progress: ALA became a more open, more tolerant, more humane organization as a result of the experience, and some of the reforms generated by the conference led to unexpected developments down the road, not least of which was the election of Eric Moon as president of the association seven years later.

University of Kentucky Library Press Institute

Atlantic City cemented Eric and Ilse's relationship. It was, in her words, "the high point of our lives." The lovebirds did not meet again until nine weeks later when they attended a workshop on the library press at the University of Kentucky in Lexington in early September. Funded by the U.S. Office of Education and officially an institute called "Upgrading the Knowledge and Skills of Editors of Regional and State-Wide Library Journals," the five-day event was hosted and administered by George Bobinski, assistant dean of the library school at Kentucky; Moon, while still at Bowker, had agreed to organize and implement it.

The institute attracted some 30 library journalists, among them the editors of the three major national professional magazines—Gerry Shields, *ALA Bulletin*; William Eshelman, *Wilson Library Bulletin*; and John Berry, *LJ*—who along with Moon served as the institute's faculty. Most of the other participants were editors of state association journals, including the *Virginia Librarian*, which sent two representatives, editor Richard Burns and his assistant editor, Ilse Webb. Registration and a welcoming dinner took place on Sunday, September 7, but Moon, who at one point had decided not to attend because of responsibilities at Scarecrow Press, did not arrive until late that evening or early the next morning. In a letter to Ilse, dated August 4, he wrote, "I told John Berry last week that I would be joining the Kentucky institute crowd after all.

He laughed, knowing why I changed my mind about not going and said, 'You're not leaving me much time to move in on your chick, are you?' I told him I'd bash him if he so much as tried. I guess he liked the back view of you from the balcony window in Atlantic City, the bastard."

When Moon did arrive, he immediately learned that Berry had indeed made a move on Ilse, though not the customary one. Moon: "I had organized the institute, and I was due to give the final summation. I got in late and before I got there John had sat Ilse down and given her a lecture. He told her not to hurt me, his friend, which we now look back on with some amusement." In his wisdom, Berry believed Moon had lost his cool over "this woman" and, because he liked Diana and sensed the affair was getting dangerously serious, John decided to step in and have a Dutch-uncle talk with Ilse. He wanted to know what Ilse's intentions were. John:

The institute was held out at this convention center [Carnahan House], which was a beautifully converted Kentucky bluegrass horse barn. We decided we would drink the drink of the region — bourbon. So we asked this old guy who ran the place what the best bourbon was and he gave us a brand name. At the liquor store all they had were half-pint bottles, so we bought cases of them and brought them out to the conference center and soon everybody was walking around the place with a half-pint bottle.

Eric and Ilse were there. Eric acted like a child, an absolutely infatuated, totally obsessed schoolboy over her. He was gaga. I began to fear for his sanity, he was so out of it over this woman. He was just totally, totally obsessive. I had never seen Eric like that before in my life. This thing just did him in; he was totally smitten by her. Never was there such a love as this.

And at the conference was this other guy who was also smitten by Ilse. He was our friend but Eric and he were pissed off at each other because of Ilse. So in addition to all the ferment of the library issues of that time, there was the underpinning of all these people locked up in this horse barn for a week with half-pints of bourbon and sex on their minds. And Eric and Ilse were acting out this melodrama with the other guy over who's going to win the fair lady. I was pissed at Eric, but I was absolutely pissed at her for leading these two guys on. I saw my friend [Eric] deteriorating into a smitten schoolboy before my eyes over this love affair.

Remember, I had a bias — I liked his wife Diana. Everybody liked Diana. Ilse had a tough time cracking that circle because people tend to take sides when there's a split. Anyway, before he arrived I confronted her. But first I had to deal with the other guy who was in love with her. I finally convinced him that the best thing for him to do was to get the hell out of there and go back home and find another woman and get on with his life. I really carried him through that thing. I set him up in a room at a Holiday Inn down the hill from the conference center. I told him, "You damn fool, it's no good sitting around here moping. Obviously Ilse's turned to Eric and you can't do anything about it; you can't make people love you." I was sick of these mewling guys and their display of total weakness in the face of this little woman. So I did Eric and Ilse a big favor by getting this other guy off their case.

So I took Ilse aside. I said to myself, by God, I'm going to have it out with her. I asked her, "What are your intentions toward my friend? Why are you messing over this great man who is clearly a basket case in your hands, and it's clearly your fault." She of course told him what I said and he was very touched actually — that I was worried and cared about him.

Ilse's recollection of John's talk with her began with the admission, "I don't think he liked me very much." She continued:

I think John thought it was getting much too serious, and that didn't fit with his image. He wanted to be the roué who worked his way through the women of the world — that's the way he wanted to live. And I think he wanted to be able to continue competing with Eric in this. Eric settling down with one woman didn't fit his picture of the way they were going to live their conference lives together. So John wanted Eric to cool it. We sat on a bench out in a garden with a bunch of concrete statuary, and he said, "Are you going to be nice to my friend?"

In the end Berry's intervention had no discernible effect on the lovers, who shared a room at a motel down the road from the conference center. Ilse's other suitor, however, did manage to make a nuisance of himself, despite Berry's best efforts. "This guy was rather upset," Eric remembered. "He knocked on our door at all hours. It was difficult and unpleasant." Gerry Shields recalled these events too: "At the University of Kentucky library school workshop for state editors staged by George Bobinski, Eric and Ilse's affair had not only blossomed, it ran rampant over the sensibilities of several people in charge of the retreat house site of the meetings. It seems there was another gentleman involved in seeking Ilse's hand, so to speak."

Still, cupid's antics did not unduly interfere with the functioning of the institute or affect its substance, which by all accounts participants found useful and provocative. A number of practical suggestions—convert state journals into newsletters; improve library news-gathering techniques at the state and regional levels; develop more effective communication between state and national editors—came out of the proceedings, and later Moon published an article on the subject called "The Library Press" that today is considered a classic. The institute prompted one other noteworthy development: the birth of the Eric Moon Flying Circus. Moon developed his "circus" as an alternative to giving speeches:

George Bobinski, who was the assistant dean at the library school, came over to the building where we were doing the workshop [institute] and said, "Eric, I've got an emergency. Will you do the colloquium speech tomorrow morning?" I said, "George, I did the colloquium speech last year at this library school and I'm fed up with doing colloquium speeches." His face dropped. I said, "Look, I don't want to let you down. I'll tell you what I'll do: I'll bring you a circus." He said, "What the hell's that?" Moon: "I don't know what to tell you." Bobinski: "You're not going to do something bad, are you?" Moon: "George, if you don't trust me, find somebody else; if you do trust me, leave it to me. I'll bring you a circus." Bobinski: "All right, but don't do anything bad."

So the next day was the school's colloquium. There was a massive turnout — the workshop editors, library school faculty and students, and librarians from the local area — and we walked into this big lecture hall and cleared the platform, took the table off the platform, took the lectern and chairs away, and we sat on the edge of the platform, about knee-high. I said, "Nobody here is going to give a speech or talk at you like they do at library school. What we're here today for is to discuss anything you want to talk about; if you don't have anything to talk about, we'll leave and go to the pub. I'll tell you who we are and then we're not going to say a word." Then I introduced John Berry, Bill Eshelman, Gerry Shields, and a couple of others. Then there was absolute silence that seemed endless—you know how long silence can seem when you're waiting. Then a guy in the back asked a question and it started.

The colloquium was scheduled from 10:00 to 11:30 in the morning, and at 1:00 PM one professor said he was canceling his classes for the day and another said so am I. And at 2:30 I said, "I hate to quit this but we have another responsibility over at the workshop and besides we need a drink." So we all went down to the bar before returning to the workshop.

I thought what a success this is, so I started what became known as the Eric Moon Flying Circus. What I did was put together four or five people who would all fight with each other, so the audience wouldn't feel it was a "we versus they" situation, and they would get involved on one side or the other. I got tired of giving speeches, so when I'd be asked I'd say no, but I'll bring you a circus. We did them all over the place.

Ilse recalled not being happy about Eric's first Flying Circus: "About the only people who didn't get to attend the circus were the state periodical editors for whom the workshop had been arranged. The editors who were the workshop leaders, thinking the circus would only take the usual short colloquium time, had set us some homework-type assignment. Then when it dragged on endlessly, they still wouldn't let us in. Oh, we were annoyed!"

Point of No Return

The University of Kentucky institute wrapped up on Friday, September 12. The next day Eric and Ilse flew to Washington, D.C., where they spent the night together before returning to their respective homes and spouses on Sunday the 14th. Diana— now a deeply suspicious Diana—found Eric's airline ticket in his coat pocket, which was, remembered Moon, "really the beginning of the breakup because by then she was sure about what was happening. After that, it simply fell apart." Several days later, in a letter dated September 17, Eric informed Ilse he had decided to leave Diana: "The deed is done. We went the whole route, from suicide threats on down." Shortly thereafter Ilse told her husband, Ken, that she was leaving him for Eric Moon, though she was not exactly sure when she would move out of their Gloucester Point home. For months the lovers had fantasized about leaving their spouses, but now fantasy was suddenly reality and they had to begin taking those grim, painful, prosaic steps necessary to undo any marriage.

Eric physically left Diana on Saturday, October 18, 1969, moving into "a one-room pad" in East Orange, a Jersey community seven or eight miles north of Elizabeth, where the Moons had lived since 1962 and Diana remained. "I just left everything," he recalled. "The thing with the kids was very difficult. Max was still in Taiwan [with the military]; we wrote to him individually. Diana worked on Alan, who was much younger— he wouldn't speak to me for several years." Meanwhile, Ilse pondered the best time to leave Ken, when to hand in her resignation at William and Mary, and what jobs might be available for her in the New York–New Jersey area.

In addition, family and friends had to be told. Ilse was especially concerned that her parents know what was going on before they left Mount Vernon for their winter vacation in Majorca. She called them, asking them to visit her in Virginia before their departure: "I knew I had to break it to them before they left. I was having a very hard time getting up my nerve to tell them. Finally my mother demanded to know what was going on — I wouldn't have insisted on the visit if something weren't up — and I told them." She told them she was leaving Ken and planned to live with and eventually marry a man named Eric Moon: "I asked Papa if he wanted to meet Eric? 'Certainly not — a man who would leave his wife and two children!' But my mother said, 'Of course I want to meet him. You can't do this without my meeting him.' So I called Eric and said you have to go and see my parents at their place in Mount Vernon. They lived in an apartment now that Sue [Ilse's sister] and I were gone. And he said, 'Alone??' And I said, 'Yeah, alone.'"

Eric vividly recalled his first meeting with Ilse's parents:

So I made a date to meet them one afternoon at their apartment. I arrived early and sat outside their building in my car editing a manuscript. There was nobody home. I got impatient and phoned Ilse at William and Mary from a telephone booth down the street. "I'm scared," I said. Eventually I saw this guy come in. I waited a bit, then rang the buzzer. A great dramatic voice with a German accent said, "WHO IS IT?" "My name is Eric Moon," I said. "COME ON UP." I went up the stairs and when he opened the door, he told me that he had two sons-in-law already and couldn't stand either of them and he didn't suppose I'd be any different. I said, "How about a drink?" He said, "Good idea." We were half sloshed [on scotch] by the time Ilse's mother got home from playing bridge.

Things were going well. They asked me to stay for dinner, but I couldn't because I was due to give a speech at Columbia University that evening. But things began to move along so well, I thought I better not break the mood, so I said, all right, I'll stay. Then Ilse's mother said, "My God, all I have are leftovers!" Still, I stayed. Suddenly during dinner Ilse's father leaned over to me and said, "Do you and Ilse plan to procreate?" Which stopped me cold. I thought about it for a minute and said, "I've done a bit of procreating already and I guess it's up to Ilse," which apparently was the right answer.

From that first meeting until they died in Florida years later, Ilse's parents looked upon Eric as their "good" son-in-law. He got along well with Fritz Bloch; they became, in Eric's words, "very good friends actually," having chess, politics, and enjoyment of wine in common; the two men also shared information about financial investments. Eric liked Ilse's mother too, though once he got in her doghouse by saying she reminded him of Mrs. Portnoy in Philip Roth's *Portnoy's Complaint*: "She went out and bought the novel and when she read it she was absolutely livid and wouldn't speak to me for weeks!"

Moon sensed that most of his family, friends, and colleagues took the breakup of his marriage in stride. His mother and brother Bryan were understanding and supportive; his great friend Ron Surridge in London was anything but shocked: "My wife and I saw the strains of Eric's first marriage emerge soon after his arrival in America. Consequent to all sorts of hearsay, Eric's own stories, and some conjecture, his divorce from Diana came as no surprise." After all, this was the swinging 1960s and marriages were crashing all over the place like dead trees in a windstorm. Moon:

I would say on the whole there wasn't a lot of reaction one way or another, partly because most people I knew were involved in some way or another themselves in the forming or breaking up of relationships or both. The two people I remember particularly who were vocal were John Berry, who never believed in serious entanglements, and Dick Bye, who constantly warned me against this sort of thing, though he was in the same situation and eventually left his wife and children. It was really a time of great change, and later on many of our friends went through the same thing and Ilse and I — as a couple who had already gone through it — became sort of an advice bureau.

In time, even those most upset by Eric leaving Diana or resentful toward Ilse as "the other woman" came to see the pair as a nearly perfectly matched couple who complemented each other's strengths and weaknesses. John Berry, for instance, admitted that it took him and Ilse a bit of time to put the events of Kentucky behind them, but they did. "I like her, she's smart," he said years later. "You see that mother approach of hers; she's the kind of person who insinuates herself into every detail of everybody's life who's anywhere near her. She has a Yiddish momma approach to life. She and I have come to love each other." And Alan Moon — Eric's younger and more vulnerable son, the person most hurt perhaps by the collapse of his parents' marriage — eventually reconciled with his father and stepmother.

Uneasy Riders

After the Kentucky institute, Eric and Ilse next saw each other in early October at a meeting of library activists in Pittsburgh. The meeting, held at the same time as the annual conference of the Pennsylvania Library Association, centered on proposals to reform ALA advanced by an ad hoc organization called Librarians for 321.8. Chaired by John Forsman, an early SRRT member, and taking its name from the Dewey Decimal number for democracy, the 321.8 group sought to have all candidates for office in ALA publicly declare their views on key issues of concern to the profession. Specifically, it called for (1) candidates' positions to be incorporated as part of the ALA election ballot; (2) publication of this information in the library press prior to the election; and (3) roll call votes on major issues before the ALA Council.

The 321.8 group also wanted a support fund for librarians involved in intellectual freedom battles, and at the Pittsburgh meeting it launched the National Freedom Fund for Librarians, a nonprofit corporation. The NFFL came about largely as a response to the firing of Ellis Hodgin the previous July; Hodgin had been director of the Martinsville (Virginia) public library until he ran into censorship problems. The Hodgin case, which became a national cause célèbre, energized competing efforts on the part of ALA and its critics (SRRT, 321.8, Moon Mafia, etc.) to establish a defense fund, something the profession had long needed but never seemed to get around to setting up. Judith Krug, head of ALA's Office for Intellectual Freedom, pushed for creation of a tax-exempt organization called the Freedom to Read Foundation, which would have the ALA imprimatur but not be subject to oversight by the association's Executive Board or Council. Moon and his friends rejected Krug's foundation, viewing it, in Moon's words, as "a little club at ALA" beholden only to Krug. They wanted a defense fund like NFFL that would be open — and accountable — to the whole profession.

After the Pittsburgh business concluded, Moon returned to New Jersey, throwing himself into his work at Scarecrow and preparing to move to his bachelor pad in East Orange in a couple of weeks. Also around this time his book, *Book Selection and Censorship in the Sixties*, a collection of articles and editorials from *LJ*, was published by Bowker. The following month brought some unexpected fallout from the Pittsburgh 321.8 meeting. Diana, now in fighting mode, happened upon a photograph in *LJ* (November 15, 1969) accompanying a news story about the meeting that set her off. "John Berry had taken some photographs and printed one that included a shot of the backs of our heads, Ilse's and mine," explained Moon. "As a result, Diana was down in his office really giving him a going over for the better part of an hour; she recognized us from the backs of our heads." Diana told John she intended to make Eric "suffer."

During this period Ilse too was busier than the proverbial bee, attending meetings of the Potomac Technical Processing Librarians, a Washington-area organization, and working hard as founding chair of VLA's Junior Members Round Table to make the new group a success, which she did. On Saturday, November 15, she and some friends drove up to Washington to join a massive protest against the Vietnam War; Eric and a like-minded group descended on the capital from the other direction, trucking down from New Jersey in a van. "Washington was an armed camp," Ilse remembered. "Andy Armitage got gassed. That was Andy. Nobody else went that far. Librarians were marching like everybody else against the war but only Andy went to the front lines where they were throwing tear gas. I believe we stayed at Jim Welbourne's. It was one of those 1960s parties—50 people crammed into somebody's house, sleeping on the floor or air mattresses or whatever."

Thanksgiving 1969 found Moon feeling lonely and at loose ends, so he decided to take Ilse up on an invitation to spend the holiday with her in Gloucester Point. She told him to bring along anyone he wished: "By this time Ken and I were on very poor terms and he said he wanted to see for himself all these very interesting people who were my new friends." Eric asked Bill Katz, also feeling low (woman trouble), to accompany him to Virginia for turkey and whatever trouble a couple of footloose middle-aged men could get into. Thus began the so-called "Easy Rider Weekend," a crazy, picaresque few days that became legend in the Eric-Ilse courtship saga.

Katz came down to New York City from Albany and the two men, joined briefly by John Berry, began by toasting the holiday with a few drinks—and then a few more. Presently Moon and Katz, now two mellow dudes, hit the road. All the time the urge to see and hold Ilse was uppermost in Eric's mind, a yearning akin to Lancelot finding and embracing the lady Guinevere. Years later Katz recalled their journey in similar terms: "We went like two slightly worn Lochinvars from New York to her southern castle. The trip took as long as we were there, and while it is all now a bit vague, I saw Eric for the first time in the role of the serious, holy man of romance."

They squeezed into Eric's Volkswagen Beetle—Katz, a tall man, sat with his knees in his chin—and headed south by southwest. Eric remembered only some of the details:

We took off very drunk and first got to Washington, D.C. There was a bar I knew in Washington where all the good progressive librarians came. Bill and I got to this bar after being detained by a policeman because we both looked like hippies; Bill looked like a decrepit Jesus Christ with hair down to his shoulders and a long beard. We got to the bar and it was totally empty. Bill said, "Jesus Eric, you really know the swinging places." Then this woman came in, and she asked the bartender, "Where are all the librarians tonight?" He said the regulars aren't here but there's a couple of visiting ones from New York over there. She came over and said, "My God, you're Eric Moon!!!" And Bill said, "And I'm Bill Katz!!!" She said hi and went on talking to me, ignoring Bill.

She asks where we were staying and says we could stay at her place, and then she takes us there. She says she has to go to a party, but calls some friends, three young women, who come right over. Bill says, "Boy, Eric, we've got it made!" We put on some music and had some drinks, but Bill says he has an uneasy feeling that things aren't going the way they ought to. It turned out that all three women were lesbians. At any rate it didn't go well and we eventually went out for a drink somewhere. When we got back our hostess still wasn't home, so we went to bed in the room she had shown us, in a double-decker bed. In the middle of the night Bill wakes up, hearing a noise. It's a hamster in a cage going round and round on a wheel: we were in her kid's room.

In the morning we left there and got on the road again and rolled on down to Ilse's place in Virginia, which was near Williamsburg. We went directly to Chowning's Tavern in the colonial part of Williamsburg and called Ilse from there. She said, "Where are you?" I said, "Chowning's Tavern." She said, "Oh my God." There was a big party at her house, so she informed her husband that these two friends from New York had arrived and were coming to the party. So we found her house and went to this party. Bill was having himself a high old time by then, dancing with every woman there and propositioning most of them.

There was one young woman he rather fancied. He was assigned a bed in the basement, and the next morning Ilse, her husband, and I were sitting around drinking Bloody Marys and Katz came up from the basement looking absolutely distraught. He said, "I have just had one of the worst experiences of my life—I woke up and felt this tongue on my cheek and I thought, ah, it's this young woman from last night and everything is coming together, and I woke up and opened my eyes and here's this big Afghan hound licking my face. I need a drink!"

This was the first time Eric met Ken Webb. Ilse recalled it as "a terrible, tense time," but it could have been worse. There were no fisticuffs, duels, or other manly displays. There was a fuss over who would have the bedroom that night, but that got resolved when Ken went off with one of his several girlfriends named Susan. (In fact, Webb ended up marrying a Susan after he and Ilse were divorced.) The next day the exhausted Lochinvars again jammed into Eric's little car, which by this time had a shattered windshield (the result of an accident only vaguely remembered), and headed north, back to Washington, back to New York, back to the grind. "That's how the thing went," mused Moon. "We drove the whole way back that day—how we stayed awake I don't know, because we had been drinking and partying for about five days. It was a wild trip."

December 1969 was a rotten month for Moon. Early in the month he received a letter from Case Western Reserve in Cleveland, inviting him to apply for the deanship of the university's library school. Jesse Shera, one of the great figures of modern American librarianship, was planning to retire as dean in 1970 and Moon had been recommended as a possible successor. Was he interested? Conflicted, Moon reluctantly wrote back explaining he had recently taken a top position at Scarecrow Press and could not consider other possibilities at this time.

In the middle of the month he had a horrendous automobile accident, a one-car wreck that left his Beetle wrapped around a telephone pole. Robbie Franklin, who worked with him at Scarecrow and visited him in the hospital, remembered "the emergency medics found Eric with his pipe still firmly clenched between his teeth even though he was virtually unconscious. He was knocked up pretty badly." Moon: "Actually I had the bowl of my pipe clutched firmly in my *hand*. I asked Al [Daub] when he came to visit me in hospital to go back to the car and see if he could find the other half of the pipe!" Daub agreed it was a bad accident: "There were pictures in the paper. The VW was totaled and so was the telephone pole. People thought he had been killed."

Then, to top off the bad month, Ilse told him she was going to spend Christmas with her husband. Moon, out of the hospital but not feeling so hot, protested. But Ilse had her logic:

I had promised Ken that I would spend Christmas with him. We hadn't been getting along all that well, but he didn't want me to leave, though I had clearly told him I was really going to go. I think he was rather shocked by my decision. He started being nice to me, giving me presents and even saying he would get rid of all his girlfriends. Eric was getting nervous that Ken would persuade me not to leave him. Both of us were getting very edgy and tense. Eric was very resentful that I was going to spend Christmas day with Ken. I was head over heels in love with Eric, but still I had been married to Ken for 18 years—he was the first man I had ever had a serious relationship with. So I agreed to spend Christmas day with him.

Moon still thought it was a lousy deal. But a new year and a new decade would be here in a twinkle, and things would be better, he felt sure. He felt it in his bruised bones.

New Year, New Decade, New Day

Eric and Ilse rang in 1970 at a merry party with library friends at a big old house Bill Katz had in rural Ghent, New York, a village half way between Albany (where Katz taught) and the Massachusetts border, just off the Taconic Parkway. "It was really out in the country," recalled Ilse, adding: "The whole weekend was a big party with lots of political discussion. It was all part of the 1960s thing. And it was snowing like hell, and Katz's house was cold. It seems to me that all of us spent a lot of time in bed that weekend!"

Truth be told, the 1960s were already slipping into history, literally and figuratively. Students of social and political trends predicted the 1970s would be much different than the previous decade, almost certainly less cacophonous, less extreme, less militant. By the end of the 1960s a general feeling of fatigue was abroad in American society; respected voices were cautioning it was time to slow down the rollicking pace of change experienced during the preceding ten years, to consolidate the decade's gains (there were many) and cut the losses (also many). Whether Eric and Ilse had a sense of these transforming currents as they saw in the New Year at Katz's place in Ghent is not known. But all outward indications suggested their lives in the 1970s would be tame in comparison with the 1960s.

After the Katz party Ilse returned to Virginia, "But only to leave my job and to clear up odds and ends and pack." Eric drove down to Gloucester Point in a rented van and moved the bulk of her belongings to East Orange. Ilse followed a day or two later, her car laden with personal items; the plan was for her to drive as far as Washington where Eric would meet her:

> Eric was going to fly to Washington to meet me, so I wouldn't have to drive the whole way to New Jersey by myself. I got up early in the morning — 4:00 or 5:00 o'clock — and the car wouldn't start. I thought Ken had put sugar in the gas tank. I finally got somebody to help me and got the car going. I got to Washington and met Eric, only a little late. I had filled up the entire car with my things; there were plants in the front seat; there was no place for him to sit. Poor Eric. The plants have been a bone of contention all our lives.

They began living together in East Orange in mid–January 1970. Eric's one-room "pad" was too small for two people — Ilse deemed it "a horrible little efficiency" — so they moved across the hall to a larger apartment. Ilse recalled, "It was meager living at first. We took a packing crate I brought and used it for a side table; we ate at a card table and had a pull-down bed."

Never happy idle, Ilse immediately began searching for a job in the area. Though she had grown to like cataloging and knew the value of her experience at William and Mary, she wanted to switch directions and do reference work. "I had always wanted to be a reference librarian," she revealed, harkening back to her work with the scientists at the marine institute on Sapelo Island. She had several interviews, including one at Rutgers University, where she hoped for a reference position but instead was offered the job of head of cataloging, which she turned down: "I didn't like the Rutgers setup. It was apparent Kidman [Roy Kidman, the library director] wanted a hatchet job done — a wholesale cleanup of the department. I didn't think I had the stomach for it. Besides, the cataloging department was in the basement; it seemed like a concentration camp."

In the end she accepted a reference position ("number two of two") at Drew University, a Methodist school with a strong theology program located in Madison (New Jersey), about a dozen miles from East Orange. She learned much at Drew but was discouraged by the "dreadfully low salary" and the fact that so much of the materials budget went into the religion collection: "I just couldn't stand it. I think the crowning blow was when we asked for a second copy of *Winchell* [*Guide to Reference Books*] and the director said we couldn't afford it but then turned around and bought a page of the *Gutenberg Bible* to show off." She left Drew after only 15 months.

Soon after Eric and Ilse set up housekeeping, Ted Waller, who had not yet met her, invited the couple to dinner. Ilse remembered the event with distaste:

> Ted liked me but that first meeting was just dreadful. We were invited to dinner at the Bull and Bear in the Waldorf Astoria in midtown New York. Eric said we really need to make a proper impression on this man, so I had a new dress for the occasion. I don't know

if Eric bought the dress or if we bought it together, but it was black velvet, cut really low in the front and, in the style of the times, quite short and tightfitting. I remember that dress very well. After we got there and had drinks, Ted says, "Oh my dear, stand up so I can see you. Now turn around." It was so he could ogle me. The boobs and the behind were well scrutinized. Why I went along with it I don't know—I guess I didn't want to make trouble. Of course Eric encouraged him.

Waller's ogle quickly melted into the past, but not so their main predicament: they needed to be free of their spouses to marry. Ilse promptly filed for and got an uncontested divorce from Ken, but Eric's case was different: he confronted a vindictive wife, a woman who sincerely believed she had been wronged. Diana let it be known she wanted revenge, his head (or some part of his anatomy) on a platter, telling mutual friends, "I'm going to make him pay, make him suffer." According, she initiated divorce proceedings against Eric early in 1970, in which she sought not only to rid herself of an unfaithful husband but to gain a settlement that would financially cripple him — possibly for the rest of his life. Eric, who retained a lawyer recommended by Al Daub to defend him, remembered, "It was touch and go for quite a few months. It was very unpleasant."

Finally, to Eric's relief, the case ended and the divorce was granted. No longer was he tied to the woman whom he had married in England 23 years earlier and for whom he no longer felt love nor now even affection. But Diana had achieved her goal—to punish him by emptying his wallet. Moon candidly admitted she took him to the cleaners:

I lost a big hunk of money in the divorce. Of course, she had a better case. After all, we had lived together for more than 20 years and had two kids. Most of time she hadn't worked, because she was not a very good bet in the job market, although I did eventually get her a job at Bowker. I wasn't too bothered by the settlement, except that I hated the open-endedness of it—it became forever. Then I find out she was doing rather well and that my money seemed to be supporting a lot of activities that I didn't think I needed to support. I was bothered about that.

It was very tough for awhile after the divorce. Ilse and I were getting clobbered by the agreement because it cost a helluva lot of money, both in division of assets and alimony and medical insurance. Eventually we got very tired of this, because we had been hearing that Diana had a boyfriend and was off skiing in Vail and swimming in Acapulco. I thought, God, they're doing all this on my money, while we're struggling. And we were struggling, because Ilse wasn't making much money—when she first came up from Virginia she couldn't find a job immediately and then went to Drew University for something like $8,000 a year.

It seems likely that Diana also got revenge in petty ways. For instance, she apparently deprived Eric of one of his treasured possessions, the rare Hunt Botanical Library type design book Hermann Zapf had given him in 1967. Moon was hurt:

That book met a fate worse than death. It was lost in the divorce. We had an agreement in the settlement that two-thirds of the book collection of my choosing was mine. I asked Al Daub to accompany me back to the house to collect the books—Al said it was one of the toughest experiences he had ever had in his life—and I kept looking for the Zapf book and it was not there. Subsequently I asked one of my sons to look through Diana's books for it but we never could determine what happened to it. It was very sad to lose it.

Ilse, on the other hand, was angry: "This was an example of Diana's meanness—she was out to get him. She was so resentful of this whole thing." One thing Diana could not do after the divorce, however, was stop Eric and Ilse from getting married, which they did in early 1971, eagerly, lovingly, joyously, emphatically, irrevocably.

Ilse Moon

Ilse Webb (née Bloch) became Ilse Moon in Paramus, New Jersey, on Saturday, March 6, 1971. A beautiful (if not blushing) bride, Ilse chose that date because it was Eric's birthday — his 48th; she was 38 at the time. Charles Reid, mayor of Paramus and a big foot in library circles, performed the ceremony. He and Moon were longtime friends, and he promised that if the marriage didn't "stick" he would "put a curse on Eric or worse." The wedding, which took place in Reid's home, was a small affair. Moon remembered it this way:

We were married by a library trustee, Charlie Reid, who became head of the National Commission on Library and Information Science, chair of the 1991 White House Conference on libraries, and was president of the American Library Trustees Association. I had known Charlie for years, and Ilse and I felt it would be a cute idea to be married by him. We had nobody except Bill Katz at the wedding other than family — Ilse's parents and sister [Sue] plus my mother, son Max, and brother Bryan and his wife Cicely. [Alan, Eric's other son, was estranged from his father at this point].

Charlie's wife Betty had bought some champagne and he was so nervous that he broke it out before the ceremony, so we were really loosened up before taking the vows. There was lots of good-natured banter. For example, Bill Katz and Ilse's father liked one another; Katz, ever curious, asked Dr. Bloch, then in his seventies, "Say, Pops, how's sex in the seventies?" Ilse's father gravely responded, "Well my boy, I don't do it as often but I still enjoy it." Katz says, "Man, you've made my day. I'm going to check back with you in your eighties!"

After the ceremony everyone drove from Paramus to Manhattan to get ready for Eric and Ilse's wedding party that evening. The newlyweds had taken the bridal suite at a hotel on the Upper East Side near the site of the party. Roughly 150 guests were expected and an entire restaurant had been booked. But at the last minute the owner informed the couple that he was awfully sorry but they could only have the top floor of the restaurant: his wife had scheduled the main floor for a meeting of the Lithuanian women's liberation movement! Mellow, Ilse and Eric agreed the top floor would be fine.

The party turned out to be a gas. Eric's mother from England, who traveled by air for the first time in her life to be there, had a grand time, helped along by at least half a dozen glasses of port and lemon, her favorite drink. Other guests included Ilse's aunt Hede Hollander, who was in her eighties and the oldest person at the party; Ilse's cousin John; most of the Moon inner circle (John Berry, Pat Schuman, Arthur Curley,

Bill Katz, Bill Eshelman); Ted Waller, Al and Marty Daub, and Robbie Franklin from Scarecrow Press; the lawyer who had handled Eric's divorce; a diverse assortment of New York area library talent ranging from Ellen Gay Detlefsen and Ollie Kirkpatrick to Bob Wedgeworth (then at Rutgers University), Jack Frantz, and Ella Yates; and of course all the family members who had been in Paramus for the wedding.

Years later Eric's recollection of the party included these vignettes:

- Ella Yates [at the time assistant director of the Montclair (New Jersey) Public Library] made her usual entrance. I was still at the hotel when Ella arrived. I had sent Bryan over to the party to look after things until Ilse and I got there. When Ella came in she looked around and asked, "Who's that man over there who looks like Eric?" Someone said that's his brother. So Ella rushed over, threw her arms around him, and said: "I think I've been making it with the wrong brother for years."

- Ollie Kirkpatrick, a Jamaican, was a union organizer at the Brooklyn Public Library and a great character. In addition to working at Brooklyn Public he published several marvelous children books. The wife of the lawyer who had handled my divorce and Al Daub's wife Marty were standing together when Ollie came over and joined them. They made polite conversation, asking Ollie where he was from and was he married? "Oh yes, she's sitting over there on the sofa. She has just come over from Jamaica." They said, "Doesn't she get lonely while you're at work?" "No," said Ollie. "I just come home every evening and give her a good fuck and she's absolutely happy!"

- I danced most of the evening with Pat Schuman, who's a terrific dancer. And Ilse's mother went over to Ilse and said, "Watch that woman!"

And a couple of Ilse's memories:

- People danced, they ate, they drank. It was a nice party. Everybody loved Eric's mother and my old Aunt Hede. I remember them sitting together kind of holding court, these two old ladies. Everybody adored them.

- The restaurant made a nice cake for us. We were getting ready to cut it when Arthur Curley grabbed this great big knife we were to cut it with from Eric. He took the knife and plunged it like a sword into the center of the cake. Everyone was in hysterics over this. Then we cut the cake and ate it.

After the party Eric and Ilse and some others went back to the hotel suite for more celebration before calling it a night. Robbie Franklin, Eric's protégé at Scarecrow, was among the revelers. Robbie recalled being quite drunk and trying to get a lady librarian in the mood and then passing out: "By 11 o'clock that evening I was blatantly feeling her tits off in the middle of the party laughing idiotically, drunk as a lord. She and I essentially passed out on a couple of beds in this big suite. Then dawn came. When I woke up, she was gone."

Later, Robbie joked that he had spent Eric and Ilse's wedding night sleeping with them, and Ilse, laughing, set the record straight: "The next morning we got up and found Robbie outside our room, passed out. He woke up and staggered in and said, 'Oh my God, I didn't spend your wedding night with you, did I?' But he had. Luckily, it was a suite of some size." Eric asked Robbie to take care of the many bottles of booze left over from the party. Robbie remembered Eric saying that it was "lucky I had hung around, because now I could take care of all the liquor that was left. So I boxed it up as Eric and Ilse motored off to the airport to go on their honeymoon."

The honeymoon — in Ocho Rios, Jamaica — was a wonderful getaway, a time to relax and savor their union. "We stayed at the most unlikely place," said Ilse, "a beautiful old hotel Playboy had bought out. The hotel had lovely gardens and a great beach. We went to Dunn's River Falls and rented a car and drove up into the mountains. The car had a flat tire, but it was fixed quickly. The people were very nice. The pianist in the bar at the hotel was from Southampton — he and Eric hit it off, of course."

– 13 –

Feeding a Scarecrow

After Bowker—What?

When Moon decided to quit *Library Journal* at the end of 1968 at age 45 after nine remarkably productive years as editor, he faced the dilemma of what to do next. What *does* one do after achieving and then leaving the pinnacle of professional success? In truth, he had no specific job in mind when he made the decision to give up the *LJ* editorship. He knew only that it was time to do something else, that he had had his shot at library journalism (and what a noise he had made), and that to stay fresh both he and the magazine needed a change.

Initially Dan Melcher provided a facile solution, enticing him to continue working for Bowker by creating a new position—head of editorial development—expressly tailored to his interests and talents. At least that was the idea. Without giving it a great deal of thought or looking elsewhere, Moon took the job, but it did not work out, chiefly because he lacked real authority. Whereas at *LJ* he had made the decisions, had been in control, in the new job he mostly pushed paper. A large part of the problem was that he no longer worked for Melcher, whose confidence he had enjoyed throughout the *LJ* years. Instead, in the new job he reported to a new man, George McCorkle, brought in by Xerox, the new owner. The Bowker Company in the late 1960s was no longer the small, close-knit business it had been when Moon first arrived on the scene. After the Xerox merger it became a cog in a giant corporation, and practically all of Bowker's top people quickly came to regret the transaction and soon most were gone; younger employees like John Berry fumed that the big boys (Melcher, Greene, Bye, Moon, et al.) had sold them and the company down the river of corporate bigness and bureaucracy. Melcher himself resigned in early 1969, his parting shot said to be a "bitter" internal memo calling the Xerox deal a "terrible mistake."

Confronted with the realization that his new job at Bowker was a dud, Moon began looking around, asking himself: what do I *really* want to do with the rest of my working life? He never seriously considered returning to library administration—Newfoundland marked the end of his days as a practicing librarian—nor were there other library magazines he wanted to edit. In the mid–1960s he and George Wieser and several other Bowker drinking buddies had kicked around various entrepreneurial schemes, including buying a publishing company and starting a new magazine to rival *Publishers Weekly*, but none of these ventures got beyond barroom palaver. Around the same time Verner Clapp, an influential figure in Amerian librarianship — he was czar of the well-heeled Council on Library Resources— approached Moon about the possibility of becoming head of Forest Press, which published the *Dewey Decimal Classification* and was then located in Lake Placid, New York. Moon liked Clapp (who was then a member of Forest Press's board of directors), finding him "an imposing, charming man," but the job did not appeal:

One time in New York Clapp invited me to where he was staying and asked me if I'd like to be president of Forest Press. I said, "Verner, they only publish one book." He pointed out how important that book was, but I said I didn't think it was my cup of tea. I recommended Esh [Bill Eshelman] to him and Esh gave him the same answer. *LJ* had made great progress under my editorship, and I guess Clapp wanted someone who would go in and shake up Forest Press— it was a moribund organization but had tons of money. It would have been a delightful sinecure — great pay, little work.

Along with editing and publishing, library education seemed a natural area for Moon to consider as a place to cap his career. Not only had he been a part-time lecturer in London in the 1950s at North-Western Polytechnic School of Librarianship and a frequent guest speaker at library schools in North America throughout the *LJ* years, he loved "playing the guru" at library association meetings, offering teacherly advice and guidance to reform-minded colleagues on how best to outmaneuver the conservative opposition. In similar fashion he had adroitly used the pages of *LJ* for nearly a decade to educate readers about the issues and problems facing the profession, often framing the discussion in dialectical terms.

Moon had a genuine reverence for knowledge (as opposed to mere information and data) and he was always eager to share his with others, whether showing the way by example or by debate or exhortation. Whatever the method or forum, his words and actions commanded attention. Simply put, Moon was a born teacher — smart, energetic, self-assured, quick-witted, humane, honest (acerbically so when necessary or provoked), charismatic, always on point, always in command of his material — and it comes as no surprise that over the years he received a number of invitations and feelers to join the ranks of library education in one capacity or another.

The most serious of these came from Lawrence Clark Powell, who shortly before retiring as dean at the UCLA library school in 1966 offered Moon a faculty appointment. "Eric was the man I wanted to give the school credibility in public library work," Powell remembered. "The only other person I wanted was Ed Castagna [longtime director of the Enoch Pratt library in Baltimore]. Moon and Castagna were role models for me. But their lack of the doctorate would have prevented a tenured appointment and a corresponding lack of security for them." Moon recalled that earlier he had visited UCLA and was a big hit as a guest lecturer, but he turned down Powell's offer, telling him, "I think I have a larger classroom at *LJ* than I could ever have at a library school. I reach 30,000 librarians twice a month; if I'm in a library school it would take half a lifetime to reach half that number."

A similar opportunity arose a few years later when the venerable Jesse Shera retired as head of the library school at Western Reserve University in Cleveland (now Case Western Reserve). Moon received a letter from the chair of the search committee indicating he had been recommended as a possible candidate for Shera's position. Shera himself, said Moon, "informally told me that he hoped I might apply for the deanship at Western Reserve." But he had just begun working at Scarecrow Press and decided not to pursue the post. A year or so later Mary Gaver, a well-known professor at Rutgers library school, retired and suggested Moon as a person who might teach some of her classes as a part-time instructor. Again he declined: "I never could stand the thought of working as an adjunct faculty member for slave wages, so I didn't do it."

It's clear that had Moon really wanted to spend his later years in the workplace as a library educator, he could have done so. True, as Powell noted, he lacked the academic credentials ordinarily required by American colleges and universities, but in special cases—and there's no doubt Moon was special—such impediments are rarely insurmountable. Still, he hung back, always finding an excuse why he could not or should not pursue this or that academic position. In reality, he had little respect for library education in North America, dismissing most of the schools as mediocre or worse—only UCLA, Rutgers, the University of British Columbia, and "maybe" Western Reserve were exceptions, and none in his opinion compared with Loughborough, his alma mater in England.

Moon's comments in the article "A Jungle Tale," published in *LJ* in 1963, typified his negative attitude toward American library education: "My own visits to library schools leave me most of the time with a depressing memory of young people with old, gray-flannelled minds, unhealthily obsessed with visions of security, concerned clinically with status, without knowing that stature is vastly more important and must come first." In interviews with this author he often characterized library educators as airy people with too much time on their hands and too little inclination for hard work or involvement in the rough-and-tumble of the real world. Ralph Blasingame, for instance, was great as the state librarian of Pennsylvania but when he left to become a library science professor at Rutgers, "he gradually faded into library school oblivion, got lazier and lazier, and did less and less." Gerry Shields did a fine job as editor of *American Libraries* but when he joined the faculty at the library school at Buffalo "something happened to him that, I suppose, happens to lots of people when they go into library education—he became very misty and vague." Another victim of library school oblivion, according to Moon, was Ellen Gay Detlefsen, "a very radical young woman, a member of the Congress for Change" in the late 1960s, but when she accepted a teaching position at Pittsburgh, "she sort of faded away rather quickly, becoming a scholarly type."

Pat Rom, who came to know Moon well after marrying his friend Bill Eshelman, explained that "Eric has a strong distaste for academic types. He doesn't like their pomposity and self-importance, and they normally don't write well." Moon himself advanced yet another reason for avoiding library education: "I simply didn't like teaching. I didn't like teaching and giving speeches because I couldn't stand the pressure on my nervous system. I got all wound up and tense and upset the digestive processes and I spent too much time in bathrooms. I couldn't see living that way. That's one of the reasons I decided against acting as a career; I was all right when I was on stage, but before was awful and afterward was awful. It was too much to put up with."

So the question remained: after Bowker — what?

Scarecrow Press

Sometime in the spring of 1969 the Moon luck struck again. He received a call out of the blue from Theodore Waller, president of Grolier Educational Corporation, inviting him to dinner to discuss a business proposition. The previous December, Grolier had acquired Scarecrow Press, a small New Jersey publisher with strong ties to the library community, and Waller was in the market for an experienced editorial hand to take over the company. Might Moon be interested? Given his unhappy situation at Bowker it was a no-brainer: yes, he was very interested.

Even before talking with Waller, Moon knew a fair amount about Scarecrow Press and its unique history and operation. Launched in 1950 by Ralph Shaw, one of modern librarianship's acknowledged geniuses as well as one of its bona fide curmudgeons, the press was dedicated to publishing small print runs (usually 500 or more copies) of worthy books on specialized topics other publishers avoided as likely financial losers due to narrow audience appeal and limited sales potential. Shaw believed such books deserved publication and, moreover, that they could be published profitably, with both publisher and author realizing a reasonable return on their investment. The trick involved keeping production costs to a bare minimum. An article (by Moon) recounting the Scarecrow story in the 1985 *Library Science Annual* provides excellent background information about Shaw's original idea and relates how the press got its name:

Before his first book was published he [Shaw] was talking one day with his friend and colleague, author-editor Earl Schenk Miers, who had been associated with the Rutgers University Press. Describing his new venture, Shaw detailed how he intended to avoid "excessive office costs, excessive editorial costs, general trade advertising and the building up of a staff, which would then continue to have to be supported." Miers broke in, "You're talking about a scarecrow: it has no overhead, it pays no rent, it is not responsible for anybody's future clothing and shelter. It's a scarecrow." And thus was Shaw's new baby christened.

A workaholic who normally slept only a few hours a night, Shaw (MLS, Columbia; Ph.D., Chicago) was fully employed at the time as director of the U.S. Department of Agriculture Library in Washington, D.C., and had his busy fingers in a myriad of other professional pies. At the outset he viewed Scarecrow strictly as a diversion, a hobby. Assisted only by his wife, Viola, he performed all editorial and most production and distribution functions himself, the press's modest physical plant conveniently located in the cellar of the Shaws' home in Alexandria, Virginia. In 1954 Shaw left the agriculture library for a professorship at the newly created library school at Rutgers University in New Brunswick, New Jersey; he became dean of the school in late 1958. Naturally

Scarecrow moved with him, the thriving little press now grown to the point that it consumed both the basement *and* garage of the Shaws' new residence on Landing Lane Road in New Brunswick.

Eventually Scarecrow grew too large for Shaw and his wife to manage alone, and in 1956 Albert Daub, a veteran bookseller and scholarly book publisher, bought a controlling interest in the press, which was then incorporated with Daub installed as the company's first president and Shaw continuing as sole editor and guiding spirit. Soon after Daub took over he moved the press's business office across the river to Manhattan, setting up shop downtown on 17th Street and Park Avenue South. In 1964 Shaw left Rutgers for the University of Hawaii in Honolulu, where he devoted much of his energy to developing a new library school. Yet he still found time to acquire and edit books for his cherished Scarecrow. In 1965 Albert Daub's son, Albert W. (known simply as Al), joined the company, and the following year the Daubs moved the press back across the river, this time settling in Metuchen, New Jersey, where Scarecrow remained for the next thirty years.

Toward the end of the 1960s the senior Daub contemplated retirement and Shaw's health — he was a confirmed chain smoker — began to deteriorate; in fact, his wife, also a smoker, died of lung cancer in 1968. That same year Daub and Shaw sold Scarecrow Press to Grolier, Inc., a major American publisher of encyclopedias and related reference products then headquartered in New York City. Scarecrow became a division of Grolier Educational Corporation, and as part of the merger agreement Albert Daub *père* retired, Shaw took over as company president, and Grolier's Ted Waller, who had negotiated the deal, assumed the position of chairman of the board. Al Daub, who replaced his father as manager of the press's business operation, remembered that Shaw insisted Grolier maintain Scarecrow's distinctive identity: "We had been given assurances from Ted Waller that the press would continue as it was, and Ted held to his promise. The deal also included my father's retirement, and Shaw, my father, and I all took stock. Shaw agreed to stay on but on a short-term basis only — his role was to find a new editor who would perpetuate the Scarecrow philosophy, as defined by Shaw."

Both Shaw and Waller actively searched for Scarecrow's next editor, who would also eventually take over the presidency of the company. A number of people were considered, including C. Edward Wall (of Pierian Press) and Padraig Walsh (editor of Bowker's *General Encyclopedias in Print*), but once Eric Moon was approached and expressed interest the search ceased. Moon recalled his initial meetings with Waller and Shaw:

I suddenly got this call from Ted Waller, who invited me out to dinner and popped the question. He told me that Ralph Shaw was dying of cancer, and that nobody had run Scarecrow the whole time of its existence except Ralph and that finding somebody to replace him was very difficult but he [Waller] thought I was the man to do it. Was I interested? I said yes, but had questions about what was involved and where I would stand vis-à-vis Ralph. After this conversation I went out to an AV conference in Portland, Oregon, with Dick Bye and George McCorkle, and while I was there I got a phone call from Ted, saying it would be helpful if I could go out and see Shaw in Hawaii, and since I was in Portland, why didn't I just hop over to Hawaii while I was there. I thought this was a good idea, so I told Dick Bye what I was doing, and flew over, saw Shaw, and was back before the end of the conference.

Moon's meeting with Shaw went well — or well enough. Moon remembered, "I had this long interview with Shaw. He said he thought I was the right person for the job because he couldn't think of anybody else in the library field who was as ornery as he was except me. I was offered the job of executive officer of Scarecrow and president in six months. I went back to Portland and told McCorkle; he was a bit shattered but congratulated me." Waller's recollection made clear that Shaw had only a veto over the decision to hire Moon: "Ralph did not oppose Eric's appointment, but it was not his choice. Ralph in effect said yes, but if he had despised Moon — and Shaw despised a bunch of people — I wouldn't have appointed him. If Shaw had thought I was dead wrong he would have said so." Al Daub remembered it somewhat differently: "It was my feeling that for us to grow the way we wanted to grow we needed someone who was dynamic, controversial. So we looked around. I guess Ted Waller takes the credit for hitting on Eric Moon — but I'm not sure he's entitled to it. Ralph Shaw also took credit for finding Eric, and he more likely is the person who started to focus on Eric."

In any event Moon accepted the position, which boiled down to replacing Shaw as Scarecrow's chief editor and, in six months or so, becoming president of the company. In the interim his title would be executive officer, and it was further agreed that he would take up his new duties on July 1, 1969, right after the much anticipated American Library Association conference in Atlantic City.

Problems

The job appealed to Moon for a number of reasons, but mainly because Scarecrow was a small, lean, well-ordered operation unencumbered by layers of bureaucracy and corporate bloat, much like Bowker had been before Xerox, and Waller promised that the press would continue to function under Grolier as it had previously. Moon especially admired the entrepreneurial ingenuity of Shaw's creation:

There's no doubt Ralph Shaw was a great man, a genius. His founding of Scarecrow was a real breakthrough. What Shaw set out to do was to start a publishing company that would publish books no one else would handle — books that needed to be read, that were contributions to scholarship, but that were not likely to sell enough copies to satisfy the requirements of the normal publishing industry. So he set it up with all kinds of money-saving devices: typewriter composition done by women in their own homes so he could substantially cut the overhead costs associated with employees in the office; standard-sized books, so the company didn't need different sizes of paper and binding; very prompt payment to suppliers like printers and binders so that the company got better terms than anybody else.

But — and in retrospect this seemed inevitable — conflicts soon developed between Moon and Shaw. Despite, or perhaps because of, his failing health, Shaw had a difficult time letting go. He had always been, in Al Daub's words, "a prickly character, feisty as hell," but now he was even more so. Brilliant and inventive, Shaw was used to being in charge and expected things to be done his way; haughty and querulous, he derived satisfaction from putting down those he identified as rivals. Lawrence Clark Powell — perceived by Shaw as a competitor (along with Jesse Shera and a few others) for the mythical title of America's foremost librarian of the postwar era — offered this telling anecdote in his autobiography, *Life Goes On*:

> Ralph Shaw was a different kind of hombre, using a machete on our [Powell's] sentimentality and needless routines. I felt it first after my ALA keynote speech, "The Alchemy of Books," given at the Waldorf in 1952. When I finished speaking to my largest audience up to then, relieved and reasonably pleased with myself, there came Shaw down the aisle holding out his hand. I extended mine, expecting congratulations such as I was receiving from all sides…. Instead he slipped me a printed card which read WHAT A LOAD OF BULLSHIT. Whereupon he vanished in the crowd with a hyena laugh.

For Moon the conflicts with Shaw were doubly distressing due to the parlous state of Shaw's health: "What made the situation much more difficult was that here was Shaw dying this hideous death — his face was all deformed and he was obviously in agony from the disease and all the treatments, and you felt like a shit quarreling with this guy. But on the other hand he was really impossible to deal with." The major disagreements centered on editorial policy, but they were ultimately about power and whose will would prevail. Al Daub remembered the tension between the two men: "Shaw and Moon were both very strong personalities, and you knew damned well that somewhere down the road there was going to be a confrontation. And you knew damned well that neither one would walk away from it thinking they had lost."

One tangible source of friction concerned the amount of attention given to editing and proofreading of manuscripts. Throughout the nearly twenty years he was Scarecrow's one and only editor, Shaw devoted minimal time to these basics, dismissing typographical errors and the like as "mouse farts." He believed it was more important to get the book out than to delay publication over something as inconsequential as a few typos or occasional errors of fact. Daub recalled one infamous instance that involved the misspelling of Shaw's wife's name: "We had this book in the page proof stage where we still had an opportunity to correct mistakes. Shaw looked at the book, which was dedicated to his first wife, Viola Leff Shaw, who had recently passed away, and the first thing he found was that her name was misspelled. Ralph's decision was, the hell with it, no one will notice. To do it over would have been an expense that he didn't think was justified."

As a result Scarecrow publications became synonymous with sloppy and indifferent editing. Moon, a stickler for editorial accuracy, brought a different standard to the press, which irked Shaw: "I started paying a little more attention to proofreading and editing. Shaw was very flip about the whole thing. He didn't care about editing; his objective was to get the book out cheap and dirty — and fast. It was a reputation that has taken Scarecrow a long time to live down."

The two men also clashed over the number and type of books Scarecrow published. Moon:

> Under Shaw, Scarecrow published a relatively small number of books per year. When I got there the largest number it had ever published in a year was thirty or so. During my first year we published if not 100 books then very close to that number. Shaw was upset that this manner of change could have taken place in one year. But if he had thought about it he shouldn't have been, because before I came Shaw did all the editing himself on a part-time basis, often

on the road, in airplanes, and so on. That first year I was full-time plus I had an assistant editor, Robbie Franklin.

Then there were a number of projects that Shaw wanted that I thought weren't worth much, and we argued about that. And there were all sorts of things I was doing that he didn't approve of—I got into a lot of social issues that Shaw wasn't interested in, such as civil rights and women's studies. E.J. Josey's *Black Librarian in America* [published by Scarecrow in 1970] was an example. So we had divisions all over the place.

Still another area where Moon and Shaw butted heads was over Moon's assistant editor, Robert (Robbie) Franklin, whom Moon had hired in August 1969, just a month after starting at Scarecrow himself. A bright, eager, verbal, well-read young man then in his mid-twenties, Franklin was the son of two Ohio librarians, a graduate of Yale University, and a Columbia University library school dropout. Eric and Robbie worked well together from the start, forming a strong master-apprentice kinship. Shaw, however, was determined to get rid of Moon's assistant editor. He professed not to like the quality of Robbie's work, but in reality he was peeved that Moon had added another full-time editor to the payroll, which violated one of Scarecrow's founding principles—no unnecessary staff. But mostly Shaw wanted to thwart Moon, to let the new guy know who really had the power; Shaw might be sick and deformed, but he still ruled.

In this instance Shaw won the battle, routing Moon, at least for the nonce. Supported by Ted Waller, who disapproved of Robbie's lack of "corporate" demeanor and "hippie" attire (he usually wore casual clothes to work), Shaw forced Moon to fire Robbie. It was a humiliating defeat for Moon, who had difficulty explaining the politics of the situation to his young colleague and friend:

Robbie was the place that Shaw decided to launch his fiercest attack. It was fairly clear to me that if I was going to fight that fight, everything else would go down the drain. So I went to Robbie and I said, "I know you're not going to understand this, but I've got to let you go. But it is only until I become president. Wherever you are, the moment I succeed to the presidency, you're back." He was very hurt, of course; he didn't understand what the hell was going on. He went off to Europe and lived for about a year with a girl and did who knows what else.

For his part Franklin says he was not hurt by the firing; on the contrary, "I took it quite well, even reassuring Eric," who was chagrined by the whole business. Franklin: "Eric was very unhappy about the situation; he was very awkward and very embarrassed about it. He was embarrassed first of all because he had to be disloyal to a person like me, and secondly he was embarrassed that he did not have the strength yet, in a corporate way, to stand up to the pressure."

All during this time Waller engaged in a juggling act, trying to keep both Shaw and Moon reasonably satisfied while making sure the two men had as little to do with each other as possible. Waller saw to it that Shaw stayed away from Metuchen and Moon never went to Hawaii after the interview trip in 1969. According to Moon, it was "a long-distance conflict. Al Daub and I ran the Scarecrow office in Metuchen and Shaw issued his dictates from Hawaii." Waller remembered, "Moon and Shaw did not have that much contact. Moon reported to me and I talked to Shaw."

This state of affairs dragged on and on, and Moon became more and more frustrated.

He had been promised the presidency of the company in six months after starting at Scarecrow in July 1969, but as 1971 drew to a close he still was not president, not in control. Shaw continued to cling to power, as alert as ever mentally though physically much debilitated, and Waller continued to stall. While tempted at times to chuck the whole business, Moon wanted to see the job through: "I never wanted to quit—I wanted to do something at Scarecrow Press, build on what had been done, leave something of a legacy. But I was angry, particularly about the contract. Here I was virtually operating without a contract for at least a year and half, because the original agreement had been abrogated." Finally, he got fed up and decided to force the issue: Waller would have to settle matters one way or another—and quickly.

Problems Resolved

Much to the surprise of those who knew them both, Moon and Waller generally got on well together, despite being totally different people. Before Scarecrow they had known each other through ALA, where both were active though almost always on opposite sides of any issue. Waller, who assiduously courted the library Establishment, recalled, "Eric was a major factor in ALA. He was a controversial character. I was not taken with his friends, but he was a bright, able fellow. I was impressed by him, but disagreed with him on ALA matters." Moon originally viewed Waller as a blustering captain of industry straight out of the pages of Sinclair Lewis, but that impression softened once they began working together:

> Theodore is a very, very complex character. On the one hand, he's an awful, pompous show-off. A lot of people really, really hate him. I remember going to a publisher's meeting sometime after I had taken the Scarecrow Press job and somebody said, "What's it like working for the biggest shit in publishing?" I did not find him that unpleasant to work with—in fact, quite the reverse. He left me pretty much alone; we got virtually no interference from Grolier headquarters; Theodore was the man who protected us from a lot of corporate bullshit that came from other parts of the corporation. He kept it that way, and we were very solid.

Toward the end of 1971, however, Moon was not feeling kindly toward Theodore. More than two years earlier he had been promised Shaw would bow out in six months and he, Moon, would become president of Scarecrow. He had been patient; he had not told Shaw to go to hell, though he had been provoked enough to do so many times; he had given Waller plenty of leeway to ease out the terminally ill Shaw, but it hadn't happened. Now he wanted the problem resolved once and for all—a problem that he saw as one entirely of Waller's making and one that only he could fix. Moon: "It seemed to me that only Ted could resolve the situation. He was the only one with the power to resolve it, and eventually he saw that. He eventually saw that it was vital to do that." Though, Moon added, Waller didn't much like the role: "It got pretty warm."

In this crisis Moon found an ally in Al Daub, Scarecrow's vice president and overseer of all business functions. Daub and Moon were poles apart politically, Daub a conservative Republican, but they developed a healthy respect for each other's professional abilities and in time became lifelong friends. Moon recalled, "Al tried not to take sides but I think it was clear that he understood that I was the future of the company and Shaw was the past. And he also understood, I think, how unreasonable Shaw could be — and was. My feeling was that Al was pretty much on my side, although he, obviously being in the middle, had to look impartial."

In late 1971 Moon and Daub met with Waller for a working lunch. Moon laid his grievance on the table, telling Waller, "This has got to stop — enough already. I need a satisfactory contract, and you've got to decide. Do you want to continue with Shaw or do you want to hand it over to me. If not, I've got to start looking somewhere else." Daub's recollection confirmed the tone and substance of the meeting: "Finally one day Eric and I had a luncheon meeting with Ted. The basic decision that had to be made that day was: was Eric going to become president and Shaw get the hell out or was Shaw going to keep his oar in the water and Eric was going to walk. It was fish or cut bait time."

Shortly thereafter Waller met with Shaw in Honolulu and by the end of the year Moon at long last became president of Scarecrow Press. "It took a long time but eventually it was resolved," said Moon, palpably relieved the struggle was over. Shaw continued, however, to labor for Scarecrow until his death in the fall of 1972, and he never stopped trying to stick it to Moon who, Shaw once complained, avoided "tackling the tough stuff." In fact, Shaw's last project — an English-language translation of Richard Muther's classic *German Book Illustration of the Gothic Period and the Early Renaissance, 1460–1530* — arguably proved to be the toughest editing assignment of Moon's career. Viewed cynically, it appeared that Shaw undertook the Muther book as a final, desperate thrust in his obsessive three-year war with Eric Moon. "One of the strange weaknesses in Shaw's character," observed Moon, "was that he seemed not to want somebody succeeding him who might be seen as a stronger figure than himself. That was part of his problem when I joined the company. I had some firm ideas about what I wanted to do and I think Shaw saw that as a threat, for some reason that I don't understand. But it was clear that was so."

Al Daub was impressed by how well Moon handled the difficult Muther assignment:

The book, which was in Old German, was translated by Shaw. It had some great woodcuts and Shaw correlated the translation with a numbering system to identify the woodcuts that went with the narrative. Eric had to work his way through the project. It wasn't going to be a significant moneymaker, but it was a massive editorial job. Shaw, who was dying [he was in the hospital during much of this time], wrote it all by hand and it was very difficult to read. Eric couldn't do the editing in the office because it would take too much time out of his schedule, so he did it on weekends and evenings. He did it for two reasons. One, he wanted to do it because he thought it was the right thing for Ralph, who was near the end. Despite their differences, Eric never lost respect or regard for Ralph. And two, he did it as a challenge, because Ralph had let it be known through Waller that he thought Eric only did the easy stuff. This was the most difficult editorial job Eric ever had at Scarecrow — and Shaw gave him no recognition in the book's acknowledgments.

Regarded as one of the pillars of the library profession in the postwar period, Ralph Shaw died of lung cancer at age 65 on October 14, 1972, in a Honolulu nursing home, where, according to a biographer, "he had, characteristically, been working almost up to the day of his death." Moon, despite their contentious relationship, remained among Shaw's staunchest admirers:

I knew Ralph pretty well before coming to Scarecrow Press and got along with him. He was a thorny character and I think he saw me as a thorny character. Inevitably his health played some part in our conflicts, but I think some of it was not unusual. I am proud to have succeeded him. In my opinion, Ralph Shaw is one of the great figures of librarianship — and nothing that happened between us at Scarecrow Press has altered that opinion. There's no doubt about it that the man was a genius — and I don't use that word loosely. I was disappointed that he didn't recognize that I was working in the best interests of the company, but life is full of disappointments.

Moon Almost Sacked

Moon scarcely had time to get accustomed to his hard-won position as president of Scarecrow before a new and potentially ruinous crisis arose, this time pitting him against the chairman of the board, Ted Waller. The problem blew up wholly unexpectedly as the result of comments Moon made at an Eric Moon Flying Circus presentation at the library school at Drexel Institute in Philadelphia. Moon's remarks, which contained a strongly worded allegation of ethical impropriety on the part of David Clift, who had just retired as ALA executive director, got back to Waller, who was not only Clift's "super great friend" but a central player in the alleged wrongdoing. Moon said the incident was not planned but had occurred spontaneously:

After the Kentucky institute [in September 1969], we did a number of Eric Moon Flying Circuses around the country. One was at Drexel at the invitation of Dorothy Bendix. On the panel that day were Peter Doiron, Pat Schuman, Arthur Curley, Ilse, me — maybe someone else. Now this was just about the time David Clift was retiring as executive director of ALA [September 1972] and Wilson [H.W. Wilson Company], Grolier, World Book, and a couple of other biggies [in the reference publishing industry] had set up a $25,000 fund to send Clift around the world on some pretext that he was going to do a report on international library management. Somebody from the audience asked Peter Doiron what did he think about this, and Peter said Eric is really the one to ask, because his company [Scarecrow, a division of Grolier] is one of those involved. And I said, "Well, it looks like a payoff to me."

So then we got into the discussion a bit more and I talked about all these publishers who contributed to Clift's trip being heavily reliant upon the kind reviews they get in *Subscription Books Bulletin* [now *Reference Books Bulletin*], published by ALA, and that indeed the whole thing smelled of a pretext. The next thing I knew a faculty member at Drexel had called ALA to say that she did not want to see ALA reviewing the publications of these companies anymore until a thorough investigation had been made because of Eric Moon's charge that this trip was a payoff! Well, this got back to David Clift, Clift called Theodore Waller, and Waller called Al Daub at his place at the beach in New Jersey at about 6 o'clock on a Sunday morning. He said, "Who are we going to replace Eric Moon with?"

Initially, Waller wanted to fire Moon, but backed off when Daub said, "Ted, I don't know what this is about, but if Eric goes, you'll have to replace me as well. If that's the direction you want to take this company, I can't live with it." Waller of course knew that he couldn't afford to lose both Moon and Daub and still maintain Scarecrow's viability — not to mention profitability (always a major concern at Grolier, which went through hard times in the 1970s).

Daub was intrigued by how the crisis was resolved:

We went to lunch with Ted in New York, where Grolier then had its headquarters. There was a debate between Eric and Ted regarding the Clift incident at lunch and then back at Ted's office. I remember sitting there listening to the debate, thinking that it was like they were working their way through Dante's circles of hell. Ted would say to Eric, "You know what you did was inappropriate, et cetera, et cetera," and Eric would say, "Well, maybe it wasn't the right thing to do but at the time it was honest and straightforward." Then Waller would say, "Well, you're going to have to make an apology, now you agree with that, don't you?" And Eric would say, "No." And with that we were all the way back down to the bottom of hell. Finally, we got to the point where Waller said, "If you had it to do over, would you do it differently?" And Eric said, "Well, maybe a little bit differently." Waller then said, "So we have an understanding that you're not going to do something like that again, right?" And Eric said, "OK, if you want me to say that I probably won't do something like that again, fine." And that was how the whole thing was left.

Around this time Moon and Daub seriously discussed leaving Scarecrow and starting their own publishing company, based on the Scarecrow model. Ilse Moon recalled that Eric "always wanted to do it, to go it alone," and that she too was all for the idea, but Al's wife, Marty, considered it "too risky." Said Ilse, "We still regret not doing it. I particularly regret it, because I could have been more involved with Scarecrow, which I wanted to be. I always wanted to work with Eric more. Maybe he didn't want me to, but I would have liked it." Ilse did, however, make it her business to now and then "pop in at Scarecrow and have a cup of coffee and chat with Al and the people in the office."

Robbie Franklin also heard the buzz about starting a new company: "I remember once Eric, Al, and I went to lunch and Eric more or less said, 'Hey, Al, hey Robbie, let's quit this jerk joint and start our own. We don't need Grolier. We don't need this bullshit. Let's do our own.' And Al was very reluctant to agree to it; his excuse was his wife wouldn't let him. Of course I was ready for anything. Eric was like a great combat leader: I would have followed him over a cliff." But for the time being everyone stayed put. Eric was not sacked, and the David Clift affair faded into Scarecrow lore. Decades later Moon and Daub still remembered the details, but Waller said he recollected nothing about it, except that the $25,000 for Clift's retirement travel "was a one hundred percent Waller project."

Inside the Scarecrow Operation

During Moon's nine and half years at Scarecrow, the press, located "in very modest quarters" at 52 Liberty Street in Metuchen, a suburban New Jersey town of 13,000, published more than 1,000 books with a total staff of never more than 25, split about evenly between full-time and part-time employees. The full-timers included Moon, Daub,

Franklin, Norma Shear (who handled publicity and promotion), Marie Devlin (in charge of billing), a couple of proofreaders, a couple of people in accounts, a shipping room person, and a secretary. Most or all of the part-timers were typists who worked out of their homes. The press's physical setup reflected the basic division of labor: "Enter the front door and go to the right and you were in Al's part of the terrain," recalled Moon. "This was where the billing, accounting, promotion — the business end — took place, all in Al's bailiwick, his half of the office. Go to the left and you were in the editorial side, where the proofreaders and editors worked. In the back was the shipping room."

Owing to the large number of books published annually — more than 100 — and the small number of personnel, there was little time for schmoozing at Scarecrow. "Everybody had to work like hell," said Moon, "but I think they all felt tremendously involved and part of the company. Our billing lady, Mrs. Devlin, a sweet woman who was one of my great favorites, used to handle the billing of every single item sold by Scarecrow, which had a lot of individual orders. It was that kind of operation." By all accounts, people enjoyed working at Scarecrow; certainly there was little turnover during the Moon years.

Luck blessed Moon with the best publishing partner he could ever have dreamed of or hoped for. Al Daub — a buoyant, perceptive, honorable, ultra-competent man who knew the book business inside out — was, according to Moon, Scarecrow's "foundation stone," the rock everyone, including himself, leaned on. From the beginning the two men clicked, creating a productive and harmonious work environment. Moon greatly valued their relationship:

The thing I think that made Scarecrow such a happy operation, at least for me, was that Al and I were as comfortable and compatible a team as any I have come across in my working career. This was really strange. Ted Waller was immensely worried about whether Al and I would get along, because he thought I would see Al as a right-wing Republican and he would see me as some wild left-wing radical. Early on Ted would call up Al and ask, "How are you getting along with Eric?" Al would say, "Fine, wonderful." Still dubious, he would then call me and ask the same thing, and I would say, "Terrific." Ted couldn't understand it.

But Al and I became extremely good friends. We loved working together because we worked out the relationship so that we were never in each other's hair. Anything that concerned editorial, Al kept his hands off, turning it over to me; anything that was financial or office related, I turned it over to Al. Al and I were a team, neither was over the other. I saw us as running the company jointly. It was a very, very happy situation.

If Moon and Daub were at the top of Scarecrow's pecking order, followed by Franklin (Moon's number two) and Shear (Daub's number two), the part-time typists were at the bottom. Yet they were absolutely essential to the functioning of the press. One of Ralph Shaw's economizing innovations involved photo-offset production of books from typescript, or typewritten copy. The typists, who had to deliver pristine copy, used high quality IBM typewriters and were paid by the page. (Shirley Lambert, the press's editorial director beginning in 1995, has described Scarecrow as "the original desk-top publisher.")

"On the whole the typewriter composition staff was fantastic," remembered Moon, though occasionally odd problems cropped up:

For example, one typist was very fast but quite strange. She was a very weird woman. She had dozens of cats in the house, and the paper we used to get good reproduction was glossy and her pages would come in with cat hairs all over them. If they went to the printer that way, there would be little black lines all through the book. I had to talk to her about that problem. Then she decided she wanted to be a writer and started writing short stories. She got friendly with my head proofreader who cajoled me into reading her stories to see if she had any talent. They were awww-ful.

Some industry wags suggested Scarecrow typists were just a step above sweatshop workers, a charge that rankled Moon:

Everybody thought we were taking advantage of these women, who did piecework paid at a set rate per unit. The fact is for many of them it was a way of getting employment when they couldn't do it any other way. Many of them had children and couldn't get out of the house, and our taking jobs to them made it possible for some highly talented women to work at home. Furthermore, at the rates they were getting, if they were any good, they could earn more than most of the people working in our office. Of course this was advantageous for us as well, in that we didn't have to pay benefits. But basically they were doing very, very well. We certainly weren't victimizing anybody. They were very happy to have those jobs.

Scarecrow's various efficiencies rendered the operation quite profitable. The press, for instance, normally printed 1000 copies of any title and was able to make money on as few as 200 copies sold. Moon liked to boast that no book published on his watch, no matter how specialized or esoteric, failed to turn at least a small profit. His closest call came with a charming little book with almost zero sales appeal called *Billy the Cartwheeler*, a memoir written in the 1920s by W. Harrison Culmer who proclaimed himself "the last of the Dickens boys"—one of the many London street urchins author Charles Dickens befriended and used as source material for his novels.

Certainly Grolier was pleased with its investment in Scarecrow. According to Waller, it represented "the most profitable single unit in Grolier based on percentage of volume" throughout the 1970s. Nevertheless, despite Scarecrow's bottom-line success, Moon and Daub constantly had to fend off those in corporate Grolier who automatically equated increased growth with increased profits. "When I was president of Scarecrow Press it was an enormously profitable company on a percentage basis—not a lot of volume, but very profitable," observed Moon, adding:

On a percentage basis it was certainly the most profitable arm of the Grolier Corporation—that is, profit against gross. But one of the fights we had continually with Grolier was the typical large corporation battle for growth. They kept saying to Al and me, "You've got to grow, Scarecrow. Grow, grow." And we kept saying one of the virtues of our size is that we have no nonproductive administrative staff. The more we grow the more administrative staff we need, the more building space we need, which increases our costs against growth. There was a running battle, which we managed to resist.

The main reason Scarecrow was able to escape the maw of the giant corporation, Moon explained, was Ted Waller, who acted as a buffer between Grolier's profit-hungry executives and little Scarecrow:

When the Grolier boys would come to Metuchen, they couldn't understand, for example, that Mrs. Devlin was doing what it took three or four people in any other department of

Grolier to do. Waller was absolutely our bastion. One felt he understood why Scarecrow should not attempt to grow by leaps and bounds. At one point virtually all of the Grolier operations were being taken to Danbury [Connecticut] so they would all be under the same corporate roof. Scarecrow was one of the few exceptions; we were left untouched, because our operation would have been lost had we been moved.

Another Surrogate Son

In the 1960s at *LJ* Moon formed a subconscious father-son bond with John Berry, and in the 1970s at Scarecrow he developed a similar relationship with Robbie Franklin, who idolized him and looked to him for both professional and personal direction and approval. "I'm 20 years and six days younger than Eric, so we have a sort of father-son relationship," Franklin once observed. "He has two sons. At the time I came to work at Scarecrow he was divorcing Di, and one of his sons was estranged as a result and the other heavily into computers, so Eric in a way turned to me, because I was a warm and affectionate type. I was full of love, and we had similar interests. On a certain level for a brief period in Eric's life I fulfilled a more ideal sonship than either of his real sons."

Robbie was a teenager in Ohio when he first met Eric, who visited the Franklin family home in Toledo soon after he had been appointed *LJ* editor. Robbie remembered,

My father [Bob Franklin, director of the Toledo Public Library] was on the magazine's advisory board, and Eric stayed overnight at our house on his way back to New York from a conference somewhere in the Midwest. I was the captain of the high school chess team, so Eric and I got into a chess game. It was assumed by my father that any visitor to our house who good-naturedly consented to play a game with me would, of course, lose. And Eric beat me!

Ten years later, shortly after Moon had signed on as Ralph Shaw's successor at Scarecrow Press, he received a letter from Bob Franklin, offering congratulations on the new job and noting that his son, Robbie, was coming home from Europe after a stint in the military and that he wanted to go into publishing. Did Eric know of any openings? Moon wrote back, "Tell him to contact me when he gets back," which Robbie did. The first thing young Franklin said to Moon when they met in Metuchen was, "You're the guy who beat me at chess!" Moon took to Robbie at once, impressed by his academic qualifications and warm personality, and offered him a position as assistant editor, which was accepted on the spot. That evening, August 1, 1969, Eric wrote to Ilse (then still in Virginia) about his new sidekick:

Today I hired my first assistant editor. As I look at the manuscripts I have piled up I breathe easier at the prospect of some help. The young man I've hired — bearded, very handsome, and attractively intense — is the son of Bob Franklin, librarian at Toledo. Robbie, the son, remembered me as the only one of his father's friends ever to visit their home who beat him (Robbie) at chess. I told him he could recuperate by becoming a better editor than I, and I really think he will take a good crack at it.

Editing on average a book apiece a week, Moon and Franklin formed a highly effective and productive team. Seated twenty feet from one another on the editorial side of the Scarecrow plant, they worked together day after day for nine-plus years, save for the time Robbie was forced out, a pawn in Ralph Shaw's campaign to undercut Moon's position at Scarecrow. But as soon as Moon won the war with Shaw and became president of the company, Robbie returned — with a promotion. Moon recalled sending him a telegram: OK, IT'S OVER. COME BACK. YOU'RE NOW SENIOR EDITOR AT SCARECROW. Robbie remembered it somewhat differently, but the fact remains he did return, resuming his old duties and close relationship with Moon.

"I saw Eric as my role model," said Franklin, who summed up his years at Scarecrow under Moon's tutelage in an interview in 1990 in the magazine *Sipapu*:

This employment was an enormous curriculum. The lessons flowed — freedom of speech, toleration and acceptance, emotional maturity, tactfulness, limpidity with authors. Good and simple habits were learned, such as do it now while it's on your mind, and keep the routine sacred by picking up all the slack yourself. Eric tried sort of second-handedly to teach me political skills too, but I never learned any. Eric taught, and teaches, largely by example. He almost never explicated anything to me. It's effective, a little like the guy who whispers to get your attention.

Franklin especially admired Moon's desire for calm in the workplace:

One of the things Eric taught me is that there's business and there's everything else. You have to understand that in a way he was an old-fashioned guy with a very rigid sense of business ethics. He was virtually never late for work, for example. And the flip side of the coin was that he almost always left the office at exactly the same time. Eric has a lot of compensating mechanisms. If he felt deficient or bad about something, he would do something else all the better and that would make up for it. One of these compensating mechanisms was his devotion to business routine. One of the deepest lessons I learned from him was how to have an office in which there is total calm — 100 percent of the time, not 99 percent. I learned this from Eric and my office is run the same way.

Franklin, who in 1979 established his own publishing company, McFarland, in Jefferson, North Carolina, believed, "I am the person most similar to Eric — he knows it and I know it." On the other hand, he had difficulty dealing with Moon's compulsive competitiveness, first witnessed by Robbie years earlier in Toledo during their famous chess game:

My relationship with Eric is not competitive, and I think that's one of the weaknesses he felt I had. I would virtually shut up when he was in one of his more flamboyant moods. He seemed to denigrate me for not joining in or holding up my end. In his eyes I failed to show the inner aggressive dynamism that would give him a better time at it — why beat somebody at a game if the other guy's not really playing? I wasn't doing it on purpose; in a way it was almost worshipful. I wouldn't dream of trying to out-pun him or anything like that.

Like Berry, Franklin had a deep, complicated, emotional tie to Moon that went beyond the workplace. Moon's influence on both younger men was far-reaching, not unlike the impact of a parent on a child. Both Berry (in journalism) and Franklin (in publishing) followed in Moon's footsteps, striving in their different ways to please him — and, of course, to top him.

Moon Leaves His Mark

Moon's general plan when he joined Scarecrow Press in 1969 was simple: to build on and expand what Ralph Shaw had so ingeniously begun. His specific objectives focused on increasing the number of titles Scarecrow published each year; improving the editorial quality of its publications, including reducing the unacceptably high number of factual and typographical errors; and broadening the scope of the press beyond its traditional emphasis on library science and related topics.

He achieved the first of these goals early on and in dramatic fashion: "In 1968, the year before I went to Scarecrow Press, it had published about 33 or 34 books. During the next three years, we averaged over a hundred books a year, which was a pretty startling increase." Scarecrow maintained or slightly exceeded this production rate throughout the Moon era, which ended in 1978 with his retirement. Efforts to meet the goal of improved editorial quality began immediately, but recognition of progress came slowly. Two decades of insouciant editing by Shaw could not be erased from the public mind in a year or two or even ten. Moon, who hated having his name associated with sloppy work of any kind, introduced a new standard of editorial accuracy at Scarecrow, yet the stigma lived on. In the early 1990s he commented:

We started the process of improving the quality of Scarecrow books, which was something Ralph Shaw studiously ignored. We tightened up proofreading and the editorial process to a great degree. Esh [Bill Eshelman, who succeeded Moon as president of Scarecrow in 1979] went much further with these improvements than when I was there. This process has been going on ever since Ralph left but today still some of the old image of Scarecrow remains, even though it is unfair. For example, the composition is no longer done by typewriter, but some people don't seem to know that. Some of the books that have been done since Shaw have been very nicely produced — and the old business of no proofreading and so on has not been true for almost 30 years now.

Moon's third and final goal — to expand Scarecrow's list into new subject areas— reflected his belief that "being primarily a library science publisher was too limiting to achieve the kind of growth we needed." The first book Ralph Shaw issued under the Scarecrow imprint back in 1950 was an English translation of Alfred Hessel's *History of Libraries*, originally published in German; its sales were encouraging and over the years Shaw pretty much hewed to the formula that any manuscript with the word "library" or derivation thereof in its title would find a ready market among librarians and hence was potentially a Scarecrow book. Moon sought to change this image, and during his first few years at the press— those years he and Shaw battled for editorial control of the company — he acquired and published a fair number of titles dealing with nonlibrary topics, such as women's studies and countries of the world.

In time he moved Scarecrow into other fertile areas, finding this not only enhanced the press's visibility but made his work as editor more interesting and challenging. For example, Moon, an inveterate movie buff dating from his youth in England, started publishing books on the subject: "I went out and through one device or another recruited people to submit manuscripts dealing with film. Over the next several years we probably published more reference books on the cinema than any other publisher in America. I remember the librarian of the British Film Institute once telling me that they automatically buy two copies of every Scarecrow movie book. It was a hobbyhorse that developed into one of our big lines."

In similar fashion the press began publishing significant amounts of material in the fields of music and parapsychology, the latter the result of Robbie Franklin's interest in the subject. Religion was another area Moon developed; here Ilse Moon, drawing on contacts at Drew University, was able to steer some major publications her husband's way, including a series of scholarly works the press published cooperatively with the American Theological Library Association. By the time Moon left Metuchen for the Florida sunshine, Scarecrow Press had moved well beyond its origins as a publisher interested primarily in works with "library" or "librarian" in their titles.

On the other hand he did not abandon or neglect the library science list, which remained a vital part of Scarecrow's identity, not to mention its bread and butter. Shaw, of course, had been a librarian, and during the Moon years all of the top people at the press— Daub, Franklin, Shear, and Moon himself— had attended library school. (Norma Shear, Scarecrow's publicist, came to the company via the library school at Rutgers, where she and Daub were students together.) With so many library pros in the organization, quality manuscripts dealing with any aspect of libraries or librarianship were always welcome at Scarecrow; Moon's forays into new fields were intended to increase the press's scope, not diminish the library science list.

In point of fact, Scarecrow's best-selling book ever is *Building Library Collections*, known to an earlier generation of librarians as "Carter and Bonk," after its original authors, Mary Carter and Wallace Bonk. The book, a guide to materials selection techniques and procedures used widely as a text in North American library schools, was developed under Shaw in the late 1950s and has undergone numerous revisions, each edition selling in the neighborhood of 12,000 copies, with total sales now well over 100,000. Moon was unhappy with the substance of the book when he arrived at Scarecrow, finding it tired and not always current. He recalled, "It was clear to me that the book needed serious overhaul and modernization, and that Bonk [Carter had retired by this time] was not at that point capable of the job. I wanted to make it less theoretical and more practical." Eventually he recruited Dorothy Broderick and Arthur Curley, both fine writers with extensive collection development experience, to undertake subsequent editions.

Moon also had a hand in originating or shaping or improving many other library science titles published by Scarecrow, but two stand out:

- *Library Lit.— The Best of [year]*. An annual introduced in 1970, *Library Lit.* featured noteworthy contributions culled from the literature of librarianship. Dreamed up by Moon and edited by his pal Bill Katz, the publication each year reprinted some thirty articles selected by a jury consisting of the president of Scarecrow Press (i.e., Moon or one of his successors), Katz, and four of their friends. Readers received an omnium-gatherum of the year's best professional writing, while the jury, which met in Katz's roomy house in Ghent, had a ball deciding exactly what was "best." Katz enjoyed the tactical nature of the selection process:

When Eric moved over to Scarecrow Press, it was his idea to start of a "Best of Library Literature" series. A novel notion, particularly as he went on to suggest I edit it. The meetings we had to select the best articles are among my fondest, and here, as always, Eric was at his best. A good in-fighter, with a strong sense of humor, if not always complete fairness, he managed to channel the votes his way. I am happy to report that the votes normally were my way as well. I suggest, then, we worked as a team which was not always appreciated by the sometimes more sober, yet well meaning jury members.

Long after Moon had retired from Scarecrow, Katz stepped down as editor of *Library Lit.*, turning the series over to Jane Hannigan, a library school professor whose chief contribution was to preside over its demise, the last volume, covering the best of 1990, appearing in 1992. Moon offered this eulogy: "I don't think there's much of library literature that I would recommend at all. One of the things Bill Katz and I were trying to do with the "Best of Library Lit" was dig out a very few crumbs from the overall mess of library literature that was worth reading. If you look back over those volumes, there are things in them that are still worth reading. In fact, we were trying to build a core of readings that incoming students and new librarians could be referred to."

- *Prejudices and Antipathies: A Tract on the LC Subject Heads Concerning People*. Written by Sanford Berman, this "tract" hit the library profession like a shock of intellectual lightning when published by Scarecrow in 1971. A masterpiece of exposé, the book denounced Library of Congress subject headings for including "racist" and "colonial" bias, the heading "Yellow Peril" being but one example. How Scarecrow came to publish this revolutionary screed reveals much about Moon and the strengths he brought to Scarecrow.

In early 1969 Sandy Berman, then working as a librarian at the University of Zambia in Lusaka, published a letter in *LJ* (February 15, 1969) that for the first time publicly set forth his core criticisms of LC subject headings. An alert editor in ALA's publishing department, sensing an opportunity, wrote to Berman in Africa asking if he might consider expanding his complaints into a monograph further explicating the problem. Three weeks later Berman sent ALA such a manuscript. Astonished, the editor took it to his superiors, but soon astonishment turned to, well, something quite different. Moon, about to enter the picture, described what happened next:

In the months that followed, ALA began to delay, first suggesting changes, then saying it would have to make certain cuts and deletions. At that point Sandy was really pissed off—he was still in Zambia. He wrote to Fay Blake [a library colleague and friend] who was in London, telling her of his terrible experience with ALA and this manuscript and wondering if there was anyone in library publishing he could trust. She wrote back, "Send it to Eric at Scarecrow." So he sent it to me with a letter saying he didn't know me from Adam but if Fay Blake said I was OK I was probably OK.

I wrote back that I liked the manuscript but wanted to reorganize it, not to cut or censor it but to make it more readable. When I got it it had these masses of footnotes on every page — there were about three or four lines of text and about 15 footnotes. I eventually decided the only way to tackle this was to cut it up with scissors and then staple it all together so that it was continuously readable. I had the equivalent of tennis elbow at the end — which I called staple elbow. Sandy was happy with the results and today the book is a classic.

In 1993 McFarland (Robbie Franklin's press) issued a paperback edition of *Prejudices and Antipathies*, with a foreword by Moon recounting the tale of the book's publication two decades earlier and praising its author as the library profession's "leading missionary, revolutionary, irritant, conscience and inspiration." For his part, Sandy Berman summed up Moon's contribution as a publisher this way: "At Scarecrow Press, he made 'intellectual freedom' a reality by publishing works — my own included — that other library presses shunned." Not a bad mark to leave.

Methods

Practically everyone who ever worked with Moon marveled at his devotion to order. Somehow a guy as interested in reform and revolution as he was (went the thinking) should keep a wild, exuberant desk, with papers, books, and scribbled notes strewn everywhere higgledy-piggledy like toys in a hyperactive child's room. But just the opposite was true. Robbie Franklin cherished Moon's "old-fashioned" business habits, exemplified by total calm in the office. Al Daub remembered Moon "never did twice what could be done once"; he had "strong concentration, a single focus"; and he "kept a clean, neat desk with a writing pad and a red ballpoint pen at the ready." Wife Ilse saw the same traits: "Eric would go into the office usually before anyone else — if the office opened at 8:30 A.M. he was there at a quarter after. If the office closed at 4:30 P.M. he walked out the door at 4:30. There was no work left over — he had done what he had to do that day. He rarely brought work home; he was compartmentalized."

Moon's methods at Scarecrow differed little from those he employed at *LJ*, partly because the jobs had so much in common. In fact, observed Moon, "I didn't see that there was a lot of difference between *LJ* and Scarecrow," adding:

I got into some of the same kinds of interests and concerns in both jobs. I dealt with authors and manuscripts at Scarecrow in exactly the same way I did at *LJ*. I always found both at *LJ* and at Scarecrow that the authors who resisted editing were usually the worst writers and the really good ones, the established people, were confident enough to understand that a good editor never hurt anybody. That was as true at *LJ* as it was at Scarecrow. People asked me wasn't it difficult to switch from running a magazine to running a book publishing operation. I said I didn't see that it was greatly different at all. In fact, I thought it was a lot easier at Scarecrow than at *LJ* because I didn't have the constant terrible deadline pressure you always have at a magazine. The publishing operation, in a sense, was much more leisurely.

Testimony regarding Moon's promptness and fairness when dealing with authors abounds. Donald Yelton, author of the superbly literate *Brief American Lives: Four Studies in Collective Biography* (Scarecrow, 1978), remembered giving the book's manuscript to Moon on April 3, 1976, at a meeting of the Rhode Island Library Association in Newport, where Moon was a guest speaker: "Eric took the typescript home and read it over the remainder of the weekend. On the Monday following (April 5) he dispatched a two-page letter to me agreeing to publish it if I would add several chapters, which I did. Throughout our negotiation both Eric and his staff proved unfailingly responsive to my queries and initiatives."

Guy Lyle, well known in his day as an authority on academic library administration, had a similar experience:

In the mid–1970s, after my retirement and my interest in library administration was limited to using the books in the stacks for my research, I compiled a little back burner entitled *Praise from Famous Men.* I wanted to write about great men and women who reached down a helping hand to newcomers trying to climb upwards. Two general publishers and my old publisher, the H.W. Wilson Company, turned it down after long months of study. I have forgotten whether ALA rejected it, but a friend of mine suggested that I send a chapter or two and the outline to Mr. Moon. Instead of waiting weeks and months for a reply, Mr. Moon took it home the weekend he received it and wrote me the following week: "Both manuscript and contents are terrific. Thank you for putting this together." I had my publisher. I mention this because he did not wait for months while the author was chewing his fingernails (most publishers move like glaciers), but he answered promptly and it did not require a meeting of subordinate editors for him to decide what he thought was worth publishing. He did not trifle. He was frank and forthright.

Moon's approach to acquiring manuscripts for Scarecrow also differed little from the way he had operated at *LJ*: plant seeds and, when possible, assist their growth. Some of the most important books he published at Scarecrow resulted from knowing and encouraging the author — E.J. Josey's seminal *The Black Librarian in America* is a prime example — or because a colleague of the author recommended Moon as a trustworthy publisher, as in the case of the Berman book. In other instances, manuscripts came Scarecrow's way because Moon had published other works on the subject, establishing a presence and sense of authority in the field. He recalled one particularly sweet coup:

Because we had a track record in the area of music, someone from McGraw-Hill called me one day, saying I have a terrific manuscript but it's not profitable for us to publish as a trade book. Would Scarecrow like to see it? I said sure, and we got a beautiful manuscript that required almost no work. And the book [*Organ Literature*, a two-volume bibliography by Corliss Arnold] turned out to be very successful. We got this manuscript simply because we had already built a good list in music. Once that process was started, it grew of its own accord; once people know you're a publisher of movie books, people start sending you movie manuscripts; it was the same with music and other areas.

Finally, some manuscripts came unsolicited — or over the transom, as publishers say. Most of these orphans lacked merit or relevance to Scarecrow's list and were rejected. In a talk presented at Rutgers University in 1977, Moon discussed the importance of finding the right publisher: "Would you believe that Scarecrow Press receives a children's book every week or two, a collection of poems about once a month? It does. And it has never published one thing that could possibly lead an author to believe that it is a likely place to send such things. Authors like that will die unpublished."

At Scarecrow, Moon had final authority over every publication produced by the press. He was an astute editor and publisher, knowing how to acquire and expeditiously evaluate raw manuscript material, how to deal with authors (always an insecure lot), and when to make editorial changes and when to keep his mitts to himself. He knew, for instance, that Berman's manuscript needed to be reorganized for readability, and he did it. Conversely, post-retirement, when editing Ronald Benge's much esteemed autobiography, *Confessions of a Lapsed Librarian* (Scarecrow, 1984), he made few if any substantive changes, giving the author his head; Benge later described Moon's chief contribution to the book: "He left me alone."

Personal Life

During the Scarecrow years Eric and Ilse courted, began living together, divorced their original spouses, married, and established happy, busy, fruitful existences that included rewarding work and a satisfying social life as an active professional couple. This phase of their lives lasted until Eric retired as president of Scarecrow at the end of 1978 at age 55. All during this time they lived in New Jersey, first in a rented apartment in East Orange, then from 1972 to 1976 in a cooperative apartment in Glen Ridge, and finally in a condominium in New Brunswick. They left for Florida in January 1979.

While Eric was making his mark at Scarecrow, Ilse had several library jobs, all reasonably close to home. From April 1970 to mid–1971 she worked as a reference librarian at Drew University; in August 1971 she joined the staff of the Montclair Public Library (then headed by friend Arthur Curley), working in both reference and technical services; and in January 1977 she became director of professional development studies at the library school at Rutgers University, a position she held until the end of 1978 when she and Eric packed up for Florida.

The biggest problem the couple faced in the early years of their marriage was alimony — specifically scads of dollars Eric was forced to pay his former wife Diana who had vowed to make him suffer, and she was as good as her word. By never remarrying she could keep the alimony spigot flowing for years to come. In time Eric learned that Diana had a boyfriend and that they were taking expensive vacations and living it up on his and Ilse's money. Grrrrr. What to do? "I said to Ilse, 'We've *got* to do something about this.'" It was lawyer time. After checking around, Moon found an attorney in Newark who was "very experienced in this area, very reliable."

The lawyer told him his best hope of getting "off the alimony hook" involved proving Diana and her lover were cohabiting as husband and wife; such evidence might be enough to induce the couple to legally tie the knot without threat of further action. Moon agonized during the ordeal and rejoiced in its salutary outcome:

I told the lawyer my story and he said, "How tough are you?" I said, "I guess I'm tough enough to do whatever is necessary," and he said, "What we have to do is hire some investigators," and I said, "Fine." The investigators came back with loads of evidence, and then the lawyer said we can go with this, but it's going to be rough — but that it was his experience that if you made it rough enough they [in this case Diana and her boyfriend] almost always got married and once they're married you're off the hook. I said, "Fine. Let's try it." It was not pleasant but eventually it went through and they did get married. So Ilse and I were off the alimony hook. We bought a magnum of champagne, went to bed, drank the champagne, called all our friends, and celebrated!

A coda to Moon's first marriage: one evening sometime in the mid–1980s at son Max's home Eric briefly saw Diana for the first time since the divorce some 15 years earlier. Moon remembered Diana was "very distant, very cold." She said, "You're looking old," and he responded gallantly, "You're not."

The saddest loss the Moons experienced during the Scarecrow years was the death of Eric's mother on April 8, 1975, in Southampton, England. Fortunately, Mum had made it to Eric and Ilse's wedding four years earlier — Robbie Franklin remembered her as "a sweet little thing" — but now at 73 Grace Moon Beatson was gone, and the circumstances of her final years and death pained both Eric and his brother Bryan. When Mum died, observed Ilse, it probably wasn't just due to illness:

There were other problems there. Eric's mother lived with a young man — a man who brightened her later years. He was her young lover; she was a woman very much interested in having a young lover. He originally was a lodger at her boarding house, after being in a tuberculosis sanitorium. Later he worked for her at the boarding house, doing laundry, cleaning, cooking, shopping, et cetera. But he wasn't real bright and he drank a good bit, and as she got older I think he met other women in pubs and began to brag about the fun he had — he was like Andy Capp, the working-class cartoon character.

Bryan, Eric's brother, had no use for this guy, whose name was Archie Donkin. Gradually Archie took money out of the household. Eric and Bryan both sent their mother an allowance every month but there was some question how that money was used. But Eric didn't care — let Archie go drink at the pub as long as he took good care of Mum and made her happy. But it gradually became apparent that he was selling off the furniture and that the money was being misused. I think he gradually starved her; there wasn't the kind of care at home that there should have been. She had always had these intestinal problems that everybody in Eric's family has. But I think if she had had a little bit better care and a lot better nutrition she would have lived longer.

Archie called and said that she was very ill and that we should come right away. We got the first plane we could. Bryan was already there when we got there. She had been in a coma and didn't recognize anyone. She died an hour before we got to the house.

On a happier note, Eric's son Max and daughter-in-law Belinda (born Pi Chu in Taiwan) made him a grandfather with the birth of Eric Lonnie Moon in 1969. (Diana reportedly was angry the child was named Eric.) Seven years later Max and Belinda produced a second son, Colin — thus continuing the Moon family tradition (or curse) of mostly male offspring. Eric's younger son, Alan, had gone to college (English and theater major), married (no children), and in the 1970s was busy scratching out a career in the highly competitive board game business, including a stint at Parker Brothers as a designer. During this time Alan, who had sided with his mother after the breakup of his parents' marriage, reconciled with Eric and met and accepted Ilse.

Creating a series of crossword and acrostic puzzles provided a pleasant diversion for the Moons, who loved wordplay, during the early years of their marriage. Published in *Wilson Library Bulletin*, their first effort, "Acrostic for Librarians with a Passion for Books," appeared in November 1973. Others included "April Flowers; or Roses by Some Other Name" (April 1974), "Points of Reference" (June 1974), "Neighborly Acrostic" (June 1975), and "Periodically Speaking" (November 1975).

The couple's social life revolved largely around close friends and colleagues in the

New York–New Jersey library community. Eric always referred to this group as The Gang but others knew it as the nucleus of the Moon Mafia or Moonies, the informal fraternity of liberal librarians that coalesced around Eric in the late 1960s and 1970s. Whatever one chose to call them, the Moons and their inner circle were a bright, gregarious bunch who worked hard but also enjoyed having a good time. They got together for numberless meetings and parties, combining business and pleasure leavened by generous amounts of gossip. Normally nothing of great import occurred at these get-togethers but every once in awhile something happened that stuck in the memory as a turning point. For instance, Robbie Franklin never forgot the 1974 Christmas party at the Moons' apartment in Glen Ridge:

I loved Eric's parties because he always had a bunch of people — there were black people there, there were some gays, and other interesting people. It was a mini-spectrum of his ALA friends. And at this particular party was this young guy, a Scarecrow author about my age, and his wife, who was very pretty in a sort of ordinary girl-next-door way. We all as usual had drunk a fair amount and there was a lot of hilarity and a lot of moving from room to room — even in a relatively small apartment Eric's parties were known for having at least five major clumps that you could make your rounds among and they were all doing something different.

So this very nice pretty wife of the Scarecrow author wound up in one of the rooms that was least populated. She began telling me that she liked this boy she was married to, that he was very nice. She described how he had deflowered her and how there had been blood all over the bed. "But you know," she said, "it's just not there anymore." Not long thereafter my hands were under her dress, and at this point her husband came in. He didn't threaten to do anything but very shortly thereafter, 30 seconds or less, Eric came into the room and practically dragged me out and gave me one of those really hard bangs in the upper arm — a serious blow that was akin to a blow to the chin. He briefly delivered a statement of grave concern and astonishment and anger. There began a very slow decline in our relationship: the blow was a metaphor for the decline.

Arthur Curley, who witnessed the incident, remembered Eric telling Robbie, "You've got to shape up. You can't seduce this guy's wife in front of him."

During the summers the Moons rented a beach house at the Jersey Shore with two other couples, including at one time or another Pat Schuman and her then husband Alan, and later Peter Doiron; Arthur Curley and Jana Varlejs; and Bill Eshelman and his then wife Eve, and later Pat Rom. Located on Long Beach Island, a narrow 18-mile strip of sand fronting the Atlantic Ocean, the shore house became a retreat from the stress and heat of the megalopolis on summer weekends.

Arthur Curley, the group's sailing enthusiast and all-around good guy, described those idyllic days:

The house was on Long Beach Island, which is in the middle of nowhere. We would be down there every weekend that we could. While we sought to get away from the pressures of work — we would be on the beach, out sailing, reading, that sort of thing — the place was also a salon. People sought it out, and they did that mainly because Eric was there. There were few weekends that someone wasn't stopping by. It was a salon: we'd be on the porch and the great issues would be discussed. I swear that Eric's influence reached across the dunes. He was the charismatic center of the group.

Pat Rom, who began coming to the shore house in 1974 after Eshelman separated from his first wife, recalled that "roughly 60 percent of the conversation involved shop and libraries," but that there was also "a sense of joy and fun—and a lot of silliness," such as playing charades (John Berry, a frequent visitor, loved the game) or the time the group got enthusiastic about collaborating on writing a novel. "A book had just been published at that time called *Naked Came the Stranger* with a naked woman on the cover who was supposedly the author," said Eric. "It turned out that a bunch of guys on Long Island, I believe, had each written a chapter. We thought it might be fun to do something similar. Our novel was to be called *Convention*, which was sort of a triple entendre, and Robbie was to do an outline and allocate the chapters among us. For some reason it never got done." Another shore house memory Eric treasured was when Pat Rom first joined the group and "the first thing she did was jump in the sea with all her clothes on."

ALA and the Structure Freak

No matter where he worked—public libraries in England and Canada or the Bowker Company and Scarecrow Press in America—Moon devoted unbelievable amounts of time and energy to professional associations. From early on he was convinced—doubtless due to growing up in a working-class environment where unions and organized labor were the real kings—that associations equal power and that the aggregate power of any association is always greater than that of any individual. Strong organizations, Moon believed, were essential for the success of any collective human endeavor, and libraries were no exception. The key word was *strong*: Moon's quarrel with library associations in both the UK and United States was that they were often too weak or timid or hidebound or narrowly focused (or all of the above) to accomplish what needed doing.

His enduring connection with the American Library Association began immediately upon his arrival at *LJ* at the tail end of 1959 and continued uninterrupted throughout his working career and long retirement. Even after he stopped attending meetings and conferences in the mid–1990s, his interest in the association never waned. Though he cared tremendously about ALA (as a parent cares for a miscreant child) and always encouraged colleagues to join it, he was among its harshest critics. In the 1960s, in the pages of *LJ*, in speeches, and at conferences, Moon blasted the association for dragging its feet in the fight to eliminate racial segregation in the nation's libraries and in ALA itself, and further for failing to take a stand on other pressing social issues, such as war and poverty. Moreover, he condemned the association's mandarin ways, exposing its policies as too often based on expedient self-interest while condemning its modus operandi as overly bureaucratic and secretive.

His aim, he said, was not to undermine or put down the organization but to strengthen it by changing it. The association's leaders did not, however, take kindly to Moon's criticisms, and they shunned him and even tried to have him muzzled or removed as *LJ* editor. An ordinary person would have given up the fight, deciding to go along to get along. But Moon kept hammering away at what he perceived to be ALA's weaknesses, and over the years more and more librarians, especially young ones who saw the world very differently than many of their elders, came to agree with him. By the time ALA members arrived in Atlantic City in the summer of 1969 for their annual conference, the library Establishment was nervous as a mouse high on library glue. Moon now had an army of sorts and he spent much of the conference briefing his troops on tactics and negotiating concessions from the powers that be. The association was never the same after Atlantic City.

During the nine and half years Moon worked at Scarecrow Press his involvement with ALA continued at the same furious pace and in certain ways it intensified, the emphasis shifting from broadside attack to organizational reform. He had been elected an at-large member of the ALA Council in 1965, a position he held until 1972. While on Council he established the so-called "backbench"—a group of like-minded councilors who sat like watchdogs at every meeting hoping to keep the Establishment honest. Early recruits to the backbench, a term borrowed from British parliamentary government, included Ken Duchac, E.J. Josey, Bill Eshelman, Pat Schuman, Arthur Curley, and Liz Futas.

Also during this period Moon worked hard, mostly behind the scenes, to create the ALA Social Responsibilities Round Table. This group, which made its presence first felt in Atlantic City, provided a base for Moon's army; for the first time there was a semblance of *organized* opposition to the ALA Establishment, a development that scared the hell out of some of the profession's graybeards. In an article entitled "Association Agonies: Life with ALA" in the April 1972 issue of *American Libraries*, Moon praised SRRT's accomplishments, suggesting they were greater than even its members realized:

… the Social Responsibilities Round Table, though not a student organized or dominated group, has the youngest leadership in the ALA — unless one counts seriously the Junior Members Round Table, which very few people do. SRRT is the most volatile group in the association, and though it loses more often than it wins, it has done much to upset the equilibrium of the upper Establishment and it has, far more than it knows, I think, changed the climate of ALA. There is a nervousness, even fear, among those who were merely complacent before, and some of the inertia has been translated into an unwilling receptivity.

Grace Stevenson, an especially venomous Moon hater who had retired as ALA deputy executive director some years earlier, responded, "Isn't it enough for *LJ* to conduct its unremitting hatchet job on ALA, as it has for several years, by fair means and foul, without *AL* [*American Libraries*] giving space to Eric Moon who mounted this hatchet job under his editorship?"

Around this time David Clift announced he was retiring as ALA's executive director, a post he had held since 1951. Nearing 65, Clift was ready to go. The last few years had been tough, especially the Atlantic City conference and trying to deal with the militant young people and that damned Eric Moon and his radical friends who persisted in stirring up the membership with talk of democracy and social responsibility. The comfortable, cozy, corseted atmosphere of the old ALA was fast disappearing, and Clift, who still had many admirers in the association, was savvy enough to call it quits while still standing; his retirement would take effect on September 30, 1972.

The minute he learned Clift was leaving, Moon saw an opportunity to influence the direction of ALA for the next decade, perhaps for the next generation, by getting the "right" person appointed the new executive director.

He and his friends, who enjoyed few things more than the ALA insider game, put their heads together to determine their choice for this key position. Eventually they hit on a person few rank-and-file librarians knew much about: Robert Wedgeworth. Who, people asked? Wedgeworth (aka "Wedge") was a tall, articulate, clearheaded black librarian (MLS, Illinois) in his mid-thirties then teaching and studying for a doctorate in library science at Rutgers University. From the perspective of Moon and The Gang, Wedgeworth seemed an ideal candidate—a youngish, good-looking minority with impressive bona fides, including the fact that Moon had once published an article by him in *LJ* on the literature of jazz, which posed the politically correct question, "Can libraries committed to the preservation and perpetuation of American culture continue to ignore jazz?" And, after a long and intense search, which began in early 1971 and included interviews with liberal Ken Duchac and conservative F. William Summers (then assistant dean at the library school at the University of South Carolina), Wedgeworth emerged as the consensus choice to succeed Clift as ALA executive director.

The Moon forces, which had high hopes for a Wedgeworth directorship, considered his appointment a signal victory, though they were only one of several power blocs within ALA that had supported his candidacy. Years later Wedgeworth explained:

> When I came under consideration for the position I was fortunate to have small pockets of influential supporters in a number of areas of the field including academic libraries, the Black Caucus of the ALA, library automation and the cataloging and classification people. And on the Executive Board that appointed me there were several influential leaders who knew me. Although the support that Eric and his associates gave to my candidacy was very important, I had an independent base of support of which I was not fully aware until after my name surfaced as a candidate. We have never discussed it directly, but I think that the presence that year on the board of three prominent and well respected African American librarians— Augusta Baker, Virginia Lacy Jones, and A.P. Marshall—was key to my being appointed.

In another breakthrough development Moon was appointed to the association's Committee on Organization (COO) in 1971 and he became its chair in 1972–1973. Established as part of the spirit of reform flowing from the Atlantic City Conference, the committee was charged with proposing structural changes in ALA's governing machinery. Though Moon failed to secure everything he wanted—for instance, he lost an effort to institute a recall procedure for members of the Executive Board and Council—the committee's work led to a number of progressive rule changes. According to a report in *LJ*, Moon's performance as COO chair was "a model of efficiency that won him a reputation as a doer as well as a critic of the association's failings." Later, in a campaign statement when he ran for ALA president, he asserted, "My long experience on Council and the chairmanship of COO have given me a certain organizational know-how."

All of this reformist activity—pressing to liberalize ALA's governance; helping to create a group within ALA (i.e., SRRT) hospitable to the ideas and discontents of young activist librarians; serving on Council and establishing the backbench to keep tabs on the conservative opposition; working to install a new executive director sympathetic to the Moon group's agenda—all of this effort was conducted strictly within the association's rules. Moon spent much time scheming to manipulate or change the ALA Constitution and bylaws to get what he wanted, but he never violated the rules. He was not an extremist, not a bomb-throwing revolutionary, not a aspiring dictator in populist robes. Rather his political methods were rooted in a deep respect for the democratic process and the procedures governing it. His road to power involved mastering the rules and using that knowledge to achieve his ends. Some of the SRRT people along with John Berry called him a "structure freak." Moon accepted the label, albeit none too happily — perhaps the word "freak" bothered him. In his "Association Agonies" article he wrote:

… some of those who seek radical change in ALA have begun to learn the uncomfortable lesson that organization and knowledge are necessary weapons to overcome the fear, the inertia, the defensiveness, and so they are learning the machinery — the Bylaws and the Constitution, the election procedures, and how they can be used to advantage. In the past few years they have pressured for the liberalization of the nomination and election machinery, the one weapon that is not locked in the establishment's arsenal. And there is now a steady input of new names on election ballots, either put there by petition or — and this is important, too — put there by those who control the nomination procedure, as a means of quelling some of the protest.

The things the change-seekers have not yet done, or certainly have not done effectively, is to go out and organize votes for those they have gotten on the ballot. It's a lot of work, but it can be done and it has to be. All current appearances and the Yippies to the contrary, successful revolutions have never been organized and won by people who want to play games, or who see chaos and turbulence as just another kind of fun. They are won by people who have a target and who go after it. If that makes me a structure freak, so be it.

His friends heard this sort of talk and they naturally asked themselves, Why isn't Eric president of ALA? He understands the issues; he knows the association's rules and how its governing machinery works; he's a persuasive communicator. In short, he's everything we desire in a leader. Let's get him to run. But Moon adamantly refused their entreaties. He was more effective, he said, providing advice behind the scenes; he was more comfortable as the loyal opposition; he was "a backbench guy." Besides, he didn't think he could win. "I kept saying no, no, no. Then they literally got me tanked to the gills until at some unguarded moment during the evening I signed this thing and there I was — on the ballot."

That's how, according to legend, Moon came to run for the ALA presidency in 1976, which he won handily over three other candidates. Ralph Shaw, Scarecrow Press's founder, had served as ALA president twenty years earlier, and Moon's election, which dominated his final years at the press, gave Scarecrow the distinction of being the only publisher ever to be headed by two ALA presidents.

Upper left: Eric with his mother, Grace, ca. 1925. *Upper right:* With his first bicycle, Southampton, early 1930s. *Lower left:* Alex Beatson, "Jock": stepfather, carpenter, scholar and mentor, early 1940s. *Lower right:* Bryan Moon, age 12, Bournemouth, 1940, an evacuee to escape the bombing of Southampton.

A

Top: Detail from class picture (28 boys), Taunton's Grammar School, Southampton, mid–1930s, EM with poaching elbow. *Lower left:* EM's father, Francis Edward (Ted) Moon, on Ocean Island, late 1920s. *Right:* EM as library assistant, Shirley Branch Library, Southampton, 1940.

B

Upper left: With Roy Stokes (left), director of the Loughborough library school and Moon's all-time favorite teacher, Vancouver, 1992. *Upper right:* Atop the Central Library in Southampton, 1946, with Dickie Denton (left), best man at EM's first wedding and Southampton Public Library colleague. *Middle left:* Southampton Public Library colleagues Bill and Paddy Graham, with Ilse Moon (right), Siesta Key, Sarasota, 1981. *Bottom:* Loughborough library school students, 1947 or '48 (from the left — Ric Taylor, Tony Rowberry, John Taylor, John Colgan, EM, Ron Surridge, Jimmy Matthews).

C

Top: Captain of the Loughborough soccer team, 1948. *Lower left:* The terrible trio of the AAL, Nottingham, 1953 (from the left — Bill Smith, Ron Surridge, EM). *Middle right:* EM being interviewed about *Lolita* by Don Jameson, czar of Newfoundland television, in 1959. *Bottom right:* EM with first wife, Diana, and younger son Alan, St. John's, Newfoundland, 1958.

D

Top: EM (center) as Otto Frank (Anne's father) in a St. John's production of *The Diary of Anne Frank,* 1959. *Middle left:* Diana Moon — and *middle right* — Alan (left) and Max Moon: at the New Jersey shore, 1962. *Bottom left:* Grandpa Eric reads to little Eric (Max's firstborn), Glen Ridge, N.J., 1972. *Bottom right:* Bowling champions, father and son (Max), New Jersey, 1965.

E

Above: The R.R. Bowker board of directors, December 1966 (from the left — Anne Richter, Dick Bye, Elizabeth Geiser, Dan Melcher standing, Louis Greene, Bud Frasca, Chandler Grannis, Mildred Smith, EM).

Left: John (Moon's successor at *Library Journal*) and Louise Parker Berry, Long Beach Island, New Jersey, 1982.

Opposite page, top: With E.J. Josey (right), a future ALA president — 60s firebrands turned late 1970s establishment. *Middle:* Wyman Jones (right), librarian, magician, jazz pianist, reluctant *LJ* columnist, calls the guru as EM awaits bafflement, at some ALA conference. *Third down:* Stalwarts of the New Jersey shore gang (from the left — Jana Varlejs, Arthur Curley, EM, Bill Eshelman), Long Beach Island, 1982.

F

G

Top: With Bill Katz (left) at the Moon group's annual gathering in New Hampshire, 1991. *Middle:* At the Wakemans' home in Great Chesterford, England, 1969 (from left—Max Moon, baby Eric Moon, Belinda Moon, John Wakeman, Hilary Wakeman. *Left* (from the left): Pat Rom, Zoia Horn, Ilse Moon, Edison, N.J., recovering from an ALA conference in New York, 1986.

H

Upper left: Ilse Bloch (Moon), age 7, and brother Ernie, Mt. Vernon, N.Y., 1939. ***Above:*** Ilse Moon at EM's inauguration as president of ALA, 1977. ***Left:*** Fritz and Kate Bloch with children Ernest and Ilse, Mt. Vernon, N.Y., ca. 1937.

I

Top: Moon activist friends years later at a Washington, D.C., ALA Midwinter meeting, 1998 (from left — Ed Beckerman, Pat Schuman, Michael Malinconico). *Middle:* The vaunted Flying Circus, a traveling talk-fest of library leaders who answered questions but gave no speeches (from the left — EM, Pat Schuman, Arthur Curley, here at Pittsburgh library school, early 1970s). *Left:* Ilse Moon flirting with Bill Eshelman, Editor's Workshop, Lexington, Ky., 1969.

Top: The Scarecrow Press leadership, mid–1970s (from left — Robbie Franklin, EM, Norma Shear, Al Daub, later Scarecrow's president). *Lower left:* Robbie Franklin ca. 15 years later, head of McFarland. *Right:* EM and sons Max (center) and Alan, Long Beach Island, 1982.

Top: John Berry (left) and EM build castles in the sand, Long Beach Island, N.J., 1984. *Middle left:* Nancy and Dick Bye with EM in Eze sur Mer, South of France, 1985. *Middle right:* Norman Horrocks (left) and EM in a pensive moment in New Hampshire, 1991. *Right:* Belinda Moon with Moon grandsons Colin and Eric, Cave of the Winds, Colorado Springs, 1980.

L

Top: Clara Jones hands over the ALA presidency to EM and looks happy about it, Detroit, 1977. *Middle:* ALA leaders EM, Clara Jones and Bob Wedgworth, Detroit, 1977. *Bottom left:* Donald Urquhart (center), director of the British Lending Library at Boston Spa and speaker at EM's ALA presidential program, 1978, flanked by EM and Norman Horrocks. *Right:* EM celebrates the end of his presidency, Chicago, 1978, dancing with Marva DeLoach (photograph by Art Plotnik, courtesy of *American Libraries*).

M

N

Facing page, top: Ilse and Eric, San Francisco, 1992, as she is honored with lifetime membership in ALISE, recognizing her services as its executive secretary. *Facing, middle:* Scottish golf tour, Edinburgh, 1990: (from left — the Moons, Dick Dougherty, Marty and Al Daub). *Facing, bottom:* Bill Eshelman (left) and EM share a laugh with Theodore Waller (center), their boss when each was president of Scarecrow Press, Portland, Oregon, 2000.

This page, top: In the Florida suite at the White House Conference on Libraries, 1991 (from left — Cecil Beach, Lydia Acosta, Pat Schuman, Ann Symons, EM). *Middle* (from the left): Ronald Benge and Edward Dudley at Benge's 80th birthday party, London, 1998 — with EM (right), three irritants to the Library Association establishment in the 1950s, all in 2002 in or near their 80s, each the recent recipient of the LA's highest award, Honorary Fellowship. *Bottom right:* Alan Moon, 1999, detail from the cover of his new CD "Dream Walkin'."

O

The Brothers. *Top*, from left: Ron Moon (age 52), Bryan Moon (73), David Moon (62), at Ron's home in Pearcedale, Australia (near Melbourne), December 2001. *Middle*, from left: Michael (Mick) Moon (67), Adelaide, Australia, December 2001, and Bryan (64) and Eric (69), on the banks of the Mississippi outside Bryan's house in Frontenac, Minnesota, 1992.

Left: Grace Moon (mother of Eric and Bryan) in 1960 when she was still managing her boarding house in Southampton.

P

– 14 –

Moving from Backbench to President

Nomination by Petition

Russell Shank and Eric Moon became petition candidates for vice president/president-elect of the American Library Association for the year July 1976–June 1977 at the association's January 1976 Midwinter meeting in Chicago. Earlier, as required by ALA's Constitution, a nominating committee appointed by the president (then Allie Beth Martin) had submitted two "official" nominations for the position: Cecil Beach and Robert Rohlf. Behind these dry facts lay years of reform and jockeying for power in the world's premier library association.

People in the know, including Moon, promptly sized up the official presidential slate for 1976–1977 as a contest between two relatively weak candidates. While both Rohlf (director, Hennepin County Library in Minnesota) and Beach (director, Florida State Library) had solid reputations as library leaders at the regional level, neither was well-known nationally. Seizing the moment, supporters of Russell Shank nominated him for president by petition, an option available to those dissatisfied with the nominating committee's candidates. Shank, a former library science professor at Columbia University and in 1976 director of the Smithsonian Institution Library in Washington, D.C., had a substantial following among librarians around the country, especially members of the Association of College and Research Libraries, the largest and most powerful division of ALA.

The Shank candidacy alarmed the Moon Mafia, which feared ACRL domination of the association; only a couple of years earlier Edward Holley, who also had deep ties to ACRL, had been president, and now it appeared, in Moon's words, "Russ Shank would waltz into the job," easily defeating two unheralded opponents. Moon winced at the prospect:

ACRL was the largest, richest, and most arrogant of the divisions at that time and tended to throw its weight around, threatening to leave ALA unless it federated or in some other way

315

satisfied ACRL's lust for more power and independence. When Shank was put up on petition against two public librarian candidates, many people saw this as another ACRL power play. Also, since Russ was very popular and had held a diversity of jobs across the country, it was clear that he would easily defeat a weak nominated slate.

Furthermore, Moon and his people wanted one of their own to succeed the current president-elect, Clara Jones, who, like them, was a liberal on social issues and very much in sync with their reform agenda. The Moonies had vigorously supported Jones's run for the presidency, and now they wanted to keep the position in friendly hands for at least another term in order to solidify their position in the association and to build on the progress that had been made toward democratizing ALA in the years since the wild Atlantic City conference in 1969. A political tactician constantly concerned with gaining and exercising power, Moon argued that winning once was nice but real success required back-to-back victories:

Over the years I had lectured (I suppose is the word) to most of the ALA opposition groups, or revolutionary groups, about the need to sustain a period of power if you were going to effect change. They — especially the early SRRT people — used to call me a "structure freak" because I kept talking about this, saying that it's not just about presenting manifestos and doing marches and so on; that you've got to get at the power base, and once you've got it, you've got to control it for awhile because one year [the length of the ALA presidential term] is not enough. You can have one year and start making changes but if you lose for the next three, all that progress is gone. What you need to do is grasp the seats of power for three, four, five years in a row — *then* you can change so much that it's irreversible for a long period of time. So having won with Clara, there was a hunger to win again.

Accordingly, the Moon Mafia decided to put up its own petition candidate for president. But who? Who indeed but Eric Moon, the group's godfather and only person thought to have enough political muscle to beat Russell Shank and thus sustain the liberal momentum while at the same time curtailing ACRL's growing clout.

Nomination by petition was increasingly popular with ALA members at this time, widespread use of the procedure growing out of the activist fervor of the late 1960s and early 1970s. Moon clearly understood the potential for change offered by the petition process:

Out of the backbench movement grew a habit of questioning the whole procedure of nomination, which was pretty much a closed-shop affair, the nominating committee consisting of maybe five people putting up two candidates each year for the presidency. The petition process had not really been used to any great extent over the years, though it was there in the rules. The earliest example of it was back in 1949 when Skip [Clarence R.] Graham of Louisville won on petition over the old gray eminence, Carl Milam [ALA's longtime executive secretary, as the position of executive director was then known]. But in the modern era there had been very few petition candidates; I think Dick Darling was one of the first and barely lost in his election. Then there was Clara Jones. Clara had been nominated by the nominating committee the first time [1974] and lost to Allie Beth Martin, then the following year she was put up on petition and won.

Jones's victory as a petition candidate made electoral diversity a reality in ALA. When the only candidates in the race were those chosen by the nominating committee, a creature of the sitting president, power naturally tended to remain in the hands of Establishment groups or cliques year after year; Moon called it a "self-perpetuating" process. But self-perpetuation became a much less certain proposition when ALA members began nominating their own candidates, which was easy enough to do: in 1976 it required nothing more than a petition form bearing the signatures of the candidate and 100 members in good standing or 25 members of Council.

But the Moon forces faced the problem of convincing their leader to run. According to Moon's recollection and that of his wife, he steadfastly resisted all appeals to enter the race, giving in only after being "shanghaied" late one night while in his cups. "They came to me," recalled Moon, "and said, my God, can't we do something about this? ACRL keeps dominating this association. Shank is going to beat these two guys in a landslide. Shouldn't we find somebody who can at least give him a battle for the job?" Moon's response: "Russell is unbeatable." But his friends persisted:

They said nobody's unbeatable; we think you could beat him. They said to me, we think we ought to put up a candidate and we think you're the one — you can beat him. But, I said, I don't want to run. Besides, I'm not sure I could beat him. I said I don't really know if I could beat him or not. I doubt it. Russell has enormous support and ACRL is the strongest division in ALA. But in any case I don't want to run. I like running the backbench — that's what I'm good at, so why don't you leave me in peace.

That was how the thing emerged. I don't think I was ever convinced I should do it; I simply got gang-tackled with the great help of Ilse. I knew what was going on but at the same time trying hard as I could to resist it. Only Ilse can testify to the degree that I was gang-tackled into doing this. I was really shanghaied, no question. I really did not want that job at all.

Ilse Moon, helpmate par excellence, confirmed the story of how her husband was dragooned into running for the ALA presidency, adding these details:

The Moon Mafia said to Eric, you're the only person who can beat Shank, but Eric resisted. So we got him really drunk at a party — I have this vague recall of being in a hotel room late at night, Eric pretty boozed up, and a delegation coming up. They had talked to me and asked, Do you think you can get him to sign this thing [the petition required his authorizing signature] and what do you think? I said I think if he signs it he'll do it. And I was for it. And somehow they and I got Eric to sign it. When he woke up in the morning I said, "Do you remember you signed this thing?" And he said, "I don't recall." But he agreed to do it.

This seems to have been the one and only time in his career that alcohol induced "hollow-leg man" Moon to do something he didn't want to do. Or was his apparent reluctance to run a bit of subconscious theater? Did the interior man enjoy being coaxed? Norman Horrocks, a Moon confidant of long-standing, furnished this unadorned account of how his friend became a candidate for high office: "I had collected 25 signatures, which was all that was needed for Eric to run as a petition candidate. I was the one who finally put the paper down in front of him and got him to sign it." Was he drunk? "No, not to my recollection. I think he wanted to run. He liked the attention of being persuaded."

In 1958 in England Moon was vice president/president-elect of the Association of Assistant Librarians, but left the country for Newfoundland before taking over as president. Now nearly two decades later he had another opportunity to become president of a library association, only this time the association was a much bigger deal. Drunk or not, disinclined to run or not, Moon must have thrilled somewhere deep inside when he signed that piece of paper triggering his candidacy: this was his chance, perhaps the only one he would ever have, to become president of the American Library Association and by so doing achieve a unique place in American librarianship.

Low-Key Campaign

John Berry observed in *Library Journal* (March 15, 1976), "This year's ALA presidential race ought to be a hot one…. Beach and Rohlf have kept low profiles, and will have an uphill battle against the visible and audible Moon and Shank." Most ALA insiders agreed the contest would be a close one, with the probable winner either Shank or Moon by a small margin. Yet by today's standards the campaign was remarkably restrained, with little overt or public display by any of the candidates. Robbie Franklin recalled, "Eric constantly claimed that he had no chance of winning and that he was running just for fun. He made it all seem so calm. You could hardly tell down at the office [Scarecrow Press] that anything was going on. He was extremely low-key about the campaign." In fact, aggressive electioneering by candidates for the ALA presidency did not begin until Thomas Galvin introduced mass mailings, telephone appeals, slogans, buttons, and other campaign hype in his race against Gerry Shields and Dick Dougherty in 1978. Some older members of ALA still refer to Galvin as "the Nixon of American library politics."

Candidate Moon — 53 and still trim, though fuller of face than when he first arrived in North America 18 years earlier — sported a mustache, long sideburns, and thick dark hair modishly brushed over the ears and curling at the collar. His pipe, artfully employed as a prop in social and platform situations, seemed permanently attached to his person, constantly in mouth or hand. The campaign, such as it was, stretched over three and half months, kicking off at the Midwinter meeting in late January when the final list of candidates was announced and wrapping up shortly after the ballots began to be mailed to members in the middle of May; ballots had to be returned to ALA headquarters by June 25, 1976, at the latest.

Moon's platform, as expressed in his "Statement of Professional Concerns" (a brief document required of all ALA candidates for elective office and mailed to members with the ballot), focused on three problem areas:

1) That while libraries' financial support is eroding daily, some ALA leaders seem more interested in tinkering yet again with the organization, leading us ever backward to the still recent days before a massive membership majority ratified the reconstituted Council, adopted new priorities, etc. Fiddling, indeed, while our Rome burns.

2) That ALA may by default begin to lose its position as THE voice of the profession in Washington (where it has hitherto been immensely effective) to the National Commission (NCLIS), which appears to be too susceptible to the importunings of the so-called information industry.

3) That membership views have great difficulty in filtering through to the policy-making levels of ALA. Broad membership views, as opposed to those of special interest groups, seem often to be received as embarrassing "nuisance" items. The principle of government by the people seems to have gone into decline.

Moon and his opponents had an opportunity to elaborate on key issues in an "If Elected I Will…" feature published that spring in both *LJ* and *SLJ*, which at the time had a combined circulation of 80,000 and doubtless reached practically every ALA member. The magazines' editors, John Berry and Lillian Gerhardt, devised ten questions for the candidates, emphasizing difficult choices facing the profession, including several devoted to hot-button social issues, a Moon specialty. In a scribbled P.S. to Moon at the end of his formal letter accompanying the questions, Berry wrote: "We ought to knock off a couple this way!" Obviously the *LJ* editor intended to help out his old boss with a few softball questions; Ilse Moon corroborated Berry's bias for candidate Moon: "John made sure that Eric's ideas got great prominence. For instance, his questions in *LJ* were carefully structured to show off Eric at his best."

Moon's basic philosophy and rhetoric resonated well among the ALA rank and file. In addition, various activist groups within the association — SRRT, the Black Caucus (led by E.J. Josey), the Task Force on Women, etc.— enthusiastically supported his candidacy and some, Moon remembered, "electioneered like crazy for me." In addition, the Moon Mafia and fellow travelers boosted his candidacy whenever and wherever they could. For instance, Gerry Shields (who by this time had left library journalism for the academic life in Buffalo) published a letter in *American Libraries* declaring his support for Moon, concluding: "I've adopted as my slogan for approaching the annual ALA ballot: *Oh-o-oh. What a little MOON light could do.*"

Sometimes, however, Moon's supporters were a mixed blessing. He recalled that when Al Daub interacted with librarians during the campaign, "Al would inevitably ask if the person was going to vote for me. One time he asked this of Roger Greer [a well-known figure in ALA at the time], who said, 'Well, I like Eric. I might even vote for him, but I can't stand all those people he runs with.'" Another prominent librarian, Jack Frantz, former director of the Brooklyn Public Library and later head of the San Francisco Public, told Moon in a letter dated May 18, "You are clearly the most intelligent and mature of the lunatic left"— hardly a ringing endorsement.

If Moon's "lunatic left" supporters made some people nervous, so did the fact that he worked not as a librarian but as an editor and publisher in the private sector. Some saw this as fertile ground for conflicts of interest should he be elected. Jack Frantz, who did end up enthusiastically supporting Moon, was one of those concerned:

 I feel a mild uneasiness over the prospect of having, as president of our principal professional association, the chief executive officer of a commercial publishing company which depends almost exclusively on the library and institutional market for its profits. If you are elected, Scarecrow would obviously benefit from the lustre and visibility of the ALA presidency. You cite the costs of serving a presidential year and I recognize that they are substantial. But this fact hardly justifies what I deem to be a dubious precedent.

Moon deflated the issue by promising to recuse himself should conflict of interest situations arise:

I think some people feared my election. I don't know what horrible things they thought I was going to do, but yeah some people were very worried about it. There was opposition on all kinds of grounds. I remember being attacked frequently over the years because I was a member of the library press and worked for a commercial company, and serving on Council while at the same time reporting what Council was doing — this was seen as a conflict of interest. When I was running for the presidency, this same conflict of interest issue came up — what will he do when issues come up that affect his other interests? I said, for example, that on the issue of copyright, should it come up, I simply will not vote on Exec Board deliberations. I said I would handle similar issues the same way.

Way back in the early 1960s when as the crusading editor of *LJ* he was persona non grata with the ALA Establishment, Moon happened to be having a drink at a conference with Ed Castagna (one of the outstanding public librarians of the day) and his wife, Rachel. At one point in the conversation, Rachel, who knew a thing or two about library politics, impulsively said, "You know, Eric, one day you're going to be president of ALA." Moon remembered, "I laughed like a drain and so did Ed. I said, 'Rachel, that's the most ridiculous thing I've ever heard you say. Here I am Public Enemy Number One of this association and you're talking about me being president!'"

But by the time balloting for the 1976 election rolled around, Rachel Castagna's prediction did not seem so far-fetched. As a matter of fact most of the Moon crowd felt certain Eric would win, though he himself remained pessimistic to the end, knowing better than anyone just how deep the anti–Moon feeling was among some influential ALA members. "When the Gang wanted me to run for president, I said, you know it's a really iffy proposition because the real question is, Are there more people out there who hate me than like me?" In May, at the time the ballots were going out, Moon told everyone that his chances of winning were "extremely doubtful." Norman Horrocks, Moon's unofficial campaign manager, also had doubts: "It's always a lottery when you have four people running. Shank was very popular with the academic library set. Eric had the support of many but he had also antagonized others. Also, it was held against him that he was not born in the United States, and that he had never worked in a U.S. library."

Moon Wins!

Bob Wedgeworth notified Moon of his victory on Wednesday, June 30, 1976, the day the election results were certified at ALA headquarters in Chicago, calling him at Scarecrow Press late that morning and following up with a confirming telegram:

> YOU HAVE BEEN ELECTED TO THE OFFICE OF PRESIDENT-ELECT.
> ELECTION COMMITTEE REPORT WILL BE IN MAIL JULY 1, 1976.
> PLEASE ATTEND AS MANY BOARD MEETINGS AS POSSIBLE DURING
> FORTHCOMING ANNUAL CONFERENCE. YOU WILL BE GUEST AT
> HEAD TABLE FOR INAUGURAL BANQUET FRIDAY, JULY 23.
>   ROBERT WEDGEWORTH EXECUTIVE DIRECTOR

The final vote: Moon 2,796; Shank 2,095; Rohlf 1,797; Beach 945.

Moon had not merely been elected but he won by a larger plurality than even his most idolatrous supporters had thought possible. In the bargain he made ALA history, becoming the first British-born president of the association, a feat made all the more remarkable by the fact that in 1976 he had lived and worked in North America for only 18 years (17 of them in the United States). And he achieved another historical footnote by becoming the second ALA president in succession to be elected via the petition route, another first.

Congratulatory letters and calls poured in from around the country and abroad. Here's a small sampling:

"I haven't been more pleased about an election since Kennedy beat Nixon."— Lillian Gerhardt, editor, *School Library Journal.*

"I cannot tell you how delighted I was to see that you have fought and won over 'City Hall' to become the new ALA president-elect."— Catharine Heinz, director, Broadcast Pioneers Library, Washington, D.C.

"It was with surprise and delight that I saw your ugly face on the front cover of the July *Record* [*Library Association Record*] and to learn that you have been elected president of the ALA. May I join the crowd who will surely be sending congratulations to you and say how delighted I am that a British librarian has attained this distinguished honour."— Jim Davey, an AAL pal from the old days.

"Congratulations and commiserations on being elected president of ALA!"— Martha Boaz, dean of the library school, University of Southern California.

"The size of your achievement can only be judged if we try to think of an American president of our association."— Eric Clough, a former president of the (British) Library Association and a Moon mentor at the Southampton Public Library in the 1940s.

"Although I have expressed my congratulations verbally to you ... I feel it still necessary for the record to express my elation and joy [in this letter]. I am also thinking of the kind of assistance that you can give to Clara [Clara Jones, incoming ALA president]. She too is very happy over your election."— E.J. Josey, Moon's longtime comrade in the struggle to overcome racism and bigotry in American librarianship.

"Hearty congratulations. It is good to know that your association with Grolier and remarkable success as head of Scarecrow have not been a commercial kiss of death in the profession. I know that the next two or three years will be most interesting."— William J. Murphy, president of Grolier, Inc.

Moon knew exactly what Murphy, Grolier's grand old man, meant. Winning the presidency was definitely not a one-year deal; it involved a year as vice president/president-elect, a year as president, and a year as immediate past president. Fulfilling his editorial and administrative responsibilities at Scarecrow, where extra help was not an option, while meeting the demands of the ALA presidency, would be an exhausting undertaking. But Moon had impressive energy reserves and seemingly unlimited self-confidence, as his reply to Murphy suggested: "The next three years are likely to be pretty tough, but with the always ready cooperation of the super Scarecrow staff I feel sure we can keep things moving onward and upward here while I tend to a few side duties. Mrs. Moon joins me in thanking you for your cordial letter."

For her part Mrs. Moon viewed her husband's victory strictly as a realist: "Of course we were glad to have won, but I don't think there was any great euphoria on our part. We had certain trepidations about the office of the presidency. We knew it was going to be a hassle. Eric saw the presidency as the hope that he could accomplish some things in a new way—but it didn't turn out that way. There was as much anxiety as there was euphoria. There was never the feeling, *Wow, now we've done it!* It was never like that."

American Libraries declared the election results a "Decisive Win for Moon," quoting the new president-elect as musing, "I'll only know if it's a victory after the war" (a sadly prophetic comment). In an article headlined "Eric Moon Elected New ALA President in Upset," *LJ* informed its readers, "The vote could be taken as an expression of lack of confidence in the association structure, or as a renewed expression of the reformist zeal that swept the association for a few years after the 1969 Conference in Atlantic City. But.... The more likely explanation [for his victory] is Moon's personal popularity as a former editor of *Library Journal* and a highly articulate debater at ALA meetings."

Moon's own analysis of why he won placed heavy emphasis on name recognition:

I had a sense that the election was between Russ Shank and me. I did not figure that the official slate [Rohlf and Beach] had any chance and that's how it turned out. I would have called the election that way but with an "if" about whether Russ or I would win—I thought probably Russ would win, quite honestly. I was somewhat surprised—I was a little surprised I won. Although most of those who were supporting me seemed not at all surprised. I don't know what that was based on except name recognition. At that time I had pretty high name recognition, and that's a very big factor in national elections—it was then and still is.

He also credited an offhand comment in the *LJ* "If Elected I Will..." piece for winning him many unexpected votes and possibly the election:

I later discovered that one of my statements that I had sort of thrown in off-the-cuff in answer to the final question [in the *LJ* Q&A] apparently garnered me a whole slew of votes from a source where I didn't really expect any at all. The final question was, "Why are you the best qualified candidate for the ALA presidency?" And I wrote back and said, given the fact that people like Frances Henne, Jesse Shera, and many other great leaders have never been president of ALA, I'm not sure that there's a good reason why any of the current candidates should be president. I went to several meetings soon after that and all kinds of school librarians came rushing up to me saying we read your statements and we're going to vote for you. I said, well thank you, that's nice, but why? And they said you were the only candidate to mention Frances Henne [influential library educator in the field of school and children's librarianship]. Just mentioning Frances Henne's name brought me hundreds of school librarian votes. But it wasn't done with that in mind at all. It was simply one of those purely fortuitous things.

Vice Presidential Year

Whether he welcomed it or not, Moon's election instantly metamorphosed him from ALA maverick to major association insider. Becoming vice president/president-elect automatically returned him to Council, ALA's large governing body, where he had previously served as an at-large member (1965–1972). His election also gained him a seat on the more exclusive and more powerful Executive Board, a 13-member directorate responsible for managing the organization's affairs. "Exec Board," as Moon called it, consisted of the president, vice president/president-elect, treasurer, immediate past president, and eight members elected from the Council, plus the executive director, the lone nonelected (and nonvoting) member. Notably, the only ALA election Moon ever lost occurred in the early 1970s when, as a member of Council, he ran for a seat on the Executive Board but was defeated, finishing fifth out of a field of six. Obviously, his political strength derived from the general membership and not the ALA Establishment.

By virtue of his new status Moon was privy to literally hundreds of internal concerns, deliberations, and pieces of information the average ALA member knew little or nothing about. He was now at the apex of the association's hierarchy, one of the decision-making elites. Some observers, including some members of the Moon Mafia, wondered how he would handle the abrupt transition from outsider to insider. Would the tiger become a pussycat? After several months on the job as vice president/president-elect and tired of hearing the speculation, Moon addressed the issue head-on in a speech to the California Library Association's annual conference in December 1976:

A lot of people, after recovering from the shock of seeing one of ALA's most vociferous critics elected as president, have asked me what I'm going to do. I tell them I don't know.... The other thing I'm asked is: now *you* are a member of the establishment, are you too just going to move around blowing the PR horn for ALA? In short, have the critical fangs been removed by this elevation to office? The answer is NO, to both questions. But I did say, even in the days of my most vitriolic sermons from the *LJ* pulpit, and shall go on saying, that ALA, for all its foibles and weaknesses, is the best political weapon the library profession has. And if you want to change it, make it better, make it do what you want, you have to join it, have to get involved. Sideline bitchers and crybabies get no free tissues from me.

Moon formally became ALA vice president/president-elect on July 23 at the conclusion of the 1976 conference in Chicago, where the association celebrated its centennial year. At the same time Clara Jones, director of the Detroit Public Library, was inaugurated as president, though she had been performing the duties of the office on an interim basis for months due to the illness and death of her predecessor, Allie Beth Martin, who succumbed to cancer that spring. The first African American to serve as ALA president and the first petition candidate to win in years, Jones welcomed Moon's election and looked forward to working with him. Though she did not know him well at this point, she knew of and appreciated his bold stand against racial intolerance and segregation in the 1960s while editor of *LJ*. During that time, said Jones years later, "I was watching and noticing and listening. Naturally, if you were involved in ALA in the 1960s, you were going to see and hear Eric Moon. So I was watching and noticing and listening to him before he knew me personally. He was a leader. He was outspoken. He was not just outspoken, he was eloquent, he was courageous."

Clara Jones and Eric Moon, kindred spirits, formed a compatible and effective leadership team, each possessing skills and interests the other lacked or had not fully developed. Moon took great pleasure in their congenial modus operandi:

One of the great joys of my presidential and vice presidential years was that Clara and I were able to work so well closely together. We had not known each other that well before, but

I had great admiration for her before and as I saw her operate it grew even more. And I believe Clara was also delighted when I came on board because we each had strengths that the other didn't. Clara said, "You have so much more background in ALA than I do, which is enormously valuable. Furthermore, I hate doing those meetings where all this procedural stuff crops up and I get lost in it, and you love doing that, you're good at that, so I'm going to hand over the chair to you whenever anything like that looks like it's coming up." So it was a great working relationship. If we went somewhere where some impromptu remarks were called for, I would say, "That's you, Clara." She's so regal and smooth — she's just beautiful. I couldn't help thinking how different it would have been if I were following somebody I couldn't get on with.

Moon's vice presidential year, which ran from July 1976 to June 1977, was filled with speeches to library groups around the country, plus numberless committee and sub-committee meetings at ALA conferences and at association headquarters in Chicago. Exec Board alone had four grueling multi-day sessions during the year, augmented by frequent correspondence and phone consultations. The board's agenda was normally full to overflowing. The American Library Association did not always accomplish a great deal, but it was a busy, busy, busy organization always aflutter with a myriad of issues and problems and disagreements and rumors— some vital, some grandiose, some cranky, some piddling, but all needing attention. It was a heavy load, and Moon took the work very seriously. After all, ALA was the profession's best hope, wasn't it, for advancing the cause of librarianship in the wider world?

In Search of a Theme

In addition to the speeches and committee work, president-elect Moon had to decide on a program for his presidential year prior to being inaugurated at the annual conference in June 1977. Presidents of ALA traditionally selected a broad, upbeat theme or cause to promote during their year in office. Often this turned out to be little more than bombast wrapped in a catchy slogan, but Moon was determined that *his* program would be one of substance, not flash. He wanted his presidency to be remembered for making a significant contribution to the profession. If he could pull it off, librarianship and ultimately the people it served would benefit, the stature of the association would be enhanced, and his place in the pantheon of memorable library leaders would be secured. No one ever accused Eric Moon of thinking small.

But first he needed to find the right issue, one that had both resonance and cachet. As he candidly admitted in his December 1976 speech to the California Library Association, he did not at that point know exactly what he wanted to do as president. He just knew it had to be something substantial that hadn't already been done or talked and studied to death — for instance, censorship. Ideally he wanted a theme that would result in a policy initiative with major ramifications for the entire library community. To help him formulate his program Moon appointed a presidential commission:

I had not decided what the thrust of the presidency would be because there were so many things that needed doing that I didn't want to decide just like that. What I did do was send out invitations to something like a hundred people to come to a gathering at the first Midwinter meeting after I was elected at which we would discuss ideas for my presidency — the theme, actual objectives, and so forth. Now I have to tell you they were not all people who would be thought of as the backbench crowd — they were a very diverse group of people. I wanted as much diversity as I could achieve.

Eventually 40 people — including wife Ilse and boss Ted Waller — agreed to serve on his presidential commission. About half were hard-core Moon supporters: Ed Beckerman, John Berry, Fay Blake, Dorothy Broderick, Arthur Curley, Bill Eshelman, Jack Frantz, Norman Horrocks, Clara Jones, Wyman Jones, E.J. Josey, Stefan Moses, Karl Nyren, Pat Rom, Pat Schuman, Gerry Shields, Jana Varlejs, John Weatherford, Billy Wilkinson and of course Ilse Moon. The other half — all of whom had amiable relations with the president-elect but were not particularly chummy — represented a laundry list of ALA doers and achievers: Barbara Anderson, Ralph Blasingame, Lillian Bradshaw, Jack Dalton, Dick Darling, Elizabeth Fast, Mildred Frary, Ervin Gaines, Michael Harris, Frances Henne, Alice Ihrig, David Kaser, Frank McKenna, Regina Minudri, Myra Nadler, Carleton Rochell, Frank Stevens, Rod Swartz, Paul Wasserman, and the afore-mentioned Waller, who was as conservative as Moon was liberal.

The commission met for the first time in early February at the 1977 Midwinter meeting, held that year in Washington, D.C. With 21 of the 40 members attending, most from the hard-core contingent, the group spent a couple of hours brainstorming about Moon's presidential program and the direction it should take. According to a summarizing memorandum Moon sent members a week after the meeting, two interrelated ideas or "motifs" emerged. First, the president's Midwinter program, due to be presented the following year in early 1978, would focus on the worldwide "information gap" and feature speakers ("heads of national departments of education, high-ranking politicians, etc.") from various countries such as Japan, Tanzania, and Sweden; and second, Moon's culminating program at the annual conference in the summer of 1978 would feature recently elected U.S. President Jimmy Carter or a top official of his administration presenting a major speech "outlining an information policy" for the nation, something Moon believed was "desperately needed." The memo concluded, "With the prior information from other countries gained at Midwinter, Carter will be able to cap the year's program at Chicago [site of the 1978 annual conference] with his plan for the U.S."

Almost to the bitter end of his ALA presidency, Moon allowed himself to believe that Carter would be amenable. Unfortunately, it didn't happen that way.

Moon now had several months to flesh out and refine his presidential program, which would be unveiled in his inaugural speech in June at the 1977 Annual conference, scheduled to be held that year in Detroit. During this time some commission members tinkered with or wanted to change the group's original suggestions, and new ideas were constantly being floated. But through it all the urgent need for a clearly defined national information policy remained firmly planted in Moon's mind, and by the spring of 1977 he had determined to make it his cause. In those heady days he had no way of knowing that an evil specter — racism — would become the real centerpiece of his presidency.

Committee Chairs and a Major Flap

Still another task to be accomplished during the vice presidential year — one that Moon eagerly welcomed — involved committee appointments. As vice president/president-elect he chaired Council's Committee on Committees, which gave him immense influence over filling committee vacancies and exclusive power to name committee chairs, though his selections were subject to pro forma approval by the Executive Board. From the outset Moon intended to use his appointments authority to the hilt. Several years earlier in his "Association Agonies" article in *American Libraries*, Moon made his feelings about ALA committees crystal clear: more people should be appointed to key committees "whose views differ radically from those of the traditional incumbents. If nothing else, the committee rooms might become less deadly places to pass a few hours if a modicum of dissident opinion were heard there. The club members, who have served endlessly and repeatedly, must be weeded out and replaced."

Moon struck quickly and decisively, replacing every chair of every committee under his control:

I figured that I only had one shot at this, and that one of the opportunities presented by the presidency was to effect change, particularly change in the thinking and attitudes of the association through the chairs of its committees. So I simply threw out all the incoming chairs and appointed new ones. This had never been done previously to this extent, and to say that some people were upset would be an understatement. There was a great furor, particularly about the Committee on Accreditation, not only because I had thrown out the old chair but suggested Guy Marco as the new chair.

In fact, the Marco appointment to head the Committee on Accreditation created a potentially explosive confrontation between Moon and a majority of the Executive Board, which threatened to withhold approval of all his appointments unless Marco's name was withdrawn. Marco, then dean of the library school at Kent State University, was roundly disliked by many library educators. Moon's friend Bill Eshelman, who was also appointed to COA, put it more bluntly: "The entire library education Establishment hated Guy Marco." Not only was Marco's doctorate in musicology and not library science, he was an outspoken critic of the Committee on Accreditation. A few years earlier, for example, he had publicly and harshly disparaged the committee, attacking its "dubious record" and calling on it to resign en masse after issuing "a formal apology ... for errors made" in one of its accreditation decisions.

As word spread that Marco was to be chair of COA, mighty howls of protest swept through the association. Moon's appointments policy, squealed library educators, was an abomination; he was out to destroy the very fabric of American library education; he had to be stopped! Even Mrs. Moon was set upon by a pack of angry academicians intent on pressing their complaint. After many strong words and much posturing, a compromise was reached and the Marco flap faded into history. Moon:

I had long had the feeling that COA was dominated by representatives of library schools and that since it was ruling on the health and future welfare of library schools, that was a bit like having self-policing. So I thought I'll make some revolutionary changes here. Fortunately

I had a year where there were four places to fill [or one third of the 12-member committee], so I nominated Guy Marco, Bill Eshelman, Fay Blake, and a guy called Tom Watson [a librarian at the University of the South]. And I named Marco as chair.

There were rumblings all over the place about what I was doing with committee nominations, but this one apparently was the capper. I remember when Ilse and I went to Midwinter [in early 1977] at which word of my nominations had already leaked from headquarters, we got to the Shoreham [hotel], went in through the swinging doors, and as I was veering off to the desk to deal with our reservations, a group of library educators grabbed Ilse and took her aside and started screaming at her: "What the HELL is wrong with your crazy husband?? What does he think he's up to??" They were really attacking her, and she said, "Why are you attacking me? Ask him!"

When I got to the Exec Board, I was told that there was so much furor over the appointment of Marco as chair of COA that the board would refuse to OK any of my appointments. So I said OK, fine, you want to fight, we'll fight. I'll take them all to the membership. Everybody was very nervous about this, so finally Tom Galvin, playing the role of great peacemaker, said "Look, Eric, this is a fight none of us can win, so I will make a deal with you: if you will give up Marco as chair of COA, I will move for unanimous approval of all of your other appointments, including the controversial ones, such as Zoia Horn for the Intellectual Freedom Committee. So I thought, OK, I'm not going to risk everything I've done on Guy Marco as chair, so I said fine, but I'm not giving up Marco's appointment as a member of COA. Galvin agreed, but on condition that the present chair continue. This was probably the last time Galvin and I ever cooperated on anything.

Years later Moon reluctantly admitted naming Marco as COA chair was not one of his best ideas. Even trusted adviser Norman Horrocks urged him not to do it. Moon: "My nomination of Marco as chair was probably a miscalculation, because in my naïveté I thought he would be considered less controversial than either Eshelman or Fay Blake. But it turned out he was more controversial than either of them."

On the positive side, Moon's slash-and-burn approach toward committee appointments brought new blood into prominent positions in the association. As E.J. Josey pointed out, "During his tenure as president, he appointed women, minorities, and young librarians to leadership positions heretofore never held by this segment of the association." In an editorial in *LJ*, John Berry applauded Moon's efforts to bring diversity to major committees: "The Moon style is beginning to show up in some appointments to those key ALA committees, such as the two urban librarians now joining the Legislation Committee, Ella Yates from Atlanta and Wyman Jones from Los Angeles. A new trio of vocal critics of ALA policies on various issues, Bill Eshelman, Guy Marco, and Fay Blake, will join that holy of holies, the Committee on Accreditation. There's a westerner on nearly every committee that Moon could influence."

Norman Horrocks, in an informative essay entitled "Decision Processes in ALA: Nudging the Dinosaur," credited Moon with a high degree of success in his exercise of the power of appointments:

As President-Elect he [Moon] moved swiftly to have his appointments made by the Midwinter meeting after his election. Customarily—and still—many committee appointments are not made until the Annual Conference. Technically the President-Elect makes recommendations which the Executive Board approves. In practice the Board usually pays the courtesy of automatic approval although it can and does raise questions, as indeed it did with a couple of Moon's choices. However, speed was not his only contribution to the process. The other, which has had longer-standing influence, was to ensure that Committee appointments went to those of similar outlook to his. The impact of this was not lost on succeeding Presidents and the art of this form of "patronage" now seems to be established within the Association.

Inauguration in Detroit

The American Library Association held its 1977 annual conference the week of June 17–23 in Detroit, much to the relief of outgoing president — and Detroiter — Clara Jones. Detroit had undergone tough times economically and socially in the 1970s and after some serious violence in 1976 in the downtown area where ALA would be meeting, there was a possibility the association might abandon the city, taking its convention elsewhere. However, assurances of adequate police protection and the lure of the brand-new Renaissance Center, a multimillion-dollar skyscraper complex featuring upscale shops, restaurants, and one of the tallest hotels in the world, the 73-story Detroit Plaza, saved the day. More than 7,000 ALA members and 2,600 exhibitors flocked to the conference.

Actually ALA was the first large group to meet at Renaissance Center ("Ren Center" to conferees), which was still not completely finished in the summer of 1977. There were occasional inconveniences, but overall the venue provided excellent conference facilities, ranging from the glittering new hotel to spacious meeting rooms; and Cobo Hall, Detroit's world-class auditorium and exhibit hall, was only a short stroll from Ren Center. The Moons were especially impressed with the presidential suite atop the Detroit Plaza. Ilse never forgot it:

It was a wonderful suite. We were the first convention to go into Ren Center. It wasn't even completely finished — the stores weren't open downstairs, so it had kind of an unfinished look to it. We had a third of the top floor of the Detroit Plaza Hotel. It was a marvelous suite with seven rooms. The rooms were weird: when someone rang a doorbell, you didn't know which door to go to, you had to check all seven! There was plush red carpeting throughout the suite with floor-to-ceiling windows. It was kind of scary — until you realized that no one could see in but you could see out.

Soon after the couple took possession of the suite and were alone, Ilse threw off her clothes and danced nude through all the rooms, a spontaneous expression of her total happiness at that moment: "It had to do with the glory of the suite and the thick, red carpet," she confided. "It was so magnificent; it was like a movie set. It was a response to the hotel, to the plushness, to being at the top." Indeed, for a few magical days in June 1977, the Moons not only resided at the top of one of world's poshest hotels, they were on top of the library world. But Eric, a case-hardened realist, knew it wouldn't last: "I remember when we got up to the suite, it was such an incredible view, and Ilse looked out those windows and said, 'Do you think anyone can see in?' So we went outside to the rooftop to check and you couldn't see in at all, so Ilse stripped and danced around the whole suite and said, 'This is marvelous, I could get used to this.' I said, 'Don't. Within two years we'll be back in a box.'"

The Moons were tightly scheduled during the conference, and their suite, unimaginatively named the Lake Ontario Suite, was too much for them to run by themselves, so Eric recruited old friends from Bowker days to manage the place and keep things running smoothly. He recalled:

We had one-third of the top floor of the hotel. One-third was Clara Jones's, one-third was Bob Wedgeworth's, and one-third was ours. The suite was huge, it went right around the building. We had a view of what seemed like half of Canada; I guess we had seven or eight rooms and two bars. We had friends staying with us—Dick Bye and his wife Nancy—because we needed help with the suite. It was very difficult because we were going to meetings all week and I was doing interviews with radio, television, and newspapers. And so somebody needed to be in control of the flow of things in the suite, and Nancy is absolutely a superb organizer of anything, everything. She operated like a chief of staff at the suite.

Busy as they were during the conference, the Moons and their friends found time for relaxation and fun. Wyman Jones, one of Eric's greatest conference buddies and an accomplished jazz musician, offered to play the piano in the Moons' suite. Fine, said Moon, but the suite had no piano. Was one available and could it be hauled up 73 stories? Right away? Moon remembered Nancy Bye did not flinch at the assignment:

Wyman called me about the first day he was in and said, "When do you want me to play the piano?" and I said, "All the time, Wyman, all the time." So he said, "Have you got a piano?" and I said no. He mentioned the kind of piano he wanted—a grand piano and the brand, which I forget now. He said it's got to be tuned before it's brought up. I said fine, I'll turn this over to my chief of staff, Nancy Bye. Nancy got on the phone to the manager of Ren Center and said President Moon wants this kind of grand piano delivered here by 3 o'clock and please tune it before it's brought up. And it was brought up. And Wyman played beautifully.

The same Wyman Jones teamed up with Arthur Curley, both inveterate pranksters, to add some levity to Moon's inaugural conference. Curley especially relished the "underwear caper":

Eric's mother used to buy him very, very colorful underwear at Marks and Spencer, the London department store. The boxer shorts type, but always very colorful. Eric would show them off—not wearing them but holding them up, saying, "Look what my mother just sent me." He thought it was charming that his mother always sent him underwear.

It was the year that Eric was incoming president of ALA in Detroit at Ren Center, and he threw his suite open to virtually all comers so people could come in and have a drink and meet the new president. Before the party, Wyman Jones and I went into his bedroom and took six or eight pairs of his underwear and hid them in all kinds of places. We opened the refrigerator, for example, and put them in the freezer. Well, sure enough, a little later Eric is holding court and among the first people to arrive are a couple of very conservative little old ladies. He says anything you want, ladies, a drink or a soft drink, just go right into the kitchen there—there's ice in the refrigerator. And the next thing he overhears is one of the ladies saying to the other, "My dear, he keeps his underwear in the freezer!"

Also, when he was presiding on the platform as president, Wyman and I got a couple pairs of his underwear, put them in a manila envelope, and on it wrote, "President Moon—URGENT OPEN AT ONCE." We sent it up by messenger and of course he opens the envelope and his underwear falls out! He gave me a couple pairs as souvenirs and I wear them only on special occasions. He takes delight in this sort of humor.

Not so amusing was an incident at the U.S.-Canadian border the night before Moon's inauguration. He and Ilse and a group of their friends—"Arthur, Jana, Norman, I don't know who else"—went over to Windsor, the well-ordered Canadian city opposite Detroit. The Gang had a pleasant evening but it took a sour turn at the border. Moon remembered everyone crossed back into the U.S. without incident except himself:

The customs guard stops me and asks if I'm a U.S. citizen and I say yes and he said, prove it. I said you didn't ask anybody else to prove it—how am I going to prove it? Oh, wait a minute, I've got a voter's registration card. But the guard says that doesn't prove anything—anyone can forge a voter's card. So we got into this horrendous argument. The others are standing down the aisle watching, laughing themselves sick. Eventually it looked as though it was going to get critical; they were going to slap me in jail. So Norman came over and explained that this man is going to be inaugurated as president of the American Library Association tomorrow night, and that this convention is bringing the city of Detroit about $20 million and if the president doesn't turn up, there's going to be hell to pay! So eventually I got through.

The next night—Tuesday, June 21—Moon's inauguration took place on schedule. The banquet, an $18 event, featured a lengthy address by the new president entitled "Data Bank Is Two Four-Letter Words." Sounding the theme of his presidency, Moon's remarks fixed on the pressing need to develop a comprehensive national information policy. He wanted to have such a policy drafted and approved well in advance of the first White House Conference ever devoted to libraries, scheduled to convene in 1979, just two years away. Moon had strong, deeply held views on information policy, and he responded with the speech of his life.

National Information Policy Launched

His eloquently crafted inaugural address called on members of ALA and the American library community to "loudly, insistently, affirm that free access to information for all is the very foundation, not only of our profession and our services, but of individual liberty." Librarians must "speak up," declared Moon:

And more than that—we must think, and having thought, move on—to action. And not action prompted by short-term expediency, but action motivated by principle. For if we do not, there is nothing more certain than that others, and particularly those who see the material potential in information as a commodity, will move before us to grab off this energy source as they have oil and gas and coal, and who will use it and develop it with perhaps no more social concern than the record from the Industrial Revolution on down should lead us to expect.

Later in the speech Moon returned to the information-as-energy metaphor, the energy crisis much on people's minds at the time: "We must argue and establish the position, I believe, that we and our institutions and services should be the citizenry's protectors in the information arena, ensuring that this vital energy source is not, as others have been, drained off into private storage tanks to which the only key is money. We must fight not only for the production of information geared to the needs of individuals at all levels of society, but for their right of unlimited access to it."

Moon contended tax-supported libraries have an obligation to make information available to *all* users without charge, rich and poor alike. Imposing fees for this "vital energy source" would be tantamount to discrimination — economic discrimination, an evil every bit as destructive as racial discrimination. To provide information only to those who can afford to pay for it would inevitably result in "a total renunciation of all the things we [librarians] have ever said we believed it: social responsibility, public access, a professional concern for the public interest, and all of our perennial holiness about intellectual freedom and the rights of the individual."

Of all the many themes or causes Moon might have embraced during his year as ALA president, formulating an egalitarian national information policy seemed to him to be far and away the most important — and most crucial: "We need, urgently, before it is too late and the scene is mangled by piracy and greed and fear, a national information policy which addresses and respects the real and multifaceted needs of all the people of our society. This is what I have determined to move toward in my presidential year because here is a matter, I believe, on which it is vital that the voice of the librarian be heard in the land." Moon wanted to formulate an information policy statement that ALA and kindred organizations such as the Special Libraries Association and the Medical Library Association could agree upon and endorse. This way the library profession could go into the much anticipated White House Conference on Library and Information Services unified by a single set of principles regarding the delivery, access, and cost of information. The ultimate goal was to promote and shape legislative action that would guarantee all Americans free access to public information.

The speech was reasonably well received and many of ALA's more thoughtful members later told Moon it had greater substance than any inaugural speech within memory. Others found it overly long, and in their conference wrap-up *LJ* editors groused that the speech was "Slow to get going, full of asides and anecdotes." Moon knew the speech was too long, but he couldn't bring himself to cut it — there was so much he wanted to say, so much that seemed essential to get on the record right at the start; after all, he had only one year, one fleeting year, to accomplish this most ambitious goal. He worked on the speech, he later said, "longer and harder than on anything else I have written," and Ilse remembered, "Eric worked on the speech constantly" prior to the Detroit conference. But all the time he worried ALA members might find information policy an unappealing topic or, as he put it, "an immediate turn-off." He was right to worry:

My theme — national information policy — was not greeted with wild enthusiasm by anybody. I think a lot of people were very disturbed that I did not choose a subject like censorship or race relations. Everyone kept saying, "What the hell's national information policy?" It was not a subject that had ever, in my experience, been discussed in ALA, at least in the big forums during my time in the association. But it seemed to me that it was perhaps the most pressing concern for us to get in on as early as possible before we were locked out by other forces that were already getting seriously involved with the topic. So I think the choice was the right one, but it was, interestingly, not one that came out of that gathering [Moon's presidential commission] which was supposed to identify the choice for me.

Moon insisted that he and he alone decided on information policy as his grand cause, and it was true that he first raised the issue, albeit obliquely, in his "Statement of Professional Concerns" at the very beginning of the presidential campaign in January 1976: "ALA may by default," he wrote, "lose its position as THE voice of the profession in Washington ... to the National Commission (NCLIS), which appears to be too susceptible to the importunings of the so-called information industry." Then after being elected, but prior to the first meeting of his presidential brain trust, Moon again attacked NCLIS — a permanent 14-member federal commission created in 1970 to advise both the President and the Congress on matters pertaining to library and information services — this time in a speech to the California Library Association. He portrayed the commission as a conservative, pro-business bureaucracy all too willing to do the bidding of profit-hungry commercial information providers. He also resented NCLIS's encroachment on what he perceived to be ALA's territory; "...the *policy* recommending voice for the future of libraries is ALA, broadly representing libraries and library service as it — and only it — always has," declared Moon, adding: "Let's get NCLIS out of the lobbying business."

All sorts of thorny policy questions about the availability, dissemination, and cost of information began to emerge in the 1970s, largely as a result of the advent of electronic publishing, then in its infancy but growing rapidly and relentlessly. Librarians were especially concerned about who would pay for information obtained via new, and pricey, online database services. Soon "free or fee" debates became commonplace within the ranks of librarianship and the information industry. The 39th annual conference of the American Society for Information Science meeting in San Francisco in October 1976, for instance, had "INFORMATION★POLITICS" as its provocative theme. A panel loaded with big-name information providers got into a heated discussion about the pros and cons of fees, and a featured speaker specifically discussed the crying need for a "national information policy" to deal with such questions. A few months later a major ruckus over fees broke out at the 1977 ALA Midwinter meeting in Washington. Zoia Horn introduced a resolution urging the association go on record supporting the people's right to information regardless of ability to pay, but the conservative Council decisively (96 to 36) voted it down.

No slouch at identifying trends in the library field — he had done it for years at *LJ* — Moon was aware of these and related developments, and by the time his presidential commission first met, he knew that information policy had (or soon would) become a front-burner issue for librarians as well as politicians, civil servants, and of course information vendors in the private sector. He quickly determined that this issue, so rich in political and professional crosscurrents, had great potential as a presidential theme. Not only was information policy of vital importance to the future of librarianship and the American people, it was a fresh and forward-looking topic that hadn't yet been talked to death. Besides, it was something he could get his teeth into. In short, information policy was an issue big and imposing enough for Moon, who thrived on big and imposing issues. Coincidentally, it complemented outgoing president Clara Jones's program at the

Detroit conference, "The Information Society: Issues and Answers." Hence by spring 1977 Moon had decided to make information policy his cause.

Accordingly, that May he appointed an Ad Hoc Committee to Draft a Statement on National Information Policy. The seven-member committee, chaired by David Kaser (distinguished professor of library science at Indiana University and a former director of Cornell University libraries) included Fay Blake, E.J. Josey, and Rod Swartz from Moon's presidential commission, plus newcomers Mary K. Chelton, S. Michael Malinconico, and Peggy Sullivan. Tom Galvin, then dean of the library school at the University of Pittsburgh, turned down an invitation to serve on the committee, which led Moon to pick Sullivan, a longtime Galvin ally, to give the committee a semblance of ideological balance.

Chelton, a young adult librarian and friend of Dorothy Broderick, remembered the committee as "a wonderful mix that worked very well." That's exactly what Moon wanted—a stimulating mix:

> I chose very bright people who didn't have an awful lot in common who came from different viewpoints and different areas of the profession to sit down and write a first stab at what ALA might want to say about national information policy. So I appointed this committee—Dave Kaser was the chair, because Dave seemed to be one of the sanest and most likable people in the profession, and probably the only one who was likely to be able to handle the crew I was going to give him. It was a very diverse bunch. It was a group of people who were calculated to blow the walls out of most rooms—they were going to argue and fight about everything. I remember after the first meeting or two they had together, Mike Malinconico [then with the New York Public Library in systems analysis and data processing] and I were having a drink together and he said, "I'm a bit disappointed about that committee." And I said, "Why's that?" And he said, "I thought I was the lefty on that committee, but now I've met Fay Blake!"

The drafting committee first met at the Detroit conference at noon on Sunday, June 19 in the Moons' suite. The president-elect told members he would "lay in some sandwiches, beer, etc. to keep us going," and by all accounts the meeting went swimmingly. The goal was to produce a "discussion document" on information policy that would be ready prior to ALA's Midwinter meeting in January 1978. Moon planned to invite the leaders of other interested associations to the meeting to react to the document, the hope being they would provide cogent criticism and in time endorse it.

Kaser delivered the final draft of the document in November 1977. His cover letter, dated November 18 and addressed to Moon with copies to Executive Director Wedgeworth and members of the drafting committee, read:

> Herewith is our document. I do not believe that any of us are totally satisfied with it, but all of us are prepared to support it. We are surprised that it is as brief as it is [a dozen typed manuscript pages], but we think that it touches in one way or another all of our concerns. It should elicit some discussion at the President's meeting, both from your invited guests and from the general audience.

After input and scrutiny by Moon, Wedgeworth, and a few trusted insiders (Moon called them his "kitchen cabinet"), the national information policy statement was sent to the heads of the American Society for Information Science, the Association of Educational Communications and Technology, the Medical Library Association, and the Special Libraries Association, all of whom agreed to respond publicly to the statement at ALA's Midwinter meeting in January in Chicago.

The drafting and distribution of the Kaser committee's discussion document completed the launch of Moon's information policy initiative. All he could do now was sit back and hope for favorable reactions from the other associations. Could all five organizations, including ALA, which had not yet officially considered the document, find common ground on a subject as complex and contentious as information policy? Could these various interest groups, each with its own demanding constituencies, come together and support the Kaser committee's statement, which espoused the idealistic principle of free and equitable information access for all? Was a united front against the hard-charging, profit-oriented information industry possible?

The Speaker: *Secret Project*

Unfortunately for Moon these questions were not uppermost in the minds of many ALA members in Detroit, nor would they be at anytime during his presidency. Instead, beginning in June 1977 and continuing well into 1978 the attention of most members was riveted on a much more emotional — and inflammatory—concern: what to do about an ALA-sponsored film called *The Speaker*, which, shades of the 1960s, again brought the association face to face with the sickening smirch of racism? Moon was nonplussed. The last thing he wanted was a great commotion diverting attention from his information policy initiative, which would be difficult enough to achieve in the best of circumstances. Yet neither he nor anyone else in the association had the power to quell *The Speaker* controversy once it raged out of control. Like a virulent disease, animus created by the film infected and overwhelmed the association in 1977 and 1978, and national information policy, never a crowd pleaser, got lost among all the angry words and hurt feelings.

Prior to the Detroit conference, the large majority of rank-and-file ALA members knew little or nothing about *The Speaker*, though several items in the library press that spring, most notably a John Berry editorial, "A Whimper for Freedom," in the June 1, 1977, issue of *LJ*, warned that the film had problems and could be trouble. In addition, some insiders, including members of the Executive Board, had viewed the film at private screenings in April and May, and there had been a festive "premiere" in California in mid–May for the cast, production crew, and invited guests. Once in Detroit, however, everyone had an opportunity to see *The Speaker* and learn the basic facts.

Subtitled *A Film About Freedom*, the 42-minute 16mm color production was completed in April 1977 and ALA, the copyright holder, began processing 150 advance orders in the middle of June, just days before the opening of the Detroit conference. The ALA Intellectual Freedom Committee sponsored the film, with Judith Krug, director of the association's Office for Intellectual Freedom, credited as executive producer. Lee R. Bobker, president of Vision Associates, the New York production company that made the film, was producer-director. Bobker also coauthored the script (originally called *Days in the Death of Freedom*) with Barbara Eisberg.

From the outset *The Speaker* project was envisioned as an exploration of the First Amendment in contemporary American society. The film's plot, originally suggested by Archibald Cox (of noble Watergate fame), involves a fictionalized account of real-life efforts to prevent Dr. William Shockley, a Nobel Prize laureate in physics, from publicly speaking about his theories on race and specifically his belief that black people are genetically inferior to whites. The fact that Shockley had been denied the right to speak at Harvard University and other college campuses in the early 1970s disturbed Cox and like-minded academics concerned about the future of free speech in America. In the film, a high school current events club invites a Shockley-like character (called Dr. Boyd) to discuss his ideas about race at a school assembly, but others at the school and in the local community are outraged and pressure the club and its adviser, history teacher Victoria Dunn (played by acclaimed actress Mildred Dunnock), to rescind the invitation. Dunn and the club refuse, but in the end the speaker, who is never actually seen or heard in the film, is banned by the school board. Filmed at Sunnyvale (California) High School near San Jose, *The Speaker* drew on the school's student body and faculty for its interracial cast.

How did a film with such a story line come to be associated with ALA, especially since the plot has nothing directly to do with libraries? How did it happen that an organization riven by excruciating racial conflict just a dozen years before came to put its imprimatur on a project built around the premise of black inferiority? Why did the controversy caused by the film dominate ALA business for practically an entire year, during which time Moon's information policy proposal was wiped off the association's radar screen? How did all of this happen? Who was responsible?

Answers to these questions lie buried in the film's often cryptic preproduction history. From its earliest glimmerings in June 1975, when ALA's Intellectual Freedom Committee and the Freedom to Read Committee of the Association of American Publishers discussed the possibility of jointly producing a First Amendment film, until the day the film was first shown in late April 1977 to the ALA Executive Board, *The Speaker* was virtually a secret project whose details, including the script, were known to only a handful of people in the ALA bureaucracy. (The Association of American Publishers withdrew from the project in 1976, well before the film was made.) Certainly the vast majority of ALA's 35,000 members had no inkling that such a film was being produced in their name; nor did Council, ALA's governing body, know anything specific about it; nor, incredibly, did some members of the IFC, the film's official sponsor. Even when they inquired about the film's progress and subject matter, committee members were brushed off with vague and evasive answers. Zoia Horn, an IFC member during 1976–1977 and committee chair the following year, recalled: "It was a strange experience being on the committee but as a member not knowing the substance of the film and not being told when I wrote and asked about the subject."

Also incredibly, the Executive Board, ALA's management team, was kept in the dark. Though technically the board had oversight responsibility for the film, early on it ceded control of the project to the IFC, which in turn delegated that authority to a small, clannish subcommittee consisting of Judith Krug and two fiercely loyal supporters, Robert Delzell, a professor of library science at the University of Illinois at Urbana-Champaign

and self-described "very close friend" of Krug and her family, and Florence McMullin, a
library trustee from the King County Library System in Seattle and IFC chair during
1976–1977. Moon, who joined the Executive Board at the time ALA and Vision Associates
were negotiating the contract to produce the film, remembered being constantly frustrated by the lack of hard information about the project:

The Speaker was a film that, according to what we were told, was supposed to be an ALA
statement on the First Amendment. It was made by Judy Krug and the OIF and a committee
attached thereto, and an independent filmmaker, whose name [Lee Bobker] I've forgotten,
maybe buried because I couldn't stand the man. I was on the Exec Board at the time, just having been elected vice president/president-elect. Clara was president. We would ask questions
about the film and we would get very vague reports. We had asked several times and got very
vague explanations; there was never any clear idea of what the film was about. We never got
to see the film until finally late in Clara's presidency [at an April 1977 meeting of the Executive Board].

   As Zoia Horn revealed in her recent memoir, Zoia!, which furnishes the first
detailed inside account of The Speaker fiasco, the Krug subcommittee not only controlled
all aspects of the film's production, it deliberately withheld crucial information from
other concerned parties until the film was in the can and therefore unable to be changed:

In this film project the total decision-making authority of the American Library Association had been assumed by this small subcommittee…. Not being aware of vital information
until the film was completed and accepted by this subcommittee cheated the ALA of its right
to examine a production that would have its name as the official producer…. I was entrapped
by ignorance that was made possible by the secrecy practiced by the director of the Office of
[i.e., for] Intellectual Freedom [Krug] and the subcommittee. Only Mrs. Krug, Mrs. McMullin and Mr. Delzell, as the "authorized" subcommittee, were privy to this information and
they did not share it with the IFC members, President Jones or the Executive Board.

   When it originally approved the project in April 1976 the Executive Board stipulated
the film had to pay for itself — in other words, said the board, don't look to the association for a subsidy. Krug understood this and immediately initiated a campaign to obtain
seed money for an "up-to-date film on intellectual freedom and the First Amendment,
specifically tailored to the needs of modern libraries" (emphasis added). She urged librarians to order and pay for the film in advance, a tricky bit of business because standard
library selection practice normally requires librarians to preview films prior to purchase.
But Krug sweetened the deal with a 20 percent discount: "We believe this film will find
a place in hundreds of libraries across the country," she burbled. "What we are asking is
that those libraries submit pre-release orders so that the film becomes a reality. At the
same time they can take advantage of a special pre-release price." Paid orders received
before September 15, 1976, would get the $400 film for $320.
   In addition to her own appeal (published in the July-August 1976 issue of American
Libraries), Krug asked acting ALA president Clara Jones to send a letter, drafted by
Krug's office, soliciting orders for the film to roughly a thousand libraries. According to
the letter the film — as yet unnamed, unscripted, and unmade — would "explain the special role of the library in preserving and disseminating controversial works" (emphasis
added). Jones, a strong advocate of intellectual freedom, was pleased to support such a

worthy endeavor and signed the letter. She had no reason to believe that Krug and her colleagues would produce anything other than an outstanding educational film that would bring credit to ALA.

Later, however, Jones would learn she had been duped by Krug, and her letter, which had helped generate nearly a hundred orders and enough money to ensure the film's production, became a source of anguish when she learned the true nature of the work she had plugged. On Wednesday, April 27, 1977, at its spring meeting in Chicago, the Executive Board finally got to view *The Speaker*, which had been hastily shot and edited earlier that year. Clara Jones recalled, "There was a dead silence at the end. I was appalled by the film. It did not carry out what Judy Krug had said it would be about and what people had agreed to by sending in their advance subscriptions." Moon had a similar reaction:

We were finally invited to see the film. I was sitting with Clara and it's not too much to say that she almost went white watching that film. We were really quite horrified, because of all of the things that could have been chosen to illustrate ALA's position on the First Amendment, to pick one that dealt with race relations and dealt with it in such a way that it obviously could be interpreted by different people in different ways, as later developments proved, seemed unconscionable. Many people did see it as a racist film. It seemed to me very destructive in view of the fact that ALA was still recovering from the battles of the 1960s during which we had finally begun to overcome that long history of racial discrimination in libraries. Those battles had largely been won over the years—but then to throw this film into the middle of the scene seemed to me to endanger ALA and set back race relations ten years at least.

The following day the Executive Board met in closed session and after a four-hour debate voted that copies of *The Speaker* "not be issued until such time as the film has been viewed by the Intellectual Freedom Committee and by the Membership" at the Detroit conference, upcoming in six weeks. The board wanted both IFC and the membership to see the film and have an opportunity to endorse or reject it. If the verdict went against the film the board presumably would sever the association's contract with Vision Associates and not release the film — or if it were eventually released it would not carry ALA's name or implied stamp of approval.

Those who created the film were stunned by the Exec Board's decision and responded swiftly and intensely. Executive Director Wedgeworth reported that IFC chair McMullin (speaking for both herself and Krug) "expressed great concern" about the board's action, as did Vision Associate's Bobker. In a long letter to Wedgeworth dated April 29 that began, "Naturally, I am both deeply disappointed and appalled at the action by your Executive Board," Bobker challenged the board's authority to block distribution of the film: "The basic point is, I think, that it was never stated to me that the Board had the power to do what they have done and the contract, so carefully negotiated by Bill North [ALA's attorney] and myself in intent and specivity [sic], clearly assigns to Judith Krug and her film committee, and only to them, the final decisions concerning this film. It was on that basis that we [Vision Associates] agreed to make the investment we have made and to defer the monies we have deferred."

Bobker also expressed concern about the fate of the film's "premiere" at Sunnyvale

High, scheduled to take place in just two weeks: "The entire community has been invited and elaborate arrangements made for a series of showings on May 12th and 13th. There is literally no way to recontact all these people who contributed so much to the film and uninvite them, and even if there were, it would cause so much embarrassment for your organization and mine that I couldn't possibly participate in such an action."

Attorney William North, in a written opinion requested by Wedgeworth, stated the Executive Board had the authority to delay or cancel the film's release but if it did there almost surely would be costly consequences, both in terms of financial liability (breach of contract) and damage to the association's good name. North made the point — a telling one — that the board's action would be interpreted by many as an attempt to censor the film. Was the board prepared for the public relations disaster that would ensue? North: "Considering the extensive publicity about [the] film, the promotional effort involved, the personal promotional appeals from Ms. Jones, first as Acting President and then as President of ALA, and the large number of pre-release orders received, I can visualize only the most extreme embarrassment to the Association and its officials were the right of cancellation and suppression to be exercised. It doubtless would be viewed as a substantial 'acting out' of the plot of the film."

Wedgeworth, whose signature appeared on the film's contract as ALA's representative, later acknowledged that he was "kept informed of the progress of the film project all along the way." Not only was he in the picture (so to speak) from the beginning, he supported the finished product, finding *The Speaker* to be "an effective test of the First Amendment," adding:

Specifically, I can also say that I knew the subject of the film and I knew the origins of the idea. I had not seen a script nor had I seen a rough cut of the film before it was previewed for the Executive Board. I was surprised to see the subject of the film acted out in reality by the members of the association. While there is some merit to the process related concerns, the real objection was to the subject matter. It was fascinating to see First Amendment advocates who found that they could not distinguish their feelings about the subject from its treatment as a First Amendment issue. While the issue was race, I believe denying the Holocaust would have produced a similar reaction.

Armed with strong negative reactions to the Exec Board's decision from the IFC chair, the film's producer-director, and ALA's attorney, plus his own conviction that the film had accomplished its mission, Wedgeworth wasted no time advising board members to reconsider their April 28 vote not to release *The Speaker*. And in a conference call on Tuesday morning, May 3, they did just that, the board voting unanimously (with one abstention) to reverse its earlier vote and immediately release the film.

The single abstention was Eric Moon. Exasperated by the furtive way the film came into being and its makers' blatant insensitivity to the association's recent racial history, Moon was already heartily sick of *The Speaker*. By abstaining on the vote to issue the film — a feeble gesture but the only means of protest available — he vented his mounting frustration with the whole business. To vote to release *The Speaker* — a work created and owned by ALA — would ipso facto imply association approval of the film's content and message; to vote against its release would doubtless be seen as a move to censor it. Moon considered both options equally repugnant.

E.J. Josey would later claim, "Krug browbeat the board into accepting the film," which may or may not be true, depending on one's reading of events. What is clear, however, is that by the time the Executive Board learned the truth about *The Speaker* it was too late — the film was a fait accompli, a done deal. In retrospect, the board had only one realistic course of action: release the film. To have jettisoned it at that point would have been both politically and financially untenable. On the bright side, the secret project was secret no more, and in six weeks "all hell broke loose" (Moon's words) in Detroit when ALA members got to see the film. Krug finally had her precious celluloid *Speaker*, but even she must have questioned whether it was worth the price.

The Speaker: *Public Uproar*

But before all hell broke loose, the pro-film forces experienced a brief period of euphoria. The Executive Board had been forced to eat humble pie on May 3, and nine days later *The Speaker* scored a public triumph at its gala premiere at Sunnyvale High School, the film's one shining moment. Krug, Bobker, and company could not have been more pleased: their creation was a hit and everyone involved felt like a Tinseltown celebrity for a day or two. Everyone that is except Zoia Horn, who came down to Sunnyvale from Berkeley (where she lived) to see the film for the first time. The screening confirmed her worst fears about *The Speaker*:

The laboratory/lecture room was filled with teachers and students who wanted to see themselves on the screen. They were all elated, they had loved acting in the film and having their school in it. Wow! After the showing there was a catered buffet, which made it even more of a Hollywood party. I was furious, resentful, and ashamed. The film was racist and mischievous in the way it contrived to test commitment to free speech. When Lee Bobker came over to speak with me, I contained my anger, but told him quietly that I did not like it and gave him some of my reasons. He became very defensive. Pointing to the enthusiastic students he assured me that I was going to be a very lonely minority of one.

Bobker could not have been more wrong. The next month at ALA's annual conference in Detroit hundreds of librarians joined Horn in opposing the film, finding it unacceptable on numerous grounds ranging from racist content to unsuccessful explication of the First Amendment to poor technical quality. But others defended it as a hard-edged case study probing the complexities of free speech in a democratic society, and cited the vigorous debate it provoked among ALA members as proof of its efficacy. "Rarely, if ever, had veteran ALA conference-goers heard so much heated discussion on a single topic. Everywhere one went — in restaurants, hotel lobbies, meeting rooms, corridors—librarians were talking about the film, usually in highly emotional terms," reported the editors of *Wilson Library Bulletin* in their conference summary.

The film's most aggressive supporters tended to be — like their heroine, Judith Krug — absolutists, or "purists," on intellectual freedom issues. They believed the First Amendment literally means what it says ("Congress shall make no law … abridging the freedom of speech, or of the press"), no ifs, ands, or buts. If some people suffer emotional or psychological hurt due to polemical "speech" — racial epithets, hateful ideas, offensive words or symbols, hard-core pornography, hooded thugs marching in sheets, whatever — tough luck, that's the price of freedom. During the yearlong turmoil over *The Speaker* the most frequently heard voices raised in the film's defense belonged to Dorothy Broderick, Florence McMullin, Grace Slocum, Robert Delzell, Elliott Shelkrot, Ella Yates (the only prominent African American to openly support the film), Kathleen Molz, Pamela Darling, Eli Oboler, Richard Buck, and Mary K. Chelton. Krug actually contributed little to the public debate but was active behind the scenes fending off attacks on the film and her own conduct.

Those most adamantly opposed to *The Speaker* were members of ALA's Black Caucus and SRRT-type social activists, including most of the Moon tribe. They believed human rights take precedence over intellectual freedom when the two are in conflict; put another way, they placed the Fourteenth Amendment, which guarantees civil rights, above a literal interpretation of the First Amendment. No one, they felt, for example, has a constitutional right to advocate slavery or genocide. Among the film's most vocal critics were Clara Jones, E.J. Josey, Zoia Horn, Miriam Braverman, Jackie Eubanks, David Weill, Geraldine Clark, Major Owens, Avery Williams, Pat Schuman, Arthur Curley, Dorothy Nyren, John Berry, Gerry Shields, and Eric Moon.

As Moon saw it, race was the key issue driving the furor over the film:

The primary opposition to *The Speaker* came from the blacks and those who understood why the blacks were upset with the film, and also those of us who felt that this was a very stupid thing for ALA to do in terms of its own racial history. It had taken us many, many decades to confront the racial problem at all in librarianship, and finally over the years we had seemingly gotten past that and the association was to a large degree healed when *The Speaker* came along and stuck a knife in it.

The opposition came from leaders like E.J. Josey and Clara Jones, along with the active support of myself and many other people. On the other side were many people who saw this as an intellectual freedom battle, who felt that what we were trying to do was censor this film. And on that side were many of my good friends too, particularly Dorothy Broderick. It was not a clear-cut thing at all, but it certainly did tear the association apart for a period of time.

I think what bothered me most was that it was not necessary, that we could have made a film that would have expressed our position on the First Amendment without doing it that way. It was not just the topic — the Shockley-type speaker, who I agree ought to be allowed to speak — but it was the presentation of the topic that was the problem. Even down to the casting you could see the problem — those demonstrating in the film were the blackest of the black; the ones who seemed most reasonable were the lightest of the blacks. Little things like that — messages like that throughout the film were really quite destructive.

The Intellectual Freedom Committee kicked off its debate over *The Speaker* at a meeting on Friday, June 17, in an atmosphere one observer characterized as "open hostility." Miriam Braverman, a library science professor at Columbia University and recent committee appointee, introduced a resolution calling on the committee to "dissociate" itself from the film, which she lambasted as a "failure" as an educational film. Braverman's motion not only produced sharp exchanges concerning the film's merits but the alarming news that Krug planned more such films. She told the committee that, because it had been "too complicated to try to explain the library role viz-a-viz [sic] the First

Amendment" in *The Speaker*, "We hope to follow up with productions on the library role." The thought of more cinematic offerings from Judith Krug must have sent shivers through Braverman and her single ally on the committee, Zoia Horn. Eventually the IFC decided not to vote on Braverman's resolution until after the membership had had an opportunity to see and discuss the film on Sunday.

Word of mouth put *The Speaker* in the conference spotlight from day one, and more than 2,000 librarians jammed Cobo Hall at the first membership meeting on Sunday evening, June 19, many simply to see what all the fuss was about. At the conclusion of the showing, which elicited both polite applause and scattered hisses, President Clara Jones invited three respected librarians—Geraldine Clark (New York City school libraries), Ervin Gaines (Cleveland Public Library), and Gerry Shields (library school at the State University of New York at Buffalo)—to the podium to offer brief assessments of the film. As it turned out, all three critiques were negative and Jones was loudly accused by Broderick and Chelton of stacking the deck against *The Speaker*, a charge Jones emphatically denied. A scheduled reception at the Detroit Public Library later that evening limited the floor discussion to about 45 minutes, but that was more than enough time for battle lines to be firmly drawn: Josey, for instance, emotionally attacked *The Speaker* as racist and insensitive while Broderick asserted it was a "superior film," adding: "I could teach an entire semester on this film."

After the meeting adjourned and most of the conferees trotted off to Detroit's main library for an hour of socializing, the IFC met again, picking up where it had left off on Friday, the hostility level just as high or now even higher. Horn ripped the Krug subcommittee for its star-chamber tactics: "How it [the making of the film] all occurred is really unknown. A subcommittee was empowered, and I asked what the subject would be. I was never permitted to find out. I was unable to be a responsible member of this committee. I couldn't get a copy of the script. I am not commenting on filmmaking, I am commenting that there was no democracy in the selection of the subject of the film, no debate on the choice." Delzell responded, defending the decision-making process, pointing out that the subcommittee, of which he was a member, had clear authority to act for the whole committee. He said he now believed in the film "more than ever.... I'm proud to have my name on it."

After much more back and forth, a weary IFC voted 7 to 2 against Braverman's motion to dissociate the committee from *The Speaker*, with only Braverman and Horn in favor. (Throughout *The Speaker* controversy, Horn and Braverman usually functioned as a minority of two within the committee. The pro-film majority especially disliked the aggressive Horn, calling her "Zoia Anti-Everything" in private and, according to Delzell, when Krug and her subcommittee got together socially in public at a restaurant or a bar, they used code names for the two women: Horn was "Tear Drop" and Braverman "Mixed Bag.") But the defeat of the Braverman resolution would not be the end of efforts to disconnect ALA from the film. While almost no one advocated banning *The Speaker* outright, many wanted the association's name expunged and sponsorship repudiated.

The question of what to do about the film dominated subsequent membership meetings in Cobo Hall on Monday evening, June 20, and Wednesday morning, June 22 — the latter convened just hours after Moon's Tuesday evening inaugural address on national information policy, a topic that seemed dense and remote compared with the combustible *Speaker* business. The mood at the membership meetings became increasingly rancorous and accusatory as positions on both sides hardened; civility, like the nation's dwindling oil supply, became a scarce commodity in Cobo Hall. Looking back, Ed Holley remembered the debate over *The Speaker* in Detroit as "a battle royal," and Dorothy Broderick, who always seemed to be in the middle of the action, recalled that the Wednesday morning meeting "came as close to creating a mob riot as any I've seen in my professional life; the meeting was a lynch mob in operation." Though she had never been chummy with Krug or part of ALA's cliquish intellectual freedom set, Broderick stepped forth to defend *The Speaker* because she believed in the film and the issues it raised. Her conscience, she said, would not allow her to be quiet: "Silence is acquiescence."

The caustic war of words revolved around two resolutions, one introduced by Nancy Kellum-Rose, a librarian at the San Francisco Public and Bay Area SRRT leader, and the other by the Black Caucus and its chairperson, Avery Williams. Both motions had the same intent — to remove ALA's name from the film — but the Black Caucus's contained additional language detailing the film's alleged racism:

WHEREAS, the Black Caucus is disturbed by the interjection of the issue of race relations which destroys the intent of *The Speaker*; and

WHEREAS, in the portrayal of the races, the characterization of the Blacks is negative and stereotyped; and

WHEREAS, *The Speaker* is condescending, simplistic, and insulting to Blacks; and

WHEREAS, the development of the theme utilizes the Black characters as victims and scapegoats; and

WHEREAS, the process by which *The Speaker* was commissioned, produced, reviewed, edited and authorized for distribution is obscure and questionable; and

WHEREAS, the subtleties and innuendos of the film contribute to deteriorating social and interpersonal relations; and

WHEREAS, *The Speaker* violates the Library Bill of Rights by failing to provide a mechanism for the discussion of both sides of a controversial issue; and

WHEREAS, the Black Caucus expresses its serious concern in the strongest terms by declaring that its members are outraged at the apparent capricious choice of the subject matter and the stereotyped depiction of Black people;

BE IT THEREFORE RESOLVED, that out of respect for its Black members and out of a real concern for the preservation of the integrity of the Association in terms of its own Library Bill of Rights, the Black Caucus requests that the American Library Association withdraw its name from the film.

Broderick and other pro-film advocates insisted, however, that adoption of either resolution would be censorship plain and simple. Withdrawing ALA's name, they maintained, would effectively kill *The Speaker*'s commercial viability and in essence kill the film. The argument rankled Moon and his friends:

The thing Dorothy Broderick liked about *The Speaker* was that the film didn't go out and attack the right — it attacked the liberals. It showed how great we were, how evenhanded we were. Well, that was pretty damn dumb, it seems to me, because that goes out as ALA's position. What I was arguing and others were arguing was, OK the film's made, let it go out, but for Christsake we don't have to put ALA's imprimatur on it. Well then we were called censors. I said we're not censoring anything. We're saying let the film go free, but not as *our* film. I was perfectly willing to write the thing off as a loss and give it to the filmmaker and let him distribute and sell it. But nevertheless we were called censors because we were trying to interfere with the health, welfare, and profit of this film.

Toward the end of the debate in Detroit, Major Owens, a member of the New York State Senate and former librarian, castigated *The Speaker* for its "secret agenda of racism," and Josey asked ALA members "to support the humanity of black people" by voting for the Black Caucus resolution. Pamela Darling, a Columbia University librarian and defender of the film, countered, "I am heartsick over the debate that I have heard over the past several days.... For we have somehow allowed the red herring of racism and the, to my mind, petty anxiety about the librarians' image to obscure the basic issue of freedom of speech in this country." Other proponents of the film suggested black members were being "overly sensitive" about the film. Richard Buck, a New York Public librarian and IFC member, was especially irritated by Josey, "who sounded like a preacher." Buck remembered Josey threatened to tear up his ALA membership card if the vote didn't go his way: "I thought, why don't you tear up your card, damnit, and never come back, go away and leave forever. That was the intensity of feeling at the time." Ultimately, was the argument over *The Speaker* about race and racial sensibilities or intellectual freedom and the First Amendment? Did racism pervade and thus negate the film's validity? Or was the charge of racism, as Darling and others suggested, a "red herring"?

On Wednesday morning, in an apparent decision to downplay or defuse the race question, members voted 385 to 197 not to consider the Black Caucus resolution, but instead to vote on Kellum-Rose's, which stressed the film's failure to explain the First Amendment and its relevance to libraries. After more than two and a half hours of bitter wrangling, the question was called. John Berry described what happened next in his account of *The Speaker* saga in Detroit entitled "The Debate Nobody Won":

> So they voted on the Kellum-Rose motion to remove ALA's name from *The Speaker*. It was a standing vote, and the tellers' count was first reported as 372 in favor of removing the ALA name, and 326 against. There was a gasp from the podium, and an embarrassed Wedgeworth said there had been an error. The actual tally was 322 for removing the ALA name, 326 against doing so. A recount changed this to 318 for removing the name, 334 against it, and so, even if they could have recalled those 150 prints [advance orders of the film sent out just days before the Detroit conference], the members voted not to do so, but the comings and goings from Cobo Hall showed that this result ... was truly inconclusive.

Yet another motion concerning *The Speaker* (called the "Sunshine" Resolution) floated around the Detroit conclave all week like a bad smell. It proposed censuring Judith Krug and the ALA Office for Intellectual Freedom for "conduct ... dangerous to the democratic process" and for "unprofessional conduct of office." Originally drafted and approved by SRRT on June 17 but rescinded three days later (why has never been entirely clear), the resolution was then submitted to the membership by Jackie Eubanks, a SRRT stalwart and strident opponent of the film. In the end, however, Eubanks's resolution was ignored and never voted on; according to a report in the *Interracial Books for Children Bulletin*, it "became a casualty of the rush of events." It's also possible Eubanks, a Brooklyn College librarian, failed to follow proper procedure when introducing the resolution. Known to friends for her motto "struggle and giggle," Eubanks, who died in 1992, had the reputation of something of a free spirit. Moon remembered that at one conference she was in charge of SRRT's hotel suite: "At the end of the week she got the bill from the hotel but instead of paying it she distributed the money to the hotel's waiters and maids and left!"

Wednesday afternoon the ALA Council met and took up *The Speaker* matter, limiting debate to 30 minutes. The Black Caucus motion to remove ALA's name from the film had been placed on the agenda and, after turning aside a move to substitute the Kellum-Rose resolution (the one narrowly defeated by the membership that morning), Council voted decisively against it. This meant that both ALA's membership and Council were now on record as supporting the controversial film. For better or for worse, *The Speaker* emerged from Detroit bearing the association's name and stamp of approval.

In an attempt at reconciliation, Ella Yates proposed that both sides get together and draft a positive statement, to be inserted in *The Speaker*'s discussion guide, clarifying the purpose of the film and explicitly disavowing any intention on the part of the film's makers to offend any racial or ethnic group. At this juncture Clara Jones, now at the end of her presidency, stepped down from the podium and spoke movingly about the pain the film had caused her and the association she led: "There is now new distrust because the black members of the association feel their humanity has been questioned ... but black people feel that their humanity is not debatable.... The film casts a pall — we have taken a backward step. Sure, ALA will survive ... but trust across racial lines has been lost here."

Yates's motion was adopted "in spirit," but angrily rejected by ALA's black leadership. Jones called the compromise "an easy cop-out" and Avery Williams, responding on behalf of the Black Caucus, said, "We have no interest in this activity. It would have little or no effect." Later Williams issued a terse formal reply, which concluded, "...mere statements *expressing* the concerns of black librarians and clarifying the *purpose* of the film are peripheral and irrelevant. Such obvious patching will neither redeem the film, appease the Black Caucus, nor restore the lost integrity of the American Library Association." Toward the end of the meeting Robert Wedgeworth told the councilors that he and the Executive Board would work to develop better oversight procedures for any similar projects ALA might undertake in the future. In other words, no more imperial subcommittees.

As the Detroit conference lurched to a close, Moon took over as president of ALA. Now *The Speaker* was his tar baby, which made him more than a little uncomfortable. His open opposition to the film irritated his friends on the other side. Mary K. Chelton, who considered herself part of the "second-generation Moon Mafiosi," remembered "lecturing Eric vehemently and pompously about *The Speaker* in some hotel conference room to his somewhat alcohol-induced bemusement." Dorothy Broderick was particularly harsh, chastising him for deserting the intellectual freedom cause and bluntly warning that his dream of a national information policy was in jeopardy. In late 1977 she sent him this note:

Dear Eric—I never thought I would have to write you a letter like this—and I just wish I knew where the Moon set that used to shine demanding librarians buy Putnam's *Race and Reason* [a once controversial pseudoscientific study of race in the Shockley mode].

Just make up your mind—give up a National Information Policy in favor of playing buddy to the Clara Jones [Joneses], or face the necessity of telling Jones and Company to go to hell and get your NIP. No way you can have both.

Moon greatly resented Broderick's "assumptions and tone" and told her so. He also told her he was "sick to death of *The Speaker*" and that "the most constructive thing we could do is forget it and get on with more productive business." These feelings helped account for the fact that Moon was not as publicly visible or out-front as many others caught up in the frenzy over the film. He felt depressed that this rotten problem should explode at precisely this time. Moon: "Because I spent so many years trying to deal with the racial problems in ALA, and then suddenly to have this—in my presidential year— blow up in my goddamn face was about as bad a thing as I can still imagine happening."

Bob Wedgeworth suggested another reason—internal conflict—for Moon's relatively muted public voice during *The Speaker* debates:

The film forced us to come to grips with intellectual freedom, but Eric did not welcome nor understand this test. Rather, he got caught in the crossfire because he was torn apart internally by his passion for civil rights on the one hand and his deep belief in intellectual freedom principles on the other. Although Eric understood *The Speaker* dilemma intellectually, he was pulled apart by it emotionally. The irony was that *The Speaker* co-opted Eric's agenda on national information policy in his great moment of triumph.

But no matter what Moon thought about *The Speaker* or how much he wished it would go away, as president of ALA he had to deal with it. His first task after the Detroit conference was to find a way to carry out Council's wish, per the Yates resolution, to add exculpatory language to the discussion guide aimed at placating black members. But black members persisted in refusing to have anything to do with what they saw as a "sop" to assuage white guilt, and at the next meeting of the Exec Board (in late July) it was determined nothing more could be done along these lines. Moon so informed Council in a letter dated August 5: "The Executive Board concluded on July 28 ... that neither the spirit nor the letter of the Yates Resolution could be implemented, and recognized that there is no alternative but to continue with the distribution of the film based on the actions of Membership and Council at the 1977 Annual Conference."

After Detroit *The Speaker* debate continued in state and regional library associations, library schools, and individual libraries around the country, many of these taking a public stand on the film, usually against it. For instance, in September the Minnesota Library Association went on record as opposing the film, declaring *The Speaker* "does not identify with sufficient clarity the issues of intellectual freedom with which it purports to be concerned." Later in the year the large and influential California Library Association rejected the film as insulting to blacks and urged ALA "to withdraw its endorsement and promotion of the film." One library educator, James Nelson at the University of Kentucky, wrote to Moon suggesting ALA produce a companion piece to *The Speaker*, "mainly as a vehicle for arbitration between the offended and offending parties who lay in the wake of our self built disaster." Moon wrote back, thanking Nelson for his idea but adding: "On reflection, though, I have to tell you that right now, I think the Board is about as likely to contemplate touching another film as it is to climb into bed with a rattlesnake."

At its fall 1977 meeting, the board again devoted hours to *The Speaker*, mostly searching for some honorable way to salve the wounds of ALA's black members. Clara Jones, still on the board as the association's immediate past president, introduced a statement from 20 distinguished black librarians offended by the film. Speaking for them, she told the board:

The American Library Association produced this film, endorsed it, and over 200 copies have been sold. [As of October 31, 1977, ALA had sold 223 of the film's 300 prints.] It's being shown all over the United States; it's going to be shown to school children now, through videotape. It would be much easier for us to leave this issue alone. It's painful. It's painful right in this room right at this moment. But if someone came into your home and invaded it and violated the members of your family you would feel that you had to stand up and defend yourself and your family. And we believe that we have been violated, that our spirit has been violated…. We too are Americans.

This film is making a statement and since it is produced and endorsed by the American Library Association, it is the American Library Association making an official statement. We do not believe that this [black inferiority] is the belief of individual members of the association. I do not believe that this is the belief of the Executive Board of the American Library Association. But it is our feeling that the members have not understood that this is a statement being made in this film. It would not be enough for you to assure me or any of your black members that you do respect their intelligence, that you respect my intelligence, to pat me on the back, to reassure me — because there that statement is. It's being made all over the country. And that is the reason we cannot ignore it. If it were not a live thing, going on and on, we could ignore it perhaps. But it is live, and it is going on and on…. It is very subtle. You know that the old signs of "Whites Only" and "No Indians and Dogs Allowed" are gone, they're down. But the subtleties are there and they are harder to deal with, much harder.

Eventually, at Jones's request, the board voted to recruit an interdisciplinary panel of experts to determine whether or not *The Speaker* "actually addresses the First Amendment." President Moon was instructed to appoint and chair an ad hoc committee to select the panel. The board also adopted a concise statement dissociating ALA from "the doctrine of racial superiority/inferiority, a concept that has long since been discredited." This statement, the board stipulated, should be "given wide dissemination" and "all purchasers [of *The Speaker*] should be asked to disseminate the statement when showing the film." Finally, the board refused to authorize anyone other than ALA to reproduce *The Speaker* in any format — this in order to limit distribution to the 300 prints originally produced. In effect, these actions by the Executive Board reopened the debate about the film.

Around this time the saga took another odd turn. Page one of the November 1977 issue of *American Libraries* announced *The Speaker* had won a Special Jury Award for Excellence at the San Francisco International Film Festival, held October 5–16. Judith Krug also trumpeted this good news in her October *Memorandum to State Intellectual Freedom Committee Chairpersons*, devoting the first two pages to the award. But Zoia

Horn — by now distrustful of anything Krug and Bobker had to say about the film — checked with the festival's sponsor, the San Francisco Council for the Performing Arts, and discovered that in fact *The Speaker* had won no such award. It had merely been listed in the festival's program as one of 214 participants; Bobker later insisted this represented a "participation award."

In their zeal to promote and sell *The Speaker*, its makers seemed willing to exaggerate, distort, and even misinform. Krug later told Horn (in a letter dated December 29, 1977) that the bogus award was an "honest mistake," but another IFC member and supporter of the film later recalled admiringly that "Judy was very good at playing innocent. She did her thing and then, with a wink, said, 'Oh my, how could this have happened?'"

Miriam Braverman, Horn's confederate, put it more bluntly: "Judy Krug was an underhanded person." *Library Journal*, in its December 15, 1977, issue, gave Krug an award of her own: "The 'grand dragon' award for ALA race relations, which consists of a boxed set of the works of William Shockley, to Judith Krug of the ALA Intellectual Freedom Office for her effort in developing and producing the ALA film *The Speaker*. This award may be cited in the promotion and sale of prints of the film." Krug's supporters were livid; Arthur Hamlin, director of libraries at Temple University, fired off a letter to *LJ*: "I was shocked at the insulting 'annual award' made by the editors ... to Judith Krug, who has been and remains an outstanding leader in intellectual freedom and other liberal causes."

All of the activity and contention involving *The Speaker* following the Detroit conference ensured it would continue to be a hot topic at the 1978 ALA Midwinter meeting in late January in Chicago. But hot became red-hot when word got out that the national media, both print and broadcast, planned to be at the conference in full force to cover the continuing rumpus over the film. Even CBS's popular *60 Minutes* television magazine program was sending a crew led by famed reporter Dan Rather to get the poop on the film that had turned freedom-loving librarians into beady-eyed censors— at least that seemed to be the media angle coming in.

In a report in *American Libraries* (March 1978), Susan Spaeth Cherry captured the circus-like atmosphere caused by the presence of so many reporters and cameras at the conference:

> The Palmer House State Ballroom resembled a scene from *Close Encounters of the Third Kind* as the Council meeting convened. Under dazzling TV floodlights and crystal chandeliers, camera crews from local television stations scurried about with space-age hardware. CBS "60 Minutes" reporter Dan Rather mingled with Council members and studied *American Libraries*, getting background material for a feature on *The Speaker* to be aired in February or March. Newspaper reporters flitted between the Council chamber and ALA's pressroom, setting up interviews with key *Speaker* advocates and opponents. Their articles later appeared in Chicago's three major dailies and on the *Los Angeles Times* wire service, supplementing *Speaker* coverage on local NBC, ABC, and CBS television stations.

Naturally the cameras stimulated a certain amount of showboating and rhetorical wind in the ballroom. John Berry (in *LJ*, April 1, 1978) described the jockeying for face time among some of the players in *The Speaker* drama:

The rush to the microphones was like the stampede in a Merrill-Lynch "bullish on America" commercial. The lineup was predictable: all the ALA Councillors you can always count on to bombast a meeting. By actual count, Eli Oboler basked in the TV lights six times, just beating out rising IFC star Richard Buck, who scored only five appearances at the microphone. Dorothy Broderick was an unwilling third with four TV shots, and Clara Jones and Kathleen Molz tied for fourth place with three appearances each. The award for best actor has to go to Broderick playing Broderick, but Oboler, who had been uncharacteristically quiet about the film until CBS showed up with cameras, played his role as "old curmudgeon for freedom" with verve.

Moon presided over the meeting, which he remembered as the toughest chairing assignment of his career:

The meeting was in a large ballroom full of people — maybe 2,000 to 3,000 people were there — and the whole meeting was conducted under the lights of the cameras of *60 Minutes*. Dan Rather's crew was there because they had heard about *The Speaker* and they expected some big explosion was going to come at this meeting. It was the most difficult meeting I ever chaired in my life.

I'm fairly good, I think, at chairing meetings — I know the procedures and I read people fairly well, and I try to inject a little humor here and there to keep the thing from growing rabid, but I couldn't see the audience at all because of the spotlights. I went down at 7:00 in the morning when they were setting up the room and I looked at this and I said to the guys, "You're not going to have these lights on all the time, are you? I've got to read this audience if I'm going to control the meeting." And they said, yes, they had to keep them on all the time, the lights take too long to warm up if switched off and on.

So the meeting was conducted that way, and I had to have people down front checking microphones for me, so I would know which order to call, because people get very pissed off if they have been at a microphone for half an hour and you keep calling other microphones and they don't get called. So we were handing out slips with the order — Microphone 7, 8, 3, 10, and so on. We had to conduct the meeting that way. It was really wild.

Dan Rather wanted to interview Moon for the *60 Minutes* segment, but it never happened. By this time Moon was in no mood to discuss *The Speaker*, which he likened to flogging a sick horse: "Rather was doing interviews with people all week in Chicago. He asked to interview me and I said I didn't want to talk with him about this film but if he wanted to talk about some of the major issues that we were concerned with in ALA I'd be glad to do an interview. So he didn't interview me at all. The ALA PR office asked me for other names to give Rather to interview — I know I gave him Zoia Horn as one, and Clara and some others."

Specific issues concerning *The Speaker* tended to get lost in the media glare at the Midwinter conference, but Council did manage to undo most of what the Executive Board had decided at its fall 1977 meeting. First, Council rescinded the board's decision to deny permission to outside groups to reproduce *The Speaker* in any format. Wedgeworth noted the issue grew out of a request by two school systems to videotape the film. Moon explained the board voted to deny such requests because no one knew how the schools intended to use the film, and there was a strong desire to avoid "exacerbating an already difficult, sensitive, and hurtful situation." But a majority of councilors disagreed, voting to allow the film to be reproduced. Council also rescinded the board's decision to establish a panel of experts to determine if *The Speaker* was indeed about the First Amendment. The general attitude was, let's not open up that can of worms. Council did, however, approve the board's statement on racial superiority/inferiority intended to accompany showings of the film.

The Midwinter session ended with a conciliatory gesture by Dorothy Broderick. After acknowledging "the deep hurt and rage" caused by *The Speaker*, Broderick asked councilors to stand and demonstrate "respect, love, and admiration" for ALA's black members. "Amid applause, the councilors stood," reported *American Libraries*, "but later a few councilors objected to their love and respect being 'legislated' in this manner." Actually, many anti-film people were put off by Broderick's heavy-handed attempt at reconciliation. Moon recalled, "Dorothy gave a disastrous speech at the end of the Midwinter session on *The Speaker*. She was trying to heal the breach somewhat but what she said completely offended those she was trying to appease."

The Speaker controversy refused to die, persisting on into the winter and spring of 1978. More library groups went on record opposing the film. The Schenectady (New York) County Public Library and the Mohawk Valley Library Association jointly resolved that the film "does not carry out the initial intent of the American Library Association to produce a film on the First Amendment," and the library science faculty of the University of Toronto gave the film an emphatic thumbs down: "Social irresponsibility has no place in librarianship." On the pro–*Speaker* side, Thomas I. Emerson, renowned Yale University Law School authority on the First Amendment, praised the film for achieving "one of the fundamental objectives of the First Amendment, which is to make us think about difficult issues and make up our own minds about them."

On Sunday evening, April 2, 1978, CBS broadcast the *60 Minutes* piece on *The Speaker*. The 15-minute report displeased *Speaker* opponents, who accused Rather of bias in favor of the film and its supporters. One group of black librarians sent CBS a strongly worded protest, calling the segment "a hatchet job" and "a travesty of fair reporting practices and ethics." Moon had much the same reaction:

I thought the *60 Minutes* piece was very disappointing because it did not use much of the material from Clara and Zoia. Zoia, I think, never appeared in the report on television and Clara only very briefly. Among the disturbing stories I heard was that when Zoia was interviewed by Rather, she said to him, "Well, Mr. Rather, you're asking me a lot of questions. I'd like to ask you one: Do you think this is a racist film?" And Rather said, according to Zoia, "Yes, I think it is." But when he reported on *60 Minutes* it came out exactly the opposite. So there are some of us who are not great admirers of Mr. Rather.

Though echoes of the acerbic debate continued for many more months (and even years), by the time ALA's annual conference rolled around in June 1978 the uproar over *The Speaker* had largely subsided. Everything that could be said had been said at least a dozen times, and most people were thoroughly tired of the whole business. Various efforts to sever the association's connection with the film had failed, as had attempts to censure or fire Judy Krug; *LJ* reported in its September 1, 1978, issue that "Krug seems to have weathered the storm." But the wounds, the anger, the bitterness remained, often just below the surface.

The Speaker: *Bitter Fruit*

It is impossible to know the full extent of the personal and professional harm done by *The Speaker* incident, but certainly, as Clara Jones once remarked, there were "no winners in the ordeal":

- The American Library Association — ripped apart by the film's offensive racial theme — was a loser;

- The Office for Intellectual Freedom — its image as a fighter against censorship soiled by the undemocratic, intellectually dishonest tactics used to produce and sell the film — was a loser;

- The Intellectual Freedom Committee — complicit in the production of the film — was a loser;

- E.J. Josey — told by Eli Oboler at one point "to shut your black nigger mouth" — was a loser;

- Dorothy Broderick — called a "bigot" by many members of the Black Caucus — was a loser;

- Clara Jones — forced as ALA's first black president to preside over a conference focused on the humiliating premise that black people are genetically inferior — was a loser;

- Zoia Horn — shunned by most members of the IFC during the year of *The Speaker* and called names behind her back — was a loser;

- Miriam Braverman — ditto Horn — was a loser;

- Robert Wedgeworth — perceived by many as ineffectual and "lacking leadership" in his handling of *The Speaker* affair — was a loser;

- Judith Krug — who during the course of getting the film approved, financed, produced, and distributed deliberately withheld information from those entitled to it, deceived the association's elected president, and used shady promotional tactics — was a loser;

- Eric Moon — his long-shot attempt to forge a national information policy engulfed and some say destroyed by the uproar over the film — was a loser.

As for *The Speaker* itself — another loser: a celluloid dirty trick. Years later, after he was retired, Moon reflected on the fate of the film: "The film fortunately seems to have gone to another place and one doesn't hear much about it anymore. My opinion, without much evidence, is that the film never really made any money for ALA. In fact it may have made a loss. I hope that is true, because I think ALA deserved to lose on this business. But I don't really know. The film is still shown occasionally but as far as I know it's no longer for sale." (A check with ALA in 2001 confirms *The Speaker* is no longer available for purchase, though it can be borrowed through the OIF for viewing by interested parties.)

National Information Policy Lost

In November 1977 the ad hoc committee Moon had appointed to draft a national information policy completed its work. Guided firmly but fairly by chairman David Kaser, the drafting committee produced a 12-page document entitled *Toward a Conceptual Foundation for a National Information Policy* that called for "free and equitable access to information" for all Americans, regardless of economic or social status. This "right," stated the document, "is not new in the American social ethic, but has, rather, been the lodestar of the American public library movement for almost a century and a half." It continued:

The nation's advancing social requirements and technical capabilities during that time, however, have resulted in vast changes in the nature of libraries, so that today they embrace not only traditional repositories of print materials but also computer-based data stores, information and reference centers, film and tape collections and services, and other similarly diverse activities, many of which are more costly to operate than were their less-complex predecessors. Whatever their cost should ultimately become, however, the cost to the nation of not so providing information to its inhabitants seems certain to be higher.

The nation must therefore reaffirm its mandate to its publicly supported libraries to seek out and deliver to all people the information they need or desire, as well in the newer, more expensive modes as in the older, more traditional ways. For out of information comes knowledge, and out of knowledge comes wisdom, and those nations that determine their actions most wisely seem destined the longest to endure.

The Kaser committee document concluded with a strong pitch for "sufficient" public support — especially federal funds— to meet these lofty goals. Moon was eager to have the ideas expressed in the document adopted as the official position of the library profession prior to the much anticipated White House Conference on Library and Information Services, scheduled to convene in 1979. As a first step in this process he invited the presidents of four other major information-oriented associations— Audrey Grosch of the American Society for Information Science (ASIS; later called the American Society for Information and Technology, or ASIST); William Grady of the Association of Educational Communications and Technology (AECT); Gilbert Clausman of the Medical Library Association (MLA); and Shirley Echelman of the Special Libraries Association (SLA)— to respond to the Kaser committee document at the president's program at the 1978 ALA Midwinter meeting in Chicago.

That meeting took place on Wednesday evening, January 25, before a generally apathetic audience of about a thousand ALA members. The day before, media coverage of *The Speaker* controversy, replete with the bright lights of *60 Minutes*, had brought drama and excitement to the conference proceedings. National information policy, on the other hand, commanded no such attention: there were no TV cameras, no reporters panting for interviews, no conga lines of librarians waiting impatiently at microphones to offer their two cents on the subject. *The Speaker* was hot, information policy was not. And Moon's presidential program got downright frosty as one by one his invited guests shot holes in the Kaser committee's work.

Grosch from ASIS, objecting mainly to the document's emphasis on free services, noted that "The post-industrial society has brought us to the point where information services may be viewed much like educational services, legal services, or other socially related services provided through both the public and private sectors. A certain amount may be obtained through tax supported programs, but beyond that, the rest must be supported through individual or institutional sources." Grady of AECT was skeptical about how the document's proposals could be translated into "plans of action." And, while conceding the importance of access to information, he wondered if "perhaps a more crucial issue facing us today is better utilization of the information resources we already have.... This will become increasingly more important as we find our dollars buying less." The MLA's Clausman, echoing Grosch, suggested the document was too idealistic: "Librarians would like to provide free service, so that the poor as well as the rich are given equal information service. But the reality is that library budgets cannot continually absorb these high costs." Neither Grosch nor Clausman mentioned the f-word—fees—but that's obviously what they had in mind.

Shirley Echelman of SLA, speaking last, offered the harshest assessment of the document. Among her complaints:

The document is not a statement of policy, but a political manifesto for public libraries. It barely recognizes other kinds of libraries and their contributions to information service—academic and school libraries, as well as special libraries. Worse than this oversight, it ignores completely the vast importance of other information resources, such as television, newspapers, and radio, which supply a far greater proportion of information on a day-by-day basis than libraries do, in formats that are much more easily accessible to the public at large.

The document, while being political in nature itself, recognizes neither the political nor economic realities of our society. It takes a simplistic view of societal priorities. If it becomes an official statement of either ALA or of several associations, it stands little chance of being taken seriously by the federal policy makers for whom we must assume it is ultimately intended.

The language of the document is inexact, and will certainly cause misunderstanding and misinterpretation.... A statement ripe for misinterpretation appears on page 8—"An information-elite is a power-elite, neither of which has any place in a democracy." If this means what it seems to mean, the document contemplates changes much more far-reaching than anything having to do only with libraries, and if that is what the writers intend, they ought to be a lot clearer about just what they have in mind.... I would like to say that the document suffers greatly, if not terminally, from a linguistic disease which I call "academo-bureaucratise," and should be submitted forthwith to Edwin Newman [a language maven] for treatment.

Librarians attending the meeting had little demonstrable reaction to the presentations or the proposed information policy itself and those who did seemed to agree with its critics. Some members of the Kaser committee were taken aback by the barrage of negative comments leveled at their handiwork. Fay Blake, an ardent proponent of free library service for all and major shaper of the document, was "devastated" by the criticisms:

Working on the Kaser committee was fun because its members were bright and diverse and articulate. But it came to an ignominious end. Naively, I hadn't expected that the drive of the profit motive was so strong and that private enterprise had already permeated the ALA so intensely. When Eric offered the committee's report for comment by special library types, they fell on it like hungry harpies. We had proposed that publicly funded libraries (public, school, university) make themselves responsible for providing information to everyone and that they be adequately funded to do so by public monies. The roof fell in! Business, corporations, private universities, medical libraries in hospitals for profit were all lined up panting at the trough and ready to provide information to everyone — who could afford the fees. The audience was worse. Those who weren't sitting like toadstools that had sprouted in the night, lapped up the elitist, undemocratic, inhumane arguments.

Later in the year a brief but savage attack on the Kaser committee document appeared in *LJ* (June 1, 1978) in a two-page article jeeringly titled "Midwinter Night's Dream or The Origin of Specious." The article's authors, Patrick Williams and Joan Thornton Pearce, pulled no punches: "We should say at the outset of this analysis that this document does not provide a conceptual foundation for anything. It is arrant nonsense and deserves to be repudiated as quickly and emphatically as possible." They viewed the draft document as little more than a crass ploy to wheedle more public funds for libraries:

The purpose all along was to associate information, democracy and libraries in a demand for cash…. It is easy to see that large quantities of money are called for. In order to convince legislators that the need is urgent, the authors have produced an irrational and ulterior fantasy. Its purpose is to persuade legislators that a vote against library support is a vote against democracy and fulfillment. This murky and confusing document is not harmless. Nor is it redeemed in any way by its arrogant pseudo-democratic tone. The document is embarrassing and makes the library profession look foolish.

The negative reception accorded the Kaser committee statement essentially doomed Moon's ambitious information policy initiative, though he undertook several damage-control measures after the Midwinter debacle, the most apparent being the appointment of a new ad hoc committee, chaired by Maurice Freedman (then a Columbia University library school professor), to redraft the original document with an eye to getting it "into shape for adoption by Council as an official ALA policy statement." This was very much a Moon pipe dream and of course never happened. In the end, he had miscalculated the immensity of the task as well as the strength of the opposition. Moreover, all the commotion created by *The Speaker* added significantly to the difficulty. Moon:

I set the document up as a dummy to be fired at at the Midwinter meeting that year and invited speakers from four associations to come in and shoot it down, in order to create discussion. The committee said, what are you doing to us? You're just putting us up on the firing line for people to shoot at, and I said, that's the idea, we want to see how people react to it; that might enable you to reshape it and hone it further. But we never really got anywhere — it was too complex to be dealt with, and with all that was going on with that film we never could get that kind of focus. So national information policy got sidetracked. Tom Galvin in fact brought much more focus to it in his presidency [1979–1980] but I don't think he had the kind of automatic support that I had in some areas, so it never really went anywhere, and it died.

Over the years many people came to believe and often repeated as fact the supposition that *The Speaker* controversy was solely or at least largely responsible for snuffing out

Moon's effort to produce a progressive national information policy the entire library profession could embrace. Moon himself believed the film was mainly to blame for destroying the effort: "The whole week of the Midwinter conference was disrupted by the presence of *60 Minutes*— it was a big event, Dan Rather was there, television cameras were there, and getting attention on anything else was virtually impossible. The debate over the film continued and escalated all through my presidency, which is one of the major reasons why I could not get any association work focused on national information policy. I believe it was killed by *The Speaker*."

Gerry Shields, a former ALA insider who was actively involved in these battles, suggested a fascinating scenario in support of the notion that *The Speaker* was the instrument that murdered Moon's information policy proposal:

Why the film project was allowed to proceed without the Executive Board having seen a proposal, an outline of the plot (at least), and a method of jobbing out the production makes one wonder. It is no secret that when Eric was editor of *LJ* he was not a favored son of the ALA Establishment (although there were members in that club who knew and liked him, they did not go out of their way to make a crusade of their position). Also, it is no secret that ALA was looking the other way on the conduct of NCLIS, taking the prone position that any agency is better than none at all no matter how partisan it may be. I assume there was consternation that Eric was interested in creating a national information policy. I can almost see the scurrying around looking under rugs for hidden motives for his agenda — all this abetted by a fear of offending NCLIS when attempts were being made to fund a White House conference.

One would like to let one's paranoia run rampant here and say that *The Speaker* was seized upon as a way to block any such attempt to forge a national coalition leading to a policy consensus. That would be fanciful indulgence. However, it can be said that when the preview of the film in Detroit [in June 1977] demonstrated that it was a highly fanciful interpretation of real-life First Amendment issues couched in the cant of the Office for Intellectual Freedom, the film was seized upon as a diversion from the very real issue Eric was trying to introduce. The resultant sideshow was a good demonstration of how ALA is an emotion-driven body able to produce bread and circuses for a handful (2,000) of its vocal membership so that the real power base (publishers) can see that only those issues of their making manage to surface.

Well, perhaps. A more likely, though less intriguing, explanation for why Moon's national information policy failed is that, because it incorporated his extreme egalitarian — some might say socialist — position on library fees and funding, it never stood a chance, especially given the conservative political and economic climate of the mid–1970s. Indeed, Moon never hid his fundamental believe that libraries "are among the preeminent examples of socialist thought and activity" in the American experience.

Unlucky Presidency

The American Library Association returned home to Chicago for its 1978 annual conference, with some members (including Moon) arriving as early as Thursday, June 22, and some (including Moon) staying through Saturday, July 1. This was Moon's presidential conference, featuring his theme, "Toward a National Information Policy," and his program, which included speeches by television newsman Daniel Schorr, media critic Ben Bagdikian, and innovative British library administrator D.J. Urquhart. Ironically, just as *The Speaker* stole the spotlight the previous year at the Detroit conference, California's Proposition 13, a draconian tax-cutting measure that presaged dire consequences for libraries, was the big racket at the 1978 Chicago conference. Poor Moon! He had been so lucky in his professional life up until the time he became ALA president. Then almost everything he touched seemed to go awry, spin out of control, turn to ashes. Lucky Eric all of a sudden became unlucky President Moon, hobbled throughout much of his term by *The Speaker* morass and now blindsided by California's Prop 13. Fumed Moon in a report to the ALA Council in Chicago: "We should have launched already— and certainly should not delay beginning beyond this week—a massive effort, through ALA, through our chapters, through alliances with other associations and unions whose members and the services they supply are in similar jeopardy—an effort to inform and persuade the public of the full and disastrous consequences of their emotional response to ill-considered populist campaigns of this kind." Poor Moon! Constantly off balance, constantly on the defensive. It was an unaccustomed posture for a man of his activist disposition.

And prior to the Chicago conference he suffered yet another frustrating setback. A year and half earlier, then in the full flush of winning the presidency, Moon set his cap on getting the newly elected U.S. president, Jimmy Carter, to be his main speaker at the Chicago conference. Part of the reason he chose national information policy as his theme was Carter's documented interest in libraries. In his inaugural speech in Detroit, Moon described the new American president in glowing terms. Carter was someone, enthused Moon,

who started his career of public service as a library trustee, who came out of Georgia with a record of support for education and libraries, who talked constantly of the need to communicate with the people, of public access to information. After years of not so benign neglect, here, we have to hope, is an opportunity to make ourselves heard, to stem the tide of degradation of our facilities and our collections; for us to lay claim to the significant contributions this profession has made, and can make, to the health, education and welfare of this nation.

In meetings and communications with the Kaser committee and others during the latter half of 1977 and early 1978, Moon constantly referred to his invitation to President Carter to speak at the ALA conference and of sending the president material "as background for his address in Chicago." When the Kaser committee completed its work, Moon promptly sent Carter a copy of the document. Getting Carter to speak at ALA and, more important, getting the president's ear in advance of the 1979 White House Conference, were crucial to Moon's grand strategy for having his vision of a national information policy eventually adopted by the fledgling Carter administration. In order to achieve his goal of "sufficient" federal support for libraries, Moon felt he had to get to President Carter before the NCLIS bureaucrats and greedy representatives of the increasingly powerful commercial information industry got there.

But like so much he attempted as president, Moon's efforts to bring Carter to Chicago in June 1978 failed. He kept trying almost to the end, giving up only a few weeks before the conference:

I wanted as my main speaker for the president's program, number one, Jimmy Carter. Jimmy was president of the U.S. but he had also started political life as a library trustee. I was extremely interested in having him. Bob Wedgeworth said the problem with getting someone like that is you're always in danger that at the last moment something else will come up and they won't be able to make it. We worked on getting Carter for quite a long time but never got a firm commitment from the Carter people. We kept the door open for as long as we could, but when we still had no commitment two or three weeks from the convention, I gave up.

To fill the void he turned to Ben Bagdikian, renowned author and journalism professor (University of California–Berkeley) whom he had met through Zoia Horn and her husband Dean Galloway. Moon recalled, "It got to the point where there was only a couple of weeks left before the conference, so I said unless there's a breakthrough during the next 24 hours, I have to find somebody who will do it on very short notice, who is a name, someone important. So I turned to a friend, Ben Bagdikian, who became one of three speakers at my three presidential programs, and he was marvelous, as always. Ben talked about the concentration of power among the providers of information, which fit well with my theme."

Still, not getting Carter was a major disappointment and in hindsight dealt the coup de grâce to his national information policy dreams. The previous year's big disappointment, the bloody fight over *The Speaker*, was not much in evidence at the Chicago conference, at least on the surface. The IFC scheduled four hours of "hearings" on Saturday, June 24, but they caused little stir, there really being nothing new to be said on the subject. Nevertheless, the deep divisions caused by the film hung over the conference like a threatening cloud, and as time ran out on his presidency, Moon insisted the film was chiefly to blame for "why my presidential year was a write-off." By the summer of 1978 he was also feeling dyspeptic about the cost of the ALA presidency, which had taken an enormous toll on his time, energy, and emotions. Al Daub believed the experience hastened his retirement from Scarecrow at the end of 1978. In addition, Moon spent an estimated $16,000 of his own money on the presidency.

He vented his feelings of disappointment, frustration, and anger in a brief farewell speech at the Chicago conference's banquet on Thursday evening, June 29. (The banquet featured the installation of Russell Shank as Moon's successor. Shank had become vice president/president-elect in 1977, beating out F. William Summers and petition candidate Dorothy Broderick, who got very little support from the Moon Mafia and other social activists, punishment for acting like "a shit" during *The Speaker* wars.) Moon's speech, which has never been published in full, was not the typical presidential farewell: "I did not give the usual kind of speech at the end of the presidency. They always go out saying how much they've enjoyed this and what a pleasure and honor it's been. I didn't intend to say those things—I did not enjoy it, my year was wrecked by this film, and it was a very painful experience."

Rarely if ever had Eric Moon been as emotionally naked in public as he was that evening in Chicago:

I want to say that it has been an honor to hold this position and to try to serve you. I wish I could add that it has been a pleasure. But despite many marvelous moments and the opportunities it gave me to meet again many old friends around the country and to acquire some new ones, it has been generally, for me personally, a frustrating, often depressing year. I have *not* enjoyed presiding over an association rent asunder by anger and hurt and insensitivity to a degree that I have not witnessed since some of our most bitter battles during the early 1960s.

I have *not* enjoyed seeing some of my closest friends and colleagues attacked, vilified, embarrassed, and slighted. And copies of some of the correspondence that have come my way can only be described as shameful. Moreover, my program and the emphasis and impetus I tried to give to a matter I believe to be of great importance to the future of libraries and library service were constantly overwhelmed by the hoopla surrounding a film and its making.... I can only hope for his and the association's sake that all of the "speakers" Russell [Shank] will have to deal with will be standing at microphones in this hall. Thank you very much.

Apparently in his mind Moon made no mistakes during this difficult time. None of the problems that transpired were due to errors or miscalculations on his part. Fault and blame in Moon's universe always rested with others, never himself. It was the mark of a truly confident — and egocentric — personality.

Presidential Perks

But not everything went wrong during Moon's presidential year. Among "the many marvelous moments" he experienced during his term as ALA's chief elected officer was the opportunity to meet famous mystery writer John D. MacDonald and influence the drinking habits of the author's legendary creation, Travis McGee. Moon:

Although Joe Lippincott [the publisher] didn't like me much, he did invite me to one party during my presidential year. It was a little party for John D. MacDonald, and it was during this party that I told MacDonald that I had read most of the Travis McGee novels on the beach during the summer. I said I liked them a lot, but... MacDonald said, "I knew there was a 'but' coming." So I asked him why McGee has to have such lousy taste. And MacDonald said, "What do you mean — lousy taste?" I said, "If there's one thing I know something about it's gin, and you have him drinking this rotgut gin, Plymouth, which no intelligent, self-respecting man like Travis McGee would drink." I told MacDonald that both my wife and Robbie Franklin had bought me bottles of this gin the previous Christmas, because they knew I was such a Travis McGee fan, and the stuff was AWFUL. He asked which I thought was the best gin and I said, "No question, Bombay and Boodles. Tanqueray's a poor third, and nothing else really counts."

That's not quite the end of the story. After being in retirement in Florida for about a month, Ted Waller called and asked, "Have you seen the latest MacDonald?" I said no. Ted said he had a copy and he sent it to me. On about page 15, Travis McGee has switched to Boodles! So I figure I have made an impact on American literature, if only in a very minor way.

Moon also took pleasure in his presidential program at the Chicago conference, even though he couldn't get Jimmy Carter: "Since I was dealing with information policy, the three speakers — Bagdikian, Schorr, and Urquhart — seemed to fit perfectly, and that

was my presidential program. It was really a pleasant part of the presidency. I got in people I liked and admired and we had time to spend together." He especially got a kick out
of racing around Chicago with Schorr in pursuit of a breaking story:

Dan Schorr and I were picked up at the hotel and we were supposed to be driven in this
limousine over to the Chicago Public Library where ALA was having a big reception for the
president and speakers and so on. As we got into the limo Dan said, "I've got to ask the driver
to take a diversion because there's a big demonstration going on in this area involving Rabbi
Kahane, the right-wing Jewish rabbi, and a march by the Nazis, and there are thousands of
cops over there. I'm still a reporter and I can't pass up something like this."

So he directed the limo over to this area and we run into barricades and cops, and the cops
tried to stop the limo but Schorr holds out his press pass and says "Press" but the cop says
you're still not coming through here, so Schorr gets out of the limo, and I said, "You're not
going without me — you're my speaker. I'm hanging on to you." So we plowed into the crowd
and people recognized Schorr and waved to him. The scene was fairly hairy with the Nazis
and the Rabbi's followers. We were around there for a fairly long time and eventually we left.
All the others had gone on to the reception — the only two people who weren't there were the
president and his speaker! We got there just in time for the program, but missed most of the
reception. It was one of those amusing, unexpected events that come up.

Moon also enjoyed the social aspects of being president, he and Ilse working hand
in glove to make people feel comfortable, whatever the occasion:

There are I don't know how many different functions the president puts on, such as luncheons and dinners, and there was a young woman in Bob Wedgeworth's executive office who
was sort of turned over to me as an assistant to help with all of this. I said to her, "You
haven't done any of this before, have you?" She said, "No, but it's very exciting." I said, "Well,
you'll learn how exciting it's going to be because you are going to be solely responsible for all
of these luncheons, four, five, or six of them — you will pick the menus, you will arrange the
rooms, you will do it all with no interference from me. Only on one thing are you required to
confer, and that is the seating. Confer with Ilse on this. I do not want old antagonists seated
next to each other and so on, and Ilse knows enough of the characters and the politics to
avoid any problems — all else you're in charge. Afterward, she said how much she enjoyed
consulting with Ilse on the seating arrangements because she didn't know all this political "in"
stuff.

And what was Moon's greatest satisfaction during his "painful" year as president?

I suppose it was the party given for me on the night when my presidency ended and Russ
Shank was inaugurated [Thursday evening, June 29]. It was something that had been planned
without my knowledge and took place in my suite. Ilse of course was involved in the planning; everybody was in on it except me. It was a kind of interesting setup, although if you
don't know the hotel it's kind of hard to picture. The Chicago Hilton has on top of its two
wings, if you look at it at a distance across Michigan Avenue, what look like two little concrete boxes that sort of face each other. I had one of these and Bob Wedgeworth had the other.
We had a shared lobby, so when you came off the elevators you went left to Wedgeworth's
suite, right to mine.

Now there was also a party in Wedgeworth's suite for Russ Shank, the incoming president
and all of the bigwigs had been invited to that. I was not there at the beginning, I was tied up
somewhere. But I was told that when people got off the elevators, they were all being directed

to Wedgeworth's suite. After a time, someone at the Wedgeworth suite looked over at the Moon suite and said, "Doesn't seem to be much going on over there," and another person replied, "Well, this is the Senate and that's just the House of Representatives."

Later, I arrived and found much to my surprise the party for me, and soon after Mitch Freedman arrived with all the music equipment; Mitch is a fiend at that stuff. And in no time at all there was rock 'n' roll going on in my suite with people dancing all over the place and the parties began to reverse — everybody began coming over to my suite. Now I had heard this earlier story and I said to someone, "Look's as though the Senate is thinning out a bit, doesn't it?" So many people came and said so many nice things to me. That had to be the time I felt best, because I had really been feeling kind of down because of all the things that had happened.

– 15 –

Taking Sherry at
Westminster Abbey

Traveling Man

The presidency of the American Library Association offered yet another fringe benefit: the opportunity to travel around the country and overseas representing the association and, by extension, American librarianship. Moon did not accept every invitation that came his way, preferring to pick his spots. He explained:

As president you do get a lot of invitations to speak. I did not fulfill many of these because I hate to speak anyway and I was too busy running the presidency and Scarecrow. Unlike, say, the director of a large library, I did not have a large staff to help out. So I did not do much of that. I asked Clara [Jones], as past president, who loved to go out and do speeches, to do many of them. She was terrific at it. And when Russ [Shank] came on board as president-elect, I asked him to do some of them.

I did go to a few. I decided that among those I would accept would be those from small or remote states or states that did not normally receive presidential visits. I accepted one from Maine, I remember. I went to Maine and I must say I've never been received like that anywhere I've ever been. They were absolutely ecstatic that I agreed to accept their invitation, saying, "Do you realize that you are the first ALA president in a hundred years to come to Maine?" They feted me. That was nice.

In addition to selected engagements in the United States, Moon led two ALA delegations abroad during his presidential year, the first to celebrate the 50th anniversary of the International Federation of Library Associations and Institutions in Brussels, and the second to participate in the centennial (or "centenary") conference of the Library Association in London. The IFLA affair turned out to be a modern day version of innocents abroad, the naif Americans outmaneuvered and outvoted by the more worldly Europeans, whereas the LA conference, which featured a major address by Moon, revealed American librarians at their best — idealistic, dynamic, diverse, democratic, progressive.

The IFLA World Congress

With President Moon at the head of the pack, a large ALA contingent attended IFLA's 50th World Congress in Brussels during the week of September 5–10, 1977. The group included Bob Wedgeworth, Dick Dougherty (a candidate for the IFLA Executive Board), Doralyn Hickey, Frank Schick, S. Michael Malinconico, Virginia Young (of ALA trustee fame), Pat Schuman, Arthur Curley, Ilse Moon, and E.J. Josey, who as chair of ALA's International Relations Committee that year had a key role in formulating U.S. policy at the IFLA Congress. Despite this array of library talent, the Americans made a dim showing in Brussels, being generally unprepared, confused, and uncertain about IFLA's customs and rules of governance, which were vastly different from ALA's. Shirley Havens covered the conference for *LJ*; her report appeared in the December 15, 1977, issue. It read in part:

Prior to the opening of the ceremonial Congress, the IFLA Council held its annual meeting to deal with business matters. Two major items on the agenda were the election of a new Executive Board and an increase in membership dues…. The dues increase for associations passed easily, but the increase for institutional members, especially in developing countries, was hotly contested. Whether through a lack of political acumen or a desire to march to their own drummers, the U.S. delegates appeared to be completely disorganized on this issue. Not only did they vote against each other, but many ended up supporting what was considered an unsubstantiated increase [32%], hitting hardest in the developing countries. The U.S. also lost its representation on the Executive Board by failing to develop sufficient backing—both internationally and institutionally—for its candidate, Richard Dougherty.

In subsequent coverage Havens branded the American performance at IFLA a "debacle." Part of the problem appeared to stem from Moon's dismissive attitude toward IFLA, which he considered a moribund, autocratic organization operated as a fiefdom by pompous Europeans: "In general I thought IFLA stuffy, dull, and under the control of a small, elite, European power group, and I've never thought it a very useful organization. I never attended again, but many ALA presidents seem to love it and make a second career out of it." Among these was Robert Vosper, whom Moon criticized for becoming an IFLA swell:

I was very friendly with Bob Vosper in the early years of the 1960s, as was Esh [Bill Eshelman]. Vosper seemed to me to be one of the better, more creative librarians in the country and he was politically progressive on the race issue. At some point, however, he began to change. I remember Vosper as the kind of guy who in the days of the ALA banquet when all the other men on the platform would be in tuxedos, Vosper would be in a sports jacket. I approved of that mightily. But then he became the stuffiest of them all when he became involved in the international circuit and IFLA, as so many past presidents of ALA do. He got enamored with things like the Royal Library of Denmark and the whole panoply. The international library community is a great clique.

For the Moons the IFLA excursion was redeemed by a side trip to Amsterdam where they "had a couple of wonderful evenings with E.J." Also, Moon recalled, there was a "grand dinner in Brussels at one of Europe's top restaurants. Pat [Schuman] had made reservations from the States months ahead and about a dozen of us were at the dinner.

But not Ilse, who was sick and confined to bed in the hotel." A dutiful husband, Eric tried to comfort his ailing spouse by bringing her a token from the restaurant, but his best intentions backfired. He relished telling the tragicomic story:

All through the festive dinner I was feeling terrible about Ilse's absence, particularly since no one enjoys a fine meal more than she. So as things drew to a close at the restaurant I called the sommelier over and asked him to let me have a couple of bottles of the best champagne he had in the house. Then I pressed all the gang present to come back to the hotel where we'd party and cheer Ilse up. I forgot one thing: glasses! Since Ilse was so infectious she could not swig out of the bottle like the rest of us. She just lay in bed and fumed — madder than ever. And who could blame her?

Moon added this footnote: "On reflection this doesn't make much sense, even though Ilse and everyone else remembers it that way. But why weren't there some glasses in the bathroom? And if there were not, why didn't I call room service? Just too sozzled, or what?"

The LA Centenary Conference

A month later, in early October 1977, Moon was off again, this time shepherding a distinguished group of American librarians to London to take part in the Library Association's centenary conference, held at the Royal Festival Hall and the city's South Bank Centre. The U.S. delegation comprised most of ALA's top elected officials along with Executive Director Wedgeworth. Moon recalled, "Bob Wedgeworth and Clara Jones and I decided that it was important to have a strong American delegation there, since it was an historic occasion. Apparently at the first LA conference [in 1877] there had been a big American delegation present."

Ilse, fully recovered from her illness in Brussels, accompanied Eric on the trip. She remembered how pleasantly it began, thanks to Ted Waller's thoughtfulness: "Ted did little niceties, like having orchids sent to me at the airport when we were going to England." Once in London the Americans "had a pretty good time," said Moon, lapsing into British understatement. On the first day of the conference (Monday, October 3) the Moons were invited to "take sherry" with Sir Frederick Dainton, the LA's president that year, in the Jerusalem Chamber of Westminster Abbey after a service of thanksgiving. Though he had lived and worked in London and environs for nearly ten years prior to emigrating to North America, this was Moon's first visit to England's most famous church:

Sir Frederick had this little reception in this room [Jerusalem Chamber] in Westminster Abbey. There had been a very beautiful religious ceremony in the Abbey itself to which we were all invited. I had never been in Westminister Abbey myself. I remember Ilse and I were sitting with Bob Wedgeworth right up front — it was an incredibly formal but rather beautiful occasion. Then we had sherry with Sir Frederick, who was not a librarian but related to the profession because of the Dainton Commission Report on British libraries issued some years earlier.

The next day the Moons joined Sir Frederick and other dignitaries for lunch following the conference's inaugural session, and that evening there was a display of British pageantry at a reception for LA members and their guests at the City of London's Guildhall. Moon never forget it:

It was a marvelous night at the Guildhall. This was invitation only. There were two kinds of invitations—the top people were ushered to a certain door, where they had to wait to be announced, and when announced you marched across this huge hall with pikemen down either side—the pikes [weapons with pointed steel heads on long wooden shafts] were 20 feet high, and at the end standing in the middle was the Lord Mayor of London with the most incredible chain around him. He looked as though he were wearing 20 million bucks. So we were announced and marched down; we shook hands with the Lord Mayor and I touched this thing he was wearing. I said, "That is some dangler you have there, Mr. Mayor," and he said, "You'd better get your hands off it, son, or you'll get one of those pikes up your ass," or words to that effect.

Another evening the visitors had a choice between the conference dinner at the Dorchester Hotel or a riverboat cruise on the Thames. Moon, who wanted an American presence at both events, easily solved the problem: "That night there was a great clash between a huge formal banquet and a trip up the Thames on a boat with the AAL with a jazz band and lots of booze. Bob said who did I think should go to which event? I said, 'Clara, who has such a magnificent presence at formal occasions, would love the formal dinner, so why don't we go on the boat?'" The cruise, which turned out to be one of the conference's liveliest functions, featured some fancy footwork by Moon, who remembered it all fondly: "I was sort of cutting it up, dancing throughout the night. One of the AAL kids said to Bob Wedgeworth, "Isn't he president of the American Library Association?" Bob said yes, and the kid said, "Do all presidents of the ALA dance like that?" And Bob said, "It's an absolute requirement!"

"Bravura Performance"

Moon delivered his speech on Wednesday, October 5, at the South Bank Centre at a packed session sponsored by the AAL, which was part of the LA and the association Moon was most identified with when he worked in British libraries in the 1950s. Actually, the AAL had invited him to the conference well before the LA did, and he let Philip Gill, the AAL's president in 1977, know how pleased he was "that the AAL can still occasionally steal a march on the LA." What Moon did not know was that a high ranking LA member, Douglas Foskett, opposed his participation in the conference. Years later Harold Smith, part of Moon's circle back in the 1950s, revealed the story:

I think Eric's lively and aggressive personality was an asset and his departure [for North America in 1958] a loss to British librarianship. That this was not the accepted view of the Establishment I can illustrate with a small, relatively unknown incident. I was elected by the London AAL to be their representative on the committee planning the 1977 centenary celebrations. When we were planning some of the programme, names of speakers were discussed and Eric's came up. This seemed reasonable to me—he was well-known in the UK, having once been prominent in professional matters here. But one of the members of the committee,

Douglas Foskett, the previous president of the LA, objected to Eric being invited, without giving any specific reason, suggesting that we instead invite the current ALA president, a black woman [Clara Jones, who by October 1977 was immediate past president of ALA]. There was an objection to this, led may I say by myself. I had general support and the objection to Eric was rejected. My view is that this was part of an Establishment move to get their own back on an erstwhile rebel. It did not succeed.

Just as he did with his inaugural address at the ALA Detroit conference in June, Moon took great pains preparing his speech to the AAL. His audience would include old friends as well as enemies, and he wanted to impress upon both that he was still the rebellious, outspoken Moon they had known and either loved or hated two decades earlier. Only now he was not merely one of a number of up-and-coming librarians in the UK, he was a famous American librarian returning to his native country as head of the most important library association in the world. Clara Jones recalled his mood: "It was especially thrilling to see Eric go back home as president of the American Library Association. You can imagine what that would do to a person! To your ego! It gave him so much joy to go back, especially as president. He was sort of king of the realm." Bob Wedgeworth noticed too that "Eric basked in his triumph."

Moon had every right to feel proud of his achievements, and his occasional prima donna behavior regarding the centenary conference was understandable. When in November 1976 Philip Gill asked him for a tentative title of his speech, Moon, ego extended, replied: "But oh, that title request! I always find this process of dreaming up a title for a speech whose content has not even been considered a little like naming the baby before it's conceived, and long before one knows what sex it might be. Let's provisionally call this unborn thing, then, THE STATE OF THE UNION, JACK. It leaves all the doors open and mildly indulges my fondness for puns."

Months later, in May 1977, Gill wrote and asked Moon for an abstract of his forthcoming speech. Moon replied, again in the same vainglorious voice:

The trouble with associations is that faced with a "great occasion" they get bureaucratic and unreasonable. And they don't appreciate a touch of mystery. Yes, let's confirm that the title will be "The State of the Union, Jack." I chose it because I like the ring of it and because it's loose enough to fit *anything* underneath it. I really don't yet have the faintest idea what I'm going to talk about, and given the fact that I am currently struggling with an inaugural address which I must deliver to ALA in a few weeks, there is no way I can contemplate a synopsis by the end of May. I don't work that way, in any case. I kinda like free flow, to let a paper develop as the typewriter gets warm. Thus, a synopsis can only follow completion.

The hour-long speech — described in the *Library Association Record* as a "bravura performance" — was part lecture, part braggadocio, part reminiscence. It began, "This is, I think, the second most difficult speech I've had to deliver in a very long time. The hardest was last June, when I was inaugurated as ALA's president. I have always been more comfortable, like Michael Foot [then leader of the Labour Party] perhaps, in opposition and the warm minority of the back bench, and I do not adjust easily to august occasions, the polite nothings of diplomacy, or the aura of history." The most controversial portion of Moon's speech dealt with the way the LA chose its presidents and the fact that it had had only one female president during its century of existence:

I find it hard to believe that there is general acceptance and equanimity about a procedure by which a small group of senior citizens of the association retires to a small, closed room, like some medieval Star Chamber, later to emerge and tell you who your next president will be. Not only do you have no voice in the matter; you aren't even offered a choice between two. It doesn't sound like the democracy for which Britain is famous. Certainly, American librarians would not sit still for anything so authoritarian. Who knows, with a more democratic system, you might even get another woman president!

Moon remembered that his speech "really did stir up a terrific rumble — it went on for the next couple of years. I felt able to say things to them that probably no other ALA president could have said, because it would have sounded like the 'ugly American' preaching to them. There was a lot of fireworks for the next several years, and I believe there have been other women presidents since then." Naturally some of the conservative librarians Moon had tangled with in the old days were not happy with him or his speech, and one of them said to him afterward, "We didn't need you back, Moon," and he shot back, "I think you did."

In addition to his very public advice to his old confederates, he and Bob Wedgeworth reinforced the message of reform in a private meeting with top British association leaders. Wedgeworth:

Eric and I in a late night private conversation with the leadership of the LA pointed out emphatically that we did not think that the LA would reach its full potential until it had the confidence to appoint one of its own professionals to the top administrative position. This did occur in the 1980s with very positive results. Although we never discussed it, I am sure Eric was especially pleased to prick the conscience of his LA colleagues by leading a delegation from the ALA that had two highly regarded African Americans. At the time there were no librarians of color in leadership positions in the LA.

Nostalgia Time

For the most part, however, AAL members welcomed Moon's speech, which received a standing ovation. Robert Usherwood, a rising star in the association, was especially complimentary afterward from the floor, noting that members had been waiting for a long time for this sort of address at an LA conference. There were also questions and comments from old friends and colleagues in the audience. Moon remembered that Margaret Amor (now Redfern), who had worked the reference desk at North Finchley with him and John Wakeman 25 years before, "stood up and said how glad she was that I had talked about sexism in British librarianship." And Flo Green, his flamboyant boss at Brentford and Chiswick, "was one of the first people up on the floor, obviously very proud of the fact that I was giving this speech, even though we argued some over what I had said."

But the strongest reaction came from Bill Smith, Moon's old journalism partner in the 1950s. Smith, who had left librarianship to become a bookseller around the time Moon took off for the wilds of North America, hadn't been to an AAL meeting in years, but Moon's speech brought him back, ready for heated public debate followed by a matey tête-à-tête at some nearby restaurant or pub. In fact, one of Moon's oft-told stories concerned his affectionate battles with Bill Smith:

> Picture the scene. It's the middle 1950's. The place is the Marlborough, a London drinking establishment, otherwise known as a pub, one block from the headquarters of The Library Association....
>
> It is late afternoon, perhaps ten minutes after opening time. I am sitting in the lounge bar, enjoying a pint of best bitter with my close friend Bill Smith (who is not a pseudonym). We are known in those days as the two terrible young turks of the library profession over there, but at that moment we are simply rehashing our perpetual argument about which of the London football teams is the best in the country.
>
> The door to the bar opens and a young woman enters. She looks around and when she spots us her face registers shock and indignation. She marches across to our table, stands over us like a judgment and pronounces, "You two are frauds." Surprised and mildly amused, we invite her to sit down, have a beer, and present her evidence for the charge.
>
> The explanation is that she has been present that afternoon at a meeting in Chaucer House, the L.A. headquarters, during which Bill and I had for a couple of hours been on opposite sides (not for the first time) of a fiery political debate, laced with what we both then thought of as the customary ingredients of invective and vituperation. At least they were common in Parliament, especially when such luminaries as Aneurin Bevan and Winston Churchill faced each other without gloves.
>
> The young woman had difficulty accepting that two people who only a short time before had been hurling insults at each other could possibly have been serious in their differences, since here they were, drinking together, obviously warm friends. The afternoon's events, clearly, had been no more than a cynical performance.

The point being that reasonable people can disagree and still be friends—something, Moon believed, Americans have a hard time doing. So the Smith-Moon act returned to the AAL stage in October 1977 for one last encore, Smith attacking and Moon slashing back. True to form, they later repaired to Rules, the historic London restaurant near Covent Garden and next to Smith's bookstore in Maiden Lane, where they drank and ate and talked and talked and talked. "Bill knew everybody there," remembered Moon. "They had one of the top wine stewards in Europe. A lovely place." Bill Smith's death from cancer in 1992 left a hole in Moon's normally unsentimental heart.

He also had nostalgic reunions with Ron Surridge (who chaired the meeting when Moon spoke), Edward Dudley, Bill Graham, Gawan Vesey, and many others, including a former student from North-West Poly. He also saw a lot of "the old timers," like Frank Gardner, who had helped him and Smith launch their innovative newsletter, *Liaison*, in 1957. Moon recalled, "Frank was one of the big names in British librarianship. He was wearing a lapel pin that signified he was a past president of the LA. I asked Wedge [Wedgeworth] to look at it. Wouldn't it be nice I said if ALA had something like that? But he never did anything about it."

Much was made of Moon's accent and how it had changed over the years. One friend remarked, "He looks like Eric but he doesn't sound like Eric," and an interviewer characterized his intonations as "more Yonkers than Yeovil." Looking back, Moon agreed his accent was "sort of untypical. It's got elements from all over the place, due to my having traveled all over the world. In England they think I'm an American or an Australian, and in America everybody thinks I'm English. I've never consciously changed my accent, but it clearly has changed."

A New Library World *Interview*

While in London for the LA centenary conference Moon did an interview with Frank Atkinson, editor of the *New Library World*, a major independent British library journal. Entitled "Moonlight at Waterloo," the two-page interview ran in the November 1977 issue. In it Moon offered a series of blunt opinions about the state of librarianship in the United States and the UK, seemingly going out of his way sometimes, as he had in his speech to the AAL, to let old friends and enemies know that success in America had not tamed him, that he was still the same tough guy he had been in England back in the 1950s.

When, for instance, Atkinson asked, "Do you regularly read any British library journals?," Moon replied, "Are there any?" Atkinson: "Just a few — about half-a-dozen." Moon: "So there are, but I rarely read them. They're terribly dull. If a professional journal doesn't take the lead on professional issues, then it is irrelevant. I see no British library journal doing that except, occasionally, *New library world*— which is also the only reasonably literate one."

Moon's response to Atkinson's next question was equally feisty — and it landed the magazine and its publisher, Clive Bingley, in a legal hassle. Atkinson: "As an ex-professional editor, I suppose you approve of the appointment of a professional journalist to edit the *Library Association record* [*LAR*, the LA's official journal]?" Moon: "The editor of a library journal must be someone deeply involved in the library profession. Otherwise he is simply a copy editor." Roger Walter, *LAR*'s editor, took offense at Moon's "copy editor" remark and threatened to bring a libel action against *New Library World* and Bingley. Toward the end of 1975 the Library Association had appointed a new editor of *LAR*, replacing Edward Dudley, a part-time volunteer editor and a librarian, with Walter, a full-time journalist and nonlibrarian who had previously worked as deputy editor of *The Teacher*, a British education magazine. Walter considered Moon's comment injurious to his reputation as an editor and an aspersion on his ability to edit *LAR* successfully.

The flap was resolved when Moon agreed — unhappily — to the publication of a retraction in the next issue (December 1977) of *New Library World*. It read: "Mr Eric Moon, President of the American Library Association, is glad to make clear that he did not intend it to be understood, from his interview with Mr Frank Atkinson published in the November issue of *New library world*, that Mr R M Walter, Editor of the *Library Association record* was incapable of or had failed to develop the deep involvement in the library profession necessary for the performance of his duties and was consequently 'simply a copy editor.'"

Bingley sent a copy of the December issue to Moon, who wrote back, "Thanks for the 'apology' issue. As an editor who has been often attacked before, it still riles me to let that ass at the *LAR* get away with stuff like this."

"Tribal Betrayal"

That Moon's 1977 visit to England ended in an acrimonious public dispute seemed entirely appropriate. When he left the country for North America at age 35 in 1958, he was disgruntled with British society and institutions. The country as a whole was too stodgy, too complacent, too insular, too class-bound, too wedded to the status quo, too reluctant to embrace progressive change to satisfy him. The postwar Labour electoral revolution, which had begun with such promise in 1945, petered out in half a dozen years, the death rattle occurring in 1951 when Nye Bevan, Moon's socialist hero, resigned his cabinet post in protest over backsliding government policies.

Moon found a very different social and political climate in America. He thrived on the freedom and opportunity that such a dynamic system afforded him. He quickly experienced success at the Bowker Company, turning a lackluster *Library Journal* into a powerhouse of a professional magazine, and in no time he had become a Bowker shareholder and member of the board of directors, and after that president of Scarecrow Press, a thriving publishing company. Such achievements would have been improbable in England at the time for a man of his education, experience, and social status. Of course, Moon found plenty wrong with his adopted country too; one colleague who worked closely with him in the 1970s remembered that Moon frequently indulged in "little anti–American comments." Still, the contrast between British and American postwar society was stark, and Moon's dissatisfaction with the country of his birth remained deeply embedded in his psyche.

Ronald Benge, one of the most thoughtful librarians of his day, was, like Moon, a British expatriate who left the UK to pursue his career abroad (in Africa and the West Indies). The two men knew one another in England and later Moon served as editor of Benge's evocative memoir, *Confessions of a Lapsed Librarian* (Scarecrow Press, 1984). Looking back, Benge theorized that he and Moon, though very different people, were both "outsiders" in England, that "from the beginning" neither felt part of or belonged to British society "in any complete sense." He continued, "In view of the fact that we both abandoned the folk back there — a kind of tribal betrayal — we both have been 'accepted' professionally in Britain only with certain unstated reservations: 'Yes, a remarkable career, but not quite *sound* perhaps — not *really* one of us.'" Both he and Moon, observed Benge, would always be viewed as renegades by those who mattered in Britain.

By 1977 Moon had been away from England for almost twenty years, and returning for the LA conference — and particularly the act of preparing his speech to the AAL — forced him to confront buried feelings about his native country. Though he returned as a great success, his deep-seated resentments at never having truly belonged or been fully accepted welled up and spilled out. He felt compelled to let members of the British Establishment know how much he disdained them, how superior he was to them. His attacks were sometimes rude but nearly always eviscerating. But in the end that "ass" at *LAR* had trumped him, robbed him of his victory. Though the public retraction galled Moon to his core, it was a fitting way to conclude his return to the mother country after so many years.

The Speaker *Abroad*

Compared with his chief problem during his year as ALA president —*The Speaker*— the flap over his "copy editor" remark in the *New Library World* was small beer and quickly faded from memory. In fact, he could not escape *The Speaker* mess even in England; it accompanied him and his ALA colleagues to London; the film seemed impossible to shake, stuck like dog shit on a shoe. Moon himself referred to the controversy in his AAL speech:

We [American librarians] are still far from home or on safe ground on racial issues. If people, whatever their heritage or colour, may now use most libraries without distinction or barriers; if any librarian may now join and attend the meetings of his or her association, we have still not achieved equal treatment in recruitment, training, hiring and promotion of librarians. White middle class people still mostly run libraries, and they naturally tend to gear their services to the needs they know. We don't have to be naive enough to believe that prejudice can be eradicated, to insist that such visible and unjust *results* of prejudice be eliminated. Worse, perhaps, after all these years of grappling with racial problems, is the degree to which otherwise intelligent people remain grossly insensitive in this area. We faced the results of such insensitivity again this year at our annual conference in Detroit, where a film called *The speaker*, made we must assume with good intentions, and with the sponsorship of ALA's Intellectual Freedom Committee, managed to split our association wide open on racial lines, to a degree we have not experienced in more than a decade.

The film was also a major source of friction between Bob Wedgeworth and Clara Jones on the plane trip to England. Wedgeworth recalled, "Clara spent the whole trip over talking about how I should have fired Judy Krug" as a result of *The Speaker* business. "I told her that this would have been the biggest mistake the association could make — it would have been interpreted to mean that ALA had repudiated its support for intellectual freedom and the First Amendment." Once in London, Wedgeworth remembered he "was impressed by the amount of ceremony" at the LA conference, but "it became hard for me to focus because of the side conversations about *The Speaker*," adding: "I've never told anyone this before, but I was so beaten down by the anti–*Speaker* sentiment that I left the conference a day early so I would not have to fly home with Clara and others who were bugging me about the film. I threw away my charter flight ticket home via New York with the group and purchased, at my expense, a direct flight to Chicago."

Travel — especially the trips abroad — added a diverting, often pleasurable dimension to the ALA presidency for Moon. But in the end he found no relief from the ghosts of the past on the road, nor did getting away make the problems of the present any less insistent or more resolvable. Oddly, at this time of greatest triumph, Moon was caught in an unlucky patch. Maybe he was right when, in his AAL speech, he confessed to being "more comfortable" in opposition than in power. After all, his greatest professional accomplishments occurred when he was fighting, not leading, the Establishment.

– 16 –

Reforming the
American Library Association

Democratic Impulse

Whereas Moon's year as president of the American Library Association was largely a failure, his long-term effort to reform — that is, democratize — the association met with considerable success, despite setbacks and discouragements toward the end of his career. Indeed, no individual in modern times worked longer or harder or with greater skill and efficacy than Moon to open up ALA's many doors to all its members, but especially its minorities, dissidents, and younger recruits— those groups that hitherto had been ignored or condescended to by association leaders. Of course change was slow and halting, challenged at every turn by entrenched bureaucrats and self-perpetuating elites. Reforming ALA proved to be difficult, often thankless, truly endless work that occupied Moon, along with many kindred spirits, for longer than thirty years, from 1960 into the 1990s.

The reform movement he led eventually transformed ALA from a cozy, parochial club catering to narrow 3 × 5 card concerns into one of the most open, vibrant, and socially responsible professional organizations in the world. He proudly enumerated this progress in his speech to the AAL at the Library Association's centenary conference in London in 1977. But by the late 1970s the appetite for reform within ALA had waned, and throughout the 1980s and into the 1990s some of the changes in association governance that Moon and his supporters had worked so hard to bring about were either reversed or whittled away. A conservative tide, reflecting the Reagan "revolution" in the country at large, swept over American librarianship, and Moon spent his final years as an active member of ALA exhorting the association not to backslide into the bad old days.

During these years he became especially disturbed by ALA's increasing tendency toward decentralization (or fragmentation), which he opposed because it reduced the association's effectiveness as *the* voice on matters concerning libraries and librarian-

370

ship. During this time ALA became essentially a federated association, meaning that its divisions—11 at last count, including the influential Association of College and Research Libraries, Public Library Association, and American Association of School Librarians—had acquired a large degree of autonomy, including the right to hold their own conferences and collect their own dues. As the divisions grew in power and influence, ALA's central authority became commensurately weaker and, in the case of the executive director, dysfunctional.

A report in the August 1994 issue of *Library Journal* neatly summarized this fundamental schism within the bosom of ALA:

> One camp clearly could be called "centrist," a loose group of members who stand for a strong Executive Board, president, and treasurer of ALA, easy action by members, and usually direct election to the board. This group wants to belong to an ALA willing to take positions on social or political issues not strictly or narrowly related to libraries. These centrists see the growing power and autonomy of ALA divisions as destructive of ALA unity. Many of them belong to the Social Responsibilities Round Table.
>
> The other apparent camp believes that the ALA divisions are basic and central to ALA, create its programs, and provide its leadership. These "federationists" want more power and autonomy for ALA's divisions to pursue their own respective interests. They maintain that through a representative Council, ALA can come together when issues require one voice. They believe members should only vote in mail votes to all members, not in less representative, poorly attended membership meetings at conferences. In general, the federationists agree that by taking positions on larger social issues, ALA loses credibility and wastes effort.

By the early 1990s Moon, an adamant "centrist," became seriously pessimistic about the association's future, and after the 1994 annual conference in Miami Beach he stopped attending ALA meetings, a drastic step for him — and for Ilse, who never ceased to enjoy the excitement and chatter of the conference life. In 1998 the death of a friend, Arthur Curley, prompted the couple to return to ALA one more time. In a letter to *LJ* (October 1, 1998), Moon shared his lugubrious thoughts about the state of the association with readers of the magazine he once edited:

> For well over 30 years I attended every ALA conference and Midwinter Meeting and never missed either a Council or membership meeting. A few years ago, following the demise of the membership meeting and the evident decay of Council, I stopped attending ALA conferences. It was just too sad to see the whole process returning to the moribund conditions it was in some 40 years ago. Spurred to return to the conference in Washington to participate in a gathering in memory of my close friend Arthur Curley, I was amazed to find that the petrifaction of Council had continued apace....

Many of the Moon Mafia—like their leader, now the old guard of the profession—felt the same way. Bill Eshelman, the faithful "Esh," who had been at Moon's side during every major reform battle in the 1960s and 1970s, became acutely disillusioned, unhappy with "ALA's fiddling around with committees and unnecessary apparatus. The thing I'm most sad about is that ALA isn't worth it. I think I wasted a lot of time." Fay Blake, also one of those in the Moon camp from the beginning, was equally gloomy: "Was Eric able to effect positive and lasting changes? The answer, lamentably, is mostly no. Not because he wavered or stumbled. He gave it a damn good try and went probably as far as was possible. But the ALA, like the AMA, represents not libraries, not library users, not librarians but the library bureaucracy, the 'managers,' whose interest is maintaining the status quo (that's how they got where they are, after all)." And Pat Schuman, a former ALA president (1991–1992) and one of Moon's most successful protégées, observed, "The bureaucrats are taking over; the association's going back to its old ways."

Still, despite these laments, ALA in the early 21st century retains the basic democratic character brought about by the reforms achieved in the 1960s and 1970s. For instance, almost all meetings remain open and opportunities now exist for members of any age, color, gender, sexual inclination, or political hue to participate fully in the affairs of the association. The problem, as the "federationists" are quick to point out, is that in recent years too few rank-and-file members have been interested in participating in general membership meetings, preferring to put their time and energy into the divisions, roundtables, and committees that directly affect them and their work. Times have changed. The social and political activism prevalent in the 1960s and 1970s has largely given way to the intense self-interest witnessed in recent decades, and the association has changed accordingly. But when (not if) the pendulum again swings leftward, the basic democratic prerogatives Moon and his colleagues fought for and implanted in ALA's shared conscience will be there, waiting to be rediscovered and redeployed.

Central Principles

Why did Moon care so passionately about ALA? What drove him to attend *every* conference and *every* Council and Membership meeting for more than thirty years? The answer: he devoted so much of himself to ALA — as he had earlier to the LA and AAL in England — because he passionately believed in strength through association. Associations, he said, "are the place where we can and should gather in force and unity. They are our political potential for change and influence. It is there that we must clarify our communal thinking and translate it into influence and action." He sought to improve the way ALA operates in order to make it a stronger, more powerful organization. When he arrived in the United States at the end of 1959, he found an ALA that he believed was weak and wasteful of its potential. Specifically, he found a national association that squelched new ideas and dissent, tacitly condoned discrimination against blacks and other minorities, avoided discussions of and positions on relevant social and political issues, and conducted its important business behind closed doors.

Moon wanted to reshape ALA into an open, inclusive, dynamic, forward-looking organization that confidently represented the broad interests of the library profession in American society generally and the councils of government specifically, where the huge infusions of dollars needed to improve the nation's libraries were most readily available. He cited the lobbying efforts of ALA's Washington Office as the association performing at its best: "The kind of funding libraries received in the 1960s would have been totally impossible without ALA and the Washington Office. For the first time libraries received quite massive federal funding. When there's real clout needed, the ALA Washington Office is the only really important library organization."

Moon was well suited to the role of reformer. It came instinctively. From his earliest days as a politically sentient young man and librarian in England he embraced reform, not revolution. He believed intuitively in working for change through the system. Though often sharply critical of institutions he was a builder, not a destroyer. Growing up in a working-class environment in the Depression in the rough port city of Southampton, he naturally allied himself with the Labour Party, which had its roots in the Fabian socialism preached by Sidney and Beatrice Webb, H.G. Wells, and George Bernard Shaw — his boyhood literary hero. Political change, argued the Fabians, must occur gradually through incremental reforms; they believed fervently in "the inevitability of gradualness." The young Moon absorbed these principles and later, when he became an association politician, used them to good advantage. Gerry Shields, who knew him well during the 1960s and 1970s, attributed Moon's success as a reformer to his British political roots:

> Eric obviously owes a considerable amount of his success in the field as editor, publisher, and eventually leader in ALA to his socialist-labor background in England. Such a traditional heritage has not been a normal part of the training and philosophy of U.S. librarians. When I became aware of him as something more than a name on the masthead of *Library Journal* he already had been an activist and a reformer for some time. However, he was always careful to assume the posture of a voice of conscience, not of a rabble-rouser or despoiler.

Russell Shank, Moon's main opponent in the 1976 race for the ALA presidency and his successor as president in 1978, remembered a telling conversation he had with Moon in the 1960s about reforming ALA: "We chatted briefly in the lobby of one of the ALA conference hotels, following a rather dull Council session (an oxymoron?). I remember Eric saying he was 'going to bring the association down.' What he was actually saying was that he was going to make the association more responsive to members and attentive to social conditions. In that, he was way ahead of the game in many (maybe all) professional associations."

Modus Operandi

And how did this transplanted Englishman — who did not arrive in the States until age 36 — go about reforming the American Library Association, the oldest, largest, wealthiest, and most prestigious organization of its kind in the world? Most obviously he did not do it alone. Applying the principle of strength through association he developed informal working relationships with other reform-minded librarians, such as members of the Black Caucus and SRRT. By joining together they had a much greater chance for success than if they fought their battles separately.

Similarly, he fashioned two loosely constructed coalitions entirely of his own invention: the backbench, a bloc of progressive councillors dedicated to monitoring and prodding a Council much inclined to rubber-stamp recommendations of an Executive Board that often assumed an imperious tone; and the Moon Mafia, a select group of liberal friends and cohorts who, à la Melvil Dewey, sought to make libraries a central force in society and librarianship a major profession in the same class as medicine, law, and teaching. While considerable overlap existed among Moon's various alliances, together they included nearly all of ALA's liberal and radical activists at any given time. These people became Moon's troops, his partisans, his guerrilla army on the march for a more democratic ALA and a stronger, better librarianship.

Moon also understood that achieving reform required thoughtful preparation for political combat. A carefully calculated battle plan was essential. In a 1981 interview with Milton Wolf in the magazine *Technicalities* he talked about the need for strategic planning:

You've got to start with whatever the natural support basis might be.... But ultimately, you've got to crack the council, and you've got to do a lobbying job in council. I think that what has gone wrong with a lot of the social efforts generated by groups like SRRT is that they have simply gone onto the firing line before they've softened up the opposition, and the opposition has come back strongly and defeated them time and time again. One of the things that Norman Horrocks is particularly good at is doing his advance political work and getting a lot of people who've never thought about an issue sympathetically tuned into it before it reaches the floor. Certainly you have to do that in the council, and you have to do it in the executive board. If you don't crack those 2 areas, you can't ever get anything into policy or operation in any way at all. Again, it's good political groundwork you have to have.

Sometimes, however, Moon's tactics seemed, at least to Ed Beckerman, "a little too clever by half." Beckerman, a prominent New Jersey public librarian and Moon mafioso, recalled, "One time in the 1970s, Eric got the idea that a point was to be made during Council elections for the Executive Board by flooding the market with unknown board candidates, and accordingly eight or ten candidates were nominated (myself included), and predictably each received token support. I don't think any of the candidates quite understood why they were running, and in retrospect I wonder if Eric ever knew. But he seemed to think some point had been made."

A few years later in an interview with Frederick Stielow, Moon underscored the need to organize as a key ingredient in the reform effort: "I remember some of the younger people in the SRRT movement used to react to me with a certain frustration and constantly call me a structure freak, because I would say protests are fine, demonstrations are fine, digging up resolutions is fine. But if you really want to do something about this association, you have to get where the power is. The only way to get where the power is, is to organize." Moon believed too that getting and using power required being conversant — in meticulous detail — with the rules of ALA governance:

The reason people think of me as a political person or leader is that many people realized I knew more about how ALA worked than almost anyone around, and how to use the machinery to get things done. Norman Horrocks is thought of in the same light; he became famous as the master of parliamentary procedure and the policy handbook. Both Norman and I knew the mechanics of the association and meetings maybe better than anybody on Council, so we were always being consulted by people who wanted to do things. Larry Burgess gave me this advice when I was 16 starting at the Southampton Public Library: if you want to get anywhere in this profession, you've got to speak and write and do them both forcefully and often. I would add to that, you've got to know how to use the machinery—you've got to know the book.

Finally, Moon's success as an ALA reformer owed much to his considerable communications skills, especially as an orator. Almost everyone, friend or foe, who experienced Moon at the microphone at an ALA meeting came away impressed by his deftness as an extemporaneous speaker. Longtime Moon watcher Ernie DiMattia: "I believe Eric's writing ability influenced his ability to speak fluidly, think on his feet, et cetera. ALA served the same outlet for his verbal communication as *LJ* did for his written communication. Eric possessed both the power of the pen and the power of oratory, and that made him formidable." Fellow journalist Art Plotnik: "To Yanks, perhaps influenced by his Brit accent and relatively debonair posture (and pipe!), Eric's style in Council and elsewhere was reasoned, diplomatic, but very tough on sensitive issues. An angry closing sentence at the microphone could shame an audience as well as E.J. Josey's impassioned admonitions. Eric wasn't a bully, but he could wear anyone down; you knew there was always going to be an opinion, beautifully organized and expressed, and as unrelenting as it seemed open." Grizzled compatriot Bill Eshelman: "Part of his success was that when he spoke at Council meetings he nearly always was one of the last people to speak, and he summarized what the problem was, what the issue was, and what the proposed solution was. And most of the time he won."

Concerns and Convictions

Over the years Moon developed a detailed knowledge of ALA's principal components but his main concerns were its governing "troika"—Membership, Council, and Executive Board—along with the key leadership positions of executive director and president. He also took a particular interest in the association's divisions, which caused him distress, and its publishing operation, which he thought poorly managed. Though not all his opinions about these and other elements of ALA gained wide acceptance among members, many did and some have had a lasting impact. Coincidentally, his deepest convictions about ALA provide a revealing window into his professional psyche.

• ALA Membership. Moon was first, last, and always a membership man. Constitutionally, ALA's membership possesses the final authority in the association. Though the Council is the *representative* policy-making body, the membership ideally functions as democracy in its purest form. It can, as stated in the ALA Constitution (Article VI, Sec. 4 [c]), "set aside" any Council action by "a three-fourths vote at any membership meeting of the Association, or by a majority vote by mail in which one-fourth of the members of the Association have voted." The Constitution also grants the membership the right to "refer any matter to the Council" with recommendations for debate and possible adoption (Article VI, Sec. 4 [a]).

Moon championed a strong, vigorous membership as a check on the powers of the Council and Executive Board. On the other hand he had no illusions about the difficulties involved in prompting the membership to exercise its ultimate authority. Its size alone, in 2001 about 57,500 members, makes decision-making a complicated and often chaotic process. Soon after taking over the editorship of *LJ*, Moon described ALA's membership as an awkward giant, a metaphor that still rings true:

The American Library Association is governed, essentially, by a very peculiarly balanced troika. One element, the smallest in size but the real apex of the power structure, is the Executive Board. The giant among the three elements, sporadically powerful when aroused but more often lethargic, muscle-bound, and uncoordinated — as giants are prone to be — is the Association's membership. The third element — the middle-sized bear — is the ALA Council, larger than the Executive Board, smaller than the membership, and most of the time less effective than either.

He also argued that ALA required a robust membership in order to speak and act effectively on behalf of the entire profession. In his view the chief threat to a strong membership came from the growing power of the divisions, which tended to fragment the association and diffuse its central authority. During his campaign for the ALA presidency in 1976 Moon repeatedly stressed this concern: "…the membership is going to have to learn more about [the governing] machinery and wield its votes more effectively if it really wants to recover some of its lost power."

Moon was always on the lookout for ways to boost the membership's political heft. For instance, he once promoted a resolution calling for election of Executive Board members not by Council, the current method, but directly by the membership, as had been done up until the late 1950s. This he believed would force the board to be more responsive to membership needs and wishes, but more important it would give liberal candidates a better shot at getting elected. He himself had once run for the board while on Council and was defeated decisively — the only election he ever lost. In fact all during his career Moon's political strength in ALA derived from the membership, as opposed to the ALA establishment, which never really cottoned to him. "You have to realize," observed Ernie DiMattia, "that when Eric ran for president and Council he wasn't elected by the people who go to ALA or the councilors of the association. He was elected by the association's population, the whole membership. The majority of that membership doesn't go to ALA conferences and meetings."

Moon also advocated for the automatic conferral of ALA membership on all those who belonged to the association's 50-plus affiliated state and regional library associations, called chapters; for example, the Florida Library Association and the New England Library Association are chapters of ALA. Because the chapters collectively have many more members than ALA, this would be a quick-and-dirty way of spiking the association's membership totals, which in turn, at least hypothetically, would increase ALA's power and influence in both the library world and society as a whole. Moon:

It seems to me there are many members of state associations out there that aren't members of ALA but should be. One of the hurdles here is dues. But I think it ought to be possible to do this, perhaps by making state associations branches of the national association [as is done in the UK], so we would all be part of one membership group. It is so important for ALA when it makes representations to government agencies, or engages in any other level of public discourse, that it be able to support the claim that it speaks for all of librarianship. If it speaks for only a quarter or a third of librarians, it is not as convincing as if it speaks for 90 percent. And it would have more clout if it speaks for 100,000 librarians rather than 50,000.

Unfortunately for Moon and other ALA centrists, these and similar efforts to enhance the membership failed or never got out of the box, and during the complaisant 1980s and 1990s the membership's role in ALA governance became less and less significant, a giant sapped of its strength. In 1994 a self-study committee chaired by F. William Summers and charged with finding ways to streamline ALA's organizational structure concluded the association "has grown too large to function effectively as both a direct and representative democracy." Agreeing, the Council *and* the membership (the latter in a rare mail vote) endorsed the committee's recommendation that the number of members required to petition for a vote to override an action of Council be increased from 200 to 1 percent of ALA's total membership — in 2001, about 575 members. The 1 percent figure also became the number necessary for a quorum to convene membership meetings at Midwinter and annual conferences. In recent years such a quorum has been unattainable and as a consequence membership meetings have dissolved into meaningless "chat" sessions.

It was at this point Moon got so upset he stopped going to ALA conferences. "Final power rests with the membership, and that's what's being destroyed," he warned at the 1994 Miami Beach conference. "Membership meetings have been strangled for many years. And now we're going to stab the body. It's a very sad conclusion." Like his old pal Eshelman, he began to wonder if his many years of working to improve ALA had been for nothing, had been a big waste of time. What's more, though not a sentimental man, he had loved those membership meetings, where *his* ALA had had its say and where he had so often ripped the enemy while rallying the troops. At membership meetings he had been through good times and bad times, times of crisis and times of hilarity. Ruminating, he recalled the painful debates over racial segregation in the profession in the 1960s and the divisive film *The Speaker* in the 1970s; then he thought of the time John Carter, a likable young rebel from Mississippi, had 'em rolling in the aisles:

John and I had become very good friends. He was a great raconteur, and he drank a lot. I remember one membership meeting when John had an item on the agenda. He was sitting next to me, and he said, "Eric, I have just got to have a piss. Do you think my item will come up?" I said go ahead, but while he was gone his item did come up and he wasn't there to present it, so it was dropped, or passed over. Well, John comes back and gets up to the microphone and says, "Mr. Chairman, I regard this as a very black day in the annals of democracy when a man cannot go out to relieve himself without his item being passed over on the agenda." The whole house broke up.

• ALA Council. During Moon's day, Council (as everyone refers to it, sans the article) was a formidable assembly. In 1975, Art Plotnik described it this way:

Sometimes it [Council] looks like a $100-a-plate dinner sponsored by the Committee to Elect Franz Kafka. They sit at four or five long tables, each with a white linen cloth and several pitchers full of ice water. No matter how many fat bundles of documents they bring with them, there are always more waiting on the tables. They start arriving early and form a quorum punctually. They take their seats, facing a greatly elevated podium of officers and parliamentarian, and they chat in low tones with a neighbor or in little political caucuses. To their right is the press table, far enough away so that reportorial wit and clicking cameras are only a minor distraction. On either side and behind the Councilors are ALA members and other observers, some 500 to 1,000.

Altogether Moon spent more than a dozen years on Council (1965–1972; 1976–1979; 1982–1986) but he rarely had a good word to say about the institution. He had two long-standing peeves about ALA's representative governing body: it too often acted as little more than a submissive servant to a domineering Executive Board; and it was usually top-heavy with "special-interest" representatives—that is, councilors elected by ALA's divisions, chapters, and other interest groups. Moon and company worked long and hard to pare down Council to just 100 members, all elected by the entire membership (or at large), and for a brief time in the 1970s they succeeded. But in time Council returned to its old ways, and today there are more than 80 special-interest councilors, another "sad" development for Moon and the reform movement:

You have to remember that Council has been through an enormous number of changes in recent times. When we had the 1960s revolution, the whole look of Council was changed. We finally achieved what some of us wanted and threw out all of what today is commonly known in politics as special interests. We threw out the chapter councilors, the division councilors, the past presidents—all that was left were the councilors at large. We reduced the Council's size from about 200 to 100 people, which made it a better working organization. The councilors were all elected at large and therefore did not represent any narrow constituency.

But over the years since, all of this reform slowly began to erode and now we again have chapter councilors, division councilors, roundtable councilors—they're all back, except for the past presidents, and some of them have run for Council on their own and have gotten elected. So once again Council's become moribund and terribly conservative and fractionated, because these councilors are all looking out for their little territory rather than looking at the whole picture and doing what is best for ALA as a whole. It's very sad.

Moon's comrade in reform, Bill Eshelman, professed a similar sadness:

I'm getting sour in my old age. It's mostly about ALA, which Eric has been trying to save all these years. The organization is sliding right back to where we started from when we were trying to reform it. The deadwood on Council, for example, has sneaked back, including the chapter and division representatives. We envisioned a Council of 100 members, all of them elected by the membership at large—that was our goal. But now public librarians want to meet only with public librarians, academic librarians with academic librarians and so on, which dilutes the strength of the profession. So when we go to lobby Congress it's really a lie to say that ALA is speaking for 50,000 or more members.

During his day, Moon's impact on Council was far-reaching. This was due not only to his impressive skills as a debater but his position as commander of the backbench, which he founded to keep an eye on business before Council. No longer could that body get away with being the Executive Board's lackey; the backbench was ever vigilant, ready to challenge every illiberal action. Moon, along with Horrocks and Eshelman, also mentored new councilors, helping them find their way through the thicket of Kafkaesque procedures and paperwork. One of these was Jeanne Isacco, a prominent government documents librarian, who remembered that when she was elected to Council in the 1970s, "Eric, Norman, and Esh took this first-time councilor under their wing and showed me the ropes." She was especially in awe of "Eric's ability to cut through the garbage Council can get caught up in."

For his part Moon had strong views about what makes a good ALA councilor:

It's someone who cares about issues, people, the profession, library service, and is not afraid to express him or herself and is able to be persuasive. What irritates me is that too many people run for Council simply in order to get something on their resume. They sit there for four years and never say anything or do anything—a total waste of time. I would say that applies to probably better than 50 percent of the councilors. Another thing that annoys me greatly is that after being elected to Council some of them don't even take the trouble to stay for the final Council meeting, which is usually on the last afternoon of the conference. It seems to me that when you're elected, you have an obligation to be there from beginning to end, and if you're not, you're not doing the job.

- ALA Executive Board. Technically the Executive Board—or Exec Board—is not a policy-making body, though it often becomes one by default. The ALA Constitution (Article VII, Sec. 3) assigns it these responsibilities: "The Executive Board shall act for the Council in the administration of established policies and programs. The Executive Board shall be the body which manages within this context the affairs of the Association, but shall delegate management of the day-to-day operation to the Association's Executive Director. The Executive Board shall make recommendations to Council with respect to matters of policy."

The smallest of ALA's governing troika, the board consists of 12 voting members (the association's elected officers—president, vice president/president-elect, treasurer, and immediate past president—plus eight members elected by Council from its own ranks) and the executive director, who sits on the board ex officio with no vote. Moon served just one three-year term (1976–79) on the board by virtue of his election as vice president/president-elect in 1976. During this time he experienced firsthand the board's complex and sometimes adversarial relationship with Council. "The Exec Board is supposed to be a management body, designed to carry out policies established by Council," explained Moon, "but there's a constant tussle about policy and power between these two groups. The issue is what's management and what's policy. Exec Board is in a powerful position on this question because board members are on top of things much more than anyone else in the association."

With the obvious exception of the many enervating hours spent trying to resolve *The Speaker* disaster that plagued his presidential year, Moon enjoyed serving on the

Exec Board. It brought him as close to the heart of the organization as any member can get, and it gave him an opportunity to work closely with his good friend Norman Horrocks, who was elected, with a little help from Moon, to the board in 1977. As ALA president-elect, Moon chaired the Council's Committee on Committees, which allowed him to select four nominees from Council to fill two open seats on the board; Moon of course made sure Horrocks was one of the nominees.

Moon and Horrocks worked extremely well together on the Exec Board. Combining their redoubtable political skills and extensive knowledge of the rules, they frequently maneuvered the board into doing their bidding. According to Moon, their favorite tactic was old-fashioned cloakroom politicking: "Norman and I were very close on ALA Council and Exec Board. We used lobbying as few other people had. When we were on the Exec Board, we were in a distinct minority on most issues, so Norman would bring down duty-free liquor from Canada and we would invite those on the other side up to his room one at a time for a drink and talk to them and see whether we could sway votes, and when we thought we had enough we would raise the issue with the board and get it through." Horrocks remembered they had a system for sounding out board members on particular issues: "Eric would always assign me the conservative members, because I was seen as an 'Establishment figure' whereas he was the 'flaming radical.' This was more a matter of style rather than substance. Actually we saw eye-to-eye on most issues."

Moon pretty much abandoned his customary attack mode while serving on the board, finding it counterproductive. Upon election as association president and board member, he ceased to be Moon the outsider, free to strike wherever and whenever he chose; his election made him an insider whether he wanted the distinction or not, which required a different set of political stratagems. To get things done it was necessary to engage in backroom persuasion (assisted of course by Horrocks's duty-free whiskey) or, failing that, seek compromise or negotiated solutions, something he had not done much of during his career as an ALA activist and reformer. He described the situation in his 1981 *Technicalities* interview:

When I was on the executive board, I had to learn to work much more closely and strenuously with people who disagreed with me than I'd ever had to do as a "back bench" operator. Before that time, it didn't matter to me particularly whether they agreed with me or not, as long as our point of view was expressed. But on the executive board, my point of view was clearly always going to be the minority point of view; and therefore we couldn't ever prevail unless we worked politically with people who didn't agree with us and tried to turn them around on a particular issue. I found myself, on one issue after another, in alliance with people who normally would have been on the opposite side of the fence from me.

A good example of such unlikely alliances involved the Huron Plaza project, a controversial plan to construct a new high-rise headquarters building for ALA in Chicago in late 1970s. Moon was wary of the complicated deal and, along with ALA treasurer William Chait, resisted endorsing it until the last minute. Moon:

At the time it seemed to some of us an enormously risky involvement. Here we were embarking on a multimillion-dollar enterprise at a time when ALA finances had been shaky for years, and some of us—including treasurer Bill Chait—were doubtful that this was the way to go. Not only were we providing expanded space for headquarters staff but becoming a landlord as well. There were differences on the Exec Board over this deal. Interestingly the two people who were the longest holdouts on the building were Bill Chait and myself. And Bill Chait was about as far right as one could imagine, so he and I were not exactly thought of as a team. And the building could not go ahead without our signatures. We finally succumbed because it was clear that both Council and membership wanted this.

- ALA Executive Director. Known as the "executive secretary" until 1958, the executive director is appointed by and serves at the pleasure of the Executive Board. The executive director manages the association's day-to-day operations, including the headquarters staff (in 2001, some 270 employees), and is arguably the single most powerful individual in the association. Elected officers come and go, but executive directors tend to stay—though this was not the case in the dysfunctional 1990s when no less than five people served in the position. Moon's years in ALA were dominated by three executive directors: David Clift (1951–1972), Robert Wedgeworth (1972–1985), and Thomas Galvin (1985–1989). To one degree or another he had contentious relations with each of these men.

Clift first welcomed Moon into the organization in 1960 but soon branded him an enemy because of his editorials and reports in *LJ* that openly criticized ALA in a manner never before experienced by American librarians. The executive director and his staff publicly snubbed Moon while behind the scenes trying to get him muzzled or removed. But as the 1960s wore on, Clift, no match for the younger, more dynamic Moon, became increasingly ineffectual and soon after the tumultuous Atlantic City conference quietly announced his retirement. Moon was obviously pleased: "Actually I thought Clift was a pretty able executive director in many respects. For instance, he built up ALA's financial strength. But one of his great abilities was to try to tone down anything that might lead to change, or at least the kind of change some of us were looking for. Like many of ALA's executive directors, he had been there too long and accrued too much power. Clearly he needed to go, and I said so."

Of all of the executive directors Moon knew and worked with, he was closest to Bob Wedgeworth. Their first contact came when Moon published an article by Wedgeworth, then assistant librarian at little Park College in Missouri, in *LJ* (May 1, 1963) on jazz record collections in libraries. In the early 1970s the two men got to know each other well in New Jersey when Moon was at Scarecrow Press and "Wedge" was at Rutgers University in the dual role of assistant professor and doctoral student in the library school. When David Clift let it be known in 1970 that he was retiring as executive director, Eric and Ilse Moon were among the first people "to put Wedge's name into the hopper" as a candidate for the job.

But once Wedgeworth got the job, relations between the two men cooled, due apparently to caution on Wedgeworth's part:

Eric may have considered me as a protégé, but I do not believe that I thought of him that way. I was a graduate of ultra conservative Wabash College [in Crawfordsville,

Indiana] and had been a protégé of A.P. Marshall [Lincoln University] and Dick Sealock [Kansas City Public Library] when I first entered the profession in Missouri. Later, I was the protégé of David Jonah, the director at Brown University, who wanted me to return and succeed him when he retired, and I was the protégé of Paul Dunkin, the cataloging and classification specialist at Rutgers, who I succeeded as editor of *Library Resources & Technical Services*.

Wedgeworth believed Moon "saw me as someone he could manipulate. But I wasn't a neophyte in management, and once I became executive director I kept a little bit of distance between me and Eric and his friends." Wedgeworth:

I had enormous respect for Eric as an intellect and a consummate association politician. But at the time I came to Rutgers I was intent on becoming a prominent academic librarian, preferably in one of the great research libraries. Eric did not fit into that construct. Moreover, I believe Eric and his friends saw me as a different person than I really was. Mine was basically a managerial focus whereas Eric's was as an issue-oriented activist. I was somewhat conservative with a strong commitment to libertarian principles. As my friend Bill Summers said once, "How could they have considered a black 1959 graduate of Wabash College to be a liberal?" But it was the late 1960s, I wore a beard and had an Afro haircut, and was prominent in a number of groups within ALA agitating for change. Therefore it's easy to see how they might not have looked beyond what they could see at the moment.

This, however, did not stop Wedgeworth from liking Moon and most of his crowd. The only one he did not care for was Eshelman, who "was a bitter person constantly looking for dirt." Wedgeworth never forgot that Eshelman publicly called him a "liar" during an ALA debate. Adding fuel to the fire, Eshelman wrote in his recent memoir *No Silence!* that Wedgeworth, soon after being named executive director, bragged at a party, "I'm going to out–Honky the Honkies." Wedgeworth emphatically denied saying this: "That's so outrageous. I tend to have a very conservative style of speaking, both in public and private. I don't use a lot of profanity. It's a matter of style and decorum. It's completely out of character for me to say something like that." Moon, who was there, remembered it as Eshelman wrote it: "I think Bob is suffering from selective memory syndrome. Certainly this is not the kind of language the present suave Wedge would use, but these were earlier days and this may have happened during a boozy party." Final word on the matter to Wedgeworth: "I categorically deny that I ever said the words attributed to me by Bill Eshelman. I would not have said such a thing to my own brother. It sounds more like something Bill Eshelman may have said. He always tried to demonstrate that he was 'hip' to the latest slang."

For his part Moon denied ever wanting or trying to manipulate Wedgeworth: "I supported him [for the executive director position] because I saw him as a smart cookie. Haven't changed my mind about that." Overall Moon gave Wedgeworth fairly high marks for his 13-year tenure as executive director:

Wedgeworth was a great outside advocate — a presence outside the profession, representing librarians in Washington, in international circles, and so forth. Wedgeworth was definitely very good at this. I do not think he was so effective as an internal director. There's been a great deal of debate about that: whether we want somebody who would be a good manager or somebody who would be a good public representative for the profession. My point of view is that there's no way to avoid having the executive director be a public representative of librarianship. It's such an important job. Some argue the ALA president should be the voice of librarianship, but like it or not in the world at large the executive director will be seen as the voice, because of continuity.

So we have to have someone in the executive director position who has that public presence, who is a great salesman. Ideally, I would like to see the executive director's number two [the deputy director] act as the manager of the association. I think Wedgeworth felt that way too, but he made such lousy appointments that he never had a very strong number two. On the whole I think he was a pretty good executive director, although he was sometimes arrogant.

When Wedgeworth left ALA in 1985 to become dean of Columbia University's library school, Thomas Galvin took over as executive director. Over the years Moon and Galvin were on opposing sides of most issues and, according to insiders like John Berry and Norman Horrocks, a "fierce rivalry" existed between the two men. In a postscript in a letter to Ben Bagdikian dated May 24, 1985, Moon commented: "Did you know that the new ALA Executive Director is to be Tom Galvin? Ugh!" Four years later Galvin's directorship ended ignominiously when he was forced out. Moon shed no tears, characterizing his rival "one of the world's natural disasters" and his term in office "a fiasco." After Galvin came a parade of executive directors— Linda Crismond, Peggy Sullivan, Elizabeth Martinez, and Mary Ghikas (acting) — none of whom had the right stuff to master or survive ALA's venomous political culture and imploding organizational structure. The book is still out on the current occupant, William Gordon, appointed in 1998.

- ALA President. The association's highest elected officer, the president serves a one-year term but election carries a three-year obligation: "The president-elect shall serve the first year after election as vice-president, the second year as president, and the third year as immediate past president" (Constitution, Article VIII, Sec. 3). Duties of the president include serving on the Executive Board and Council, developing a presidential agenda and program, presiding at meetings, and representing ALA at meetings of other library associations in the United States and abroad.

Despite not achieving his big goal as president (a viable national information policy), Moon took satisfaction in knowing that he had aimed high. In addition he performed the routine responsibilities of the office conscientiously and with considerable proficiency. Especially noteworthy was the way he conducted Council and Membership meetings, which received plaudits even from people who disliked him. He remembered one time he turned to chair over to Russell Shank, the vice president: "And something erupted, I forget what, and Russ got more and more bothered by the situation, and finally he said in an angry voice, 'Listen, we can settle all this if you will only do what I tell you to do.' We finally had to call a five-minute break, and all kinds of people from the audience came up and said, 'Eric, take over, for God's sake, take over.' So I took over after the break, and it was all right." Moon believed few people know how difficult chairing a large meeting can be:

You're on the platform, you've got the dais, you've got the big prompt book, you've got papers galore, you've got the executive director on one side whispering in your ear, the parliamentarian on the other side, various people coming around, and you've got all these people at microphones that you've got to keep tabs on. It's damned hard work. Most people don't have any idea how hard it is. But if you ever look as if you're losing control, you're dead. You're absolutely dead. I used to enjoy chairing; that was the part of the thing I liked.

What frustrated him most about the presidency — and this has been true of other ALA presidents in recent times — was the lack of real power inherent in the office. An activist by nature, Moon used every ounce of presidential power available to him (most dramatically in the area of committee appointments), but in the long run he accomplished precious little, considering the energy expended. He summed it up this way: "There's some power there [in the presidency], but it depends of course on the individual, and how much the individual is prepared to use what power there is. But it's inevitable that the executive director and headquarters staff will have more power because they are permanent. The staff holds tremendous power, simply by virtue of being permanently in place, and also having years and years to build up a support network."

How might the presidency be strengthened? The Summers self-study committee criticized recent presidents for lacking a sense of continuity: "Each presidency has been like a circus that puts on its show, then takes down its tents and leaves." Obviously one year is not sufficient time to develop and implement major policy initiatives. What about increasing the length of the president's term? Wouldn't this improve continuity and give the president more power vis-à-vis the ALA bureaucracy? Moon:

Theoretically it would be a good idea to lengthen the term of the president but practically I would say it's virtually impossible and in some respects undesirable. It's undesirable because it would limit even more the number of people who could compete for the position, because they couldn't be away from their library job that long. And even those who could run would resist serving more than a year because of the amount of time involved. The term is, in essence, three years. You spend a year as president-elect, during which you're doing all the appointment process and preparing your program and a variety of other stuff, including lots of travel around the country; then you have a year of actually being president; and then you have a year of being immediate past president, during which you're still on the Exec Board — that year is a real comfort after the other two, but nevertheless it's still one with lots of responsibilities. If you lengthen the term, it gets even more impossible.

What about a paid — as opposed to volunteer — president? For instance, when Dick Dougherty was president (1990–1991) he proposed establishing "a well-funded Office of the President of ALA." Moon:

I remember that both Ed Holley and I at various times argued there is a need for a fund to support the presidency, that it could go to the person's authority for release time, expenses, or whatever. Being ALA president is a very expensive proposition, and for most members of the association it's not even a feasible thing to think about. If you're not in a large system or a library school it's very difficult to manage because of the amount of time involved off of the job and also the amount of travel. Ilse and I calculated that the presidency cost us— out of our own pocket — something like $16,000, and that was back in 1977-78. This was not money spent on the campaign but money spend performing the duties of the office — travel, et cetera.

- ALA Divisions. Moon never disguised his strong conviction that in their desire for autonomy and a distinct identity ALA's divisions do great harm to the association's central authority. Here Moon made a distinction between "library" divisions (those representing types of libraries, such as the Association of College and Research Libraries), which he believed are the real culprits, and "activity" divisions (those representing types of library service, such as the Reference and User Services Association), which he viewed more benignly. Given a free hand to change ALA any way he wanted, Moon said, "One of the things I would want to get rid of, more than anything else, would be the library divisions."

Moon also believed that in addition to weakening ALA at the core the library divisions foster an unhealthy class consciousness among librarians:

Even the word "division" implies what's wrong: what we need is unity, not division. I don't think the library divisions we have help the profession much at all; in fact they tend to perpetuate the kind of class structure that has existed in librarianship for a long time. At the top are the academic and research librarians, somewhere in the middle are the public librarians, and at the bottom are the school librarians. The divisions perpetuate the sort of iron curtains that exist among these types of libraries. It's very difficult to move across these library boundaries in the association and in the workplace. It seems to me ALA should be in the business of breaking down these barriers, not building them up. I'm not too hot for the activity divisions either — I'm not very hot for divisions altogether — but I think they're less damaging than the library divisions.

But much as the divisions annoyed him, it distressed him more when leaders of ACRL or one of the other library divisions made noises about breaking completely with ALA, as they periodically did (and still do): "I thought it was already a tragedy that we had lost the special librarians, the medical librarians, and some others. In fact I wrote a number of times that this profession is not strong enough to afford disunity. The biggest and most powerful voice we have is ALA. What we've got to do is make ALA represent the things we believe in, but certainly not leave it or try to set up some opposition organization, which I think would be foolish." Carla Stoffle, a well-known academic librarian, recalled that when she became president-elect of ACRL, "Eric challenged me to bring ACRL leadership into ALA leadership positions. He challenged me to show that we could all be one association and work together for the best of librarianship."

- ALA Publishing Services. Another facet of ALA that came under Moon's close scrutiny was its publishing operation, which as recently as the early 1990s he criticized as inefficient and underperforming. Moon:

Certainly financially the publishing department ought to be a major, major source of income for the association and it is not. Its profit against gross is something that would have got me fired from *Library Journal* and Scarecrow Press. It publishes about one-third what I was publishing at Scarecrow with five times the staff. It also overprints, printing 10,000 copies of a book that will sell only 2,000 copies, on theory of keeping cost per copy down. Which means they have to eat a large inventory. Overprinting has traditionally plagued the university presses, and ALA does the same thing. Scarecrow, on the other hand, keeps the copy cost low by printing short runs, and reprinting as necessary, which is a much more effective way of cutting costs.

ALA publishing has all the advantages— all those magazines where they can advertise free, and they have membership support, but still the performance is dismal. Another problem is ALA publishing uses the committee system to decide what to publish. This is too cumbersome and involves too many delays. The publishing operation ought to be providing several million dollars a year to support programs— but it barely breaks even. This is an area ripe for reform in ALA.

Soon after Wedgeworth became executive director in 1972, Moon offered to take over the association's publishing enterprise, promising big profits: "I advised Wedge to look to ALA publishing, pointing out that there's the place you can get a lot of the income you need to run the association, if it's done right. I made him an offer at the time, which I would not have made to anybody else: I said if you could guarantee me no committees and absolutely no interference from anybody, I could, as head of ALA publishing, earn you a million dollars a year clear profit within the first two years and three million dollars a year within five years." This was not simply Moon bluster. By this time he had full control of Scarecrow Press and was highly knowledgeable about the economics of the publishing business. But could he have made ALA millions? We'll never know.

Obviously Wedgeworth did not take Moon up on his offer. Moon later heard via the grapevine that Wedgeworth had said, "ALA doesn't have room for both Moon and me," to which Moon responded, "Bob was always scared of competition, which is why I think he made so many bad appointments. He appointed people who would be no threat to him." But Wedgeworth retorted that Moon "never offered directly to come and work for ALA. Eric is not a person who would make such an offer directly. Any offer to work for ALA — if there was any such offer — was implied, not stated directly."

As for his appointments, Wedgeworth said, "It is true that I am not a competitive person in the sense that Eric would see it. I have always measured myself more in terms of my own goals. Contrary to what Eric says, I have been enormously successful in attracting great talents to work with me in many capacities because they are confident that they will receive strong support and full credit for their accomplishments. When they are successful I am successful. The record speaks for itself!"

Later Moon confessed, "I knew there was no possibility of my taking over ALA publishing. I was trying to make a point and trying to urge Bob to get someone who would run it that way and so he would know what the possibilities were. My offer was meant as a challenge." But, he added, if Wedgeworth had taken up the challenge, "I might have considered it."

"Card-Carrying Reformer"

On more than one occasion Moon testified that "ALA has played a major role in my life." Equally true is the fact that Moon played a major role in the life of ALA. He was made aware of his singular contribution to the association at a luncheon for past presidents in 1987: "It was in San Francisco. I had just received the Honorary Membership award [ALA's highest honor]. When I came into the room, Keith Doms congratulated me and said aloud to the entire table, 'You know, of all the people in this room, it's really appropriate that Eric should receive the award because he probably has done more to change things in ALA and the profession than any of us.' These were all the past presidents and this was very nice to hear in that assembly."

In his efforts to change/reform/democratize ALA, he did not win every battle. Far from it. But with the help of talented, committed colleagues—Horrocks, Josey, Eshelman, Curley, Schuman, and scores of others—he made his mark. Perhaps David Kaser put it best: "He was a card-carrying reformer, and he got much reformed, most of which has resulted in the strengthening of the American library political system."

– 17 –

Retiring in the Sun

Goodbye Workplace

In an interview with the editor of the *New Library World* while in England in the fall of 1977 for the Library Association's centenary conference, Moon dropped a cryptic hint about his retirement plans: "I'm thinking of retirement — well, sort of retiring — pretty soon. I've got lots of things planned." He was 54 at the time and had never made a secret of his desire to quit the workplace early. Years before in Newfoundland he publicly announced (in a playbill, presumably tongue in cheek) that his ambition was to retire at age 37. Later while toiling as president of Scarecrow Press — a demanding job made tougher by heavy responsibilities with the American Library Association — he told Ilse, Robbie Franklin, and others close to him that because "the Moon men die young," he wanted to retire early in order to have at least a few years to enjoy himself before departing this world. But scrutiny of his family history reveals the claim of early death in the Moon line to be baseless, a small fib concocted possibly as a convenient way of cutting off further discussion about why he wanted to pack it in so soon. Around the time he repeated these statements, Moon knew nothing about the longevity of his paternal antecedents, including his long lost father, Ted Moon. Only years later, in 1999, did he learn that Ted died in Australia at age 62 — not old but not young either.

In any event, intimates were not surprised when he retired from Scarecrow at the end of 1978 at age 55. Al Daub, the press's vice president and one of the people most affected by his decision, believed the ALA presidency took a lot out of him and hastened his retirement by at least a couple of years. Moon denied this:

The fact is I always had a hankering to retire early because it seemed to me that as large a portion of your life as possible ought to be reserved for yourself. In fact, theater programs from Newfoundland always noted that Eric Moon's sole ambition was to retire by 37; I didn't retire until 55 — or 18 years behind schedule. But I really wanted to retire to use that part of my life for myself. And I've never regretted retiring when I did. I've had some comfortable years in which to enjoy myself.

So I went to Al and said, "I think I'm finished. I'm going to spend some time for me now." It wasn't sudden; I'd been thinking about it for several years; I'd had enough of work; I wanted to be lazy and have some fun. I don't think it grew out of the ALA presidency or frustration with Scarecrow. It was just something I wanted to do and had wanted to do for a long time. I would have done it earlier but for Ilse. We discussed retirement a number of times and she [nearly ten years younger than he] was by no means ready to retire. So I said OK, I will not do it until you tell me when. Finally — maybe the presidency did have something to do with it — she said OK, I think I'm ready. At that point I made the decision.

Though Moon retired as head of Scarecrow, he continued to work part-time as an editor for the press and as a consultant for Grolier, the parent company. Both Al Daub and Grolier's Ted Waller helped smooth the transition. Moon:

I wasn't particularly looking to continue with Scarecrow Press after retirement, but Al and Theodore set it up to make things easier for me in retirement. It was a kindhearted effort by them to make my life more comfortable — and to maintain a contact that still had some usefulness to them, since it was not that long after the ALA presidency and my name still had some currency. I was supposed to be on something like one-third time at one-third salary — I got a flat annual fee. This situation lasted for about six years, until I went on Social Security. That was the idea, to help tide me over until I got Social Security at 62.

I did whatever they asked me to do: editing manuscripts, giving them ideas for projects for Scarecrow, giving them names of people, that kind of thing. I also did a number of things for Grolier. I remember one year Ted asked me to go up to Danbury [in Connecticut where Grolier had moved its corporate headquarters] and examine all of the Grolier editorial departments and write a report for him on my findings. Another year I was asked to go to the Frankfurt Book Fair looking for new project ideas for Grolier. Ilse and I went and really wore our feet to the ground — the fair is held in five gigantic halls about the size of the Roman Colosseum, just packed to the gills with books. I spoke to Italian publishers, French publishers, et cetera and got a bundle of ideas, and when I got back I wrote a voluminous report, suggesting to Grolier what I thought were good, viable projects. And I never heard a word about any of them. This was very frustrating. The terrible thing about working on a consultant basis for Grolier was that I never really heard back. I would make proposals but never hear the results.

Moon handpicked his successor at Scarecrow, longtime friend Bill Eshelman. Esh, who left the editorship of *Wilson Library Bulletin* to take over the presidency of Scarecrow at the beginning of 1979, remembered the deal had been in the works for several years:

At Wilson I thought it would be time to move on after five or seven years [Eshelman started as editor of *WLB* in 1968] because editors especially are hard put to keep the old vigor after a time. You know, the burnout factor. So I was looking around and of course Eric knew it. He kept saying, "Why don't you follow me. I'm going to retire early, so why don't you wait a bit and follow me at Scarecrow." As time went on and I didn't find anything I wanted, Eric spoke to Ted Waller of Grolier. Then he introduced me to Waller and kept laying the groundwork. Finally in 1976 it was all arranged that I would follow Eric. Then I pointed out to Ted that if I stayed at the Wilson Company through 1977 I would have the ten years required for pension rights. So it was all carefully arranged that as soon as my pension rights were secured, I would go to Scarecrow. So in October 1978 I worked side-by-side with Eric until the end of the year and then took over at the beginning of 1979.

Robbie Franklin, Moon's loyal number two at Scarecrow during most of the 1970s, had mixed feelings about this turn of events. Moon: "When I retired I think Robbie expected to take over for me. I did not think Robbie was ready for the presidency and in any case I would not have appointed him over Al [Daub]. I thought we needed someone with much more background and context in the profession, so Esh got the job." Franklin said he "absolutely did *not*" expect to become Scarecrow's head man but that he had hoped for more than he got, which was nothing:

It never occurred to me that I would take precedence over Al. I think Eric finally decided that I was a Karl Nyren—a number two. The closest I came was the fantasy that Al would become president and I would become either vice president or something called editorial director. And in pursuit of that fantasy, a couple of times I thought I clearly demonstrated to Eric and Al, and also to Ted Waller, that in Eric's absence I could run the entire editorial operation absolutely just as well without exception. When Eric was out with his back problems—he was out for more than two months—I made damn certain that we kept pace and more than that, that we went up just a notch or so, so that I could communicate to anyone that I could do it. But as for being the top guy, it had not occurred to me.

But Franklin did want recognition for his hard work and loyalty over the years. So he asked for a raise, more as a sign of his worth to the company than a desire for money qua money. Making $19,000 a year at the time, he requested a healthy increase to $25,000, effective January 1979, which would coincide with Eshelman's taking over. Franklin recalled that Moon, Eshelman, and Daub invited him to lunch to render their decision:

I think one or more of the trio—Eric, Al, and Esh—was worried that there might be a big emotional blowup of some kind. I think they were actually worried—they were a little stiff-legged, like dogs; they were hyperaware, their antennae quivering. We went out to a local deli, two cars, four guys, bought big fat sandwiches and drove over to Esh's house, because they wanted to have my emotional breakdown happen in private. They didn't want it to happen in a public restaurant or at Scarecrow, and I think they were a little surprised to discover that I was at least as calm or calmer than the three of them. And they said to me, we're sorry but we're not able to meet your request. No counteroffer was forthcoming, so I said, "Well, I'll stay on for a few months if you would like, but then I'll take off." And that was that.

Franklin left Scarecrow in March 1979 and immediately began planning the launch of his own house, McFarland & Company, Inc., Publishers (McFarland being his middle name). Based on the Scarecrow model and located in Jefferson, North Carolina, McFarland published its first six books by September 1980, and not many years later Franklin's company had grown to roughly the size of the Scarecrow he had left. Today McFarland, with an admirably diversified list, has developed a strong presence in American publishing. Moon, Franklin's mentor, expressed pleasure about the way it all worked out: "I think actually Robbie is grateful now that he did leave when he did, because he's really done more good for himself on his own than he would have had he stayed at Scarecrow."

Hello Florida

Originally the Moons contemplated retiring to a foreign paradise. "Some years before Eric actually retired we embarked on this plan of looking for some warm, cheap place where we could afford to retire," recalled Ilse. "We wanted to be near the sea, and considered the Greek islands or the Canaries, romantic places like that. I opted for the Canaries because I figured Spanish was an easier language than Greek. I really didn't want to retire to a place where I not only had to learn a new language but a new alphabet!" In the mid–1970s the Moons spent a vacation in the Canary Islands (which lie off the northwest coast of Africa but have been part of Spain since the late 15th century), and not only did they have a smashing time, they impulsively brought a retirement house on Tenerife, the largest of the islands. Ilse:

We had an absolutely wonderful holiday. We looked at real estate and bumped into this little two-bedroom house in the Spanish style that had been owned by two widowed sisters. Tenerife is beautiful, especially the mountains, and the bedrooms overlooked Mount Teide [Pico de Teide], a beautiful snowcapped mountain. The house was up the mountain from the city [Puerto de la Cruz] and the living room looked down over a banana plantation. It was lovely. The only problem was the garden had been concreted over by the old ladies. The house was not all that expensive, so we bought it.

The financial transaction had to be completed pronto, and Eric turned to Robbie Franklin back at Scarecrow in New Jersey for help. Franklin had to use his ingenuity to come up with the necessary funds on short notice and have them transferred to a Tenerife bank. He remembered the caper well: "Al wasn't available, so I forged his signature on a Scarecrow check because anything over a certain amount had to have a double signature — Al's and Eric's. I did Al's and right under it I did a perfect Eric Moon. My Al was not very good but my Eric was spot on. I took the check down to the bank and cashed it, then I hopped on the train and went into New York, where I went to the Spanish bank of blah-blah and had the money wired to Eric in the Canary Islands."

The Moons arranged to rent the house until such time as they were ready to take up permanent residence on Tenerife. But Casa Moon soon developed some nasty — and costly — problems. During the first year, for instance, it sank an inch or two and faulty electrical wiring blew out three refrigerators in rapid succession, which of course the Moons had to replace. They also discovered their estate agent was, in Ilse's words, "somewhat less than honest." By the time retirement became a reality in 1978 the couple had had enough of Tenerife and their little dream house, and eventually they sold it.

Meanwhile, for quite practical reasons, Florida became their retirement destination. Ilse explained:

My parents by this time were living in Cape Coral, Florida [just south of Fort Myers on the Gulf coast]. My father had retired and wasn't very well. In the last years before he retired they became snowbirds in Florida, then they settled in pretty much fully retired in a condominium. I got more and more uncomfortable about retiring to the Canaries. I know Eric: I was the one who was going to have to deal with things around the house, the electricity and plumbing — the things that went wrong. And there was the language problem. And it was an isolated place, a long way from the U.S. and our friends. And my parents were getting elderly. So it seemed reasonable to be closer to them.

In January 1979 the Moons moved to Florida, staying with Ilse's parents for six weeks or so until they found their own place. "We looked up and down the coast from Naples to Tampa and finally decided that Sarasota had the most to offer culturally," recalled Ilse. "And it was close enough to my parents that we could help them if needed, but not so close that my mother would be running our lives, which she would try to do if she could." Eric remembered that he and Ilse took off for Florida like a couple of carefree spirits chasing the sun:

Ilse's parents were becoming quite aged by that time, and she felt that if we retired it would be well for us to be somewhere close to them so that we could deal with anything that came up. So we simply decided to take off for Florida and see what happened. What we did essentially was sell or give away everything that we had in our New Jersey home except for some books and pictures and stuff that we stored in the Eshelmans' basement. We filled the car with whatever we were going to take with us, drove to Washington [D.C.] for the ALA Midwinter meeting, and then simply drove south to Florida, free as birds.

That was it. We were retired! We had nowhere to live, we were on the road. We went down to Cape Coral, saw her parents, dumped all our stuff there, and began looking for a place to live on the west coast. Soon it became clear Sarasota was the place, because it was probably the least redneck place we had seen in Florida — in fact, it's sort of the cultural capital of Florida. And so we settled there. I also wanted to spend a lot of time playing golf, so we wanted a place on a golf course.

The Moons ended up settling in Palm Aire, an upscale, almost exclusively white subdivision of Sarasota with a well-tended golf course and other amenities of the good life. They have been there ever since, largely happy with their lot. Eric:

I love the weather here but I hate the political climate. I don't like too many of the people, although I have some golf friends. I live here because I like to play golf and the weather's terrific and everything's fine, except that it's kind of an elite society. There's something that niggles me about that but I don't know what to do about it because I'm really very happy here. I've avoided involvement in the Sarasota community. Ilse once suggested I get involved in the local theater. I didn't want to do that — it would interfere with my retirement. I am really seriously in pursuit of laziness. I like it. The only structure in my life is golf. I have regular golf days; everything else is entirely loose.

Senior Statesman

While golf became a mainstay in retirement, Moon never lost interest in the library profession, remaining active through writing, speaking, and especially participation in a host of organizations. He spent three years (1979–1981) on the advisory board of the Library of Congress's Center for the Book, five years (1980–1985) on the board of directors of the Council for Florida Libraries, and a year (1980–1981) as a member of the Florida Library Association's Intellectual Freedom Committee. In 1987 he joined the board of the Friends of the Selby Public Library in Sarasota, and in 1991 he served as a delegate to the White House Conference on Library and Information Services. He even accepted an invitation to join the advisory board of the Maurice F. Tauber Foundation, established in 1981 to honor Tauber, a longtime professor at the library school at Columbia University who had died the previous year. Ironically, Moon disliked Tauber: "Maury was a bum with a big reputation. I once had a terrible run-in with him at an Archons [of Colophon] meeting, where he tried to attack me physically. We didn't like each other much." The Tauber Foundation lasted only a short time but for years Moon's résumé included his connection with it.

Naturally, ALA was the organization that received the lion's share of his attention during the retirement years. In fact, Moon contributed more to ALA *after* he retired than most members do during the course of an entire career. And in certain ways his influence in the association actually increased during this period. In retirement he took on the aura of elder statesman, achieving a kind of avuncular acceptance he had never had (nor aspired to) in the contentious 1960s and 1970s. Moon could not help but wonder: who had changed, he or "they"? He struggled with the conundrum:

You will find people who would say that I grew less radical with the passage of time, that I became far more reasonable and inclined to soft-pedal than in the past. I don't know if that's true or not, but I did start noticing a difference in attitude toward me. In the early days when I got to the microphone in ALA, the chances are that, if I were addressing Council, they would overwhelmingly vote against anything I spoke for. Later, frequently if they were in a hassle and I got up and said something, it resolved the problem. There was a real difference in attitude. Maybe it was the senior statesman syndrome. I didn't feel that I had changed but that it was they who had changed to my point of view. My message hadn't changed at all. Also, many people who were not connected with the ALA Establishment just saw me as a past president, ergo a figure rather than a person. These were inevitable changes in perception, but I hope they were not an indication that my attitudes had changed.

In addition to continuing to attend ALA Annual conferences and Midwinter meetings during the retirement years, he served on the Nominating Committee (1980–1981), had yet another stint on Council (1982–1986), chaired the Intellectual Freedom Committee (1984–1985), and put in three years (1991–1994) as an ALA Endowment Trustee (elected to the position by the Executive Board). He also remained a force in ALA politics, working mostly behind the scenes. As he explained in an interview in the magazine *Technicalities* in 1981, "I've gone to senior citizen's back-room status. I'm not out there at the microphones on the floor anymore or organizing in council. I'm working, if at all, in the smoke-filled rooms." He was especially active in the presidential campaigns of E.J. Josey, Pat Schuman, and Arthur Curley, all of whom won, as well as those of Norman Horrocks, who lost twice.

Helping Josey win the ALA presidency in 1983 was among his proudest achievements:

I was E.J.'s campaign manager. We had a very strenuous nationwide campaign with committees in every state and well organized telephone and letter-writing campaigns. E.J.'s opponent was a friend of Ilse's and mine but we couldn't see supporting anybody other than E.J. Much as I love and admire Clara Jones, I still somehow feel it's a pity that E.J. wasn't the first black librarian elected president of ALA. More than any other single individual, he was recognized as the real leader in the breakthrough for minorities in librarianship. He's a very quiet, low-key individual, except when he's embarked on a battle. He's a warm, pleasant person, very religious. And he works himself to death; he works harder than anybody I know. Now retired, he's important today as a mentor and role model for young black librarians. He's the Jackie Robinson of librarianship.

Josey appointed Moon chair of the Intellectual Freedom Committee for the association year 1984-85, an assignment that once again brought him face to face with the controversial subject of national information policy. In the early 1980s, ALA president Carol Nemeyer (who had defeated Horrocks for the job) created a high-level commission to study and make policy recommendations on such politically sensitive issues as fees for access to electronic databases; private-sector publication of information generated by the government agencies; censorship by governmental entities at all levels (local, state, and federal); and the future of the Fairness Doctrine, the federal equal time provision that regulated political content in the broadcast media.

The commission — officially the ALA Commission on Freedom and Equality of Access to Information but commonly called the Lacy Commission, after its chair, Dan Lacy — included both librarians and nonlibrarians. Lacy, for instance, came from trade publishing (McGraw-Hill) and Ben Bagdikian, another member, was a well-known media analyst and journalism professor (and coincidentally Moon's good friend). Librarians on the commission included Bob Wedgeworth, Thomas Galvin, Brooke Sheldon, Kenneth Dowlin, and of course Nemeyer. The commission issued a draft report in early 1985 that Moon found alarming, not only due to its pro-business stance but the fact that many of its recommendations contradicted long-standing ALA policy. In February 1985 he expressed his deepest fears in a letter to Bagdikian: "NCLIS has in many respects sold out to the information industry, and the Lacy Commission, if one is to judge by this draft, is headed in the same direction.... From the beginning this operation has given every appearance of railroading (somewhat like the production of the film, *The Speaker*) and it is one of the things about the Commission that most worries and angers many of us at ALA."

Moon, in his role as IFC chair, delivered a damning critique of a minimally revised version of the Lacy Commission Report a few months later at ALA's annual conference in July, and years later he summed up the business this way: "This report created much controversy at the time, mainly because so much of it was in opposition to existing ALA policy — despite the presence on the body of an all-star delegation of librarians. The principal defender of ALA policy, and of what many of us regarded as socially responsible positions, was, interestingly enough, none of those librarians but the distinguished journalist Ben Bagdikian, whose minority opinions remain a pleasure to read." In the end the Lacy Commission and its report had minimal impact, ending up in a file drawer somewhere, another muddled — and failed — effort to patch together a national information policy acceptable to both public and private interests.

Highest Honors

Moon's final years of active participation in ALA focused on trying to halt the association's seemingly irrepressible slide toward division and balkanization. The decline of the association's membership as a political force hit him hardest. He had always regarded a vigorous, enlightened membership as essential to ALA's governance and ultimately its being. When the collective power of the membership faded to almost nothing in the early 1990s he decided the time had come to leave center stage. The circus was moving on. New venues, new acts, new performers required new leaders. Accordingly, after the 1994 Miami Beach conference, he bowed out. "We've finally done it," he reported. "I am now finally out of everything." Eager to underscore his resolve, he added: "I've resigned from everything, I've refused appointments to anything new, and we are no longer going to ALA." Of course this did not stop him and Ilse from following the library spectacle from afar, which they did — avidly.

Before his exit from the stage Moon received ALA's highest honors: the Joseph W. Lippincott Award (in 1981) and Honorary Membership for life (in 1987). Of all of the association's numerous awards— more than 100 are doled out each year — the Lippincott and Honorary Membership are the most prestigious, reserved for librarianship's crème de la crème.

The Lippincott Award, which consists of a citation of achievement and a cash prize of $1,000, annually recognizes a prominent librarian "for distinguished service to the profession." Moon used half the money for golf clubs and donated (anonymously) the other half to a library education scholarship at Rutgers University. The citation, written by his friend Bill Eshelman, provides an adulatory (and occasionally fanciful) summary of Moon's career:

Librarian, champion of civil liberties, social critic, journalist, editor, and suave politician, Eric Moon has worked for the betterment of librarianship for more than four decades. That he chose our profession over his youthful enthusiasms— acting and professional soccer — is cause for rejoicing. Forged in England and tempered in Newfoundland, his wit and will were ready when the call came to revivify *Library Journal*.

As editor he stimulated librarians to look beyond housekeeping and focus on service. He commissioned the seminal article exposing the ugly spectacle of segregation in libraries and library associations and led the fight to get the American Library Association to expel those chapters still practicing segregation.

As mentor he influenced thousands of students with editorials and in rap sessions.

As publisher he trebled the output of Scarecrow Press, extending its range and fearlessly accepting manuscripts too controversial for other publishers.

Rising from the back bench to the American Library Association presidency, as virtual conscience of the profession, he inspired in an entire generation of librarians a humanistic and socially progressive philosophy of library service. As American Library Association president, he opened up its committees to young people and minorities and persuaded other library associations to cooperate in drafting a National Information Policy. Even The International Federation of Library Associations and the Library Association have felt his liberating influence.

Honorary Membership for life is the crowning tribute ALA can bestow on an individual, and in 1987 Moon became only the 90th person so honored. He was of course elated: "Honorary Membership is the top ALA award. In fact, during ALA's history the number receiving the award works out to be less than one a year. And many of those are not librarians but people like Barbara Bush and members of the U.S. Congress who have been great library supporters. There are relatively few librarians. It's a very select group." When he received the Honorary Membership (at the opening session of the 1987 annual conference in San Francisco at the Moscone Convention Center), photos representing different periods of his life were flashed on a large screen. It was a fitting moment for a man who gave so much of himself to the association over the years.

As is the case with most ALA business, politics plays a large part in the awards selection process. Moon offered this behind-the-scenes account of the competition for the Lippincott the year he won:

What happens usually is a bunch of friends will decide, hey, why don't we nominate so-and-so for this award this year. Who started the campaign for me for the Lippincott I'm not entirely sure. It might have been E.J. [Josey] or Norman [Horrocks] or Arthur [Curley]—who knows? Wyman Jones was the chair of the Lippincott jury that year, which is why I think they decided to nominate me that year, because they figured I had a better chance with Wyman as chair than if we had one of the ALA conservatives who still probably disapproved mightily of me.

Anyway, whoever it was eventually got in touch with me, because they discovered that Margaret Monroe [an eminent library educator known for her innovative work in the area of adult services] was also nominated that year. They contacted me and asked for suggestions about people they should contact to write letters on my behalf. I said, look, you're not going to be able to compete with Margaret Monroe on numbers—there aren't that many people who are going to write letters for me, so why don't we compete on name value, and get real big names. So they got Bill Katz and about 25 other impressive supporters. Apparently there were hundreds of letters for Margaret against my two dozen or so, but mine were so powerful that I got the nod.

Another example of how important letters of support are in the ALA awards business occurred when Moon nominated Lawrence Clark Powell for Honorary Membership. Moon explained:

That year E.J. [Josey] was chair of the Executive Board subcommittee that deals with awards. He wrote to me asking if there was anyone I thought we should put up for Honorary Membership and I said Larry Powell. Here was one of the great people of the profession; for God's sake, let's get Larry Powell, I said. So I wrote a nominating letter and got others to write in support. And E.J., who didn't know the situation and without consulting me, contacted Bob Vosper, one of Powell's protégés, a person who owed his career to Powell, and asked whether he would write a letter supporting Powell's nomination. And Vosper wrote a rotten letter saying that Larry Powell had never done anything for ALA and didn't deserve this. E.J. sent this to me in a panic and I said, "Bury it. You should never have written to this person in the first place."

In October 2000, Moon received yet another high honor: an Honorary Fellowship of the (British) Library Association bestowed in recognition of his "long and distinguished service in promoting the objects of the Association by encouraging the highest standards of professional practice and library service." In his acceptance letter Moon wrote, "For someone who has been so long an expatriate, it is heartwarming to be not only remembered but so honored by The Library Association, which was a major shaping force early in my professional career." Harold Smith was especially pleased: "I did suggest the Honorary FLA for Eric. He was a thorn in the Establishment of yesteryear, but why not try? And it came off. He does deserve it — there aren't many British librarians who have gone to the States and become president of the ALA — and I think the award rather tickles him."

White House Conference

Another big moment for Moon during the retirement years occurred in 1991 when he served as a delegate to the White House Conference on Library and Information Services, held in Washington, D.C., the week of July 9–13. It was an experience he almost missed because of a bureaucratic snafu:

I got a call from the White House Conference staff asking if I'd be interested in being a delegate, and I said yes, I'd like to be. I sent in all the appropriate forms and so forth but heard nothing more. Just before going off to ALA in June [1991] I called the conference office to check on my status but nobody knew anything about me or my being a delegate. So I go off to ALA [in Atlanta] and on the first night I'm sitting in a restaurant with Tom Featherstone [a British librarian] and his wife and three tables away is Charlie Reid, who's chairman of the National Commission [NCLIS] and of the White House Conference. Charlie's an old friend of mine and Ilse's, the one who married us. He comes over to my table and I tell him the story about not getting an answer about my status from the conference office. A half an hour later Peter Young and Mary Alice Resnick of the White House Conference staff come over to the table saying there must be some mistake, I'm a delegate. This of course was all bullshit but eventually I am a delegate, all because of Charlie. It was a pure fluke, bumping into Charlie.

Moon loved being part of this high-profile event, only the second such conference ever held (the first was in 1979). It featured 700 delegates and 254 alternates, a mix of both librarians and nonlibrarians representing every state of the union and all relevant interest groups. They came together for five days in the nation's capital to explore the big issues facing libraries and other information providers in the electronic age. The debate was intensely political, combative, and often frenetic. Moon was in his element:

I was a delegate-at-large. There were 10 or 12 panels or discussion groups, and I went onto the panel on national information policy. Each group had to elect two of their members to serve on the Conference Recommendations Committee, which already had nine members appointed by the National Commission [NCLIS], including Pat Schuman [who was president of ALA that year], Bob Wedgeworth, and a lot of information industry people. Out of our group, I was elected along with Senator Garn [U.S. Senator Jake Garn, a conservative Republican from Utah]. The committee was up all night two nights in a row battling to reduce 172 resolutions to something reasonable, and I was fighting like hell with Garn and other people to keep out all the stuff on privatization and fees. Pat Schuman was doing the same. We were battling like crazy to stop all that and in fact we won.

It was an interesting experience, but what a mess that whole operation was. Just dreadful — the conference was chaotic. I'm not personally a fan of White House Conferences. I think they're political exercises in futility. It's like having an elephant crack walnuts. I doubt that very much came out of the 1991 conference, though one encouraging thing about it was that the delegates from around the country were very supportive of ALA's stand opposed to fees and privatization. Nothing about fees and privatization appears in the report, despite great pressure from the Republicans and the information industry to promote these concepts.

Writing and Speaking in Retirement

When Moon left Scarecrow he intended to stop writing for publication. "Retirement means giving up work," he declared, "and the most work of all is writing. Now if I keep writing I may as well not be retired at all." Similarly, he vowed to reject all speaking invitations that came his way; they too would interfere with his retirement regimen. But these resolutions were easier to announce than to keep and, as in the case of his involvement with library organizations, he soon found himself doing more writing and speaking in retirement than most librarians do in a professional lifetime.

Among his varied output during this period: "To Disagree Is Not to Destroy," a speech delivered in 1981 at a University of Alabama symposium on the First Amendment organized by Dorothy Broderick; "The Issues That Confront Us Now," a speech delivered in 1984 at a meeting of the New Jersey Black Librarians Network honoring E.J. Josey; "The Library Press and Eric Moon," a 1984 interview with Moon conducted by Frederick J. Stielow for publication in *Activism in American Librarianship, 1962–1973*, edited by Mary Lee Bundy and Stielow (Greenwood Press, 1987); "Our Commission, Our Omissions," a much quoted article on NCLIS published in *Library Journal* (July 1984); a foreword to Lawrence Clark Powell's memoir *Life Goes On: Twenty More Years of Fortune and Friendship* (Scarecrow Press, 1986); "Living the Library Bill of Rights," a speech to the ALA Intellectual Freedom Round Table delivered at the association's 1990 annual conference; "A 'Chapter' Chapter: E.J., ALA, and Civil Rights," an essay published in *E.J. Josey: An Activist Librarian*, a festschrift honoring Josey edited by Ismail Abdullahi (Scarecrow Press, 1992); and a foreword to the paperback reissue of Sandy Berman's classic *Prejudices and Antipathies: A Tract on the LC Subject Heads Concerning People* (McFarland, 1993).

Moon capped his career with the publication of a 442-page sampler of his writings and speeches entitled *A Desire to Learn: Selected Writings* (Scarecrow Press, 1993). Dedicated to E.J. Josey and Dorothy Broderick, two of Moon's closest colleagues who became estranged over *The Speaker*, the collection consists of 50 items ranging from an early article ("Critics, Awake!") originally published in the British periodical *The Library Assistant* in 1951 to the 1992 essay in the Josey festschrift. *A Desire to Learn* received much critical praise in both the United States and Britain, David Gerard's review an especially thoughtful example:

> The book is a compendium of editorials, articles and speeches delivered on a variety of occasions in Moon's long career as a polemicist and *provocateur*, a record of a campaigner, an eloquent and persistent campaigner, in support of some very unpopular causes previously deemed unsuitable for ventilation in the library press. Here in Britain we tend to think of Americans as stridently assertive of their rights (didn't they coin a Bill of Rights?) and everywhere and always noisily re-emphasizing their addiction to freedom. It is not often appreciated what a weight of conservatism, inertia, equivocation and malignant prejudice poisons progress in the USA, because we are treated to wide coverage of Civil Rights marches. Such visual highlights blind us to the underlying presence of a large majority which resists social evolution and feels menaced by any threats to its status. Moon's efforts to align the profession with the currents of change which were discernible on the political scene in the 1960s led to internal dissensions. Openly, explicitly, in continued advocacy he brought the racial problem, Vietnam, the status of women in libraries, the endemic urge towards censorship of thought in print — all these explosive themes into the columns of a traditionally conservative professional journal, and equally he broadcast his convictions on public platforms, at library conferences, on the stump the length and breadth of the country. It required courage, and resulted in threats to his person, but he wrote and spoke as he saw, and in doing so brought a professional body out of the era of pallid self-effacement into the hot blood and sand of our late twentieth century. It was an achievement which finds its reward in the pages of this book.

The book complements two other collections—*Book Selection and Censorship in the Sixties* (R.R. Bowker, 1969) and *Library Issues: The Sixties* (R.R. Bowker, 1970)— that include many of Moon's *LJ* articles, surveys, and editorials.

One writing assignment Moon adamantly refused to undertake was his autobiography or memoirs— this despite being urged to do so by Bill Eshelman (when Esh was president of Scarecrow Press) and despite the fact that while Moon was head of Scarecrow he initiated a series devoted to the lives of notable British and American librarians, including Ronald Benge, Martha Boaz, Ralph Ellsworth, David Gerard, Guy Lyle, and Will Ready. "I never seriously considered doing an autobiography," confessed Moon. "One morning I sat down to play with it and never went back to it. I just decided it would be more work than I wanted to do." And off he went to polish his putting game.

Team Moon

When Moon retired from full-time work at the end of 1978 at age 55, Ilse was only 46. For her the move to Florida meant giving up a rewarding job in New Jersey as director of Professional Development Studies at the library school at Rutgers University, a position she had held for just two years. Though Ilse enjoyed aspects of

Sarasota and Palm Aire, and being within easy reach of her elderly parents was a solace, life in Florida required some difficult adjustments concerning her career. For a number of years she did not seek professional work, opting instead to fill her days with a variety of suburban housewifely activities, but eventually tedium set in: "I was going bananas doing mostly volunteer work for the public library and the League of Women Voters. It got to the point that I was spending the whole morning reading the newspaper over coffee." She did briefly try her hand at writing for *Current Biography* (the H.W. Wilson reference publication), contributing profiles of such newsworthy people as Eleanor Smeal (then head of the National Organization for Women) and Neil Goldschmidt (Jimmy Carter's transportation secretary), but the pay was poor and in the end she concluded "it just wasn't worth it."

In 1988 Ilse went back to work, becoming executive secretary of the Association for Library and Information Science Education, a national organization of library educators affiliated with (but not part of) ALA. The job, which allowed her to work at home in Palm Aire, was officially a part-time position but during certain months she put in full-time hours and more. Motivated by a genuine interest in library education and the people involved, she did stellar work for ALISE, and the job suited her assertive personality and eagerness to be in the know. "The part of the job I liked best," she recalled, "was being in constant contact with the deans and faculty — being kind of a nerve center."

Eric tried to be a good sport about Ilse's job. For instance, at ALISE's annual conferences he tended bar, and one year he was given (humorously) a bartender's badge and bow tie to wear. Ed Holley, an active member of the association and noted bow tie guy, remembered Moon quipping, "I never thought I'd see the day when I would be competing with Ed Holley for bow ties!" However, the job soon caused friction in the Moon household. "The ALISE job hasn't put a strain on our relationship," said Eric at the time, "but it's clearly something that we have different points of view on. It's very unfortunate: part of the enjoyment of retirement is being able to decide at the drop of a hat that let's tomorrow go to, say, Tahiti."

Ilse or course understood his frustration and reluctantly decided to give in: "I think Eric will be much happier when I get rid of this job so we can pick up and travel. This job has many restrictions; it's difficult to go away for a month at a time. From the beginning the ALISE job has been an annoyance to Eric, because it interfered with playtime."

Finally after four years with ALISE, Ilse called it quits. At her last conference as executive secretary, in January 1992, she received plaques, flowers, and a standing ovation; the minutes of the business meeting reported:

Moon said that her four years with ALISE were among the most enjoyable and productive in her professional life. She said that she accomplished most of the goals she had when hired: to improve communication, foster better relations with practitioners, increase membership, strengthen ALISE's ties with other associations, encourage members' participation in legislative efforts, and create a sound financial situation. While looking forward to spending more time with her husband and friends, Moon said that she would miss the daily challenges and people with whom she has worked.

Notwithstanding whatever stresses Ilse's ALISE job might have put on the relationship, the Moons' marriage was always a close and happy one, an enduring partnership based on mutual love, respect, and interests. People who knew the couple well often commented that Eric and Ilse made "a great team" (Pat Schuman) and that they functioned together "like hand and glove" (Clara Jones). Evie Wilson-Lingbloom, a librarian friend of the Moons for many years, observed, "I know this sounds hokey, but from my observations of them together, I think Ilse and Eric *really* love each other." Another frequent observation concerned Ilse's key role in facilitating Eric's career as a library politician. Norman Horrocks offered this perspective: "I think Diana [Moon's first wife] didn't have the same intensity; her interests were not the same as Eric's, and she wasn't a librarian. Ilse on the other hand, who is a librarian, has always been interested in the political process, so from a political and professional standpoint they make a good team. Ilse has supported him in a way that Di was unable to or chose not to." Carla Stoffle pointed out, "Ilse broadens Eric's perspective and helps him see other viewpoints and angles," and Bob Wedgeworth added, "Ilse is a strong person in her own right. She smooths out some of Eric's rough edges. He can be abrupt and insensitive at times and she often helps him achieve his objectives."

On a more personal level Dick Bye observed, "All I know is that when Eric met Ilse he settled down and stopped talking like a schoolboy on the prowl." And Mary K. Chelton had this to say about team Moon: "Given his intellect, I suspect she keeps him from being an arrogant prick at times, and I think any male, no matter how enlightened, can benefit from constant exposure to a feminist bed partner."

Retirement Pleasures

A welcome aspect of retirement for Moon was freedom from the stuffy decorum of the business world. Retirement meant complete casual living, as in no coats and ties. Well, almost. One time after leaving Scarecrow but while still working as a consultant to Grolier, he had business at the publisher's corporate headquarters in Connecticut, and he and Ilse decided to drive up leisurely from Florida. About 500 miles into the trip he turned to her and exclaimed, "God!" Alarmed, she asked, "Eric, What's wrong?" "I got so used to being retired," he said, "I didn't even bring a suit." He had to stop and buy one along the way. But retirement had little effect on Moon's sartorial style at ALA, which was almost always conspicuously casual, even when casual was not the fashion rage it is today. Gerry Shields saw Moon's informal attire as part of a calculated facade: "Eric's style was that of a good actor in a professional touring company. His role was as sage in an unbuttoned shirt. He seldom if ever appeared in the suit and tie affected by his peers. Polo shirts and sweaters were the costume. They were never loud or tasteless—just informal and insistent in promoting a relaxed old-shoe image. It was not until he became ALA president that he made a few concessions to traditional costume."

In addition to sharing life with Ilse and never (or rarely) having to dress up, Moon's chief pleasures in retirement were golf, travel, reading, films, and family, not necessarily in that order, though golf, oddly, assumed a special place in his putatively socialist heart. (The game of golf is still looked upon by some proletariat types as a reactionary hobby that requires an unconscionable amount of desirable land for the frivolous enjoyment of an elite few). Mostly he played the Palm Aire Country Club course, located near the Moon's villa, though every now and then he tackled other courses in and out of Florida. For instance, he and Dick Dougherty and Al Daub made two trips abroad, to Scotland and later Ireland, to play some of the world's most famous holes; Dougherty remembered Moon as "a ferocious competitor," adding: "He will do his best to hustle a stroke, if he can get away with it. I can almost hear him now telling Al and me how old and decrepit he is and how many strokes we simply have to give him." Moon especially looked forward each year to March when Daub and his wife Marty usually visited the Moons and the two men would team up for Palm Aire's annual invitational tournament, which they won in 1992.

The Moons did some serious recreational travel in the 1980s, including trips to England with Bill Eshelman and Pat Rom; the south of France with Dick and Nancy Bye (an area, enthused Moon, "I loved so much I could have retired there"); and the Canary Islands (during which time they divested themselves of the little house they had bought there some years before.) But it wasn't until the 1990s, after Ilse gave up the ALISE job, that they really spread their wings. Among the highlights: Ireland in 1992 with the Daubs and Doughertys, which featured golf for the men and sightseeing for the women; Asia in 1994, including stops in Hong Kong, Bangkok, Java, Bali, and Manila; an Alaska cruise in 1995; Mexico in 1995 with the Byes; England in early 1998 to fête Ronald Benge on the occasion of his 80th birthday (a gala event attended among others by actress Julie Christie, who told Moon, "I wish I could speak like you"; he gallantly replied, "I wish I could do anything like you"); a European tour in the fall of 1998 with Eshelman and Rom (Moon was mugged on this trip in Amsterdam); and a Panama Canal cruise in 1999. A major trip in the new century occurred in early 2001 when the couple visited a number of islands in the South Pacific in the Tahiti area.

Always a prolific reader, Moon in retirement averaged about six books a week, many of them mysteries. "About half the time I spend reading detective stories now," he reported. Lest anyone criticize him for wasting time on pap, he quickly added, "As a matter of fact it's my considered opinion that the best writers of literature today are writing in that genre. They are considerably better, many of them, than the name writers that get big reviews in *The New York Times Book Review* and everywhere else." In 1984 Dallas hosted ALA's annual conference and the city's public library asked association leaders to indicate their favorite books for a display. Moon identified *The Collected Plays of Bernard Shaw* as having "the greatest impact upon me as a young person" and then named "the three most important books of my adult years": Ralph Ellison's *Invisible Man*, J.D. Salinger's *Catcher in the Rye*, and Doris Lessing's *Golden Notebook*. "These three great novels," he explained, "deal with three of the most oppressed and misunderstood groups in our society: blacks, young people, and women." At last count his personal library contained roughly a thousand books, each title evoking a memory that "means something" to him.

Moon also indulged his love for the cinema during the retirement years, continuing a passion that began as a young man in Southampton and later prompted him to establish a line of books on the subject at Scarecrow. Arthur Curley considered Moon "a genuine authority on the movies." As anecdotal evidence, Curley told this story: "Once when my daughters were young I was in a restaurant in Gloucester, Massachusetts, with the two of them. We were talking about movies and because we were in Gloucester the film *Captains Courageous* came up, and immediately we were trying to recall who played the little kid in that film. Finally I said to the girls I knew where I could find out in a second. I went to a phone, called Eric in New Jersey [this was in the 1970s], and said, "I can't remember the name of the little kid in *Captains Courageous*," and without a halt, he said, "Freddie Bartholomew." In the retirement years he and Ilse built a substantial home library of favorite films.

Family Bonds

During his years in the workplace in England, Canada, and the United States, Moon normally put career ahead of family, but after retiring he made efforts to renew or strengthen relations with his two sons and brother and their families. Max, Moon's first son, himself an early retiree (from AT&T at age 50), moved with wife Belinda to Osprey, Florida, a town a few miles south of Sarasota. Moon took a grandfatherly interest in Max and Belinda's children, Eric Lonnie (born 1969) and Colin (born 1977). Belinda recalled that when the boys were young, "My father-in-law would read to them before bedtime, and he took them out on the golf course and let them drive the golf cart." In 1998 he and Ilse attended Eric Lonnie Moon's marriage in Hershey, Pennsylvania, which, he said, made him feel old.

Alan, his younger son, found challenging work in the international board game business. Estranged from his father for a period after his parents' divorce in the early 1970s, Alan eventually came to grips with that hurt and reconciled with his father. "Four years in college from age 23 to 27 [after military service that included a tour in Vietnam] turned out to be my time of healing," confided Alan. "It was then that I first began to realize how much my father had influenced my feelings and beliefs. Without my consciously knowing it, my father had passed on his simple philosophy of the value of freedom, of how to be happy, of how to enjoy life. He had also hidden a timed release bomb in my head, a bomb full of liberal political views, compassion, and respect for the rights of others."

Eric and his brother Bryan also became closer, reconnecting both fraternally and geographically. As adults, the brothers were never on bad terms (though Eric's divorce caused some tension) but their careers took much different paths and until the 1990s they saw each other only rarely. Bryan, a retired airline executive and highly successful artist, and wife Cicely have lived in Minnesota since the 1960s, where they raised their two sons, Christopher and Howard, and he had his studio. Like many successful Midwesterners, they began coming to Florida in the frigid months, naturally gravitating to the Sarasota area where brother Eric lived, and in 1999 they bought a winter home in Palm Aire quite near Eric and Ilse. For the first time since their youth in Southampton the Moon brothers were experiencing sibling togetherness.

Crossing the Bar

Moon, who turned 79 on March 6, 2002, remains mentally sharp and in reasonably good physical condition for a man his age. The hair has naturally thinned and the mustache is now white, but the frame is still trim and the carriage erect. He quit smoking in 1990 (mainly for social reasons) and, though he continues to drink, his alcohol intake has been considerably reduced from years past. To be sure, there are assorted health problems, though none life-threatening. Since birth he had been plagued with a bad digestive system, a Moon family malady apparently inherited from Mum; and he developed a chronic back condition (herniated disk) that dated back to bowling with his sons in the 1960s in New Jersey. In the 1990s he suffered from a swallowing disorder called achalasia, which was successfully treated by Dr. H. Worth Boyce, a prominent specialist in Tampa.

"I've really enjoyed most of my life," reflected Moon, who, being a realist, knew that time was growing short. As he aged, inquired his biographer, had he grown more spiritual? Did he derive strength or comfort from any religious faith? Moon, an atheist, would have none of it:

I have declared frequently publicly and privately that the world's two greatest enemies are religion and nationalism. Get rid of both of those and you would get rid of the cause of nearly every war that has ever broken out. I really regard religion as a kind of mythology and folklore that has been built up to support an illegitimate profession. I really don't want anything to do with it. I can't abide it. The satisfactions there are in life come from people who do things that inspire or help or improve the lives of other people, and in that group, supreme for me, are the artists, the writers, the actors—people whose imaginations help improve the imaginations of others.

And his attitude toward death? "I'm not for it! I guess my attitude is that it's inevitable, though one needn't be too pleased about it." He was "very much in favor of the right to die; you should have a right to decide for yourself." He revealed he will be cremated, and jokingly said he'd like to have his ashes scattered in one of the sand traps on the Palm Aire golf course.

– 18 –

Summing Up Eric Moon

The Record

Moon's remarkable library career, which began in 1939 on the eve of World War II, took him from a junior assistant (or clerk) position in his hometown of Southampton, England, to the heights of the profession in the United States in the raucous 1960s and 1970s. Among his major accomplishments: rejuvenation of a stale, foundering *Library Journal*, North America's foremost library periodical; creation of a fresh, honest, dynamic library journalism that changed the way librarians perceive themselves and their world; transformation of Scarecrow Press from a back-pocket operation into a formidable publishing enterprise; and election as president of the American Library Association, the world's largest and most influential library organization.

In addition, Moon's leadership was instrumental in exposing and eliminating institutional racism in American librarianship, and in democratizing ALA, hitherto the preserve of a narrow, conservative elite. He also contributed substantially to the debate on intellectual freedom and censorship in libraries, adopting the final sentence of *The Freedom to Read Statement* as his credo: "Freedom is a dangerous way of life, but it is ours."

Moon's impact on the profession as teacher and mentor was less readily apparent than his other achievements but no less significant. Except briefly in the 1950s when he lectured part-time at North-Western Polytechnic School of Librarianship in London, he did little formal teaching, resisting several opportunities to join library school faculties in the United States after gaining prominence as editor of *Library Journal*. Yet he was an inveterate teacher, his passion to educate infusing everything he did professionally. During Moon's editorship of *LJ*, for instance, the magazine took on the character of a lively national tutorial on the major issues confronting contemporary librarianship, with himself as master (or head tutor) and *LJ*'s readers his students. In similar fashion, during the campaign to reform ALA in the late 1960s and early 1970s, he assumed the role of "guru," instructing young militants in tactics about how best to achieve their — and his— aims. Later he created the Eric Moon Flying Circus, a sort of traveling college of librarianship. His protégés—Arthur Curley, Pat Schuman, John Berry, Robbie Franklin, Judy Serebnick, John Wakeman, et al.—attest to his mentoring powers.

Moon did not win every battle nor slay every dragon. But neither did he shrink from taking on the truly tough problems. In the case of his most public defeat—an ambitious but ill-fated effort to promulgate an egalitarian national information policy during his ALA presidency—the failure was due as much to bad luck (the eruption of the protracted *Speaker* affair) as to his own miscalculations. Moreover, like the strongest leaders, Moon refused to let defeat discourage or stop him. In the case of information policy, he continued to champion the cause long after his term as ALA president was over, battling against privatization and fees, which he considered forms of economic censorship, as recently as the 1991 White House Conference.

The Philosophy

At core, Moon was (by American definition) a liberal activist who advocated progressive change in the library field and society as a whole. His social and political conscience grew out of his English working-class roots. As a young man he embraced Fabian socialism, a movement that preached socioeconomic reform through democratic means and provided the philosophical underpinnings of the British Labour Party, which he resolutely supported during his years in England.

Like the political hero of his youth, ex-coal miner and Labour stalwart Aneurin Bevan, Moon believed in representative democracy, human equality, and public sector solutions to social needs and problems. He empathized with the underclasses, the weak, the poor, society's outsiders, and especially its rebels, of which he was one. Conversely, he had no love for the upper classes, the well born, royalty, or the Establishment, which he distrusted and disparaged as stuffy, snotty, complaisant, and politically retrograde.

Moon believed fervently in the Fabian axiom, "The way to truth is through argument." From early on he relished debate and controversy, always certain that his position was the correct one and that through persuasion others would ultimately see the light. Part of his strategy involved keeping the lines of communication open with those who disagreed with him. While unwilling to compromise principle, he rarely turned down an opportunity to meet and negotiate with an adversary, preferably over a drink.

Perhaps more than any other American library leader in the second half of the 20th century (he became a United States citizen in 1965), Moon articulated a clear and expansive vision of what the profession could—and should—be. He advocated a librarianship fully immersed in the world, not one that feared or shrank from it; a librarianship that viewed libraries and librarians as central to the society they serve; a socially responsible librarianship that confronted rather than ignored society's ills, such as war, poverty, racial and sexual discrimination, and censorship. He had no time for those who looked upon the library profession as a refuge from the real world.

In 1983, after retiring to Florida and toward the end of his active career, Moon summarized his philosophy about the profession in a letter to a younger colleague, Jeanne Isacco, then teaching in the library school at Texas Woman's University in Denton: "If you can persuade your students that nothing they are likely to do as librarians will have any meaning unless it is done with understanding of people's individual needs, and with caring for those needs, you will have done something much more important than teaching them 'administration' or cataloging. This is the road to the kind of change that is mandatory if our profession and our library services are to make the contribution that they should and can render society." He continued:

I always enjoyed my rap sessions with library school students because there at least one had a chance of finding a few minds not yet set in concrete. But the young people coming into the profession must be prepared to take chances, to be unorthodox, to challenge the "accepted." And they must know that it will take courage to do so. It's risky, but life's more interesting that way (as the famous last sentence of *The Freedom to Read Statement* suggests). The major breakthroughs are nearly always achieved by the risk-takers. We haven't had nearly enough of them, which is perhaps the principal reason why we haven't progressed as far as we should have.

Isacco was not only impressed by Moon's wise words but "bowled over" that he took the time to address her students, which "made a tremendous impact on them."

The Personality

The circumstances of Moon's birth and formative years in England provide *a* key — possibly *the* key — to understanding his character and motivations. He grew up poor in the economically depressed 1930s, and though gifted intellectually and blessed with impressive mental stamina, his general education ended at age 16 upon completion of grammar school, the British equivalent of American high school. Unable to afford to go to college, let alone consider "the extravagance of elite and expensive institutions like Oxford and Cambridge," the teenage Moon entered the workforce, taking the first job offered. As luck would have it that job was a position at the local public library. It paid a pittance, but it launched one of the storied library careers of our (or any) time.

Librarianship took him light-years beyond his mother's modest boardinghouse near the Southampton docks. Yet no matter how high he rose professionally or how well off he became materially, psychologically he remained a needy boy from the British working-class who understood, with total certitude, that nothing would be handed to him, that he would have to fight and scrape and scheme for everything he got in life.

Deep in his psyche he scorned the privileged people who automatically went to the best universities, who relied on their family name and Old Boy connections to get the best jobs, the comfortable deals, the fine fruits of the good life. Normally the system in prewar Britain expected little of lads like him except that they stay in their place and be satisfied with minimal education, grunt jobs, occasional titillation in the tabloid press, a rooting interest in the local football club, and enough beer to remain harmlessly anesthetized through the nights and weekends until they crossed the bar. Moon wanted more than this bleak future, and early on he subconsciously developed a set of defense mechanisms that would help him escape the laboring-class fate and cope with the insecurities and hurts that were innately part of his heritage.

These mechanisms—a relentless, competitive drive to achieve, to excel, to win, to dominate; a constant quest for recognition and ways to project himself as special or superior; and a compulsive urge to control his environment, including the actions of others—were at the governing center of Moon's life at every stage, from childhood to old age. They colored practically every aspect of his personality, which included these less than admirable traits:

- great difficulty admitting mistakes or apologizing for errors;
- a penchant for finding fault and putting others down: Russell Shank recalled, "It took a lot of forbearance on the part of those of us who were part of the profession he wanted to change to be able to tolerate Eric. The impression that he gave me was that he considered many of us—including me—to be lightweights";
- the use of guile and manipulation to get his way: Edward Dudley called this trait in Eric a fondness for "plots, ploys, and stratagems";
- an obsessive need to turn everything into a contest, even the most mundane transactions: "Eric's overly competitive about everything," observed John Berry;
- a tendency to exaggerate his own importance or accomplishments: according to Ron Surridge, "he could 'shoot a very good line' with stories well stretching the truth";
- an unmitigated egotism; his son Alan described the condition:

If my father has a major character flaw, it is his ego. He knows he is good at the things he does. But instead of letting other people sing the praises of his talents and accomplishments, he often takes on that role himself. Many times I have listened to him tell a same few stories about how wonderful he was at something or how important his role was in something. The specifics aren't important, at least not to me, as I always found this immodesty to be embarrassing. Maybe I wanted my opinion of how good he was to be more important than his own. Maybe I just didn't want him to have any faults or at least such a visible fault. Maybe I should have just told him to stop being such a pompous bore.

It must be noted that Moon's defense mechanisms and the personality traits they engendered were central to his professional success. Without them he doubtless would not have achieved what he did: without the impulse to get ahead or the need to be considered special or the affinity for plots, ploys, and stratagems—without these coping devices it is unlikely Moon would have become a star student at the library school at Loughborough College or would have gone on to be a great presence in the AAL or the crusading editor of *Library Journal* or the transformational figure at Scarecrow Press or the president of ALA or the author of numerous publications and or the giver of countless speeches or...

His son Alan added this: "I kept hoping someone—Bill Eshelman?—would tell my father to shut up. But maybe the fact he didn't, that no one did, is just an indication of one of my father's other talents. He is loved by those who have been a part of his life. And love allows people to overlook many faults."

Melvil's Heir

Few students of library history would disagree that Melvil Dewey was the American profession's most prominent pioneer, the 19th-century prime mover who among many other accomplishments devised the enduring Dewey Decimal Classification system, founded *Library Journal*, started the first library school in the United States, and played an indispensable part in establishing the American Library Association and the New York Library Association. Who among all the great and famous librarians since Dewey — Lester Asheim, Augusta Baker, Verner Clapp, Robert Downs, Michael Gorman, Frances Henne, Virginia Lacy Jones, E.J. Josey, Anne Carol Moore, Lawrence Clark Powell, Frances Clarke Sayers, Ralph Shaw, Jesse Shera, Louis Shores, Joseph Wheeler, Robert Wedgeworth, to name but a few — is Dewey's natural heir? Who is the 20th-century Melvil Dewey?

A case can be made that Eric Edward Moon is that person.

Dewey (1851–1931) stood out as the commanding figure in American librarianship during the last thirty years of the 19th century (actually his career as a practitioner ended in 1905), a period of enormous youthful zeal and growing pains for the new profession. Moon (born in 1923) made his mark as American librarianship's most influential and durable leader during the 1960s and 1970s, a period of profound change at least equal in intensity to that experienced during Dewey's day. Dewey and Moon claimed center stage at very different times in the history of the profession and quite understandably confronted very different circumstances, issues, and challenges. On the other hand the two men were quite similar in their philosophies and leadership styles.

Both men were passionately committed to their profession, viewing it not as work or a job but a high calling; both were generalists who believed librarians must take a leading role in shaping the intellectual and cultural destiny of their respective communities; both were activists/innovators/reformers whose deeds had a major impact on the future of the profession; both were journalists/editors/publishers whose words moved their colleagues; both were teachers whose opinions and arguments inspired the next generation; both were committed to associations as a means of advancing the profession; both possessed an astute business sense; both were brash and courted controversy; both were hyper-industrious and keenly competitive — when ALA was formed in Philadelphia in 1876 Melvil rushed to sign the register, "Number one, Melvil Dewey"; both loved women; both were egocentric and boastful; both were leaders par excellence.

Of course there were differences between them too. Moon, for instance, believed in human equality and Dewey, a bigot, clearly did not; Moon adamantly opposed censorship in any guise and Dewey, who saw the librarian as an agent for moral betterment, did not; Moon never sexually harassed women and Dewey apparently did; Moon was not especially interested in classification whereas Dewey built his career around it. But these and any other differences Dewey and Moon might have had are historically insignificant: both men were giants who enlarged the profession by their presence; both had that quintessential quality — some call it gravitas — that marks a born leader.

    The last word goes to another great librarian, Lawrence Clark Powell, who died in 2001 at age 94 and will be missed. In a letter he wrote dated January 6, 1981, recommending Moon for the Lippincott Award, Powell said: "I now judge him [Moon] as one of the few creative librarians of our time, along with such as Ralph Shaw, Verner Clapp, and Keyes Metcalf. In a larger perspective I class Moon with Dewey and [John Cotton] Dana. He is truly one of our great ones, towering above the housekeepers, glorified and lesser, that librarians almost invariably are, God help us all!"

Notes

Brief citations to *published* material quoted in this book are provided here. Full citations are found in the Bibliography (see next section). *Unpublished* interviews, correspondence, and internal documents quoted in the book are identified in the text by personal or institutional name but not cited here. This source material, along with other of Eric Moon's papers, will eventually be deposited in the American Library Association Archives at the University of Illinois–Urbana, and thus accessible to any interested person.

Abbreviations used in these notes:

AL	*American Libraries*
DTL	*A Desire to Learn* (by Eric Moon)
LJ	*Library Journal*
NYTBR	*New York Times Book Review*
WLB	*Wilson Library Bulletin*

Preface

page xv   "It is perhaps": Strachey, *Eminent Victorians*, 1988, p. 7.

xv   "the professional burglar": Malcolm, *The Silent Woman*, 1994, p. 9.

xv   "Voyeuristic and invasive": Breslin, "Terminating Mark Rothko," *NYTBR*, July 24, 1994, p. 19.

xvi   "biography is not merely": Zoglin, "The First Lady and the Slasher," *Time*, April 22, 1991, p. 69.

xvi   "Uninterpreted truth": Clarke, "Biography Comes of Age," *Time*, July 2, 1979, p. 86.

xvi   "pathography": Oates, "Jean Stafford: Biography as Pathography" in *Where I've Been, and Where I'm Going*, 1999, p. 145.

xvi   "there is properly no history": Emerson, "History" in *Essays of Ralph Waldo Emerson*, 1945, p. 6.

xviii   "a degree of trouble": "Advertisement to the First Edition" in *The Life of Samuel Johnson*, 1992, p. 3.

xviii   "to maintain his own freedom": Strachey, *Eminent Victorians*, 1988, p. 8.

Chapter 1: Growing Up in Southampton

page 3   "a poor boy": Moon, "Education Without Libraries =Catastrophe" in *DTL*, 1993, p. 54.

9   "If I could bring": Moon, "Education Without Libraries = Catastrophe" in *DTL*, 1993, pp. 53–54.

16 "Southampton was very much": Gadd, *Southampton Through This Century*, 1988, p. 31.

19 "At my private school": Carpenter, *The Brideshead Generation*, 1990, p. 152.

20 "These were the thirties": Moon, "Education Without Libraries = Catastrophe" in *DTL*, 1993, p. 54.

Chapter 2: Entering Librarianship

page 22 "I left school": Moon, "Education Without Libraries = Catastrophe" in *DTL*, 1993, p. 54.

25 "The system": Kister, "A Yank in Sherwood Forest," *LJ*, November 15, 1965, p. 4914.

27 "that odd, dead period": Carpenter, *The Brideshead Generation*, 1990, p. 340.

28 "broken in spirit": Hennessy, *Never Again*, 1994, p. 34.

29 "pylon boys": Carpenter, *The Brideshead Generation*, 1990, p. 303.

29 "ganged up": *ibid.*, p. 304.

30 "addicted to beer": Arlott, *Basingstoke Boy*, 1990, p. 88.

Chapter 3: Defending Home and Country

page 33 "My individualism": Benge, *Confessions of a Lapsed Librarian*, 1984, p. 23.

39 "a levelling up": Carpenter, *The Brideshead Generation*, 1990, p. 383.

40 "I felt empty": Benge, *Confessions of a Lapsed Librarian*, 1984, pp. 84–85.

Chapter 4: Learning at Loughborough

page 46 "educational buccaneer": Cantor & Matthews, *Loughborough*, 1977, p. 108.

46 "On the morning": *ibid.*

51 "I thought back": Moon, Foreword to Powell's *Life Goes On*, 1986, p. viii.

Chapter 5: Advancing in British Libraries

page 63 "had changed the very spirit": Cole, *A.J.P. Taylor*, 1993, p. 227.

63 "vermin in ermine": "Bevan, Aneurin" in *The New Caxton Encyclopedia*, 1977, p. 674.

63 "the Minister of Disease": Laybourn, "Bevan, Aneurin" in *Twentieth-Century Britain*, 1995, p. 73.

63 "a sheep in sheep's clothing": Douglas-Home, *The Way the Wind Blows*, 1976, p. 98.

83 "This job cannot": Moon, "A Stock-Editor's Viewpoint," *North-Western Polytechnic School of Librarianship: Occasional Papers*, October 1957, p. 7.

Chapter 6: Ruffling Establishment Feathers

page 89 "parish pump politicians": Moon, "Letter from America," *Assistant Librarian*, July 1960, p. 147.

89 "an uneasy stepmother": Jones, "Past, Present, and Future," *Assistant Librarian*, July 1960, p. 138.

91 "an AAL member": Moon, "Letter from America," *Assistant Librarian*, July 1960, p. 147.

91 "always Moon": Moon, "Moonlight at Waterloo," *New Library World*, November 1977, p. 208.

91 "I can well remember": Jones, "Past, Present, and Future," *Assistant Librarian*, July 1960, p. 135.

92 "A little over a year ago": Moon, "The State of the Union, Jack," *The Library Association Centenary Conference: Proceedings*, 1977, p. 75.

94 "wings clipped": Moon, "Letter from America," *Assistant Librarian*, July 1960, p. 147.

94 "I find it hard to believe": Moon, "The State of the Union, Jack," *The Library Association Centenary Conference: Proceedings*, 1977, p. 78.

96 "You don't have to": Lancour, "McColvin Festschrift," *LJ*, March 1, 1969, p. 963.

99 "I had heard": Moon, Foreword to Powell's *Life Goes On*, 1986, p. xi.

100 "When dealing with serious matters": Jones, "Letters," *Assistant Librarian*, July 1956, p. 118.

100 "I want *assistants*": Moon, "Letters—Reply," *Assistant Librarian*, July 1956, pp. 118–19.

Chapter 7: Rabble-Rousing in Canada

page 109 "virtually a voyage": Moon, "The Province Nobody Knows," *Atlantic Advocate*, April 1959, p. 29.

110 "You will surely": *ibid.*

110 "Having fought through": *ibid.*

115 "Before us were": *ibid.*, p. 31.

116 "It would be overstating": Moon, "The Gosling Memorial Library" in *The Story of Newfoundland*, 1959, pp. 70–71.

118 "Newfoundland's library missionary": Penney, "Library Services for the People: Newfoundland," *Third World Libraries Interest Group Newsletter*, November 1992, p. xxii.

118 "The butter is": Moon, "The Gosling Memorial Library" in *The Story of Newfoundland*, 1959, p. 71.

119 "the old-time Maritime": Smallwood, "The Truth about Newfoundland," *Atlantic Advocate*, April 1959, p. 33.

122 "The whole problem": Redmond, "We Need Them — Where Do They Fit?," *APLA Bulletin*, Spring 1959, p. 54.

122 "a medium for": Richards, "FALANA — A New Association," *LJ*, May 1, 1960, p. 1751.

Chapter 8: Reviving Library Journal

page 129 "invented trade bibliography": Berry, "Born-Again Bowker," *LJ*, October 1, 1996, p. 6.

130 "a mouser in musty": Dewey, "The Profession," *American Library Journal*, September 30, 1876, p.6.

130 "the librarian is in": *ibid*.

130 "It is not now enough": *ibid.*, pp. 5–6.

130 "In a word": Dewey, "Editorial Notes," *American Library Journal*, September 30, 1876, p. 13.

131 "The plan of": *ibid.*, p. 12.

132 "There comes a time": Wessells, "Editor's Farewell," *LJ*, April 1, 1957, p. 920.

133 "His friends know": "Lee Ash to Be Lj's New Editor," *LJ*, May 1, 157, p. 1170.

133 "One of my favorite": Gerhardt, "F.G.M.," *Journal of Youth Services in Libraries*, Winter 1988, p. 141.

134 "So, what makes you": Moon, Foreword to Powell's *Life Goes On*, 1986, p. xi.

138 "with substantial literature": Moon, review of Cleland's *Memoirs of a Woman of Pleasure*, *LJ*, July 1963, p.2725.

138 "our daddy": Rudin, "An Anniversary," *School Library Journal*, September 1963, p. 38

143 "flat conformity and dullness": Moon, "The Library Press," *LJ*, November 15, 1969, p. 4106.

143 "looked tired and middle-aged": Moon, "The Issues That Confront Us Now" in *DTL*, 1993, p. 99.

145 "Early in the conference": Eshelman, **No Silence!**, 1997, p. 113.

147 "That mediocre value judgements": Broderick, "Librarians and Literature," *LJ*, August 1960, p. 2710.

147 "literature experts": *ibid.*, p. 2709.

147 "If we want status": *ibid.*, p. 2712.

147 "If librarians": Moon, "The Uninvited," *LJ*, January 15, 1960, p. 210.

148 "to a number of Lj readers:" "Opinion," *LJ*, August 1960, p. 2713.

148 "Frankly, we expected": *ibid*.

148 "a barrage of correspondence": "Librarians and Literature: Aftermath of an Article," *LJ*, p. 3621.

148 "I would suggest": *ibid.*, p. 3623.

148 "What we librarians": *ibid.*, p. 3624.

149 "Apparently Miss Broderick": *ibid.*, p. 3625.

149 "Now that Dorothy": Neufeld, "Second Thoughts on Selection Tools," *LJ*, November 1, 1960, p. 3882.

149 "The changes can": Broderick, "The New Fiction Catalog," *LJ*, March 15, 1961, p. 1099.

149 "physically but not mentally retired": Broderick, "Turning Library into a Dirty Word: A Rant," *LJ*, July 1997, p. 42.

150 "Miss Evelyn Smart": "Women on the March," *LJ*, May 1, 1960, p. 1760.

151 "An article on segregation": Moon, "The Danville Story," *LJ*, November 1, 1960, p. 3943.

Chapter 9: Exploding the Silent Subject

page 153 "two-thirds of the Negro": "US Commission on Civil Rights Reports on Southern Libraries," *LJ*, January 15, 1962, p. 188.

153 "As I began to move": Moon, "The Issues That Confront Us Now" in *DTL*, 1993, p. 99.

154 "shockingly cruel and feudal": Kunitz, "The Roving Eye: The Spectre at Richmond," *WLB*, May 1936, p. 592.

154 "Since there has been": "The Roving Eye," *WLB*, June 1936, p. 672.

155 "Books should be open": "Faulkner Condemns Closing of Libraries in the South," *LJ*, July 1960, p. 2559.

155 "*Library Journal*, I felt": Moon, "The Issues That Confront Us Now" in *DTL*, p. 100.

155 "how best to explode": *ibid*.

156 "How has the American": Wakeman, "Talking Points: Segregation and Censorship," *WLB*, September 1960, p. 63.

157 "An article on segregation": Moon, "The Danville Story," *LJ*, November 1, 1960, p. 3943.

157 "the Association cannot": Wakeman, "Talking Points: Segregation and Censorship," *WLB*, September 1960, p., 63.

157 "So far no library": Estes, "Segregated Libraries," *LJ*, December 15, 1960, p. 4418.

157 "Many librarians": *ibid.*, p. 4419.

157 "An editorial": *ibid.*, p. 4420.

158 "If only this passage": *ibid.*, p. 4419.

158 *"Dear Madam"*: Wright, "The Freedom to Read," *LJ*, December 15, 1960, p. 4421.

158 "It is common knowledge": Moon, "The Silent Subject," *LJ*, December 15, 1960, p. 4436.

158 "years of vacuum": *ibid.*

158 "It is encouraging": *ibid.*

159 "With Mr. Estes": *ibid.*

159 "local jurisdiction": *ibid.*, p. 4437.

159 "How actively does the profession": *ibid.*

159 "whose services": *ibid.*

159 "really launched publicly": Moon, *DTL* ("Introduction" to Part II), 1993, p. 85.

160 "I would like to congratulate": "Segregation in Libraries," *LJ*, February 15, 1961, p. 734.

160 "What a fresh breeze": *ibid.*

160 "Rice Estes' clear summons": *ibid.*

160 "It is embarrassing": *ibid.*, p. 732.

160 "It is difficult": *ibid.*, pp. 732, 734.

161 "All the correspondence": Moon, "A Survey of Segregation," *LJ*, March 15, 1961, p. 1110.

161 "had to be stopped": Moon, "The Library Press and Eric Moon" in *Activism in American Librarianship*, 1987, p. 102.

161 "were urged to cool it": Moon, "Association Agonies," *AL*, April 1972, p. 397.

161 "as much a public enemy": Moon, "A 'Chapter' Chapter" in Abdullahi's *E.J. Josey*, 1992, p. 44.

161 "A number of librarians": Moon, "On Editorials," *LJ*, August 1961, p. 2618.

163 "only vaguely aware": Eshelman, "Editorial," *California Librarian*, January 1961, p. 23.

163 "We violently oppose": Berry, "A Question," *Bay State Librarian*, April 1963, p. 7.

163 "Some readers seem": Moon, "Internal Integration," *LJ*, June 1, 1961, p. 2060.

164 "a small but vocal element": Smith, "ALA and the Segregation Issue," *ALA Bulletin*, June 1961, p.485.

164 "terribly negative": Moon, "On Editorials," *LJ*, August 1961, p. 2618.

164 "Not only do we": Moon, "Internal Integration," *LJ*, June 1, 1961, p. 2060.

165 "came more and more": Moon, "A 'Chapter' Chapter" in Abdullahi's *E.J. Josey*, 1992, p. 46.

165 "considerable study": Spain, "ALA and Integration," *LJ*, April 1, 1961, p. 1344.

165 "The rights of an individual": McNeal, "Integrated Service in Southern Public Libraries," *LJ*, June 1, 1961, p. 2046.

165 "I was amazed": Spain, "ALA and Integration," *LJ*, April 1, 1961, p. 1342.

166 "every appropriate action": Moon, "Integration and Censorship," *LJ*, March 1, 1962, p. 904.

166 "be required to state": *ibid.*

166 "drastic action": *ibid.*, p. 905.

166 "a monstrously cynical": *ibid.*, p. 904.

166 "If we're a professional": *ibid.*, p. 906.

166 "Even the Council": Moon, "A 'Chapter' Chapter" in Abdullahi's *E.J. Josey*, 1992, p. 46.

166 "Urge libraries": Moon, "A Concern for Users," *LJ*, July 1962, p. 2496.

166 "may request of the Council": *ibid.*

166 "What has finally emerged": *ibid.*, p. 2495.

167 "Pursue with diligence": *ibid.*, p. 2496.

167 "precisely": Moon, "A Survey of Segregation," *LJ*, March 15, 1961, p. 1110.

167 "freedom of access": Moon, "Dues and Rights," *LJ*, August 1961, p. 2587.

167 "electrified the conference": Moon, "Two Kinds of Access," *LJ*, August 1963, p. 2849.

167 "immune from 'de facto'": "'Access Study' Advisory Committee Has Second Thoughts on Branches," *LJ*, November 1, 1963, p. 4176.

168 "This study will be": Moon, "Bastille Day and After," *LJ*, September 1, 1963, p. 3008.

168 "It seems that you need": *ibid.*

168 "The fault lies": Moon, "The Process of Dilution," *LJ*, December 15, 1963, p. 4711.

168 "where it was clear": *ibid.*, p. 4710.

168 "While rooting for malpractice": *ibid.*, p. 4711.

168 "disaster": *ibid.*, p. 4712.

170 "That editorial alone": Josey, "The Civil Rights Movement and American Librarianship" in *Activism in American Librarianship*, 1987, pp. 15–16.

170 "It is unfortunate": Wakeman, "Segregation in Libraries," *WLB*, May 1961, p. 708.

170 "War ... had thus been": Moon, "A 'Chapter' Chapter" in Abdullahi's *E.J. Josey*, 1992, p. 46.

171 "That all ALA officers": Moon, "Two Stars from Georgia," *LJ*, August 1964, pp. 2921.

171 "hothead" and "troublemaker": Berry, "The Role of the Radical," *LJ*, September 15, 1997, p. 6.

171 "I exploded!": Josey, "A Dreamer" in *The Black Librarian in America*, 1970, p. 314.

171 "The motion set off": Moon, "Two Stars from Georgia," *LJ*, August 1964, p. 2921.

172 "help all the states": *ibid.*

172 "This quiet declaration": *ibid.*

172 "The membership of the American": Moon, "President vs. Parliamentarian," *LJ*, March 1, 1965, p. 1066.

172 "thunderous applause": *ibid.*, p. 1065.

173 "Any library or": Moon, "Fiscal and Federal," *LJ*, August 1965, p. 3188.

173 "It seemed clear": *ibid.*

173 "that we … are no longer": Moon, "Discrimination at Detroit," *LJ*, August 1965, p. 3224.

174 "several errors": Oboler, "Discrimination at Detroit," *LJ*, November 1, 1965, p. 4648.

174 "After time to reflect": Moon, "Follow the Bouncing Ball," *LJ*, March 1, 1966, p. 1174.

175 "The fallout from this": Moon, "A 'Chapter' Chapter" in Abdullahi's *E.J. Josey*, 1992, p. 48.

175 "brigade of southern": Moon, "The Library Press and Eric Moon" in *Activism in American Librarianship*, 1987, p. 103.

175 "such epithets": *ibid.*, p. 111.

175 "local totalitarianism": Moon, "The Central Fact of Our Time," *Alabama Librarian*, October 1965, p. 4.

176 "sensitized the library": "Savannah State College Award to Virginia L. Jones & Lj Editor," *LJ*, May 1, 1966, p. 2300.

Chapter 10: Remaking Library Journalism: Techniques

page 180 "kettle of mush": Burns, "Nuggets and Mush," *LJ*, February 1, 1962, p. 2650.

181 "Access … lies not only": Moon, "The Benefit of the Doubt," *WLB*, April 1965, p. 27.

181 "Maybe the 'censors'": Dollen, "Freedom All Over the Place," *LJ*, February 15, 1961, p. 764.

181 "I am sure Lj": Griffin, "Freedom to Protest," *LJ*, April 15, 1961, p. 1494.

181 "The lopsided rationale": Burns, "Freedom to be Wrong," *LJ*, April 15, 1961, p. 1496.

182 "The time *was*": Dewey, "The Profession," *American Library Journal*, September 30, 1876, p. 6.

183 "Most of the crucial problems": Moon, "A Decade Minus One," *LJ*, December 15, 1968, p. 4597.

183 "For whatever it may be worth": Kilpatrick, "Censorship Debate," *LJ*, August 1961, pp. 2580–81.

183 "He is simply confused": Downs, "Censorship Debate," *LJ* August. 1961, p. 2582.

184 "There has been much ado": Moon, "The Uninvited" (editorial), *LJ*, January 15, 1960, p. 210.

184 "Reading this … in the privacy": Broderick, "Librarians and Literature," *LJ*, August 1960, p. 2709.

184 "I agree with Harold": Moon, "The Benefit of the Doubt," *WLB*, April 1965, p. 38.

184 "quick and dirty": Moon, "The Library Press and Eric Moon" in *Activism in American Librarianship*, 1987, p. 109.

185 "When it comes to": Fiske, *Book Selection and Censorship*, 1959, p. 64.

185 "might become controversial": *ibid.*

185 "the public's allegedly": *ibid.*, pp. 109–10.

185 "I suppose it was Marjorie": Moon, "The Benefit of the Doubt," *WLB*, April 1965, p. 30.

186 "How many librarians": Moon, "'Problem' Fiction," *LJ*, February 1, 1962, p. 484.

186 "practices and principles": *ibid.*, p. 496.

186 "While I have been": Jackson, "Problem Nonfiction," *LJ*, March 1, 1962, p. 858.

186 "The report of the survey": Ross, "To Read and Ponder," *LJ*, May 15, 1962, p. 1824.

186 "Too often we spend": Sampson, "Blank Generation," *LJ*, April 1, 1962, p. 1342.

186 "That every public library": Greenaway, "No Substitute," *LJ*, April 1, 1962, p. 1342.

186 "The fact is": Bloss, "Easiest Way Out," *LJ*, April 1, 1962, pp. 1342; 1344.

187 "The February 1 issue": Moon, "Book Rejection," *LJ*, June 15, 1962, p. 2298–99.

187 "To lead or to follow": Broderick, "'Problem' Nonfiction, *LJ*, October 1, 1962, p. 3378.

187 "It was no more than": Moon, "The View from the Front," *LJ*, February 1, 1964, p. 570.

187 "While seven out of eight": Moon, "On the Shelf," *LJ*, January 15, 1964, p. 205.

188 "the most important": Moon, "Balance in Boom-Time," *LJ*, January 1, 1960, p. 58.

188 "should be on the shelves": Moon, "In, Out, or Neglected" (Part I),*LJ*, January 1, 1966, p. 57.

188 "see how the theories": *ibid.*, p. 64.

189 "The title should be": Moon, "The Library Press," *LJ*, November 15, 1969, p. 4108.

191 "We … may as well confess": Moon, "Who Cares About the Code?," *LJ*, May 1, 1961, p. 1744.

191 "The case for the prosecution": Moon, "The Case *for* Code Revision," *LJ*, September 1, 1961, p. 2739.

191 "If you are laboring": Hickey, "Invitation to a Ball," *LJ*, September 15, 1961, p. 2902.

193 "It seemed to me": Moon, "The Library Press," *LJ*, November 15, 1969, p. 4106.

194 "We have been as strong": Moon, "Whose Opinion?," *LJ*, April 1, 1961, p. 1368.

194 "There is little genuine": Angoff, "End National Library Week," *LJ*, April 1, 1961, p. 1365.

195 "an assistant professor": Anon., "I Love Librarians!," *LJ*, January 1, 1962, p. 45.

195 "I would list the sins": *ibid.*, 47.

195 "She will not wear": King, "The Bookworm," *LJ*, February 1, 1963, p. 512.

195 "The above is the slogan": Spavin, "'We Represent the Library's Interest'," *LJ*, December 15, 1964, p. 4871.

195 "but, like the two similarly": *ibid*.

196 "the large number": Molesworth [Stevens], "Uncritical Editing of Who's Who," *LJ*, March 1, 1967, p. 945.

196 "Nigel Molesworth was": Shera, "'Playboy' Substitute," *LJ*, April 15, 1967, p. 1550.

197 "How long has": Tate, "Fiction Tomfoolery," *LJ*, February 1, 1965, p. 416.

197 "I never too much minded": Moon, "A Conspiracy Against the Laity?" in *DTL*, 1993, pp. 266–67.

198 "spokesperson for the Right": Hillard, "Right of Center," *WLB*, September 1977, p. 75.

198 "notorious liberal sentiments": Hillard, "'Coolie' Labor," *LJ*, May 1, 1964, p. 1893.

198 "It will be hard": *ibid*.

199 "let me render my objection": Shepard, "Dissent from Dissent," *LJ*, December 1, 1967, p. 4305.

199 "meetings of those state": Moon, "Problems of Consistency," *LJ*, August 1964, p. 2966.

199 "*Wyman Jones's column*": Moon, "Problems of Consistency," *LJ*, August 1964, p. 2966.

200 "I never believed": Moon, "The Library Press and Eric Moon" in *Activism in American Librarianship*, 1987, p. 107.

200 "alone speaks *for* the magazine": Moon, "The Library Press," *LJ*, November 15, 1969, p. 4107.

200 "a platform for those": Moon, "Practical Convention Programs," *LJ*, June 15, 1960, p. 2378.

202 "I asked Larry": Moon, Foreword to Powell's *Life Goes On*, 1986, p. xii.

203 "virtually empty": Moon, "The Library Press," *LJ*, November 15, 1969, p. 4106.

203 "This is a good test": *ibid*.

203 "Ninety per cent of our photographs": Moon, "The Paucity of Pictures," *LJ*, February 1, 1960, p. 506.

204 "I have just read": Taylor, "Covering the Candidates," *LJ*, March 15, 1960, p. 1048.

204 "We cannot guarantee": *ibid*.

204 "I am a librarian": Johnson, "Tasteless Cover," *LJ*, January 1, 1968, p. 15.

204 "Magazines of many other professions": Moon, "A ClearChoice," *LJ*, October 15, 1964, p. 3927.

205 "to brainwash some idiots": Berry, "End of the Story," *LJ*, December 15. 1964, p. 4872.

205 "primarily a book review": "Attempt to Censure Bowker Company Fails," *LJ*, November 15, 1964, p. 4490.

Chapter 11: Remaking Library Journalism: Triumphs

page 208 "It seems years": Hillard, "To the Foggy Isles?," *LJ*, October 15, 1963, p. 3780.

209 "Will it make": "Bowker Company Moves," *LJ*, April 15, 1963, p. 1642.

211 "Two of the group": Moon, "On the Road," *LJ*, November 15, 1963, p. 4332.

212 "We have been tempted": Moon, "A Rebirth," *LJ*, September 1, 1962, p. 2850.

212 "in dealing with this truly": *ibid*.

212 "If you think": *ibid*.

213 "Is it responsible": Moon, "Questioning a Question," *LJ*, July 1963, p. 2644.

213 "naive audacity": Berry, "Editorial Policy," *LJ*, January 1, 1969, p. 15.

213 "It is my contention": Moon, "Questioning a Question," *LJ*, July 1963, p. 2645.

217 "raised Republican": Berry, "The Corruption of Popular Information," *LJ*, February 1, 1996, p. 8.

218 "When I went to talk": Moon, "A Priori Censorship" in *DTL*, 1993, p. 153.

219 "part of the machinery": Berry, "Who's Underdeveloped?," *LJ*, November 15, 1964, p. 4488.

220 "Moon is a disappointment": Katz, "Day at Lj," *LJ*, June 15, 1966, pp. 3111–12.

221 "It was past 10 A.M.": *ibid.*, p. 3111.

223 "for excellence in Educational": "Lj Wins 1964 Edpress Award," *LJ*, August 1964, p. 2974.

223 "For some time I have": Holley, "Change and Challenge," *LJ*, July 1965, p. 2918.

223 "began, for the first time": Berry, "Bowker, R.R., Company" in *Encyclopedia of Library and Information Science*, Vol. 3, 1970, p. 143.

224 "fat, golden years": Moon, "A Potpourri of P's" in *DTL*, 1993, p. 284.

225 "a contributing editor": "Major Changes Announced in Lj Editorial Staff," *LJ*, October 1, 1966, p. 4590.

225 "delivered so well": Moon, "A Living Library," *LJ*, April 15, 1963, p. 1632.

226 "He was a fine writer": Berry, "In Memoriam: Karl Nyren," *LJ*, September 1, 1988, p. 94.

226 "We shall go on": Moon, "Accentuate the Physical," *LJ*, September 15, 1961, p. 2900.

227 "Lj's last redesign": Moon, "The Living End," *LJ*, December 15, 1966, p. 6049.

227 "Lj, uniquely among": *ibid.*

227 "move to a considerably": *ibid.*

228 "Before every national": Oboler, "Oboler Dicta," *LJ*, February 15, 1967, p. 742.

228 "scared pup": "New Orleans Librarian Reinstated," *LJ*, August 1967, p. 2698.

228 "It makes the prospects": Lorenz, "The Format Change," *LJ*, February 1, 1967, p. 507.

228 "Magnificent": Bradshaw, *ibid.*

228 "I like the new *LJ* format": Mason, *ibid.*

230 "As editor of *LJ*": Moon, "The State of the Union, Jack" in *The Library Association Centenary Conference: Proceedings*, 1977, p. 77.

232 "it looks as though": Nyren, "A Bowl of Rain," *LJ*, June 1, 1969, p. 2179.

232 "We have noticed": Moon, "Voices on Vietnam?," *LJ*, October 15, 1967, p. 3577.

233 "Thank you for reprinting": Tweedy, "Moon's Misguided Minions," *LJ*, July 1992, p. 8.

235 "I met Eric Moon": Futas, Review of Moon's *DTL*, *Library Quarterly*, July 1994, p. 341.

235 "Moon Bunch": Eshelman, *No Silence!*, 1997, pp. 223–24.

240 "remarkably like a wiser": Katz, "A Day at Lj," *LJ*, June 15, 1966, p. 3112.

242 "principal erotica book": Moon, "The Library Press and Eric Moon" in *Activism in American Librarianship*, 1987, p. 109.

243 "I began as a reviewer": Moon, *DTL* ("Introduction" to Part VIII), 1993, p. 396.

248 "Despite the high hopes": Berry, "Oryx at 20," *LJ*, February 15, 1995, p. 129.

249 "an ideal time": Moon, "A Decade Minus One," *LJ*, December 15, 1968, p. 4597.

250 "President Nixon opened": Berry, "National Library Wake," *LJ*, May 15, 1969, p. 1927.

251 "Looking back over *Library Journal*": Nyren, "Introduction" to *Library Issues: The Sixties*, 1970, pp. xiii–xiv.

mid-1970s

Chapter 12: Capturing Ilse's Heart

page 263 "on the Social Responsibility": Duchas, "A Plea for Social Responsibility," *LJ*, August 1968, p. 2798.

264 "controlled by old people": Blasingame, "ALA: Problems and Proposals," *LJ*, August 1968, p. 2809.

264 "Forty years ago": Moon, "Business—Not Quite As Usual," *LJ*, August 1968, p. 2807.

265 "like the Olympic trials": Moon, "The Library Press and Eric Moon" in *Activism in American Librarianship*, 1987, p. 106.

266 "[E]very effort should": Smith, "Kansas City Stirring," *LJ*, October 1, 1968, p. 3483.

266 "This group wants": Freiser, "The Bendix-Duchac Establishment," *LJ*, September 15, 1968, p. 3105.

266 "I'll back you in every way": "Social Responsibility Group Meets in Philadelphia," *LJ*, October 15, 1968, p. 3729.

267 "Its activists are young": Berry & Havens, "Wait 'Til Atlantic City," *LJ*, March 15, 1969, p. 1111.

267 "less than splendid": Berry, "The New Constituency," *LJ*, August 1969, 2725.

267 "For an entire year": Berry, "The New Constituency," *LJ*, August 1969, p. 2731.

267 "a hoop-skirted old maid": Berry, "No Answers Yet," *LJ*, August 1969, p. 2709.

267 "to fatten the cats": Berry, "The New Constituency," *LJ*, August 1969, p. 2729.

268 "a legitimate and unavoidable": Moon, "A 'Chapter' Chapter" in Abdullahi's *E.J. Josey*, 1992, p. 51.

269 "Atlantic City was probably": Moon, "The Library Press and Eric Moon" in *Activism in American Librarianship*, 1987, pp. 106–07.

271 "timid, frugal, and clandestine": "ALAiad; or, A Tale of Two Conferences," *WLB*, September 1969, p. 87.

271 "were simply not accepted": *ibid.*, p. 88.

273 "The old order": Berry, "The New Constituency," *LJ*, August 1969, p. 2739.

Chapter 13: Feeding a Scarecrow

page 289 "My own visits": Moon, "A Jungle Tale," *LJ*, January 15, 1963, p. 182.

290 "Before his first book": Moon, "The Scarecrow Press" in *Library Science Annual*, 1985, p. 3.

293 "Ralph Shaw was": Powell, *Life Goes On*, 1986, pp. 98–99.

297 "he had, characteristically": Stevens, "Shaw, Ralph Robert" in *Dictionary of American Library Biography*, 1978, p. 476.

299 "foundation stone": Moon, "The Scarecrow Press" in *Library Science Annual*, 1985, p. 4.

302 "This employment was an enormous": Franklin, "The Publisher in Ashe County," *Sipapu*, Fall 1990, p. 4.

306 "leading missionary": Moon, Foreword to Berman's *Prejudices and Antipathies*, 1993, pp. 3–4.

307 "Would you believe": Moon, "Hook, Line and Sinker" in *DTL*, 1993, p. 370.

312 "the Social Responsibilities Round Table": Moon, "Association Agonies," *AL*, April 1972, p. 399.

312 "Isn't it enough": Stevenson, "Alter Moon?," *AL*, September 1972, p. 861.

313 "a model of efficiency": "Eric Moon Elected New ALA President in Upset," *LJ*, August 1976, p. 1577.

314 "some of those who seek": Moon, "Association Agonies," *AL*, April 1972, pp. 398–99.

Chapter 14: Moving from Backbench to President

page 318 "This year's ALA presidential race": Berry, "The Participation Problem," *LJ*, March 15, 1976, p. 785.

319 "*Oh-o-oh. What a little MOON*": Shields, "A Moonlighting Member," *AL*, April 1976, p. 195.

322 "I'll only know if it's a victory": "Decisive Win For Moon," *AL*, July-August 1976, p. 456.

322 "The vote could be taken": "Eric Moon Elected New ALA President in Upset," *LJ*, August 1976, p. 1577.

323 "A lot of people": Moon, "A Matter of Values" in *DTL*, 1993, p. 32.

326 "whose views differ radically": Moon, "Association Agonies," *AL*, April 1972, pp. 399–400.

326 "dubious record": "ALA Accreditation Committee Should Resign," *LJ*, April 1, 1973, p. 1069.

327 "The Moon style is beginning": Berry, "Issues in Detroit," *LJ*, May 15, 1977, p. 1081.

327 "As President-Elect he": Horrocks, "Decision Processes in ALA" in *Library Education and Leadership*, 1990, p. 95.

330 "loudly, insistently": Moon, "Data Bank Is Two Four-Letter Words" in *DTL*, 1993, p. 52.

330 "speak up": *ibid.*, p. 43.

330 "We must argue": *ibid.*, p. 48.

331 "a total renunciation": *ibid*, p. 51.

331 "We need, urgently": *ibid*, p. 43.

331 "Slow to get going": "The Key Word was Access," *LJ*, August 1977, p. 1556.

331 "longer and harder": *DTL*, 1993, p. 2.

332 "the *policy* recommending voice": Moon, "A Matter of Values" in *DTL*, 1993, p. 37.

332 "national information policy": Martin, "Information, Politics, & Money," *LJ*, December 15, 1976, p. 2547.

336 "In this film project": Horn, *Zoia!*, 1995, p. 205.

336 "up-to-date film on intellectual freedom": "Color Film on First Amendment Needs $$ Votes of Librarians," *AL*, July-August 1976, p. 458.

336 "We believe this film": *ibid.*

336 "*explain the special role*": Horn, *Zoia!*, 1995, p. 203.

339 "The laboratory/lecture room": *ibid.*, p. 207.

339 "Rarely, if ever, had veteran": Eshelman, "Head-onCollision," *WLB*, September 1977, p. 33.

340 "open hostility": Berry, "The Debate Nobody Won," *LJ*, August 1977, p. 1574.

340 "dissociate": *ibid.*

340 "failure": *ibid.*, p. 1575.

340 "too complicated to try": *ibid.*

341 "superior film": *ibid.*, p. 1576.

341 "How it ... all occurred": *ibid.*, p. 1577.

341 "more than ever": *ibid.*

343 "secret agenda of racism": Chambers,

"The Selling of 'The Speaker'," *Interracial Books for Children Bulletin*, Vol. 8, Nos. 4 & 5, 1977, p. 17.

343　"to support the humanity": Berry, "The Debate Nobody Won," *LJ*, August 1977, p. 1579.

343　"I am heartsick": Eshelman, "Head-on Collision," *WLB*, September 1977, p. 36.

343　"So they voted on": Berry, "The Debate Nobody Won," *LJ*, August 1977, p. 1579.

344　"became a casualty": Chambers, "The Selling of 'The Speaker'," *Interracial Books for Children Bulletin*, Vol. 8, Nos. 4 & 5, 1977, p. 17.

344　"There is now new distrust": *ibid.*

344　"but black people feel": Berry, "The Debate Nobody Won," *LJ*, August 1977, p. 1573.

344　"an easy cop-out": *ibid.*, p. 1579.

345　"sop": Eshelman, "Head-on Collision," *WLB*, September 1977, p. 36.

345　"does not identify": "ALA's 'The Speaker' Nixed in Minnesota," *LJ*, December 1, 1977, p. 2382.

345　"to withdraw its endorsement": "Presidential Timbre," *LJ*, March 1, 1978, p. 522.

347　"participation award": Horn, *Zoia!*, 1995, p. 218.

347　"THE 'GRAND DRAGON' AWARD": "LJ's Annual Awards," *LJ*, December 15, 1977, p. 2459.

347　"I was shocked": Hamlin, "About 'LJ' Awards," *LJ*, June 1, 1978, p. 1094.

347　"The Palmer House": Cherry, "Take 2," *AL*, March 1978, p. 150.

348　"The rush to the microphones": Berry, "The Dominant Issue was Race," *LJ*, April 1, 1978, p. 716.

348　"exacerbating an already difficult": Cherry, "Take 2," *AL*, March 1978, p. 151.

349　"the deep hurt and rage": *ibid.*, p. 152.

349　"Amid applause": *ibid.*

349　"Krug seems to have": "'The Speaker' Debate Goes On," *LJ*, September 1, 1978, p. 1550.

350　"no winners": Jones, "Reflections on The Speaker," *Wilson Library Bulletin*, September 1977, p. 55.

351　"free and equitable access": ALA Ad Hoc Committee to Draft a Statement on National Information Policy, "Toward A Conceptual Foundation for a National Information Policy," *WLB*, March 1978, pp. 545–46.

351　"sufficient": *ibid.*, p. 548.

353　"We should say at the outset": Williams & Pearce, "Midwinter Night's Dream," *LJ*, June 1, 1978, p. 1137.

353　"The purpose all along": *ibid.*, p. 1138.

354　"are among the preeminent": Moon, "Money in the (Data) Bank" in *DTL*, 1993, p. 63.

355　"We should have launched already": Berry, "Tax Revolt," *LJ*, August 1978, p. 1470.

355　"who started his career": Moon, "Data Bank Is Two Four-Letter Words" in *DTL*, 1993, p.43.

Chapter 15: Taking Sherry at Westminster Abbey

page 361　"Prior to the opening": Havens, "IFLA Turns Fifty," *LJ*, December 15, 1977, p. 2484.

361　"debacle": Berry, "Tax Revolt," *LJ*, August 1978, p. 1479.

364　"bravura performance": "LA's 'Medieval Star Chamber'," *Library Association Record*, November 1977, p. 625.

364　"This is, I think": Moon, "The State of the Union, Jack," *The Library Association Centenary Conference: Proceedings*, 1977, p. 73.

365　"I find it hard to believe": *ibid.*, p. 78.

366　"Picture the scene": Moon, "To Disagree Is Not to Destroy" in *DTL*, 1993, pp. 138–39.

366　"more Yonkers than Yeovil": Moon, "Moonlight at Waterloo," *New Library World*, November 1977, p. 208.

367　"Do you regularly read": *ibid.*, p. 209.

367　"As an ex-professional editor": *ibid.*

367　"Mr Eric Moon": "R M Walter, Esq," *New Library World*, December 1977, p. 228.

369　"We … are still far from home": Moon, "The State of the Union, Jack," *The Library Association Centenary Conference: Proceedings*, 1977, p. 76.

369　"more comfortable": *ibid.*, p. 73.

Chapter 16: Reforming the American Library Association

page 371　"One camp clearly": Berry, "ALA in Miami Beach," *LJ*, August 1994, p. 44.

371　"For well over 30 years": Moon, "The Caucus 'Disease'," *LJ*, October 1, 1998, p. 8.

372　"are the place where we can": Moon, "The State of the Union, Jack," *The Library Association Centenary Conference: Proceedings*, 1977, p. 78.

374　"You've got to start": Moon, "A Conversation with Eric Moon," *Technicalities*, April 1981, p. 6.

374　"I remember some of the younger": Moon, "The Library Press and Eric Moon" in *Activism in American Librarianship*, 1987, p. 106.

375　"troika": Moon, "Follow the Bouncing Ball," *LJ*, March 1, 1966, p. 1172.

375　"set aside": Barber & Hodges, *ALA Handbook of Organization 1999-2000*, 1999, p. 22.

376   "refer any matter": *ibid.*

376   "The American Library Association is governed": Moon, "Follow the Bouncing Ball," *LJ*, March 1, 1966, p. 1172.

376   "the membership is going to have to learn": "If Elected I Will," *LJ*, April 15, 1976, p. 982.

377   "has grown too large": Flagg, "In Hot Miami Beach," *AL*, July-August 1994, p. 678.

377   "Final power rests with": Berry, "ALA in Miami Beach," *LJ*, August 1994, p. 42.

377   "Membership meetings have been": Flagg, "In Hot Miami Beach," *AL*, July-August 1994, pp. 677–78.

378   "Sometimes it looks like": Plotnik, "Nonagenarian Guest-Stars in 'Streets of San Francisco'," *AL*, September 1975, p. 476.

379   "The Executive Board shall": Barber & Hodges, *ALA Handbook of Organization 1999-2000*, 1999, p. 22.

380   "when I was on the executive board": Moon, "A Conversation with Eric Moon," *Technicalities*, April 1981, p. 6.

382   "I'm going to out–Honky": Eshelman, *No Silence!*, 1997, p. 245.

383   "The president-elect shall": Barber & Hodges, *ALA Handbook of Organization 1999-2000*, 1999, p. 22.

384   "Each presidency has been like a circus": "Self-Study Report Finds ALA Lacking an Overall Vision," *LJ*, November 15, 1993, p. 14.

384   "a well-funded Office": Berry, "Money, Politics, and Freedom at ALA Midwinter," *LJ*, March 1, 1991, p. 52.

Chapter 17: Retiring in the Sun

page 388   "I'm thinking of retirement": Moon, "Moonlight at Waterloo," *New Library World*, November 1977, p. 209.

393   "I've gone to senior citizen's": Moon, "A Conversation with Eric Moon," *Technicalities*, April 1981, p. 9.

394   "This report created much controversy": Moon, *DTL* ("Introduction" to Part VI), 1993, p. 306.

399   "The book is a compendium": Gerard, Review of *DTL*, *Library Review*, Vol. 43, No. 1, 1994, p. 49.

400   "Moon said that her four years": "Association News and Views," *Journal of Education for Library and Information Science*, Spring 1992, p. 142.

Chapter 18: Summing Up Eric Moon

page 407   "the extravagance of elite": Moon, "Education Without Libraries = Catastrophe" in *DTL*, 1993, p. 54.

Bibliography

Abdullahi, Ismail, ed. *E.J. Josey: An Activist Librarian*. Metuchen, NJ: Scarecrow Press, 1992.

"'Access Study' Advisory Committee Has Second Thoughts on Branches," *Library Journal*, November 1, 1963, p. 4176.

"ALA Accreditation Committee Should Resign, Says Marco," *Library Journal*, April 1, 1973, p. 1069.

ALA Ad Hoc Committee to Draft a Statement on National Information Policy (chaired by David Kaser). "Toward a Conceptual Foundation for a National Information Policy," *Wilson Library Bulletin*, March 1978, pp. 545–49.

"The ALAiad; or, A Tale of Two Conferences" (conference report) *Wilson Library Bulletin*, September 1969, pp. 80–91.

"ALA's 'The Speaker' Nixed in Minnesota," *Library Journal*, December 1, 1977, p. 2382.

Angoff, Allan. "End National Library Week — A Librarian's Minority Opinion," *Library Journal*, April 1, 1961, pp. 1364–66.

Arlott, John. *Basingstoke Boy*. London: Collins, 1990.

Atlas, James. "Choosing a Life," *New York Times Book Review*, January 13, 1991, pp. 1; 22–23.

"Attempt to Censure Bowker Company Fails at Southwestern LA Meeting," *Library Journal*, November 15, 1964, p. 4490.

Barber, Peggy, and Gerald G. Hodges, eds. *ALA Handbook of Organization 1999–2000*. Chicago: American Library Association, 1999.

Benge, Ronald. *Confessions of a Lapsed Librarian*. Metchen, NJ: Scarecrow Press, 1984.

Berry, John N., III. "Accreditation Freeze" (editorial), *Library Journal*, April 15, 1973, p. 1225.

_____ [and others]. "ALA in Miami Beach: Summer Bummer"(conference report), *Library Journal*, August 1994, pp. 40–47.

_____. "Born-Again Bowker" (editorial), *Library Journal*, October 1, 1996, p. 6.

_____. "Bowker, R.R., Company" in *Encyclopedia of Library and Information Science* (ed. by Allen Kent and Harold Lancour; New York: Marcel Dekker, 1970), Vol. 3, pp. 133–48.

_____. "The Corruption of Popular Information" (editorial), *Library Journal*, February 1, 1996, p. 8.

_____. "A Day at Library School," *Library Journal*, January 1, 1965, pp. 72–75.

_____. "The Debate Nobody Won" (conference report), *Library Journal*, August 1977, pp. 1573–80.

_____. "The Dominant Issue was Race" (conference report), *Library Journal*, April 1, 1978, pp. 716–20.

_____. "Editorial Policy" (editorial), *Library Journal*, January 1, 1969, p. 15.

_____. "End of the Story" (editorial), *Library Journal*, December 15, 1964, pp. 4872; 4881. (Reprinted in Moon & Nyren's *Library Issues: The Sixties*, pp. 104–06.)

_____. "In Memoriam: Karl Nyren, 1921–1988" (editorial), *Library Journal*, September 1, 1988, p. 94.

_____. "'International by Definition'," *Library Journal*, November 15, 1964, pp. 4469–72.

_____. "Issues in Detroit" (editorial), *Library Journal*, May 15, 1977, p. 1081.

_____. "The 'Lessons' of Detroit" (editorial), *Library Journal*, August 1977, p. 1543.

_____. "Money, Politics, and Freedom at ALA Midwinter" (conference report), *Library Journal*, March 1, 1991, pp. 50–52.

_____. "National Library Wake" (editorial), *Library Journal*, May 15, 1969, p. 1927.

_____. "The New Constituency" (conference report), *Library Journal*, August 1969, pp. 2725–39.

_____. "No Answers Yet" (editorial), *Library Journal*, August 1969, p. 2709.

_____. "Oryx at 20: Steckler's Secrets," *Library Journal*, February 15, 1995, pp. 128–29.

_____. "The Participation Problem" (conference report), *Library Journal*, March 15, 1976, pp. 784–89.

_____. "A Question" (editorial), *Bay State Librarian* (bulletin of the Massachusetts Library Association), April 1963, p. 7.

_____. "The Role of the Radical" (editorial), *Library Journal*, September 15, 1997, p. 6.

_____ [and others]. "Tax Revolt — The Library Defense" (conference report), *Library Journal*, August 1978, pp. 1469–80.

_____. "To Catch a Thief," *Library Journal*, April 1, 1965, pp. 1617–21.

_____. "A Whimper for Freedom" (editorial), *Library Journal*, June 1, 1977, p. 1227.

_____. "Who's Underdeveloped?" (editorial), *Library Journal*, November 15, 1964, pp. 4488; 4498. (Reprinted in Moon & Nyren's *Libary Issues: The Sixties*, pp. 290–92.)

_____, and Shirley Havens. "Wait 'Til Atlantic City" (conference report), *Library Journal*, March 15, 1969, pp., 1104–11.

"Bevan, Aneurin" in *The New Caxton Encyclopedia* (London: Caxton Publishing Company, 1977), Vol. 3, p. 674.

Blake, Fay M. "Librarians and Labor," *Library Journal*, November 1, 1961, pp. 3733–35.

Blasingame, Ralph, Jr. "ALA: Problems and Proposals," *Library Journal*, August 1968, pp. 2809–10.

Bloss, Meredith. "Easiest Way Out" (letter), *Library Journal*, April 1, 1962, pp. 1342; 1344.

Boswell, James. *The Life of Samuel Johnson.* Everyman's Library edition. New York: Knopf, 1992. (*The Life of Samuel Johnson* was first published in 1791.)

"Bowker Company Moves," *Library Journal*, April 15, 1963, p. 1642.

Bradshaw, Lillian M. "The Format Change" (letter), *Library Journal*, February 1, 1967, p. 507.

Breslin, James E.B. "Terminating Mark Rothko: Biography is Mourning in Reverse," *New York Times Book Review*, July 24, 1994, pp. 3+.

Broderick, Dorothy M. "Librarians and Literature," *Library Journal*, August 1960, pp. 2709–12. (Reprinted in Moon's *Book Selection and Censorship in the Sixties*, pp. 225–29.)

_____. "The New Fiction Catalog," *Library Journal*, March 15, 1961, p. 1099.

_____. "'Problem' Nonfiction," *Library Journal*, October 1, 1962, pp. 3373–78. (Reprinted in Moon's *Book Selection and Censorship in the Sixties*, pp. 59–66.)

_____. "Turning Library into a Dirty Word: A Rant," *Library Journal*, July 1977, pp. 42–44.

Brown, H. Glenn. "Tea and Houris" (letter), *Library Journal*, March 1, 1962, p. 862.

Burns, Richard K. "Freedom to be Wrong" (letter), *Library Journal*, April 15, 1961, p. 1496.

_____. "Nuggets and Mush" (letter), *Library Journal*, August 1962, p. 2650.

Bundy, Mary Lee, and Frederick J. Stielow, eds. *Activism in American Librarianship, 1962–1973.* Westport, CT: Greenwood Press, 1987.

Cantor, Leonard M., and Geoffrey F. Matthews. *Loughborough: From College to University; A History of Higher Education at Loughborough, 1909–1966.* Loughborough, England: Loughborough University of Technology, 1977.

Carmichael, James V., Jr. "Ahistoricity and the Library Profession: Perceptions of Biographical Researchers in LIS Concerning Research Problems, Practices, and Barriers," *Journal of Education for Library and Information Science*, Spring 1991, pp. 329–56.

Carpenter, Humphrey. *The Brideshead Generation: Evelyn Waugh and His Friends.* Boston: Houghton Mifflin, 1990.

Chambers, Brad, and others. "The Selling of 'The Speaker'," *Interracial Books for Children Bulletin*, Vol. 8, Nos. 4 & 5, 1977, pp. 15–17.

Cherry, Susan Spaeth. "Take 2: *The Speaker*, Highlights/Spotlight" (conference report), *American Libraries*, March 1978, pp. 150–52.

Clarke, Gerald. "Biography Comes of Age," *Time*, July 2, 1979, pp. 83; 86.

Cole, Margaret. *The Story of Fabian Socialism*. Stanford, CA: Stanford University Press, 1961,

Cole, Robert. *A.J.P. Taylor: The Traitor Within the Gates*. New York: St. Martin's Press, 1993.

"Color Film on First Amendment Needs $$ Votes of Librarians," *American Libraries*, July-August 1976, p. 458.

Dear, I.C.B., ed. *The Oxford Companion to World War II*. New York: Oxford University Press, 1995.

"Decisive Win for Moon," *American Libraries*, July-August 1976, p. 456.

Dewey, Melvil. "Editorial Notes," *American Library Journal*, September 30, 1876, pp. 12–14. (Reprinted in *Library Journal*, March 15, 1951, pp. 463–65.)

_____. "The Profession," *American Library Journal*, September 30, 1876, pp. 5–6. (Reprinted in *Library Journal*, March 15, 1951, pp. 457–59.)

Dollen, Charles. "Freedom All Over the Place" ("Viewpoint" column), *Library Journal*, February 15, 1961, pp. 764–65.

Douglas-Home, Alec. *The Way the Wind Blows: An Autobiography*. New York: Quadrangle, 1976.

Downs, Robert B. "Apologist for Censorship," *Library Journal*, June 1, 1961, pp. 2042–44. (Reprinted in Moon's *Book Selection and Censorship in the Sixties*, pp. 251–54.)

_____. "Censorship Debate: Between Two Stools," *Library Journal*, August 1961, pp. 2581–82. (Reprinted in Moon's *Book Selection and Censorship in the Sixties*, pp. 256–58.)

Duchac, Kenneth. "A Plea for Social Responsibiity," *Library Journal*, August 1968, pp. 2798–99. (Reprinted in *Library Journal*, May 1, 1992, pp. S6–7.)

Emerson, Ralph Waldo. "History" in *Essays of Ralph Waldo Emerson* (New York: Literary Classics, 1945), pp. 1–30.

"Eric Moon Becomes Editor of Library Journal," *Library Journal*, October 15, 1959, pp. 3094–95.

"Eric Moon Elected New ALA President in Upset," *Library Journal*, August 1976, p. 1577.

Eshelman, William R. "Editorial" (on library segregation), *California Librarian*, January 1961, pp. 23–24.

_____ [and others]. "Head-on Collision: ALA in Motor City" (conference report), *Wilson Library Bulletin*, September 1977, pp. 30–42.

_____. *No Silence! A Library Life*. Lanham, MD: Scarecrow Press, 1997.

_____. "Social Responsibility and the Library Press," *Wilson Library Bulletin*, May 1972, pp. 804–12.

Estes, Rice. "Segregated Libraries," *Library Journal*, December 15, 1960, pp. 4418–21.

"Fabianism" in *Key Ideas in Human Thought* (edited by Kenneth McLeish; New York: Facts on File, 1993), pp. 269–70.

"Faulkner Condemns Closing of Libraries in the South," *Library Journal*, July 1960, p. 2559.

Fiske, Marjorie. *Book Selection and Censorship: A Study of School and Public Libraries in California*. Berkeley: University of California Press, 1959.

Flagg, Gordon, and others. "In Hot Miami Beach ALA's Temperature Went Way Down" (conference report), *American Libraries*, July-August 1994, pp. 672–83.

"Former 'LJ' Editor to Head Scarecrow," *Library Journal*, June 15, 1969, pp. 2381; 2384.

Franklin, Robert. "The Publisher in Ashe County" (interview by Noel Peattie), *Sipapu*, Fall 1990, pp. 1–6.

Freedman, Russell. "On Telling the Truth," *Booklist*, September 15, 1998, pp. 224–25.

Freiser, Leonard H. "The Bendix-Duchac Establishment" ("Viewpoint" column), *Library Journal*, September 15, 1968, p. 3105. (Reprinted in *Library Journal*, May 1, 1992, p. S8.)

Futas, Elizabeth. Review of *A Desire to Learn: Selected Writings* by Eric Moon, *Library Quarterly*, July 1994, pp. 341–42.

Gadd, Eric Wyeth. *Southampton Through This Century*. Southampton, England: Paul Cave Publications, 1988.

Gerard, David. Review of *A Desire to Learn: Selected Writings* by Eric Moon, *Library Review*, Vol. 43, No. 1, 1994, pp. 48–50.

Gerhardt, Lillian. "F.G.M.," *Journal of Youth Services in Libraries*, Winter 1988, pp. 139–42.

Green, Larry. "Life Imitates Art in Fight Over Librarians' Censorship Film," *Washington Post*, December 26, 1977, p. 3-A.

Greenaway, Emerson. "No Substitute" (letter), *Library Journal*, April 1, 1962, p. 1342.

Griffin, Lloyd W. "Freedom to Protest" (letter), *Library Journal*, April 15, 1961, p. 1494.

Hamlin, Arthur T. "About 'LJ' Awards" (letter), *Library Journal*, June 1, 1978, p. 1094.

Havens, Shirley. "IFLA Turns Fifty" (conference report), *Library Journal*, December 15, 1977, pp. 2482–84.

Hennessy, Peter. *Never Again: Britain, 1945–1951.* New York: Pantheon Books, 1994.

Hickey, Mary E. "Invitation to a Ball" ("Viewpoint" column), *Library Journal*, September 15, 1961, p. 2902.

Hillard, James M. "'Coolie' Labor" (letter), *Library Journal*, May 1, 1964, p. 1893.

_____. "Right of Center" (column), *Wilson Library Bulletin*, September 1977, pp. 74–75.

_____. "To the Foggy Isles?" (letter), *Library Journal*, October 15, 1963, p. 3780.

Holley, Edward G. "Change and Challenge" (letter), *Library Journal*, July 1965, 2918.

_____. "Neglect of the 'Greats'," *Library Journal*, October 1, 1963, pp. 3547–51.

Hopkins, Eric. *The Rise and Decline of the English Working Classes, 1918–1990: A Social History.* New York: St. Martin's Press, 1991.

Horn, Zoia. *Zoia! Memoirs of Zoia Horn, Battler for the People's Right to Know.* Jefferson, NC: McFarland, 1995.

Horrocks, Norman. "Decision Processes in ALA: Nudging the Dinosaur" in *Library Education and Leadership: Essays in Honor of Jane Anne Hannigan* (ed. by Sheila S. Intner and Kay E. Vandergrift; Metuchen, NJ: Scarecrow Press, 1990), pp. 85–97.

"I Love Librarians!," *Library Journal*, January 1, 1962, pp. 45–47.

"If Elected I Will…," *Library Journal*, April 15, 1976, pp. 975–84.

International Research Associates, Inc. *Access to Public Libraries.* Chicago: American Library Association, 1963.

Jackson, Robert B. "Problem Nonfiction" (letter), *Library Journal*, March 1, 1962, p. 858.

Johnson, M.D. "Tasteless Cover" (letter), *Library Journal*, January 1, 1968, p. 15.

Johnston, Wayne. *Baltimore's Mansion: A Memoir.* New York: Doubleday, 2000.

_____. *The Colony of Unrequited Dreams.* New York: Doubleday, 1999.

Jones, Arthur. "Letters," *Assistant Librarian*, July 1956, p. 118.

_____. "Past, Present, and Future: The Presidential Address to the A.A.L. of A.C. Jones, F.L.A.," *Assistant Librarian*, July 1960, pp. 135–43.

Jones, Clara S. "Reflections on *The Speaker*," *Wilson Library Bulletin*, September 1977, pp. 51–55.

Jones, Wyman. "Keep Talking" ("On the Grindstone" column), *Library Journal*, August 1964, p. 2967.

Josey, E.J., ed. *The Black Librarian in America.* Metuchen, NJ: Scarecrow Press, 1970.

_____, ed. *The Black Librarian in America Revisited.* Lanham, MD: Scarecrow Press, 1994.

_____. "The Civil Rights Movement and American Librarianship: The Opening Round" in *Activism in American Librarianship, 1962–1973* (ed. by Mary Lee Bundy and Frederick J. Stielow; Westport, CT: Greenwood Press, 1987), pp. 13+.

_____. "A Dreamer — With a Tiny Spark" in *The Black Librarian in America* (ed. by E.J. Josey; Metuchen, NJ: Scarecrow Press, 1970), pp. 297–323.

_____. "A Mouthful of Civil Rights and an Empty Stomach," *Library Journal*, January 15, 1965, pp. 202–05.

Katz, Bill. "A Day at Lj," *Library Journal*, June 15, 1966, pp. 3110–16.

"The Key Word was Access" (conference report), *Library Journal*, August 1977, pp. 1555–72.

Kilpatrick, James Jackson. "Censorship Debate: Polemicist at Work," *Library Journal*, August 1961, pp. 2580–81. (Reprinted in Moon's *Book Selection and Censorship in the Sixties*, pp. 255–56.)

King, Alexander. "The Bookworm," *Library Journal*, February 1, 1963, p. 512.

Kister, Kenneth. "A Yank in Sherwood Forest," *Library Journal*, November 15, 1965, pp. 4914–20.

Kniffel, Leonard, Peggy Sullivan and Edith McCormick. "100 of the Most Important Leaders We Had in the 20th Century," *American Libraries*, December 1999, pp. 38–48.

Kunitz, Stanley. "The Roving Eye" (editorial note), *Wilson Library Bulletin*, June 1936, p. 672.

_____. "The Roving Eye: The Spectre at Richmond" (editorial), *Wilson Library Bulletin*, May 1936, pp. 592–93.

Lancour, Harold. "McColvin Festschrift" (review of *Libraries for the People: International Studies in Librarianship, in Honor of Lionel R. McColvin*, 1968), *Library Journal*, March 1, 1969, p. 963.

"LA's 'Medieval Star Chamber'," *Library Association Record*, November 1977, p. 625.

Laybourn, Keith. "Bevan, Aneurin 'Nye' (1897–1960)" in *Twentieth-Century Britain: An Encyclopedia* (ed. by F.M. Levental; New York: Garland, 1995), pp. 72–73.

"Lee Ash to Be Lj's New Editor" (editorial), *Library Journal*, May 1, 1957, p. 1170.

Leventhal, F.M., ed. *Twentieth-Century Britain: An Encyclopedia*. New York: Garland Publishing, 1995.

"Librarians and Literature: Aftermath of an Article" (letters), *Library Journal*, October 15, 1960, pp. 3621–25; 3634.

"LJ Leads Library Magazines in Recent Reader Study," *Library Journal*, May 15, 1967, p. 1886.

"Lj Wins 1964 Edpress Award for Excellence in Journalism," *Library Journal*, August 1964, p. 2974.

"LJ's Annual Awards" (editorial), *Library Journal*, December 15, 1977, p. 2459.

Lorenz, John G. "The Format Change" (letter), *Library Journal*, February 1, 1967, p. 507.

"Major Changes Announced in Lj Editorial Staff," *Library Journal*, October 1, 1966, pp. 4590; 4592.

Malcolm, Janet. *The Silent Woman: Sylvia Plath and Ted Hughes*. New York: Knopf, 1994.

Martin, Susan K. "Information, Politics, & Money: The 39th Annual Conference of ASIS," *Library Journal*, December 15, 1976, pp. 2546–49.

Mason, Ellsworth. "The Format Change" (letter), *Library Journal*, February 1, 1967, p. 507.

McNeal, Archie L. "Integrated Service in Southern PublicLibraries," *Library Journal*, June 1, 1961, pp. 2045–48.

Molesworth, Nigel [pseud. of Norman Stevens]. "Uncritical Editing of Who's Who" (letter), *Library Journal*, March 1, 1967, p. 945.

Moon, Eric. "A Priori Censorship" in Moon's *A Desire to Learn* (Metuchen, NJ: Scarecrow Press, 1993), pp. 151–54. (Originally published as part of "Speak Out on A Priori Censorship" in the *Newsletter on Intellectual Freedom*, September 1985, pp. 169–71.)

_____. "Accentuate the Physical" (editorial), *Library Journal*, September 15, 1961, p. 2900.

_____. "Air Race from Newfoundland: The Story of the Alcock and Whitten-Brown Flight Forty Years Ago," *Atlantic Advocate*, July 1959, pp. 45–56.

_____. "Association Agonies: Life with ALA," *American Libraries*, April 1972, pp. 395–400. (Reprinted in slightly revised form in Moon's *A Desire to Learn* as "Library Association Agonies: Or, Life with ALA and its Brothers and Sisters," pp. 309–20.)

_____. "Balance in Boom-Time" (editorial), *Library Journal*, January 1, 1960, p. 58. (Reprinted in Moon & Nyren's *Library Issues: The Sixties*, pp. 59–60.)

_____. "Bastille Day and After" (conference report), *Library Journal*, September 1, 1963, pp. 3004–17.

_____. "The Benefit of the Doubt," *Wilson Library Bulletin*, April 1965, pp. 27–31; 38. (Reprinted in Moon's *A Desire to Learn*, pp. 130–37.)

_____, ed. "Book Rejection: Is It Censorship" (symposium), *Library Journal*, June 15, 1962, pp. 2298–2304; 2353. (Reprinted in Moon's *Book Selection and Censorship in the Sixties*, pp. 12–21.)

_____, ed. *Book Selection and Censorship in the Sixties*. New York: Bowker, 1969.

_____. "Business—Not Quite As Usual" (conference report), *Library Journal*, August 1968, pp. 2797–2809.

_____. "The Case *for* Code Revision" symposium, *Library Journal*, September 1, 1961, p. 2739.

_____. "The Caucus 'Disease'" (letter), *Library Journal*, October 1, 1998, p. 8.

_____. "The Central Fact of Our Time," *Alabama Librarian*, October 1965, pp. 3–8. (Reprinted in Moon's *A Desire to Learn*, pp. 10–20.)

_____. "A 'Chapter' Chapter: E.J., ALA, and Civil Rights" in *E.J. Josey: An Activist Librarian* (ed.

1977

by Ismail Abdulllahi; Metuchen, NJ: Scarecrow Press, 1992), pp. 44–52. (Reprinted in slightly revised form in Moon's *A Desire to Learn*, pp. 110–16.)

_____. "A Clear Choice" (editorial), *Library Journal*, October 15, 1964, pp. 3926–27. (Reprinted in Moon & Nyren's *Library Issues: The Sixties*, pp. 102–04; also reprinted in Moon's *A Desire to Learn*, pp. 4–7.)

_____. "A Concern for Users: ALA Highlights from Miami Beach," (conference report), *Library Journal*, July 1962, pp. 2494–97.

_____. "A Conspiracy Against the Laity?" *Texas Library Journal*, Summer 1969, pp. 61–72. (Reprinted in Moon's *A Desire to Learn*, pp. 264–79.)

_____. "A Conversation with Eric Moon" (interview by Milton Wolf), *Technicalities*, April 1981, pp. 1–9.

_____. "The Danville Story," *Library Journal*, November 1, 1960, pp. 3942–43.

_____. "Data Bank Is Two Four-Letter Words" in Moon's *A Desire to Learn* (Metuchen, NJ: Scarecrow Press, 1993), pp. 42–52.

_____. "A Day in Bedford Stuyvesant," *Library Journal*, October 1, 1964, pp. 3689–93.

_____. "A Decade Minus One" (editorial), *Library Journal*, December 15, 1968, p. 4597. (Reprinted in Moon & Nyren's *Library Issues: The Sixties*, pp. 248–49.)

_____. *A Desire to Learn: Selected Writings*. Metuchen, NJ: ScarecrowPress, 1993.

_____. "Discrimination at Detroit" (editorial), *Library Journal*, August 1965, p. 3224. (Reprinted in Moon & Nyren's *Library Issues: The Sixties*, pp. 146–48.)

_____. "Dues and Rights" (conference report), *Library Journal*, August 1961, pp. 2583–99.

_____. "Education Without Libraries = Catastrophe" in Moon's *A Desire to Learn* (Metuchen, NJ: Scarecrow Press, 1993), pp. 53–60.

_____. "Eric Moon Interviewed" (interview by William Eshelman), *Wilson Library Bulletin*, October 1969, pp. 140; 142.

_____. "The Fighting Women of Foxtrap," *Atlantic Advocate*, March 1959, pp. 39–43.

_____. "Fiscal and Federal" (conference report), *Library Journal*, August 1965, pp. 3184–95.

_____. "Follow the Bouncing Ball, or, Fiddling While Clapp Burns" (conference report), *Library Journal*, March 1, 1966, pp. 1172–80.

_____. Foreword ("Here's Looking at You, Katz!") to *Library Lit. 18 — The Best of 1987* (ed. by Bill Katz; Metuchen, NJ: Scarecrow Press, 1988), pp. vii–ix.

_____. Foreword to *Life Goes On: Twenty More Years of Fortune and Friendship* by Lawrence Clark Powell (Metuchen, NJ: Scarecrow Press, 1986), pp. vii–xvi. (Reprinted in Moon's *A Desire to Learn* as "Who's Larry Powell?," pp. 295–302.)

_____. Foreword to *Prejudices and Antipathies: A Tract on the LC Subject Heads Concerning People* by Sanford Berman (revised ed.; Jefferson, NC: McFarland, 1993), pp. 1–4.

_____. "The Generation Gap" (editorial), *Library Journal*, August 1968, p. 2775. (Reprinted in Moon & Nyren's *Library Issues: The Sixties*, pp. 370–72.)

_____. "The Gosling Memorial Library" in *The Story of Newfoundland* by A.B. Perlin (St. John's, Newfoundland: privately published, 1959), pp. 70–71.

_____. "High John," *Library Journal*, January 15, 1968, pp. 147–55. (Reprinted in Moon's *A Desire to Learn*, pp. 245–63.)

_____. "Hook, Line and Sinker or, Fishing for a Publisher" in Moon's *A Desire to Learn* (Metuchen, NJ: Scarecrow Press, 1993), pp. 369–76.

_____. "In, Out, or Neglected," *Library Journal*, January1, 1966 (Part I), pp. 57–64; and February 1, 1966 (Part II), pp.633–37. (Reprinted in Moon's *Book Selection and Censorship* in the Sixties, pp. 91–109.)

_____. "Integration and Censorship" (conference report), *Library Journal*, March 1, 1962, pp. 904–08; 937.

_____. "Internal Integration" (editorial), *Library Journal*, June 1, 1961, p. 2060. (Reprinted in Moon & Nyren's *Library Issues: The Sixties*, pp. 121–22.)

_____. "The Issues That Confront Us Now" in Moon's *A Desire to Learn* (Metuchen, NJ: Scarecrow Press, 1993), pp. 98–109.

_____. "A Jungle Tale," *Library Journal*, January 15, 1963, pp. 179–85. (Reprinted in Moon's *A Desire to Learn*, pp. 218–27.)

_____. "The Lacy Commission Report" in Moon's *A Desire to Learn* (Metuchen, NJ: Scarecrow Press, 1993), pp. 335–42.

_____. "Letter from America," *Assistant Librarian*, July 1960, p. 147.

_____. "Letters—Reply," *Assistant Librarian*, July 1956, pp. 118–19.

_____. "The Library Press," *Library Journal*, November 15, 1969, pp. 4104–09. (Reprinted in Moon's *A Desire to Learn*, pp. 352–65.)

_____. "The Library Press and Eric Moon: An Interview" (interview by Frederick J. Stielow) in *Activism in American Librarianship,1962–1973* (ed. by Mary Lee Bundy and Frederick J. Stielow; Westport, CT: Greenwood Press, 1987), pp. 99–111. (Reprinted in Moon's *A Desire to Learn*, pp. 377–91.)

_____. "The Living End" (editorial), *Library Journal*, December 15, 1966, p. 6049. (Reprinted in Moon & Nyren's *Library Issues: The Sixties*, pp. 245–46.)

_____. "A Living Library" (editorial), *Library Journal*, April 15, 1963, p. 1632. (Reprinted in Moon & Nyren's *Library Issues: The Sixties*, pp. 239–40.)

_____. "Living the Library Bill of Rights," *Newsletter on Intellectual Freedom*, September 1990, pp. 181–85. (Reprinted in Moon's *A Desire to Learn*, pp. 155–65.)

_____. "London's First World Book Fair: Trade Show or Public Fair?" *Publishers Weekly*, July 27, 1964, pp. 24–29.

_____. "A Matter of Values" in Moon's *A Desire to Learn* (Metuchen, NJ: Scarecrow Press, 1993), pp. 32–41.

_____. "Money in the (Data) Bank or, User, Can You Spare Ten Bucks?" in Moon's *A Desire to Learn* (Metuchen, NJ: Scarecrow Press, 1993), pp. 61–68.

_____. "Moonlight at Waterloo: An Interview with Eric Moon" (interview by Frank Atkinson), *New Library World*, November 1977, pp. 208–09.

_____. "Movement in Mobile" (editorial), *Library Journal*, June 1, 1965, p. 2509. (Reprinted in Moon & Nyren's *Library Issues: The Sixties*, pp. 145–46.)

_____. "A National Organization or a Private Club?" (editorial), *Library Journal*, April 1, 1963, p. 1429. (Reprinted in Moon & Nyren's *Library Issues: The Sixties*, pp. 355–57.)

_____. "Newfoundland Revisited," *Library Journal*, July 1969, pp. 2562–66.

_____. "No Place for Ladies," *Atlantic Advocate*, May 1959, pp. 75–80.

_____. "On Editorials" (editorial), *Library Journal*, August 1961, pp. 2618–19. (Reprinted in Moon & Nyren's *Library Issues: The Sixties*, pp. 122–24.)

_____. "On the Road" (editorial), *Library Journal*, November 15, 1963, p. 4332. (Reprinted in Moon & Nyren's *Library Issues: The Sixties*, pp. 267–69.)

_____. "On the Shelf" (editorial), *Library Journal*, January 15, 1964, p. 205. (Reprinted in Moon's *Book Selection and Censorship in the Sixties*, pp. 67–68.)

_____, ed. "Opinion … Readers' Views on Dorothy Broderick's Article" (symposium), *Library Journal*, August 1960, pp. 2713–17. (Symposium accompanies Broderick's "Librarians and Literature.")

_____. "An Orange Nightmare, or The Heady Grapes of Roth," *Library Journal*, March 1, 1961, p. 964–65.

_____. "Our Commission, Our Omissions," *Library Journal*, July 1984, pp. 1283–87. (Reprinted in *Library Journal*, July 1993, pp. S1–4; also reprinted in Moon's *A Desire to Learn*, pp. 69–82.)

_____. "The Paucity of Pictures" (editorial), *Library Journal*, February 1, 1960, p. 506.

_____. "A Potpourri of P's" in Moon's *A Desire to Learn* (Metuchen, NJ: Scarecrow Press, 1993), pp. 280–94.

_____. "Practical Convention Programs" ("Viewpoint" column boxed announcement), *Library Journal*, June 15, 1960, p. 2378.

_____. "President vs. Parliamentarian" (conference report), *Library Journal*, March 1, 1965, pp. 1063–66.

_____. "'Problem' Fiction," *Library Journal*, February 1, 1962, pp. 484–96. (Reprinted in Moon's *Book Selection and Censorship in the Sixties*, pp. 41–58.)

_____. "Problems of Consistency" (editorial), *Library Journal*, August 1964, pp. 2966–67. (Reprinted in Moon & Nyren's *Library Issues: The Sixties*, pp. 143–45.)

_____. "The Process of Dilution" (editorial), *Library Journal*, December 15, 1963, pp. 4710–12. (Reprinted in Moon & Nyren's *Library Issues: The Sixties*, pp. 138–42; also reprinted in Moon's *A Desire to Learn*, pp. 91–95.)

_____. "The Province Nobody Knows," *Atlantic Advocate*, April 1959, pp. 29–31. (Reprinted in Moon's *A Desire to Learn*, pp. 397–401.)

_____. "Questioning a Question — And Some of the Answers" (editorial), *Library Journal*, July 1963, pp. 2644–47. (Reprinted in Moon & Nyren's *Library Issues: The Sixties*, pp. 131–36.)

_____. "Reading the Lessons" (editorial), *Library Journal*, February 15, 1964, p. 817. (Reprinted in Moon & Nyren's *Library Issues: The Sixties*, pp. 142–43.)

_____. "A Rebirth" (editorial), *Library Journal*, September 1, 1962, p. 2850. (Reprinted in Moon & Nyren's *Library Issues: The Sixties*, pp. 235–36.)

_____. Review of *Memoirs of a Woman of Pleasure* by John Cleland, *Library Journal*, July 1963, pp. 2724–25.

_____. "The Right to Write" (editorial), *Library Journal*, August 1960, p. 2750. (Reprinted in Moon & Nyren's *Library Issues: The Sixties*, pp. 36–37; also reprinted in Moon's *A Desire to Learn*, pp. 121–22.)

_____. "RTSD and the Big Wide World," *Library Resources & Technical Services*, Winter 1966, pp. 5–12. (Reprinted in Moon's *A Desire to Learn*, pp. 235–44.)

_____. "Satisfaction Point" (editorial), *Library Journal*, May 15, 1968, p. 1947. (Reprinted in Moon & Nyren's *Library Issues: The Sixties*, pp. 87–88.)

_____. "The Scarecrow Press" in *Library Science Annual*, (Littleton, CO: Libraries Unlimited, 1985), Vol. 1, pp. 3–7.

_____. "The Silent Subject" (editorial), *Library Journal*, December 15, 1960, pp. 4436–37. (Reprinted in Moon & Nyren's *Library Issues: The Sixties*, pp. 117–19; also reprinted in Moon's *A Desire to Learn*, pp. 87–90.)

_____. "The State of the Union, Jack" in *The Library Association Centenary Conference: Proceedings* (London: The Library Association, 1977), pp. 73–78. (Reprinted in the *Assistant Librarian*, November 1977, pp. 166–72; also reprinted in Moon's *A Desire to Learn*, pp. 321–34.)

_____. "A Stock-Editor's Viewpoint," *North-Western Polytechnic School of Library Science: Occasional Papers*, October, 1957, pp. 1–9. (Reprinted in Moon's *A Desire to Learn*, pp. 189–98.)

_____. "A Survey of Segregation" (editorial), *Library Journal*, March 15, 1961, p. 1110. (Reprinted in Moon & Nyren's *Library Issues: The Sixties*, pp. 119–21.)

_____. "To Disagree Is Not to Destroy" in Moon's *A Desire to Learn* (Metuchen, NJ: Scarecrow Press, 1993), pp. 138–50.

_____. "Two Kinds of Access" (editorial), *Library Journal*, August 1963, p. 2849. (Reprinted in Moon & Nyren's *Library Issues: The Sixties*, pp. 136–38.)

_____. "Two Stars from Georgia" (conference report), *Library Journal*, August 1964, pp. 2919–28.

_____. "The Uninvited" (editorial), *Library Journal*, January 15, 1960, p. 210. (Reprinted in Moon & Nyren's *Library Issues: The Sixties*, pp. 325–26.)

_____. "The View from the Front," *Library Journal*, February 1, 1964, pp. 570–74. (Reprinted in Moon's *Book Selection and Censorship in the Sixties*, pp. 69–74.)

_____. "Voices on Vietnam?" (editorial), *Library Journal*, October 15, 1967, p. 3577. (Reprinted in Moon & Nyren's *Library Issues: The Sixties*, pp. 108–09; also reprinted in *Library Journal*, May 1, 1992, p. S4; also reprinted in Moon's *A Desire to Learn*, pp. 8–9.)

_____. "Walking…" (letter), *American Libraries*, September 1972, p. 862.

_____. "Who Cares About the Code?" *Library Journal*, May 1, 1961, p. 1744. (Reprinted in Moon & Nyren's *Library Issues: The Sixties*, pp. 173–74.)

_____. "Who's Out of Step?" (editorial), *Library Journal*, March 1, 1962, pp. 936–37. (Reprinted in Moon & Nyren's *Library Issues: The Sixties*, pp. 125–27.)

_____. "Whose Opinion?" (editorial), *Library Journal*, April 1, 1961, p. 1368–39. (Reprinted in Moon & Nyren's *Library Issues: The Sixties*, pp. 225–27.)

_____, and Karl Nyren, eds. *Library Issues: The Sixties*. New York: Bowker, 1970.

"Moon, Eric" in *The ALA Yearbook 1977: A Review of Library Events 1976* (Chicago: American Library Association, 1977), p. 62.

"Moon, Eric" in *The ALA Yearbook of Library and Information Services 1988: A Review of Library Events 1987* (Chicago: American Library Association, 1988), p. 74.

"Moon, Eric" in *Directory of Library & Information Professionals* (Woodbridge, CT: Research Publications in collaboration with the American Library Association, 1988), Vol. 1, p. 857.

"Moon, Ilse" in *Directory of Library & Information Professionals* (Woodbridge, CT: Research Publications in collaboration with the American Library Association, 1988), Vol. 1, p. 857.

Neufeld, John. "Second Thoughts on Selection Tools" (letter), *Library Journal*, November 1, 1960, pp. 3882; 3884.

"New Orleans Librarian Reinstated, But Penalized," *Library Journal*, August 1967, p. 2698.

Nyren, Karl. "A Bowl of Rain" (editorial), *Library Journal*, June 1, 1969, p. 2179.

_____. "A Dime-Store Paul Revere," *Library Journal*, October 1, 1967, pp. 3380–84. (Reprinted in Moon's *Book Selection and Censorship in the Sixties*, pp. 347–55.)

_____. "Introduction" to *Library Issues: The Sixties* (ed. by Eric Moon and Karl Nyren; New York: Bowker, 1970), pp. xiii–xiv.

_____. "A New Breed of Cat," *Library Journal*, September 15, 1968, pp. 3091–95.

_____. "Trustees in the Age of Consensus," *Library Journal*, September 15, 1965, pp. 3550–52.

Oates, Joyce Carol. "Jean Stafford: Biography as Pathography" in *Where I've Been, and Where I'm Going: Essays, Reviews and Prose* by Oates (New York: Penguin, 1999), pp. 145–52.

Oboler, Eli M. "Discrimination at Detroit" (letter), *Library Journal*, November 1, 1965, pp. 4648; 4650.

_____. "Oboler Dicta," *Library Journal*, February 15, 1967, p. 742.

_____. "Running..." (letter), *American Libraries*, September 1972, pp. 861–62.

Packard, Jerrold M. *Farewell in Splendor: The Passing of Queen Victoria and Her Age*. New York: Dutton, 1995.

Penney, Pearce. "Library Services for the People: Newfoundland," *Third World Libraries Interest Group Newsletter*, November 1992, pp. xxii–iv.

Plotnik, Arthur, and others. "Nonagenarian Guest-Stars in 'Streets of San Francisco'" (conference report), *American Libraries*, September 1975, pp. 473–84.

Powell, Lawrence Clark. *Life Goes On: Twenty More Years of Fortune and Friendship*. Metuchen, NJ: Scarecrow Press, 1986.

_____. "Of Those Who Were Truly Great" ("On the Grindstone" column), *Library Journal*, October 1, 1962, p. 3404.

"Presidential Timbre: The 79th Annual Conference of the California Library Association," *Library Journal*, March 1, 1978, pp. 520–23.

"R M Walter, Esq" (correction), *New Library World*, December 1977, p. 228.

Redmond, D.A. "We Need Them — Where Do They Fit?" *APLA Bulletin* (journal of the Atlantic Provinces Library Association), Spring 1959, pp. 54; 56.

Richards, Vincent. "FALANA — A New Association," *Library Journal*, May 1, 1960, p. 1751.

Rose, Jonathan. "Fabian Society" in *Twentieth-Century Britain: An Encyclopedia* (ed. by F.M. Levental; New York: Garland, 1995), pp. 277–78.

Rose, Phyllis. "Confessions of a Burned-Out Biographer," *Civilization*, January-February 1995, pp. 72–74.

Ross, Virginia L. "To Read and Ponder" (letter), *Library Journal*, May 15, 1962, p. 1824.

Rudin, Ellen. "An Anniversary" (editorial), *School Library Journal*, September 1963, p. 38.

Samek, Toni. *Intellectual Freedom and Social Responsibility in American Librarianship, 1967–1974.* Jefferson, NC: McFarland, 2001.

Sampson, Dorothy H. "Blank Generation" (letter), *Library Journal*, April 1, 1962, p. 1342.

"Savannah State College Award to Virginia L. Jones & LJ Editor," *Library Journal*, May 1, 1966, pp. 2300–01.

"Segregation in Libraries" (letters), *Library Journal*, February 15, 1961, pp. 730–36.

"Self-Study Report Finds ALA Lacking an Overall Vision," *Library Journal*, November 15, 1993, p. 14.

Sheldon, Brooke. *Leaders in Libraries: Styles and Strategies for Success.* Chicago: American Library Association, 1991.

Shepard, Marietta Daniels. "Dissent from Dissent" (letter), *Library Journal*, December 1, 1967, p. 4305.

Shera, Jesse H. "'Playboy' Substitute" (letter), *Library Journal*, April 15, 1967, p. 1550.

Shields, Gerald R. "A Moonlighting Member" (letter), *American Libraries*, April 1976, p. 195.

Smallwood, Joseph R. "The Truth about Newfoundland: Ten Years with Canada," *Atlantic Advocate*, April 1959, p. 33.

Smith, Eldred. "Kansas City Stirring" (letter), *Library Journal*, October 1, 1968, p. 3483.

Smith, Samray. "ALA and the Segregation Issue" (editorial), *ALA Bulletin*, June 1961, pp. 485–87.

"Social Responsibility Group Meets in Philadelphia," *Library Journal*, October 15, 1968, p. 3729.

Spain, Frances Lander. "ALA and Integration" (letter), *Library Journal*, April 1, 1961, pp. 1342; 1344.

Spavin, George (pseud.). "We Represent the Library's Interest," *Library Journal*, December 15, 1964, p. 4871.

The Speaker: A Film About Freedom. Chicago: American Library Association, 1977.

"'The Speaker' Debate Goes On: Cheers & Jeers," *Library Journal*, September 1, 1978, p. 1550.

Stevens, Norman D. "Shaw, Ralph Robert (1907–1972)" in *Dictionary of American Library Biography* (ed. by Bohdan S. Wynar; Littleton, CO: Libraries Unlimited, 1978), pp. 476–81.

_____. *See* Molesworth, Nigel.

Stevenson, Grace T. "Alter Moon?" (letter), *American Libraries*, September 1972, p. 861.

Strachey, Lytton. *Eminent Victorians: The Illustrated Edition.* New York: Weidenfeld & Nicolson, 1988. (*Eminent Victorians* was first published in 1918.)

Tate, Vernon D. "Fiction Tomfoolery" (letter), *Library Journal*, February 1, 1965, p. 416.

Taylor, Edith W. "Covering the Candidates" (letter), *Library Journal*, March 15, 1960, p. 1048.

Tweedy, Patrick. "Moon's Misguided Minions" (letter), *Library Journal*, July 1992, p. 8.

"US Commission on Civil Rights Reports on Southern Libraries," *Library Journal*, January 15, 1962, pp. 188–91.

Wakeman, John, ed. "Segregation in Libraries: Negro Librarians Give Their Views" (symposium), *Wilson Library Bulletin*, May 1961, pp. 707–10.

_____. "Talking Points: Segregation and Censorship"(editorial), *Wilson Library Bulletin*, September 1960, pp. 63–64.

Wessells, Helen E. "Editor's Farewell" (editorial), *Library Journal*, April 1, 1957, p. 920.

Wiegand, Wayne. *Irrepressible Reformer: A Biography of Melvil Dewey.* Chicago: American Library Association, 1996.

_____. "This Month 93 Years Ago … American Library Leader," *American Libraries*, October 1998, p. 87.

Williams, Patrick, and Joan Thornton Pearce. "Midwinter Night's Dream or The Origin of Specious," *Library Journal*, June 1, 1978, pp. 1137–38.

"Women on the March," *Library Journal*, May 1, 1960, pp. 1760–61.

Wright, Richard. "The Freedom to Read: An Author's View of a Library" (excerpt from Wright's *Black Boy*, 1945), *Library Journal*, December 15, 1960, p. 4421.

Ziegler, Philip. *London at War, 1939–1945.* New York: Knopf, 1995.

Zoglin, Richard. "The First Lady and the Slasher," *Time*, April 22, 1991, pp. 64–69.

Index

Capital letters in **boldface** *refer to plates of photographs between pages 314 and 315.*

AAL *see* Association of Assistant Librarians
Access Study *see Access to Public Libraries* (ALA)
Access to Public Libraries (ALA) 167–69
Acosta, Lydia **O**
advocacy journalism 182, 205–06, 251–52
Agler, Raymond 188
ALA *see* American Library Association
ALA Bulletin 132, 156, 164, 227, 238, 269, 273
Alabama Library Assoc. 171–72, 175–76
Alexander, Shana 183
ALISE *see* Association for Library and Information Science Education
Altman, Ellen 267
American Assoc. of School Librarians *see* American Library Assoc.
American Booksellers Assoc. 129
American Libraries 132, 227, 289, 312, 322
American Library Association 130–31, 153–174, 185, 229–31, 261–73, 278, 311–66, 369–87, 393–97, 409, **M**; *Access to Public Libraries* (Access Study) 167–69; American Assoc. of School Libarians 371; American Library Trustees Assoc. 284; Association of College and Research Libraries 315–17, 371, 385; awards by 395–97; Black Caucus 313, 319, 340, 342–44,

373; chapters (affiliated associations) 170–72, 376–77; Committee on Accrediation 326–27; Committee on Committees 326, 380; Committee on Organization 313; conferences *see* Richmond ALA conference (1936); Montreal ALA-CLA conference (1960); Cleveland ALA conference (1961); Miami Beach ALA conference (1962); Chicago ALA conference (1963); St. Louis ALA conference (1964); Detroit ALA conference (1965); Kansas City ALA conference(1968); Atlantic City ALA conference (1969); Detroit ALA conference (1977); Chicago ALA conference (1978); San Francisco ALA conference (1987); Miami Beach ALA conference (1994); Constitution 173–74, 314–15, 375–76, 379, 383; Council 166–67, 172–74, 229, 231, 268, 278, 312–13, 318, 320, 322–23, 332, 335, 344–45, 348, 353, 355, 371–81, 383, 393; divisions 371–72, 375–76, 385; elections and nomination procedures 278, 314–17, 374; Executive Board 166–67, 172–74, 229, 278, 313, 320, 323–24, 326–27, 334–39, 344–46, 348, 354, 371, 374–76, 378–81, 384, 393, 396; executive director 312–13, 323, 371, 375, 379, 381–84; Freedom to Read Foundation 278; Honorary Membership 387,

395–97; Huron Plaza 380–81; Intellectual Freedom Committee 165–67, 173, 334–35, 337–38, 340–41, 346, 350, 356, 369, 393–94; Intellectual Freedom Round Table 398; International Relations Committee 361; Junior Members Round Table 265, 279, 312; Lacy Commission and Report (Commission on Freedom and Equality of Access to Information) 394–95; Lippincott (Joseph W.) Award 395–96, 410; meetings (opening up) 230, 372; membership and membership meetings 165, 229, 263, 341–43, 371–72, 375–77, 383–84, 395; Moon as backbench founder and leader 312–14, 316–17, 364, 374, 379–80; Moon as chair of meetings 348, 383–84; Moon committee appointments as president 326–28, 384; Moon as Committee on Committees chair 326, 380; Moon as Committee on Organization chair 313; Moon as Council member 231, 268, 312, 320, 322–23, 376, 378–80, 393; Moon as Endowment Trustee 393; Moon as Executive Board member 320, 323–24, 326–27, 336–38, 344–46, 348, 379–81; Moon farewell speech as president 356–57; Moon inaugural speech as president 325, 330–31, 341, 355; Moon as

431

Intellectual Freedom Committee chair 393–94; MOON as membership advocate 263, 318–19, 373, 395; MOON as Nominating Committee member 393; MOON as president 23, 325, 328–65, 369–70, 380, 383–85, 388–89, 397,401,405, 408, M; MOON as presidential candidate 313–20, 332; MOON presidential commission and program 324–25, 332, 354–56, M; MOON as reformer 229–31, 238, 263, 268–70, 311–19, 370–87, 405; MOON as vice president/president-elect 320–28, 336; Nominating Committee 315–16, 393; Office for Intellectual Freedom 278, 334, 336, 343, 350, 354; petition candidates for elective office 314–17, 321, 323; presidency 315–17, 375, 383–85; Public Library Assoc. 371; publishing services 305, 375, 385–86; racism and 153–75, 192, 213, 229–30, 311, 334–50, 369; Reference and User Services Assoc. 385; Social Responsibilities Round Table 235, 263–70, 312–14, 316, 319, 343–44, 371, 373–74; *Speaker* controversy 325, 334–54, 356–57, 369, 377, 379, 394, 399, 406; staff of 381, 384; Task Force on Women 319; Washington Office 372–73
American Library Directory 132
American Library Journal 130, 223, 251
American Library Trustees Assoc. *see* American Library Assoc.
American Society for Information Science 332, 334, 351
American Society for Information Science and Technology 351
American Theological Library Assoc. 304
Amis, Kingsley 106
Amor, Margaret 75, 365
Anderson, Barbara 325
Anderson, Maxwell 29, 41
Angoff, Allan 193
Angry Young Men movement 106, 178
Annual American Catalogue 129
Antioch College 256–57
Archer, Leonard 184
Archons of Colophon 242, 393
Arlott, John 30, 41
Armitage, Andy 237, 279
Armstrong, Dora 49
Army Institute of Education 102
Ash, Lee 133, 160
Asheim, Lester 212, 409
Ashmore, Sted 49

Assistant Librarian 89, 93, 98–100, 104
Association for Library and Information Science Education 400–01, N
Association of American Publishers 335
Association of Assistant Librarians 24, 88–93, 95, 178, 372, 408; MOON as officer of 90, 317; MOON at centenary conference (1977) 99, 363–67, 370; relationship with Library Assoc. 89–90; visit (1963) to U.S. by 209–11
Association of College and Research Libraries, *see* American Library Assoc.
Association of Educational Communications and Technology 334, 351
Association of Research Libraries 230–31
Atkinson, Frank 367
Atlantic Advocate 110, 123
Atlantic City ALA conference (1969) 232, 265–73, 292, 312–13, 316, 322, 381
Atlantic Provinces (Canada) 111
Atlantic Provinces Library Assoc. 121, 123
Attlee, Clement 39, 63
Auden, W.H. 29
Austin, Derek 49, 58, 61
Austin, Mary 61, 66–69
Ayre, Anthony (Tony) 113–14, 121
backbench *see* American Library Assoc.—MOON as backbench founder and leader
Bagdikian, Ben 194, 355–57, 383, 394
Baker, Augusta 313, 409
Baker, Ray Stannard 206
Baraka, Amiri 243
Barber, Peggy 238
Barnes, Johnnie Givens 238
Bartlesville (Okla.) Public Library 160
Bay State Librarian 163, 165, 212–13
Beach, Cecil 315, 318, 320, 322, O
Beatson, Alexander (Jock) (stepfather) 7–11, 28–29, A
Beatson, Grace Emily Scott Moon (mother) 4–8, 10–11, 13–16, 28, 277, 284–85, 309, A, P
Beckerman, Ed 238, 325, 374, J
Bedford Stuyvesant (Brooklyn, N.Y.) 219
Bendix, Dorothy 160, 167, 171, 218, 237, 263, 266, 297
Benge, Ronald 33, 40, 96–97, 101–02, 308, 368, 399, 402, O

Bennett, Dorothy 149
Berman, Sanford 305–07, 398
Berninghausen, David 184
Berry, John N., III vii–ix, 114, 163, 165, 200, 211–21, 225–26, 230–31, 235–37, 239, 241–45, 248–52, 266–68, 270–71, 273–75, 278–79, 284, 287, 301–02, 311, 314, 318–19, 325, 327, 334, 340, 343, 347, 383, 408, F, L
Berry, Louise Parker F
Berton, Pierre 120
Bevan, Aneurin (Nye) 63–64, 80, 77, 97, 106, 366, 368, 406
Billy the Cartwheeler (Culmer) 300
Bingley, Clive 367
Biography xv–xix
Black Boy (Wright) 157–58, 164
Black Caucus *see* American Library Assoc.
The Black Librarian in America (Josey) 294, 307
Blackpool (England) 32–34
Blake, Fay 149–50, 237–38, 305, 325, 327, 333, 352–53, 371–72
Blasingame, Ralph 264, 289, 325
Bloch, Ernest I
Bloch, Fritz 253–57, 277, 284, 392, I
Bloch, Ilse *see* Moon, Ilse
Bloch, John 254
Bloch, Kaethe (Kate) 253–57, 277, 284–85, 392, I
Bloch, Susan 254
Blood and Sand (Blasco) 84
Bloss, Meredith 186
Boaz, Martha 238–39, 321, 399
Bob, Murray 150
Bobinski, George 273, 275
Bobker, Lee 334, 336–37, 339, 347–48
Bonk, Wallace 304
Bonny, H.V. (Harold) 23–24
book selection *see* collection development
Book Selection and Censorship (Fiske) 185
Book Selection and Censorship in the Sixties (Moon) xvii, 250, 279, 399
Bookguide 101
Books and Bookmen 99–100
Books in Print 129, 139, 142, 246, 248
Boston Public Library 210, 234
Boswell, James xviii
Bowker, Richard Rogers 129–30, 132, 142, 162
Bowker, R.R., Co. 125–26, 129, 162, 192–93, 205, 208–09, 224–25, 246–48, 287, 368, F; MOON as director of editorial development 249–50, 265, 271, 287
Bowker suite *see* Library Journal

Bowron, Albert (Al) 68–69, 120, 144, 212
Boyce, H. Worth 404
Bradshaw, Lillian 144, 228, 237, 325
Brahm, Walter 150, 201
Braine, John 100, 106
Braverman, Miriam 340–41, 347, 350
Brennan, William J. 184
Brentford (England) 79
Brentford and Chiswick Public Libraries 62, 70, 78–81, 86, 90, 102, 122
Brief American Lives (Yelton) 306
Brighton (England) 42
Bristow, John 24, 32
British Broadcasting Corp. 101
British Council 78
British Library Assoc. *see* Library Assoc. (British)
British Ministry of Education 46
British National Bibliography 91
British Phosphate Commission 5, 7
Broderick, Dorothy 147–49, 160, 162, 179, 184, 187, 235–36, 238, 304, 325, 333, 340–45, 348–50, 356, 398
Brooklyn (N.Y.) 135, 219, 254
Brooklyn Public Library 219, 222
Brown, James Duff 20, 51
Brown, Karl 132–33, 135, 140, 144
Brown, Richard (Dick) 237
Brown, Robert W. 167–68
Brown, Ruth W. 160
Browne charging system 25–27, 91
Brussels (Belgium) 361
Bryant, Douglas 190
Buck, Richard 340, 343, 348
Building Library Collections 304
Bulletin of the American Library Association 132
Bundy, Mary Lee 149, 175, 219, 237, 241
Burgess, Lawrence 24, 375
Burke, Gordon 237
Burns, Richard K. (Dick) 181, 237, 262, 265, 273
Burroughs, William 184
Bush, Barbara 396
Bushey (England) 66–67
Bushey Public Library *see* Hertfordshire County Libraries
Butlin (Billy) holiday camps 87
Butt, Bert 115, 124
Butt, Grace 115, 124
Bye, Nancy 270, 329, 402, **L**
Bye, Richard (Dick) 126, 143, 208–09, 232, 241, 247–48, 270, 278, 287, 291, 329, 401–02, **F**, **L**
Caldwell, Erskine 184
California Librarian 145, 163, 213

California Library Assoc. 266, 323–24, 332, 345
Calne (England) 36
Campbell, Harry 120, 122, 127
Canada 107–08, 112, 117
Canadian Broadcasting Corp. 116, 123–24
Canadian Library Assoc. 85, 107, 114, 117, 121, 123, 250
Canary Islands 391–92
Cape Coral (Fla.) 392
Carnegie, Andrew 131, 193
The Carpetbaggers (Robbins) 186
Carter, Jimmy 325, 355–57
Carter, John 238, 377
Carter, Mary 304
Case Western Reserve University library school 280, 289
Castagna, Edwin 184, 288, 320
Castagna, Rachel 320
cataloging and classification 191
censorship *see* intellectual freedom and censorship
Center for the Book (Library of Congress) 393
Chait, William 380–81
Changi (Singapore) 38–39
The Chapman Report (Wallace) 186
chartered librarians *see* professional qualifications
Chelton, Mary K. 333, 340–41, 344, 401
Cheney, Frances Neel 230
Cherry, Susan Spaeth 347
Chicago ALA conference (1963) 213–14
Chicago ALA conference (1976) 323
Chicago ALA conference (1978) 325, 354–59
Chicago Hilton 358
Chicago Public Library 203, 358
Chiswick (England) 79
Chiswick Press 81
Chivers Company 84
Christie, Julie 402
Churchill, Winston 27, 30, 32, 39–40, 63, 77, 106, 366
Civil Rights Act (1964) 171–72
civil rights movement *see* racism in libraries and associations
CLA *see* Canadian Library Association
Clapp, Verner 173, 272, 288, 409–10
Clark, Geraldine 340–41, 344
Clarke, Esmé *see* Vesey, Esmé
class system in Britain 1–3, 20, 105–06, 368
Clausman, Gilbert 351–52
Cleveland ALA conference (1961) 145, 165–66, 173
Clift, David 145, 161, 229–30, 273, 297–98, 312–13, 381

Clough, Eric 23, 32, 78, 321
Cobb, Mary Lou *see* Cobb-Corbett, Mary Lou
Cobb-Corbett, Mary Lou 261–62, 264–65
Cobo Hall (Detroit) 328, 341–43
Colburn, Edwin 148
Coleman, Jean 238
Coles, Tony 210
Colgan, John 49, 58, **C**
collection development 68–69, 73–74, 82–84, 184–89
College & University Business 223
College of William and Mary library 261, 265
Columbia University library school 131, 259–60, 383, 393
Comilla (India [Bangladesh]) 37–38
Commission on Freedom and Equality of Access *see* American Library Assoc.— Lacy Commission and Report
Committee on Accreditation *see* American Library Assoc.
Committee on Committees *see* American Library Assoc.
Committee on Organization *see* American Library Assoc.
communism in libraries 96–97, 189
Communist Party (British) 96–97
Confessions of a Lapsed Librarian (Benge) 33, 308, 368
Congress for Change 267–69, 289
Conservative Party (British) 2–4, 39–40, 63, 106
Cooley, Lesley 132, 138–40, 142
Cooley, Margaret 132, 137–38, 140, 148, 221–22
Copeland, Charles 212
Council *see* American Library Assoc.
Council for Florida Libraries 393
Council on Library Resources 173, 185, 288
Cousins, Norman 243
Cox, Archibald 335
Cox, John 51
Cram, Mona 115
Crane, Leila 77, 210
Crane, Stanley 76–77, 90, 135, 210
Crawford, Miriam 238
Cricklewood (England) 86–88
Crismond, Linda 383
Croneberger, Robert 218, 237
Curley, Arthur 234–37, 240, 242, 284–85, 297, 304, 308, 310, 312, 325, 329, 340, 361, 371, 387, 393, 396, 403, **G, J**
Current Biography 400
Cushman, Jerome 148, 184

Cuttack (India) 37
Cutter, Charles 51, 131
Cuyahoga County (Ohio) Public Libraries 121
Dainton, Sir Frederick 362–63
Dalton, Jack 209–10, 325
Dana, John Cotton 51, 410
Danville (Va.) Public Library 151, 155, 158
Darling, Pamela 340, 343
Darling, Richard 316, 325
Daub, Albert (father of Al Daub) 291
Daub, Albert W. (Al) 208, 272, 281, 285, 291–300, 304, 306, 319, 356, 388–90, 402, **K, N**
Daub, Marty 272, 285, 298, 402, **N**
Davey, Jim 209–10, 321
Davis, Joe 136
Days in the Death of Freedom 334
De Grazia, Edward 184, 243
De John, Bill 237, 266, 268
Delaney, Terry 23, 30
DeLoach, Marva 238, **M**
Delzell, Robert 335–36, 340–41
Denton, Dickie 26, 42, **C**
A Desire to Learn (Moon) xvii, 100, 398–99
Detlefsen, Ellen Gay 235, 237, 285, 289
Detroit 328
Detroit ALA conference (1965) 173
Detroit ALA conference (1977) 325, 328–34, 337, 339–45
Detroit Plaza Hotel 328–29
Devlin, Marie 299–300
Dewey, Melvil 20, 51, 126–28, 130–31, 374; Moon compared with xix, 126, 178, 182, 223, 249, 251–252, 394, 409–10
Dewey Decimal Classification 190, 288, 409
Dewton, Johannes 191
DiMattia, Ernest A. 236, 375–76
Dix, William 269, 273
Doiron, Peter 237, 297, 310
Dollen, Charles 181, 199
Doms, Keith 237, 272, 387
Donkin, Alfred (Archie) 11, 309
Dorothy Canfield Fisher Library Awards 213
Dougherty, Richard (Dick) 318, 361, 384, 402, **N**
Dowlin, Kenneth 394
Downs, Robert 150, 181, 183–84, 409
Drew University library 282–83, 304, 308
Drexel Institute of Technology library school 160, 266, 297
Drysdale, Richard 247

Duchac, Ken 237, 263, 266, 312–13
Dudley, Edward 64, 74, 78–79, 91–92, 96–97, 100, 103–04, 366–67, 408, **O**
Dunkin, Paul 150, 190–91, 201, 382
Dunnock, Mildred 335
Durrell, Lawrence 184
Dylan, Bob 207
E.J. Josey: An Activist Librarian (Abdullahi) 398
East Orange (N.J.) 188, 244, 276, 279, 282, 308
East Orange Public Library 188
Easy Rider Weekend 279–80
Echelman, Shirley 351–52
Edgewater Beach Hotel 240
Edpress Award 223
Edwardian Age 2, 17
Eisberg, Barbara 334
Eisenhower, Dwight 151–53, 177
Elementary and Secondary School Education Act 224
Eliason, Margaret *see* Cooley, Margaret
Elizabeth (N.J.) 136, 243–44
Ellsworth, Ralph 150, 230–31, 399
Emerson, Ralph Waldo xvi
Emerson, Thomas I. 349
Eminent Victorians (Strachey) xv
Endowment Trustee *see* American Library Assoc.—Moon as Endowment Trustee
Eric Moon Flying Circus 275–76, 297, 405–06, **J**
Esdaile, Arundell 59–60
Eshelman, Eve 310
Eshelman, William (Esh) 5, 145, 163, 165, 167, 213, 226, 230, 235–37, 251, 271, 273, 275, 285, 288–89, 303, 310–12, 325–27, 361, 371, 375, 377–79, 382, 387, 389–90, 392, 395–96, 399, 402, 408, **G, J, N**
Estes, Helena 162
Estes, Rice 151, 155–60, 162–63, 169
Eubanks, Jackie 237, 340, 343–44
Evans, Charles 131
Evans, Luther 144, 146
Executive Board *see* American Library Assoc.
executive director *see* American Library Assoc.
Fabian Society 2, 8, 10, 40, 178, 217, 373, 406
Fanny Hill (Cleland) 138, 180, 242
Fanwood (N.J.) 136, 243–44
Fast, Elizabeth 325
Faulkner, William 29, 41, 58, 101, 154–55
Featherstone, Tom 210, 397

federal aid to libraries *see* libraries (American)
Feinberg, Renee 237
Fellows and Associates of the Library Association in North America 122
Fellowship of the Library Association *see* Library Assoc. (British)
Fiction Catalog 147–49, 160, 179, 184
Finchley (England) 71
Finchley Public Libraries 62, 71–77, 135–36, 142, 365
The First Freedom (Downs) 181
Fisher Library Awards *see* Dorothy Canfield Fisher...
Fiske, Marjorie 185
Fiske Report see Book Selection and Censorship (Fiske)
Florida Library Assoc. 376, 393
Flying Circus *see* Eric Moon Flying Circus
Forest Press 288
Forsman, Carolyn 237, 262
Forsman, John 237, 262, 278
Forster, E.M. 2
Fortune and Friendship (Powell) ix
Foskett, D.J. 96–97, 363–64
Francis, Sir Frank 105, 272
Franklin, Hardy 219, 238, 268
Franklin, Robert D. (Bob) 134, 144, 150, 301
Franklin, Robert (M.) (Robbie) 193, 251, 260, 281, 285–86, 294, 298–99, 301–02, 304, 306, 310–11, 318, 357, 388, 390–91, **K**
Frantz, Jack 285, 319, 325
Frary, Mildred 325
Frasca, Bud **F**
Freedman, Maurice (Mitch) 237, 353, 359
Freedom to Read Committee (Association of American Publishers) 335
Freedom to Read Foundation *see* American Library Assoc.
The Freedom to Read Statement (ALA) 405, 407
Freiser, Leonard 201, 266
Fry, Roger 2
Further Education and Training Scheme *see* library education in Britain
Futas, Elizabeth 235, 237, 312
Gadsden, Sidney 101
Gaines, Ervin 184, 234, 325, 341
Galloway, Dean 356
Galvin, Thomas 213–15, 235–37, 318, 327, 333, 353, 381, 383, 394
Gardner, Frank 51, 98, 366
Garn, Jake 398
Gaver, Mary 289

Geiser, Elizabeth 142, 193, 224, 248, **F**
Geller, Evelyn 239, 251
Georgia Library Assoc. 164, 170–72
Gerard, David 97, 180, 399
Gerhardt, Lillian 133, 249, 319, 321
German Book Illustration of the Gothic Period and the Early Renaissance… (Muther) 296
Ghikas, Mary 383
Gilbert and Ellice Islands 5
Gill, Philip 363–64
Ginsberg, Allen 243
Ginzburg, Ralph 243
Givens, Johnnie *see* Barnes, Johnnie Givens
Glazer, Fred 238, 265
Glen Ridge (N.J.) 308, 310
Gloucester Point (Va.) 259, 261, 279, 282
Goddard, Joan 238
Goldwater, Barry 204–05, 217
Gordon, William 383
Gore, Daniel 150, 222–23
Gorman, Michael 409
Gosling Memorial Library *see* Newfoundland Public Libraries
Grady, William 351–52
Graham, Clarence R. (Skip) 316
Graham, Paddy Martin 24, 30, **C**
Graham, T.W. (Bill) 18, 22–25, 30–32, 41–44, 47–49, 55–57, 70, 87, 209–10, 212, 366, **C**
Grannis, Chandler 126, 142–43, **F**
Grapes of Wrath (Steinbeck) 58
Gray, Duncan 54
Greater London Division *see* Library Assoc. (British)
Green, Esmé 49
Green, Florence (Molly; Flo) 79–81, 365
Greenaway, Emerson 168, 186
Greene, Louis 208–09, 248, 287, **F**
Greenville (S.C.) Public Library 155
Greer, Roger 319
Griffin, Agnes 238
Griffin, Lloyd 181
Griffin, Marjorie 144
Grolier, Inc. 290, 389, 401
Grolier Educational Corp. 290–92, 295, 297–98, 300
Grosch, Audrey 351–52
Grove Press 242–43
Gunnersbury (England) 79
Guy Fawkes Day 135
Hacker, Harold 146, 237
Hagelin, Daniel 160
Hamlin, Arthur 347
Hannigan, Jane 305
Hanoi 38

Hardy, Thomas 4, 29, 41
Haro, Roberto (Bob) 237, 262
Harris, Michael 325
Harrison, Dean 104
Harrison, J. Clement (Clem) 218
Hatfield (England) 65
Havens, Shirley 133, 135–37, 200, 211, 219, 221, 251, 361
Haycraft, Howard 99
Heinz, Catharine 321
Hemel Hempstead (England) 65
Hemingway, Ernest 29, 41, 58
Henne, Frances 149, 322, 325, 409
Hertfordshire (England) 62, 65
Hertfordshire County Libraries 61–62, 65–69; MOON at Bushey Public Library 66–67; MOON at Oxhey Public Library 67–69
Hickey, Doralyn 361
Hickey, Mary 191
High John 219
Hill, Benny 18
Hillard, James M. 198–99, 203, 208
Hinchliff, Bill 237
History of Libraries (Hessel) 303
Hodges, T. Mark 122, 210
Hodgin, Ellis 265, 278
Hoduski, Bernadine 237
Hogarth, William 79, 81
Hollander, Hede 284–85
Holley, Edward 223, 315, 342, 384, 400
Holliday, Stan 82
Honorary Fellowship *see* Library Assoc. (British)
Honorary Membership *see* American Library Assoc.
Horn, Zoia 200, 236–37, 327, 332, 335–36, 339–41, 347–50, **H**
Hornback, Miriam 208
Horrocks, Norman 47–48, 78, 90, 92–93, 218, 234, 236–37,

245, 317, 320, 325, 327, 330, 374–75, 379–80, 383, 387, 393–94, 396, 401, **L, M**
Horwood, Harold 119
Hotline see Library Hotline
Htutt, Htan 49
Hudson, W.C. 114
Humby, Hubert (Bumble) 23, 30–31
Hunt Botanical Library 228, 283
Huron Plaza *see* American Library Assoc.
IFLA *see* International Federation of Library Associations and Institutions
Ihrig, Alice 325
In Dubious Battle (Steinbeck) 58
India 37–38
Indiana University library school 222
information policy *see* national information policy
intellectual freedom and censorship 67, 91, 120–21, 180–88, 278, 335–40, 369, 405
Intellectual Freedom Committee *see* American Library Association
Intellectual Freedom Office *see* American Library Assoc.— Office for Intellectual Freedom
Intellectual Freedom Round Table *see* American Library Assoc.
International Federation of Library Associations and Institutions 360–61
International Relations Committee *see* American Library Assoc.
International Research Associates 167–68
Invisible Man (Ellison) 402
Isacco, Jeanne 379, 407
Isherwood, Christopher 29
Jackson, Robert B. 186
Jackson (Miss.) Public Library 155
Jacques Cattell Press 248
Jameson, Don 120, **D**
Jefferson, Mona *see* Stokes, Mona
Jews (discrimination against) 253–55
Johnson, Alfred (Fred) 46, 51–52
Johnson, Lyndon xvi, 131, 171, 189, 204, 232, 261
Johnson, M.D. 204
Jonah, David 382
Jones, Arthur 89, 91, 94–95, 97, 100, 103

1988 or 1989

Jones, Clara 208, 316, 321, 323–25, 328, 332, 336–38, 340–41, 344–46, 348–50, 360, 362–64, 369, 394, 401, **M**
Jones, LeRoi *see* Baraka, Amiri
Jones, Virginia Lacy 144, 164, 170, 313, 409
Jones, Wyman 150, 199, 201–02, 238, 325, 327, 329, 396, **G**
Josey, Elionne (E.J.) xviii, 150, 169–72, 175–76, 230, 235–37, 252, 294, 307, 312, 319, 321, 325, 327, 333, 339, 340–41, 343, 350, 361, 375, 387, 393–94, 396–98, 409, **G**
journalism *see* advocacy journalism; library journalism
Junior Libraries 138, 141
Junior Members Round Table *see* American Library Assoc.
Kansas City ALA Conference (1968) 232, 235, 262–66, 269
Karnac, Harry 83
Kaser, David 325, 333–34, 351, 387
Kaser committee and report *see* national information policy
Katz, William (Bill) 148, 150, 188, 220–21, 228, 240, 251, 279–82, 284–85, 304–05, 396, **H**
Kazan, Elia 184
Kellum-Rose, Nancy 342–44
Kennedy, John F. 141, 151, 153, 177, 203–04, 207
Kennedy, Robert 261
Kensington (England) 81–82
Kensington Public Libraries 62, 82–86, 102, 107
Kent, Allen 201
Kidman, Roy 282
Kilpatrick, James J. 183–84, 199
King, Coretta Scott 256
King, Horace M. 18
King, Martin Luther, Jr. 153, 177, 207, 256, 261
Kirkpatrick, Oliver (Ollie) 238, 285
Krug, Judith 278, 334–37, 339–43, 346–47, 349–50, 369
Kumilla *see* Comilla
Kunitz, Stanley 153–54
LA *see* Library Assoc. (British)
labor unions and libraries 102–03, 189, 204
Labour Party (British) 2–4, 8, 20, 39–40, 63–64, 68, 97, 105–06, 178, 217, 368, 373, 406
Labrador 111
Lacy, Dan 212, 394
Lacy Commission and Report *see* American Library Assoc.
Ladenson, Alex 203
Lady Chatterley's Lover (Lawrence) 180, 186

Laich, Katherine 146
Lambert, Shirley 299
Lancour, Harold 133, 146, 218, 228
Langleybury 70
LAR see *Library Association Record*
Lawrence, D.H. 2, 29, 184
Lee, Luther 175–76
Lessing, Doris 106
Leypoldt, Frederick 129–31, 142
Liaison 98–100, 136, 178, 184, 366
Liberal Party (British) 2
librarian qualifications *see* professional qualifications…
Librarians for 321.8 (organization) 278
libraries (American) 130–31, 351–53; federal aid to 189, 224, 232, 250, 351–53, 355, 373
libraries (British) 63–69, 71–85, 91
libraries (Canadian) 117
The Library Assistant 100, 399
Library Assistants' Assoc. 89
Library Association (British) 44–46, 64, 88–91, 93–99, 102–03, 178, 321, 360, 362–69, 372, 388; Associateship of the Library Assoc. 45, 57, 122; chartered librarians 44; examinations 24, 42–45, 57–60, 90, 94, 101, 122; Fellowship of the Library Assoc. 45, 57, 59–60, 71, 122; Greater London Division 89–90, 92; Honorary Fellowship of the Library Assoc. 397, **O**; London and Home Counties Branch 94, 103; MOON at centenary conference (1977) 99, 230, 360, 362–68, 370; MOON as reformer 93–95, 229, 364–65; MOON as member of Register and Examinations Executive Committee 94, 105; Register and Examinations Executive Committee 60, 94, 105; relationship with Association of Assistant Librarians, 89–90
Library Association Record 98–100, 136, 321, 367
Library Bill of Rights 157, 165, 342, 398
Library Bureau 131
library education in Britain 44–61, 178, 289; Further Education and Training Scheme 45, 57
library education in U.S. 44, 289, 326–27
Library for the Blind 219
Library Hotline 226
Library Issues: The Sixties (Moon and Nyren) xvii, 250–51, 399
Library Journal 125–252, 322,

347, 368; advertising in 138–39, 179, 186, 223–24, 227, 249; awards and recognition 149, 223–25; Ash (Lee) as editor 133; Berry (John) as editor 250, 252; bias in 198–200, 252; Brown (Karl) as editor 132–33; book reviews in 132, 137–38, 198; book selection and collection development (coverage of) 184–89; business side of 179, 186, 223–24, 227, 252; circulation of 131–32, 162, 179, 227, 249, 319; columns and columnists in 191, 199–202, 228; conference reports in 146, 229; covers of 179, 189, 203–05, 217; "Days at…" series 219–21; Dewey (Melvil) as editor 130–31, 223; editorial consultants to 144, 200, 208; editorials (purpose of) 182, 200, 204; format and design 226–28; frequency of 132; history of 129–33, 409; humor in 194–97; intellectual freedom and censorship (coverage of) 180–88; letters to the editor in 148–49, 159–60, 202–03, 205, 233; *Library Journal* suite 236–42, 262–63, 268–69; MOON as editor 134–252, 287, 306, 368, 405, 408; MOON editorials in xvii, 147–48, 158–59, 164, 169–70, 173–74, 184, 191, 193–94, 198, 204–05, 211–14, 227, 229, 232–33, 251–52; MOON leaves 248–51; news gathering and coverage in 145, 150, 170, 228, 239, 252; photographs and illustrations in 189, 198, 203–05; *Publishers Weekly* (competition with) 141–43, 218–19, 224, 227, 288; racism in libraries and library associations (coverage of) 151–76, 189, 213–14, 251; social and political issues (coverage of) 179–80, 189, 198, 203–06, 231–33, 250–52; staff of 136–39, 211–15; titles and headlines 189; Vietnam War (coverage of) 189, 198, 231–33, 251; Wessells (Helen) as editor 132; Xerox merger 246–48, 287; writers for 146–50, 184
library journalism 98–101, 129–252, 273, 275, 405
Library Lit.— The Best of [year] (Katz) 304–05
Library of Congress 190, 393
Library Public Relations Council 242
Library Resources & Technical Services 382

Library Services and Construction Act 163, 224
Library/USA project (New York World's Fair 1964) 219
Library World 51
Life Goes On (Powell) 51, 99, 202, 293, 398
Linden, Maurice 271
Linowitz, Sol 247
Lippincott, Joseph 357
Lippincott (Joseph W.) Award *see* American Library Association
Literary Market Place 129, 142
LJ see Library Journal
Llandudno (Wales) 93
Loizeaux, Marie 135
Lolita (Nabokov) 120, 186, **D**
London (England) 62–65, 362–63
London and Home Counties Branch *see* Library Assoc. (British)
London County Council 65
Long Beach Island (N.J.) shore house 310–11, **F, G, K, L**
Lord, Milton 54, 210
Lorenz, John 228
Loughborough (England) 46–47
Loughborough College library school 43–44, 46–61, 178, 289, 408, **C, D**; MOON as student at 47–48, 54–60, 90
Louisiana Library Assoc. 171–72
Lubetzky, Seymour 191
Lyle, Guy 307, 399
Lynn, Robert (Bob) 24–25, 32, 41, 47, 57
Lynn, Ron 24, 32, 41
MacDonald, John D. 19, 357
Machrihanish (Scotland) 35
Madden, Henry 184
Mailer, Norman 184, 243
Maine Library Assoc. 360
Malinconico, S. Michael 237, 333, 361, **J**
Malraux, André 29, 41, 75–76
Manchester College of Science and Technology library school 48, 93
Marco, Guy 326–27
Marshall, Albert (A.P.) 174, 313, 382
Marshall, Joan 235, 237
Martelle, Marty 237
Martin, Allie Beth 315–16, 323
Martin, Kingsley 206
Martin, Lowell 234, 272
Martin, Paddy *see* Graham, Paddy Martin
Martinez, Elizabeth 383
Mason, Ellsworth 228
Massachusetts Library Assoc. 212, 215
Matta, Seoud 238

Matthews, Jimmy 49–50, **C**
McCarthyism and libraries 97, 189
McColvin, Ken 78, 82, 96
McColvin, Lionel 51, 54, 95–96, 100
McCorkle, George 248, 250, 287, 291–92
McDonough, Roger 146, 238, 263–64, 266, 269, 273
McFarland & Company, Inc. 302, 306, 390
McKenna, Frank 325
McMorrow, Diana Simpson Moon (first wife) xviii, 3, 60, 70, 86–88, 108–11, 113, 127, 135–36, 241, 243–46, 271, 274, 276–79, 301, 308–09, 401; miscarriage 88; MOON divorce from 283–84, 308–09; MOON marriage to 42, 60, 70, 86–88, 112–13, 136, 243–46, 276–78, 283–84; **D, E**
McMullin, Florence 336–37, 340
McNeal, Archie 167, 171–72, 272–73
McShean, Gordon 238
Medical Library Assoc. 331, 334, 351
Melcher, Daniel (Dan) 124–28, 133–34, 136, 139–41, 143–47, 156, 161–62, 194, 200, 208, 211, 220–21, 224, 246–49, 287, **F**
Melcher, Frederic G. (Fred) 125–26, 132–33, 139–41, 161, 193–94, 208–09
Melcher, Margaret Saul 138, 146
Melcher, Marguerite 125
Melcher, Peggy 125
Memoirs of a Woman of Pleasure (Cleland) 138, 180, 242
Mencken, H.L. 158, 162, 206
Mercer, Faith 115
Metcalf, Keyes 235, 410
Metuchen (N.J.) 291, 298
Mews, Marjorie 115
Miami Beach ALA conference (1962) 166–68
Miami Beach ALA conference (1994) 371, 377, 395
Miele, Madeline 271
Miers, Earl Schenk 290
Mifflen, Jessie 115–17, 208
Milam, Carl 316
Miller, Henry 101, 184
Minnesota Library Assoc. 345
Minudri, Regina 325
Mississippi Library Assoc. 171–72
Mohawk Valley (N.Y.) Library Association 349
Mohrhardt, Foster 264
Molesworth, Nigel *see* Stevens, Norman D.
Molz, Kathleen 164, 202, 340, 348

Monroe, Margaret 396
Montclair (N.J.) 125
Montclair Public Library 285, 308
Montreal ALA-CLA conference (1960) 145–46, 155, 157
Moon, Alan (son) 13, 70, 87, 108–09, 113–14, 244–45, 276, 278, 284, 309, 403, 408, **D, E, K, O**
Moon, Belinda (daughter-in-law) 309, 403, **H, L**
Moon, Bryan (brother) 5, 7, 10–14, 28, 87–88, 225, 277, 284–85, 309, 403, **A, P**
Moon, Christopher (nephew) 7, 12, 403
Moon, Cicely (sister-in-law) 284, 403
Moon, Colin (grandson) 309, 403, **L**
Moon, David (half brother) 7, 88, **P**
Moon, Diana *see* McMorrow, Diana
Moon, Edward George (grandfather) 4
Moon, Eric Edward vii–ix, xvi–xix, **A–H, J–P**; accent of 146, 366–67, 375; accidents by 14–15, 123–24, 280–81; as actor and entertainer 30–34, 41, 87–88, 102, 123, 193, 246, 290, **E**; advocacy journalism (practiced by) 182, 205–06, 251–52; as American Library Assoc. member and leader *see* American Library Assoc.; American literature (interest in) 29–30, 55, 58; as Angry Young Man 104–06, 178; as argumentative person xvii, 10, 56, 239, 406; as Association of Assistant Librarians member and leader *see* Association of Assistant Librarians; at Atlantic City ALA conference (1969) 265–73; autobiography and 399; automobiles of 113, 136, 279–81; awards received by 176, 395–97; backbench *see* American Library Assoc.— MOON as backbench founder and leader; bicycles and 9–10, 16, **A**; birth of 3–4; in Blackpool (England) 32–34; as book reviewer 138, 242–43; *Book Selection and Censorship in the Sixties* (book by) xvii, 250, 399; books (interest in and favorites of) 19, 184, 402; at Bowker as member of board of directors and director of editorial development *see* Bowker, R.R., Co.; as bowler 404, **E**; as

(Moon, Eric Edward, *continued*)
boxer 8, 30; at Brentford and Chiswick Public Libraries as deputy chief *see* Brentford and Chiswick Public Libraries; British versus American library education (attitude toward) 122, 289; brothers of *see* Moon, Bryan; Moon, David; Moon, Michael; Moon, Ron; at Bushey Public Library as regional librarian *see* Hertfordshire County Libraries; business acumen of 252, 409; at Butlin (Billy) holiday camp 87; in Calne (England) 36; Canadian–U.S. border disputes by 146, 330; as Canadian Library Assoc. member *see* Canadian Library Assoc.; censorship issues and 67, 120–21, 180–88; in Changi (Singapore) 38–39; chairing meetings by 348, 383–84; as checkers player 38; as chess player 301; at Chicago ALA conference (1963) 213–14; at Chicago ALA conference (1976); at Chicago ALA conference (1978); childhood of 5–20; children of *see* Moon, Alan; Moon, Max; class system in Britain (attitude toward) 20, 368; at Cleveland ALA conference (1961) 145; clothes (favored by) 134, 220, 244, 401; collection development and 68–69, 73–74, 82–84, 184–89; in Comilla (India [Bangladesh]) 37–38; as Committee on Organization (ALA) chair; communism (attitude toward) 97; as competitive person xvii, 55, 86, 142, 194, 241, 244, 301, 402, 406, 408–09; controversy (use of by) 144, 149, 160–61, 181–82, 184, 186, 406, 409; as cricket player 87, 244; in Cricklewood (England) 86–88; critics of 174, 197–99, 203; crossword puzzles by 309; in Cuttack (India) 37; dancing by 42, 285, 359, 363, **M**; as darts player 8, 59; daughter (wish for) 88; death (attitude toward) 22, 404; *A Desire to Learn* (book by) xvii, 398–99; at Detroit ALA conference (1965) 173–74; at Detroit ALA conference (1977) 328–31, 333–34, 339–45; at Detroit Plaza Hotel 328–29; Dewey (Melvil) and xix, 126, 178, 182, 223, 249, 251–52, 374, 409–10; at Drexal Institute of Technology library

school as visitor 297; drinking by 37, 49–50, 110–11, 113, 117, 123–24, 239, 317, 357; driving by 38–39, 113–14; drunk driving by 123–24, 178, 225; in East Orange (N.J.) 244, 276, 279, 282, 308; Eastern Brothers and 33–34; Easy Rider Weekend and 279–80; editorial methods of 178–206, 251, 306–08; education (formal) of 17–20, 44–61; ego of 86, 182, 238, 357, 364, 408–09; in Elizabeth (New Jersey) 136, 243–44; England (attitude toward) 210–11, 368; Eric Moon Flying Circus 275–76, 297–98, 405–06, **J**; in Fanwood (New Jersey) 136, 243–44; as father 60, 70, 244–45, **D, E, K**; father of *see* Moon, Francis Edward George (Ted); films (love of) 303–04, 402–03; at Finchley Public Libraries as district librarian *see* Finchley Public Libraries; floods (experienced by) 70, 81, 244; in Florida 391–404; as Florida Library Assoc. member *see* Florida Library Assoc.; at Frankfurt Book Fair 389; in Glen Ridge (N.J.) 308, 310; as golfer 392, 395, 401–02, 404, **N**; as grandfather 309, 403, **E**; in The Group 29–31, 33, 41; Guy Fawkes Day and 135; at Happy World Cabaret 39; at Hertfordshire County Libraries as regional librarian *see* Hertfordshire County Libraries; Honorary Fellowship (LA) received by 397; Honorary Membership (ALA) received by 387, 395–96; humor (sense of) 194, 329–30, 348; illnesses of 390, 404; in India 37–38; influences on 1–3, 8–10, 30, 61, 63, 206, 402; intellect of 18, 55–56; intellectual freedom (attitude toward) 180–81, 306, 405; at International Federation of Library Associations and Institutions World Congress (1977) 360–61; job interviews by 21–22, 77–79, 114, 121, 125–27, 290–92; at Kansas City ALA conference (1968) 262–65; at Kensington Public Libraries as stock editor *see* Kensington Public Libraries; labor unions and 102–03, 189; in Langleybury (England) 70; leadership qualities of xvii, 103, 235, 298, 374, 406, 409; as *Liaison* editor *see* *Liaison*; as Library Assoc. member *see*

Library Assoc. (British); library associations (attitude toward) 88, 230, 311, 372; library education (attitude toward) 122, 288–89, 405; *Library Issues: The Sixties* (book by) xvii, 250–51, 399; as *Library Journal* editor *see* *Library Journal*; at *Library Journal* suite 236–42, 269; as library journalist 98–101, 134–252, 405; lineage of 4–5, 13; Lippincott Award received by 395–96, 410; in Llandudno (Wales) 93; at Long Beach Island (N.J.) shore house 310–11, **G, K, L**; in London (England) 62–65, 362–63; at Loughborough Library School as student *see* Loughborough Library School; luck of 14–15, 32, 128, 290, 355, 369; in Machrihanish (Scotland) 35; management style of 220–22, 302; manipulation of others by 6, 64, 66–67, 73–74, 80, 104, 192–94, 238, 314, 382, 408; marriages of *see* McMorrow, Diana; Moon, Ilse; as mediator 11, 269; at Miami Beach ALA conference (1962) 166–67; at Miami Beach ALA conference (1994) 371, 377, 395; mistakes by (reluctance to admit) 141, 174, 357, 408; at Montreal ALA-CLA conference (1960) 145–46; Moon Mafia 315, 371, 374; in Morecambe (England) 36; Morse Code and 33, 35–36; mother of *see* Beatson, Grace Emily Scott Moon; muckrakers and 206; at Muelhbach Hotel (Kansas City, Mo.) 238, 262–63; national information policy (advocated by) *see* national information policy; nervous system of 102, 289–90; in New York City 178, 211; in Newfoundland (Canada) 109–24, 127–28, 178, 211, 250–51, **D**; at Newfoundland Public Libraries as director *see* Newfoundland Public Libraries; at North Finchley branch library as district librarian *see* Finchley Public Libraries; at Ocean Island (Pacific Ocean) 5–6, 178; at Oxhey Public Library as regional librarian *see* Hertfordshire County Libraries; in Palm Aire (Fla.) and Palm Aire Country Club 392, 402, 404; personality of 6, 62, 86, 103–06, 192–94, 220–21, 208,

246, 357, 368,407–08; physical appearance of 134, 220, 318, 404; political philosophy and beliefs of 8–9, 40, 63, 97, 178, 217, 314, 354, 373, 402, 406; political tactics of 103–04, 314, 316, 374–75, 380, 405; as public speaker 102, 375, 398; publishers' parties (attended by) 242–43; *Publishers Weekly* and 141–43, 218–19; racism in libraries and library associations (fight against) 151, 153–76, 192, 213–14, 229–30, 311, 323, 325, 334, 337–38, 340, 342–50, 369, 405; as raconteur 26, 104, 194, 408; reading by 19, 402; as reformer 93–95, 263, 311–14, 370–87, 405; at Regent's Park Elementary School 17; religion (attitude toward) 404; at Renaissance Center (Detroit) 328–29; retirement by 123, 356, 388–404; in Royal Air Force 11, 24, 31–41; at Rules (London restaurant) 366; rules and procedures (knowledge and mastery of) 92, 314, 374–75; at St. Louis ALA conference (1964) 171–72; at San Francisco ALA conference (1987) 396; Savannah State College Library Award received by 176; at Scarecrow Press as president and editor *see* Scarecrow Press; as senior library statesman 392–95; sex life of 17, 31, 34–35, 39, 88, 92, 105, 123–24, 180, 240–41, 245, 263, 270–71; at Shirley branch as library assistant *see* Southampton Public Library; in Singapore 38–39; smoking by 23, 109, 134, 220, 244, 318, 375, 404, **E, J, K, L, M, N**; as soccer (football) player 16, 32, 37, 39, 41, 56, 70, 244; social and political awareness in libraries and librarianship (advocate of) 95, 155, 178–80, 189, 198, 229, 231–33, 235, 238, 251, 263, 268–70; 311, 370, 373–74, 406; socialist convictions of 8–9, 40, 63, 97, 178, 217, 354, 373, 402, 406; in Southampton (England) 3–8, 13–17, 27–29, 178, 373; at Southampton Public Library as library assistant *see* Southampton Public Library; *Speaker* controversy (involvement in) 325, 334, 337–38, 340, 342–50, 353–57, 369, 379, 394, 406; speeches and papers by 20, 83–84, 181, 185, 197–98,

230, 307, 323, 330–32, 355–57, 360, 363–65, 369–70, 398; stepfather *see* Beatson, Alexander (Jock); as "structure freak" 314, 316, 374; superiority (feelings of) 6, 10, 104–05, 357, 368; as table tennis player 30, 32, 36–37, 39, 244; tape recorder (use of) 221; at Taunton's School 17–19, 178; as teacher and mentor 36, 101–02, 182–83, 185, 238, 251, 262, 268, 288–90, 302, 405–407; telephone (use of) 146–47, 221; in Tenerife (Canary Islands) 391; as tennis player 18–19, 30, 37, 56, 244; travel by in retirement 402; at Traymore Hotel (Atlantic City, N.J.) 268, 270; typewriter (use of) 36; U.S. citizenship (acquired by) 225; at University of Kentucky library press institute 273–76; at University of Pittsburgh library school as visitor; Vietnam War (attitude toward) 199, 231–33, 243; White House Conference on Library and Information Services 393, 397–98, 406; as wireless (radiotelegraphy) operator 32–37; at Woolston branch as library assistant *see* Southampton Public Library; work habits of 220–21, 302, 306; working-class roots and resentments of 1–3, 20, 40, 66, 106, 134, 178, 192, 244, 311, 368, 373, 406–08; at World Book Fair (London) 218; during World War II 21–22, 26–41; as writer 29–30, 41, 98, 128, 221, 375, 398–99; writers and authors (relations with) 146–50, 251, 306–08; Xerox Corp. and 246–48; in Yeovil (England) xvii, 3–5
Moon, Eric Lonnie (grandson) 309, 403, **E, H, L**
Moon, Francis Edward George (Ted) (father) 4–7, 13, 88, 388, **B**
Moon, Gladys (stepmother?) 7
Moon, Grace *see* Beatson, Grace
Moon, Howard (nephew) 403
Moon, Ilse Bloch Webb (second wife) xvii–xviii, 5, 39, 236–37, 245–46, 253–86, 297–98, 304, 306, 308–09, 317, 319, 321–22, 325–328, 331, 357–58, 361–62, 371, 381, 388–89, 391, 399–401, **C, H, I, J, N**; at Antioch College 256–57; as Association for Library and Information Science Education executive secretary 400–01, **N**; at Atlantic

City ALA conference (1969) 268, 270–71, 273; childhood and adolescence of 253–56; at Columbia University library school as student 259–60; at Detroit ALA conference (1977) 328–30; at Drew University as reference librarian 283–83, 304, 308; at Kansas City ALA conference (1969) 262–64; at *Library Journal* suite 237–38, 262–63; at Montclair (N.J.) Public Library as reference and technical services librarian 308; MOON courtship of 238, 248, 262–65, 270–71, 273–84; MOON marriage to 284–86, 308–11, 391–92, 399–401; at Muelhbach Hotel (Kansas City, Mo.) 238, 262–63; parents of 253–57, 259, 276–77, 284–85, 392, 400, **I**; at Rutgers University library school as director of professional development studies 308–09; at Sapelo Island (Georgia) 258–60, 282; at University of Kentucky library press institute 273–76; Webb (Ken) marriage to 257; at William and Mary College library as cataloger 261, 276, 282
Moon, Louisa Ann Sumsion (grandmother) 4
Moon, Maxwell (Max) (son) 39, 58, 60, 70, 87, 108–09, 113, 209, 233, 244–45, 276, 284, 309, **E, H, K**
Moon, Michael (Mick) (half brother) 7, 88, **P**
Moon, Ron (half brother) 7, **P**
Moon, Ted *see* Moon, Francis Edward George (Ted)
Moon Mafia xviii, 233–42, 310, 315–16, 319, 323, 371, 374
Moonies *see* Moon Mafia
Moore, Anne Carol 409
Moore, Everett 145, 184
Morant, Joe 23
Moravia, Alberto 184
Morecambe (England) 36
Morton, Elizabeth 107
Moses, Richard 238
Moses, Stefan 325
Mosley, Oswald 14, 97
Mounce, Marvin A. 228
Mount Vernon (N.Y.) 254, 257
muckrakers 206
Muelhbach Hotel (Kansas City, Mo.) 238, 262–63
Mumford, L. Quincy 99, 190
Murphy, Dennis 149
Murphy, William J. 321
Murrow, Edward R. 206
Nabokov, Vladimir 120, 184

Nadler, Myra 325
National Assoc. of Local Government Officers 102–03
National Commission on Libraries and Information Science 284, 318, 332, 354–55, 394, 397–98
National Defense Education Act 224
National Freedom Fund for Librarians 278
national information policy 325, 330–35, 342, 345, 350–57, 383, 394–95, 397–98, 406; Ad Hoc Committee to Draft a Statement on National Information Policy (Kaser committee) 333–34, 351; *Toward a Conceptual Foundation for a National Information Policy* (Kaser committee report) 351–53
National Library Week 180, 193–94
National Medal for Literature 243
NCLIS *see* National Commission on Libraries and Information Science
Neiswender, Rosemary 148
Nelson, Jack 184
Nelson, James 345–46
Nelson, Truman 212, 214
Nemeyer, Carol 394
Neufeld, John 149
New Brunswick (Canada) 111
New Brunswick (N.J.) 111
New England Library Assoc. 376
New Jersey shore house *see* Long Beach Island (N.J.) shore house
New Library World 51, 367, 369, 388
New Towns Act (1946) 65
New York City 178, 211
New York Library Assoc. 409
New York Library Club 210, 242
New York Public Library 132, 222, 235
Newell, Harold 115–16, 118, 127
Newfoundland (Canada) 107–114, 118–19, 123–24, 127–28, 178, 211, 250–51
Newfoundland Public Libraries 62, 107, 114–21, 127, 193, 287; Gosling Memorial Library 115, 118, 120; outport libraries 115–17, 119
1960s *see* The sixties
Nix, Lucile 172
Nixon, Richard M. 153, 232, 250, 318
Nominating Committee *see* American Library Assoc.
North, William (Bill) 337–38
North Finchley branch library *see* Finchley Public Libraries

North-Western Polytechnic School of Librarianship 85, 101–02, 288, 366,405
Nova Scotia (Canada) 111
Nuremberg (Germany) 253–54
Nyren, Dorothy 150, 237, 242, 340
Nyren, Karl 200, 221, 225–26, 228, 232, 237, 241–42, 249–51, 262–63, 325, 390
Oboler, Eli 167, 173–74, 203, 228, 340, 348
Ocean Island (Pacific Ocean) 5–7, 10, 178, **B**
Ocho Rios (Jamaica) 286
Odets, Clifford 29
Odum, Eugene 258
Office for Intellectual Freedom *see* American Library Assoc.
O'Hara, John 184
Orne, Jerrold 144, 150
Osborne, John 106
Owens, Major 340, 343
Oxhey (England) 65–68
Oxhey Public Library *see* Hertfordshire County Libraries
Palm Aire (Fla.) and Palm Aire Country Club 392, 402, 404
Palmer, Bernard 68, 96
Panizzi, Anthony 51
Paperbound Books in Print 142
Pearce, Joan Thornton 353
Penney, Pearce 127
Pennsylvania Library Assoc. 278
Pentagon library 219
Perez, "Judge" Leander 175
Peters, Jean 197
Petersburg (Va.) Public Library 155, 158
Pine, John 150, 184, 186
Plaquemines Parish (La.) 175
Players Club 209
Plimpton, George 242
Plotnik, Arthur 225, 235, 238, 251, 260, 375, 378
Poole, William 131
Potomac Technical Processing Librarians 279
Powell, Benjamin 157
Powell, Lawrence Clark ix, 51, 99, 134, 144, 148, 166, 201–02, 222, 243, 288–89, 292–93, 396–98, 409–10
Precious, Maureen 49
Prejudices and Antipathies (Berman) 305–06, 398
Previews 250
Prince Edward Island (Canada) 111
professional qualifications for librarians (UK and North America) 24, 42–45, 85, 105, 107, 122
Proposition 13 (California) 355

Public Library Assoc. *see* American Library Assoc.
The Publishers' and Stationers' Weekly Trade Circular 142
Publishers Trade List Annual 129
Publishers Weekly 125–26, 129, 131–32, 141–43, 218–19, 224, 227, 247, 288
Putnam, Herbert 51
qualifications for librarians *see* professional qualifications…
Queens (N.Y.) Public Library 222
Quinn, Patsy 31
Quorn (Australia) 7
Quorn (England) 58–59
Race and Reason (Putnam) 345
racism in libraries and library associations 151, 153–76, 192, 213–14, 229–30, 311, 323, 325, 334–50, 357–58, 365, 369, 405
racism in U.S. society 152–53
Rackham, Joyce 30–31
RAF *see* Royal Air Force
Randall, Ann 260
Rather, Dan 347–49, 354
Rayward, Boyd 237
Reader's Adviser 142
Ready, Will 145, 399
Redfern, Margaret *see* Amor, Margaret
Redmond, D.A. 122
Reference and User Services Assoc. *see* American Library Assoc.
Reference Books Bulletin 297
reference service in libraries 71, 74–76, 91
Regent's Park Elementary School 17
Register and Examinations Executive Committee *see* Library Assoc. (British)
Reid, Betty 284
Reid, Charles E. 284, 397
Renaissance Center (Detroit) 328–29
Resnick, Mary Alice 397
Reynolds, J.D. (John) 71, 76, 79, 135–36
Reynolds, Richard J., Jr. 258
Reynolds, R.J., Tobacco Company 258
Rhode Island Library Assoc. 306
Rice, Elmer 29
Richards, Vincent 122
Richmond ALA conference (1936) 154
Richter, Anne 126, 142, 215, 225, **F**
Robbins, Ruth K. 228
Roberts, Bill 265
Roberts, Don 238
Rochell, Carleton 325

Rohlf, Robert 146, 315, 318, 320, 322

Rom, Patricia 5, 236, 289, 310–11, 325, 402, **H**

Roosevelt, Eleanor 152, 175

Roosevelt, Franklin D. 152, 175

Rose, Maureen 139

Ross, Virginia 186

Rosset, Barney 242

Roth, Harold 188

Rowberry, Tony 49, 58–59, **C**

Royal Air Force 11–12, 31–40

Rutgers University libraries 282

Rutgers University library school 219, 289–90, 304, 308, 395, 399

St. John's (Newfoundland) 109–16, 123–24

St. John's University (New York) 147–48

St. Louis ALA conference (1964) 171–72

Sampson, Dorothy 186

San Francisco ALA conference (1987) 396

San Francisco Council for the Performing Arts 347

San Francisco International Film Festival 346

Sapelo Island (Ga.) 258–60, 282

Sarasota (Fla.) *see* Palm Aire (Fla.)

Saturday Review 243

Saul, Margaret *see* Melcher, Margaret Saul

Saunders, Lelia B. 187

Savage, Ernest 51

Savannah (Ga.) Public Library 155

Savannah State College Library Award 176

Sayers, Frances Clarke 409

Scarecrow Press 250, 271–72, 290–308, 314, 318–21, 368, 388–91, **K, N**; economics of 298–301, 386; history of 290–92; MOON almost fired from 297–98; MOON as head of 249, 293, 296, 301–08, 321, 399, 405, 408; MOON retires from 308, 356, 388–91; staff of 298–301

Schenectady (N.Y.) County Public Library 349

Schick, Frank 361

Schofield, Herbert 46–47, 50

School Library Journal 133, 138, 141, 224, 227, 239, 319

Schorr, Daniel 355, 357–58

Schuman, Alan 310

Schuman, Patricia Glass 235–37, 260, 266, 284–85, 297, 310, 312, 325, 340, 361, 372, 387, 393, 398, 401, **J, O**

Scott, Clara Ellen (grandmother) 5, 11

Scott, James (great-grandfather) 5

Scott, James Albert (grandfather) 4–5, 11

Scott, Stanley (Scott or Scotty) (uncle) 8, 13–14

Scott, William (great-great-grandfather) 5

Sealock, Richard 382

segregation *see* racism in libraries and library associations; racism in U.S. society

Selby Public Library (Sarasota, Fla.) 393

Sellen, Betty-Carol 235, 237

Sellers, Rose 150

Serebnick, Judith 137, 142, 222

Severance, Robert 175

sex discrimination in librarianship 22, 89, 189, 364–65

Shaffer, Kenneth vii, 213–15

Shank, Russell 260, 272, 315–18, 320, 322, 356–58, 360, 373, 383, 408

Sharify, Nassar 218

Shaw, George Bernard 2, 9–10, 19, 29, 373, 402

Shaw, Ralph 144, 219, 290–97, 302–03, 314, 409–10

Shaw, Viola Leff 290, 293

Shear, Norma 299, 304, **K**

Sheldon, Brooke 394

Shelkrot, Elliott 340

Shepard, Marietta Daniels 199, 203, 268

Shera, Jesse vii, 150, 196, 280, 289, 292, 322, 409

Sherman, John 198–99

Sherman, Stuart 184

Shields, Gerald (Gerry) 194, 237–38, 240, 268–69, 273, 275, 289, 318–20, 325, 340–41, 354, 373, 401

Shirley branch library *see* Southampton Public Library

Shockley, William 335, 340, 345, 347

Shores, Louis 409

Sillitoe, Alan 106

Simmons College library vii, 212–14

Simmons College library school 212–14

Simpson, Diana *see* McMorrow, Diana

Sinclair, Upton 206

Singapore 38–39

The sixties 177, 180, 224, 240, 251, 281–82

60 Minutes (television show) 347–49, 351, 354

Slocum, Grace 340

Smallwood, Joseph 112, 117–21, 127

Smith, Carol 49

Smith, Eldred 238, 262, 266, 268

Smith, Hannis 144

Smith, Harold 64, 94, 97, 104–05, 108, 363–64, 397

Smith, Mildred 142–43, 248, **F**

Smith, Ray 184, 186

Smith, Roger 143

Smith, Samray 164

Smith, W.G. (Bill) 78, 92–93, 97, 98–101, 104, 108, 212, 216, 365–66, **D**

The Smut Peddlers (Kilpatrick) 183

social and political awareness in libraries and librarianship 95, 155, 178–80, 189, 198, 229, 231–33, 235, 238, 251, 263, 268–70, 311, 370, 373–74, 406

Social Responsibilities Round Table (ALA) *see* American Library Assoc.

socialism (British) 1–3, 8–10, 39–40, 105–06, 178, 373, 402, 406

Somerset (England) 4

Soskice, Sir Frank 102

South Oxhey (England) 65, 67

Southampton (England) 3–8, 11, 13–17, 27–29, 178, 373

Southampton College of Art 11

Southampton Public Library 21–31, 41, 57, 375; MOON at Shirley branch library 26–27, **B**; MOON at Woolston branch library 26, 42

Southwestern Library Assoc. 205

Spain, Frances Lander 165

Spalding, C. Sumner 191

Spanish Civil War 8–9

The Speaker (ALA film) xviii, 325, 334–57, 369, 377, 379, 394, 399, 406

Special Libraries Assoc. 331, 334

Spender, Stephen 29

State University of New York at Buffalo library school 289

Stead, William 206

Steffens, Lincoln 206

Steinbeck, John 29, 41, 58, 101, 184

Stevenage (England) 65

Stevens, Frank 325

Stevens, Norman D. 196–97

Stevenson, Gordon 150

Stevenson, Grace 161, 229, 312

Stielow, Frederick 175, 200, 374, 398

Stockham, Ken 65, 105

Stoffle, Carla 385, 401

Stokes, Mona Jefferson (Jeff) 49

Stokes, Roy 46–48, 50–61, 71, 90, 105, 201, 238, **C**

Strachey, Lytton xv–xvi, xviii

Subject Collections (Ash) 133

Subject Guide to Books in Print 142

Subscription Books Bulletin 297

Sullivan, Peggy 333, 383

Summers, F. William 268, 313, 356, 377, 382, 384
Sunnyvale (Calif.) High School 335, 337–39
Surridge, Ronald 48–50, 52, 55–56, 58–60, 64, 78–79, 87–89, 91, 97, 100, 103–04, 107–08, 136, 209–10, 212, 277, 366, 408, C, D
Swartz, Rod 325, 333
Symons, Ann O
Tamblyn, Eldon 188
Tarbell, Ida 206
Tate, Binnie 237, 241, 262
Tate, Vernon D. 197
Tauber, Maurice F. 260, 393
Tauber (Maurice F.) Foundation 393
Taunton's College 18
Taunton's School 17–19, 21, 25, 178, B
Taylor, Edith W. 204
Taylor, John 49–50, 55, C
Taylor, Ric 49, C
Technical Bookguide 101
The Tee Pee 134, 144
Tenerife (Canary Islands) 391
Texas Library Assoc. 197
Thatcher, Margaret 71
Thomas, Alan 243
Times Literary Supplement (*TLS*) 79, 103, 107
Tomlinson, Tommy 74
Toronto Public Library 120
Toward a Conceptual Foundation for a National Information Policy (Kaser committee report) 351–53
Town and Country Planning Act (1947) 65
Tropic of Cancer (Miller) 180, 184, 186
Truman, Harry 152, 262
Tucker, Harold 184, 237
Tweedy, Patrick 233
Tynemouth, Bill 209–10
Ulrich's International Periodical Directory 129, 142, 244
Ulveling, Ralph 167–68, 272
United Nations library 219
University of British Columbia library school 289
University of California at Los Angeles (UCLA) library school 222, 288–89
University of Georgia marine institute 257–59
University of Hawaii library school 291
University of Kentucky library press institute 273–76, J
University of Kentucky library school 273

University of London library science curriculum 45
University of Maryland library school 219, 267
University of Pittsburgh library school 218, 228, 234, 289
University of Toronto library school 349
Urquhart, D.J. (Donald) 355, 357, M
Usherwood, Robert 365
Varlejs, Jana 237, 240, 310, 325, 330, G
Vesey, Esmé Clarke 49
Vesey, Gawan 49, 52, 67, 69, 106, 366
Victoria (British queen) 1–2, 82
Victorian Age 1–2, 17
Vietnam 38
Vietnam War 189, 199, 207, 231–33, 243–44, 251, 261, 267–68, 279
Virginia Institute of Marine Science 259
Virginia Librarian 265, 273
Virginia Library Assoc. 261–62, 265, 279
Vision Associates 334, 336–37
Vladimirov, Lev 219
Vosper, Robert 361, 396–97
Voting Rights Act (1965) 172
VOYA (*Voice of Youth Advocates*) 149
Wagman, Frederick 203
Wain, John 106
Wakeman, Hilary 135, H
Wakeman, John 71–77, 125, 127–28, 134–35, 140, 146, 155–57, 160–64, 170, 206, 212, 230, 240, 365, H
Wall, C. Edward 291
Wallace, Irving 184, 243
Waller, Theodore 208, 271–72, 282–83, 285, 290–92, 294–301, 325, 357, 362, 389–90, N
Walling, Ruth 172
Walsh, Maurice E. 205
Walsh, Padraig 291
Walter, R.M. (Roger) 367
Wang, Arthur 126
Wasserman, Paul 219, 325
Watkins, David 191
Watson, Tom 327
Weatherford, John 150, 201, 325
Webb, Beatrice 2, 373
Webb, Ilse *see* Moon, Ilse
Webb, Kenneth 257–59, 276, 279–81
Webb, Sidney 2, 373
Wedgeworth, Robert 208, 238, 268, 285, 313, 320, 329, 333, 337–38, 343–45, 348, 350, 356, 358–59, 361–66, 369, 381–83,

386, 394, 398, 401, 409, M
Weill, David 340
Welbourne, Jim 237, 262, 267, 279
Wells, H.G. 2, 373
Wessells, Helen 132
Westchester (N.Y.) Library Association 181, 185
Western Reserve University library school *see* Case Western Reserve University library school
Westminster Abbey 362
Wheeler, Joseph 51, 160, 409
White House Conference on Libraries and Information Science (1979) 330–31, 351, 354–55
White House Conference on Libraries and Information Services (1991) 284, 393, 397–98, 406, O
Wieser, George 139, 143, 212, 224, 230, 237, 240–41, 288
Wilkin, Binnie *see* Tate, Binnie
Wilkinson, Billy 325
William and Mary College library *see* College of William and Mary library
Williams, Avery 340, 342, 344
Williams, Patrick 353
Williamsburg (Va.) 259, 261, 280
Wilson, H.W., Co. 147–48, 154, 156, 237, 297
Wilson Library Bulletin 77, 132, 134–35, 153–59, 163–65, 227, 309, 389
Wilson, H.W., Library Periodical Award 145, 212–13
Wilson-Lingbloom, Evie 401
Winsor, Justin 51, 131
WLB see Wilson Library Bulletin
Wolf, Milton 374
Wolfe, Thomas 58
Woods, Bill 209–10
Woolf, Leonard 2
Woolf, Virginia 2
Woolston branch library *see* Southampton Public Libraries
World Book, Inc. 237, 297
World War I 2
World War II 11–12, 16, 20–22, 26–41, 63, A
Wright, Richard 157–58, 169
Xerox Corp. 246–48, 250, 287
Yates, Ella 237, 284, 327, 340, 344–45
Yelton, Donald 306–07
Yeovil (England) xvii, 3–5, 7
Young, Peter 397
Young, Virginia 361
Zapf, Herman 228, 283
Zeitlin, Jake 184